Dedication

This book is dedicated to the memory of Chief Robert A. Shields of the Southgate, Kentucky Police Department. Bob began his career with the Ft. Thomas, Kentucky Police Department and served with the Delhi Township, Ohio Police Department and the Pasco County Sheriff's Department in Florida before coming to Southgate. He was appointed Police Chief in Southgate in 1978 where he served until his untimely death in 1993. He was an influential member of Kentucky's law enforcement community. He served as President of the Northern Kentucky Chief's Association and the Kentucky Association of Chiefs of Police. Chief Shields was an innovative chief, and he was one of the first police executives in the United States to issue laptop computers to patrol officers. These efforts were unique because he raised money in the community to computerize his department. As police chief he implemented community policing and crime prevention programs, better liaison between the police and the business community as well as public and parochial schools. He also initiated one of the first D.A.R.E. programs in Kentucky.

What is unique about Chief Shields' accomplishments is that he was able to do a great deal with limited resources. His department had only four full-time officers. He implemented as many or more programs than much larger departments. Chief Shields was a leader and brought his small department to the forefront of modern policing. He proved that the small police department was as viable and active as the large department, a point often lost when police administration is discussed.

Chief Shields would unselfishly give his time to the community by working nights, weekends and holidays. To his fellow officers and colleagues, he was known for his professionalism and willingness to assist others. He always encouraged others to seek training and knowledge, and was a proponent of technology and advancement in law enforcement. Bob truly was a professional and an important friend. He is missed by his friends and colleagues.

Preface

Policing in America is grounded in tradition. That tradition is best understood by examining the teachings and writings of O.W. Wilson, who served as chief of the Chicago Police Department in the 1960s. Traditional policing is bureaucratic in nature. Managers assume that police operations must be provided uniformly and great effort must be exerted by management to ensure that this uniformity exists. As such, police administrators placed great emphasis on management and control systems and little consideration was given to how the police actually went about providing or delivering police services.

Police operations were viewed simplistically. There was a patrol unit that responded to calls for service and attempted to control crime through omnipresence. Traffic was usually the responsibility of a traffic unit. The traffic unit generated revenue by writing large numbers of traffic tickets. Offense and location selection for the issuance of tickets were generally based on ease (duck ponds or cherry picking as the vernacular goes) rather than traffic officers attempting to tackle a specific enforcement problem. Traffic officers also investigated traffic accidents and wrote citations at locations where the department received large numbers of citizen complaints. Finally, detectives investigated crimes. Traditionally, investigating crimes was considered an art, and detectives had a substantial amount of latitude when structuring their investigations. Although department size affected the exact configuration of a department's operational units, this was the basic structure.

The 1960s brought the beginning of a slow revolution in the way police services are rendered to the public. The considerable public disorder resulting from the Vietnam War and the Civil Rights Movement caused the public, government, and police officials to rethink what the police did and how they did it. The police-community relations movement was launched at Michigan State University. The due process revolution—the culmination of a series of cases rendered by the Warren Court—placed substantial limits on how police officers conducted criminal investigations and generally interacted with people. Later in the 1970s, many departments experimented with new organizational arrangements, which changed how police services were provided. There were a number of team policing experiments that placed a new emphasis on how the police responded to calls for service and crimes.

The 1980s and 1990s, with the advent of community policing, brought an all-out assault on traditional policing. Community policing necessitated that law enforcement make a 180-degree shift in its thinking relative to providing police services. Basically, police operational units must form a partnership with the citizenry. This partnership must mutually come to an understanding as to what a neighborhood's problems are and how these problems should be addressed. The police can no longer be call takers where they merely respond to a call, take the most expeditious action possible, and return to service. The police must take the time and exert the energy to attempt to rectify the situation or solve the problem at hand. In other words, police work gained substance, and substance began to have more importance than form.

This anthology traces the evolution of police operations from the traditional, bureaucratic model to our current understanding of how the police should deliver services. It has been an evolution because our quest for and acquisition of knowledge about police operations has been incremental. Our current understanding is the result of years of analysis and experimentation. It has not been an easy feat to achieve this level of understanding. There have been numerous failures and dead ends.

Section I provides an overview of policing. It attempts to better clarify the nature of the police relative to the public, and it touches on the contemporary understanding of police operations. Many issues and topics explored in greater detail in later chapters, such as the effectiveness of the police in controlling crime and the relative merits of reactive versus proactive policing, are introduced in this section.

Section II, *Patrol,* traces the historical analysis of patrolling. It examines the nature of patrol work, the Kansas City patrol study, response time studies, specialized patrol, and differential responses. These interdependent research areas form the core of contemporary thinking regarding how patrol should be managed. In essence, there is no universal or standardized way of dealing with police problems, but departments must deploy a matrix of patrol tactics or strategies to tackle specific problems or groups of problems. This section provides a foundation for understanding how this may be accomplished.

Section III, *Criminal Investigation,* looks at our understanding of the criminal investigation process. As noted above, criminal investigation was considered by many to be an art, and individual detectives were given substantial discretion in how they applied their craft. The criminal investigation process is examined in an effort to discern how crimes are solved and how effectively the police solve them. Of particular interest is whether cases are solved as a result of routine investigations or if departments need to deploy special or more sophisticated investigative procedures. Undercover work, a staple in all but the smallest police agencies as a result of the nation's drug problem, is examined to determine how such investigations contribute to solving criminal

Police Operations

Analysis and Evaluation

Gary W. Cordner
Eastern Kentucky University

Larry K. Gaines
Eastern Kentucky University

Victor E. Kappeler
Eastern Kentucky University

anderson publishing co.
p.o. box 1576
cincinnati, oh 45201-1576

Police Operations: Analysis and Evaluation

ISBN 0-87084-118-1
Library of Congress Catalog Number 96-84653

 The text of this book is printed on recycled paper.

Elisabeth Roszmann Ebben *Editor*   *Editor in Chief* Kelly Grondin

cases. Finally, modern criminal investigations, with an emphasis on DNA testing and automated fingerprint systems, are examined.

Section IV looks at special operations in law enforcement. For the most part, police organizations have created special operational units or made innovative assignments to counter special problems that develop in the community. This section highlights some of the more troublesome problems confronting law enforcement today. Repeat offender programs are examined in an effort to describe how some departments have attempted to focus on criminals who commit a disproportionately high number of crimes. Along these same lines, *hot spots*—locations with high police activity—are examined in terms of attempting to understand the crime problem. Finally, drug enforcement, domestic violence, and DUI enforcement each are addressed in separate chapters. These are high-profile problems from the perspective that they generate a substantial amount of police activity and they result in dangerous situations within the community. They are problems that the police must confront effectively.

Finally, Section V examines community policing and problem solving. As noted above, community policing is the overarching framework used today to coordinate police operations. Community crime prevention, an essential ingredient to community policing, is discussed in terms of its role in the overall police operational picture. The police must work with the community on a number of levels to create a partnership to reduce crime. Problem solving, another key ingredient in community policing, is examined as a method of dealing with crime and disorder. The police must go beyond answering calls and taking actions that solve problems and bring about closure for situations. This section also provides a model for understanding community policing. This is important because there are many perceptions and operational definitions of community policing. Finally, community policing is placed in perspective by raising questions about its effectiveness and applicability.

The authors would like to thank their families for many years of love and support. They also greatly appreciate the assistance and advice of their editor, Elisabeth Roszmann Ebben.

Contents

I. OVERVIEW

How police see their social function and what they actually do has been driven by a commonsense understanding of crime, criminals and the appropriate police responses to crime. Traditionally, the police thought of themselves as a single and unified crime-fighting institution. They also thought of crime as a generic problem that could be solved with the application of a few simplistic tactics. Criminals were conceptualized with similar simplicity. That is to say, many of the tactics and strategies used by the police were premised on commonsense beliefs about crime, criminals and effective police solutions. All crime and criminals were cut from the same cloth and all crime problems could be addressed from a deterrence, apprehension and punishment strategy. The effectiveness of police strategies and tactics in addressing this generic crime problem was often supported by the personal impressions and individual experiences of police officers and their administrators.

In the 1970s, the approach to the crime problem began to change. With the application of the scientific method to police tactics, administrators became aware that their traditional thinking about crime and the proper police response to it might have been misplaced. Due in part to evaluation research conducted in the early 1970s, innovative police administrators began to rethink the nature of the crime problem and the appropriate police response to crime. Crime and criminals were no longer seen as a generic problem, and police tactics and strategies were no longer thought of in a singular and simplistic sense. Increasingly, the traditional approach to crime control, patrol, rapid response and investigation came under attack when subjected to empirical evaluation. Police administrators and social scientists alike were forced back to the drawing board to rethink their most basic assumptions about crime and its control.

1

In the section that follows, two chapters provide the background for rethinking our traditional notions about crime and its control. First, Mark Moore, Robert Trojanowicz and George Kelling consider the relationship between crime and policing. They raise many fundamental issues that must be addressed when considering the police response to crime. These authors provide a discussion of the "commonsense" approach to crime control and then raise issues concerning the uniqueness of crime, criminals and the police response to both. In short, these authors instruct that crime, criminals and police responses to crime must be carefully defined and their uniqueness must be understood in order to realistically achieve any measure of crime control.

In the second chapter, Lawrence Sherman introduces the reader to the laboratory of criminal justice. The reader is first walked through the idea of scientific problem-solving as it pertains to police crime-control operations. Sherman then takes the opportunity to prescribe some approaches police should consider when addressing crime from a scientific perspective. Sherman stresses the importance of evaluation and application of the scientific method to discover what is effective in crime control.

Both articles in this section provide a foundation for many of the issues and evaluations presented later in the text. Readers should notice that the issues of proactive and reactive policing, community-oriented policing, domestic violence, DUI enforcement and apprehending violent criminals are all touched upon as viable specimens for the criminal justice laboratory. In the remaining chapters of the text, many of these issues are placed under the evaluator's microscope.

CRIME AND POLICING   1

Mark H. Moore, Robert C. Trojanowicz
& George L. Kelling

The core mission of the police is to control crime. No one disputes this.
Indeed, professional crime fighting enjoys wide public support as the
basic strategy of policing precisely because it embodies a deep commitment
to this objective. In contrast, other proposed strategies such as problem-
solving or community policing appear on the surface to blur this focus.[1] If
these strategies were to leave the community more vulnerable to criminal
victimization, they would be undesirable alternatives. In judging the value
of alternative police strategies in controlling crime, however, one should not
be misled by rhetoric or mere expressed commitment to the goal; one
must keep one's eye on demonstrated effectiveness in achieving the goal.

Professional crime-fighting now relies predominantly on three tactics: (1) motorized patrol; (2) rapid response to calls for service; and (3) retrospective investigation of crimes.[2] Over the past few decades, police
responsiveness has been enhanced by connecting police to citizens by
telephones, radios, and cars, and by matching police officer schedules
and locations to anticipated calls for service.[3] The police focus on serious
crime has also been sharpened by screening calls for service, targeting
patrol, and developing forensic technology (e.g., automated fingerprint systems, computerized criminal record files, etc.).[4]

Although these tactics have scored their successes, they have been
criticized within and outside policing for being reactive rather than proactive. They have also been criticized for failing to prevent crime.[5]

Reactive tactics have some virtues, of course. The police go where
crimes have occurred and when citizens have summoned them; other-

Source: Mark H. Moore, Robert C. Trojanowicz and George L. Kelling (1988). "Crime and Policing."
Perspectives on Policing, 2:1-13. Reprinted by permission of the National Institute of Justice.

wise, they do not intrude. The police keep their distance from the community, and thereby retain their impartiality. They do not develop the sorts of relationships with citizens that could bias their responses to crime incidents. These are virtues insofar as they protect citizens from an overly intrusive, too familiar police.

Moreover, the reactive tactics do have preventive effects—at least in theory. The prospect of the police arriving at a crime in progress as a result of a call or a chance observation is thought to deter crimes.[6] The successful prosecution of offenders (made possible by retrospective investigation) is also thought to deter offenders.[7] And even if it does not deter, a successfully prosecuted investigation incapacitates criminals who might otherwise go on to commit other crimes.[8]

Finally, many police forces have developed proactive tactics to deal with crime problems that could not be handled through conventional reactive methods. In drug dealing, organized crime, and vice enforcement, for example, where no immediate victims exist to mobilize the police, the police have developed special units which rely on informants, covert surveillance, and undercover investigations rather than responses to calls for service.[9] In the area of juvenile offenses where society's stake in preventing crimes seems particularly great, the police have created athletic leagues, formed partnerships with schools to deal with drug abuse and truancy, and so on.[10] It is not strictly accurate, then, to characterize modern policing as entirely reactive.

Still, the criticism of the police as being too reactive has some force. It is possible that the police could do more to control serious crime than they now achieve. Perhaps research will yield technological breakthroughs that will dramatically improve the productivity of police investigation. For now, however, the greatest potential for improved crime control may not lie in the continued enhancement of response times, patrol tactics, and investigative techniques. Rather, improved crime control can be achieved by (1) diagnosing and managing problems in the community that produce serious crimes; (2) fostering closer relations with the community to facilitate crime solving; and (3) building self-defense capabilities within the community itself. Among the results may be increased apprehension of criminals. To the extent that problem-solving or community strategies of policing direct attention to and prepare the police to exploit local knowledge and capacity to control crime, they will be useful to the future of policing. To explore these possibilities, this paper examines what is known about serious crime: what it is, where and how it occurs, and natural points of intervention. Current and proposed police tactics are then examined in light of what is known about their effectiveness in fighting serious crime.

SERIOUS CRIME

To individual citizens, a serious crime is an offense that happened to *them*. That is why police departments throughout the country are burdened with calls requesting responses to offenses that the police regard as minor. While there are reasons to take such calls seriously, there is also the social and administrative necessity to weigh the relative gravity of the offenses. Otherwise, there is no principle for apportioning society's indignation and determination to punish; nor is there any basis for rationing police responses. The concept of serious crime, then, is necessarily a *social* judgment—not an individual one. Moreover, it is a *value* judgment—not simply a technical issue. The question of what constitutes serious crime is resolved formally by the criminal code. But the criminal code often fails to give precise guidance to police administrators who must decide which crimes to emphasize. They need some concept that distinguishes the offenses that properly outrage the citizenry and require extended police attention from the many lesser offenses that pose less urgent threats to society.

Like many things that require social value judgments, the issue of what constitutes serious crime is badly neglected.[11] Rather than face a confusing public debate, society relies on convention, or administrative expertise, or some combination of the two, to set standards. Yet, if we are to assess and improve police practice in dealing with serious crime, it is necessary to devote some thought to the question of what constitutes serious crime.

DEFINING SERIOUS CRIME

The usual view of serious crime emphasizes three characteristics of offenses. The most important is physical violence or violation. Death, bloody wounds, crippling injuries, even cuts and bruises increase the severity of a crime.[12] Sexual violation also has a special urgency.[13] Crime victims often suffer property losses as well as pain and violation. Economic losses count in reckoning the seriousness of an offense. Still, society generally considers physical attacks—sexual and nonsexual—as far more serious than attacks on property.[14]

A second feature of serious crime concerns the size of the victim's losses. A robbery resulting in a murder or a permanent, disfiguring injury is considered worse that one that produces only cuts, bruises, and fears. An armored car heist netting millions is considered more serious than a purse-snatching yielding the price of a junkie's next fix.

Third, the perceived seriousness of an offense is influenced by the relationship between offenders and victims. Commonly, crimes against strangers are viewed as more serious than crimes committed in the context of ongoing relationships.[15] The reason is partly that the threat to society from indiscriminate predators is more far-reaching than the threat from offenders who limit their targets to spouses, lovers, and friends. Moreover, society judges the evil intent of the offender to be more evident in crimes against strangers. In these crimes, there are no chronic grievances or provocations in the background to raise the issue of who attacked whom first and in what way. The crime is an out-and-out attack, not a mere dispute.[16]

These characteristics—violence, significant losses to victims, predatory strangers—capture much of what is important to societal and police images of serious crime. The intuitive appeal of these criteria is reflected in the categories of the FBI's Uniform Crime Reports. Murder, rape, robbery, burglary, aggravated assault, and auto theft (most presumably committed by strangers) are prominently reported as Part I Offenses. This key, national account of crime not only reflects, but anchors society's view of serious crime as predatory street crime.

While this notion has the sanction of intuitive appeal, convention, and measurement, it also contains subtle biases which, once pointed out, might cause society and the police to adjust their traditional views. First, the accepted image of crime seems to downplay the importance of crime committed in the context of ongoing relationships. From the perspective of the general citizenry, such offenses seem less important because they do not pose a *general* threat to society. From the perspective of the police (and other criminal justice officials), such crimes are less clear-cut because the existence of the prior relationship muddies the distinction between offender and victim and increases the likelihood that a case will be dropped when the antagonists resolve the dispute that produced the offense.

From the victim's point of view, however, the fact of a relationship to the offender dramatically intensifies the seriousness of the offense. A special terror arises when one is locked into an abusive relationship with a spouse or lover. A date that turns into a rape poisons a victim's psyche much more than an attack by a stranger. And, as Boston Police Commissioner Mickey Roache found when he was heading a unit dealing with interracial violence in Boston, serious interracial intimidation and violence did not appear in crime reports as robberies or burglaries. Rather, the serious crimes appeared as vandalism. What made the vandalism terrifying was that it was directed at the same address night after night.

Second, the view of serious crime as predatory violence tends to obscure the importance of fear as a separate, pernicious aspect of the crime problem. To a degree, the issue of fear is incorporated in the conventional view of serious crime. Indeed, fear is what elevates predatory street crimes above crimes that occur within personal relationships. What the conventional view misses, however, is the empirical fact that minor offenses and incivilities trigger citizens' fears more than actual crime victimization. Rowdy youth, abandoned cars, and graffiti frighten people, force them to restrict their movements, and motivate them to buy guns, locks and dogs. To the extent that the conventional view of serious crime deflects attention from fear and the offenses that stimulate fear, it may obscure an important opportunity for the police to contribute to the solution of the serious crime problem.

Third, defining serious crime in terms of the absolute magnitude of material losses to victims (without reference to the victim's capacity to absorb the loss, or the implications of the losses for people other than the victim) introduces the potential for injustice and ineffectiveness in targeting police attention. In the conventional view, a jewel theft at a swank hotel attracts more attention than the mugging of an elderly woman for her Social Security check. Yet it is clear that the stolen Social Security check represents a larger portion of the elderly woman's wealth than the losses to the hotel's well-insured customers. The robbery of a federally insured bank would attract more attention than the robbery of an inner-city convenience store. But the robbery of the ghetto store could end the entrepreneurial career of the owner, drive the store from the area, and, with the store's departure, deprive the neighborhood of one of its few social underpinnings.

Fourth, to the extent that the conventional view of crime emphasizes the reality of individual criminal victimization, it underplays crimes that have symbolic significance. The current emphasis on child sexual abuse, for example, is important in part because it sustains a broad social commitment to the general care and protection of children. The current emphasis on domestic assault, among other things, helps to sustain a normative movement that is changing the status of women in marriages. The interest in white-collar economic crimes and political corruption can be explained by the desire to set higher standards for the conduct of those in powerful positions. The social response to these offenses is important because it strengthens, or redefines, broad social norms.

In sum, the view of crime as predatory, economically significant violence stresses the substantial losses associated with street offenses. It obscures the losses to society that result from offenses that poison relationships, transform neighborhoods into isolated camps, and undermine important social institutions. It misses the terror of the abused spouse or molested child, the wide social consequences of driving merchants out of business, the rot that drug dealing brings to an urban community, and the polarizing effects of fear. An alternative view of serious crime would be one that acknowledged violence as a key component of serious crime but added the issues of safety within relationships, the importance of fear, and the extent to which offenses collapse individual lives and social institutions as well as inflict individual losses. This enlarged conception rests on the assumption that the police can and should defend more social terrain than the streets. Their challenge is to preserve justice and order within the institutions of the community.

LEVELS, TRENDS, AND SOCIAL LOCATION OF SERIOUS CRIME

It is no simple matter to represent the current levels, recent trends, and social location of serious crime. Still, several important observations can be made.

First, in any year, a noticeable fraction of American households is touched by serious crime. In 1986, 5 percent of American households experienced the violence associated with a rape, robbery, or assault. Almost 8 percent of households were touched by at least one serious crime: rape, robbery, aggravated assault, or burglary.[17] When considering the likelihood that a household will be victimized sometime in the next 5 years, these figures increase dramatically, for a household faces these risks *each year*. Thus, most American households have first- or second-hand experience with serious crime.

Second, from the mid-1960's to the mid-1970's, the United States experienced a dramatic increase in the level of serious crime. In fact, the level of serious crime reached historic highs. Since the mid-seventies, the level of serious crimes has remained approximately constant, or declined slightly.[18]

Third, criminal victimization is disproportionately concentrated among minority and poor populations in the United States. Homicide is the leading cause of death for young minority males living in metropolitan areas.[19] Black households are victimized by violent crimes such as robbery, rape, and aggravated assault at one and a half times the frequency of white families. The poor are victimized at one and a half times the rate of the wealthy.[20] These numbers probably underestimate the real differences in the losses—material and psychological—experienced by rich and poor victims, since those who are black and poor have fewer resources to deal with the losses associated with victimization.

PRECIPITATING CAUSES OF SERIOUS CRIME

In searching for ways to prevent or control serious crime, the police look for precipitating causes. While it may be useful to examine what some call the root causes of crime (e.g., social injustice, unequal economic opportunity, poor schooling, weak family structures, or mental illness), such things are relatively unimportant from a police perspective since the police exercise little influence over them.[21] The police operate on the surface of social life. They must handle incidents, situations, and people as they are now—not societies or people as they might have been. For these reasons, the immediately precipitating causes of serious crime are far more important to the police than are broader questions about the root causes of crime. Four precipitating causes of crime seem relevant to policing: (1) dangerous people; (2) criminogenic situations; (3) alcohol and drug use; and (4) frustrating relationships.

One way the police view serious crime is to see the precipitating cause in the character of the offender. A crime occurs when a predatory offender finds a victim. One could reduce such events by teaching potential victims to avoid situations and behavior that make them vulnerable. And, to some degree, the police do this. But the far more common and attractive part for controlling predatory crime is to identify and apprehend the predators. Thus, dangerous offenders can be seen as a precipitating cause of serious crime and an important focus of police attention.[22]

Recent research on criminal careers provides a firm empirical basis for this view.[23] Interviews with convicted criminals conducted by the Rand Corporation indicate that some criminal offenders committed crimes very frequently and sustained this activity over a long career.[24] Moreover, these violent predators accounted for a substantial amount of the serious crime.[25] Now, an investigation of the root causes of such patterns of offending might disclose strong influences of social disadvantage and psychological maltreatment in shaping the personalities of such offenders. Moreover, the influence of these factors might reasonably mitigate their guilt. One might also hold out some hope for their future rehabilitation (through the natural process of aging if nothing else). So, the criminal proclivities of violent predators need not be viewed as either inevitable or unchangeable. From the vantage point of the police, however, the presence of such offenders in the community can reasonably be viewed as an important precipitating cause of crime. Controlling such offenders through incapacitation or close surveillance thus becomes an important crime control strategy.

Having noted the role of dangerous offenders in producing serious crime, it is worth emphasizing that such offenders account for only a portion of the total amount of serious crime—far more than their share, but still only about half of all serious crime.[26] The necessary conclusion is that a significant portion of the serious crime problem cannot be attributed to determined attacks by career criminals or to predatory offenders. These crimes arise from quite different causes.

Some of these crimes might be produced by situational effects. Darkness and congestion around a subway exit may create an attractive location for muggings. An after-hours bar may host more than its share of fights. A rock house from which crack is being sold may become a magnet for violence. Closing time in a popular disco may produce fights among teenagers leaving the scene. In sum, there are some places, times, and activities that bring people together in ways that increase the likelihood of serious crime.

The fact that this occurs is knowable to police. By analyzing calls for service, they can observe that there are repeated calls made from certain places and at certain times.[27] These "hot spots" become important targets of police attention.[28] For example, patrol units might be dispatched just to sit and observe at the appropriate times. There may also be other solutions including permanent changes in the criminogenic situations. For example, the subway area could be lighted; the attention of a neighborhood watch group could be directed to the troublespot; the after-hours bar could be put out of business; aggressive street-level enforcement could be directed against the rock house; or transportation could be arranged for the kids leaving the disco so the crowd thins out more quickly.[29]

Crimes are also significantly related to alcohol or drug abuse.[30] It is now quite clear that: (1) a surprisingly high percentage of those arrested for serious crimes are drug or alcohol users;[31] (2) many offenders have drunk alcohol or taken drugs prior to committing crimes;[32] and (3) victims as well as offenders are often intoxicated or under the influence of drugs.[33] What is unclear is exactly how alcohol and drugs produce their criminogenic effect. Four hypotheses have been advanced to explain this phenomenon.[34]

The first is that physiological effects stimulate or license the person to commit crimes. The theory of stimulation may be appropriate to methamphetamines or PCP, which sometimes seem to produce violent reactions among consumers. The theory of licensing or disinhibition seems more appropriate in the case of alcohol where the release of inhibitions is arguably the mechanism that permits offenses to occur.[35]

Second, dependence or addiction forces users to spend more money on purchasing drugs, and they turn to crime in a desperate effort to maintain their habits. This is a powerful theory in the case of heroin (under conditions of prohibition), and perhaps for cocaine. It is far less powerful for alcohol or marijuana.

Third, drug use gradually demoralizes people by putting them on the wrong side of the law, bringing them into contact with criminals, and gradually weakening their commitment to the obligations of a civil society. Again, this seems more appropriate for those who become deeply involved with drugs and alcohol over a long period of time, and therefore relies more on the dependence-producing attributes of drugs rather than on the immediate intoxicating effects.

Fourth, intoxicated people make particularly good victims. In some cases, intoxication makes people vulnerable to victimization.[36] In other cases, it causes victims to provoke their attackers.[37] In either case, a serious crime can result.

Whichever theory, or theories, is correct, the close association among drugs, alcohol, and serious crime suggests that the amount of serious crime might be decreased by reducing levels of alcohol and drug use, or by identifying those offenders who use drugs intensively and reducing their consumption.[38]

Finally, the fact that many serious offenses occur in the context of ongoing relationships suggests that some relationships may be criminogenic. Relationships can cause crime because they create expectations. If the expectations are not met, the resulting disappointment produces anger. Anger may lead to vengeance and retaliation. In such cycles, the question of who caused the ultimate crime becomes confused. Usually, the offender is the one least damaged after the fight. A court may conclude that the crime stemmed from the evil intentions of the person identified as the offender. But this may not be the best way to view the problem from the vantage point of crime control or crime prevention.

It might be more suitable to see the crimes as emerging from a set of relationships that are frustrating and provocative. The proper response might be to work on the relationship through mediation, restructuring, or dissolution. Indeed, this is often the challenge confronting the police when they encounter spouse abuse, child abuse, and other sorts of intrafamily violence. In such situations, arrests may be appropriate and effective in deterring future crime and in restructuring the relationship.[39] There are many other crimes which emerge from less obvious relationships: the personal relationships of neighbors and friends; the economic relations of landlord and tenant or employer and employee; or transient relations that last just long enough to provoke a quarrel or seed a grudge. Seen this way, many serious crimes—including murders, robberies, rapes, and burglaries—are disputes and grievances among people rather than criminal attacks.

CONTROLLING SERIOUS CRIME

Currently the police fight serious crime by developing a capacity to intercept it—to be in the right place at the right time so that the crime is thwarted, or to arrive so quickly after the fact that the offender is caught. Reactive crime fighting is intuitively appealing to both the police and those to whom the police are accountable. It is unclear, however, whether the reactive response really works. Over the last two decades, confidence in the reactive approach has been eroded by the accumulation of empirical evidence suggesting that these tactics are of only limited effectiveness. It is not that the approach fails to control crime. (It would be foolish to imagine that levels of serious crime would stay the same if police patrols and investigations were halted.) Rather, the limits of the reactive strategy are now becoming apparent. Further gains in police effectiveness in dealing with serious crime must come from different approaches. Key research findings suggesting the limitations of the reactive approach are these.

First, the Kansas City Preventive Patrol Study found that levels of serious crime were not significantly influenced by doubling the number of cars patrolling the streets.[40] This cast doubt on the potential for reducing serious crime simply by increasing the level of preventive patrol.

Second, a study of the effectiveness of rapid response to calls for service (also in Kansas City) found that the probability of making an arrest for most serious crimes was unaffected by the speed with which the police responded. The crucial factor was not the speed of the police response, but the speed with which citizens raised the alarm. If citizens did not notice the crime, or did not call the police quickly, no amount of speed in the police response helped much.[41]

Third, studies of the investigative process revealed that the key factor in determining whether a crime was solved was the quality of the information contributed to the investigation by victims and witnesses about the identity of the offender.[42] If they could not be helpful, forensic wizardry generally was not up to solving the crime.

It is important to understand that these weaknesses appeared in precisely those areas of crime control where the reactive strategy should have been particularly strong: i.e., in dealing with crimes such as murder, rape, robbery, assault, and burglary. These crimes could be expected to produce alarms; they also were interceptable and solvable by a vigilant police force waiting to be mobilized by outraged citizens.

There are, of course, many other kinds of serious crimes for which the reactive police strategy is much more obviously inappropriate.[43] It cannot, for example, deal with consensual crimes such as drug dealing behind closed doors. Nor can it deal with crimes such as extortion and loan sharking where the victims are too afraid to report the crimes. A reactive strategy cannot deal with sophisticated white collar crimes or political corruption where the losses associated with the crimes are so widely distributed that people do not notice that they have been victimized. Finally, a reactive strategy cannot deal even with traditional street crimes in those parts of cities where confidence in the police has eroded to such a degree that the citizens no longer call when they are victimized.

Although these findings and intrinsic limitations of the reactive strategy have not unseated the intuitive appeal of the wide experience with the reactive crime fighting strategy, they have added to a growing sense of frustration within police departments. Confronted by high levels of crime and limited budgets, the police felt a growing need for initiative and thoughtfulness in tackling serious crime. Working within the logic of their current approaches, but reaching for additional degrees of effectiveness, during the 1970's the police developed new proactive tactics.

DEVELOPMENTS IN PROACTIVE CRIME FIGHTING

To deal with serious street crime, the police developed the tactic of directed patrol. Sometimes these patrols were aimed at locations that seemed particularly vulnerable to crimes, such as branch banks, convenience stores, and crowded bars. Other times, the patrols were focused on individuals who, on the basis of past record or recent information, were thought to be particularly active offenders.[44]

The police sought to attack street robberies and muggings through anti-crime squads that sent decoys into the streets to prompt active muggers into committing a crime in the full view of the police. The police also sought to control home robberies and burglaries through sting operations involving undercover officers who operate as fences to identify and gather evidence against the offenders.

Finally, the police sought to enhance the effective impact of their enforcement efforts by increasing the quality of the cases they made. Quality Investigation Programs[45] and Integrated Criminal Apprehension Programs[46] were adopted by many departments to increase the likelihood that arrests would be followed by convictions and long prison sentences.

For the most part, each of these innovations produced its successes. The perpetrator-oriented patrols, sting operations, and quality investigation efforts were a little more successful than the location-oriented directed patrols and the undercover operations directed against street robbery. Nonetheless, the police did demonstrate that concentrated efforts could increase arrests, clearances, and convictions. These efforts did not show that these programs alone—without the support of courts and corrections and the involvement of the community—could reduce aggregate levels of serious crime in the cities in which they were tried.

Moreover, insofar as each program took a more aggressive and proactive approach to crime, it also troubled those who were concerned that the police not become too intrusive. Perpetrator-oriented patrols, for example, raised the question of whether it was appropriate to target offenders rather than offenses, and if so, on what evidentiary basis.[47] The use of undercover tactics to deal with both robbery and burglary raised important questions about entrapment.[48] And the emphasis on producing convictions from arrests prompted worries that the police might be motivated to manufacture as well as simply record and preserve evidence. Arguably, these civil liberties concerns were inappropriate at a time when the police seemed unable to deal with high crime rates. The fact that these concerns arose, however, indicated that the police were, in fact, using their authority more intensively than they had when they were relying principally on reactive strategies. Such concerns must be reckoned a cost of the new efforts.

The police also made substantial investments in their ability to deal with those crimes that could not be handled through routine patrol or investigative operations, either because the crimes were too complicated to handle with ordinary arrest and investigative methods, or because the routine operations would not disclose the crime. In terms of dealing with especially demanding crimes, like hostage taking or well-armed offenders, the police developed Special Weapons and Arrest Teams. They also enhanced their capacities to deal with riots and demonstrations. And at the other end of the spectrum, the police developed special procedures for dealing with deranged and disordered offenders who often looked violent (and sometimes were) but mostly were simply mentally disturbed.

To deal with crimes that were not always revealed through the ordinary procedures of complaints by victims and witnesses, the police developed special units skilled in investigating the sensitive areas of child sexual abuse, rape, and domestic assault. They also created special investigative units to deal with high-level drug dealing, organized crime, arson, and sophisticated frauds. These units often relied on special intelligence files as well as special investigative procedures, such as the recruitment of informants, electronic wiretaps, and sustained undercover investigations. These programs also scored their successes and enhanced the ability of the police to deal with serious crime.

MISSED OPPORTUNITIES IN CRIME FIGHTING?

These innovations demonstrated the resourcefulness and creativity of the police as they faced the challenge of high crime rates with limited financial resources, diminished authority, and constrained managerial prerogatives. With the benefit of hindsight, however, some crucial oversights are apparent.

First, there was little appreciation of the crucial role that better information from the community could play in strengthening police performance.[49] It was not that the police were unaware of their dependency on citizens for information. Long before it was demonstrated that the success of rapid response to crime calls and retrospective investigation depended on the willingness of victims and witnesses to report crimes and aid in their solution, the police had mounted campaigns mobilizing citizens to support their local police.

The real problem was that the police did not adequately consider what was needed to attract that support. They thought that their interest and ready availability would be sufficient. They did not understand that citizens felt vulnerable to retaliation by offenders in the community and needed a closer connection with the police if they were going to help them solve the crime. Nor did the police understand that a partnership with the community could be constructed only from the material of daily encounters with the public; in particular, by taking seriously the public's concern with less serious offenses. In short, while the police knew that they were dependent on the community for information about crime, they never asked the public what was needed to obtain help beyond setting up 911 systems.

Second, the police rarely looked behind an offense to its precipitating causes. Nor did they think about crime prevention in terms of managing the precipitating causes. They knew, of course, that much crime was being produced by dangerous offenders, criminogenic situations, alcohol and drug abuse, and aggravating relationships. But they were ambivalent about acting on that knowledge. They tended to limit their responsibilities to applying the law to incidents to which they were summoned; they did not think in terms of applying instruments of civil law or the capacities of other city agencies to work on the proximate causes of crime. Criminal investigations emphasized legal evidence of guilt or innocence—not the question of precipitating causes.

There were many reasons to maintain this narrow focus on law enforcement. To a degree, it protected police organizations from criticisms that they were lawless and out of control. The police could explain that they merely enforced the laws and that they exercised no discretion beyond this basic function. The narrow focus on law enforcement also protected the organization from failure in its basic crime control mission. If the police role was limited to applying the criminal law to offenses rather than to the more challenging goal of actually preventing and controlling crime, the police could succeed even if crime were not controlled. They could blame the other parts of the criminal justice system for their failures to deter and incapacitate the offenders whom the police had arrested. Finally, the narrow focus was consistent with the training and aspirations of the police themselves. Arresting people and using authority was real police work; mediating disputes, mobilizing communities, and badgering other city agencies for improved services was social work.

Whatever the reasons, the police remained reluctant to develop the internal capabilities needed to make their anecdotal impressions of precipitating causes systematic and powerful. Crime analysis sections merely kept statistics or characterized the location of crime; they did not identify dangerous offenders or trouble spots and avoided examining the role of alcohol and drugs in the serious crime problem. Nor did they propose alternative methods for dealing with crime problems. From the perspective of the police, it was far better to stay at the surface of social life and respond to crimes as they occurred rather than to intervene more widely and actively to manage the immediate conditions that were producing crimes.

Third, the police never fully exploited the self-defense capacities of the community itself. They did offer advice to merchants and citizen groups about how they could protect themselves from criminal victimization. And they helped organize neighborhood watch groups. But the main efforts went into helping the communities become more effective operational auxiliaries to the police departments. Citizens were encouraged to mark their property not only because it helped the police solve the crime, should the item be stolen, but also because it allowed the police to return the property to the owners. Crime watch groups were instructed to call the police rather than to intervene themselves. This was consistent with the desires of the police to maintain their monopoly on both expertise and operational capability in dealing with crime. They did not really want any growth in private security—whether it took the form of volunteer associations such as the Guardian Angels or commercial operations such as Burns Security Guards. Because of that interest, police commitment to building a community's self-defense capacities was always ambivalent. And, because they were ambivalent, the police did not think through the question of whether and how such efforts could actually help them control serious crime.

PROBLEM-SOLVING AND COMMUNITY APPROACHES TO CRIME CONTROL

In the 1980's, police departments throughout the country have begun to explore the crime-fighting effectiveness of tactics that build on previous approaches, but seek to extend them by looking behind offenses to the precipitating causes of crimes, building closer relations with the community, and seeking to enhance the self-defense capacities of the communities themselves. These efforts are guided mostly by a theory of what might work and some illustrative examples. The theory is that the effectiveness of existing tactics can be enhanced if the police increase the quantity and quality of their contacts with citizens (both individuals and neighborhood groups), and include in their responses to crime problems thoughtful analyses of the precipitating causes of the offenses. The expectation is that this will both enhance the direct effectiveness of the police department and also enable the police department to leverage the resources of citizen groups and other public agencies to control crime.

Some examples, drawn from recent experiences, suggest the ways in which these new approaches can lead to enhanced crime control.

Enhanced police presence. From its inception, patrol has sought to prevent crime through the presence, or potential presence, of a conspicuous officer. Patrolling in cars is only one way to communicate police presence, however. Activities such as foot patrol, visiting citizens in their homes, and attending group meetings also increase the awareness of police to which all citizens respond—those intent on crime as well as those not. This presence both deters potential offenders from committing crimes and affords officers the opportunities to note criminal acts in progress.

Example: A youth walking down a street in a small business section of town sees an unlocked automobile with the key in the ignition. He is tempted to steal it. Glancing around, he notes a police officer a short distance away walking down the street. The youth decides not to enter the car for fear of being caught by the officer.

Example: An officer, through crime analysis, becomes aware of a pattern of burglaries in a neighborhood. Increasing her patrol in alleyways, she notes a youth attempting to enter the back window of a residence. She makes an arrest.

Although the success of foot patrol tactics in controlling crime is counter-intuitive to those accustomed to patrol by automobile, confidence in this approach is common in England. There, when an anticrime unit is sent in to deal with a serious crime problem, as often as not it consists of foot patrol. The approach is successful because foot patrol officers have access to areas unavailable to officers in cars: walkways and areas between houses, for example. Unpublished work by Glenn Pierce suggests that some crimes, such as burglary, tend to be patterned within limited geographical and chronological space. If this is true, when combined with what is known about how burglars enter homes and businesses, properly targeted foot patrol might be the strongest potential anticrime tactic to deal with such crimes.

Better surveillance and deterrence of dangerous offenders. From the outset, police have sought to control crime through close surveillance of those who have committed crimes in the past. The problem has been to accurately identify those offenders. Police officers who work closely with a neighborhood are in a position to learn who behaves in criminal or delinquent ways within the community. By stationing themselves in particular locations, officers can surveil known troublemakers and forestall criminal behavior.

Example: Police investigation of a rash of robberies committed by juveniles involved house-to-house interviews of the neighborhood. In these interviews, photographs of suspects were shown to residents. While no information about the crimes was produced, the word rapidly spread through the neighborhood that the police were keeping close tabs on specific individuals. The robberies stopped without an arrest.

It is also legally and procedurally possible to consider assigning neighborhood police officers to the surveillance of probationers and parolees. Such surveillance would be more immediate and regular than that now provided by probation or parole officers. Aware that neighborhood police officers had easier access to information about their activities, people who were in the community on a conditional basis might be deterred from committing illegal acts.

Example: Paroled sexual offenders in a conservative state regularly move to a community known for its relatively open values. A plan is worked out between local police and the state correctional agency. Upon parole, all sexual offenders returning to this community are interviewed by the chief of patrol and the neighborhood officer policing the area in which the parolee is to live. An offender known for attacks on teenage girls returns to the community. Regular contacts between the officer and parolee are scheduled to enable the police officer to oversee the parolee's behavior while in the community. The police officer discovers that the parolee is now working in the local fast food restaurant—a workplace which regularly hires teenage girls. The officer, in conjunction with the parole officer, requires that the parolee find a different job, one in which young girls are not always present.

Increased access to information. Community policing emphasizes the development of close communication between citizens and police. This communication helps police gather information for both *preventing* and *solving* crime.

Example: In an area frequented by many street people, a street person approaches a neighborhood police officer to inform him that a stranger from another neighborhood is attempting to recruit assistance to commit a street robbery. The street person describes the newcomer to the police officer. Shortly afterwards while patrolling, the officer notices a person on the street who matches the description. The officer approaches the person, questions him, tells him that he (the officer) is aware of what he is planning, and instructs him to leave the area.

Example: Shortly after leaving her church a woman is mugged on the street. She appears to be seriously injured as a result of being knocked to the ground. Police and medics are called. The neighborhood officer responds by foot. She is approached by several children and their parents. The children were playing in an open space in the public housing project across the street from the church and saw the youth mug the woman. They know the youth and where he lives. Accompanied by a neighborhood entourage, including the parents and children who identified the youth, the officer proceeds to the apartment and makes the arrest.

Familiarity with the social and physical characteristics of their beats also helps neighborhood police officers to understand linkages between various pieces of information gathered from their own observations and from other disparate sources.

Example: Parents have complained to a neighborhood police officer about an increase of drug availability in their neighborhood. Several parents have found drugs in their children's possession. In addition, the officer has noticed many youths congregating around an entrance to a second-story apartment over several stores. The officer contacts the drug unit and informs them of his suspicion that drugs are being sold to children from that apartment. The drug unit arranges an undercover "buy" and then "busts" the dealers.

Work by Pate,[50] Greenwood, Chaiken and Petersilia,[51] Eck,[52] and Skogan and Antunes[53] suggests that use of information gathered by patrol officers is one of the most important ways in which police can improve their ability to apprehend offenders. In 1982, Baltimore County, Maryland initiated a Citizen Oriented Police Enforcement unit (COPE), designed to bring the police into closer contact with the citizens and reduce their fears. A 1985 study showed that not only had COPE reduced fear, but also it has apparently produced a 12 percent reduction in the level of reported crime.[54]

Early intervention to prevent the escalation of disorder into crime. In a widely read article, Kelling and Wilson argue that there is an important causal link between minor instances of disorder and the occurrence of serious crime.[55] Disorderly behavior—youths congregating, drunks lying down, prostitutes aggressively soliciting—left untended, can escalate into serious crime. The implication is that intervention by police to stop uncivil behavior keeps it from escalating.

Example: Youths panhandle in a subway station. Citizens give money both out of charitable motives and because they are fearful. Youths, emboldened by citizen fear, intimidate and, finally, threaten and mug subway users. Intervention by police to end panhandling by youths reduces threatening and mugging of citizens.

Although this argument has intuitive appeal, little direct empirical evidence exists about exploiting its anticrime potential.

Crime prevention activities. An important part of community policing is providing anticrime consultation to citizens, businesses, and other community institutions. The recommendations range from home target hardening (locks, strengthened doors, etc.) to street and building design.

Example: Residents of a neighborhood have been troubled by daytime burglaries. In addition to planning a police response, police consult with homeowners about ways in which they can make their homes more secure from burglars. Suggestions include moving shrubs away from doorways, strengthening locks, securing windows, and taking other burglary prevention precautions.

A 1973 evaluation of Seattle's Community Crime Prevention Program, which used this approach, found a significant reduction in burglaries.[56]

Shoring up community institutions. Institutions of neighborhood social control include families, churches, schools, local businesses, and neighborhood and community organizations.

In many communities, the corrosive effects of social disorganization have seriously weakened such organizations. Police, working with such institutions and organizations, can reinforce their normative strength in a community.

Example: Drug dealing is a serious problem in an inner-city neighborhood. Drug dealers not only have dealt drugs freely, but also have intimidated residents to the extent that they are afraid to complain to police. A local church decides that the problem is so serious that an organized effort must be made to attack the problem. Church officials contact the police and ask them to work closely with the neighborhood group. Citizens demonstrate against drug dealing, getting both police protection and great publicity. Citywide and local political leaders, as well as other public and private agencies, become concerned about the problem and develop a concerted effort to reduce drug dealing and intimidation. Sustained street-level enforcement ends drug dealing in that location.

Example: Using up-to-date technology, police are able to identify the patterns of a burglary ring which is moving through a neighborhood. Police contact the local neighborhood anticrime group and inform its members of the patterns so that they can be alert and watch their own and each others' homes.

Example: A woman who lives in public housing has been troubled by attempts of local gangs to recruit her youngest son. Up to now, his older brother has been able to protect him. Now, however, the older brother is going into the service. Approached by the mother, the neighborhood police officer now keeps an eye out for the youngster on the way to and from school as well as on the playground.

Example: A local school is plagued by dropouts who continually hang around the school intimidating both students and teachers. Crime has increased in and around the school. The principal decides to crack down on the problem. The neighborhood police officer becomes involved in the efforts. He teaches a course in youth and the law, increases his surveillance of the grounds, consults with the teachers about handling problems, and invokes other agencies to become involved with the youths who have dropped out of school.

Although promising, it is unclear what impact the strengthening of community institutions has on serious crime. It is an attractive idea, however.

Problem solving. Police have historically viewed calls for service and criminal events as individual incidents. Many such incidents are part of a chronic problem amenable to diagnosis and preventive intervention by either police or other agencies.

Example: Police and citizens note an increase in daytime burglaries in a particular neighborhood. This neighborhood has also been characterized by high rates of truancy. Suspecting that many burglaries are committed by truants, police, citizens, and school officials plan a carefully integrated anti-truancy campaign. Daytime burglaries drop.

Problem solving appears to be a promising approach to deter crime. When, in 1985, the Newport News Police Department turned to problem-oriented policing as an approach to dealing with crime, it was successful in dealing with three stubborn crime problems that had beset the community: a series of prostitution-related robberies; a rash of burglaries in a housing project; and larcenies from vehicles parked in downtown areas. In each case, the problem was solved not simply by solving the crimes and arresting offenders, nor by increasing levels of patrol (though both were done), but also by operating on the immediate conditions that were giving rise to the offenses.[57]

These ideas, examples, and results lend plausibility to the notion that problem-solving or community policing can enhance the crime control capabilities of professional crime fighting. They do not prove the case, however.

A STRATEGIC VIEW OF CRIME FIGHTING

While police executives can produce increased levels of arrest and local reductions in crime through the creation of special programs, they are frustrated because they do not know how to produce reductions in citywide levels of crime. The main reason for this might be that their main force is not engaged in a serious crime-fighting effort even though it seems that it is. After all, it would be unreasonable to imagine that any single small program, typically engaging less than 5 percent of the force, could have much impact on aggregate levels of crime. The important question is what is the remaining 95 percent of the force doing? For the most part, the answer is that they are deployed in patrol cars, responding to calls for service and investigating crimes after they have occurred. These tactics have only limited effectiveness.

What remains unanswered is the consequence of shifting a whole department to a radically different style of policing. Moreover, the answer is hard to determine, since the period of transition would be quite awkward. In the short run, were officers taken from patrol and detective units to do problem-oriented or community policing, it is almost certain that response times would lengthen—at least until the problem-solving efforts reduced the demands for service by eliminating the precipitating problem that was producing the calls for service.[58] And even though an increase in response times does not necessarily indicate a real loss in crime-fighting effectiveness, it would be perceived as such because the public and the police have learned to equate rapid response to crime calls with crime control effectiveness.

What is tempting, of course, is to avoid choosing among these strategies, and to adopt the strengths of these various approaches while avoiding their weaknesses. This would be reflected in decisions to establish special units to do problem-solving or community policing within existing organizations whose traditions and main forces remained committed to reactive patrol and retrospective investigation.

But it may not be this easy. Indeed, experience demonstrates that it is not. Previous initiatives with team policing or split-force policing succeeded in building capacities for both styles of policing within the same department, but tended to foster eventual competition and conflict.[59] The problem-solving and community policing aspects have usually eventually yielded to administrative demands to keep response times low, or to officers' desires to avoid the demanding engagement with the community. The reason seems to be partly a matter of resources—there has never been enough manpower to maximize performance in both domains at once. But it also seems to be a matter of administrative style and structure. Problem-solving and community policing both require a greater degree of decentralization than does the current policing strategy. They depend more on the initiative of the officers. And they reach out for a close rather than a distant relationship with the community. These are all quite different than the administrative emphases of the current strategy which prescribe centralization, control, and distance from the community.

So while logic and evidence suggest the crime control potential of adding problem-solving and community policing to the concept of rapid response and retrospective investigation, it is hard to add these functions without increasing the resources and significantly changing the administrative style of a police organization. That is hard for a police chief to decide to do without convincing evidence that it would work. The only things that make such a move easy to contemplate are: (1) a deep sense that the current strategy and tactics have reached their limits; (2) the plausibility of the idea that increased effectiveness lies in working on proximate causes and mobilizing communities; and (3) the little bit of evidence we have that the alternative approach works. A few departments, such as Houston, Newport News, Baltimore County, and Philadelphia, have committed themselves to these alternative approaches. If they succeed over the next 3 to 5 years in reducing serious crime as well as in attracting citizen support, then the field will know that it has a better strategy of policing available than is now being used.

NOTES

1.   For descriptions of these alternative strategies, see Robert C. Trojanowicz, "Community Policing vs. 'High Tech' Policing: What's in a Name?" (Unpublished paper, Michigan State University, April 1987); Herman Goldstein, *The Urban Police Function* (Cambridge, Massachusetts: Ballinger Publishing, 1977); John Eck and William Spelman, "Solving Problems: Problem-Oriented Policing in Newport News" (Washington, DC: Police Executive Research Forum, January 1987).

2.   George L. Kelling and Mark H. Moore, "From Political to Reform to Community: The Evolving Strategy of Police" (Program in Criminal Justice Policy and Management, John F. Kennedy School of Government, Harvard University, Cambridge, 1987), Working Paper #87-05-08.

3. President's Commission on Law Enforcement and Administration of Justice, *Task Force Report: Science and Technology* (Washington, D.C.: U.S. Government Printing Office, 1967). Jan M. Chaiken and Warren Walker, *Patrol Car Allocation Model* (Santa Monica: The Rand Corporation, 1985). Richard C. Larson, *Police Deployment From Urban Public Safety Systems,* Vol. I (Lexington, Massachusetts: Lexington Books, 1978). David M. Kennedy, "Patrol Allocation in Portland, OR, Part A: PCAM in the Bureau," Case #C95-88-818.0 and "Patrol Allocation in Portland, OR, Part B: PCAM in the City," Case #C95-88-819.0 (Cambridge: Case Program, John F. Kennedy School of Government, 1988).

4. J. Thomas McEwen, Edward F. Connors III, and Marcia Cohen, *Evaluation of the Differential Police Response Field Test* (Washington, D.C.: U.S. Government Printing Office, 1986). Richard P. Grassie and John A. Hollister, *Integrated Criminal Apprehension Program: A Preliminary Guideline Manual for Patrol Operations Analysis* (Washington, D.C.: LEAA, U.S. Department of Justice, 1977).

5. James Q. Wilson, "The Police and Crime," in *Thinking About Crime* (New York: Vintage Books, 1975), Chapter 4. Larson, *Police Deployment From Urban Public Safety Systems.*

6. Orlando W. Wilson, *The Distribution of the Police Patrol Force* (Chicago: Public Administration Service, 1941).

7. Alfred Blumstein et al., *Deterrence and Incapacitation: Estimating the Effects of Criminal Sanctions on the Crime Rate* (Washington, D.C.: National Academy of Sciences, 1978).

8. Ibid.

9. Mark H. Moore, *Buy and Bust: The Effective Regulation of an Illicit Market in Heroin* (Lexington, Massachusetts: Lexington Books, 1977). Peter K. Manning, *The Narc's Game: Organizational and Informational Limits on Drug Law Enforcement* (Cambridge: MIT Press, 1980). Mark H. Moore, "Invisible Offenses: A Challenge to Minimally Intrusive Law Enforcement," in Gerald M. Caplan, ed., *Abscam Ethics* (Washington, D.C.: Police Foundation, 1983). Gary Marx, "Who Really Gets Stung? Some Issues Raised by the New Police Undercover Work," in Caplan, *Abscam Ethics.*

10. George L. Kelling, "Juveniles and Police: The End of the Nightstick," in Francis X. Hartmann, ed., *From Children to Citizens,* Vol. 2: *The Role of the Juvenile Court* (New York: Springer-Verlag, 1987).

11. The exception is Marvin Wolfgang's work devoted to measuring crime seriousness as perceived by citizens. See Marvin E. Wolfgang and Thorsten Sellin, *The Measurement of Crime Seriousness* (New York: Wiley Publishing, 1964). See also Mark H. Moore et al., *Dangerous Offenders: The Elusive Target of Justice* (Cambridge: Harvard University Press, 1984), Chapter 2.

12. Bureau of Justice Statistics, *The Severity of Crime* (Washington, D.C.: U.S. Department of Justice, January 1984), p. 5.

13. Susan Estrich, *Real Rape* (Cambridge: Harvard University Press, 1987).

14. Bureau of Justice Statictics, *The Severity of Crime.*

15. Ibid.

16. For a view of crime as a dispute rather than an attack, see Donald Black, *The Manners and Customs of the Police* (New York: Academic Press, 1980), Chapter 5. For important empirical evidence, see Vera Institute of Justice, *Felony Arrests: Their Prosecution and Disposition in The New York City Courts* (New York, 1981).

17. Bureau of Justice Statistics, "Households Touched By Crime 1986," *BJS Bulletin* (Washington D.C.: U.S. Department of Justice, June 1987).

18. Bureau of Justice Statistics, *Report to the Nation on Crime and Justice* (Washington, DC: U.S. Department of Justice, 1983).

19. Patrick W. O'Carroll and James A. Mercy, "Patterns and Recent Trends in Black Homicide," in Darnell F. Hawkins, ed., *Homicide Among Black Americans* (Lanham, Maryland: University Press of America, 1986).
20. Bureau of Justice Statistics, "Households Touched by Crime."
21. James Q. Wilson, "Criminologists," in *Thinking About Crime* (New York: Vintage Books, 1975), Chapter 3.
22. For a discussion of this concept and its importance to police strategies, see Moore et al., *Dangerous Offenders,* Chapter 7.
23. Alfred Blumstein et al., *Criminal Careers and Career Criminals,* Vol. 1 (Washington, D.C.: National Academy Press, 1986).
24. Jan Chaiken and Marcia Chaiken, *Varieties of Criminal Behavior* (Santa Monica, California: The Rand Corporation, August 1982).
25. Peter W. Greenwood and Sue Turner, *Selective Incapacitation, Revisited for the National Institute of Justice* (Santa Monica, California: The Rand Corporation, 1987).
26. Moore et al., *Dangerous Offenders.*
27. Glenn Pierce et al., "Evaluation of an Experiment in Proactive Police Intervention in the Field of Domestic Violence Using Repeat Call Analysis" (Boston, Massachusetts: The Boston Fenway Program, Inc., May 13, 1987).
28. Lawrence W. Sherman, "Repeat Calls to Police in Minneapolis" (College Park, Maryland: University of Maryland, 1987).
29. This example of youth transportation comes from Christine Nixon's experience in New South Wales, Australia. For other examples, see John Eck and William Spelman, "Solving Problems: Problem-Oriented Policing."
30. Mark H. Moore, "Controlling Criminogenic Commodities: Drugs, Guns, and Alcohol," in James Q. Wilson, ed., *Crime and Public Policy* (San Francisco: Institute for Contermporary Studies Press, 1983).
31. Eric Wish, "Drug Use Forecasting System" (Unpublished working paper at the National Institute of Justice, Washington, D.C., January 1988).
32. Ibid.
33. Marvin E. Wolfgang, *Patterns in Criminal Homicide* (Montclair, New Jersey: Patterson Smith Publishing, 1975). James Collins, *Alcohol Use and Criminal Behavior: An Executive Summary* (Washington, D.C.: U.S. Department of Justice, 1981).
34. Mark H. Moore, "Drugs and Crime: A Policy Analytic Approach," Appendix to Report of the Panel on Drug Use and Criminal Behavior, *Drug Use and Crime* (Washington, D.C.: The National Institute on Drug Abuse and Research Triangle Institute, 1976).
35. David Levinson, "Alcohol Use and Aggression in American Subcultures," in Robin Room and Gary Collins, eds., *Alcohol and Didingibition: Nature and Meaning of the Link* (Washington, DC: U.S. Department of Health and Human Services, 1983).
36. Moore, "Controlling Criminogenic Commodities."
37. Wolfgang, *Patterns in Criminal Homicide.*
38. M. Douglas Anglin and Yih-Ing Hser, "Treatment of Drug Abuse," manuscript to be published in Michael Tonry and James Q. Wilson, eds., *Drugs and Crime,* a special volume of *Crime and Justice: A Review of Research* (Chicago: University of Chicago Press, forthcoming).
39. Sherman, "Repeat Calls to Police in Minneapolis."
40. George L. Kelling, *Kansas City Preventive Patrol Experiment: A Summary Report* (Washington, D.C.: Police Foundation, 1974).
41. *Response Time Analysis* (Kansas City, Missouri: Kansas City Police Department, 1977).

42. Peter W. Greenwood, Jan M. Chaiken, and Joan Petersilia, *The Criminal Investigation Process* (Lexington, Massachusetts: D.C. Heath, 1977). John Eck, *Managing Case Assignments: Burglary Investigation Decision Model Replication* (Washington, D.C.: Police Executive Research Forum, 1979).
43. Moore, "Invisible Offenses."
44. Antony Pate, Robert Bowers, and Ron Parks, *Three Approaches to Criminal Apprehension in Kansas City: An Evaluation Report* (Washington, D.C.: Police Foundation, 1976).
45. Jerome E. McElroy, Colleen Cosgrove, and Michael Farrell, *Felony Case Preparation: Quality Counts,* Interim Report of the New York City Police Department Felony Case Preparation Project (New York: Vera Institute of Justice, 1981).
46. Grassie and Hollister, *Integrated Criminal Apprehension Program.*
47. Moore et al., *Dangerous Offenders,* Chapter 7.
48. Marx, "Who Really Gets Stung?"
49. Wesley G. Skogan and George E. Antunes, "Information, Apprehension, and Deterrence: Exploring the Limits of Police Productivity," *Journal of Criminal Justice,* 1979, No. 7, pp. 217-242.
50. Pate et al., *Three Approaches to Criminal Apprehension.*
51. Greenwood et al., *The Criminal Investigation Process.*
52. Eck, *Managing Case Assignments.*
53. Skogan and Antunes, "Information, Apprehension, and Deterrence."
54. Philip B. Taft, Jr., "Fighting Fear: The Baltimore County COPE Project" (Washington, D.C.: Police Executive Research Forum, February 1986), p. 20.
55. James Q. Wilson and George L. Kelling, "Broken Windows," *Atlantic Monthly,* March 1982, pp. 29-38.
56. Betsy Lindsay and Daniel McGillis, "Citywide Community Crime Prevention: An Assessment of the Seattle Program," in Dennis P. Rosenbaum, ed., *Community Crime Prevention: Does It Work?* (Beverly Hills, California: Sage Publications, 1986).
57. Eck and Spelman, "Solving Problems: Problem-Oriented Policing."
58. Calls for service declined in Flint, Michigan, after foot patrol was established and officers were handling less serious complaints informally. Robert Trojanowicz, *An Evaluation of the Neighborhood Foot Patrol Program in Flint, Michigan* (East Lansing: Michigan State University, 1982), pp. 29-30.
59. George L. Kelling and Mary Ann Wycoff, *The Dallas Experience: Human Resource Development* (Washington, D.C.: Police Foundation, 1978). James Tien et al., *An Alternative Approach in Police Patrol: The Wilmington Split-Force Experiment* (Cambridge, Massachusetts: Public Systems Evaluation Inc., 1977).

POLICE IN THE LABORATORY OF CRIMINAL JUSTICE   2

Lawrence W. Sherman

POLICE THINKING ABOUT VIOLENT CRIME

Traditional police thinking about crime has put the cart before the horse: it has tried to make crime problems respond to police strategies, rather than crafting strategies to fit the crime problems. Ever since Patrick Colquhoun's eighteenth century treatise[1] laid out the basic strategy of uniformed civilians patrolling the streets to deter crime by the threat of arrest, police have attempted to apply that strategy to all forms of crime. For those crimes that police did not observe and intercept in progress, the even older strategy of detective investigations was the preferred approach. For almost two centuries Anglo-American police work has been little more than these two strategies in search of problems. Just as the eighteenth century physicians prescribed leeching out bad blood for almost all kinds of diseases, eighteenth century police thinkers prescribed patrol and investigations as the cures for all kinds of crime. When it became apparent that leeching did not work with all diseases (if any) physicians moved beyond this crudely simple approach to test more refined and specific strategies for curing different diseases. But the spirit of scientific inquiry that guided the physicians bypassed the police, leaving them with little else but eighteenth century theories until about 1970. Only as a result of federal and foundation funding was scientific diagnosis, theory-building and experimentation brought to bear on police strategies for fighting crime.

Even then, however, the research and testing was driven by basic strategies rather than by diagnosis of the problems. One study, for exam-

Source: Lawrence W. Sherman (1983). "Police in the Laboratory of Criminal Justice." In Kenneth Feinberg (ed.), *Violent Crime in America*. Washington, DC: National Policy Exchange.

ple, tested the effects of preventive patrol on hundreds of types of crime as well as on public perceptions of safety—and found it lacking.[2] We have tested the ability of detectives to solve all kinds of crimes and arrest suspects—and found it lacking.[3] But only recently have we implemented the "crime-specific" or problem-oriented philosophy first suggested a decade ago, testing what police can do about robbery of the elderly, violence between married couples or burglaries of detached houses unoccupied during business hours.

The traditional failure to begin with problems, rather than received strategies, is part of our more general tendency to confuse two very different problems: how to reduce *crime* and what to do about *criminals*. The two problems have been commingled on the mistaken assumption that punishing criminals is the primary, or perhaps only, method of reducing crime. It is not. There is much more to preventing crime than deterring potential criminals. Reducing opportunities for criminal access to vulnerable places, people and things is probably far more important for preventing crime and should be a major factor in constructing specific police strategies for specific crime problems. But if one begins with strategies focused only on the apprehension and punishment of criminals, the potential for crime prevention may never be fulfilled. Traditional police thinking is analogous to a strategy for reducing cancer that relies solely on surgery and treatment of those who already have cancer, with no attention to reducing cigarette smoking or other factors predisposing people to cancer.

Reformers have tried for years to improve police effectiveness at fighting crime. But the focus on strategies rather than specific problems produced a misguided reform agenda. Rather than trying new and different strategies for fighting crime, police reformers devoted most of their energy to altering the inputs for those strategies. Like most other thinkers in the era of good government reform, they believed in making government more "businesslike." They blamed the failure of patrol and investigations on poorly educated police officers, inadequately trained police managers, inflexible civil service systems, weak disciplinary controls and political interference.[4] To be sure, all of these inputs are major organizational problems in policing. But even with the best inputs possible, it is by no means clear that the two very blunt and general strategies of patrol and investigations are the best ways to deal with the myriad of crime problems that have very different causes and characteristics.

Consider motorized police patrol. Patrol may be a good way to deter strong arm robberies on the street and enforce minimal standards of civility in public places (such as not urinating on walls). But patrol makes little sense as a strategy for combating rape by a victim's acquaintance inside a house or robberies in office building elevators. Police *can* address these problems of violent crime in private places, but not through patrol.

A more sensible approach to policing violent crime would conform to the following model:

- Map out the nature of the problems, classifying them into different categories and sub-categories according to their most important characteristics.

- Determine the possible *causes* of each sub-category of a violent crime problem, separating those causes that police can affect and those causes that are beyond police control.

- List all of the possible police tactics or strategies that could affect any of the causes of the specific crime problem and develop an overall strategy that focuses on what appear to be the most potent (yet tractable) causes.

- Conduct field experiments to test the strategy and measure its effect on the specific crime problem.

THINKING MORE ABOUT THE CRIME PROBLEM

Just as biology describes each specific genus and species, a science of crime control must differentiate all the types of crime. Legal labels are not sufficient. The different behaviors encompassed within the legal definition of robbery, for example, are far too diverse for designing a robbery reduction strategy. All of them involve the use of force to obtain property from a victim. But there are many types of robberies: purse snatching by juveniles, bank robberies with bomb threats, midnight liquor store holdups with sawed off shotguns and planned ambushes of armored cars.

Each of these specific types of robberies may have different specific causes. Purse snatching by juveniles may be caused by the breakdown of the family in poor neighborhoods. The bank robberies may be caused by layoffs at a local factory or other short run economic problems. The liquor store and armored car holdups may be caused, in part, by the easy traffic in illicit weapons.

Some of the causes are clearly beyond police control: poverty, broken families, factory layoffs. They are the kinds of "intractable" factors that some people have accused sociologists of emphasizing in developing causal models. While these factors may have the greatest explanatory power in accounting for violent crime, it is pointless for the police to consider them in developing a crime reduction strategy. All police can do is focus on factors they have some ability to control, even if those factors are further down the list of leading causes of that type crime. Intercepting the traffic in weapons, for example, may help reduce the frequency of holdups using heavy armament, even though economic factors may be the major cause of such crimes.

To be sure, the causes of crime are by no means clear for any type of crime, let alone their rank order of importance. But it is not necessary (although it is certainly helpful) to know the causes of crime in order to reduce it. By making informed guesses about the causes of a type of crime and intervening in accord with those guesses, the police may discover what works to reduce that type of crime.

The process of breaking crime problems down into categories can proceed along several dimensions relevant to both causation and control. The nature of the relationships between victims and offenders, for example, provides a dimension along which most legal categories of crime can be subdivided: family, acquaintances and strangers. Police have almost no difficulty in apprehending suspects in family homicides, but they have great difficulty in apprehending suspects in stranger homicides. Another characteristic is the place in which crimes occur: public, semi-private (offices or commercial establishments) or private; high crime or low crime area, and locations in which cash is kept. A third characteristic, one that the law relies on heavily, is the tool of violence that is used in the crime: gun, knife, bomb, fist, club. Many other characteristics may be important for particular types of offenses.

The exact combinations of these characteristics vary widely within and across cities. Some cities have almost no homicide or arson; others are plagued with it daily. Some parts of a city may almost never see a robbery while other parts suffer almost all the robberies in the city. That is why there can be no one national or city-wide strategy to reduce crime. Rather, police strategies for reducing violent crime must be highly localized. What is appropriate for one neighborhood—or even one block—may not be appropriate for another area.

Police thinking about violent crime should begin with a crime analysis of small areas. Unfortunately, crime analysis has been concentrated at the city-wide level, since the only purpose of crime statistics has been to provide political accountability of the police department as a whole. Police precinct commanders, district sergeants and beat patrol officers have only recently (and only in some police agencies) been able to gain access to computerized data analysis of crime problems in their localized areas. Even now, the statistical categories into which crimes are grouped are not informative enough to help design a crime reduction strategy. The relationship between the victim and offender, for example, is often omitted from statistical tabulations for many types of crime. The absence of these breakdowns can be dangerously misleading. An overall decline in aggravated assault, for example, may mask a sharp increase in knife fights between Laotian and Cuban immigrants.

Manual analysis of crime reports, however, can pick up almost any important characteristic. If enough models of this procedure are created and publicized, police managers will be able to perform their own detailed crime analysis and draw on a range of tested crime reduction strategies, just as doctors draw from a range of tested treatments of disease based on their diagnoses of patients' symptoms. The crime analysis and diagnosis is the easy part. The hard part is developing and testing the crime reduction strategies.

THINKING ABOUT CRIME PREVENTION

Even though patrol and investigations are blunt tools, we should not be too quick to abandon them. One reason is that it is hard to think of many alternative approaches that do not embody the basic ideas of patrol and detective work. Another reason is that the number of studies suggesting the ineffectiveness of these strategies is too small to be conclusive. Finally, even if patrol and investigations are indeed ineffective as they are currently organized and performed, that does not mean that they cannot be effective if they are performed differently.

For thousands of years, human societies have used three basic crime prevention strategies: watching, walling and wariness. The tactics have varied enormously, but the basic theory of each strategy has remained constant. *Watching* a potential crime target is an attempt to deter potential criminals by the threat of immediate apprehension, as well as a way of making sure that apprehension takes place—often (but not always) before the attempt to commit a crime can be completed. Some people (like the President) or places (like Fort Knox) are watched all the time; others (like suburban homes) are watched infrequently and haphazardly by public police, although with increasing intensity by volunteer neighbors or paid private police. *Walling* is the use of physical devices to try to bar potential criminals from access to potential crime targets. *Wariness* is any change in someone's life-style or behavior intended to reduce their risk of criminal attack.

Historically, police have concentrated their efforts on watching. But their approach to watching has changed drastically over the past thirty years arguably to great detriment. On the other hand, they have recently taken a more active role in helping private citizens pursue strategies of walling and wariness.

The decline of police watching was an almost inevitable response to the suburbanization of America and the rise of the automobile. As the population spread into lower density housing, police patrols on foot became less efficient as a means of watching people and property. The police adopted automobile patrol as a way of watching more locations during each tour of duty. But there is no way to watch as many suburban homes and people simultaneously as could the foot patrol officers in high density neighborhoods.

Not only do police subject homes and people to less watching in cars than they did on foot, they employ a very different kind of watching. Patrol officers on foot among citizen pedestrians learn a great deal about the social context of the events they watch: the bondings of friendship, love, jealousy, kinship, gang membership, business and other relationships that can prevent or give rise to crime. Patrol officers in cars do not take the time to chat about such gossip nor do they develop the personal relationships with storekeepers, members of the clergy and others who can supply such information. With a rich knowledge of the social context of what they are watching, foot patrol officers have an excellent basis for determining what is suspicious and requires investigation. Patrol officers in cars do not know enough of the social context of an area to distinguish the normal from the abnormal, the mundane from the suspicious. The watching police provide in cars, stripped of contextual knowledge of the area, is necessarily so superficial that one may question whether it is truly watching at all.

It is not surprising that there is strong public support in many cities for a return to more foot patrol—to police officers you can get to know and talk to on the street rather than faceless uniforms inside a passing car. The growth in car patrols has coincided with an apparent decline in public confidence in the public police. At a time when private police companies are booming, selling their services to neighborhoods wanting extra watching services, voters have generally turned down propositions to increase local taxes to hire more public police. But in Flint, Michigan, a city suffering a serious unemployment problem, voters approved a tax increase to continue an experimental foot patrol program that had been funded for several years by the Mott Foundation.

Yet the police are deterred from a widespread reassignment of personnel to foot patrol by an equally strong public demand: that police respond to requests for emergency assistance within two to five minutes of citizen phone calls. Maintaining this rapid response, "dial-a-cop" capacity can only be accomplished by assigning most patrol officers to stay in their cars most of the time to wait for a call to come in. The emphasis on rapid response has several unfortunate consequences. It destroys police interest in watching as a crime prevention strategy, displacing it with *waiting* for an emergency call as the primary purpose of patrol. A great deal of time is wasted as a result. Just as firemen relax waiting for a fire, police often pass the time of day or run errands while waiting for a call. When a call occurs, they attempt to "handle" the call as quickly as possible and return to their cars to await the next call. This fosters a view of police work as merely a matter of managing situations and their immediate consequences, rather than focusing on the long-term implications of a situation for future crimes in the same relationship or location.

Ironically, the calls the police spend so much time waiting to occur are very rarely reports of serious crime. Many of them are minor problems of disorder or requests for police service that police label "garbage" calls. They are not the "real" police work of catching criminals. A good case can be made for the prospect that many of these minor problems could turn into serious crime and that police could take advantage of these situations to prevent it. Nonetheless, maintaining the rapid response capacity for a large number of minor calls, and only rarely for true emergencies, is a wasteful, inefficient and expensive policy. If the police are to improve their performance at *preventing* crime, they will have to find a way to wean the public from rapid police response to non-emergency calls.

Although police have been forced by the telephone and the automobile to abandon the traditional watching strategy, they have made some progress in helping the public do better at walling out access to criminals and developing wariness in their life-styles to prevent crime. Special crime prevention officers have taken advanced courses on locks, windows, landscaping, lighting and other aspects of physical security. Some of them have also been exposed to suggestions for what citizens should do if they are attacked by burglars, muggers or rapists, and how to avoid such attacks in the first place. These specialists convey the information on request at civic meetings, in schools and to families that have been victimized.

Three major limitations hinder this work as a crime prevention strategy. First, these public education officers are defined as public relations people whose primary job is to sell the police department. Since public relations is a marginal function, very few officers are assigned to it (in order to preserve resources for the rapid response to non-emergencies). Secondly, the advice they give citizens may well be wrong. There is little evidence, for example, that better locks or burglar alarms reduce the risks of burglary. Much more research is needed before any advice on walling or wariness can be given with more confidence. Third, the advice is rarely grounded in localized crime analysis, anchoring it to the specific kinds of crimes recently occurring in a particular block or neighborhood. Without a focus on the precise nature of local crime problems, citizens may be misguided into preventing the wrong kind of crime for their neighborhood.

Lack of analysis plagues police efforts at catching criminals as well as preventing crime. The most wasteful police activity aimed at apprehending criminals—detective investigations—was guided by almost no analysis until very recently. Most cases received roughly equal levels of effort, regardless of the likelihood of their leading to an arrest. Research produced a list of "solvability factors" that let detectives decide very quickly whether they should try to investigate a burglary or close the case as unsolvable, and this decision model has been widely adopted.[5] But most police efforts to catch criminals are still reactive to events on a case by case basis, with little focus on the setting of priorities for specific places, suspects or victims.

Research has shown, for example, that a small proportion of criminals account for a large portion of all violent crimes. But few cities have even attempted to identify the local major repeat offenders, let alone focus police resources on apprehending them. There is a national "ten most wanted criminals list," but few cities or police precincts maintain such a list of *local* criminals. The prevailing approach to criminal investigations is dominated by a reactive philosophy: handling the most recent event is the highest priority. Attempting to intercept criminals in the act based on analysis of past crimes is, in most agencies, a very low priority.

POLICING AND PREVENTING VIOLENT CRIME

Given this diagnosis of the flaws in current police strategies for reducing violent crime, what prescriptions can be offered? It is very hard to make any promises that different strategies will work better. But many new ideas for both preventing violent crime and catching violent criminals deserve to be tested. All of them presume a much greater level of analysis, planning and setting of priorities than police currently employ.

Following the approach described earlier, there are at least three different ways for police to focus their efforts at preventing violent crime in highly localized areas. Each of them is both a cause and a predictor of violence. One is violent or potentially violent *relationships* among people. Another is *places* that have a high potential for violent crimes. A third is the injuries caused by violent attacks committed with *weapons*, such as handguns or while the perpetrator is under the influence of alcohol.

VIOLENT RELATIONSHIPS

The victim-offender relationships in violent crime are often distinguished by whether they were *acquaintances* or *strangers*. Acquaintance crimes generally appear to be caused by passion rather than the desire to obtain some other goal, such as theft. Acquaintance violence is an end in itself, while stranger violence is more often a means to an end. To this dichotomy we can add "business" violence, which often takes place among acquaintances for the instrumental purposes of enforcing discipline or collecting debts.

Acquaintance Violence

If police assume that most acquaintance violence is an expression of passionate emotions, then they can use police data to predict many relationships that become violent. They are in the best position to do this with domestic disputes, child abuse and other crimes which produce a series of calls to police over a long period of time. They are less well equipped to do this with crimes that develop out of more transient relationships, such as youth gang rivalries or unpleasant encounters in public taverns leading to threats of violence. They are least able to do this with newly formed relationships, such as a blind date that can turn into rape. These differences in sources of intelligence suggest different methods for identifying and intervening in potentially violent (or already violent) relationships.

Domestic Violence. Lover's quarrels are a classic source of homicides and serious assaults. But police see the quarrels often many times, long before they turn violent. Research by Kansas City (Mo.) police found that 85 percent of the homicides among cohabitating men and women had been preceded by at least one police intervention in a domestic quarrel, and that some 50 percent of the couples had five or more police interventions in their quarrels.[6] These figures suggest a tremendous potential for police to take action to prevent a homicide or serious assault. But it is hard to say exactly how this can be done without more research on two key issues: identifying which couples may become seriously violent and determining which forms of intervention are most effective (under different circumstances) in reducing the likelihood of violence.

The fact that most incidents of domestic violence have been preceded by police intervention does not mean that most police interventions will be followed by serious violence. There are no reliable studies of the question, but available evidence suggests that most couples police visit as a result of a domestic disturbance call do not develop into serious violence. If this is generally true then it would be hard to justify police or other agencies taking any more intrusive action than they already do. Unless the specific couples likely to become more violent can be predicted with a high level of accuracy, then intrusive interventions (such as frequent visits to the home) would be applied to many couples for whom the interventions are unnecessary and unwarranted by any balancing test of individual freedom and the protection of others. Even if the violence-prone couples could be identified with great accuracy, there would be substantial civil liberties questions about any interventions (such as long jail terms for a third simple assault) that would not be applied to others guilty of the same offenses who had not been classified into a high risk group.

Perhaps the best police can do is deal with each situation as it occurs. But there is substantial disagreement on how to do even that. Police officers have historically preferred to do little, if anything, about domestic situations, even when minor violence has occurred. In the late 1960s and early 1970s many police officers were exposed to training by clinical psychologists in "family crisis intervention." During that training they were urged to take an active role as mediators or arbitrators of the disputes. The psychologists providing the training urged the police not to make arrests if at all possible, since an arrest might leave a more lasting scar in the relationship. But in the mid 1970s, some feminist groups began to lobby for police to use their arrest authority much more often. Where the legal constraints requiring police to witness misdemeanors before making arrests posed an obstacle, these groups lobbied the state legislatures to pass specific exceptions to that rule for domestic violence.[7]

None of these debates over the best response to domestic violence, however, produced any hard evidence to support any of the positions. Police argued that arrests could backfire and cause more serious violence as soon as the couple was reunited, but they could only offer anecdotes as evidence. The psychologists only offered theory, and no data, to support their recommendation for mediation. The feminists cited the deterrence principle to support their claims for arrest, assuming that punishment would reduce rather than encourage violence. In the court of public policy analysis, the cases of all three positions were weak and unproven.

This debate is a prime example of the vital need for research on police methods and particularly for experimental research. With a similar debate over medical treatments, the customary practice would be to conduct experiments in which three equivalent groups of couples would each receive one of the three treatments. A follow-up study would then measure the seriousness and frequency of violence in the couples' relationships in each treatment group. The treatment that produced the lowest average level of violence would "win" the test and the debate, at least until the experiment was replicated or modified under different conditions.

This kind of experiment would not have been conducted by an American police agency ten years ago. But from early 1981 to mid 1982, the Minneapolis Police Department conducted just such an experiment with the Police Foundation under funding from the National Institute of Justice. And when the results are available in mid-1983, the research will provide the basis for national recommendations about how police can be most effective in reducing long-term violence in domestic relationships among lovers.

Child Abuse. Child abuse could be the subject of similar research except for the fact that there is little debate over police policy. Few clear alternatives have been formed. Much child abuse never gets seen by police, hospitals or teachers. When cases come to police attention, they are usually so serious that prosecution is warranted if the parent can be identified as the cause. But for younger children who cannot talk, the cause may be ambiguous. The child "fell down the steps," for example, and no witnesses can dispute the parent's claim in that particular case.

A pattern of serious injury to an infant or older child, however, could provide the basis for court intervention. The problem is creating the data system that would compile evidence of such a pattern. Cooperation of police, hospitals and perhaps schools would be required to produce comprehensive injury histories of children. With data from these multiple sources, it might be possible to produce a list of high risk cases that police should investigate.

Here again, however, there are major civil liberties questions. Many people would resist the privacy intrusions a "child abuse data system" would constitute. The potential for mistaken investigation of nonviolent parents of accident-prone children should not be taken lightly. Even though such a system might literally prevent many children from being murdered, we should think long and hard before mounting such a widespread surveillance net encompassing parents and children.

Moreover, once a case is identified as a likely child abuse problem, the possible interventions are not at all clear. The consequences of removing a child from home are serious and far-reaching. It is hard for police or judges to assess whether the risks of parental violence outweigh the risks of parental deprivation. A major long-term research effort would be needed to answer the question, and even that would raise a host of moral issues concerning the rights of human subjects of research.

Youth Gangs. A large proportion of violent crime is committed by juvenile males in groups. Some of it is committed against other gangs, some of it is committed against targets of extortion, such as shopkeepers and some of it is committed against targets who are strangers to the gangs. The likely targets of gang violence can vary over relatively short time spans, and police need to keep current on these changes.

In cities where gangs have created major violence problems, such as New York and Chicago, special gang units have been established to monitor their activity. Some of these units have attempted to deter gang violence through harassment, with little success. Even when gang leaders have been locked up, the gangs have persisted despite, or perhaps because of, visible police monitoring.

What appears to be a less common approach could be tested for its possibly greater effectiveness: covert monitoring of gang plans, followed by interception of gang crimes in the act. The use of paid informants, while common for narcotics enforcement, has rarely been applied to gathering intelligence about gang violence. It is doubtless a high risk strategy, given the penalties a gang would levy against an informant. But secrecy provisions in gangs are less than airtight; girlfriends, relatives and others may come to possess information the police could purchase to stop gang violence from happening. Whether the strategy would work can only be determined by trying it out experimentally.

Taking Threats Seriously. Many crimes among acquaintances are committed as "punishment." The criminal's motive is to punish the victim for the victim's affront to the criminal's honor. Bar patrons ejected for intoxication, for example, often retaliate by bombing or setting fire to the bar. Indeed, a large part of the arson problem is arson-for-revenge, not arson-for-profit. Another example is ambush homicides, which can result from a fight in which one party loses badly but lives to settle the score.

Police often witness threats to carry out those offenses. Police may be present when the bar patron is evicted, or they may break up a fight that the aggrieved party was losing. They are accustomed to hearing the threats and think little of them. Threats are just a way of blowing off steam, of saving face in public. Most of the time the police may be right. Most threats may be idle talk, with no subsequent attempt to implement them. But some threats are carried out and that may be sufficient reason for police to stop ignoring them and start taking threats seriously.

Police need not be able to distinguish real and fake threats to take action. They could simply establish a data bank for "threat control," and let the fact be widely known in the community. Any time someone makes a threat to commit violence, they would be (minimally) cited for the common law offense of assault, which is technically just a threat. The incident would generate a threat report that would be filed by the names of the threatener and the target, and by the nature of the threat (shoot, bomb, knife, or whatever). If anything happens to the target, or if a crime embodied in the threat occurs (like a bombing), then the threatener will be a prime suspect. If police warn the threatener as soon as the threat is made, the mere existence of the data bank may deter the crime.

The development of a threat control data bank would also provide the basis for sophisticated analyses of the circumstances under which threats are likely to be carried out. This kind of analysis could lead to formulas guiding police to take more active intervention with high risk threats. Guarding the target or putting the threatener under surveillance are obvious, if expensive, forms of intervention that could prevent a homicide. They may only be needed until tempers cool down. A threat control data bank could provide enough analysis to plan the intervention with minimal waste of police resources.

Once again, this plan may raise civil liberties concerns. But since a threat is a crime in itself, it is hard to object to police keeping records of past crimes. If there is no trial and conviction, there are appropriate concerns about accuracy and dissemination of these records. But all citizens could be given the right to review any file involving themselves and the data could be strictly limited to this and no other purpose.

Acquaintance Rape. This crime best exemplifies the challenge to police of no advance warning of a potentially violent relationship. A large portion of all rapes—over half by some estimates—occur among acquaintances. Blind dates, sister's (or mother's) boyfriends, classmates and even husbands are all potential rapists. Police have no way of monitoring all of these relationships (which is as it should be) nor of predicting which of them might lead to a rape. What then can they do to prevent such rapes?

Public education in "wariness" strategies is the most likely answer, despite the problems noted earlier. Common sense advice—like meeting blind dates in a public place or avoiding private situations with friends and relatives might be very helpful. Less reliable is advice about what to do if a rape attempt begins, since there is no good evidence about the relative risks of resisting or cooperating. But the various schools of thought could be presented to allow women to make up their own minds.

One may deplore the breakdown of male-female trust that a public education effort on this topic might engender. But any effort to make people more wary of potential criminal attack necessarily asks them to trust others less: lock your doors, don't talk to strangers, don't pick up hitchhikers. The message that acquaintances may be more dangerous than strangers is a tragic but important message to convey.

Stranger Violence

Stranger-to-stranger violence is probably harder for police to predict and prevent than acquaintance violence. Most of what the police can do should come from a different analytic focus: on violent places or tools or on catching violent criminals. But there is a great deal they can do to prevent opportunities for stranger violence. Once again, the most effective strategy may be public education.

The municipal police command an enormous amount of respect for their expertise about how people can protect themselves from crime. If they were to use that prestige in an extensive public education campaign, they might be able to make many people more wary and better walled. No one medium would be sufficient. Donated television time, newspaper space, community group meetings, church fellowships, boy scouts and other social networks should all be used. Even free classes at the local police station could be offered on a regular basis. The message should be broad but it should also be sophisticated. A dog taking a bite out of crime, the focus of one current national public relations effort, does not inform citizens in very much detail about how to protect themselves.

The problems that remain are the substance of the message. Our knowledge is incomplete on many key questions. Until more research is done, police would have to be very careful to avoid topics lacking reliable data. There are, however, enough clearly supported recommendations to fill a public education campaign, such as:

- lock your doors and windows
- try to have someone stay in your home as much as possible
- do not walk outside alone after 11:00
- live on a side street, not a main thoroughfare

VIOLENT PLACES

Police could gain considerably by focusing their limited enforcement efforts on violent places. Violent crime analysis showing the location of the most violent places would help to set priorities. The analysis could be done in several different ways: by specific address, by type of structure or establishment, or by neighborhood.

Violent Bars

An analysis of all licensed bars in a city might reveal that five or ten of them account for half of the major assault incidents occurring in bars. If this is the case then the police might be able to ask the alcoholic beverage control authorities to revoke the liquor licenses on those premises.

An analysis might also show a relatively high frequency of weapons crimes (both robbery and assault) in bars generally. Such findings might enable police to ask the city council to legislate a requirement that all licensed premises with a certain minimum history of violent offenses install an airport-style metal detector entry gate, with a guard monitoring the gate and searching anyone who trips the detector buzzer. The old western saloons required that all guns be checked at the door. Some of our modern saloons are no less violent and no less armed.

Violent Cash Repositories

The same requirement might be imposed upon places that are well known sources of cash: banks, all-night grocery stores, liquor stores. Any location that has had at least two holdups in the past year might be required by law to install metal detectors, if only as a protection for employees and customers. Whether the metal detectors should be monitored by armed, unarmed or any guards at all is an issue of economics as well as safety, since convenience stores often operate with only one employee on duty. But the law mandating the gun screening could be tested on a provisional basis with an early initial expiration date.

In addition to preventing holdups of cash repositories, police could refine their methods of interception of such robberies through stakeout techniques. Police have conducted surveillance on repeat holdup locations with waxing and waning enthusiasm for years. Great doubts persist about whether the long hours of waiting are a waste of time, and whether the interruption by police creates more violence than would otherwise have occurred. But when a rash of holdups occurs, it is one of the most tangible responses a police manager can make to the pressure to "do something."

The questions about the costs and benefits of stakeouts can be easily resolved through a field experiment. Using local crime analysis, police could compile a list of repeat holdup locations that would be eligible for a stakeout team to monitor, from either inside or outside. Half of the list could then be randomly selected to receive stakeouts (although not all at once) and the others would receive no extra police attention. After a given period, the costs and benefits associated with the stakeout group and the control group could be measured and compared: lives lost, injuries, police personnel costs, arrests and convictions, funds lost from the establishments. If this experiment were replicated, police nationally would have a fairly reliable basis for judging whether to employ stakeout units in their own communities.

Homes

The most promising approach to preventing stranger attacks in homes is organizing citizens to watch each other's homes for suspicious circumstances. A high level of surveillance of homes by neighbors who call the police if circumstances warrant can increase the chances that a burglary will be intercepted by police, preventing loss of property. There are many more citizens than police, and their volunteered eyes and ears cost the taxpayer nothing.

The major problem with this approach is maintaining citizen interest in watching out for crime. Since the invention of the television, citizens have had a more stimulating alternative to looking out the window at life on the street. Watching for crime is boring enough in the center city, let alone in low-density suburbs. Citizen watches have been organized (by police or civilian community organizers) without assigning specific responsibilities for specific days and times to specific people. Since everyone is responsible for watching all the time, it can happen that no one is responsible for watching any of the time. The programs are often organized in the wake of some particularly serious local crime that stirs citizen interest. As the fear produced by that event fades away, so may the volunteer efforts to watch out for crime.

Police might be able to solve the maintenance of interest problems in citizen watch by taking a stronger leadership role in organizing citizen efforts. Each crime watch block club could be assigned one police officer to work with on a permanent basis. The officer would meet with the club several times a year to help plan specific watching schedules for each resident, discuss local crime problems and give a report on most recent crime analysis for that block and neighborhood. These officers could be called the "cop-of-the-block" and could be evaluated on how well they stimulate and maintain citizen interest in watching each other's homes.

This idea, like all the ideas presented so far, requires a rigorous evaluation before police departments should invest substantial resources in such a strategy. An experimental design comparing the burglary rates of blocks with a cop-of-the-block to blocks without one would demonstrate the benefits. The costs would be eight to twelve officer hours per year per block. Not all blocks would be appropriate for this strategy, but a careful experimental evaluation would distinguish the types of blocks and areas for which the strategy might make the most sense.

Disorderly Neighborhoods

Just as individual criminals and victimized places (such as bank locations) have careers and histories in crime, so do neighborhoods. A neighborhood may begin its existence as a low-crime neighborhood and stay that way for years. But with changes in a city's housing stock and economy, a low-crime neighborhood may "decay" into a high-crime neighborhood.

One of the main harbingers of a transition to a high crime rate may be a rise in public disorder.[8] Wilson and Kelling have argued that the appearance of disorder, which has been demonstrated to cause public fear of crime, may undermine a neighborhood's defenses to serious crime itself. A neighborhood full of panhandlers, prostitutes, inebriates, rowdy juveniles and recently released mental patients may soon become a neighborhood full of armed robbers, auto thieves and rapists. Kobrin and Schuerman's study of historical trends in crime rates in Los Angeles communities supports this thesis, showing that the "tipping point" into a high crime rate condition is typically preceded by a surge in minor juvenile offenses—the kind of offenses that produce a public appearance of disorder.[9]

What can the police do to reduce public disorder and keep neighborhoods from attracting serious crime? The specific strategies may vary depending on the type of order problem. The important point is to focus on the problem analytically as neighborhood careers in crime. The most productive investments may be in neighborhoods in which a new disorder problem has appeared. Whatever the problem, there is a response that can at least be tried and tested:

- *Prostitutes*—Police might set up roadblocks to keep non-residents' cars out of the streets the prostitutes are "invading," cutting off their customers and their incentives to cruise there.

- *Panhandlers*—Police could aggressively enforce harassment statutes, letting potential panhandlers know they should stay clear of this area.

- *Inebriates*—Police could examine the sources of the liquor, and enlist local bars' and liquor stores' support in refusing to sell liquor to known public inebriates.

- *Drug Dealers*—Police could assign foot patrols to the prime drug dealing locations, conspicuously watching for any attempts to conduct business.

With support from the National Institute of Justice, the Police Foundation will soon be planning a series of experiments in which police attempt to make disorderly neighborhoods orderly. These other approaches will be tested for their short-range effectiveness at reducing disorder, as well as for their long-range effectiveness in minimizing any increase in the crime rate.

Another approach police should consider in preventing crime in neighborhoods is redesign of street traffic patterns. Recent research suggests that areas with through traffic are associated with higher crime than quieter areas more isolated from main thoroughfares. Not all areas can be sheltered from traffic, or else transportation would be snarled. But crime analysis could guide a series of recommendations to the city council for changes in traffic engineering that could reduce opportunities for crime.

One of the most striking examples of this approach was evaluated in Hartford.[10] Entire blocks were closed off to all but the residents, creating much greater familiarity and social control. In combination with several other crime prevention strategies, blocking off the streets was credited with a significant reduction in the burglary rate.

TOOLS OF VIOLENCE

Police can also find ways to prevent violent crime by focusing on the "tools" used in committing the crimes or the factors that predispose people to committing a crime. Two of the most powerful criminogenic tools or substances are guns and alcohol. Police can do much more to control both and thereby reduce violent crime.

Carrying Guns

It is fairly clear that an attack with a gun is more likely to be fatal than an attack with a knife or lesser weapon. Regardless of the right to *own* guns, the right to *carry* concealed guns in public places has been restricted in many areas precisely because of this greater killing power. The mandatory one-year sentence for mere illegal *carrying* (regardless of use) of a concealed weapon in Massachusetts appeared to deter both carrying and the frequency of the crimes committed with guns.[11] These findings suggest that an aggressive police enforcement effort aimed at gun carrying might have an even greater impact on gun crime.

Unfortunately, the police have taken a very reactive posture towards the detection of illegally carried concealed weapons. They may seize such weapons if discovered in the course of an interrogation for another offense, but rarely do police go out looking for people carrying guns. Given our constitutional rights regarding unreasonable searches, many would no doubt applaud this reactive posture.

But there are ways the police can look for illegal guns without violating the Constitution. They may be able to train dogs, who now smell luggage for drugs, to smell the gunpowder and oil in guns. The dogs need not be German shepherds or Dobermans; poodles and other non-threatening breeds can suffice. When a dog (on a leash) has identified a pedestrian with the tell-tale smell, the police officer would then have probable cause to ask for a concealed weapon license and conduct a search.

Another approach would be to give police administrative powers to conduct hand-held metal detector searches for concealed guns on a random, nondiscriminatory basis but without probable cause. The fruits of such searches would be seized and destroyed but no criminal charges would be pressed. The constitutional protection would therefore probably not apply and no record or penalty would be created. Just as housing inspectors conduct random inspections without a warrant to enforce the housing code (for compliance, not punishment) police could use this procedure to reduce the threat of concealed weapons in public.

The least intrusive and most preferred approach to gun detection would be the development of a new hand-held instrument that would tell police whether a person is carrying a concealed weapon. This kind of device would help inform police in general enforcement situations who is carrying a gun. It would also help police patrol the streets in plainclothes (with uniform backup) looking for people carrying concealed weapons. The basic sonar technology for such a device now exists. All it lacks is venture capital or federal funding to apply the technology to this particular problem.

Driving with Alcohol

We should not hesitate to call drunken driving a violent crime. The results of this behavior kill some 26,000 people a year, far more than those killed by "intentional" homicide. If police can reduce the number of drunken drivers on the highways, as they have in several European countries through aggressive enforcement, then they can save thousands of lives.

The licensing of auto driving gives police a legal basis for highly intrusive enforcement efforts. One of the most controversial is the roadblock sobriety check. In Montgomery County, Maryland police have used this approach with conflicting judicial opinions about its legality. By asking each driver a few questions, police can make an initial sobriety determination and move on to a more precise measure, such as breathanalyzer tests, if the facts warrant it. If such roadblocks were widely used in the evenings or other prime drunk driving times, they would greatly increase the drinking driver's chances of getting caught. If general deterrence theory is correct, this would reduce the frequency of drunk driving. The only way to test the theory is to experiment.

INCARCERATING VIOLENT CRIMINALS

The police can make substantial gains in apprehending criminals as well as in preventing crime. Moreover, assuming that incarcerating criminals reduces crime through general deterrence and incapacitation of the repeat offender, police should help crime reduction by doing more to insure that the criminals they arrest are convicted and sentenced. To do that, police need to develop better ways of identifying and catching violent criminals, as well as developing the evidentiary basis needed for a conviction.

IDENTIFYING VIOLENT CRIMINALS

If police are going to focus limited resources on a small group of violent repeat offenders then it is extremely important that they pick the right offenders. Previous police methods have been inadequate to the task. One approach has been to pick people suspected of recent dramatic crimes, such as a child molester. This approach ignores the repeat offender who may commit two hundred mundane robberies a year. Another approach, slightly more systematic, looks at the number of felony arrests or convictions local suspects have acquired over the past six months or year. This approach may reveal little more than the number of times the suspects were caught and may miss entirely some of the more active criminals.

Other methods of identifying violent offenders might include use of informants or general intelligence gathering from citizens. Parole notifications to local police about the release of repeat convicts returning to the area may also provide more names for the pool. The problem is not in getting the names of possible repeat offenders but in picking out the ones who are committing the most crimes and who deserve the highest priority.

One other possible solution to this problem is to test several different methods of selecting targets, interview all of the targets and then compute the average rate of self-reported crime per week for each group of targets.

APPREHENDING VIOLENT CRIMINALS

Once they have identified violent criminals, police must be able to catch them with evidence of their crimes. This is no easy matter. Witnesses are often reluctant to testify and they may leave little physical evidence behind. The best evidence can be obtained by having police observe them commit (or attempt) crimes in progress so that the police themselves can offer eyewitness testimony. But efforts to "tail" career criminals covertly have been largely unsuccessful to date.

The first evaluated program for watching repeat offenders was the Kansas City (Mo.) Police Department's "Perpetrator-Oriented-Patrol." This program suffered from department rules calling for short haircuts for the officers conducting the surveillance, the necessity of driving "obvious" unmarked police cars that could only be refueled at the police garage and other obstacles to maintaining secrecy.[12] A recent program in New York City, the surveillance teams of the Felony Augmentation Project, suffered from similar difficulties. White middle-aged men in Harlem trying to follow around black males have some clear problems in maintaining their covers.

A more promising version of the 24-hour-a-day offender surveillance strategy is the Repeat Offender Project of the Washington, D.C. police. This project seems to have solved most of the logistic and personnel problems of maintaining secrecy. But it also confronts the standard problems of surveillance: boredom, high manpower costs, difficulties in locating the targets. It is unclear yet whether ROP will produce more arrests of targeted repeat offenders. But a Police Foundation evaluation funded by the National Institute of Justice will soon address that question.

There are other methods short of following suspects around the clock with a specialized unit. A police precinct in Brooklyn has started its own "most wanted" list, with pictures on the station house wall. Minneapolis has mounted a targeted criminal program on a city-wide basis. These strategies involve all patrol officers in looking for serious criminals against whom arrest warrants have already been issued. Their effectiveness awaits careful evaluation.

MAKING CHARGES STICK

Police have historically viewed their responsibilities as ending when they have made an arrest. Recent research suggests, however, that what police do both before and *after* an arrest has a substantial impact on the likelihood of the arrest resulting in a conviction. A study of the Washington, D.C. police showed that some 15 percent of the officers made over half the arrests resulting in convictions.[13] A follow-up study in several cities suggested that the high arrest rate officers did much more work in seeking out witnesses, safeguarding physical evidence and preparing cases for prosecution. Conversely, most officers do very little of these tasks in their initial investigations and most of their felony arrests fail to result in a conviction. The "fallout" rate of arrests is substantial and perhaps unnecessarily high.

The New York City police have addressed this problem in two different programs. One is a specialized, city-wide felony arrest case augmentation team. Each time a career criminal on a pre-determined list is arrested for any offense, a special investigatory team gathers all the evidence possible in order to try to insure that a conviction and prison sentence will result. This approach has yet to be rigorously evaluated. The other program is a precinct level strategy for all arrests, designed to improve the quality of case preparation before the case is submitted to the prosecutors. This experimental program in the Bronx has been evaluated by the Vera Institute of Justice.[14] It appears to produce greater effectiveness in obtaining prosecution and convictions compared to the normal procedures in a comparison precinct. Either of these projects could become models for other police agencies around the country.

INCENTIVES FOR INCARCERATION

It is not surprising that few police officers have paid any attention to whether their arrests resulted in conviction or incarceration. It made no difference in salaries, promotions, evaluations or peer group perceptions. Until very recent improvements in court information systems, police supervisors had no way of even knowing their officers' "success" rates in court—nor did the officers themselves.

The advent of PROMIS (Prosecution Management Information Systems) has made it possible to examine convictions in evaluating police officers. But few police agencies have moved to incorporate such data in personnel evaluations—nor should they without thinking it through very carefully. Convictions are not unambiguously a good thing. Convictions for minor offenses may clog the system and use up precious resources needed for targeting more serious criminals. Convictions or cases involving minor disputes may be counterproductive to the reduction of further violence. We must avoid the temptation of blindly rewarding all arrests resulting in convictions and incarceration, just as we must move away from blindly rewarding all arrests.

Nonetheless, police managers can do much more to stem the hemorrhaging of arrests of serious criminals from the prosecution process. Better attention to case building and constitutional criminal procedure should result in more convictions of repeat offenders. Police organizations should find some way to reward such good work.

PUBLIC POLICY CONCLUSIONS

This agenda for police action against violent crime is comparatively modest. It calls for no new expenditures of local or federal funds. It calls for no difficult-to-pass legislation, such as a national handgun ban. It asks for no Supreme Court decisions removing restraints on police conduct. It merely calls for a careful and thorough testing of new ways of doing police work.

VIOLENT RELATIONSHIPS

Domestic Violence. State legislatures should exempt domestic violence from the "in-presence" requirement for police to make misdemeanor arrests. Police should analyze their repeat call data and arrest histories to identify repeat offenders and experiment with different strategies of forestalling serious violence.

Child Abuse. Police, hospitals and schools should consider pooling their information to produce a list of high risk cases police might investigate but with great sensitivity to the civil liberties problems such a list would create.

Youth Gangs. Police should experiment with using paid informants to give advance warning of gang crimes.

Threats of Violence. Police should establish a record of all threats of violence, making the threatener a prime suspect if the threatened arson, bombing or murder actually occurs.

Acquaintance Rape. Police should mount public education campaigns to make women more wary of private encounters with acquaintances.

VIOLENT PLACES

Violent Bars and Stores. Police should ask legislative authorities to require the installation of metal detectors at the entrances to business premises with a recent history of violent incidents. These violence-prone businesses should also be subjected to police stakeouts but with careful experimental evaluations to assess the costs and benefits of this technique.

Disorderly Neighborhoods. Police should try to counteract the tendency of disorderly neighborhoods to attract violence by reducing disorder. Foot patrols and other special efforts should be used to combat prostitutes, panhandlers, drunks and drug dealers.

TOOLS OF VIOLENCE

Concealed Weapons. Police should try using dogs to patrol public places sniffing for people carrying concealed weapons illegally. Police might also seek administrative authority to conduct searches for concealed weapons with hand-held metal detectors. The goal would be to seize the guns rather than arrest the carriers.

Drunken Driving. Police should try frequent roadblocks to determine whether each driver checked is sober.

CAREER CRIMINALS

Identifying Career Criminals. Police should test the effectiveness of different methods of identifying career criminals to see which methods are most effective in selecting the most active and violent offenders for special attention.

Apprehending Career Criminals. Police should experiment with surveillance, decoys, "most wanted" lists and other ways of focusing atten-

tion on the repeat violent offenders who account for a disproportionately large share of violent crime.

Convicting Career Criminals. Police should emphasize initial investigations more in order to increase the chances of arrests resulting in convictions. Post arrest investigations for career criminals should also be
tried to overcome any weaknesses in case preparation.

Two public policy choices must be made to support this agenda and see
it through. First, the funding for the National Institute of Justice must be
maintained if any of these new ideas are to be tested. Discretion in policing provides boundless opportunities for experimentation. This, in turn,
holds out the promise of establishing a scientific practice of police work.

The other public policy choice implicit in this agenda is far more difficult. It is an issue for municipal politics, one that few police chiefs or may-
ors would be eager to take on. That choice is the abandonment of the
wasteful dial-a-cop system, in which waiting for a call is made the highest
priority of a policy agency. This agenda demonstrates the wide range of
proactive police strategies that can be substituted for the dial-a-cop system.
Research may show them all to be ineffective. But the present system
seems to do so little to fight violent crime that alternatives seem to be well
worth exploring.

Even this choice is objectively quite modest. All it requires is a cutback
of current patrol (and perhaps detective) strength by about two-thirds. The
police must retain some reactive capacity for life-threatening emergencies.
But they can well afford to abandon house call service for filling out
crime reports—if the public will permit it. The resources freed up by that
cutback could be tightly managed and sharply focused to attack specific
crime problems, guided constantly by updated crime analyses. That small
portion of the population which calls the police would not get as much
hand holding, but the entire population might benefit from much lower
crime rates.

This choice is not a precondition for testing these ideas. None of the
ideas, taken separately, requires much manpower. But if many of the separate ideas work, a police agency reorganized for proactive crime fighting
will be able to make the best use of them.

One final note. This agenda addresses the actual incidence of violent
crime and not the fear of violence. Fear is a separate and in some ways
equally important problem. Many of the strategies suggested here for
reducing crime (such as public education campaigns) may have the para-
doxical effect of increasing the fear of crime, at least in the short run. Others, such as foot patrol, may be more successful at reducing fear than at
reducing the actual incidence of crime.

As long as fear affects decisions about where to live and the general
quality of life, we must not lose sight of it in choosing strategies to combat crime. Evaluation research should continue to measure the effects of

new strategies on fear as well as crime. And where tradeoffs may exist between reducing one or the other, we must be prepared to make difficult choices.

NOTES

1. P. Colquhoun, *Treatise on the Police of the Metropolis* (7th ed. London 1806 & photo. reprint 1969).
2. G. L. Kelling, T. Pate, D. Dieckman & C. Brown, *The Kansas City Preventive Patrol Experiment* (Police Foundation, 1974).
3. P. Greenwood, *The Criminal Investigation Process*, (The Rand Corporation, 1975).
4. This critique draws heavily on the writings of University of Wisconsin Law Professor Herman Goldstein. See also R. Fogelson, *Big City Police* (1977).
5. J. E. Eck, *Managing Case Assignments: The Burglary Investigation Decision Model Replication*, (Police Executive Research Forum, 1979).
6. Police Foundation, *Domestic Violence and the Police: Studies in Detroit and Kansas City* (Police Foundation, 1977).
7. For an up-to-date list of the states which have enacted this change, contact the Center for Women's Policy Studies, 2000 P St., N.W., Washington, D.C. 20036.
8. J. Q. Wilson & G. L. Kelling, "Broken Windows: The Police and Neighborhood Safety" (*Atlantic Monthly*, Vol. 243, March 1982).
9. S. Kobrin & L. Schuerman, *Interaction Between Neighborhood Change and Criminal Activity: Interim Report* (Social Science Research Institute, University of California, 1981).
10. F. J. Fowler, *Reducing Residential Crime and Fear: The Hartford Neighborhood Crime Prevention Program* (National Institute of Justice, 1979).
11. D. Rossman, et al., *The Impact of the Mandatory Gun Law in Massachusetts* (Boston University School of Law, 1979).
12. T. Pate, et al., *Three Approaches to Criminal Apprehension in Kansas City* (Police Foundation, 1976).
13. B. Forst, et al., *What Happens After Arrest?: A Court Perspective of Police Operating in the District of Columbia* (Institute for Law and Social Research, 1977).
14. E. McElroy, C. A. Cosgrove & M. Farrell, *Felony Case Preparation: Quality Counts* (Vera Institute, 1981).

II. PATROL

Patrol is the largest and most significant individual unit in the police organization. It is the largest unit because patrol officers are the first responders to most crimes or emergencies. As such, patrol officers are strategically deployed throughout a jurisdiction to reduce the time it takes to respond to a crime or emergency. Such deployment, especially over a 24-hour period, requires large numbers of patrol officers. Also, preventive patrol, in which officers observe for crimes, suspicious persons and suspicious activities, constitutes one of policing's primary tactics for combating crime and disorder. Patrol officers must be strategically deployed to accomplish this task.

Patrol is the most significant unit in the police organization because, theoretically, all other units support patrol. Even though most citizens view detectives as more important than patrol officers, detectives were created to allow patrol officers to remain on patrol rather than leave their beats to investigate crimes. Furthermore, the workloads of other units increase when patrol does not function at a maximum level. Patrol officers, as a result of their patrolling activities, should be able to reduce crime, enhance citizen perceptions of safety, reduce traffic crashes, and take actions to eliminate situations that lead to disorder and criminality. Thus, patrol officers can have a very significant impact on a community's well-being and the activities of other units in the police organization.

This section examines the patrol function. Although there appears to be a fairly clear understanding of what patrol should do and how patrol officers should do it, over the years there has been a substantial amount of discussion and disagreement along these lines. The first chapter, "What is Patrol Work?" provides an overview of what patrol officers do. By examining what patrol officers do, a better understanding of their function can be obtained. The Whitaker article attempts to reduce some of these misunderstandings and the mystique surrounding patrol.

Historically, the patrol function has constantly evolved. The foundation for understanding the patrol function is vested in the bureaucratic model of policing, which postulated that patrol's primary function was crime reduction through omnipresent patrolling. However, this premise was questioned and substantially discarded after the Kansas City patrol study, which is the topic of the second chapter in this section. The Kansas City patrol study attempted to validate the effectiveness of patrol in reducing crime. The researchers found that patrolling had little impact on criminal activity or other measurable conditions. The study was the beginning of a quiet revolution in the way the police respond to crime and disorder. Today, police administrators attempt to tailor police responses to the nature and specifics of problems confronting their departments and communities, instead of simply spreading police presence throughout the jurisdiction.

The third chapter, "Calling the Police," by Spelman and Brown investigates the practicality of a rapid police response to crimes. Traditional wisdom was that there was a direct relationship between police response time and criminal apprehension. This philosophy substantially affected police management of operations. Administrators tended to evaluate patrol productivity by average response times, and response time became a critical element in the decision-making process when allocating police officers. However, Spelman and Brown found that response time had little direct impact on criminal apprehension. Indeed, given a best-case scenario, an efficient and rapid response potentially would affect only a small number of cases. They found that for the most part, offenders were long gone before the victim called the police. A de-emphasis of response time provided administrators greater latitude when deciding how to assign officers. It also changed the way police departments responded to non-emergency and non-crime calls for service.

The Kansas City patrol study and the various response time studies formed the foundation for developing new strategies to combat crime. Basically, police administrators came to understand that a singular tactic would not be effective in reducing crime, but police agencies would have to apply a matrix of tactics to be successful. "Specialized Patrol" by Gaines examines the various tactics that have been used by the police. Specialized patrol refers to the deployment of officers in configurations that are not randomized patrol assignments. There are perpetrator-oriented strategies that include field interrogations, perpetrator-oriented patrol and repeat offender programs. This group of tactics represents an effort by police officers to identify and target criminals who are committing a disproportionately high number of crimes. If high-activity criminals can be apprehended and incarcerated, there should be a significant impact on a jurisdiction's crime rate. Location-oriented tactics include stakeout and decoy units, split-force patrols, location-oriented patrol, directed patrol, crackdowns and problem-solving. Location-oriented tactics are designed to attack a problem that is concentrated in a specific location. Hence, administrators may examine the jurisdiction, identify several problem areas or *hot spots,* and then deploy a variety of tactics to counter the crime and disorder in each location. These tactics are discussed in terms of their usefulness and applicability.

Finally, Worden examines the efficacy of differential police responses in "Toward Equity and Efficiency in Law Enforcement: Differential Police Response." In a continued effort to free up police officers to assign to specialized patrol, administrators examined the effects of different responses to police calls for service. Traditionally, administrators believed that patrol officers had to be dispatched to every call for service, regardless of how insignificant the call was. For example, it is questionable whether an officer should be dispatched to the scene of a stolen bicycle. Consequently, police researchers and managers began to look for other ways to handle certain calls. Today, a number of departments take reports by telephone, have victims come to police headquarters to report minor crimes, refer citizens to other agencies that are better equipped to handle their problems, and in some cases refuse to provide services for minor incidents. These types of activities, usually considered differential police responses, free up officers' time so that they can be assigned to special operations or more critical functions. Worden examines how a differential response strategy affected the quality of law enforcement in Lansing, Michigan. He found that it was effective and did not adversely affect citizen attitudes toward police services.

WHAT IS PATROL WORK?   3

Gordon P. Whitaker

As Goldstein notes, most police departments themselves have little systematic information about how their officers spend their time or the
range and frequency of actions they take toward citizens. Even for patrol,
which constitutes the largest part of almost all police departments' operations, there is little systematic data available about what officers do.
Research on police patrol activities has begun to shed additional light
on what goes on in some departments, but these studies are reported in
scattered places. The most comprehensive review is by Cordner (1979).
That review does not include some of the most detailed, more recent
studies of patrol work. This paper reviews a number of the more detailed
recent studies and contrasts their findings with those from observations of
patrol operations in 24 other departments, which have not been previously
reported.

This overview of patrol work is organized in three sections: how officers spend their time on patrol; what problems patrol officers deal with in
their encounters with citizens and what actions officers on patrol take to
control some citizens and help others. Throughout, the categories used by
each of the different research teams have shaped the sorts of data that are
available from their studies. Because they used different categories and definitions, it is often difficult to make exact comparisons of patrol work in
the various departments. Despite this limitation, it is possible to compare and contrast these studies to expand our understanding of the content of police patrol operations. In addition to previously reported data, this
paper also makes use of data from the Police Services Study.[1] These data on

Source: Gordon P. Whitaker (1982). "What is Patrol Work?" *Police Studies,* 4(4):13-22. Reprinted
by permission of MCB University Press Ltd.

patrol operations in 60 neighborhoods served by 24 departments were collected using a standard set of categories and definitions and consistent observation and recording procedures. The departments studied were in the Rochester, New York; St. Louis, Missouri; and Tampa-St. Petersburg, Florida, metropolitan areas. The study was conducted during the summer of 1977. These data increase considerably the confidence we can place in the general picture of patrol work which emerges from this review.

HOW OFFICERS SPEND THEIR TIME

Answering assigned calls and conducting general surveillance by "patrolling" are the two most time-consuming sorts of patrol activity. There is great variation in the amount of time officers on patrol spend answering assigned calls. In most places, however, assigned calls take considerably less than half of officers' work time. Patrolling the beat usually occupies a higher proportion of officers' time. However, "patrolling" also typically takes less than half of the time of officer assigned to patrol.

Most studies of how officers spend their time are based on calls for service (or dispatch) records and consequently focus primarily on time answering calls for service. Dispatch records from Wilmington, Delaware, for example, indicate that patrol officers in that city spent almost three hours (174 minutes) of every eight-hour shift answering calls for service (Tien et al., 1978:4-15). In contrast to average time on calls for service in four other departments, the Wilmington figures seemed rather high to Tien and his colleagues. They calculated that average time on calls for service per eight-hour shift was 134 minutes in Worcester, Massachusetts; 96 minutes in St. Louis, Missouri; 89 minutes in Kansas City, Missouri; and only 72 minutes in Arlington, Massachusetts (pp. 4-19). They concluded that:

> Wilmington has the highest known unit utilization factor ["fraction of time a patrol unit is responding to calls for service during an eight-hour tour"]. The paucity of available workload or productivity-related data suggests that an intensive national effort should be undertaken to fill this important gap (pp. 4-20).

In fact, however, the range of time on assigned calls is even greater than Tien et al. described. Another study which appeared about the same time indicates a substantially higher percentage of patrol officer time spent on calls for service. In their study of patrol staffing in San Diego, Boydstun and colleagues (1977:53) found that officers averaged more than 270 minutes (four and a half hours) on calls for service per eight-hour shift. These figures were obtained from dispatch records for San Diego's Central

Division where the staffing study was conducted.[2] Although over half of each eight-hour shift in San Diego's Central Division was, on the average, devoted to calls for service, this high average was not characteristic of the city as a whole. Boydstun and Sherry (1975:60), in their study of the Community Profile Project, report that only about 120 minutes (2 hours) of each eight-hour shift were spent answering calls for service in San Diego's North Division. The Community Profile Project was conducted two years before the patrol staffing study, but it is unlikely that the average time spent on calls for service more than doubled in that period. It is more probable that differences between the areas being policed account for the differences in how officers spent their time.

Calls for service or dispatch records usually do not provide a complete account of the time officers on patrol spend on encounters with citizens. Calls records are maintained by the dispatcher, who does not know about (or knows about, but does not record) many encounters which are initiated by officers or citizens "in the field." Field interrogations, for example, are often excluded from calls for service records. Traffic stops are also frequently not recorded by the dispatcher unless a citation is issued. On the other hand, dispatch records may include meal breaks, errands, maintenance stops, and dispatched runs in which no police encounter with a citizen resulted. Thus the total time accounted for on these records may miss some encounter time and include some non-encounter time. Practices vary from department to department.

Another source of inaccuracy in dispatch records of officers' use of time arises from self-reporting of the time spent on each call. Because the officer's report that an encounter is ended indicates that the officer is free for reassignment, an incentive exists for officers to delay such reports. This management use of the report that an encounter is ended conflicts with its use as a source of data about time devoted to encounters.

Two other sources of data on patrol officers' use of time are available: officer logs and observer reports. Both may be freer of bias than dispatch records because they are less likely to be used for management of individual officers. Officer logs from Wilmington, Delaware, indicate that officers there spent an average of 166 minutes (two and three-quarter hours) per eight-hour shift on both field-initiated and dispatched encounters with citizens in 1976 (Tien *et al.*, 1978:4-18). This is quite similar to the average of 174 minutes per shift calculated from Wilmington calls for service records, suggesting that in Wilmington officers either tend to report all field-initiated encounters to the dispatcher or else fail to record on their own logs encounters which they do not report to the dispatcher. Another piece of information from officer logs is the amount of time spent on administrative and personal activities (and thus not spent patrolling). Officers in Wilmington reported an average of about 90 minutes per eight-hour shift on meals, breaks, car checkups, arrest processing, phone calls, and so forth (Tien *et al.*, 1978:4-18).

Observer reports are a more expensive form of data collection, but they can also give a fuller picture of police activities They remove the bias often present in officer self-reporting, yet, if carefully conducted, avoid interfering with officer activities. Observers in the Kansas City Preventive Patrol Experiment indicate that almost 40 percent of each shift was spent on encounters with citizens (both dispatched and field-initiated) (Kelling et al., 1974:500). Thus about 190 minutes (just over three hours) of every eight-hour shift were, on the average, spent on citizen-police encounters. Another 75 minutes per shift were devoted to report writing and other administrative tasks. An average of 73 minutes per eight-hour shift were spent on personal breaks and errands (see pp. 504-509). This is considerably more time on administrative and personal activities reported for Kansas City than for Wilmington, but it is important to remember that the Kansas City estimates are from observer records while the Wilmington estimates are from officer logs. Some difference is probably due to variation in police practices between the two cities, but some of the difference is also likely to result from officers' tendency to be quite conservative in reporting how much shift time they spend on personal errands.

Observers using consistent coding rules and observation techniques in several different departments can provide data which permit a better estimate of the extent to which the activities of officers in different departments differ. In the Police Services Study (PSS), observers recorded how officers spent their time and what they and citizens did in encounters for approximately 120 hours in each of 60 residential neighborhoods. Officers from 24 departments were observed. In each case, observations were made for 15 shifts at the same time of day and day of the week in each neighborhood.[3] With these data it is possible to compare officer activities across neighborhoods within the same department's jurisdiction as well as to compare officer activities across departments. It is important to note that these data relate to patrol in residential areas where commercial activity varied from moderate to nil.

Officers in all 60 PSS neighborhoods devoted considerably less than half their time to assigned calls and field-initiated encounters. The average for all neighborhoods was 128 minutes (just over 2 hours) per shift. On the average there were 6 encounters per shift, for an average encounter length of just over 20 minutes. The most time spent on encounters was an average of 217 minutes (over three and a half hours) per eight-hour shift. The least time spent on encounters was an average of 53 minutes per eight-hour shift. In half of the neighborhoods officers averaged less than 130 minutes (two hours and ten minutes) per eight hours on encounters with citizens. There was also considerable variation within departments in officers' use of time. In the city with the highest overall average, time on encounters ranged from 217 minutes to 103 minutes per shift for the neighborhoods studied.

It is useful to divide time on encounters according to whether the encounter was assigned or officer initiated. On average, 96 minutes per eight-hour shift were spent on encounters resulting from assigned calls. These findings suggest that Tien and colleagues were correct in asserting that Wilmington's average time on assigned calls is high. The national norm is likely to be between an hour and a half and two hours per eight-hour shift on encounters resulting from assigned runs.

Administrative activities, report writing, and police assignments other than calls for service took an average of 68 minutes per eight-hour shift in the 60 PSS neighborhoods. This compares with an average of 75 minutes on such activities in Kansas City during the Preventive Patrol Experiment. Again, there is considerable difference among the 60 neighborhoods in the Police Service Study. In one lower income neighborhood of a large city, an average of 153 minutes per eight-hour shift was devoted to report writing, administration, and other assignments besides calls for service. This was the highest average PSS observed. In a middle-class neighborhood in another large city, officers averaged only 34 minutes per eight-hour shift on these kinds of activities. This was the lowest average observed.

The amount of time officers have available for "proactive" police work also varies considerably from place to place. If we combine the time officers spend answering assigned dispatches and the time they spend on reporting and other administrative duties, we get the total "assigned time" they have. For the 60 PSS neighborhoods, assigned time averaged 167 minutes per eight-hour shift. This left an average of 313 minutes per eight hours (or two thirds of a shift, on the average) "unassigned." It is this unassigned time which officers use for initiating encounters in the field, for conducting general surveillance "patrolling"), and for meals and other personal activities. The least unassigned time for the 60 neighborhoods was an average of 202 minutes less than three and a half hours) per eight-hour shift. The most was 398 minutes more than six and a half hours) per eight-hour shift. The average of 67 percent unassigned time found in the PSS study is considerably higher than the 55% "uncommitted" time reported by Cordner for a midwestern city and also higher than the 60% reported by Kelling *et al.* for Kansas City.

About 10 percent of officers' *unassigned* time was spent on officer-initiated encounters with citizens in the 60 neighborhoods observed by PSS. An average of 29 minutes per eight-hour shift was allocated to encounters which officers themselves initiated. Most of these were traffic stops. Overall, PSS observers reported an average of one traffic stop per shift. In five neighborhoods, officers averaged more than two traffic stops per shift, while in two other neighborhoods PSS observers noted only a single traffic stop in the 15 shifts studied. Officers in the 60 neighborhoods were less likely to stop people for reasons other than traffic or vehicle violations. PSS observers recorded non-traffic stops in an average of two out of three shifts. In one neighborhood there were nearly two such stops per shift; in another neighborhood there was only one in the 15 observed shifts. An average of once every two shifts, patrol officers observed by PSS themselves initiated a follow-up investigation of a problem or case they had dealt with before. In four neighborhoods there was an average of at least one such encounter per shift, while in another neighborhood no officer-initiated follow-up investigations were observed. Officers provided unassigned assistance to fellow officers an average of about once every five shifts. In only one neighborhood was there an average of one such encounter per shift. In seven neighborhoods no officer-initiated backup was observed.

Much less unassigned time is used by officers in response to requests they receive directly from citizens: an average of only five minutes per eight-hour shift. Overall, PSS observers noted one encounter of this type for every two observed shifts. In three neighborhoods there was an average of more than one encounter of this kind per shift, but in another there was none. In general, about one encounter in six is initiated by an officer or citizen (on the street). Five in six are dispatched.

Making security checks and issuing parking tickets are two other activities officers may perform during unassigned time. Officers conducted security checks of commercial buildings in all of the 60 PSS neighborhoods, but at substantially different rates. In only three neighborhoods did officers average one commercial security check per hour of unassigned time. In 15 of the neighborhoods officers averaged fewer than one commercial security check in every 10 hours of unassigned time. The PSS neighborhoods were primarily residential and varied in the extent to which they included commercial areas. Some of the difference in frequency of commercial security checks is therefore due to less opportunity for these activities in neighborhoods with very few commercial structures. But while all 60 neighborhoods afforded ample opportunity for residential security checks, these were much less frequent than commercial checks. No residential security checks at all were observed in 10 of the 60 neighborhoods. In only three neighborhoods was there more than one residential security check per two hours of unassigned time. Officers issued parking tickets even less frequently. Obviously, residential security checks and parking control in residential areas are not high priorities in most of these areas.

The major part of *unassigned* time is spent patrolling. This consists of driving about the beat, looking for problems which may require police action and demonstrating the presence and ready availability of police. These activities are usually not directed either by supervisory personnel or by conscious planning of the patrol officers themselves. In some neighborhoods as few as two hours per eight-hour shift were spent patrolling, but the average for the 60 PSS neighborhoods was 214 minutes (about three and a half hours) per shift. In one neighborhood an average of more than five hours in eight were spent this way. Thus, undirected patrol takes more time than any other activity in most departments, although often less than half of a patrol officer's time is spent this way.

In the 60 neighborhoods observed by PSS, patrol officers spent an average of 65 minutes per eight-hour shift on meals and other personal activities. This is about 8 minutes less per shift than Kelling *et al.* (1974) report for Kansas City and about the same as Cordner reports for an anonymous midwestern city. There was considerable variation both among and within the 24 PSS departments. In three neighborhoods officers averaged more than 100 minutes per eight-hour shift on meals and personal activities. In two neighborhoods officers averaged less than 30 minutes per shift on these activities. The highest average time (109 minutes per eight hours) was recorded in a middle-income neighborhood of a large city. In another neighborhood of that same city, officers averaged only 43 minutes of meal and personal activity time per eight-hour shift. The lowest average time (19 minutes per eight-hour shift) was recorded in an inner city neighborhood in another large city. In that city the highest average time on these same activities was recorded at 54 minutes per eight hours.

Overall, officers assigned to patrol spend about one third of their time on specific assignments: responding to dispatches and carrying out administrative duties. The remaining two-thirds of their time is spent on patrolling the beat, officer-initiated encounters with citizens (mostly traffic stops), citizen-initiated encounters (begun directly on the street), and personal business of the officer. Patrolling accounts for most of this unassigned time. These overall averages conceal a wide variation, however. Not only do individual shifts vary greatly from each other, but the pattern of officers' use of time varies by beat and by jurisdiction. Data from one department, or even averages from a number of departments, can not be used to estimate how officers do or should spend their time in another department. The kinds of problems areas present vary so greatly that wide variation in officers' use of time is to be expected.

THE KINDS OF PROBLEMS OFFICERS DEAL WITH IN ENCOUNTERS

In general, crime is involved in a minority of the calls police are assigned to handle. Webster (1970:95) reports that fewer than 17 percent of the "dispatches" in "Baywood" involved crime. This contrasts with almost 40 percent of all "dispatches" which were for "administration." Another 17 percent were for "social services," 7 percent for "traffic," and 20 percent "on view." This is a striking statement of the extent to which police patrol involves work on non-crime matters. It is an overstatement. Webster's classification of all incidents in which the officer took a report of a crime under the heading "administration" reduces the percentage of calls classified as dealing with crime. Moreover, Webster includes in "administration" (and hence in the total number of "dispatches" on which all the percentages are based) officers' meals, errands, and court time. Bearing those classifications in mind, Webster's report for types of calls in Baywood does not differ greatly from that of Boydstun *et al.* (1977) for the Central Division of San Diego. They suggest that while only about 20 percent of all calls assigned involved "current" Part I and Part II crimes, another 15 percent involved taking reports of crimes which had already occurred and 8 percent involved checking on suspicious persons or circumstances (pp. 22, 28). Thus, a total of about 43 percent of the calls for service answered by San Diego's Central Division patrol officers involved crime. About 30 percent of the San Diego Central Division calls were related to peace-keeping, 10 percent to traffic, 10 percent to medical emergencies, and 7 percent to other miscellaneous problems. Officers' meals, breaks, and errands are not included in these figures.

Wilmington, Delaware, appears to be an exception. Records show the majority of calls there concerned crime. Tien and colleagues (1978:4-4) use a somewhat different classification in reporting types of problems dealt with by Wilmington patrol officers. Table 3.1 presents the breakdown they report. Note that they show 63 percent of all calls involved crime in 1974-75, and 57 percent in 1976. These percentages exceed those reported for both Baywood and San Diego. The coding rules are different, but there may also be real differences among the cities. Certainly there appears to have been a decrease in Part II crimes dealt with by patrol officers in Wilmington in 1976. This may be partly due to a change in classification. Note that traffic calls became less numerous, while miscellaneous calls increased substantially. It seems possible that at least some of the kinds of calls which were classified as Part II crimes and traffic in 1974-75 were included in the miscellaneous category in 1976.

We have seen that from 43 to 63 percent of the calls police handled in Wilmington and Central Division San Diego were related to crime. These estimates are based on dispatch records. Difference in coding from one city to another may account for much of the apparent difference in the kinds of problems their patrol officers deal with, but it is also possible that differences in coding rules make an apparent difference less than it actually is. Without data collected in some standard way, we do not know. Patrol observer reports using a standard set of categories shed some light on the range of problems patrol officers actually work on. PSS researchers observed a total of 5,688 encounters between citizens and officers in the 60 neighborhoods they studied. Each encounter concerned one or more "problems" which occasioned police action.

Table 3.1
Average Daily Calls for Service Dispatched in Wilmington, Delaware

Types of Calls Assigned to Primary Patrol Units	1974-75		1976	
	Daily Average	Percentage	Daily Average	Percentage
Part I crime	24.4	16.3	25.8	16.7
Part II crime	70.0	46.9	62.2	40.2
Traffic	28.7	19.2	21.0	13.6
Medical	3.1	2.1	5.2	3.4
Alarm	12.9	8.6	12.2	7.9
Miscellaneous	10.4	7.0	28.1	18.2
Total per day	149.4		154.6	

Source: Adapted from James M. Tien et al., An Alternative Approach in Police Patrol: The Wilmington Split-Force Experiment (Washington, DC: U.S. Government Printing Office), 1978.

Crime was the primary problem in only 38 percent of the encounters observed by PSS. This is considerably less than the proportion reported for Wilmington and also less than the proportion reported for San Diego. Comparisons of the kinds of problems officers deal with on patrol are difficult to make when they must rely on reports from different sources. In general, however, it appears that patrol observers record more traffic-related encounters than are found in dispatch records. Thus, the total number of encounters includes more traffic encounters and this reduces the proportion of all encounters which concern crime. As Table 3.2 shows, one fourth of all encounters observed by PSS involved traffic accidents or violations. (For 22 percent of all encounters, traffic was the primary problem in the encounter.) Observers record more traffic encounters because these are officer-initiated and not reported to dispatchers. Only 20 percent of these traffic encounters were dispatched runs: 77 percent were officer-initiated, and the rest were initiated by citizens in the field.

Another source of the difference may be the information requests. Citizens' requests for information from officers were the sole basis for six percent of the PSS encounters. Eighty percent of these requests were initiated by citizens in the field. Such encounters were probably rarely if ever included in the San Diego or Wilmington data. It is also possible that some of the incidents Tien and his colleagues classified as Part II Crime in Wilmington would be classified as interpersonal disputes or nuisances in PSS categories.

The lower proportion of crime-related encounters in the PSS study may thus be due in part to including more traffic and information encounters in the total number of encounters on which the percentages are based, as well as to differences in categories. But there are also differences in the kinds of problems officers confront in different places.

A clearer picture of the extent to which police patrolling different areas deal with different types of problems can be gained by closer examination of the PSS data. Table 3.3 presents the median and range for types of problems in the 60 neighborhoods. In two of the 60 neighborhoods, over half of all encounters between patrol officers and citizens involved crime. In one neighborhood about 54 percent of the encounters concerned crime as defined by the PSS typology; in another, 51 percent concerned crime. The lowest percentage of encounters concerning crime was recorded in a middle-income suburb. There were also considerable differences within jurisdictions. In the city where 54 percent of the encounters dealt with crime in one neighborhood, only 27 of the encounters in another neighborhood dealt with crime.

Table 3.2
Kinds of Problems Dealt With by Police in Their Encounters With Citizens
(Police Services Study)

Problem Category	Percentages of All Encounters With Any Problem of This Type		Percentages of All Encounters With This Primary Type of Problem
Crime	39%		38%
Violent crime		4%	
Non-violent crime		18	
Morals offense		2	
Suspicious person/ circumstances		11	
Other (warrants, assist officers, etc.)		4	
Disorder	23		22
Interpersonal dispute		10	
Nuisance		13	
Service	26		18
Medical		4	
Dependent persons		6	
Information request only		6	
Other assistance		10	
Traffic	26	__	22
Total	114%		100%
Total Number of Encounters	5,688		5,688

*Does not sum to 100% because some encounters involved two or three types of problems.

In one of the 60 neighborhoods PSS studied, 46 percent of all encounters dealt primarily with traffic. Officers assigned to patrol in that city devote a substantial part of their efforts to traffic. (In the two other neighborhoods which PSS observed in that same city, 31 percent and 37 percent of all encounters involved traffic problems.) In contrast, 9 of the 60 neighborhoods had fewer than 10 percent of all encounters in which traffic was the primary problem. In two of the study neighborhoods in a large city, only 5 percent of the encounters dealt with traffic problems. There was considerable variation within that city, however, since in another of its neighborhoods, PSS observers found that 28 percent of the encounters concerned traffic.

The percentage of encounters where officers dealt with disorders ranged from 43 percent in one PSS neighborhood to 8 percent in another. Encounters dealing primarily with services other than those concerning crime, traffic, and disorder accounted for a high of 33 percent of all encounters in one neighborhood and a low of 8 percent in another. Clearly, police officers assigned to patrol deal with a great variety of problems, and in only a few areas is crime their most common problem.

Table 3.3
Kinds of Problems Dealt With by Police in Their Encounters With Citizens:
Differences Among Residential Neighborhoods

Problem Category	Percentage of Encounters With This as Primary Problem		
	Minimum Neighborhood	*Median Neighborhood*	*Maximum Neighborhood*
Crime	22%	38%	54%
Disorder	8	20	43
Service	8	18	33
Traffic	5	23	46

OFFICER ACTIONS TO CONTROL AND HELP CITIZENS

Officers' actions during encounters with citizens are an important aspect of their work. A wide variety of actions are involved in dealing with suspects, and with witnesses, victims, and others who need police assistance. Table 3.4 presents the percentages of encounters observed by PSS in which officers took some common actions.

Information gathering was the most frequent officer activity. Both those who were to be helped and those who were to be controlled were the subject of police inquiry. Officers interviewed witnesses or persons requesting services in about two-thirds of all encounters involving crime, disorder, or service. In almost three-quarters of all traffic-related encounters but in less than half of the crimes and disorders officers interrogated suspects. The high percentage of interrogations for traffic encounters reflects the circumstances of these encounters. Most of these involve stopping drivers suspected of traffic violations. The others are investigations of traffic accidents where one or more of the drivers present was suspected of violations.

Searches and visual inspections were less common, but occurred in over 40 percent of all encounters dealing with crime.

Police use several techniques to control citizens' behavior. Officers threatened or used force in about 14 percent of all encounters PSS observed. The threat of force is much more common than its use, however. Force was used in only about 5 percent of all encounters. Most of this was an officer handcuffing or taking a suspect by the arm. Most of the encounters where force was used concerned crime or disorder.

More often than threatening or using force, police lectured people whose behavior they wanted to change. In over 40 percent of the disorder and traffic encounters observed by PSS, police lectured or threatened legal sanctions. Persuasion is another technique officers use in attempting to change citizens' behavior. Officers used persuasion in about 23 percent of all disorders observed by PSS.

Arrests were observed in about 5 percent of the PSS encounters, including over 4 percent of all traffic and disorder incidents, as well as about 7 percent of all encounters dealing with crimes. The most common instigation of legal proceedings observed by PSS was not arrests, but the issuance of tickets. Tickets were issued in more than one-third of all traffic encounters. On the average, one traffic ticket was issued for every two eight-hour shifts observed. The number of tickets over the 15 observed shifts ranged from one (in one large city neighborhood) to 22 (in another large city neighborhood). A few tickets of various kinds were issued to participants in other kinds of encounters as well. These were misdemeanor tickets for offenses against municipal ordinances.

Overall, officers in the 60 PSS neighborhoods made arrests in somewhat fewer encounters and gave tickets in somewhat more encounters than did the officers observed in the Kansas City Patrol Study. There, officers made arrests in 6.8 percent of all encounters and issued tickets in 6.8 percent of all encounters (Kelling et al., 1974:466). Boydstun et al. (1977) report San Diego arrests in about 5.6 percent of incidents for which there were dispatch records (pp. 29-30). This is quite close to the PSS average.

Arrests are relatively infrequent occurrences for patrol officers. On the average about one encounter in 20 observed by PSS involved an arrest. Officers observed by PSS averaged a little over six encounters per eight-hour shift. On the average, then, each patrol officer in the 60 neighborhoods was involved in one encounter where an arrest was made once every three working days. Arrests are considerably more frequent in some areas than in others, however. Two of the 6, 0. PSS neighborhoods, 13 arrests were observed in the 15 shifts studied. In contrast, six of the 60 neighborhoods had only one arrest during the 15 observed shifts. Many police officers (especially those working "quiet" neighborhoods) may go for months without making an arrest. Forst et al. 1978:48) report that 46 percent of all sworn officers in the Washington, D.C. department, made no arrests in 1974. Most of these were patrol officers.

Officers do not use legal sanctions at every opportunity, of course. In 10 percent of all encounters, officers remarked to PSS observers that they could have instigated legal action against a participant, but did not do so.

Officers also provide comfort and assistance to those who are distraught or without other sources of help. In almost one-fourth of all encounters PSS observed, an officer reassured someone. This sort of police activity was most common in encounters dealing with disorder. It was observed least often in encounters involving traffic problems. Police gave information in more than one-fourth of the encounters PSS observed. They rendered some sort of physical assistance other than medical help in more than 10 percent of the encounters and gave medical assistance in about 2 percent of all encounters.

Table 3.4
Officer Actions Taken in Encounters Involving Each Type of Problem
(Police Services Study)

Type of Problem Dealt With in Encounter	Percentages of Encounters in Which an Officer Took This Action											
	Interviewed a Witness or Person Requesting Service	Interrogated a Suspect	Conducted a Search or Inspection	Used Force or Threat of Force	Lectured or Threatened (other than threat of force)	Used Persuasion	Made an Arrest	Gave a Ticket	Gave Reassurance	Gave Information	Gave Assistance	Gave Medical Help
Any Crime	64%	34%	43%	17%	19%	7%	7%	1%	28%	24%	8%	1%
Disorder	68	45	15	15	41	23	5	1	30	26	11	2
Service	66	6	18	2	7	2	*	2	22	39	20	5
Traffic	26	74	28	16	48	2	4	35	9	24	8	*
All Encounters	57	40	29	14	28	8	5	9	23	27	11	2

*Less than .5%.

We have seen that in most neighborhoods police patrol officers are assigned to spend substantial portions of their time in encounters dealing with situations that do not involve crime. Often a majority of their encounters involve non-crime matters. Moreover, in most places police institute formal legal proceedings in only a fraction of the encounters they have with citizens. Many of the encounters in which legal proceedings are begun concern traffic problems or disorders rather than crime. But what police routinely do in one locality is frequently quite different from what they do elsewhere. Both the mixture of problems which confront police and the kinds of police actions taken to deal with those problems vary considerably from neighborhood to neighborhood, even within a single department's jurisdiction.

LEARNING MORE ABOUT ACTIVITIES OF OFFICERS ON PATROL

How an officer assigned to patrol uses the work time of any given shift depends on department and personal priorities and on the kinds of public problems that come to police attention during that shift. The particular actions an officer takes in dealing with citizens depend on the same sort of personal, departmental, and public factors. We have not attempted here to isolate the contributions each of these factors make to the activities of officers on patrol. Rather, our purpose was to describe the range of patrol officer activities.

Despite their importance for performance measurement and planning, many police activities receive little attention and are not known in any systematic way by public officials, the courtroom workgroup, or the public at large. Indeed, most police departments themselves have no standard reporting procedures or other means for systematically describing what their own officers do. Thus, all too often police themselves, as well as the various other constituents of police performance, have an inaccurate picture of officers' activities.

The few systematic studies which have been reported suggest that police deal regularly with many kinds of problems other than crime. These problems need to be acknowledged in assessing what police accomplish. Police officers also conduct a variety of activities which are neither highly visible nor the subject of much police training. Whether they should continue to do these things (and if so whether they can be helped to do them better) are questions that can only be answered after further careful study of what police do now and how it affects those to whom it is done.

While it is clear that the content of patrol work varies from beat to beat, department to department, and by shift and day, it is also possible to offer some generalizations about its central tendencies. On the average, about five hours of an officer's eight-hour shift are allocated at the officer's discretion. while three hours are spent on assigned tasks. An average of over three hours in eight are spent by officers driving around "on patrol." About an hour is spent on personal business. Half an hour is spent on officer-initiated contacts with citizens. An hour and a half more are spent on contacts with citizens which originated as dispatched to the officer. Almost an hour and a half are also spent on administrative matters.

The problems police deal with on patrol are often complex and difficult to neatly categorize. Moreover, they also differ from place to place and time to time. In general, however, it appears that only about 40 percent clearly involve a response to some reported or suspected crime. The other 60 percent of the problems police deal with are roughly equally divided among disorders, traffic problems, and requests for various other sorts of assistance not relating to crimes.

Police assigned to patrol take a wide variety of actions with the citizens they encounter. Asking questions is perhaps their most common activity. Threats of force are considerably more common than the use of force or the exercise of arrest powers. More commonly, however, officers lecture or seek to persuade those whose behavior they seek to change. Officers also commonly provide reassurance, information, or some form of physical assistance. A patrol officer needs to have a wide repertoire of actions available to deal with the diverse situations he or she is asked to handle.

NOTES

1. The Police Services Study was conducted by Elinor Ostrom and Roger B. Parks of Indiana University in Bloomington and Gordon P. Whitaker of the University of North Carolina at Chapel Hill under funding provided by the National Science Foundation, Grant No. 43949.
2. Boydstun *et al.* (1977:47) report the mean number of calls and minutes per call for one officer and two-officer units. The figure of 270 minutes per shift was calculated using these data and the total number of calls for each type of unit.
3. Gay *et al.* (1977) document the patterns of peaks and valleys in calls for service which recur over a week's time. Spreading observations over various shifts and days of the week is necessary to obtain a balanced view of patrol work.

REFERENCES

Boydstun, John E.; and Michael E. Sherry. *San Diego Community Profile. Final Report.* Washington, D.C.: Police Foundation, 1975, 39-66.

Boydstun, John E.; Michael Sherry; and Nicholas P. Moelter. *Patrol Staffing in San Diego.* Washington, D.C.: Police Foundation, 1977.

Cordner, Gary W. "Police Patrol Work Load Studies: A Review and Critique." *Police Studies* (Summer 1979), 50-60.

Forst, Brian; Judith Lucianovic; and Sarah J. Cox. *What Happens After Arrest?* Washington, D.C.: U.S. Government Printing Office, 1978.

Gay, William G.; Theodore H. Schell; and Stephen Schack. *Improving Patrol Productivity, Volume 1: Routine Patrol.* Washington, D.C.: U.S. Government Printing Office, 1977.

Goldstein, Herman. *Policing a Free Society.* Cambridge, Massachusetts. Ballinger, 1977.

Kelling, George L.; Tony Pate; Duane Dieckman; and Charles E. Brown. *The Kansas City Preventive Patrol Experiment: A Technical Report.* Washington, D.C, Police Foundation, 1974.

Tien, James M.; James W. Simon; and Richard C. Larson. *An Alternative Approach in Police Patrol: The Wilmington Split Force Experiment.* Washington, D.C.: U.S. Government Printing Office, 1978.

Webster, John A. "Police Task and Time Study." *The Journal of Criminal Law, Criminology and Police Science* LXI, 1970, 94-100.

THE KANSAS CITY PREVENTIVE
PATROL EXPERIMENT   4

George L. Kelling, Tony Pate, Duane Dieckman
& Charles E. Brown

I. INTRODUCTION AND MAJOR FINDINGS

Ever since the creation of a patrolling force in 13th century Hangchow, preventive patrol by uniformed personnel has been a primary function of policing. In 20th century America, about $2 billion is spent each year for the maintenance and operation of uniformed and often superbly equipped patrol forces. Police themselves, the general public, and elected officials have always believed that the presence or potential presence of police officers on patrol severely inhibits criminal activity.

One of the principal police spokesmen for this view was the late O.W. Wilson, former Chief of the Chicago Police Department and a prominent academic theorist on police issues. As Wilson once put it, "Patrol is an indispensable service that plays a leading role in the accomplishment of the police purpose. It is the only form of police service that directly attempts to eliminate opportunity for misconduct...." Wilson believed that by creating the impression of police omnipresence, patrol convinced most potential offenders that opportunities for successful misconduct did not exist.

To the present day, Wilson's has been the prevailing view. While modern technology, through the creation of new methods of transportation, surveillance and communications, has added vastly to the tools of patrol, and while there have been refinements in patrol strategies based upon advanced probability formulas and other computerized methods, the general principle has remained the same. Today's police recruits, like virtually all

Source: George L. Kelling, Tony Pate, Duane Dieckman and Charles E. Brown (1974). "The Kansas City Preventive Patrol Experiment." In *The Kansas City Preventive Patrol Experiment: A Summary Report.* Washington, DC: The Police Foundation. Reprinted with permission.

those before them, learn from both teacher and textbook that patrol is the "backbone" of police work.

No less than the police themselves, the general public has been convinced that routine preventive patrol is an essential element of effective policing. As the International City Management Association has pointed out, "for the greatest number of persons, deterrence through ever-present police patrol, coupled with the prospect of speedy police action once a report is received, appears important to crime control." Thus, in the face of spiraling crime rates, the most common answer urged by public officials and citizens alike has been to increase patrol forces and get more police officers "on the street." The assumption is that increased displays of police presence are vitally necessary in the face of increased criminal activity. Recently, citizens in troubled neighborhoods have themselves resorted to civilian versions of patrol.

Challenges to preconceptions about the value of preventive police patrol were exceedingly rare until recent years. When researcher Bruce Smith, writing about patrol in 1930, noted that its effectiveness "lacks scientific demonstration," few paid serious attention.

Beginning in 1962, however, challenges to commonly held ideas about patrol began to proliferate. As reported crime began to increase dramatically, as awareness of unreported crime became more common, and as spending for police activities grew substantially, criminologists and others began questioning the relationship between patrol and crime. From this questioning a body of literature has emerged.

Much of this literature is necessarily exploratory. Earlier researchers were faced with the problem of obtaining sufficient and correct data, and then devising methodologies to interpret the data. The problems were considerable, and remain so.

Another problem facing earlier investigators was the natural reluctance of most police departments to create the necessary experimental conditions through which definitive answers concerning the worth of patrol could be obtained. Assigned the jobs of protecting society from crime, of apprehending criminals, and of carrying out numerous other services such as traffic control, emergency help in accidents and disasters, and supervision of public gatherings, police departments have been apprehensive about interrupting their customary duties to experiment with strategies or to assist in the task of evaluation.

It was in this context that the Kansas City, Missouri, Police Department, under a grant from the Police Foundation, undertook in 1972 the most comprehensive experiment ever conducted to analyze the effectiveness of routine preventive patrol.

From the outset the department and the Police Foundation evaluation team agreed that the project design would be as rigorously experimental as possible, and that while Kansas City Police Department data would be used, as wide a data base as possible, including data from external measurements, would be generated. It was further agreed that the experiment would be monitored by both department and Foundation representatives to insure maintenance of experimental conditions. Under the agreement between the department and the foundation, the department committed itself to an eight-month experiment provided that reported crime did not reach "unacceptable" limits within the experimental area. If no major problems developed, the experiment would continue an additional four months.

The experiment is described in detail later in this summary. Briefly, it involved variations in the level of routine preventive patrol within 15 Kansas City police beats. These beats were randomly divided into three groups. In five "reactive" beats, routine preventive patrol was eliminated and officers were instructed to respond only to calls for service. In five "control" beats, routine preventive patrol was maintained at its usual level of one car per beat. In the remaining five "proactive" beats, routine preventive patrol was intensified by two to three times its usual level through the assignment of additional patrol cars and through the frequent presence of cars from the "reactive" beats.

For the purposes of measurement, a number of hypotheses were developed, of which the following were ultimately addressed:

1. crime, as reflected by victimization surveys and reported crime data, would not vary by type of patrol;

2. citizen perception of police service would not vary by type of patrol;

3. citizen fear and behavior as a result of fear would not vary by type of patrol;

4. police response time and citizen satisfaction with response time would vary by experimental area; and

5. traffic accidents would increase in the reactive beats.

The experiment found that the three experimental patrol conditions appeared not to affect crime, service delivery and citizen feelings of security in ways the public and the police often assume they do. For example,

• as revealed in the victimization surveys, the experimental conditions had no significant effect on residence and non-residence burglaries, auto thefts, larcenies involving auto accessories, robberies, or vandalism—crimes traditionally considered to be deterrable through preventive patrol;

• in terms of rates of reporting crime to the police few differences and no consistent patterns of differences occurred across experimental conditions;

- in terms of departmental reported crime, only one set of differences across experimental conditions was found and this one was judged likely to have been a random occurrence.
- few significant differences and no consistent pattern of differences occurred across experimental conditions in terms of citizen attitudes toward police services;
- citizen fear of crime, overall, was not affected by experimental conditions;
- there were few differences and no consistent pattern of differences across experimental conditions in the number and types of anti-crime protective measures used by citizens;
- in general, the attitudes of businessmen toward crime and police services were not affected by experimental conditions;
- experimental conditions did not appear to affect significantly citizen satisfaction with the police as a result of their encounters with police officers;
- experimental conditions had no significant effect on either police response time or citizen satisfaction with police response time;
- although few measures were used to assess the impact of experimental conditions on traffic accidents and injuries, no significant differences were apparent;
- about 60 percent of a police officer's time is typically non-committed (available for calls); of this time police officers spent approximately as much time on non-police related activities as they did on police-related mobile patrol; and
- in general, police officers are given neither a uniform definition of preventive patrol nor any objective methods for gauging its effectiveness; while officers tend to be ambivalent in their estimates of preventive patrol's effectiveness in deterring crime, many attach great importance to preventive patrol as a police function.

Some of these findings pose a direct challenge to traditionally held beliefs. Some point only to an acute need for further research. But many point to what those in the police field have long suspected—an extensive disparity between what we want the police to do, what we often believe they do, and what they can and should do.

The immediate issue under analysis in the preventive patrol experiment was routine preventive patrol and its impact on crime and the community. But a much larger policy issue was implied: whether urban police departments can establish and maintain experimental conditions, and whether such departments can, for such experimentation, infringe upon that segment of time usually committed to routine preventive patrol. Both questions were answered in the affirmative, and in this respect the preventive patrol experiment represents a crucial first step, but just one in a series of such steps toward defining and clarifying the police function in modern society.

What the experiment did not address was a multitude of other patrol issues. It did not, for example, study such areas as two-officer patrol cars, team policing, generalist-specialist models, or other experiments currently underway in other departments. The findings of this experiment do not establish that the police are not important to the solution of crime or that police presence in some situations may not be helpful in reducing crime. Nor do they automatically justify reductions in the level of policing. They do not suggest that because the majority of a police officer's time is typically spent on non-crime related matters, the amount of time spent on crime is of any lesser importance.

Nor do the findings imply that the provision of public services and maintenance of order should overshadow police work on crime. While one of the three patrol conditions used in this experiment reduced police visibility in certain areas, the condition did not withdraw police availability from those areas. The findings in this regard should therefore not be interpreted to suggest that total police withdrawal from an area is an answer to crime. The reduction in routine police patrol was but one of three patrol conditions examined, and the implications must be treated with care.

It could be argued that because of its large geographical area and relatively low population density, Kansas City is not representative of the more populous urban areas of the United States. However, many of the critical problems and situations facing Kansas City are common to other large cities. For example, in terms of rates of aggravated assault, Kansas City ranks close to Detroit and San Francisco. The rate of murder and manslaughter per 100,000 persons in Kansas City is similar to that of Los Angeles, Denver and Cincinnati. And in terms of burglary, Kansas City is comparable to Boston and Birmingham. Furthermore, the experimental area itself was diverse socio-economically, and had a population density much higher than Kansas City's average, making the experimental area far more representative and comparative than Kansas City as a whole might be. In these respects, the conclusions and implications of this study can be widely applied.

II. DESCRIPTION OF THE PREVENTIVE PATROL EXPERIMENT

The impetus for an experiment in preventive patrol came from within the Kansas City Police Department in 1971. While this may be surprising to some, the fact is that by that year the Kansas City department had already experienced more than a decade of innovation and improvement in its operations and working climate and had gained a reputation as one of the nation's more progressive police departments.

Under Chief Clarence M. Kelley, the department had achieved a high
degree of technological sophistication, was receptive to experimentation
and change, and was peppered with young, progressive and professional
officers. Short and long-range planning had become institutionalized,
and constructive debates over methods, procedures and approaches to
police work were commonplace. By 1972, this department of approximately 1,300 police officers in a city of just over half a million—part of a
metropolitan complex of 1.3 million—was open to new ideas and recommendations and enjoyed the confidence of the people it served.

As part of its continuing internal discussions of policing, the department
in October of 1971 established a task force of patrol officers and supervisors in each of its three patrol divisions (South, Central and Northeast), as well as in its special operations division (helicopter, traffic,
tactical, etc.). The decision to establish these task forces was based on the
beliefs that the ability to make competent planning decisions existed at all
levels within the department and that if institutional change was to gain
acceptance, those affected by it should have a voice in planning and
implementation.

The job of each task force was to isolate the critical problems facing
its division and propose methods to attack those problems. All four task
forces did so. The South Patrol Division Task Force identified five problem areas where greater police attention was deemed vital: burglaries,
juvenile offenders, citizen fear, public education about the police role,
and police-community relations.

Like the other task forces, the South task force was confronted next
with developing workable remedial strategies. And here the task force met
with what at first seemed an insurmountable barrier. It was evident that
concentration by the South Patrol Division on the five problem areas
would cut deeply into the time spent by its officers on preventive patrol.
At this point a significant thing happened. Some of the members of the
South task force questioned whether routine preventive patrol was effective, what police officers did while on preventive patrol duty, and what
effect police visibility had on the community's feelings of security.

Out of these discussions came the proposal to conduct an experiment which would test the true impact of routine preventive patrol. The
Police Foundation agreed to fund the experiment's evaluation.

As would be expected, considerable controversy surrounded the experiment, with the central question being whether long-range benefits out-
weighed short-term risks. The principal short-term risk was seen as the
possibility that crime would increase drastically in the reactive beats;
some officers felt the experiment would be tampering with citizens' lives
and property.

The police officers expressing such reservations were no different
from their counterparts in other departments. They tended to view patrol

as one of the most important functions of policing, and in terms of time allocated, they felt that preventive patrol ranked on a par with investigating crimes and rendering assistance in emergencies. While some admitted that preventive patrol was probably less effective in preventing crime and more productive in enhancing citizen feelings of security, others insisted that the activities involved in preventive patrol (car, pedestrian and building checks) were instrumental in the capture of criminals and, through the police visibility associated with such activities, in the deterrence of crime. While there were ambiguities in these attitudes toward patrol and its effectiveness, all agreed it was a primary police function.

Within the South Patrol Division's 24-beat area nine beats were eliminated from consideration as unrepresentative of the city's socio-economic composition. The remaining 15-beat, 32-square mile experimental area encompassed a commercial-residential mixture, with a 1970 resident population of 148,395 persons and a density of 4,542 persons per square mile (significantly greater than that for Kansas City as a whole, which in 1970 with only 1,604 persons per square mile, was 45th in the nation). Racially, the beats within this area ranged from 78 percent black to 99 percent white. Median family income of residents ranged from a low of $7,320 for one beat to a high of $15,964 for another. On the average, residents of the experimental area tended to have been in their homes from 6.6 to 10.9 years.

Police officers assigned to the experimental area were those who had been patrolling it prior to the experiment, and tended to be white, relatively young and somewhat new to the police department. In a sample of 101 officers in the experimental area taken across all three shifts, 9.9 percent of the officers were black, the average age of the officers was 27 years and average time on the force was 3.2 years.

The 15 beats in the experimental area were computer matched on the basis of crime data, number of calls for service, ethnic composition, median income and transiency of population into five groups of three each. Within each group, one beat was designated reactive, one control, and one proactive. In the five reactive beats, there was no preventive patrol as such. Police vehicles assigned these beats entered them only in response to calls for service. Their non-committed time (when not answering calls) was spent patrolling the boundaries of the reactive beats or patrolling in adjacent proactive beats. While police availability was closely maintained, police visibility was, in effect, withdrawn (except when police vehicles were seen while answering calls for service).

In the five control beats, the usual level of patrol was maintained at one car per beat. In the five proactive beats, the department increased police patrol visibility by two to three times its usual level both by the assignment of marked police vehicles to these beats and the presence of units from adjacent reactive beats.

Other than the restrictions placed upon officers in reactive beats (respond only to calls for service and patrol only the perimeter of the beat or in an adjacent proactive beat), no special instructions were given to police officers in the experimental area. Officers in control and proactive beats were to conduct preventive patrol as they normally would.

It should be noted, however, that the geographical distribution of beats (see Figure 4.1) avoided clustering reactive beats together or at an unacceptable distance from proactive beats. Such clustering could have resulted in lowered response time in the reactive beats.

Figure 4.1
Schematic representation of the 15-beat experimental area.

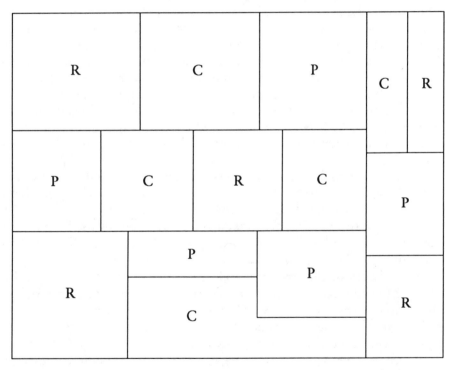

P = Proactive
C = Control
R = Reactive

It should also be noted that patrol modification in the reactive and proactive beats involved only routine preventive patrol. Specialized units, such as tactical helicopter and K-9, operated as usual in these beats but at a level consistent with the activity level established the preceding year. This level was chosen to prevent infringement of these specialized units upon experimental results.

Finally, it should be noted that to minimize any possible risk through the elimination of routine preventive patrol in the reactive beats, crime rate data were monitored on a weekly basis. It was agreed that if a noticeable increase in crime occurred within a reactive beat, the experiment would be suspended. This situation, however, never materialized.

While the Kansas City experiment began on July 19, 1972, both department and Police Foundation monitors recognized by mid-August that experimental conditions were not being maintained, and that several problems had arisen. Chief Kelley then saw to it that these problems were rectified during a suspension of the experiment.

One problem was manpower, which in the South Patrol Division had fallen to a dangerously low level for experimental purposes. To correct this problem additional police officers were assigned to the division and an adequate manpower level restored. A second problem involved violations of the project guidelines. Additional training sessions were held, and administrative emphasis brought to bear to ensure adherence to the guidelines. A third problem was boredom among officers assigned to reactive beats. To counter this, the guidelines were modified to allow an increased level of activity by reactive-assigned officers in proactive beats. These revisions emphasized that an officer could take whatever action was deemed necessary, regardless of location, should a criminal incident be observed. The revised guidelines also stressed adherence to the spirit of the project rather than to unalterable rules.

On October 1, 1972, the experiment resumed. It continued successfully for 12 months, ending on September 30, 1973. Findings were produced in terms of the effect of experimental conditions on five categories of crimes traditionally considered to be deterrable through preventive patrol (burglary, auto theft, larceny—theft of auto accessories, robbery and vandalism) and on five other larcenies). Additional findings concerned the effect of experimental conditions on citizen feelings of security and satisfaction with police service, on the amount and types of anti-crime protective measures taken by citizens and businessmen, on police response time and citizen satisfaction with response time, and on injury/fatality and non-injury traffic accidents. The experiment also produced data concerning police activities during tours of duty, and police officer attitudes toward preventive patrol.

III. DATA SOURCES

In measuring the effects of routine preventive patrol, it was decided to collect as wide a variety of data from as many diverse sources as possible. By so doing, it was felt that overwhelming evidence could be presented to prove or disprove the experimental hypotheses.

To measure the effects of the experimental conditions on crime, a victimization survey, departmental reported crime, departmental arrest data, and a survey of businesses were used. While reported crime has traditionally been considered the most important indicator of police effectiveness, the accuracy of both reported crime and arrest data as indicators of crime and police effectiveness has come under scrutiny in recent years. Both types of data are subject to wide degrees of conscious and unconscious manipulation, and to distortion and misrepresentation. Because of these, a criminal victimization survey was used as an additional source of data.

Victimization surveys were first used by the President's Commission on Law Enforcement and Administration of Justice. These surveys revealed that as much as 50 percent of crime was unreported by victims, either from neglect, embarrassment, or a feeling that the crimes were not worth reporting. Although victimization surveys also have their limitations, they can be an important way of measuring crime. Thus a victimization survey was used by the experiment to measure this key outcome variable.

To measure the impact of experimental conditions on community attitudes and fear, attitudinal surveys of both households and businesses (in conjunction with the victimization surveys) and a survey of those citizens experiencing direct encounters with the police were administered. Estimates of citizen satisfaction with police services were also recorded by participant observers.

Overall, in collecting data for the experiment, the [sources listed on the following page] were used.

Because many of these sources were used to monitor the degree to which experimental conditions were maintained or to identify unanticipated consequences of the experiment, only findings derived from the following data are presented in this report:

COMMUNITY SURVEY

The community survey, which measured community victimization, attitudes and fear, was taken on a before and after basis. A sample of 1,200 households in the experimental area (approximately 80 per beat) was randomly selected and interviewed in September of 1972. In September of 1973, 1,200 households were again surveyed, approximately 600 chosen from the same population as the 1972 survey (for a repeated sample) and 600 chosen randomly from the experimental area (for a non repeated sample). Since 11 cases had to be excluded because of missing data, the 1973 sample totalled 1,189.

COMMERCIAL SURVEY

The commercial survey involved interviews conducted both in 1972 and 1973 with a random sample of 110 businesses in the experimental area to measure victimization rates and businessmen's perceptions of and satisfaction with police services.

ENCOUNTER SURVEY
(BOTH CITIZEN AND PARTICIPANT OBSERVERS)

Because household surveys tend to interview relatively few citizens who have experienced actual contact with the police, citizens in the three experimental areas who experienced direct encounters with police officers were interviewed Although three survey instruments were developed (one to elicit the response of the citizens, a second for the police officers and a third for the observers riding with the officers) only the observer and citizen responses were analyzed. Identical questions were used as often as possible. The survey was conducted over a four-month period (July through October, 1973). Interviewed were 331 citizens who were involved in either an officer-initiated incident (car check, pedestrian check or a traffic violation) or citizen-initiated incident (one in which the citizen called for police service: burglary, robbery, larceny, assault, etc.).

Surveys and questionnaires

1	Community Survey victimization attitudes rates of reporting	5	Encounter Survey—Observer attitudes perceptions
2	Commercial Survey victimization attitudes rates of reporting	6	Noncommitted Time Survey
		7	Response Time Survey observers
3	Encounter Survey—Citizens attitudes perceptions	8	Response Time Survey citizens
		9	HRD Survey
4	Encounter Survey—Officers attitudes perceptions	10	Officer Questionnaire

Interviews and recorded observations

1	"Player" Observations	3	Participant Observer Interview
2	Officer interviews	4	Participant Observer Transaction Recordings

Departmental data

1	Reported Crime	4	Computer Dispatch Data
2	Traffic Data	5	Officer Activity Analysis Data
3	Arrest Data	6	Personnel Records

PARTICIPANT OBSERVER TRANSACTION RECORDINGS

While the community encounter survey focused on the location of the police-citizen contact, the observer transaction recordings focused on police-citizen interactions in terms of the assignment of the officer involved (reactive, control or proactive beats). These data were obtained by observers while riding with officers assigned to the experimental area, and involved observer estimates of citizen satisfaction as a result of direct contact with the police. Observations covered all three watches in all 15 beats. As a result, 997 incidents of police-citizen transactions were systematically recorded.

REPORTED CRIME

Monthly totals for reported crime by beat over the October 1968 through September 1972 (pre-experimental) period and over the October 1972 through September 1973 (experimental) period were retrieved from departmental records. Time-series analyses were then performed on these data to produce the findings.

TRAFFIC DATA

Two categories of traffic accidents were monitored: non-injury and injury/fatality. Monitoring was maintained over two time periods, October 1970 through September 1972 for the pre-experimental period, and October 1972 through September 1973 for the experimental period.

ARREST DATA

Arrest data by month and beat for the experimental year and the three preceding years were obtained from departmental records.

RESPONSE TIME SURVEY

Police response time in the experimental area was recorded between May and September 1973 through the use of a response time survey completed by the participant observers and those citizens who had called the police for service. In measuring the time taken by the police in responding to calls, emphasis was placed on field response time (i.e., the amount of time occurring between the time a police unit on the street received a call from the dispatcher and the time when that unit contacted the citizen involved). In measuring citizen satisfaction with response time the entire range of time required for the police to answer a call was considered (i.e., including time spent talking with the police department operator, police dispatcher, plus field response time).

METHODOLOGY AND MAINTENANCE OF EXPERIMENTAL CONDITIONS

Because multiple dimensions of the possible effects of the experiment were examined, differing methods of analysis were applied to the data generated. Detailed discussions of these and other factors concerning the experiment's methodology, including a discussion of the sampling error, can be found in the technical report and its appendices. A discussion of the methods used to determine the extent to which desired levels of patrol coverage were achieved, the degree to which experimental conditions were maintained, and whether the criminal world realized that routine patrol strategies had been modified and to what extent patterns of behavior changed as a result can be found in Chapter 111 of the technical report. In summary, the data sources used to analyze these factors point to the overall maintenance of experimental conditions.

SPILLOVER EFFECT

One major concern in an experiment of this type is the so-called spillover or displacement theory, i.e., that as crime decreases in one area due to increased police presence, it will increase in other, usually contiguous, areas. This would mean that the effect of the experiment within the experimental area would be offset by counter-effects in other areas. To test this, various correlations between contiguous beats were calculated and analyzed. Except for auto theft, there were no noticeable alterations in the correlations of crime levels. These results, combined with an examination of the actual monthly crime figures, tend to indicate that, in general, there was no spillover effect. Results of the calculations can be found in the appendices to the technical report.

IV. EXPERIMENTAL FINDINGS

The essential finding of the preventive patrol experiment is that decreasing or increasing routine preventive patrol within the range tested in this experiment had no effect on crime, citizen fear of crime, community attitudes toward the police on the delivery of police service, police response time, or traffic accidents. Given the large amount of data collected and the extremely diverse sources used, the evidence is overwhelming. Of the 648 comparisons made to produce the 13 major findings that follow, statistical significance occurred only 40 times between pairs in approximately 6 percent of the total. Of these 40, the change was greater 15 times in reactive beats, 19 times in control beats, and 6 times in proactive beats.

Findings of the experiment are presented in terms of the impact that the range of variation in preventive patrol used in this experiment had upon the following:

- community victimization
- departmental reported crime
- rates of reporting crime to the police
- arrest trends
- citizen's fear of crime
- protective measures used by citizens
- protective measures used by businesses
- community attitudes toward the police and the delivery of police services
- businessmen's attitudes toward the police and delivery of police services
- citizen attitudes toward the police as a result of the encounters with the police
- estimation of citizen-police transactions
- police response time
- traffic incidents

The tables used in this document to illustrate the findings are summary tables which compress elaborate amounts of data. Presentation of the data in this form presents numerous problems in that much information is lost in summary. For example, actual numbers, direction of the findings, and discussion of those methodologies used for analyses are not included. Because of this, the findings are considered in their most generalized form; the sole issues are statistical significance and whether or not routine preventive patrol, within the range of variation tested, had an impact on the experimental area. The details of that impact are not presented. Consequently, as mentioned earlier, the findings outlined here cannot be used for specific planning purposes.

On the other hand, presentation in this manner allows for an overview, and focuses on only the most significant findings. Given the importance of the issue and the difficulties inherent in proving the effects of such experiments, emphasis is placed on the large amounts of data collected from diverse sources, and the overwhelming tendency of the data to point in a single direction.

KEY TO TABLES

These tables present three kinds of information: (1) the matter being studied, (2) the probability that a finding is statistically significant (as opposed to numerically different by chance) and (3) if significance is found, the direction of that significance. Table 4A, for example, reports on findings in the area of citizen estimates of victimization by robbery with no distinction as to whether the robbery occurred inside or outside a structure.

In Table A, column I indicates that citizens were asked whether they had been robbed, and that the robberies were subsequently categorized as "no distinction between inside and outside" since respondents were unable to, or did not, indicate whether the robbery had taken place inside or outside a structure.

The "N" and "R" in column 2 indicate whether the information was derived from the non-repeated sample (N) or the repeated sample (R).

Column 3 indicates overall "P" or probability value, i.e., how likely it is that differences of this size between pairs of experimental conditions could have been the result of happenstance rather than of the effects of the experimental conditions. Social science generally cites ".05" as the required level of significance, meaning that there is only a 5 percent likelihood that the results could have occurred by chance (or a 95 percent chance that the results were the effect of experimental conditions). Column 3, therefore presents the overall P in terms of the statistical presentation p .25. Symbols > and < indicate which of the two items in an equation is the larger. Just as "a = b" indicates that a and b equal each other, "a > b" shows that a is greater than b, while "a < b" shows that a is less than b. Thus the presentation p > .25 means that the probability that the findings could have occurred by chance is greater than 25 percent. Using the standard that a finding is "statistically significant" only when it could have occurred by chance no more than 5 percent of the time, this finding would not be considered significant.

Since there are so few findings of statistical significance in the results, it has been decided not to clutter the tables in this summary report with numerical values in this column except when significance is achieved. Therefore column 3 is left blank in all tables except when a statistically significant difference between pairs of experimental conditions was found.

A statistically significant finding can be found in Table 4.3 (page 90) under the category "Residence Burglary" and appears in column 3 as follows:

$$.025 < p < .05$$

This means that the probability of the observed differences occurring by chance is greater than 2.5 out of a hundred but less than 5. Thus, the traditional level of statistical significance (.05) has been achieved, and it can be assumed that the observed differences are not due to random fluctuations.

Columns 4, 5, and 6 in Table 4A present the statistical relationship between the three experimental conditions (reactive, control and proactive). Column 4 compares the findings in the reactive and control beats, column 5 compares the findings in the reactive and proactive beats, and column 6 compares findings in the control and proactive beats. Each column contains three possibilities. For example, in column 4, the following possibilities exist:

Table 4A
Victimization

(1)	(2)	(3)	(4)	(5)	(6)
Crime type		Overall P	R,C	R,P	C,P
Robbery—no distinction	N	p > .25	R = C	R = P	C = P
between in or outside	R	p > .25	R = C	R = P	C = P

R = C	(meaning that statistically speaking, changes in the reactive and control beats between 1972 and 1973 were the same)
R > C	(meaning that statistically speaking, either the increase was greater or the decrease was smaller in the reactive beats than in the control beats)
R < C	(meaning that statistically speaking, either the increase was smaller or the decrease was greater in the reactive beats than in the control beats)

EFFECTS ON CRIME, REPORTING AND ARRESTS

FINDING 1: VICTIMIZATION

The Victimization Survey found no statistically significant differences in crime in any of the 69 comparisons made between reactive, control and proactive beats.

This finding would be expected for such categories as rape, homicide and common or aggravated assault. For one thing, these are typically impulsive crimes, usually taking place between persons known to each other. Furthermore, they most often take place inside a building, out of sight of an officer on routine preventive patrol. The spontaneity and lack of high visibility of these crimes, therefore, make it unlikely that they would be much affected by variations in the level of preventive patrol.

Given traditional beliefs about patrol, however, it is surprising that statistically significant differences did not occur in such crimes as commercial burglaries, auto theft and robberies.

Nonetheless, as measured by the victimization survey, these crimes were not significantly affected by changes in the level of routine preventive patrol. Table 4.1 shows data and findings from the Community and Commercial Surveys in regard to victimization.

FINDING 2: DEPARTMENTAL REPORTED CRIME

Departmental Reported Crimes showed only one statistically significant difference among 51 comparisons drawn between reactive, control and proactive beats.

Statistical significance occurred only in the category of "Other Sex Crimes." This category, separate from "Rape," includes such offenses as molestation and exhibitionism Since this category is not traditionally considered to be responsive to routine preventive patrol, however, it appears likely that this instance of significance was a statistically random occurrence.

Table 4.2 presents reported crime data and findings.

FINDING 3: RATES OF REPORTING CRIME

Crimes citizens and businessmen said they reported to the police showed statistically significant differences between reactive, control and proactive beats in only five of 48 comparisons, and these differences showed no consistent pattern.

Of the five instances of statistical significance, three involved vandalism and two residence burglary. But where statistical significance was found, no consistent pattern emerged. On two occasions the change was greater in the control beats, on two occasions greater in the proactive beats, and once it was greater in the reactive beats. Given the low number of statistically significant findings combined with a lack of consistent direction, the conclusion is that rates of reporting crimes by businessmen and citizens were unaffected by the experimental changes in levels of patrol.

Table 4.3 shows the data and findings.

Table 4.1
Victimization
Community and Commercial Survey

Crime type	Overall P	R,C	R,P	C,P
Robbery—no distinction between in or outside	N	R = C	R = P	C = P
	R	R = C	R = P	C = P
Robbery—inside (commercial)	R	R = C	R = P	C = P
Common assault	N	R = C	R = P	C = P
	R	R = C	R = P	C = P
Aggravated assault	N	R = C	R = P	C = P
	R	R = C	R = P	C = P

continued

Table 4.1 continued

Crime type		Overall P	R,C	R,P	C,P
Other sex crimes	N		R = C	R = P	C = P
	R		R = C	R = P	C = P
Residence burglary	N		R = C	R = P	C = P
	R		R = C	R = P	C = P
Non-residence burglary (commercial)	R		R = C	R = P	C = P
Auto theft	N		R = C	R = P	C = P
	R		R = C	R = P	C = P
Vandalism (community)	N		R = C	R = P	C = P
	R		R = C	R = P	C = P
Vandalism (commercial)	R		R = C	R = P	C = P
Larceny—auto accessory	N		R = C	R = P	C = P
	R		R = C	R = P	C = P
Larceny—all other	N		R = C	R = P	C = P
	R		R = C	R = P	C = P
All crimes combined	N		R = C	R = P	C = P
	R		R = C	R = P	C = P
Rape	N	•			
	R				
Homicide	N	•			
	R				

•Too few cases to justify statistical analysis

Table 4.2
Departmental Reported Crime

Crime type	Overall P	R,C	R,P	C,P
Robbery—inside		R = C	R = P	C = P
Robbery—outside		R = C	R = P	C = P
Common assault		R = C	R = P	C = P
Aggravated assault		R = C	R = P	C = P
Larceny—purse snatch		R = C	R = P	C = P
Rape		R = C	R = P	C = P
Other sex crimes	$.01 < p < .025$	R > C	R = P	C = P
Homicide		R = C	R = P	C = P
Residence burglary		R = C	R = P	C = P

continued

Table 4.2 continued

Crime type	Overall P	R,C	R,P	C,P
Non-residence burglary		R = C	R = P	C = P
Auto theft		R = C	R = P	C = P
Vandalism		R = C	R = P	C = P
Larceny—auto accessory		R = C	R = P	C = P
Larceny—theft from auto		R = C	R = P	C = P
Larceny—bicycle		R = C	R = P	C = P
Larceny—shoplift		R = C	R = P	C = P
Larceny—theft from bldg		R = C	R = P	C = P

FINDING 4: ARREST PATTERNS

Police arrests showed no statistically significant differences in the 27 comparisons made between reactive, control and proactive beats.

While arrest totals for 16 categories of crime were determined, it will be noted that in seven categories—common assault, larceny-purse snatch, homicide, non-resistance burglary, auto theft, larceny-auto accessory, and larceny-bicycle—either the number of arrests was too small to allow for statistical analysis, or the pre-experimental pattern of arrests was so distorted that statistical significance could not be determined. On the basis of the comparisons that could be made, however, the conclusion is that arrest rates were not significantly affected by changes in the level of patrol.

Table 4.4 shows the data and findings.

EFFECTS ON COMMUNITY ATTITUDES

Citizen Fear of Crime

The experiment measured community attitudes toward many aspects of crime and police performance to determine whether varying levels of routine preventive patrol—reactive, control, proactive—had any significant effect upon these attitudes. Previous investigators, including Roger Parks and Michael Maltz, have shown that citizens can recognize, or at least sense, changes in levels of service or innovations in policing.

Table 4.3
Rates of Reporting Crimes
Community and Commercial Survey

Crime type		Overall P	R,C	R,P	C,P
Robbery—no distinction	N		R = C	R = P	C = P
between in or outside	R		R = C	R = P	C = P
Common assault	N	•			
	R		R = C	R = P	C = P
Aggravated assault	N	•			
	R	•			
Other sex crimes	N		R = C	R = P	C = P
	R	•			
Residence burglary	N	.025 < p < .05	R > C	R = P	C < P
	R		R = C	R = P	C = P
Non-residence burglary					
(commercial)	R		R = C	R = P	C = P
Auto theft	N		R = C	R = P	C = P
	R		R = C	R = P	C = P
Vandalism (community)	N		R = C	R = P	C = P
	R	.001 < p < .005	R < C	R < P	C > P
Vandalism (commercial)	R		R = C	R = P	C = P
Larceny—auto accessory	N		R = C	R = P	C = P
	R		R = C	R = P	C = P
Larceny—all other	N		R = C	R = P	C = P
	R		R = C	R = P	C = P

•Too few cases to justify statistical analysis

Thus, through the Community and Commercial Surveys which provided the victimization information used in the previous section of this summary, citizen attitudes toward crime and police were also measured before and after the experiment.

The first attitude measured was citizen fear of crime, determined by (1) a series of questions in the Community Survey designed to probe levels of fear; (2) a series of questions in the Community Survey regarding protective and security measures taken by citizens; and (3) questions in the Commercial Survey about protective and security measures used by businessmen at their place of business.

Table 4.4
Arrests

Crime type	Overall P	R,C	R,P	C,P
Robbery—no distinction between in or outside		R = C	R = P	C = P
Common assault	•1			
Aggravated assault		R = C	R = P	C = P
Larceny—purse snatch	• 2			
Rape		R = C	R = P	C = P
Other sex crimes		R = C	R = P	C = P
Homicide	• 2			
Residence burglary		R = C	R = P	C = P
Non-residence burglary	•1			
Auto theft	•1			
Vandalism		R = C	R = P	C = P
Larceny—auto accessory	•2			
Larceny—theft from auto		R = C	R = P	C = P
Larceny—bicycle	•1			
Larceny—shoplift		R = C	R = P	C = P
Larceny—theft from bldg.		R = C	R = P	C = P

•1 Not statistically analyzed because of the nature of the variations in the data in the pre-experiment period.
•2 Number of arrests is too small to allow for statistical analysis.

FINDING 5: CITIZEN FEAR OF CRIME

Citizen fear of crime was not significantly affected by changes in the level of routine preventive patrol.

In the Community Survey, citizen estimates of neighborhood safety and perceptions of violent crimes were obtained. Citizens were then asked what they thought the probability was that they might be involved in various types of crime, including robbery, assault, rape, burglary and auto theft.

Of the 60 comparisons made between experimental areas, statistical significance was found in only five cases. Three involved the probability of being raped, one the probability of being robbed, and one the probability of being assaulted. The change in the level of fear was greater in reactive beats four times and greater in proactive beats once.

Yet when statistical significance is found, the patterns are inconsistent. For example, all cases in which the change in the reactive beats are significantly higher than in other beats are found in the repeated sample. These findings are not confirmed by the non-repeated sample, however. The one area in which control registered the higher change occurs in the non-repeated sample, but this is not confirmed by the repeated sample.

The findings thus lead to the conclusion that citizen fear is not affected by differences in the level of routine preventive patrol.

Table 4.5 shows the data and findings.

Table 4.5
Citizen Fear of Crime
Community Survey

		Overall P	R,C	R,P	C,P
Estimate of neighborhood safety	N		R = C	R = P	C = P
	R		R = C	R = P	C = P
Perceptions of violent crimes	N		R = C	R = P	C = P
	R		R = C	R = P	C = P
Probability of being robbed	N	.01 < p < .025	R = C	R = P	C < P
	R		R = C	R = P	C = P
Probability of being assaulted	N		R = C	R = P	C = P
	R	.01 < p < .025	R = C	R > P	C = P
Probability of being raped on the street	N		R = C	R = P	C = P
	R	p < .001	R > C	R > P	C = P
Probability of being raped in residence	N		R = C	R = P	C = P
	R	p < .001	R = C	R > P	C = P
Resident being burglarized when home	N				
	R		R = C	R = P	C = P
Resident being burglarized when absent	N		R = C	R = P	C = P
	R		R = C	R = P	C = P
Probability of auto theft	N		R = C	R = P	C = P
	R		R = C	R = P	C = P
Mean probability of being victimized	N		R = C	R = P	C = P
	R		R = C	R = P	C = P

Table 4.6
Protective Measures (Citizens)
Community Survey

		Overall P	R,C	R,P	C,P
Have you installed or do you have special or extra locks on doors.	N		R = C	R = P	C = P
	R		R = C	R = P	C = P
Have you installed or do you have special locks or bars on windows.	N		R = C	R = P	C = P
	R		R = C	R = P	C = P
Have you installed or do you have additional outside lighting.	N		R = C	R = P	C = P
	R	$.025 < p < .05$	R > C	R > P	C = P
Have you installed or do you have burglary alarms or security alarms.	N	$.025 < p < .05$	R < C	R < P	C > P
	R		R = C	R = P	C = P
Do you own a dog for protection.	N		R = C	R = P	C = P
	R		R = C	R = P	C = P
Do you try not to go out during the daytime.	N		R = C	R = P	C = P
	R		R = C	R = P	C = P
Do you try not to go out at night.	N		R = C	R = P	C = P
	R		R = C	R = P	C = P
Do you have guns in the house.	N		R = C	R = P	C = P
	R		R = C	R = P	C = P
Do you load guns that you have always had in the house.	N		R = C	R = P	C = P
	R	$.01 < p < .025$	R > C	R = P	C < P
Do you carry a gun.	N		R = C	R = P	C = P
	R		R = C	R = P	C = P
Do you carry a knife to protect yourself.	N	$p = .001$	R < C	R = P	C > P
	R		R = C	R = P	C = P
Do you carry a club, baseball bat, lead pipe or anything else like that.	N	$.025 < p < 05$	R < C	R = P	C > P
	R		R = C	R = P	C = P
Do you carry a chemical repellant like tear gas or mace.	N		R = C	R = P	C = P
	R		R = C	R = P	C = P
All protective measures.	N		R = C	R = P	C = P
	R		R = C	R = P	C = P

FINDING 6: PROTECTIVE MEASURES (CITIZENS)

Protective and security measures taken by citizens against the possibility of being involved in crime were not significantly affected by variations in the level of routine preventive patrol.

The questions asked of citizens in the Community Survey on this subject dealt with the installation of such devices as bars, alarms, locks and lighting, the keeping of various types of weapons or dogs for protection, and the taking of certain actions, such as staying inside, as preventive measures.

Here, 84 comparisons were made between experimental areas, with statistical significance occurring 11 times. The significance occurred most often (6 times) in those beats where preventive patrol had not changed, that is, in control beats. The change in the reactive beats showed significance three times, and in the proactive beats twice. There is no apparent explanation for the fact that the use of protective measures supposedly increased in the control beats relative to the other two conditions. For the most part the findings are inconsistent and occur either in the non-repeated sample or the repeated sample but never uniformly in both.

Thus, as measured by the use of protective and security measures, experimental preventive patrol conditions did not significantly affect citizen fear of crime.

Table 4.6 shows the data and findings.

FINDING 7: PROTECTIVE MEASURES (BUSINESSES)

Protective and security measures taken by businesses in the experimental area to protect offices or other places of business did not show significant differences due to changes in the level of routine preventive patrol.

In the Commercial Survey, businessmen were asked such questions as whether they had installed alarm systems or reinforcing devices such as bars over windows, whether they had hired guards, or whether they kept watchdogs or firearms in their places of business.

All told, 21 comparisons were made and statistical significance was found once, where the change in the control beats was the greater as compared with the reactive beats.

Because this was a telephone survey, however, some problems with the findings were evident. Briefly, some businessmen were reluctant to talk about protective measures over the phone to persons unknown to them. This is discussed more fully in the technical report.

The conclusion remains, however, that preventive variations seem to have little effect on fear of crime as indicated by protective measures taken by commercial establishments.

Table 4.7 shows the data and findings.

Citizen Attitudes toward Police
In addition to investigating citizen fear of crime and criminals, the preventive patrol experiment delved into citizen attitudes toward the police. Residents in the experimental area were asked, for instance, about the need for more police officers, about variations in patrol, police officer reputations and effectiveness, police treatment of citizens, and about their satisfaction with police service.

Table 4.7
Protective Measures (Businesses)
Commercial Survey

Crime type	Overall P	R,C	R,P	C,P
Outside alarm systems		R = C	R = P	C = P
Central alarm systems		R = C	R = P	C = P
Reinforcing measures		R = C	R = P	C = P
Guard or watchman		R = C	R = P	C = P
Watchdog		R = C	R = P	C = P
Keeping firearms in place of business		R = C	R = P	C = P
All protective measures	.025 < p < .05	R < C	R = P	C = P

Table 4.8
Citizen Attitudes toward Police

		Overall P	R,C	R,P	C,P
Need for more neighborhood police officers.	N		R = C	R = P	C = P
	R		R = C	R = P	C = P
Need for more police officers in the entire city.	N	.025 < p < .05	R > C	R = P	C = P
	R		R = C	R = P	C = P
Perception of time neighborhood officers spend on car patrol.	N		R = C	R = P	C = P
	R		R = C	R = P	C = P
Preference for amount of time police should patrol.	N		R = C	R = P	C = P
	R		R = C	R = P	C = P
Perceived amount of time police spend on aggressive patrol.	N		R = C	R = P	C = P
	R		R = C	R = P	C = P
Amount of time community prefers police spend on aggressive patrol.	N	.001 < p < .005	R < C	R = P	C = P
	R		R = C	R = P	C = P

continued

Table 4.8 continued

		Overall P	R,C	R,P	C,P
Perception of neighborhood police-community relations.	N		R = C	R = P	C = P
	R		R = C	R = P	C = P
Perception of neighborhood police officers reputation.	N	.025 < p < .05	R < C	R = P	C = P
	R		R = C	R = P	C = P
Reputation of Kansas City police officers.	N	.025 < p < .05	R = C	R = P	C > P
	R		R = C	R = P	C = P
Respect for neighborhood police.	N	.001 < p < .005	R < C	R = P	C > P
	R		R = C	R = P	C = P
Effectiveness of neighborhood officers in fighting crime.	N		R = C	R = P	C = P
	R		R = C	R = P	C = P
Effectiveness of Kansas City police in fighting crime.	N	.01 < p < .025	R = C	R = P	C > P
	R		R = C	R = P	C = P
Police treatment of whites.	N		R = C	R = P	C = P
	R	.025 < p < .01	R = C	R = P	C < P
Police treatment of minorities.	N		R = C	R = P	C = P
	R		R = C	R = P	C = P
Harassment by neighborhood police officers.	N	.001 < p < .005	R < C	R = P	C > P
	R	.001 < p < .005	R < C	R = P	C = P
Harassment by Kansas City police officers.	N	.01 < p < .025	R > C	R = P	C = P
	R	.001 < p < .005	R > C	R > P	C = P
Change in neighborhood police officers.	N	.001 < p < .005	R = C	R > P	C > P
	R		R = C	R = P	C = P
Satisfaction with police service.	N		R = C	R = P	C = P
	R	•			
Neighbors' respect for neighborhood officers.	N		R = C	R = P	C = P
	R		R = C	R = P	C = P

• Number of persons who called the police both years were too small for analysis.

The attitudes of businessmen toward police were studied in the course of the preventive patrol experiment for a variety of reasons. One was simply that businessmen's attitudes have seldom been studied in the past, although these people are often affected by crime in ways more crucial to their survival than are citizens in general. It is not only the businessman's personal comfort and safety that may be involved, but also the ability to remain in business that may be affected by crime. At the same time, businessmen are often influential in their communities. For these reasons, assessing their attitudes is often crucial to the development of new policing programs. Therefore, businessmen were asked similar questions about police effectiveness, treatment of citizens and so forth.

While the study of such attitudes is valuable in obtaining the impressions of a significant cross-section of the community, most of the citizens and businessmen interviewed were unlikely to have experienced recent actual contact with the police. Thus, another part of the preventive patrol experiment focused on determining citizens' responses to actual encounters with police officers. To determine such responses, citizens themselves, the police with whom they came in contact, and trained observers were all asked to complete reports on the encounter. Citizens were interviewed as soon as possible after the incident. Separate questionnaires were used, depending on whether the encounter was initiated by an officer or by a citizen.

Finally, a fourth measure was used to determine citizen attitudes. Here, in what has been given the title "Police-Citizen Transactions," the trained observers focused on the outcome of police-citizen interactions in terms of the patrol assignment of the officer involved, that is, reactive, control or proactive.

The next findings deal with citizen attitudes toward police, businessmen's attitudes toward police, police-citizen encounters initiated either by citizens (calls for service) or police (traffic arrests, suspect apprehension, etc.) and finally police-citizen transactions.

FINDING 8: CITIZEN ATTITUDES TOWARD POLICE

Citizen attitudes toward police were not significantly affected by alterations in the level of preventive patrol.

A large number of questions in the Community Survey were designed to measure citizen attitudes toward the police. As a result, more comparisons were made here than in other cases and more instances of statistical significance were found. Altogether, 111 comparisons were made and statistical significance occurred 16 times. Items with significant differences included the need for more police officers in the city, the reputation of police officers, citizens' respect for police, police effectiveness, harassment, and change in neighborhood police officers.

Of the 16 instances of significance, the change in reactive beats was greater five times, in control beats ten times, and in proactive beats once, demonstrating no consistent pattern of statistical significance. The indication is that there was little correlation between level of patrol and citizen attitudes.

Table 4.8 shows the data and findings.

FINDING 9: BUSINESSMEN'S ATTITUDES TOWARD POLICE

Businessmen's attitudes toward police were not significantly affected by changes in the level of routine preventive patrol.

Like citizens in the Community Survey, businessmen in the Commercial Survey were asked about their attitudes toward police. Some of the questions in the Commercial Survey were similar to those in the Community Survey and some specially selected with regard to businessmen's interests.

In all, 48 comparisons were made to measure differences in businessmen's attitudes, but no statistically significant differences were found or even approached. The clear indication here is that variations in the level of preventive patrol have no effect on businessmen's attitudes.

Table 4.9 shows the data and findings.

FINDING 10: POLICE-CITIZEN ENCOUNTERS

Citizen attitudes toward police officers encountered through the initiative of either the citizen or the officer were not significantly affected by changes in patrol level.

Citizen attitudes were measured by both questions asked of citizens themselves and observations of trained observers. Citizens and observers alike were asked about such items as response time, characteristics of the encounter, the attitude and demeanor of officers in the encounter, and citizen satisfaction. Observers in officer-initiated encounters also recorded things not likely to be noted by citizens, including the number of officers and police vehicles present.

Including both citizen-initiated and officer-initiated encounters, a total of 63 comparisons were made and no statistically significant differences were found.

Tables 4.10 and 4.11 show the data and findings.

Table 4.9
Businessmen's Attitudes Toward Police

	Overall P	R,C	R,P	C,P
Safety of neighborhood		R = C	R = P	C = P
Crime in neighborhood as compared to previous years		R = C	R = P	C = P
Effectiveness of Kansas City police in fighting crime		R = C	R = P	C = P
How good a job the neighborhood police are doing in fighting crime		R = C	R = P	C = P
Relationship between the police and businessmen in neighborhood		R = C	R = P	C = P
Reputation of police in neighborhood		R = C	R = P	C = P
Reputation of Kansas City police		R = C	R = P	C = P
Respect for neighborhood police		R = C	R = P	C = P
Number of police needed in neighborhood		R = C	R = P	C = P
Number of police needed in Kansas City		R = C	R = P	C = P
Amount of time spent by police in car patrol activities		R = C	R = P	C = P
Amount of time that should be spent by police in car patrol activities		R = C	R = P	C = P
Satisfaction with police investigation		R = C	R = P	C = P
Satisfaction with courtesy and concern during an investigation		R = C	R = P	C = P
Amount of time spent by police questioning and searching		R = C	R = P	C = P
Amount of time police should spend questioning and searching		R = C	R = P	C = P

Table 4.10
Police-Citizen Encounters
(Citizen-initiated Encounters)

(Citizen response)	Overall P	R,C	R,P	C,P
Response time evaluation		R = C	R = P	C = P
Demeanor of officer citizen spoke to most		R = C	R = P	C = P
Attitude of officer citizen spoke to most		R = C	R = P	C = P
Characteristics of the encounter		R = C	R = P	C = P
Satisfaction with encounter		R = C	R = P	C = P
Evaluation of Kansas City Police Dept.		R = C	R = P	C = P
(Observer response)				
Response time evaluation		R = C	R = P	C = P
Demeanor of officer citizen spoke to most		R = C	R = P	C = P
Character of officer citizen spoke to most		R = C	R = P	C = P
Characteristics of the encounter		R = C	R = P	C = P

Table 4.11
Police-Citizen Encounters
(Officer-initiated Encounters)

(Citizen response)	Overall P	R,C	R,P	C,P
Attitude of officer citizen spoke to most		R = C	R = P	C = P
Demeanor of officer citizen spoke to most		R = C	R = P	C = P
Characteristics of the encounter		R = C	R = P	C = P
Citizen general satisfaction with police		R = C	R = P	C = P
(Observer response)				
Number of police vehicles at incident scene		R = C	R = P	C = P
Number of uniformed officers at the incident		R = C	R = P	C = P
Demeanor of officer citizen spoke to most		R = C	R = P	C = P

continued

Table 4.11 continued

(Observer response)	Overall P	R,C	R,P	C,P
Attitude of officer citizen spoke to most		R = C	R = P	C = P
Character of the officer citizen spoke to most		R = C	R = P	C = P
Characteristics of the encounter		R = C	R = P	C = P
Satisfaction with the encounter		R = C	R = P	C = P

FINDING 11: POLICE-CITIZEN TRANSACTIONS

The behavior of police officers toward citizens was not significantly affected by the officers' assignment to a reactive, control or proactive beat.

The finding is distinct from the previous finding in that the focus here is upon the police-citizen interaction in terms of the beat assignment of the officer rather than on the location of the contact. (Many police contacts with citizens take place outside of the officer's beat.) Data were recorded by participant observers riding with the officers.

In all, 18 comparisons were made between experimental areas, and no statistically significant differences were found.

Table 4.12 shows the data and findings.

OTHER EFFECTS

EXPERIMENTAL FINDINGS IN REGARD TO POLICE RESPONSE TIME

The time it takes police officers to respond to a citizen call for assistance is usually considered an important measure of patrol effectiveness. The general principle is that the lower the response time, the more efficiently the police are doing their job.

But there are difficulties in determining how to measure response time given the numerous possible segments involved. For instance, is the response time cycle complete when the first officer arrives at the scene? Or when the last of several officers dispatched reaches the scene? Or when the first officer contacts the person making the call? For the purposes of the preventive patrol experiment, response time was defined as the time between receipt of a call from a dispatcher to the point when that unit contacted the citizen involved. In measuring citizen satisfaction with response time, the entire range of time required was considered, beginning with the citizen's contact with the police switchboard operator.

Response time was studied to see if experimental conditions would have any effect on the amount of time taken by police in answering citizen calls for service. Before the experiment began, the hypothesis was that experimental conditions would affect response time, particularly in the proactive beats. It was believed that since more officers were assigned to proactive beats, response time would be significantly reduced in those beats.

Table 4.12
Police-Citizen Transactions
(Observer Records)

	Overall P	R,C	R,P	C,P
Citizen satisfaction with disposition of all transactions		R = C	R = P	C = P
Citizen satisfaction with officer in all transactions		R = C	R = P	C = P
Citizen satisfaction with disposition of officer-initiated transactions		R = C	R = P	C = P
Citizen satisfaction with disposition of citizen-initiated transactions		R = C	R = P	C = P
Citizen satisfaction with officer in citizen-initiated transactions		R = C	R = P	C = P

FINDING 12: RESPONSE TIME

The amount of time taken by police in answering calls for service was not significantly affected by variations in the level of routine preventive patrol.

To obtain the finding, data were gathered on such matters as distance from the police car to scene of incident, mean time from receipt of calls to start of call, mean time from receipt of call to arrival at scene, and observer's estimate of patrol car speed. Citizen estimates of time and satisfaction were also measured.

In the area of response time, a total of 42 comparisons were made between patrol conditions. Statistical significance occurred only once: in the number of officers present at the scene of incidents in the reactive beats. The reason for this is unclear, but it can be theorized that police officers were exhibiting their concern for the safety of fellow officers and citizens in reactive beats.

While variations in the level of patrol did not significantly affect police response time, the Kansas City findings suggest that more research is necessary. It appears that response time is not only the result of rate of speed and distance, but also reflects the attitude of the officers involved and possibly other variables not investigated in this study.

Table 4.13 shows the data and findings.

Table 4.13
Response Time

	Overall P	R,C	R,P	C,P
Distance from location where call was received to location of incident		R = C	R = P	C = P
Mean time from receipt of call to start of call		R = C	R = P	C = P
Mean time from receipt of call to arrival at incident		R = C	R = P	C = P
Mean time from receipt of call to arrival of second officer		R = C	R = P	C = P
Mean time from receipt of call to citizen contact		R = C	R = P	C = P
Observer's estimate of speed		R = C	R = P	C = P
Number of other officers present at incident scene	.025 < p < .05	R = C	R > P	C = P
Citizen estimate of time spent speaking to police department operation		R = C	R = P	C = P
Citizen estimate of time spent speaking to police dispatcher		R = C	R = P	C = P
Citizen satisfaction with police dispatcher		R = C	R = P	C = P
Citizen estimate of time from call for service to arrival of patrol car		R = C	R = P	C = P
Citizen satisfaction with response time		R = C	R = P	C = P
Citizen estimate of time officer spent at incident		R = C	R = P	C = P
Citizen's overall satisfaction with job officer did		R = C	R = P	C = P

Experimental Findings in Regard to Traffic Accidents

Does the police visibility through routine preventive patrol have an effect upon traffic accidents? A common hypothesis is that it does, that reduction in patrol, for instance, will be followed by an increase in traffic accidents. Therefore the preventive patrol experiment involved some study of the presumed relationship.

The finding in this area is presented with considerable caution, however, since traffic patterns played no role in the selection of the experimental beats. It is possible (and in fact likely, given the area involved) that traffic patterns in the experimental area are not representative, and thus would not allow for reliable findings. In addition, the findings involved only accidents reported to the department by citizens and do not take into account accidents which occurred but were not reported.

FINDING 13: TRAFFIC ACCIDENTS

Variations in the level of routine preventive patrol had no significant effect upon traffic accidents.

A total of six comparisons were made in this area, with statistical significance not occurring in any.

Table 4.14 shows the data and findings.

Table 4.14
Traffic Accidents

	Overall P	R,C	R,P	C,P
Non-injury accidents		R = C	R = P	C = P
Injury & fatality accidents		R = C	R = P	C = P

SUMMARY AND CONCLUSION: EXPERIMENTAL FINDINGS

Of the 648 comparisons used to produce the major findings of the preventive patrol experiment, statistical significance between pairs occurred 40 times representing approximately 6 percent of the total. Of these 40 findings, the change in the reactive beats was greater 15 times, in the control beats 19 times, and in the proactive beats 6 times. Given the large amount of data collected and the extremely diverse sources used, the overwhelming evidence is that decreasing or increasing routine preventive patrol within the range tested in this experiment had no effect on crime, citizen fear of crime, community attitudes toward the police on the delivery of police service, police response time or traffic accidents.

CALLING THE POLICE   5

William Spelman & Dale K. Brown

Rapid police response may be unnecessary for three out of every four serious crimes reported to police. The traditional practice of immediate response to all reports of serious crimes currently leads to on-scene arrests in only 29 of every 1,000 cases. By implementing innovative programs, police may be able to increase this response-related arrest rate to 50 or even 60 per 1,000, but there is little hope that further increases can be generated.

These are the major findings of the Forum's three-year study of citizen-reporting and police response. These outcomes unequivocally support conclusions reached by the Kansas City (MO) Police Department in its 1977 study of police response to serious crimes: that citizen-reporting time, and not police response time, most affects the possibility of on-scene arrest; and, that, when citizens delay in reporting crimes, efforts to reduce police response times have no substantial effect on arrest rates.

The Forum's study is based on interviews with over 4,000 victims, witnesses and bystanders in some 3,300 serious crimes of the following six types: aggravated assault, auto theft, burglary, larceny, rape and robbery. The study was conducted in four American cities: Jacksonville, Florida; Peoria, Illinois; Rochester, New York; and San Diego, California. These cities were selected because of their differences; each represented a singular mix of populational, regional and police agency characteristics. Nonetheless, the outcomes from city to city were almost identical, which would tend to indicate that the findings apply to other cities across the nation.

The results of this study and the related implications for police department policy concerning rapid response to citizen calls for service must be

Source: William Spelman and Dale K. Brown (1981). "Calling the Police." In *Calling the Police: Citizen Reporting of Serious Crime*, xix-xxxvi. Washington, DC: Police Executive Research Forum. Reprinted with permission.

kept in proper perspective. The findings of this study focus only on citizen delays in the reporting of serious crimes (Part I crimes except homicide and arson) and the effect these delays have on *on-scene, response-related* arrests by the police. The effect of rapid police response on less serious crimes was addressed in the aforementioned Kansas City study. Also, previous studies have examined the effects of rapid police response on citizen satisfaction, availability of witnesses and crime scene evidence, and the handling of medical emergencies. These related issues are considered in the literature review but are not the subject of empirical analysis in this study. The effects of rapid police response on other types of citizen calls for police service, including non-crime calls, calls to maintain order, and calls which can prevent crime, have not been studied here. All of these issues must be taken into consideration along with the findings concerning response-related arrests when reviewing a police department's general policy on responding to citizen's calls for service. It would be consistent with the results of this study, for example, to have a policy requiring rapid response in a "suspicious person" call while providing for less than immediate response in a burglary discovered after the fact.

Some details of the major findings of the study are summarized in the next few pages, but a thorough understanding can only be gained by reading the full report. The page numbers listed in the margins indicate those sections of the report which relate to the findings described only briefly in this summary. (Analytic methods are described in the separate Technical Appendices.)

REPORTING TIME, RESPONSE TIME AND ARREST

For at least half a century, police have considered it important to cut to a minimum their response times to crime calls. The faster the response, they have reasoned, the better the chances of catching a criminal, at or near the scene of the crime. In the cities we studied, however, *arrests that could be attributed to fast police response were made in only 2.9 percent of reported serious crimes.*

Why is the response-related arrest rate so low? The major reason is that about 75 percent of all serious crimes reported are discovery crimes—crimes that are discovered after they have been completed, and in which offenders have had time to escape without police interference. The remaining 25 percent are *involvement* crimes—those in which the victim is directly confronted by the offender. In this study, citizen reporting time for discovery crimes averaged between ten minutes and ten-and-one-half minutes in the four cities, or between 40 and 60 percent of total response time, which includes citizen reporting time, police dispatch time and police travel time. Consequently, because "suspect get-away time" even before the crime is discovered is likely to be long, and citizen reporting time after discovery of the crime is also long, there is virtually no chance that discovery crimes will result in response-related arrests. This common sense conclusion is verified by previous research and is confirmed by the results of this study. *Therefore, in only about 25 percent of all reported serious crimes, namely those that are not discovery crimes but, rather, are involvement crimes, can fast response make a difference.*

But how fast does response to these involvement crimes have to be to make a difference? Since the late 1930's, police scientists have asserted that fast response can lead to arrest only if the police arrive while the crime is still happening or within two to three minutes after it has been completed. In this study, average citizen reporting time for *involvement crimes* ranged between four minutes and five and one-half minutes or between 28 and 47 percent of total response time. Thus, even for involvement crimes the likelihood of response-related arrest is relatively low. When citizens delay even a few minutes, the suspect has usually left the crime scene and no on-scene arrest is likely. *This was found to be true in each of the four cities surveyed.*

Of all involvement crimes reported to police, 54 percent were reported within five minutes of their occurrence.

- Thirteen percent were reported while still in-progress. Under these circumstances, the chances of response-related arrest were very good: about 35 percent.

- An additional 14 percent were reported within the first minute after the crimes had been committed. When reported within a few seconds, the chances of response-related arrest were about 18 percent; if reported 60 seconds after the crime, the chances were only about 10 percent.

- For the remaining 27 percent reported between one and five minutes after the crimes had been committed, the chances of response-related arrest were about seven percent.

Regarding the remaining reports of involvement crimes, when citizens delayed for a full five minutes, they might as well have delayed for an hour: the chances of arrest were no better for five-minute delays than for 60-minute delays.

So it is not surprising that only three percent of all reports of serious crimes led to response-related arrests: only about 25 percent of these reports were likely to be reports of involvement crimes in which fast response could make a difference; and, what is more, only 54 percent of these reports of involvement crimes were likely to be made in time enough, that is within five minutes, to afford police a reasonable opportunity to make on-scene arrests.

The findings are clear. Most serious crimes reported to the police are discovery crimes for which there is virtually no chance for response-related arrests. For the remaining crimes, those in which there is citizen involvement, the citizen must call the police within one minute, or the likelihood of response-related arrest drops dramatically.

What can police do to cut reporting times and increase the opportunities for arrest? They must focus their efforts on addressing the reasons for delay.

WHY CITIZENS DELAY

When citizens do not report crimes immediately, it is either because they decide to call the police only after they have taken some other action in response to the crime, or because they have trouble in communicating their reports to police after they have decided to call—or both.

There are three basic reasons for not deciding immediately to report crimes:

- Citizens sometimes want first to verify that a situation does indeed involve a crime, that is, they try to resolve ambiguity in the situation. To do this they take actions, some of which include:

  Observing the situation and/or investigating the crime scene. Such actions delayed reporting in just over 25 percent of the crimes studied, resulting in an average delay of two minutes.

  Telephoning someone not at the scene to acquire additional information, or seeking such information by talking to another person at the scene. One or the other of these actions was taken in about 6.6 percent of crimes studied, resulting in an average delay of three minutes for a telephone call or 90 seconds for a face-to-face conversation.

- Sometimes citizens take actions to help themselves *cope with problems the crime has created* for them. Such actions include:

  Leaving the scene of the crime. This occurred in over 19 percent of the cases studied, resulting in an average delay of about 90 seconds.

  Speaking with or telephoning someone to obtain assistance or support. One or the other of these occurred in 16.5 percent of our crime sample, resulting in average delays of about 90 seconds and three minutes, respectively.

  Chasing or restraining a suspect. Such actions occurred in about 6.4 percent of crimes studied and delayed reporting, on average, by 30 seconds.

Caring for physical injury. This occurred so infrequently in our sample (just over one percent of all cases) that no reliable estimate of delay is possible.

- Many citizens experience *conflict* as to whether or not to call the police, and they try to avoid making immediate decisions. In such cases citizens may:

    Procrastinate, hopeful that the decision will become easier. This occurred in 9.5 percent of the sample of serious crimes and caused delays that averaged 11 minutes.

    Talk to someone at the scene or telephone someone to get advice that may help in resolving the conflict. Face-to-face conversations occurred two percent of the time for an average delay of 90 seconds; telephoning occurred in only slightly above one percent of our sample, resulting in an average delay of about three minutes.

Most citizens who delay in making decisions do so for reasons they believe are very good: they may want to avoid the consequences of their calling the police about suspicious events that turn out not to involve crime; for some, coping with emotional trauma or with personal conflict may seem more urgent than reporting crime. *To prevent these decisionmaking delays, police must offer to citizens good reasons to report immediately, reasons that will override citizens' inclinations to delay.*

In undertaking to meet this objective, it is important to distinguish the three basic causes of decisionmaking delays; because of the distinctions, the methods police use in attacking the causes will necessarily differ.

When citizens *do* decide to report crimes, problems in communicating their reports to police sometimes arise. In our study, three such communications problems led to reporting delays.

- *A phone was not readily available.* This problem presented itself in only seven percent of our crime sample, resulting in an average delay of about 45 seconds.

- *The caller did not know the police telephone number* and had to look it up or call directory assistance. This problem touched 23 percent of our respondents, resulting in delays that averaged about one minute and forty-five seconds if the telephone directory was used but only a few seconds if the call was placed through the telephone company operator. Regarding the most urgent cases, the majority of people who did not know the police number dialed "0" rather than searching the directory.

- *The caller has trouble communicating with the police com-plaint taker.* This problem gave rise to reporting delays in 10 to 12 percent of the cases in our sample, resulting in an average delay of about 35 seconds.

People occasionally encountered other problems: a pay phone may have been out of order; the caller may have had no change for a pay phone; the caller may have dialed the wrong agency by mistake; but these problems arose so infrequently that, if somehow they all were eliminated, still, few if any additional arrests would ensue.

Of the six important causes of citizen-reporting delay reviewed above (three involving decisionmaking problems and three involving communications problems), on which should police focus to trim the most minutes from reporting time and to make the most arrests? To find out, we estimated the number of additional on-scene, response-related arrests police would make if each cause of delay were *eliminated*. To actually eliminate any of these causes of reporting delays is probably impossible; in general, they are susceptible to alleviation, not to elimination. Our purpose in using this method is to identify those causes of delay that have the greatest potential for increasing arrests.

The results, shown in Figure 5A, indicate that causes of decision-making delays hold significantly greater potential for increasing arrests than do causes of communications delays. Moreover, it is abundantly clear that the chief cause of reporting delay—the cause which, if removed, would have the greatest potential for increasing response-related arrest rates—is conflict as to whether or not to call the police. A program completely successful in relieving such conflict would increase the number of response-related arrests from 2.9 to 4.8 percent, an increase of 19 arrests per thousand serious crimes. Much smaller but still significant increases would be made if other causes of delay were eliminated.

What can police and local governments do to alleviate these decisionmaking and communications problems?

PROGRAMS THAT PROBABLY WILL REDUCE CITIZEN REPORTING TIME

Cut the Cost of Reporting a Crime. Citizens experience conflict because they believe, whatever they do, there will be high costs, either emotional or financial. On the one hand, reporting crimes may be inconvenient; victims may fear that police will hold them responsible for precipitating the crimes; victims may fear that offenders will take reprisals against them. On the other hand, not reporting crimes greatly reduces the chances that citizens will ever recover their property or see offenders brought to justice. Citizens in conflict feel they cannot win, so they avoid making decisions about reporting crimes: they procrastinate or ask others to make decisions for them.

Figure 5A
Potential Increases in Response-Related Arrests as a Result of Removing Each of Several Important Causes of Delay

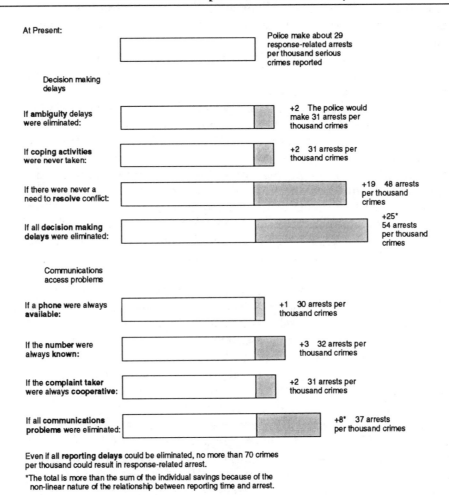

At Present:

Police make about 29 response-related arrests per thousand serious crimes reported

Decision making delays

If ambiguity delays were eliminated:

+2 The police would make 31 arrests per thousand crimes

If coping activities were never taken:

+2   31 arrests per thousand crimes

If there were never a need to resolve conflict:

+19   48 arrests per thousand crimes

If all decision making delays were eliminated:

+25* 54 arrests per thousand crimes

Communications access problems

If a phone were always available:

+1   30 arrests per thousand crimes

If the number were always known:

+3   32 arrests per thousand crimes

If the complaint taker were always cooperative:

+2   31 arrests per thousand crimes

If all communications problems were eliminated:

+8*   37 arrests per thousand crimes

Even if all **reporting delays** could be eliminated, no more than 70 crimes per thousand could result in response-related arrest.

*The total is more than the sum of the individual savings because of the non-linear nature of the relationship between reporting time and arrest.

In any efforts to root out this cause of delayed reporting and non-reporting, police must examine their procedures to ensure that costs of reporting are kept to a bare minimum. The inconvenience of reporting might be mitigated by offering to victims and witnesses assistance in getting to police stations and, when necessary, to court houses. Patrol officers could be trained to educate victims and witnesses in crime prevention techniques and to emphasize to these citizens the benefits that can accrue to them as a result of their implementing these practices. Then, too, citizens who fear reprisals deserve protection and reassurance; some police departments have instituted victim-witness protection units to prevent reprisals.

Because delays caused by conflict turn less on the *actual* costs, of reporting than on potential, often unknown, costs, it is possible that some gains can be made simply by advertising how infrequently offenders take reprisals against victims and witnesses and how convenient police procedures already are.

Distribute Phone Stickers Displaying the Police Department's Emergency Number. In the four cities we studied, most people distinguished emergency and non-emergency situations relatively well, but many people called phone company operators or dialed police administrative numbers because they did not know police emergency numbers. If stickers for telephones were distributed (perhaps along with monthly phone or electric bills) and people were encouraged to post the stickers on or near their personal and work phones, more people would use correct numbers. Regarding citizens who do not post numbers on their phones or who use phones beyond the reach of sticker distribution systems, they should be encouraged to dial phone company operators in emergencies and to refrain from searching directories. Though most people who do not know emergency numbers follow this procedure already, it should be encouraged for the benefit of the few who do not.

Implement Community-Based Neighborhood Anti-Crime Programs. Additional, but less considerable, increases in numbers of quickly reported crimes and response-related arrests can be realized by alleviating delays caused by ambiguity. If citizens are to recognize crimes while the crimes are being committed, citizens need to know what a crime looks like and where it is likely to occur: to provide such knowledge is the goal of programs like Neighborhood Watch. When Neighborhood Watch works, it is because citizens share information about each other's habits and activities. A man who sees a woman rummaging in a neighbor's house may think little of it; but, if he knows that his neighbor is on vacation he may recognize that a burglary is in progress and call the police. Neighborhood Watch programs in several jurisdictions have been shown to be effective in reducing delays due to ambiguity and in increasing the number of in-progress calls and response-related arrests.

Train Police Operators to Screen Calls for Service. One possible consequence of training police operators to screen calls would be a reduction in the occurrence of communications problems between complaint takers and reporting citizens; this reduction represents a potential gain of two arrests per thousand crimes. Nevertheless, other potential consequences have more significance.

If all the programs reviewed thus far were implemented, and they were to work perfectly, the maximum possible gain in response-related arrests would be no more than about 30 arrests per thousand. Though this would amount to a doubling of the response-related arrest rate, it is important to maintain perspective: the vast majority of crimes will continue to be discovered after they have been committed and will not require immediate police response.

No matter what else the police departments do, they can realize immense efficiency gains by screening calls for service: prioritizing them according to seriousness and how urgently police response is needed. Some kinds of calls will demand simply that reports be taken by phone; civilians can be sent to cold burglaries. In turn, this will free patrol resources to conduct more comprehensive on-scene investigations; it will make way for increased use of surveillance, decoy and other directed patrol activities; it will permit utilization of suspect "escape route blocking" tactics in cases of quickly reported crimes; it will allow officers to perform duties they are now unable to discharge because at present they must go back into service to handle non-urgent calls.

The programs surveyed at this point are all likely to result in reductions in citizen reporting times and increases in arrest rates. In contrast, our analysis shows that certain other programs, though frequently proposed, will probably *not* work.

PROGRAMS THAT PROBABLY WILL NOT REDUCE CITIZEN REPORTING TIME

911. In the cities we studied, one of which had an operational 911 system, there was nothing to show that installing 911 results in significant cuts in citizen reporting times. Where 911 is available, people who use it do so in situations in which they would otherwise dial police departments' seven-digit emergency numbers or call phone company operators. When people call operators instead of 911, delays increase by only about 10 seconds: not a significant figure within the general context of typical reporting times of five minutes or more. A 911 system would cut reporting times if people would not look up numbers in phone books when they should be using 911, but ironically, 911 seems to encourage people to look up numbers in phone books. This is because departments, in their attempts to keep the number of 911 calls under control, *encourage* people to use 911 only for emergencies; in our sample, a few people in every city mistook in-progress crimes and crimes in which a victim had been injured—very urgent situations—to be non-emergencies and, so, looked up numbers in phone books. This happened most frequently in Peoria, the only city in our

study which had installed 911. Extensive publicity accompanying 911 there may have backfired, causing slower reporting times.

More Pay Phones and "Dime-Free" Pay Phones. Some delays in reporting occur because phones are not available. Small increases in numbers of arrests could be expected if phones were always available to people who want to call police. Installing more pay phones, however, or allowing citizens to use police call boxes will not significantly alleviate this cause of delay. Moreover, to cut by one-half the number of delays that derive from this cause would require between two and four times the number of pay phones currently in place—clearly a very expensive proposition. Only nine of over 3,300 crimes studied involved delays owing to callers' having no change for pay phones, and such callers were rarely delayed for more than a few seconds. Permitting citizens to call police numbers or phone company operators for free may be useful with respect to public relations and may contribute to arrests in a few extraordinary cases but will not cause perceptible changes in arrest rates.

Mass Media Advertising. Finally, there is no evidence whatever that television and radio advertising, urging people to call the police immediately because "it's the right thing to do," will have any effect on reporting delays or arrest rates. When people delay, they do so for what they see as being good reasons. If the police hope to encourage faster reporting, they will have to give the public good reasons not to delay.

SPECIALIZED PATROL   6

Larry K. Gaines

Patrol has traditionally been viewed as the backbone of a police department. Patrol generally is the largest unit within the police department, with half or more of a department's personnel assigned there. Patrol officers are the first responders to the majority of calls received by a police department. When people have problems and they have no other way of dealing with them, they usually call the police. Patrol officers are then expected to handle problems ranging from a citizen dispute over a barking dog to a missing person. Patrol officers make more arrests than any other unit in the department. Although detectives receive more attention for their investigations, patrol officers make more felony arrests than do their investigator colleagues.

Historically, patrol was conceptualized as an omnipresent force that would reduce crime by eliminating opportunity. If patrol officers patrolled randomly, they could give the appearance of being everywhere all the time. Potential criminals, upon seeing this facade of omnipresence, theoretically would be deterred from their criminal acts for fear of being observed and apprehended. Additionally, as a result of being assigned to patrol beats or areas throughout the jurisdiction, patrol officers were in the best position to respond to citizen calls for service. Patrol, essentially, was a simple, easy strategy by which to attack a multitude of police problems.

In 1972 and 1973, the Police Foundation conducted the Kansas City patrol experiment that is reported in the chapter by Kelling et al. in this volume. The Kansas City patrol experiment attempted to test the efficacy of routine preventive patrol in reducing crime. As Kelling and his colleagues report, the experiment's results indicated that neither eliminating nor doubling the level of patrol had much, if any, impact on crime. The experiment's authors did not, however, suggest that routine patrol be eliminated. They recognized that it was the most effective method by which to deploy officers for answering citizens' calls for service. But they also suggested that police administrators search for more effective strategies to deal with crime.

The results of the Kansas City patrol experiment were vigorously attacked by the police community. Edward Davis, who later became police chief in Los Angeles, and his colleague, Lyle Knowles (1975), wrote a scathing attack and rebuttal to the experiment in *Police Chief* magazine. Others examined the experiment and found methodological problems with the research (Larson, 1975). However, the underlying problem and cause of the controversy was that the results questioned a basic police strategy that theretofore had been used by every department in the country. Police administrators had to rethink police operational strategies.

The Kansas City patrol experiment, although the best known, was not the first attempt to gauge the effectiveness of routine preventive patrol. In 1954, the New York City Police Department implemented Operation 25, in which patrol deployment was doubled for four months in the Twenty-fifth Precinct, one of the city's high-crime areas. Police officials touted the program as successful and pointed to a number of reduced crime statistics. Critics, however, charged that officials manipulated reported crime in order to achieve the desired outcomes and that the methodology was flawed. A second such experiment was conducted in New York City in 1965 when the number of police officers on its subways was increased from 1,200 to 3,100. After an initial decline in the number of reported robberies, they increased sixfold by 1970. It was later discovered that the police had manipulated the crime statistics in order to justify additional personnel. In 1966, the New York City Police Department conducted another patrol experiment in the Twenty-fifth Precinct. Patrol officers assigned to the Precinct were increased by 40 percent. The results again showed significant decreases in crime. Again, however, the methodology was flawed and the results were viewed as tenuous (Chaiken, 1978; Wilson, 1985; Walker, 1993).

Although controversial, the Kansas City patrol study did cause police administrators to rethink their crime-fighting tactics, and it eventually led to specialized patrol strategies. Routine preventive patrol was not abandoned, but departments began to supplement routine patrol with special units that targeted precise areas or specific crime problems.

SPECIALIZED PATROL AND STAFFING REQUIREMENTS

The Kansas City patrol study resulted in administrators re-evaluating patrol deployment and staffing patterns. If specialized patrols were to supplement routine patrol, additional personnel had to be obtained. Because most cities could not afford to hire additional personnel, officers had to be taken from other units within the department. Many departments initiated staffing studies in an attempt to determine the best way to allocate and deploy existing personnel.

A number of studies, including the Kansas City patrol study, indicated that patrol units in many departments were overstaffed. In Kansas City, it was found that 60 percent of officers' patrol time was uncommitted. Less than 25 percent of this uncommitted time was devoted to routine patrol activities such as observing for suspicious persons or watching buildings (Kelling et al., 1974). Similarly, Cordner (1982) investigated patrol time in an unnamed medium-sized city and found the level of uncommitted time to be 46 percent, and Whitaker (1982) examined the patrol time for 24 different departments and found that about two-thirds of the patrol time was uncommitted. Combined with the findings of the Kansas City experiment that patrol apparently had little effect on crime, these studies indicate that the number of patrol officers in some jurisdictions can be sharply reduced and officers assigned to specialized patrol units to attack crime.

It might be surmised that reducing patrol and reassigning patrol officers to specialized units or directed patrol activities will result in a lowered police response time and thus adversely affect citizen attitudes about police effectiveness and crime control. Untimely delays by the police do negatively affect public perceptions of police effectiveness (Percy, 1980; Pate et al. 1976). However, citizen impressions of their police can be properly managed by alerting citizens to any delays and by explaining the workload of officers.

Another consideration is that patrol officers' workloads would be substantially increased to the point that overall police effectiveness would be reduced. However, Bayley (1994) notes that police officials at all levels frequently complain about burdensome work loads, but studies seldom substantiate their complaints. Some police departments, some areas within many police jurisdictions, and some periods of time have large workloads, but generally the police do not have a workload that is unreasonable. McEwen et al. (1986) found that the police could effectively manage their work should it become too heavy. The police do not necessarily have to respond immediately to all calls for service. Many calls, especially minor complaints, can be handled by telephone, referral to other agencies, visits to police headquarters, or by having officers make appointments with citizens.

THE IMPACT OF THE POLICE ON CRIME

Before examining how police officers might be deployed to attack crime and criminals, the overall impact of the police on crime should be explored. The development and deployment of specialized patrol assumes that the police can have an impact on crime. This assumption should be proven before specific strategies are discussed. Furthermore, if how the police influence crime is understood, then better specialized patrol strategies can be implemented.

Criminologists and police administrators alike have for a number of years speculated on the effects of the police on crime. For example, a number of researchers have found a negative relationship between crime rates and arrest rates indicating that aggressive police practices relate to reduced crime rates (Sjoquist, 1973; Tittle & Rowe, 1974; Wilson & Boland, 1976). The results of these types of studies are tenuous because high crime rates may affect police ability to respond to crime. Thus, the outcomes may be reflective of police work overload as opposed to police effectiveness.

Others have refined this methodology and attempted to evaluate the effects of the police on crime by examining police activities, crime rates, and socioeconomic characteristics (Wilson & Boland, 1981; Sampson & Cohen, 1988). These studies indicate that if departments assume a legalistic philosophy (see Wilson, 1968) that emphasizes aggressive police patrol strategies, there is a greater effect on crime.

Wilson and Boland (1976) postulate that aggressive policing can have an impact on crime, in two ways. First, aggressive policing increases an offender's risk of arrest. They note, "By stopping, questioning, and otherwise closely observing citizens, especially suspicious ones, the police are more likely to find fugitives, detect contraband (such as stolen property or concealed weapons), and apprehend persons fleeing from the scene of a crime" (p. 373). If the real probability of arrest is increased, offenders may be less inclined to commit criminal acts. Second, if the police more aggressively enforce the law, they send a message to citizens that they are more likely to be arrested when committing a criminal act. Thus, if the perceived probability of arrest is increased, persons are less likely to commit crimes.

Wilson and Boland's ideas about aggressive patrol and crime reduction dovetail with community building and the reduction of social disorder in neighborhoods. Skogan and Maxfield (1981) and Wilson and Kelling (1982) have discussed how neighborhood disintegration results in increased fear of crime. Greenberg et al. (1985, p. 82) go a step further, noting that disintegration results in increased crime, "assuming that residents are so indifferent to what goes on in their neighborhood that they will not be motivated to confront strangers, intervene in a crime, or call the police." Such a situation most assuredly will result in criminals gaining self-confidence in their ability to avoid apprehension when committing a criminal act. Also, minor criminality and disorder attract more serious crime. For example, Weisburd, Maher and Sherman (1991) found in their Minneapolis study found that one of the strongest correlates of robbery calls was drunk calls. Furthermore, Goldstein (1990) points to a police responsibility to assist neighborhoods in building communities and solving problems as a method of reducing crime. Community building and problem solving are central parts of today's community policing.

Thus, the police can have both a direct and indirect effect on crime. To maximize their effectiveness in crime reduction, the police should adopt aggressive patrolling techniques as well as community building and problem solving.

SPECIALIZED PATROL STRATEGIES: AN EVALUATION AND DISCUSSION

Over the years, police departments have experimented with a variety of specialized patrol strategies. Some of these strategies have focused on individual suspects, while others concentrated on geographical areas that were experiencing elevated levels of crime and disorder. Still others focused on certain types of criminal acts such as robberies or muggings. The following sections describe some of the major forms of specialized patrol strategies. They are divided into two groupings: perpetrator-oriented strategies and place- or location-oriented strategies.

PERPETRATOR-ORIENTED STRATEGIES

Perpetrator-oriented strategies are those in which the police identify specific individuals or classes of individuals for investigation or targeting. The idea is that some people commit a disproportionate number of crimes, and if they can be targeted and stopped or incarcerated, the overall crime rates can be dramatically changed. Perpetrator-oriented strategies include: field interrogations, person-oriented patrol, and repeat offender programs.

Field Interrogations. Field interrogations (FI) historically have been an indispensable part of police efforts to control street crime and disorder. Police officers routinely interrogate suspicious persons as a method of possibly gaining suspect information on crimes that have already been committed and to send a message to individuals who may be desirous of committing a crime. The FI is an interpersonal contact between the police and potential lawbreakers in which the police attempt to reduce an individual's desire to commit a crime through intimidation and information gathering or reduce the opportunity to commit a crime through omni-presence.

In 1973, the Police Foundation, in cooperation with the San Diego Police Department, examined the effects of field interrogations. The study tested three forms of FI: (1) traditional FI practices, (2) FIs in which officers received training in human relations skills to minimize the friction between officers and persons interrogated, and (3) suspension of all FI activities. The study attempted to discern how the three experimental practices affected (1) crimes which were considered suppressible, (2) total arrest rates, and (3) police-community relations (Boydstun, 1975).

In terms of suppressible crimes, the results showed that FIs had a significant impact on these types of crimes. Suppressible are crimes that are observable by patrolling police officers, such as street crime. Suppressible crimes increased when FIs were suspended and decreased when FIs were resumed. However, Boydstun was unable to pinpoint the specific suppressible crimes that were most amenable to suppression by means of FIs. The experimental conditions did not have an effect on monthly arrest frequencies, but officers attributed 17 percent of their total arrests to FIs. Also, FI arrests primarily were for persons who did not reside in the area where the FI took place. The experimental practices did not result in any differences of citizen attitudes toward the police. In fact, most citizens felt the police FIs were justified and properly conducted.

Perpetrator-Oriented Patrol. Perpetrator-oriented patrol (POP) involves the surveillance of specific persons suspected of committing high levels of criminal activity or who commit individual crimes that have a significant cost in terms of property or personal injury. Such a strategy is common sense. Veteran police officers who are experienced in the streets generally know who these offenders are. If they can be removed from the streets, the overall crime rates can be affected.

POP was actually an extension of police departments' time-honored practice of issuing photographs of suspected felons and wanted persons to officers. Rather than providing officers with photographs and directions to "watch for these people," officers target and observe identified offenders until they commit a crime. For example, the Wilmington, Delaware Police Department established a six-officer robbery squad which targeted known robbers. They used stakeouts and infiltrated suspects' hangouts. The squad was able to make a number of arrests, primarily for firearms violations. At one point, 210 out of 418 state prisoners were arrested by the unit (Pate, Bowers, and Parks, 1976).

In August 1972, the Police Foundation, in cooperation with the Kansas City Police Department, examined the effects of POP. The study ran through January 1974. Two tactical squads composed of five or six-officers and a sergeant were deployed. The squads focused on robbery and burglary suspects. However, during the initial stage of the study, it was determined that the squad observed many more violations for other crimes such as narcotics violations which posed a dilemma for officers, because narcotics were not a part of their assignment. Later, the squads' format was changed to collect intelligence that could be used by other units to make arrests.

Evaluation of the POP consisted of comparing the arrest activity of officers in the POP district to the activity of officers in another district. The results indicated that POP contributed to higher levels of arrests, especially arrests of targeted individuals. POP officers averaged seven burglary and robbery arrests over the two-year program while regular patrol officers averaged one such arrest. Also, POP produced a significant level of criminal intelligence that was used by other officers to make arrests. It appears that an added benefit may have been that officers in the district not assigned to the program became more aggressive in targeting and arresting felons (Pate, Bowers, and Parks, 1976).

However, there are drawbacks to the POP strategy, especially if it is not supervised correctly. Milton et al. (1977) examined the STRESS unit (Stop the Robberies—Enjoy Safe Streets) in Detroit. The unit consisted of detectives who intimidated robbery suspects. They found the unit had an unusually high rate of use of deadly force where numerous suspects and non-suspects were shot by police officers. The unit became an issue in the mayoral campaign and was largely responsible for Detroit electing its first African-American mayor.

Repeat Offender Programs. Repeat offender programs (ROPs) were implemented in the 1970s and early 1980s and were extensions of POP. ROPs attempted to identify and arrest high-rate offenders. Research indicates that approximately ten percent of offenders commit about 50 percent of the crimes (Spelman, 1986), and their criminality rates are 40 to 50 times higher than regular criminals (Chaiken and Chaiken, 1982). Furthermore, these high-rate offenders do not specialize, but commit all sorts of crimes that result in property losses and injuries to citizens. Thus, if a higher proportion of this ten percent could be selectively incarcerated, the overall crime rate should decrease significantly.

A 1984 survey of police departments revealed that 33 departments had implemented ROP units (Spelman, 1990). These programs fell into one of the following categories:

1. *Pre-arrest Targeting* in which officers used surveillance and stakeouts to apprehend suspects before or while committing a criminal act.

2. *Warrant Services* in which officers tracked down parole or probation violators or suspects wanted on warrants.

3. *Post-Arrest Enhancement* in which officers would enter a case after a suspect had been arrested. Officers would select cases in which repeat offenders had been arrested, then assist other officers in developing a stronger case by re-examining physical evidence and re-contacting witnesses and victims.

ROPs have been implemented in a number of jurisdictions. The program in Washington, D.C. has received the most examination. Initially, ROP officers in Washington were to spend half their time on surveillance and the remaining half on serving warrants. After six months, surveillance only produced 14 percent of the unit's arrests. The unit then implemented more proactive tactics such as stakeouts, buy-busts, stings, decoys, and other covert means. A Police Foundation evaluation of the program found that target offenders were eight times more likely to be arrested relative to non-target offenders, and although ROP officers made fewer arrests than other officers, they were quality arrests for index, drugs, and weapons crimes. Also, ROP arrestees had criminal records that were approximately double the average (Martin and Sherman, 1986).

Several problems with ROP and offender-oriented strategies exist. First, Spelman (1990) notes that although there is a group of repeat offenders who commit a considerable number of criminal acts, it is difficult to identify specifically which ones to target. Even when factors such as drug use, past criminal record, employment and family record, and offense characteristics are considered, it is difficult to pare the resultant sample down to a manageable and meaningful target group. Second, Sherman (1992) notes that in order for ROPs to be successful, targeted offenders would have to be "lone wolves" or criminals who work alone, and co-offending would very likely defeat the program. Reiss (1988) occasions some co-offenders as "Typhoid Marys" who are not necessarily ringleaders in criminogenic groups, but they do provide a motivating force in getting others to commit crime. When arrests are made, but co-offenders or the Typhoid Marys remain, the overall impact on criminal behavior may be nonexistent.

LOCATION-ORIENTED STRATEGIES

Just as crime is not equally distributed across people, it is also not equally distributed across space or locations. Indeed, research in Minneapolis by Sherman (1989) shows that geographical concentrations of crime and disorder, or *hot spots,* exist.

> Three percent of the estimated 115,000 addresses and intersections in Minneapolis were the subject of 50 percent of the 321,174 calls to police between December 15, 1985 and December 15, 1986. Sixty percent of the addresses and intersections produced no calls to police at all. Of the 40 percent with any calls, the majority (52%) had only one call, while 84 percent had less than five. The top 5 percent of the locations with any calls produced 48.8 percent of the calls (p. 150).

If the police could devise successful location-oriented strategies for some of these high call rate locations, the overall workload for the police and the crime rate could be lessened. To this end, several strategies have been attempted. They include: stakeouts and decoy units, split-force patrol, location-oriented patrol, directed patrol, crackdowns, and problem solving. All of these strategies involve saturating a problem area with police officers.

Stakeouts and Decoy Units. Although this section deals with location-oriented strategies, two specific tactics—stakeouts and decoy units—deserve some discussion. First, stakeouts and decoys were used by police agencies to attack location problems long before police administrators even considered spatial distributions of crime and calls. Second, stakeouts and decoys remain important tactics that are used in several of the strategies discussed below.

An early study of stakeouts and decoys was the evaluation performed on New York City's Street Crime Unit (SCU) (Halper and Ku, n.d.). The SCU deployed officers in specific high-crime areas with the objective of arresting perpetrators during the commission of criminal acts. Officers used all sorts of clothing and activities to blend into the environment. In some cases they appeared as workmen, while other officers appeared as drunks or derelicts. Officers assumed one of two roles: that of potential victim or surveillance-backup officer. An evaluation of the project showed that crime rates could be lowered by the SCU, and that the SCU produced more arrests than did regular patrol officers.

Split-Force Patrol. An early innovative location-oriented approach was split-force patrol in Wilmington, Delaware. Split-force patrolling necessitated that the patrol force be divided into two distinct units: a patrol unit and a criminal suppression unit. The patrol unit conducted routine patrol functions including answering calls for service. When not answering calls, the patrol units had assignments that included security checks, monitoring of schools at opening and closing times, and traffic enforcement. The crime suppression unit was charged with attempting to intercept criminals in the act of committing their crimes. In addition to responding to crimes in progress, they used high-visibility saturation patrol, covert patrolling, and decoy operations. Activities were guided by crime analysis information.

Although the patrol and criminal suppression units represented a coordinated effort within a geographical area, conflict developed between the two units. The patrol officers saw themselves as being relegated a secondary function relative to the criminal suppression units while the latter group took on a pretentious and condescending view toward the patrol units. The patrol officers felt that the crime suppression officers received all the good or interesting assignments while they were left with the routine assignments (Gay, Schell, and Schack, 1977).

Location-Oriented Patrol. Location-oriented patrol (LOP), implemented in Kansas City, was a companion program with perpetrator-oriented patrol (POP). The goal of LOP was to place officers in high-crime areas, especially where robberies and burglaries were occurring, to intercept criminals in the act of committing a crime. An example of a LOP assignment was an area that had 28 burglaries in approximately a one-month period. Once they received an assignment, the autonomous LOP squads determined how they would attack a specific area.

> Dress could vary from police uniforms to business suits, casual clothes, or service worker uniforms. Vehicles might be police cars, rental cars, or such novel vehicles as soft drink, phone company, or pollution control trucks. Tactics might include frequent car and pedestrian checks, roving surveillance, or stationary surveillance from places as bizarre as the top of a telephone pole. The area of assignment might be a specific address, several blocks along a major thoroughfare, an area several blocks square, a single beat, or an entire sector (Pate, Bowers, and Parks, 1976: 9).

LOP produced higher levels of arrests of targeted offenders than POP and regular patrols. However, POP officers were able to provide the department with more intelligence information than LOP officers. Also, the quality of these arrests were higher than average. A higher percentage of the LOP arrests resulted in charges being filed by the prosecutor.

Directed Patrol. Directed patrol is where officers are assigned to patrol or work a specific location for a given period. For example, a department may be experiencing a large number of traffic accidents at a particular intersection between 10:00 A.M. and 11:00 A.M. An officer may be asked to park at the intersection for 15 minutes sometime between 10:00 A.M. and 11:00 A.M. in an effort to reduce the number of accidents. The same type of assignment can be used for a high-crime or disorder area. Officers when working the high-crime or disorder area would make as many arrests as possible to emphasize the police presence. Warren, Forst, and Estrella (1979) note that directed patrol programs seem to have four common elements:

1. directed patrol is aggressive and proactive

2. directed patrol officers use their non-committed time to engage in specific law enforcement activity

3. directed patrol officers are given specific instructions directing their aggressive patrol activities

4. instructions are the result of crime analysis efforts

Warren, Forst, and Estrella (1979) tested the effects of directed patrol on burglaries in Martinez, California. During a one-year period, two officers were assigned to patrol potential burglary targets in an area. The program resulted in a substantial reduction in burglaries. In a second study, McCampbell (1983) examined the effects of directed patrol on robberies during the Christmas season in Arlington County, Virginia. Crime analysis of data from the previous Christmas season showed that the robberies primarily occurred in four districts. Directed patrol units randomly moved from one target location to another to reduce the robberies through high visibility. The program resulted in a reduction in robberies. Finally, in a third more comprehensive study, Cordner (1981) examined the effects of directed patrols in Pontiac, Michigan. He found that when directed patrol officers used aggressive patrol tactics such as field interrogations, vehicle stops, and proactive arrests, there was an appreciable decrease in several crime areas. He also found that extending the amount of time that patrol units spent at a particular location was not particularly cost-effective. Only minimal changes in arrests and deterrence effects were found when directed patrol times were increased.

Crackdowns. Crackdowns go beyond merely saturating an area with additional officers. Crackdowns refer to a sudden increase of officers in an area with the objective of aggressive patrolling and elevated numbers of arrests. In some instances, crackdowns are for specific violations or crimes. There have been crackdowns on drunk driving, prostitution, and drug dealing. In other instances, the crackdowns have been general where officers make massive numbers of arrests for any and all offenses. General crackdowns, or street sweeping, as it is sometimes called, have been used in areas where substantial, unwieldy levels of crime and disorder exist. Officers sweep through the area, arresting as many people as possible. The idea is to restore some semblance of order by shocking disorderly persons and criminals into a higher level of conformity.

Sherman (1990) identifies two effects that crackdowns have on crime and disorder. First, they increase the perceived risk of apprehension. When the police make massive numbers of arrests in an area, potential offenders quickly determine that they are more likely to be arrested relative to the period before the police presence. Second, it increases the level of uncertainty about arrest. Prior to the crackdown, offenders had a high level of assuredness that they would not be arrested. Crackdowns remove this assuredness and increase the degree of uncertainty, which also has a deterrent effect.

Examples of crackdowns abound. In some cases, the crackdowns are for specific offenses such as parking (Sherman et al., 1986), drugs (Kleiman, 1988; Zimmer, 1990), drunk driving (Ross, 1981), and prostitution (Matthews, 1986). In other cases, the crackdown may be for a specific area. Examples include public housing (Weisel, 1990; Webster and Connors,

1992), neighborhoods (Zimmer, 1990), or a whole city (Robinson, 1986; Reuter et al., 1988). Crackdowns are very flexible and can be used to counter most crime and disorder problems confronting a department.

Crackdowns can have an extraordinary, short-term impact on a problem, but in most cases, the police cannot maintain the elevated levels of enforcement for extended periods. Once enforcement returns to previous levels, the problem tends to return (Sherman, 1990). Further, evaluations of crackdowns indicate that they result in displacement of crime to other areas and the resurgence of the problem once the crackdown is completed (Bouza, 1988; Robinson, 1986; Zimmer, 1990). However, Sherman (1990) postulates that crackdowns result in residual improvements. That is, crime and disorder levels do not immediately increase to prior crackdown levels once the crackdown is terminated, but fear of arrest and uncertainty remain for a period with crime and disorder gradually increasing to higher levels. Sherman speculates that multiple, intermittent crackdowns over an extended period could be useful in maintaining crime and disorder at lowered levels for extended periods.

Problem-Solving. Problem-solving is situational policing in which officers identify a specific condition, usually a location with an associated high volume of calls or crime, and take actions to ameliorate the conditions that cause the problem. The police response does not necessarily require enforcement actions, but may entail the deployment of other governmental or private services such as nuisance abatement, city engineers, etc. Eck and Spelman (1987) pioneered the problem-solving approach in Newport News, Virginia. They provided several examples of how the police can use non-traditional strategies to reduce or eliminate traditional problems. Since their original work, problem-solving has become a central part of community policing.

Problem-solving obviously has the potential to assist the police in alleviating problems that result in an increase in workload. Eck and Spelman (1987) provide several examples of its success. However, problem-solving should not be viewed as a panacea. Buerger (1991) examined 100 attempts by Minneapolis police officers to use problem-solving. He found there were as many failures as successes. The problem is that officers are confronted with a diverse number of problems, many of which do not have plausible answers. Regardless, problem-solving remains a viable method by which to attack locational problems.

A strategy overlapping problem-solving is situational crime prevention (SCP) (Clarke, 1992) or natural crime prevention (Felson, 1994). SCP is a proactive police response whereby the police deploy crime prevention strategies to specific problems. Clarke notes that SCP is directed at specific forms of crime whereby environmental changes are made to enhance the risks of crime or reduce the rewards as perceived by offenders. SCP has been used to attack a variety of crime problems: burglary (Griswold,

1992), convenience store robberies (Hunter and Jeffrey, 1992), and graffiti (Sloan-Howitt and Kelling, 1992) to name a few. SCP dictates that the police evaluate environmental conditions and attempt to alter conditions that are conducive to criminality and, where possible, institute changes that make the commission of crime more difficult. Clarke notes that SCP is more effective when specific crimes are identified and specific responses are implemented. Specific responses allow for better evaluation and adjustments when desired outcomes are not achieved.

CONCLUSION

The preceding sections examined perpetrator-oriented and location-oriented strategies such as specialized patrol. A number of conclusions emerge as a result of this discussion. First, the police can have an impact on crime and disorder. Second, specialized patrol strategies are more effective in dealing with crime and disorder problems than routine preventive patrol. Third, if the police are to have an impact on crime and disorder, their strategies must be well-designed and carefully implemented. Strategies must be designed to meet the problem. Fourth, police specialized patrol operations must be guided by crime analysis. The police planner must know precisely the extent and nature of problems before an effective strategy can be devised and implemented.

Finally, whenever the police implement specialized patrol strategies, they should be aware that there is the potenital for displacement. Repetto (1976) and Barr and Pease (1990) have discussed crime displacement in terms of (1) time, (2) location, (3) tactical or mode of crime commission, (4) target, (5) type of crime, and (6) perpetrator. Barr and Pease note that the crime pattern for a particular location at a given time is the result of a pattern of crime prevention and criminal opportunities. The police and other forces in a community such as environmental design, private security, or citizen crime prevention efforts tend to deflect crime from one location or victim to another. They go further to speculate that prevention efforts may not have any impact whatsoever on overall crime rates because of displacement or deflection. Crime prevention efforts seldom focus on desire, only on opportunity.

This extreme position is questionable. It is predicated on criminals being guided by determinism rather than rational choice. Eck (1994) notes that the literature is mixed with regard to the existence and scope of displacement. Even if and when displacement occurs, it is seldom 100 percent, and therefore, prevention and enforcement programs have some level of effectiveness regardless of displacement. The existence of displacement may largely depend on the nature of the criminal activity.

One way to deal with displacement is the implementation of incapacitation programs. The police can attempt to remove offenders from society through interception and arrest. Removal of offenders from the streets through arrest incapacitates them for at least some duration of time. There is also some evidence that departments that aggressively arrest offenders have reduced levels of crime in their communities, general deterrence (Sampson, 1986). Thus, police managers should attempt to couple situational crime prevention and enforcement programs together. The police response to crime and disorder can be viewed as a matrix where a variety of programs are implemented situationally.

REFERENCES

Bayley, D. H. (1994), *Police for the Future*. New York: Oxford University Press.

Boydstun, J.E. (1975). *San Diego Field Interrogation: Final Report*. Washington, DC: Police Foundation.

Bouza, A. (1988). "Evaluating street-level drug enforcement." In M. Chaiken (ed.), *Street-Level Drug Enforcement: Examining the Issues*. Washington, DC: National Institute of Justice, pp. 43-48.

Buerger, M. (1991). *Repeat Call Policing: The RECAP Casebook*. Washington, DC: Crime Control Institute.

Chaiken, J.M. and Chaiken, M.R. (1982). *Varieties of Criminal Behavior*. Santa Monica, CA: Rand Corporation.

Chaiken, J.M. (1978). "What is known about deterrent effects of police activities." In J. Cramer (ed.), *Preventing Crime*. Beverly Hills, CA: Sage Publishing, pp. 109-136.

Clarke, R.V. (1992). *Situational Crime Preventon: Successful Case Studies*. New York: Harrow and Heston.

Cordner, G.W. (1982). "While on routine patrol: What the police do when they're not doing anything." *American Journal of Police*, 1(2): 94-112.

Cordner, G.W. (1981). "The effects of directed patrol: A natural quasi-experiment in Pontiac." In J. Fyfe (ed.), *Contemporary Issues in Law Enforcement*. Beverly Hills, CA: Sage Publishing, pp. 37-58.

Davis, E. and Knowles, L. (1975). "An evaluation of the Kansas City preventive patrol experiment." *Police Chief*, (June): 22-27.

Eck, J. (1994). "The threat of crime displacement." In (R. McNamara, ed.). *Crime Displacement: The Other Side of Prevention*. East Rockaway, NY: Cummings & Hathaway.

Eck, J. and Spelman, W. (1987). *Problem Solving: Problem-Oriented Policing in Newport News*. Washington, DC: Police Executive Research Forum.

Felson, M. (1994). *Crime and Everyday Life: Insights and Implications for Society*. Thousand Oaks, CA: Pine Forge Press.

Gay, W., Schell, T., and Schack, D. (1977). *Improving Patrol Productivity: Routine Patrol*. Volume 1. Washington, DC: Law Enforcement Assistance Administration.

Goldstein, H. (1990). *Problem-Oriented Policing*. New York: McGraw-Hill Book Co.

Greenberg, S., Rohe, W. and Williams, J. (1985). *Informal Citizen Action and Crime Prevention at the Neighborhood Level: Synthesis and Assessment of the Research*. Washington, DC: GPO.

Griswold, D.B. (1992). "Crime prevention and commercial burglary." In R. Clarke (ed.), *Situational Crime Prevention: Successful Case Studies*. New York: Harrow and Heston, pp. 205-215.

Halper, A. and Ku, R. (n.d.). *New York City Police Street Crime Unit*. Washington, DC: National Institute of Law Enforcement and Criminal Justice.

Hunter, R. and Jeffrey, C.R. (1992). "Preventing convenience store robbery through environmental design." In R. Clarke (ed.), *Situational Crime Prevention: Successful Case Studies*. New York: Harrow and Heston, pp. 194-204.

Kelling, G., T. Pate, D. Dieckman, and C. Brown. (1974). *The Kansas City Preventive Patrol Experiment: A Summary Report*. Washington, DC: The Police Foundation.

Kleinman, M. (1988). "Crackdowns: The effects of intensive enforcement on retail heroin dealing." In M. Chaiken (ed.), *Street Level Drug Enforcement: Examining the Issues*. Washington, DC: National Institute of Justice.

Larson, R. (1975). "What happened to patrol operations in Kansas City?" *Journal of Criminal Justice*, 3(4): 273.

Martin, S. and Sherman, L. (1986). "Selective apprehension: A police strategy for repeat offenders." *Criminology*, 24(1): 155-173.

Matthews, R. (1986). *Policing Prostitution: A Multi-Agency Approach*. London: Middlesex Polytechnic, Centre for Criminology.

McCampbell, M.S. (1983). "Robbery reduction through directed patrol." *Police Chief*, 50(2): 39-41.

McEwen, J., Connors, E. and Cohen, M. (1986). *Evaluation of the Differential Police Response Field Test*. Washington, DC: National Institute of Justice.

Milton, C.H., Halleck, J., Lardner, J. and Abrecht, G. (1977). *Police Use of Deadly Force*. Washington, DC: Police Foundation.

Pate, T., R.A. Bowers, and R. Parks. (1976). *Three Approaches to Criminal Apprehension in Kansas City: An Evaluation Report*. Washington, DC: Police Foundation.

Pate, T., Ferrara, A., Bowers, R. And Lorence, J. (1976). *Police Response Time: Its Determinants and Effects*. Washington, DC: Police Foundation.

Percy, S. (1980). "Response time and citizen evaluation of the police." *Journal of Police Science and Administration*, 8(1): 75-86.

Reiss, A. (1988). "Co-offending and criminal careers." In M. Tonry & N. Morris (eds.), *Crime and Justice: A Review of Research*. Volume 10. Chicago, IL: University of Chicago Press.

Reuter, P., Haaga, J., Murphy, P. and Praskac, A. (1988). *Drug Use and Drug Programs in the Washington Metropolitan Area*. Santa Monica, CA: Rand Corporation.

Robinson, E. (1986). Clean sweep doesn't work: Taking the broom to drugs just moves dirt. *Washington Post*, December 21, Section D, p. 5.

Ross, H. (1981). *Deterring the Drinking Driver: Legal Policy and Social Control*. Lexington, MA: Heath.

Sampson, R.J. (1986). "Crime in cities: The effects of formal and informal social control." In A. Reiss & M. Tonry (eds.), *Communities and Crime*. Chicago, IL: University of Chicago Press, pp. 271-312.

Sampson, R.J. and Cohen, J. (1988). "Deterrent effects of the police on crime: A replication and theoretical extension." *Law and Society Review*, 22(1): 163-189.

Sherman, L. (1992). "Attacking crime: Police and crime control." In M. Tonry & N. Morris (eds.), *Modern Policing*. Chicago, IL: University of Chicago Press.

Sherman, L. (1990). "Police crackdowns: Initial and residential deterrence." In M. Tonry & N. Morris (eds.), *Crime and Justice: A Review of Research*. Volume 12. Chicago, IL: University of Chicago Press.

Sherman, L. (1989). "Repeat calls for service: Policing the 'hot spots.'" In D. Kenney (ed.), *Police and Policing: Contemporary Issues*. New York: Praeger, pp. 150-165.

Sherman, L., Roschelle, A., and Gartin, P., Linnell, D. and Coleman, C. (1986). *Cracking Down and Backing Off: Residual Deterrence*. Report submitted to the National Institute of Justice by the Center for Crime Control, University of Maryland.

Sjoquist, D.L. (1973). "Property crime and economic behavior: Some empirical results." *American Economist*, 63: 439.

Skogan, W. and Maxfield, M. (1981). *Coping with Crime: Individual and Neighborhood Reactions*. Beverly Hills, CA: Sage Publications.

Sloan-Howitt, M. and Kelling, G. (1992). "Subway graffiti in New York: 'getting up' vs. 'meanin it and cleanin it.'" In R. Clarke (ed.), *Situational Crime Prevention: Successful Case Studies*. New York, NY: Harrow and Heston, pp. 239-248.

Spelman, W. (1990). *Repeat Offender Programs for Law Enforcement*. Washington, DC: Police Executive Research Forum.

Tittle, C.R. and Rowe, A.R. (1974). "Certainty of arrest and crime rates: A further test of the deterrence hypothesis." *Social Forces*, 52: 455.

Walker, S. (1993). *The Police in America*. New York: McGraw-Hill.

Warren, J.W., Forst, M.L. and Estrella, M.M. (1979). "Directed patrol: An experiment that worked." *Police Chief*, (July): 48, 49, 78.

Webster, B. and Connors, E.F. (1992). "The police, drugs, and public housing." *Research in Brief*. Washington, DC: National Institute of Justice.

Weisburd, D., L. Maher, and L. Sherman. (1991). "Contrasting crime-general and crime specific theory: The case of hot spots of crime." In *Advances in Criminological Theory*, Vol. 5. New Brunswick, NJ: Transaction Press.

Weisel, D. (1990). *Tackling Drug Problems in Public Housing: A Guide for Police*. Washington, DC: Police Executive Research Forum.

Whitaker, G.P. (1982). "What is police work?" *Police Studies*, 4(1): 13-22.

Wilson, J.Q. (1985). *Thinking about Crime*. New York, NY: Vintage Books.

Wilson, J.Q. (1968). *Varieties of Police Behavior*. Cambridge, MA: Harvard University Press.

Wilson, J.Q. and Boland, B. (1981). "The effects of the police on crime: A response to Jacob and Rich." *Law and Society Review*, 16: 163.

Wilson, J.Q. and Boland, B. (1976). "Crime." In W. Gorham & N. Glazer (eds.), *The Urban Predicament*. Washington, DC: The Urban Institute.

Wilson, J.Q. and Kelling, G. (1982). "Making neighborhoods safe." *Atlantic Monthly*, 29 (March): 29-38.

Zimmer, L. (1990). "Proactive policing against street-level drug trafficking." *American Journal of Police*, 9(1): 43-74.

Toward Equity and Efficiency in Law Enforcement: Differential Police Response   7

Robert E. Worden

Differential police response (DPR) strategies involve efforts to sys-tematically differentiate among requests for police service in terms of the forms of police response that are optimal. DPR strategies provide for a wider range of response options than the traditional one of dispatching a patrol officer as quickly as possible. Response alternatives include delayed responses by patrol officers to some types of calls, as well as a variety of "relief" responses: dispatching civilian personnel instead of sworn officers, taking reports of some types of crimes by telephone, or asking com-plainants to walk- or mail-in their reports (see Farmer, 1981). The adop-tion (or extension) of DPR is typically prompted by increases in the demand for service relative to patrol resources, which result in an inabil-ity to respond quickly to all calls for service.[1] Indeed, differential response is one means of strategically managing cutbacks in police service (cf. Levine, 1978, 1979, 1985a), as it identifies classes of service requests for which an immediate mobile response is not essential—for people's health and safety, for protecting property, or for the apprehension of offenders— and for which a delayed or some other kind of response is adequate. Furthermore, a DPR strategy is, under most circumstances, an essential prerequisite to the implementation of proactive police technologies, such as directed patrol, community policing, or problem-oriented policing, because it enables administrators to not only expand but restructure patrol officers' time so that they may engage in other tasks interrupted only by urgent calls.[2] The objective of DPR strategies, then, is to use police

---

Source: Robert E. Worden (1993). "Toward Equity and Efficiency in Law Enforcement: Differential Police Response." *American Journal of Police,* 12(1):1-32. Reprinted by permission of MCB University Press Ltd.

resources more efficiently, in that police service may be performed equally well (or perhaps better) with fewer resources.

However, police administrators who contemplate the use of a DPR strategy are often concerned about the receptivity of the public to any but immediate mobile responses by sworn officers. Citizen satisfaction with the police is of intrinsic importance, of course; it might also have implications for the levels of citizen cooperation and coproduction on which the police can draw, and which are essential in order for the police to accomplish their objectives (see Whitaker, 1980; Rosenbaum, 1988:370-375). Thus when police administrators adopt elements of DPR, they often do so with misgivings, assuming that citizens are satisfied with nothing less than rapid responses. Moreover, the potential benefits of DPR may not be fully realized, insofar as delayed or relief responses are not used for problems for which they may be appropriate.

Furthermore, one thoughtful critique of DPR points out that the efficiency of DPR may be purchased at the price of equity, inasmuch as delayed or relief responses may represent a greater burden for low-income or minority groups than for other socioeconomic groups (Mastrofski, n.d.:25-26, 28). If this is true, then decisions about whether and how to implement DPR must take into account a trade-off between efficiency and equity (cf. Thurow, 1970).

The purpose of this paper is to further clarify the nature of the trade-offs between efficiency and equity that may be involved in implementing a DPR strategy. It first outlines the empirical and normative questions that must be addressed in an assessment of the trade-offs, and briefly reviews the extant empirical evidence that bears on these questions. It then presents new empirical evidence that bears on these issues, based on an evaluation of DPR tactics in one police department. It concludes that DPR is both efficient and equitable according to reasonable standards.

EFFICIENCY, EQUITY, AND DPR

EFFICIENCY

The efficiency with which police services are provided has both quantitative and qualitative dimensions, which (roughly) correspond to objective and subjective dimensions (cf. Ostrom, 1973). The quantitative dimension of police efficiency encompasses activities and outputs, which can (usually) be enumerated. The qualitative or subjective dimension of efficiency reflects the value of police activities and outputs to society, which is very difficult to quantify. Surveys that ask citizens to evaluate police services provide some information about this dimension.[3] The efficiency of DPR strategies can be assessed—albeit rather loosely—on both of these dimensions. DPR enables a police agency to perform the same level of activities at a lower cost, if it must (or chooses to) cut back on its patrol force. Or an agency could conceivably perform more activities, responding to a larger volume of calls for service, or having its officers undertake more activities on their own initiative, with no greater expenditures. Along this quantitative dimension of activity, then, DPR could be expected to enhance efficiency. If citizens' evaluations of police activities, which include but are not limited to handling calls for service, improve or remain the same, then DPR would have either a positive or neutral effect along a qualitative dimension of efficiency; if citizens' evaluations decline, *ceteris paribus*, then DPR would have a negative effect along this dimension.

The efficiency of DPR strategies is supported by a substantial body of empirical research. Indeed, DPR strategies, in their most fully developed forms, build on previous research to match each of several different kinds of police responses with important features of citizens' calls for service. First, previous research has shown that a rapid police response is rarely instrumental in apprehending offenders, locating witnesses, or preventing serious injury, due largely to the time that elapses between an incident (such as a crime) and the report thereof by a citizen (Pate, et al., 1976; Kansas City Police Department, 1978; Spelman & Brown, 1981; Cordner, Greene, & Bynum, 1983). Other research, furthermore, indicates that citizens' satisfaction with police service is affected less by response time as such than by the response time relative to citizens' expectations (Pate, et al., 1976; Percy, 1980); this has been taken to suggest that citizens will accept response delays if they are told to expect a delay (Farmer, 1981:8-9; McEwen, Connors, & Cohen, 1986:41-42). One could therefore expect that in many cases, delayed responses by patrol units can be provided with little or no degradation of objective or subjective service quality; given limited resources, some calls inevitably will be delayed, and a DPR strategy serves to identify those for which delays are least (if at all) costly.

Second, previous research has also shown that reported crimes are unlikely to be solved unless the victim or a witness can offer a description of the offender or some other leads (Greenwood & Petersilia, 1975). In many departments, cases for which such information is lacking are not even assigned to detectives for follow-up investigation (Eck, 1983). Those cases can thus be handled without dispatching a patrol officer, either by taking the crime report by phone or by having the citizen submit the report in person or through the mail, with little or no cost in forgone apprehensions. Reducing in this way the volume of calls for service to which patrol units must respond may mean that they can respond more quickly to those calls for which a rapid response is needed, especially as the ratio of calls to patrol personnel—and with it the likelihood of call saturation—increases. It also means that officers will have more time for proactive work.

Citizen satisfaction with such relief responses depends on their expectations. Some research indicates that crime victims tend to be better satisfied when they see police officers conduct a thorough search of the crime scene, and when the police complete a report of the offense (Parks, 1976; cf. Poister & McDavid, 1978; Percy, 1980); this suggests that "an important aspect of fair treatment [as citizens see it] in citizen-police encounters is the extent to which the police take actions that conform with their role as public servants and with the role of citizens as clients who have a legitimate right to certain services" (Tyler and Folger, 1980). However, other research shows that victims' expectations of police depend on the nature of the offense: among victims of less serious property crimes, such as crimes that are typically eligible for relief responses, 69 percent were satisfied with a low level of investigative effort, while among victims of serious property crimes, such as burglary, only 45 percent were satisfied with a low level of effort (Brandl & Horvath, 1991:300).[4]

Third, although extant research provides no systematic evidence on the matter, one could reasonably suppose that some types of calls for service can be handled as well by non-sworn personnel as by certified police officers. For example, the Santa Ana (CA) Police Department uses "police service officers" (PSOs) to perform a number of functions, such as traffic investigation, that are performed by sworn personnel in other departments; but PSOs, whose salaries and benefit levels are lower than those of police officers, do the work at a cost savings of 40 percent (Skolnick & Bayley, 1986:25-28). Similarly, the Greensboro (NC) Police Department has "community service specialists" dispatched to handle noise and other disturbances, public drunkenness, and reports of missing children and runaways (McEwen, Connors, & Cohen, 1986:94-95). Other examples of civilian personnel who can be dispatched in lieu of patrol officers are evidence technicians and animal control officers.

Finally, many calls to the police can be—and routinely are—referred by operators to specialized police units or to other agencies, although in many police departments administrators exercise little control over the use of referrals (Scott, 1981). DPR procedures can formalize and structure this practice, providing information and direction to operators; police administrators might thereby be able to standardize and extend the use of referrals.

The most comprehensive empirical evaluation of DPR strategies is based on a field test sponsored by the National Institute of Justice and implemented in Greensboro, North Carolina, Toledo, Ohio, and Garden Grove, California (McEwen, Connors, & Cohen, 1986).[5] The evaluation was as methodologically rigorous as the results were favorable. Utilization of relief responses—and thus the savings in patrol officers' time—varied across the three sites: in Garden Grove, 22.3 percent of the calls for service (exclusive of those in which the caller wanted only information) were eligible to be handled through some form of relief response, while comparable estimates in Greensboro and Toledo were 19.4 percent and 15.5 percent, respectively. The evaluation estimated that in Garden Grove, the use of relief responses for selected types of calls could have spared patrol officers nearly 500 hours on those calls during a one-month period, while other personnel would have spent 162 hours handling those calls. The staffing for relief responses is not costless, of course, but at all three sites, staffing for the relief responses was less expensive and more productive than patrol personnel.

Furthermore, the implementation of DPR at these sites seems to have had little or no adverse effect on citizen satisfaction. At each of the three test sites, citizens whose calls for police service were eligible for a delayed or relief response were interviewed by phone to ascertain their satisfaction with call takers and with other personnel with whom they had contact. Some of those citizens had received an immediate mobile response by sworn officers, and their levels of satisfaction represent benchmarks against which the responses of other citizens can be compared. Analyses of these survey data show that about 90 percent or more of the citizens were satisfied or very satisfied with how their calls were handled, regardless of the form of police response—immediate mobile responses, delayed mobile responses, telephone reports, civilian responses, or even walk-in reports.[6] Levels of satisfaction did vary some across forms of police response: citizens who received a delayed or relief response were less likely to be *very* satisfied, and more likely to be merely satisfied; they were also slightly more likely to be dissatisfied. The more striking result, however, was that such small proportions of citizens were dissatisfied.

EQUITY

DPR strategies raise intriguing but thorny issues of equity. The implementation of DPR could be expected to have distributional consequences—i.e., it might affect the level of service provided to different social groups. When some types of calls are designated to receive delayed or relief responses, the people who make these calls are given what is arguably a reduced level of service. If some racial and income groups are disproportionately represented among those who make these types of calls, then DPR might impose a greater burden on those groups than it does on others. Or, if some groups are less satisfied with alternative responses than other groups are, then DPR would represent a greater burden for those groups. Such consequences are often overlooked by administrators, whose service delivery decisions are usually based on technical professional criteria (see Levy, Meltsner, & Wildavsky, 1974; Lineberry, 1977; Mladenka & Hill, 1978; Jones, et al., 1978; see also Aberbach, Putnam, & Rockman, 1981; Gruber, 1987).

The traditional "first call, first served" practices of police departments result in a distribution of police resources—socially and spatially—in proportion to the levels of calls for service, both as service is provided to individuals who ask for it and, because patrol deployment schemes usually seek to equalize workload across districts or beats, as patrol units are allocated among neighborhoods. Such distributional consequences have, on their face, a distinctly democratic character; Mladenka (1977) calls it direct-dialing democracy. As Mastrofski (n.d.:30) points out:

> With the possible exception of fire and emergency medical service, there is no more client-oriented local government undertaking than police patrol. For the cost of a phone call virtually anyone can summon one of the state's most powerful agents. It is one of the few aspects of government service where both the poor and the wealthy have a roughly equal probability of getting public service at their doorsteps. The telephone has become the most powerful grassroots mechanism for shaping the allocation of police resources, because the bureaucratic decision rules for patrol assignment are designed in most departments to equalize the workload and thus distribute officers in direct proportion to demand. As the "invisible hand" that parcels out police service, the reactive approach serves a far more diverse and "representative" clientele than any of the alternative strategies proposed. To the extent that this clientele "misrepresents" the general population, it does so on the basis of direct and more-or-less unambiguous expressions of need.

According to this line of argument, to abandon the traditional response practice is to undermine the democratic character of police resource allocation.

But this democratic appearance is belied by a quasi-market reality, since demand does not reliably reflect need (cf. Jones & Kaufman, 1974). Some needs for police service are never voiced in a call for service (or in any other form). Moreover, any call for service represents a demand, but different types of calls represent different levels of need for intervention by a sworn police officer; some calls for service can be handled—i.e., some needs can be met—by other personnel either at the scene or at the station, and other calls can probably be handled as well or better by other agencies.[7] A choice among standards of equity is a normative one, and an adequate treatment of those issues is beyond the scope of this paper. But with respect to police services, a compelling case can probably be made for the standard of need.

Moreover, this critique of DPR is predicated partly on the assumption that police service is provided only to individuals in the contexts of police-citizen encounters. It consequently emphasizes those police services whose benefits are predominantly private in nature, to the exclusion of those whose benefits are more collective in nature. Elinor Ostrom (1973:100) has observed that "some police services are received primarily by a particular individual and are not simultaneously available to other individuals. Thus, the benefits produced are relatively separable." But she adds that:

> [S]ome types of police output are available for joint consumption only. When a patrolman stops a speeding motorist or arrests a suspected bookie, the service is not provided to a particular person or family. There is no victim or special beneficiary. No separable benefits exist (Ostrom, 1973:101).

Similarly, many of the benefits of proactive policing accrue to a collectivity rather than separate individuals or households.

It is difficult to trace the distributional consequences of police services that are of a collective nature, because it is difficult (for both social scientists and citizens) to ascertain the impacts of such services.[8] But the distributional consequences of DPR do not depend upon the ways in which departments use the patrol resources that are thereby saved. Whether the savings are used to absorb cutbacks or to facilitate the implementation of proactive police strategies, these are separate decisions—decisions made possible by the implementation of DPR. The equity of DPR does not hinge on the equity of community policing, or Drug Abuse Resistance Education, or any police program to which resources might be diverted. DPR makes it feasible to direct police resources to problems of greater need.

There is, however, another basis for concern about the equity of differential police response: that not all socioeconomic groups are equally receptive to delayed or relief responses. Unfortunately, as Mastrofski (n.d.:26, 28) points out, the evaluation of the NIJ field test failed to adequately explore this possibility. The evaluation included "baseline" (pretest) surveys of people whose calls for service had been classified as non-emergencies, in order to establish a benchmark level of satisfaction and to ascertain callers' receptivity to alternative responses. Respondents' prospective willingness to accept alternatives was analyzed in terms of their demographic characteristics, including age, income, sex, and length of residence; each characteristic bore a statistically significant relationship to the willingness to accept one or more of the individual alternatives in at least one site, although many of the differences were not substantively large (McEwen, Connors, & Cohen, 1986:ch. 11). Regrettably, data on respondents' race were not collected. The omission of race from the survey instrument is especially unfortunate in view of the substantial evidence that blacks' expectations and evaluations of police differ from those of whites; there is ample reason to hypothesize that blacks would be less receptive than whites to the response alternatives (e.g., Jacob, 1971; Schuman & Gruenberg, 1972; Furstenberg & Wellford, 1973; Durand, 1976; Flanagan, 1985). Furthermore, respondents' (retrospective) satisfaction with alternatives during the test phases was not analyzed in terms of any demographic characteristics, so one can only speculate about the extent to which different social groups evaluate their experiences with DPR differently.[9]

DPR IN ONE CITY

We may be able to gain insight into the trade-offs that DPR strategies actually entail through an empirical examination of the use and consequences of DPR tactics in one city—Lansing, Michigan. The empirical analysis replicates the evaluation of the NIJ field test, in that it measures and analyzes citizen satisfaction with delayed mobile responses to calls for service and with telephone reporting of crimes. The research design is not as sophisticated as the NIJ evaluation was, because the study was originally undertaken primarily to provide post-hoc information on the basis of which one agency could assess its procedures. Nevertheless, analyses of these data shed further light on the issues discussed above.

Lansing is a medium-sized city, with a population of approximately 130,000. As the capital of Michigan, Lansing is home to many state agencies, but the city also has a broad (if eroding) industrial base, of which Oldsmobile has been the mainstay. According to the 1980 census, 80 percent of the city's population is white, and 14 percent is black; the median age is 26.9; 28 percent of the city's households have incomes below $10,000, and an additional 30 percent have incomes below $20,000; and 69 percent of the housing units are single-family structures. One-fifth of the labor force is employed in manufacturing, one-fifth in wholesale or retail trade, and one-fourth in professional and related services.

The number of calls for service handled by the Lansing Police Department (LPD) has increased steadily and significantly. The LPD recorded 53,928 calls for service in 1973, 68,181 in 1978, 84,127 in 1983, and 116,835 in 1988.[10] During the same period, the authorized number of sworn personnel has decreased, from 261 in 1973 to 253 in 1988 (after peaking at 283 in 1979).[11]

In June of 1988, the LPD revised its call classification system and operational procedures, in order to refine the criteria on the basis of which calls were prioritized, and to expand the types and numbers of calls that were eligible for delayed responses. Call priorities are now based largely on the seriousness of the reported problem, whether the problem is in progress and, if it is not, the length of the reporting delay, and the potential for death, injury, or property loss. Thus, calls eligible for delayed mobile responses include, for example, less serious personal crimes that occurred 15 minutes or more before the report, property crimes that occurred five minutes or more before the report, noise disturbances, parking violations, and some requests for assistance. Civilian complaint board operators (CBOs) are expected to inform callers that a police unit will arrive at the scene within approximately one hour. The patrol unit that is assigned to the district in which the call originates is dispatched as soon as it is available; if it is not available when the call is received, then the call is "stacked" on that unit. When response delays exceed one hour, CBOs are expected to recontact callers, as circumstances allow, and advise them of a further response delay.

The department's procedures also provide for a method of taking telephone reports of some types of crimes, particularly larceny and vandalism. Reports of these crimes may be taken by CBOs when citizens call, provided that the amount of property damage or loss is under $1,000 and that there are no known suspects, no witnesses, no descriptions of suspects or their vehicles, and no other evidence. These reports are among those classified as NRF (No written Report Forthcoming), meaning that they receive no follow-up investigation by detectives. (Reports of these and some other types of crimes that are taken by patrol officers in the field are also classified as NRF if they meet the criteria above.) There is, then, no separate telephone report unit (TRU), as there is in Toledo and in Greensboro, which would require that TRU staff recontact callers; hence no additional staffing is required, and no delay in this form of police response is necessary.[12]

METHODS

Most of the data for this analysis were collected through a telephone survey of people who called the LPD between March and May of 1989, and whose calls were eligible either to be treated as NRF complaints or for delayed response. On selected days of each week during the data collection period, all of the identifiable parties whose reports of crimes were classified as NRF were drawn for the NRF sample; the sample thus includes those whose reports were taken by officers as well as those whose reports were taken by CBOs. Of the 452 cases sampled, interviewers contacted 302, of whom 243 completed the interview; 179 of the respondents had had their reports taken over the phone by a CBO.[13] On days selected for the delayed response sample, calls that had been assigned a low priority were drawn from each of two strata: calls for which the response delay exceeded 30 minutes, and calls for which the delay was 30 minutes or less. All of the former and (roughly) an equal number of the latter were included in the sample. Of the 785 cases drawn for the delayed response sample, interviewers contacted 454, of whom 325 completed the interview.[14] Since the delayed response sample intentionally overrepresents calls for which the delay was relatively long, the cases in that sample are weighted for analysis to render the sample representative of the population of calls from which the sample was drawn. The natural variation in response delays (many calls eligible for a delayed response need not be stacked and patrol units are dispatched quickly) permits one to construct a comparison group, consisting of calls to which the police response was—in effect—immediate.

The survey instruments provided for a brief interview that focused on the nature of the problem about which the respondent called the police, how the call was handled by the operator and (in appropriate cases) by the officer(s), the respondent's satisfaction with how the call was handled by the operator and the officer(s), and the demographic characteristics of the respondent.

EFFICIENCY

Delayed Responses. In practice, most calls that are eligible for delayed responses are for "cold" crimes (especially property crimes), public nuisances (especially noise and other disturbances), and traffic problems (especially parking violations). Together these types of calls comprise more than two-thirds of the calls that are assigned a low priority.

According to LPD data on the times of call receipt, dispatch, and arrival, the median delay for low-priority calls is 16 minutes.[15] Response times are less than ten minutes in over one-third of the calls, and between 10 and 20 minutes in an additional one-fourth; delays exceed 45 minutes for 15 percent of the calls, and 60 minutes for only nine percent of the calls.[16] It is clear, then, that while the operational procedures for call prioritization and dispatch allow for routine delays of up to one hour, delays of such length are not routine. Indeed, it is probably a mistake to assume that delayed response procedures will ineluctably result in lengthy delays for a substantial number of calls.[17]

Most citizens whose calls are assigned a low priority are satisfied with the ways in which their calls are handled. More than 90 percent of the survey respondents expressed satisfaction with the performance of the CBO, and over 80 percent expressed satisfaction with the performance of the officer(s) (see Table 7.1). Of those who were dissatisfied with either the CBO or the officer, no more than one-fifth (or less than three percent of all respondents) cited poor response time as a reason for their dissatisfaction.[18]

These results are largely congruent with those of the NIJ field test. Comparisons of satisfaction levels in Lansing with those reported for the NIJ field test sites must be made cautiously, since there are (known and unknown) differences across the cities in the composition of the populations and, moreover, there are differences across departments in the types of calls eligible for delayed response and hence in the characteristics of the people surveyed; these differences could have significant effects on aggregate levels of satisfaction. To the extent that such comparisons can be validly made, they show fairly consistent support for the inference that response delays per se do not detract significantly from citizens' satisfaction. Satisfaction with operators in Lansing is nearly identical to that in Greensboro and quite comparable to that in Garden Grove; compared with respondents in Toledo (which is demographically the most similar to Lansing), more respondents in Lansing were very satisfied (33.8 percent to 14.7), fewer were merely satisfied (59 to 82), and more were dissatisfied (7.3 to 3.3). Satisfaction with officers in Lansing was substantially lower than it was in any of the NIJ test sites, where the percentage of dissatisfied respondents ranged from 3.9 to 7.3. In light of the reasons for dissatisfaction cited by the Lansing respondents, these differences could be quite plausibly attributed to what officers do—and do not do—after their arrival, rather than to any delay in arrival.[19]

Table 7.1
Delayed Responses: Citizen Satisfaction and Reasons for Dissatisfaction

	Raw Frequency	Raw Percentage	Weighted Percentage
Satisfaction with operator			
Very satisfied	107	34.4	33.8
Satisfied	175	56.3	59.0
Dissatisfied	22	7.1	5.8
Very dissatisfied	7	2.3	1.5
Don't know	5	—	—
Refused	1	—	—
Not applicable	8	—	—
Satisfaction with officer(s)			
Very satisfied	119	45.2	46.2
Satisfied	94	35.7	34.5
Dissatisfied	31	11.8	12.9
Very dissatisfied	19	7.2	6.4
Don't know	9	—	—
Not applicable (e.g., no contact)	53	—	—

continued

Table 7.1 continued

	Raw Frequency	Raw Percentage	Weighted Percentage
Reasons for dissatisfaction with operator*			
Had to argue to get desired response	4	13.8	15.0
Operator unconcerned, disinterested	5	17.2	24.6
Operator asked too many questions	2	6.9	11.3
Poor response time	7	24.1	21.8
Operator discourteous	5	17.2	12.4
Other	7	24.2	14.9
Reasons for dissatisfaction with officer(s)*			
Not courteous	10	20.0	20.4
Not able to solve problem	9	18.0	22.2
Incompetent, didn't know what he/she was doing	1	2.0	1.0
Used poor judgment, did wrong thing	10	20.0	5.0
Didn't care, not understanding	16	32.0	39.9
Poor response time	3	6.0	3.3
Could have done more	6	12.0	12.7
Other	4	8.0	7.2

*Total percentages exceed 100 because some respondents identified multiple reasons.

Furthermore, as previous research has shown, while citizens' satisfaction bears some relationship to response time, it is much more strongly related to the response time *relative to citizens' expectations*. Table 7.2 shows a cross-tabulation of respondents' satisfaction by police response time and by respondents' expectations—i.e., whether the police response time was slower, faster, or about the same as they had expected. Citizens who expected the police to arrive more quickly were substantially less satisfied than were those whose expectations were either met or exceeded by the celerity of the officers' arrival. This finding underscores the importance of having operators inform callers of the length of anticipated delays. It also suggests that, so long as callers are told what to expect, satisfaction levels could remain high even if a larger proportion of calls received delays of up to an hour.

Table 7.2
Delayed Responses: Citizen Satisfaction and Police Response Time*

| | Satisfaction with Operator | | | |
	% Very Satisfied	Satisfied	Dissatisfied	% Very Dissatisfied
Response time was . . .				
Slower than expected (72)	17.2	58.8	17.5	6.5
About the same (125)	31.7	64.8	3.5	0.0
Faster than expected (73)	46.6	49.0	3.0	1.4
Police response time				
30 minutes or less (141)	32.1	63.0	3.9	0.9
31 - 60 minutes (75)	39.8	48.2	8.0	4.0
More than 60 minutes (60)	35.0	46.4	15.2	3.4

| | Satisfaction with Officers | | | |
	% Very Satisfied	Satisfied	Dissatisfied	% Very Dissatisfied
Response time was . . .				
Slower than expected (70)	19.3	41.2	23.1	16.5
About the same (119)	42.6	38.0	13.0	6.4
Faster than expected (71)	67.1	25.0	7.3	0.6
Police response time				
30 minutes or less (126)	46.9	33.7	14.2	5.2
31 - 60 minutes (62)	43.4	40.6	9.5	6.5
More than 60 minutes (53)	54.8	24.4	11.4	9.4

* All percentages are weighted. Unweighted sample Ns are in parentheses.

Telephone Reports. Telephone reporting procedures in the LPD serve to divert a substantial number of offense reports from the dispatch queue. (All but a tiny fraction of the offense reports that are taken by CBOs concern either a larceny or vandalism; larcenies comprise 59.2 percent of the sampled reports, and vandalism comprises 39.7 percent.) Based on the data collected for this study, one would estimate that approximately 320 calls per month are handled by CBOs as NRF complaints. If the average larceny or vandalism call consumes about 30 to 45 minutes of a patrol unit's time, the diversion of these calls from the dispatch queue "saves" 180 to 240 unit-hours per month.[20]

These figures reflect the degree to which this DPR tactic has been implemented by CBOs. CBOs seldom fail to take offense reports over the phone when, according to existing procedures, they may be handled in that fashion. Of the 221 respondents whose reports were taken by either officers or CBOs and classified as either larcenies or vandalism, 177 told the interviewers that they had sustained losses under $1,000 and that they had no information about the perpetrator(s). Of those 177 cases, 154 (or 87 percent) were handled by CBOs over the phone. Some of the remainder might not have been eligible to be taken by phone (e.g., if there was evidence to be processed at the scene). Moreover, some errors in classification are inevitable, given the fragmentary and ambiguous information that sometimes is all that is available to CBOs, and it is certainly better to err by dispatching a unit than to err by failing to dispatch a unit.[21] Full implementation of DPR is impossible (and undesirable) given the ambiguity and uncertainty of the task environment, and patrol units will be dispatched for some calls that could be handled over the phone (cf. McEwen, Connors, & Cohen, 1986: 202); but this tactic can nevertheless divert a substantial number of calls for service.

Most callers whose problems can be treated as NRF complaints, and whose calls are handled over the phone, are satisfied with the ways in which their calls are handled (see Table 7.3), and very few are dissatisfied because an officer is not dispatched.[22] Again, comparisons with the results of the NIJ field test must be made cautiously, all the more so given the procedural differences between Lansing (where CBOs take reports themselves) and the other cities (where call takers refer the calls to other units). Satisfaction with telephone reporting is somewhat lower in Lansing than it is elsewhere. The proportion of Lansing respondents who were very satisfied is equal to or less than those in the test sites, while the proportion that was dissatisfied is slightly higher.

Table 7.3
Telephone Reports: Citizen Satisfaction and Reasons for Dissatisfaction

	Frequency	Percentage
Satisfaction		
Very satisfied	63	35.6
Satisfied	99	55.9
Dissatisfied	10	5.6
Very dissatisfied	5	2.8
Don't know	1	—
Not applicable	1	—
Reasons for dissatisfaction		
Did not send an officer	6	42.9
Operator unconcerned, disinterested	4	28.6
Other	5	35.7
No reason given	1	—

EQUITY

Delayed Responses. About 20 percent of the calls eligible for a delayed response were placed by representatives of institutions—convenience stores and a variety of other business establishments, schools, etc. The rest of the calls were placed by private individuals, who as a group are demographically similar to the adult population of the city as a whole: 77 percent white and 17 percent black; 28.7 percent had incomes under $10,000, and an additional 26.2 percent had incomes under $20,000, while 26.6 percent had incomes over $30,000. Thus the most immediate consequences of the procedures for delayed responses are distributed proportionately across demographic groups.

When levels of citizen satisfaction are broken down by the characteristics of citizens, as in Table 7.4, one can determine which groups of people are more or less satisfied with delayed responses; one can thereby begin to examine the distribution of perceived costs across demographic strata. Minorities were about as likely as whites were to be less than satisfied with the operator, but somewhat more likely to be very dissatisfied; also, minorities were less likely to be very satisfied, and correspondingly more likely to be merely satisfied. A similar observation can be made about those in the lowest income group (although the highest level of dissatisfaction is found in a higher income group). These results indicate that satisfaction with the operator varies across demographic groups primarily in the intensity of satisfaction rather than in the proportions satisfied or dissatisfied. But these patterns hold regardless of response times, and are not attributable to delays. The correlation between satisfaction with operators and income is .08, while the partial correlation, controlling for response time, is .09. The correlations between satisfaction and dummy variables for blacks and other minorities, respectively, are .08 and .10, while the partial correlations are .09 and .08.

Satisfaction with officers displays greater variation but less covariation; that is, while larger proportions of respondents were dissatisfied or very dissatisfied with officers than with operators, the breakdowns by demographic groups show few consistent patterns. Whites and blacks were about equally satisfied with the officers, although other ethnic groups—mostly those of Spanish origin and American Indians—were considerably less likely to be very satisfied, and considerably more likely to be very dissatisfied. Respondents at either end of the income scale expressed the greatest dissatisfaction with officers. But again the differences are not a result of response times; the partial correlations of satisfaction with income and race are virtually identical to the first-order correlations (both -.065 for income, -.03 for black, and .10 for other race).

Telephone Reports. Compared with those whose calls receive a delayed response, and with the population of the city, callers whose complaints are handled over the phone are disproportionately white and affluent: 87 percent white and 6.8 percent black; 31.7 percent with incomes under $20,000, and 41.1 percent with incomes over $30,000. Thus the burden of this relief response is not borne disproportionately by minorities or by those with lower incomes; to the contrary, it is borne disproportionately by whites and those with higher incomes.

Table 7.5 shows cross-tabulations of citizens' satisfaction by their characteristics. Blacks were more satisfied, and other ethnic groups less satisfied, than whites were (but the percentages for nonwhites are based on small numbers). The lowest income group was appreciably more dissatisfied than higher income groups were. Otherwise no significant patterns emerge from this analysis.

Table 7.4
Delayed Responses: Citizen Satisfaction By Characteristics of Callers*

| | Satisfaction with Operator | | | |
	% Very Satisfied	Satisfied	Dissatisfied	% Very Dissatisfied
Individual (258)	33.7	58.3	6.4	1.6
Institution (53)	33.9	62.4	2.7	1.0
Race				
White (193)	36.2	55.7	7.1	0.9
Black (43)	25.7	65.5	4.8	4.0
Other (14)	15.0	74.7	5.2	5.0
Family Income				
Less than $10,000 (69)	22.4	71.7	3.3	2.6
$10,000 - $20,000 (59)	42.3	51.0	4.8	1.8
$20,001 - $30,000 (45)	32.4	49.6	16.6	1.4
Over $30,000 (64)	42.5	50.7	6.9	0.0
Gender				
Male (91)	39.1	51.2	6.9	2.7
Female (166)	31.1	61.7	6.2	1.0
Age				
5 and under (60)	26.0	62.7	8.1	3.2
26 - 35 (93)	32.8	59.8	6.2	1.2
36 - 55 (75)	35.0	58.1	6.2	0.7
Over 55 (27)	53.4	36.9	7.3	2.5

continued

Table 7.4 continued

	Satisfaction with Officers			
	% Very Satisfied	Satisfied	Dissatisfied	% Very Dissatisfied
Individual (221)	46.1	33.0	13.6	7.4
Institution (42)	47.0	42.4	9.4	1.2
Race				
White (168)	48.1	31.5	13.4	7.0
Black (36)	41.3	36.1	17.4	5.2
Other (14)	19.9	51.9	5.2	23.0
Family Income				
Less than $10,000 (57)	44.5	29.8	22.6	3.0
$10,000 - $20,000 (55)	52.1	31.6	5.2	11.1
$20,001 - $30,000 (37)	44.0	38.5	9.7	7.8
Over $30,000 (56)	47.8	28.2	16.4	7.5
Gender				
Male (76)	45.9	35.9	13.0	5.2
Female (145)	46.1	31.5	13.8	8.6
Age				
25 and under (54)	40.2	43.5	12.1	4.2
26 - 35 (85)	40.2	27.9	22.6	9.3
36 - 55 (59)	50.4	36.9	6.3	6.4
Over 55 (24)	59.1	30.8	2.5	7.6

* All percentages are weighted. Unweighted sample Ns are in parentheses.

Table 7.5
Telephone Reports: Citizen Satisfaction By Characteristics of Callers

	Satisfaction			
	% Very Satisfied	Satisfied	Dissatisfied	% Very Dissatisfied
Race				
White (141)	35.7	55.7	5.7	2.9
Black (11)	27.3	72.7	0.0	0.0
Other (10)	10.0	60.0	20.0	10.0
Family Income				
Less than $10,000 (28)	18.5	59.2	14.8	7.4
$10,000 - $20,000 (23)	30.4	65.2	4.4	0.0
$20,001 - $30,000 (32)	34.4	56.2	6.2	3.1
Over $30,000 (65)	38.5	53.8	4.6	3.1
Gender				
Male (85)	34.5	58.3	4.8	2.4
Female (87)	36.8	52.9	6.9	3.4
Age				
25 and under (40)	30.8	66.7	2.6	0.0
26 - 35 (49)	26.5	55.1	10.2	8.2
36 - 55 (52)	38.5	53.8	5.8	1.9
Over 55 (18)	38.9	55.6	5.6	0.0

EQUITY *AND* EFFICIENCY?

Differential police response makes it possible for the Lansing Police Department to use its resources more efficiently. They enable the LPD to handle a growing volume of calls for service with no increase in patrol resources, as some calls are diverted from the dispatch queue, and the remaining calls—to which immediate responses cannot be assured—are prioritized to ensure that rapid responses are given to calls for which they are necessary.

Furthermore, it is fairly clear that DPR in Lansing has had no significant detrimental effect on citizens' satisfaction with the police responses to their requests for assistance.[23] Most citizens whose calls for service are eligible to receive delayed responses by patrol units are not dissatisfied, even if response delays are an hour or more. Also, most citizens whose crime reports are taken by operators over the phone are not dissatisfied with this form of response. Moreover, of those (few) citizens who are dissatisfied, most are dissatisfied for reasons that are not directly related to DPR procedures. Hence it appears that DPR, as it is currently practiced in Lansing, has no substantial effect on the qualitative dimension of police efficiency.[24]

DPR in Lansing is also equitable. Calls for service are prioritized on the basis of need: some calls require the intervention of a sworn officer, and some of those require immediate intervention, while others can be handled over the phone by CBOs. The resulting distributions of delayed and non-mobile responses are not skewed against disadvantaged segments of the population. Delayed responses are distributed equally among demographic groups—i.e., in proportion to their representation in the population, while telephone reporting is a burden (if it is a burden at all[25]) that is borne disproportionately by white and especially by affluent people. Furthermore, while there are differences among demographic groups in satisfaction with police service, these differences are apparently not the results of DPR.

To allow demands for police service (in the form of 911 calls) to determine the allocation of police resources is not, under the most likely circumstances, equitable. Demands are not all equally needful, and some needs are never translated into demands; when police resources are not sufficient to meet all needs, demand-driven allocation is likely to result in inequities.[26] This is especially true, perhaps, for agencies, like police agencies, that deliver services both to individuals and to collectivities. Private markets supply public goods at socially suboptimal levels because the effective demand understates the social value of those goods. Similarly, police agencies would provide services with collective benefits at socially suboptimal levels if they sought only to meet demand in the form of calls for service. Police agencies cannot rely on market-like mechanisms to allocate scarce resources.

The alternative is for police administrators to play a more active role in establishing priorities and distributing resources accordingly. When administrators are given (or assume) such a role, they are obliged to make decisions that are responsive to collective interests or preferences. Their judgments may not promote the welfare of their agencies over the welfare of their clientele.

One way to inject public input, and a measure of public influence, into the management of calls for police service is to make call classification the subject of administrative rule making. This would require that proposed procedures for classifying calls for service be made available for public comment, whereupon the procedures could be revised as necessary. Administrative rule making has been seen as a means of promoting the development and systematization of police expertise, and of structuring the involvement of citizens in the formulation of police policy (see Goldstein, 1977:116-122). Perhaps no other area of police operations can build on so substantial a body of systematic research as the management of calls for service. This research has illuminated the outcomes associated with alternative responses to different types of calls for service, and thus it has formed the basis for developing criteria for differential treatment, i.e., for defining needs. Many departments have built, directly or indirectly, on that body of research, but few if any have opened their procedures to public scrutiny. Some degree of confidentiality is no doubt necessary, since the publication of some procedures would invite abuses.[27] As Goldstein (1977:120) points out, it might be possible in these cases to substitute review by the judiciary or a specially constituted body (such as a police commission). In any case, structured input from the public, or its representatives, can enhance police accountability and thereby protect against the (witting or unwitting) application of overly narrow professional criteria in defining need.

The implementation of DPR may pose other challenges to police administrators. First, expanding the range of response options also expands the breadth of operators' discretion, and it makes their judgments more significant in that they spell the difference between an immediate response, a delayed response, or no mobile response at all. Operators inevitably exercise discretion in characterizing the events described by callers (see Antunes & Scott, 1981; Percy & Scott, 1985; Manning, 1988; Gilsinan, 1989). DPR procedures structure operators' discretion by specifying the terms in which events should be characterized and the criteria in terms of which calls should be prioritized (cf. Goldstein, 1977). But in many departments the introduction or expansion of DPR may require the recruitment and retention of more highly qualified personnel, more and better training, and closer supervision (Scott, 1981; McEwen, Connors, & Cohen, 1986).

Second, police administrators must realize that the results of this evaluation, and the results of the evaluation of the NIJ field test, might not be generalizable to other cities. Thus, administrators should seek to obtain systematic information on the operation and impact of DPR programs in their own agencies by conducting (or contracting for) evaluations. Useful evaluative research can be designed around virtually any DPR program (see Worden & Mastrofski, forthcoming).

Third, if DPR is not used merely to absorb cutbacks, then administrators must determine how to use the patrol resources that DPR frees. The organizational slack that DPR generates sets the stage for innovation, but innovation carries some risk. Innovative strategies may fail; at a minimum, innovative strategies, by their nature, have yet to establish their worth and legitimacy. Furthermore, the implementation of proactive policing would probably require changes both in internal management and in external relations (Goldstein, 1987; Greene & Mastrofski, 1988).

Hence DPR creates both an opportunity and an obligation for police administrators. It creates an opportunity to more deliberately and strategically direct how police resources will be used, and thus not only to "do more with less," but also to identify and address the most pressing needs. It also creates an obligation for administrators to make difficult choices without sacrificing accountability for expediency. If it is developed and implemented properly, DPR can contribute to both equity and efficiency in policing.

NOTES

Author's note: A previous version of this paper was prepared for delivery at the Region VI Conference of the American Society for Public Administration, East Lansing, Michigan, September 27-29, 1989, and at the Annual Meeting of the Midwestern Criminal Justice Association, Chicago, Illinois, October 11-13, 1989. I am grateful for the cooperation of the Lansing (MI) Police Department and Chief Charles E. Reifsnyder (who has since retired). Special thanks must go to Charles R. Bauer, Director of the LPD's 911 Operations Center, for his interest in the study and his generous efforts to facilitate the research; to the other members of the 911 Operations Center for cheerfully tolerating my requests for assistance and other intrusions into their workdays; and to Lt. Fred Roush, formerly of LPD's Records Unit and now retired, for his assistance in accessing and interpreting records of offense reports. I am grateful also for the support of the School of Criminal Justice of Michigan State University, and the assistance of Ted Whalen and Sean Patterson. Finally, thanks to Steve Mastrofski, Jim Frank, and David Bayley for their comments on an earlier draft.

1. Most departments that serve cities of at least 50,000 population now use some type of call prioritization system, and many use relief responses—telephone, walk-in, or mail-in reporting—for certain types of complaints. See Farmer (1981) and Levine (1985b).
2. On proactive policing see Sherman (1983); Skolnick and Bayley (1986, 1987); Eck and Spelman (1987); Goldstein (1990); and Sparrow, Moore, and Kennedy (1990). Each of these expositions cites the utility of managing the demand for police service.
3. The validity of citizens' evaluations as measures of public performance, on which policy choices might be based, has been the subject of some debate. See Stipak (1977, 1979); Mastrofski (1981); Brudney and England (1982a, 1982b); Parks (1982, 1984); Brown and Coulter (1983); and Percy (1986).

4. Police were considered to have made a low level of investigative effort if they failed to perform two or more of the following activities: search the crime scene; examine evidence; attempt to locate or question witnesses; and make out a report.

5. But also see Cahn and Tien (1981), as well as Maxfield (1982) and the sources cited in McEwen, Connors, and Cohen (1986:42-45).

6. As the evaluation report points out, none of the departments implemented strategies that would exploit the time made available to patrol units; consequently, a very small proportion of the calls eligible for delayed mobile response actually resulted in substantial delays (i.e., longer than 30 minutes). The use of DPR along with, say, problem-oriented policing, which requires that officers spend more time "out of service" and thus unavailable to respond immediately to calls, would mean that a larger proportion of calls would result in substantial delays.

7. George Frederickson's Compound Theory of Social Equity distinguishes among several conceptions of equality (Frederickson, 1990). Police responses based on demand could be said to reflect "prospect equality," because everyone who calls for service receives (roughly) the same response. Responses based on need could be said to reflect segmented equality, because everyone with the same need receives the same response, but those with different needs receive different responses.

8. If citizens are better able to evaluate the quality of the service provided to them as individuals than they are to evaluate the quality of service provided to them as parts of a collectivity, then aggregate levels of reported satisfaction will probably not reflect accurately the value of the collective benefits of police services.

9. In view of the very small proportions of respondents who were dissatisfied, it is most likely that any differences across demographic groups would be limited to the intensity of satisfaction (i.e., whether callers were very satisfied or merely satisfied).

10. These numbers are of questionable reliability, because until a Computer Aided Dispatch system was installed, complaint board operators manually recorded the number of calls that they received. It was then commonplace for CBOs to "estimate" the number of calls at the ends of their shifts, rather than record them as they came in, and to base their estimates (at least partly) on workgroup norms about proper workloads.

11. At the time of this study, Lansing's 40 square miles were carved into 14 police districts (or beats). The call-for-service workload across districts had become somewhat unbalanced over time, and the department was considering alternative district configurations to achieve a better balance.

12. The director of the LPD's communications center reported that his counterparts in other agencies are incredulous when they are told that CBOs take the reports themselves, assuming that such procedures would impair CBOs' capacity to handle emergency calls. At the LPD, an alarm sounds if all of the lines are busy when a 911 call is received, whereupon a CBO handling a less urgent call—such as a crime report—puts that caller on hold to attend to the emergency call. Thus, the LPD reportedly suffers no degradation of its emergency response capacity as a result of this practice.

13. The sample was drawn from 28 daily lists of NRF complaints, four for each day of the week. Cases in which the complainant was identified only as an institution (e.g., a department store) were excluded. The completion rate was 54%. Forty-eight people refused to participate in the survey; nine people could not remember the incidents about which they had called the police, and two others indicated that they had not called the police.

14. The sample of days slightly overrepresents the busier days, as it included three each of Mondays, Tuesdays, Wednesdays, and Sundays, and four each of Thursdays, Fridays, and Saturdays. Cases in which the caller could not be identified were excluded, as were calls from police sources (e.g., the detention facility); one call was excluded due to the extremely sensitive nature of the incident. One hundred and seventy-two cases in which

no phone numbers were available were included in the original sample, and they were included in analyses that do not rely on survey data. The completion rate was 41.4%; exclusive of the cases for which phone numbers were unavailable, the completion rate was 53%. One hundred and eight people refused to participate; seventeen indicated that they could not remember the incidents about which they had called; three people claimed not to have called the police. The completed interviews underrepresent some types of problems: e.g., people who called to report disturbances were more likely than others to remain anonymous, and so were not drawn for the sample; people involved in traffic accidents, who called from public phones or nearby businesses, and for whom no home phone number was available, were less likely to be contacted; and people who called to report assaults were more likely to refuse to complete the interview. People who were too impoverished to have phones, and whose calls for service were placed from other locations, are almost certainly underrepresented.

15. Times for call receipt and dispatch are recorded when CBOs and dispatchers, respectively, make their entries into the CAD system. Times of arrival at the scene are recorded when patrol units signal their arrival, and herein lies a source of some error. Officers may signal that they have reached their destination before they actually arrive, or they might neglect to signal at all.

16. The mean delay is 25 minutes, but because the distribution of response times is so skewed, the median is a better measure of central tendency. The survey data tend to corroborate these estimates: according to respondents' recollections, the typical response delay was about 20 minutes, and the delay exceeded 45 minutes in 22 percent of the calls.

17. Many of the longer delays are the result of call stacking. About one-fourth of all low-priority calls are stacked; the median dispatch time for stacked calls is 24 minutes, and the median response time is 32 minutes. For calls that are not stacked, the median dispatch time is three minutes, and the median response time is 12 minutes. Even so, 43 percent of the calls for which the response delay exceeds 45 minutes are not stacked, and 41.2 percent of the calls for which the dispatch delay exceeds 45 minutes are not stacked. This is all the more remarkable in light of the fact that the LPD had instituted a form of community policing (if only on a small scale).

18. Almost 40 percent of those who were dissatisfied with the operator had called either about an interpersonal conflict or to report a personal crime, and dissatisfaction is substantially higher in those two event categories than in any other. The respondents who had called about such events and who were dissatisfied tended to cite as their reasons either poor response time or having had to argue to get the desired response.

Eighty-five percent of those who were dissatisfied with the officer had called about one of four types of events: personal crime reports, property crime reports, public nuisances, or assistance. Almost all of these respondents cited their treatment by the officer(s) as the reasons for their dissatisfaction—what the officer did or failed to do, the officer's concern about the problem, or the officer's courtesy; with few exceptions, any delay in the officer's response was not the principal source of dissatisfaction.

19. Some part of these differences could also be due to differences in the design of the questionnaires and the construction of individual items.

20. The estimated number of reports taken by CBOs does not include most cases of retail fraud, which were not included in the sample because the complainant was identified only as an institution; therefore, the true number is actually quite a bit larger—perhaps half again as large. Furthermore, the number of calls that are diverted from the dispatch queue will vary from month to month as the number of offenses varies. Thus, the number of diverted calls is probably larger than this estimate during the summer months, when other demands on patrol units are also greater. The price for this savings is, of course, the time that CBOs spend taking reports.

According to the data on low-priority calls to which patrol units are dispatched, the average larceny or vandalism call consumes 52 minutes of a patrol unit's time, including travel time and time at the scene. These calls presumably are somewhat more time-consuming because they may involve taking information, talking to witnesses, and so on.

21. Some errors of the latter type were also made, and thus one cost of taking offense reports over the phone is information loss. Thirty-eight respondents to the survey (or 15.7 percent) told interviewers that they had some information about the perpetrator(s): six said that they had seen the perpetrator(s) and knew who they were, nine others said that they had seen the perpetrator(s) and could describe them, 18 said that they had not seen anyone but had some idea of who the perpetrator(s) were, and five said that they had other information. In 16 of these 38 cases the report was taken over the phone; moreover, in seven of the 15 cases in which the callers said that they had seen the perpetrator(s) and either knew who they were or could describe them, the report was taken over the phone. The cases in which callers claim to have information about perpetrators represent a very small fraction (four percent) of the total number of offense reports taken by phone, and any information that is lost by taking the report over the phone may be of little value; future research should examine call takers' practices in discriminating among these calls.

22. Satisfaction levels are almost identical among those whose complaints were taken by officers, although the reasons for dissatisfaction are obviously different.

23. A post-hoc design, like this one, does not generally lend itself to causal inference. Even so, it is very likely that levels of satisfaction were substantially higher before the introduction of DPR. Unfortunately, this design makes it impossible to assess the impact of DPR on citizens' more general evaluations of police service in Lansing.

24. The limits of this assertion are readily apparent, and would require further evaluative research. If, say, response delays were routinely two hours, four hours, or even longer, then one might well observe a significant decline in citizen satisfaction. Or if relief responses were provided to some categories of calls to which they are not now provided—if, say, assault reports were taken over the phone—then one might find significantly lowered levels of satisfaction among the citizens who place such calls. As Mastrofski has observed (in a personal communication with the author), the "dosage" of the DPR treatment might have an important bearing on citizen satisfaction. That is, citizens might be much less satisfied if the magnitude of the service reduction is greater than it has been in the evaluated DPR programs, and extant research does not provide a sound basis for extrapolating.

25. One respondent, whose call for service prompted the dispatch of a patrol officer even though it was eligible for a telephone report, said she would have preferred to give her report to the operator rather than wait for the officer.

26. Some might argue that police resources are sufficient to meet needs. They could point out that much of the time that patrol officers spend on patrol is not occupied with calls for service or other tasks (see Whitaker, 1982). But this is predicated on the assumption that there is nothing useful that officers can and should do at their own initiative.

27. Police officials would be understandably reluctant to publish procedures that provide for taking telephone reports of larcenies so long as the loss does not exceed $1,000, lest they thereby invite less-scrupulous citizens to file fraudulent reports of thefts.

REFERENCES

Aberbach, J., R. Putnam and B. Rockman (1981). *Bureaucrats and Politicians in Western Democracies*. Cambridge, MA: Harvard University Press.

Antunes, G. and E. Scott (1981). "Calling the Cops: Police Telephone Operators and Citizen Calls for Service." *Journal of Criminal Justice*, 9:165-179.

Brandl, S. and F. Horvath (1991). "Crime-Victim Evaluation of Police Investigative Performance." *Journal of Criminal Justice*, 19: 293-305.

Brown, K. and P. Coulter (1983). "Subjective and Objective Measures of Police Service Delivery." *Public Administration Review*, 43 (January/ February):50-58.

Brudney, J. and R. England (1982a). "Analyzing Citizen Evaluations of Municipal Services: A Dimensional Approach." *Urban Affairs Quarterly*, 17 (March):359-369.

Brudney, J. and R. England (1982b). "Urban Policy Making and Subjective Service Evaluations: Are They Compatible?" *Public Administration Review*, 42 (March/April):127-135.

Cahn, M. and J. Tien (1981). *An Evaluation Report of an Alternative Approach in Police Response: The Wilmington Management of Demand Program*. Cambridge, MA: Public Systems Evaluation.

Cordner, G., J. Greene and T. Bynum, (1983). "The Sooner the Better: Some Effects of Police Response Time." In R. Bennett (ed.), *Police at Work: Policy Issues and Analysis*. Beverly Hills, CA: Sage Publications.

Durand, R. (1976). "Some Dynamics of Urban Service Evaluations Among Blacks and Whites." *Social Science Quarterly*, 56 (March):698-706.

Eck, J. (1983). *Solving Crimes: The Investigation of Burglary and Robbery*. Washington, DC: Police Executive Research Forum.

Eck, J. and W. Spelman (1987). *Problem-Solving: Problem-Oriented Policing in Newport News*. Washington, DC: Police Executive Research Forum.

Farmer, M. (ed.) (1981). *Differential Police Response Strategies*. Washington, DC: Police Executive Research Forum.

Flanagan, T. (1985). "Consumer Perspectives on Police Operational Strategy." *Journal of Police Science and Administration*, 13:10-21.

Frederickson, G. (1990). "Public Administration and Social Equity." *Public Administration Review*, 50 (March/April):228-237.

Furstenberg, F. and C. Wellford (1973). "Calling the Police: The Evaluation of Police Services." *Law & Society Review*, 7: 393-406.

Gilsinan, J. (1989). "They is Clowning Tough: 911 and the Social Construction of Reality." *Criminology*, 27 (May):329-344.

Goldstein, H. (1977). *Policing a Free Society*. Cambridge, MA: Ballinger.

Goldstein, H. (1987). "Toward Community-Oriented Policing: Potential, Basic Requirements, and Threshold Questions." *Crime and Delinquency*, 33:6-30.

Goldstein, H. (1990). *Problem-Oriented Policing*. New York, NY: McGraw-Hill.

Greene, J. and S. Mastrofski (1988). *Community Policing: Rhetoric or Reality?* Westport, CT: Praeger Publishers.

Greenwood, P. and J. Petersilia (1975). *The Criminal Investigation Process Volume 1: Summary and Policy Implications*. Santa Monica, CA: RAND Corporation.

Gruber, J. (1987). *Controlling Bureaucracies: Dilemmas in Democratic Governance.* Berkeley, CA: University of California Press.

Jacob, H. (1971). "Black and White Perceptions of Justice in the City." *Law & Society Review,* 6:69-89.

Jones, B., S. Greenberg, C. Kaufman and J. Drew (1978). "Service Delivery Rules and the Distribution of Local Government Services: Three Detroit Bureaucracies." *Journal of Politics,* 40 (May): 332-368.

Jones, B. and C. Kaufman (1974). "The Distribution of Urban Public Services: A Preliminary Model." *Administration and Society,* 6 (November):337-360.

Kansas City Police Department (1978). *Response Time Analysis: Executive Summary.* Washington, DC: U.S. Department of Justice.

Levine, C. (1978). "Organizational Decline and Cutback Management." *Public Administration Review,* 38 (July/August):316-325.

Levine, C. (1979). "More on Cutback Management: Hard Questions for Hard Times." *Public Administration Review,* 39 (March/April):179-183.

Levine, C. (1985a). "Police Management in the 1980s: From Decrementalism to Strategic Thinking." *Public Administration Review,* 45 (Special Issue):691-700.

Levine, C. (1985b). *Fiscal Stress and Police Services: A Strategic Perspective.* Washington, DC: National Institute of Justice.

Levy, F., A. Meltsner and A. Wildavsky (1974). *Urban Outcomes: Schools, Streets, Libraries.* Berkeley, CA: University of California Press.

Lineberry, R. (1977). *Equality and Urban Policy.* Beverly Hills, CA: Sage Publications.

Manning, P. (1988). *Symbolic Communication: Signifying Calls and the Police Response.* Cambridge, MA: MIT Press.

Mastrofski, S. (n.d.). "The New Autonomy of American Police: Review and Critique of a Contemporary Reform Program." Unpublished paper, Pennsylvania State University.

Mastrofski, S. (1981). "Surveying Clients to Assess Police Performance: Focusing on the Police-Citizen Encounter." *Evaluation Review,* 5 (June):397-408.

Maxfield, M. (1982). "Service Time, Dispatch Time, and Demand for Police Services: Helping More by Serving Less." *Public Administration Review,* 42 (May/June):252-263.

McEwen, T., E. Connors III and M. Cohen (1986). *Evaluation of the Differential Police Response Field Test: Research Report.* Washington, DC: National Institute of Justice.

Mladenka, K. (1977). "Citizen Demand and Bureaucratic Response: Direct Dialing Democracy in a Major American City." *Urban Affairs Quarterly,* 12 (March):273-290.

Mladenka, K. and K. Hill (1978). "The Distribution of Urban Police Services." *Journal of Politics,* 40 (February):112-133.

Ostrom, E. (1973). "On the Meaning and Measurement of Output and Efficiency in the Provision of Urban Police Services." *Journal of Criminal Justice,* 1:93-112.

Parks, R. (1976). "Police Response to Victimization: Effects on Citizen Attitudes and Perceptions." In W. Skogan (ed.), *Sample Surveys of the Victims of Crime.* Cambridge, MA: Ballinger.

Parks, R. (1982). "Citizen Surveys for Police Performance Assessment: Some Issues in Their Use." *The Urban Interest,* (Spring):17-26.

Parks, R. (1984). "Linking Objective and Subjective Measures of Performance." *Public Administration Review,* 44 (March/April):118-127.

Pate, T., A. Ferrara, R. Bowers and J. Lorence (1976). *Police Response Time: Its Determinants and Effects*. Washington, DC: Police Foundation.

Percy, S. (1980). "Response Time and Citizen Evaluation of Police." *Journal of Police Science and Administration*, 8 (March):75-86.

Percy, S. (1986). "In Defense of Citizen Evaluations as Performance Measures." *Urban Affairs Quarterly*, 22 (September):66-83.

Percy, S. and E. Scott (1985). *Demand Processing and Performance in Public Service Agencies*. University, AL: University of Alabama Press.

Poister, T. and J. McDavid (1978). "Victims' Evaluation of Police Performance." *Journal of Criminal Justice*, 6:133-149.

Rosenbaum, D. (1988). "Community Crime Prevention: A Review and Synthesis of the Literature." *Justice Quarterly*, 5 (September):323-395.

Schuman, H. and B. Gruenberg (1972). "Dissatisfaction with City Services: Is Race an Important Factor?" In H. Hahn (ed.), *People and Politics in Urban Society*. Beverly Hills, CA: Sage Publications.

Scott, E. (1981). *Calls for Service: Citizen Demand and Initial Police Response*. Washington, DC: National Institute of Justice.

Sherman, L. (1983). "Patrol Strategies for Police." In J. Wilson (ed.), *Crime and Public Policy*. San Francisco, CA: ICS Press.

Skolnick, J. and D. Bayley (1986). *The New Blue Line: Police Innovation in Six American Cities*. New York: The Free Press.

Skolnick, J. and D. Bayley (1987). "Theme and Variation in Community Policing." In M. Tonry and N. Morris (eds.), *Crime and Justice: A Review of Research*, Volume 10. Chicago, IL: University of Chicago Press.

Sparrow, M., M. Moore and D. Kennedy (1990). *Beyond 911: A New Era for Policing*. New York: Basic Books.

Spelman, W. and D. Brown (1981). *Calling the Police: Citizen Reporting of Serious Crime*. Washington, DC: Police Executive Research Forum.

Stipak, B. (1977). "Attitudes and Belief Systems Concerning Urban Services." *Public Opinion Quarterly*, 41 (Spring):41-55.

Stipak, B. (1979). "Citizen Satisfaction With Urban Services: Potential Misuse as a Performance Indicator." *Public Administration Review*, 39 (January/February):46-52.

Thurow, L. (1970). "Equity versus Efficiency in Law Enforcement." *Public Policy*, 18 (Summer):451-462.

Tyler, T. and R. Folger (1980). "Distributional and Procedural Aspects of Satisfaction With Citizen-Police Encounters." *Basic and Applied Social Psychology*, 1.

Whitaker, G. (1980). "Coproduction: Citizen Participation in Service Delivery." *Public Administration Review*, 40 (May/June):240-246.

Whitaker, G. (1982). "What Is Patrol Work?" *Police Studies*, 4:13-22.

Worden, R. and S. Mastrofski (1992). *Differential Police Response: A Program Evaluation Package*. Huntsville, TX: Law Enforcement Management Institute.

III. CRIMINAL INVESTIGATION

Surprisingly, criminal investigation has received much less attention from researchers than have patrol and community policing. This may be due to the fact that detectives usually comprise only 10 to 20 percent of the sworn personnel in a police agency, or that investigations are shrouded in more secrecy and mystery than are patrolling, call-handling and street-level enforcement. The situation in our popular culture, though, is exactly the opposite of this research situation. Few characters of any type are more prominent than detectives in novels, movies and television programs. From Sherlock Holmes (invented by Arthur Conan Doyle in 1891) to Sam Spade, Philip Marlowe and Lew Archer (famous fictional private eyes of the "hard-boiled" era of the 1930s, 40s, and 50s) to Sergeant Joe Friday (of *Dragnet* fame) to *Homicide, NYPD Blue,* and innumerable other recent offerings, the secrecy, mystery, and drama of investigative work have captured the public imagination. Thanks to so much attention in the popular media, we all probably think we know a lot more than we really do about the actual practice and effectiveness of criminal investigation.

The first systematic empirical study of detective work and crime solving, completed in 1975, is summarized in Chapter 8, "The Criminal Investigation Process." This research was conducted by members of the Rand Corporation, and has since been known simply as "the Rand study." Because this study concluded, among other things, that the detective contribution to crime solving is rather modest, it was instantly controversial. It is widely credited with having destroyed the "detective mystique," thereby bringing detectives down off their pedestals and under the control of police supervisors and managers. The Rand study ultimately gave rise to a number of new practices, including formal case screening, solvability factors, and enhanced patrol officer investigations.

The picture of criminal investigation revealed by the Rand study's primarily quantitative and cross-sectional approach is complemented in the next chapter by William Waegel's qualitative description of detective work in one city. Certainly, each and every case is unique—however, if detectives have heavy workloads, they tend to put cases into categories, such as "pork chop burglaries" and "morning-after rapes," that guide the amount and type of investigating they will do. The author concludes that:

> Investigative work in the department studied was vigorous and methodical in only a small percentage of the cases handled. Indeed, an image of detective work as involving a special arsenal of sophisticated techniques is substantially misleading for most ordinary criminal investigations. If the victim or witnesses are able to provide potentially identifying information in burglary and robbery incidents, the case will be vigorously pursued. In the great majority of cases, such information is not available, and minimal effort is devoted to the case.

"Solving Crimes" by John Eck reports on a replication and extension of the earlier Rand study. Eck's research was based on a careful analysis of case characteristics and investigative activity in over 3,000 burglaries and robberies handled by three police agencies. He used these data to test the traditional *Effort-Result Hypothesis* (that detective efforts determine the results of investigations) versus the Rand-inspired *Circumstance-Result Hypothesis* (that case characteristics determine the results of investigations). He found support for both hypotheses, thus in a sense restoring detectives to a position of some legitimacy in the realm of criminal investigation. He also identified several specific investigative techniques that were more likely than others to produce useful information for crime solving.

The first three chapters in this section focus primarily on so-called "reactive" criminal investigation, in which detectives follow up on crimes reported to the police. The next chapter, "Observations on Police Undercover Work," pertains more to "proactive" investigation, in which the police attempt to witness crime as it is happening or even to instigate crime as a means of apprehending offenders. Undercover police work can occasionally be applied to the solution of "normal crimes" such as homicide or burglary, of course, but it is more often used against so-called victimless or consensual crimes such as gambling, prostitution and illegal drugs. George Miller distinguishes light-cover and deep-cover situations and discusses selection, training and supervision issues, as well as the dangers and temptations inherent in this type of police work.

In the final chapter in this section, Gaines and Cordner attempt to round out the discussion of criminal investigation by identifying developments over the last decade, especially in the area of forensic science. At least since Sherlock Holmes became our most famous detective 100 years ago, the ideal of crime solving through *science,* rather than through deception, interrogation, informants or brute force, has had very strong appeal. Until recently, however, the practical evidentiary value of physical evidence and forensic science has been much more limited than the general public realized. Fingerprints could confirm a suspect, for example, but could almost never to be used to identify him or her in the first place. Similarly, analysis of blood or other human tissue could demonstrate that it might have come from the suspect, but not that it definitely did. The limitations in these two examples have now been overcome by computerized fingerprint scanning and DNA testing. In general, scientific evidence continues to become more and more conclusive, perhaps justifying some optimism that, in the future, criminal investigation will be both more effective and more just.

THE CRIMINAL INVESTIGATION PROCESS   8

Jan Chaiken, Peter Greenwood & Joan Petersilia

Criminal investigation is one of the more important functions of municipal and county police departments. Yet many police administrators know little about the nature or effectiveness of their own department's investigative operations, and even less about the situation in other departments.

At the request of the National Institute of Law Enforcement and Criminal Justice, the Rand Corporation undertook a nationwide study to fill some of these gaps in knowledge. The objectives of the two-year study were—

- to describe, on a national scale, current investigative organization and practice;

- to assess the contribution of police investigation to the achievement of criminal justice goals;

- to ascertain the effectiveness of new technology and systems that are being adopted to enhance investigative performance;

- to determine how investigative effectiveness is related to differences in organizational form, staffing, procedures, and so forth.

While the objectives were broad, many questions of potential interest had to be excluded from consideration in order to have a study of manageable size. In particular, the study focused on Part I crimes[1], thereby excluding analysis of how misdemeanors and vice, narcotics, and gambling offenses are investigated. Also, little attention was paid to personnel practices such as selection, promotion, and motivation of investigators.

Source: Jan Chaiken, Peter Greenwood and Joan Petersilia (1975). Originally appeared as "The Rand Study of Detectives." *Journal of Policy Analysis and Management*, 3(2):187-217. Reprinted by permission of John Wiley & Sons, Inc.

DESIGN OF THE STUDY

Several principles guided our study design. First, the research had to be conducted with the participation and oversight of experienced police officials from around the country. Second, information had to be collected from many police departments: single-city studies had already been conducted, and their lack of persuasiveness stemmed from the possibility that the host department was unique in some way. Third, in as many departments as possible, information had to be obtained through direct on-site interviews and observations.

We secured the participation of the law enforcement community by appointing a suitable advisory board, retaining a prosecutor and retired federal and local investigators as consultants, and assembling a panel of currently working investigators. The advisory board reviewed and vigorously criticized our research approach, data-collection instruments, findings, and interpretations of the findings. The consultants assisted in designing data instruments and participated with Rand staff in on-site interviews in many locations. The panel of working investigators commented on the validity of our observations in other cities, by comparing them with their own daily experiences and highlighted important issues that could not be captured by numerical data.

We collected data from a large number of departments by developing a comprehensive survey questionnaire and distributing it to all municipal or county law enforcement departments that had 150 or more full-time employees or that served a jurisdiction whose 1970 population exceeded 100,000. This survey produced extensive information from 153 jurisdictions (of the 300 solicited) on such topics as departmental characteristics, investigators' deployment, investigators' training and status, use of evidence technicians, nature of specialization, evaluation criteria, police-prosecutor interaction, case assignment, use of computer files, and crime, clearance, and arrest rates.[2] For example, the number of officers assigned to investigative units was found to average 17.3 percent of the police force. Thus, the investigative function in the United States costs about $1 billion per year—about the same as the cost of the entire court system.[3]

On-site interviews were conducted in more than 25 of the 153 police agencies. Many of these were selected because they were known to have implemented novel investigative practices that were reportedly successful; others were selected on the basis of their survey responses indicating interesting programs or data resources and a desire to participate. Project staff and consultants visited each of these departments, observing and participating in the operations of the investigative units and discussing their procedures with personnel at various departmental levels. In some cities, Rand staff monitored individual investigators and their supervisors continuously over a period of several days to obtain realistic profiles of their activities.

Some departments gave us previously prepared written evaluations of their investigative programs. In addition, several departments cooperated closely with the Rand staff and provided access to data that were subsequently used in one of the component studies.

One useful data source, located and made available during the course of the survey, was the Kansas City (Missouri) Detective Case Assignment File, which had been maintained since 1971. This unique computer file contained daily information submitted by individual detectives, permitting us to determine, for each investigator and each investigative unit, the time spent on various activities, the number of cases handled, and the number of arrests and clearances produced. The file greatly facilitated our analyses of how detectives spend their time and to what purposes and effects.

Additional sources of information included a computer-readable file of 1972 Uniform Crime reporting data provided by the FBI and a limited telephone survey of robbery and burglary victims.

FINDINGS

ARREST AND CLEARANCE RATES

Several earlier studies, each conducted in a single city or in a small number of neighboring cities, had shown that *department-wide clearance*[4] and arrest statistics are not suitable measures of the effectiveness of investigative operations. Our own study, using data from cities across the country, confirmed this observation in several different ways. The implication is that measures of effectiveness related to solving crimes must be defined carefully and can only be interpreted in conjunction with other information related to prosecution of arrestees, public satisfaction with the police, deterrence effects, and so forth.

In a study in New York City, published in 1970, Greenwood found that the average number of clearances claimed for each burglary arrest varied from 1 to 20 across the city's precincts, depending primarily on how frequently clearances were credited on the basis of *modus operandi* only.[5] Similarly, Greenberg's 1972 study in six California departments found wide variation in clearance rates because of differences among departments in the strictness with which FBI "exceptional clearance" guidelines were applied.[6] Our own study[7] using 1972 data from all departments with 150 or more employees, showed that the average number of clearances claimed for each arrest for a Part I crime ranged from a low of 0.38 to a high of 4.04, a factor of over 10. The ratio from high to low was even larger for each individual crime type, such as robbery or auto theft. Some departments claim a clearance for an auto theft whenever the vehicle is recovered, while others will not claim a clearance unless the perpetrator is arrested and charged for the instant offense. Clearance statistics are also affected by the amount of effort devoted to classifying reported crimes as "unfounded" when the police find no evidence that a crime was actually committed. This practice both reduces reported crime rates and increases reported clearance rates.

With administrative discretion playing such a large role in determining a department's clearance rates, any attempt to compare effectiveness among departments using clearance rates is evidently meaningless. Even comparisons over time within a single department are unreliable unless steps are taken to assure that no change occurs in administrative practices concerning clearances and classification of crimes. Arrest rates, too, are unreliable measures of effectiveness, since arrests can be made without resulting in any clearance.[8] The frequency of such events can be judged from the fact that, in half of all departments, the number of arrests for Part I crimes exceeds the number of clearances.[9]

Quite apart from their unreliability is the fact that arrest and clearance rates reflect activities of patrol officers and members of the public more than they reflect activities of investigators. Isaacs,[10] Conklin,[11] and our own study showed that approximately 30 percent of all clearances are the result of pickup arrests by patrol officers responding to the scene of the crime.[12] In roughly another 50 percent of cleared crimes (less for homicide and auto theft), the perpetrator is known when the crime report is first taken, and the main jobs for the investigator are to locate the perpetrator, take him or her into custody, and assemble the facts needed to present charges in court (see table 8.1). This means that around 20 percent of cleared crimes could possibly be attributed to investigative work, but our own study showed that most of these were also solved by patrol officers, or by members of the public who spontaneously provided further information, or by routine investigative practices that could also have been followed by clerical personnel.[13]

In fact, we estimate that no more than 2.7 percent of all Part I crime clearances can be attributed to special techniques used by investigators. (These are called "special action cases" in table 8.2.) The remaining 97.3 percent of cleared crimes will be cleared no matter what the investigators do, so long as the obvious routine follow-up steps are taken. Of course, included in the 2.7 percent are the most interesting and publicly visible crimes reported to the department, especially homicides and commercial burglaries. But the thrust of our analysis is that all the time spent by investigators on difficult cases where the perpetrator is unknown results in only 2.7 percent of the clearances.

This finding has now been established for enough departments to leave little doubt of its general correctness, with some variation, for all departments. By establishing a restricted interpretation of what constitutes "routine processing" a department might find that investigative skill or "special action" contributes to as many as 10 percent of all its clearances. Even so, the basic conclusion remains the same. Only in cases of homicide, robbery, and commercial theft did we find that the quality of investigative effort could affect the clearance rate to any substantial extent. Conversely, the contribution of victims, witnesses, and patrol officers is most important to the identification and apprehension of criminal offenders.

Table 8.1
Cleared Cases Having Initial Identification of Perpetrator
(As a Percentage of All Cleared Cases)

Crime type	Kansas City				
	Arrest at scene	Complete ID by victim or witness	Uniquely linking evidence	Total Initial ID[b]	Total initial ID from five other departments
Forgery/fraud	30.6	20.0	39.7	90.3	90.9
Auto theft	38.5	12.7	<7.8	>51.2[a]	47.4
Theft	48.4	8.6	17.2	74.2	70.0
Commercial burglary	27.4	16.9	16.9	58.2	80.0
Residential burglary	26.7	42.7	<6.2	>81.7[a]	80.0
Robbery	28.4	20.9	10.6	59.9	53.4
Felony morals	25.8	27.8	27.8	81.4	72.8
Aggravated assault	28.6	63.4	7.9	94.1[a]	100.0
Homicide	28.3	34.8	10.9	74.0	42.9

Note: Numbers may not add to total because of rounding errors.

[a]If no cases of uniquely linking evidence were found in the sample or if there were no cases other than those with initial identification 95 percent confidence points are shown.

[b]I.e., the sum of the three preceding columns.

[c]Berkeley, Long Beach, and Los Angeles, California; Miami, Florida; and Washington, D.C.

Table 8.2
Special Action Cases (Percentage of All Cleared Cases)

| | Kansas City | | Five other departments[a] | |
Crime type	Sample estimate	Maximum estimate at 95% confidence	Sample estimate	Maximum estimate at 95% confidence
Forgery/fraud	0	5.7	0	12.7
Auto theft	0	6.9	0	14.6
Theft	0	3.2	0	25.9
Commercial burglary	4.9	12.4	10	39.4
Residential burglary	0	3.5	0	13.9
Robbery	7.1	16.6	9.5	15.6
Felony morals	0	14.5	9.1	36.4
Aggravated assault	0	5.9	0	25.9
Homicide	10.2	37.3	0	34.8
All types[b]	1.3	2.7		

[a]Berkeley, Long Beach and Los Angeles, California; Miami, Florida and Washington, D.C.
[b]This figure is shown for Kansas City only and reflects the relative numbers of cleared cases of each type in that city. The maximum estimate for the total is lower than the estimate for any single crime type, because the sample size is larger.

VARIATIONS WITH DEPARTMENTAL CHARACTERISTICS

Once the nature of investigators' contributions to arrest and clearance rates is understood, it must be anticipated that variations in these rates among departments will be explained primarily by characteristics that have nothing to do with the organization and deployment of investigators. This is in fact what we found from our survey data.[14] The three most important determinants of a department's arrest and clearance rates are the department's size, the region of the country it is located in, and its crime workload.

Large departments (measured by number of employees, budget, or population of the jurisdiction) claim more clearances per arrest in all crime categories than do smaller departments. However, the arrest rates of large and small departments do not differ.

Departments in the South Central states claim higher clearance rates than those in other regions, which follow in the order of North Central, South Atlantic, Northeast, and West. However, arrest rates vary in almost exactly the reverse order. Evidently, these differences reflect administrative practices or patterns of crime commission rather than differences in effectiveness.

In regard to crime workload, we found that departments having a large number of reported crimes per police officer have lower arrest rates than other departments. This relationship works in the following way: The annual number of arrests per police officer rises nearly (but not quite) in direct proportion to the number of reported crimes per police officer until a certain threshold is reached. Beyond this threshold, increasing workload is associated with very small increases in the number of arrests per police officer. The thresholds are at approximately 35 Part I crimes per police officer per year and 3.5 crimes against persons per police officer per year. These thresholds are fairly high, as only about 20 percent of departments have greater workload levels.[15]

These findings are consistent with the assumption that a city can increase its number of arrests or decrease the number of crimes (or both) by increasing the size of its police force, but the effect of added resources would be greatest for cities above the threshold.

In regard to clearance rates, the data showed that departments with high crime workloads tend to claim more clearances per arrest than cities with low crime workloads. As a result, clearance rates are less sensitive to workload than arrest rates are. Although clearance rates for every crime type were found to decrease with increasing workload, the decreases were not significant for some types of crimes.

These workload relationships apply to all police officers, not just investigators. Although investigators are known to make more arrests per year than patrol officers, and our data confirmed this, the effect is small: we could not find a significant variation in arrest or clearance rates according to the fraction of the force in investigative units. In other words, if the total number of officers in a department is kept fixed, switching some officers into or out of investigative units is not likely to have a substantial effect on arrest or clearance rates.

Aside from the effects of size, region of country, and workload on clearance and arrest rates, we did find a few smaller effects of possible interest. Departments that assign a major investigative role to patrolmen have lower clearance rates, but not lower arrest rates, than other departments. This appears to reflect the fact that patrolmen cannot carry files around with them and therefore do not clear old crimes with new arrests. Departments with specialized units (concentrating on a single crime, such as robbery) were found to have lower arrest rates, but not lower clearance rates, for the types of crimes in which they specialize, as compared with departments having generalist investigators. Departments in which investigators work in pairs had lower numbers of arrests per officer than those in which they work singly. Since we did not collect data permitting a comparison of the quality of arrests produced by solo and paired investigators, this finding must be interpreted with caution. Still, the practice of pairing investigators, which is common only in the Northeast, is brought into sufficient question to warrant further research.

Most other characteristics of investigators were found to be unrelated to arrest and clearance rates. These include the nature and extent of the investigator's training, their civil service rank or rate of pay, and the nature of their interactions with prosecutors. However, the lack of correlation probably indicates more about the inadequacies of arrest and clearance rates as measures of effectiveness than about the inherent value of training and other characteristics.

HOW THE INVESTIGATOR'S TIME IS SPENT

From an analysis of the Kansas City (Missouri) computer-readable case assignment file, and from observations during site visits, we determined that, although a large proportion of reported crimes are assigned to an investigator, many of these receive no more attention than the reading of the initial crime incident report. That is, many cases are suspended at once. The data show that homicide, rape, and suicide invariably result in investigative activity, and that at least 60 percent of all other serious types of cases receive significant attention (at least half an hour of a detective's time). Overall, however, less than half of all reported crimes receive any serious consideration by an investigator, and the great majority of cases that are actively investigated receive less than one day's attention. Table 8.3 shows, for several crime types, the percentage of cases that detectives worked on during the study period (1 May 1973 to 30 April 1974).

The net result is that the average detective does not actually work on a large number of cases each month, even though he may have a backlog of hundreds or thousands of cases that were assigned to him at some time in the past and are still theoretically his responsibility. Table 8.4 shows the number of worked-on cases per detective per month in the various units of the Kansas City Police Department.[16] Except in the case of the Missing Persons Unit, the number of worked-on cases per detective is generally under one per day. If we imagine that each case is assigned to a particular investigator as his responsibility, the table shows the average number of cases that an investigator would be responsible for and work on in a month.

Our data revealed that most of an investigator's casework time is consumed in reviewing reports, documenting files, and attempting to locate and interview victims. For cases that are solved (that is, where a suspect is identified), an investigator spends more time in postclearance processing than in identifying the perpetrator.

Table 8.3
Percentage of Reported Cases That Detectives Worked On

Type of Incident	Percentage
Homicide	100.0
Rape	100.0
Suicide	100.0
Forgery/Counterfeit	90.4
Kidnapping	73.3
Arson	70.4
Auto theft	65.5
Aggravated assault	64.4
Robbery	62.6
Fraud/embezzlement	59.6
Felony sex crimes	59.0
Common assault	41.8
Nonresidential burglary	36.3
Dead body	35.7
Residential burglary	30.0
Larceny	18.4
Vandalism	6.8
Lost property	0.9
All above types together	32.4

Source: Kansas City Case Assignment File, cases reported from May through November 1973.

Table 8.4
Average Number of Worked-On Cases Per Detective Per Month

Unit	Number of Cases
Crimes against persons	9.2
Homicide	11.2
Robbery	7.7
Sex crimes	6.2
Crimes against property	16.9
Auto theft	19.5
Nonresidential burglary	9.4
Residential burglary/larceny	22.9
General assignment	18.6
Incendiary	7.8
Forgery/fraud/bunco	10.4
Shoplifting/pickpocket	20.9
Youth and women's	26.0
Missing persons	88.4

Source: Kansas City Case Assignment File.

For Kansas City, we found the following breakdown of investigators' time. About 45 percent is spent on activities not attributable to individual cases—doing administrative assignments, making speeches, reading teletypes, making general surveillances (of junkyards, pawnshops, gathering spots for juveniles, and the like), and occupying slack time (for example, in a unit that is on duty at night to respond to robberies and homicides). The remaining 55 percent of the time is spent on casework. Of this, 40 percent (or 22 percent of the total) is spent investigating crimes that are never solved; just over 12 percent (7 percent of the total) is spent investigating crimes that are eventually solved; and nearly 48 percent (26 percent of the total) is spent on cleared cases after they have been solved.[17] These figures, of course, apply only to Kansas City. But after reviewing them (and more detailed tabulations) with investigators from other cities, and after comparing them with our observational notes, we concluded that they are approximately correct for other cities, with variations primarily in the areas of slack time (if investigators are not on duty at night) and time spent in conference with prosecutors.

Thus, investigators spend about 93 percent of their time on activities that do not lead directly to solving previously reported crimes. How are they to be judged on the quality of these activities? The time they spend on cases after they have been cleared serves the important purpose of preparing cases for court: this activity will be discussed below. The time they spend on noncasework activities serves a general support function for casework and therefore may be useful in ways that are difficult to quantify. The time they spend on crimes that are never solved can only be judged in terms of its public relations value and possible deterrent value, because most of these crimes can be easily recognized at the start. (They are primarily the ones where no positive identification of the perpetrator is available at the scene of the crime.) Police administrators must ask themselves whether the efforts devoted to investigating crimes that are initially unsolved are justified by either the small number of solutions they produce or the associated public relations benefits.

COLLECTING AND PROCESSING PHYSICAL EVIDENCE

A police agency's ability to collect and process physical evidence at the scene of a crime is thought to be an important component of the criminal investigation process. In our study, however, we analyzed only one aspect of the collection and processing of physical evidence—their role in contributing to the *solution* of crimes, as distinguished from their value in proving guilt once the crime is solved.

Earlier studies have shown that evidence technicians are asked to process the crime scene in only a small number of felony offenses.[18] And, even when the crime scene is processed, a significant portion of the available evidence may not be retrieved.[19] Police administrators, aware of these deficiencies, have begun to experiment with a variety of organizational changes designed to increase the number of crime sites processed for physical evidence.

Our analysis of the collection and processing of physical evidence in six police departments that employ different procedures[20] confirmed that a department can achieve a relatively high rate of recovery of latent prints from crime scenes by investing sufficiently in evidence technicians and by routinely dispatching these technicians to the scene of felonies. The latent print recovery rate is also increased by processing the crime scene immediately after the incident has been reported, rather than at a later time. Some of our data supporting these conclusions are shown (for burglary cases) in the first three lines of table 8.5.

The last line of table 8.5, however, shows that the rate at which fingerprints are used to identify the perpetrator of a burglary is essentially unrelated to the print recovery rate. From 1 to 2 percent of the burglary cases in each of three departments were cleared by identification from a latent print, despite substantial differences in operating procedures. In Richmond, evidence technicians are dispatched to nearly 90 percent of the reported burglaries and recover prints from 70 percent of the scenes they process, but the fraction of burglaries solved by fingerprints is about the same as in Long Beach or Berkeley, where evidence technicians are dispatched to the scene less frequently and lift prints less often.

Why does lifting more prints not result in a higher rate of identification? The most plausible explanation seems to be that police departments are severely limited in their capability for searching fingerprint files. If a suspect is known, there is little difficulty in comparing his prints with latent prints that have been collected. Thus, latent prints may help to confirm a suspect's identification obtained in other ways. But in the absence of an effective means of performing "cold searches" for matching prints (where the suspect is unknown), the availability of a latent print cannot help solve the crime.

From a comparison of the fingerprint identification sections in Washington, Los Angeles, Miami, and Richmond, we determined that, for all these departments, from 4 to 9 percent of all retrieved prints are eventually matched with those of a known suspect. However, the number of "cold-search" matches produced per man-year differed substantially among departments, according to the size of their inked print files and the attention devoted to this activity. In some departments, technicians performing cold searches produced far more case solutions per man-year than investigators.

Table 8.5
Productivity Of Crime Scene Processing Of Fingerprints,
Residential Burglary Sample[a]

Item	Long Beach	Berkeley	Richmond
Percentage of cases where technicians were requested	58.0	76.6	87.6
Cases where prints were recovered, as percentage of cases where a technician was requested	50.8	42.0	69.1
Cases where prints were recovered, as percentage of total cases	29.4	32.2	60.5
Cases where perpetrator was identified as a result of lifted prints, as percentage of total cases	1.5	1.1	1.2

[a]The sample comprises 200 randomly selected residential burglary cases (cleared and uncleared) from each of three departments.

We infer that an improved fingerprint *identification* capability will be more productive of identifications than a more intensive print collection effort. Although some techniques and equipment currently available to police departments were found to enhance identification capability, the technology needed to match single latent prints to inked prints is not fully developed and appears to us to be of high priority for research.

PREPARING THE CASE FOR PROSECUTION

Police investigation, whether or not it can be regarded as contributing significantly to the *identification* of perpetrators, is a necessary police function because it is the principal means by which all relevant evidence is gathered and presented to the court so that a criminal prosecution can be made. Thus, police investigators can be viewed as serving a support function for prosecutors.

Prosecutors frequently contend that a high rate of case dismissals, excessive plea bargaining, and overly lenient sentences are common consequences of inadequate police investigation. The police, in response, often claim that even when they conduct thorough investigations, case dispositions are not significantly affected. We undertook a study to illuminate the issues surrounding this controversy about responsibility for prosecutorial failure.

On the basis of discussions with prosecutors, detectives, and police supervisors we developed a data form containing 39 questions that a prosecutor might want the police to address in conducting a robbery investigation. When we used this form to analyze the completeness of robbery investigations in two California prosecutors' offices, chosen to reflect contrasting prosecutorial practices in felony case screening but similar workload and case characteristics,[21] we found that the department confronted by a stringent prosecutorial filing policy ("Jurisdiction A") was significantly more thorough in reporting follow-on investigative work than the department whose cases were more permissively filed ("Jurisdiction B"). Yet, even the former department fell short of supplying the prosecutor with all the information he desired: each of 39 evidentiary questions that prosecutors consider necessary for effective case presentation was, on the average, covered in 45 percent of the cases in Jurisdiction A. Twenty-six percent were addressed by the department in Jurisdiction B. (Table 8.6 lists the 39 questions. The summary entries indicate the percentage of cases where a question could be answered from information in the documents provided by the police to the prosecutor.)

We then determined whether the degree of thorough documentation of the police investigation was related to the disposition of cases, specifically to the rate of dismissals, the heaviness of plea bargaining, and the type of sentence imposed. Our analysis showed differences between the two jurisdictions. For example, none of the sampled cases was dismissed in Jurisdiction A; furthermore, 60 percent of the defendants pled guilty to the charges as filed. By comparison, in Jurisdiction B about one-quarter of the sampled cases were dismissed after filing, and only one-third of the defendants pled guilty to the charges as filed.

A comparison of the two offices' heaviness of plea bargaining is shown in table 8.7. Although plea bargaining appears to be lighter in Jurisdiction A, this may simply reflect that the gravity of criminal conduct was less in the A than the B cases; that is, special allegations were considerably more frequent to begin with in B. One cannot conclude that only the quality of documentation of the police investigation accounted for the difference.

A similar conclusion applies to the type of sentence imposed: while there were differences in sentencing, the variations in other case characteristics indicate that these differences might not necessarily be related to thoroughness of documentation. This analysis leads us to suggest that the failure of police to document a case investigation thoroughly *may* contribute to a higher case dismissal rate and a weakening of the prosecutor's plea bargaining position.

RELATIONS BETWEEN VICTIMS AND POLICE

Many investigators, as well as top-ranking police officials, have defended the investigative function, not because it contributes significantly to the identification of perpetrators, but because it is one of the principal contacts the police maintain with the victims of serious crimes. But, despite these verbal espousals of the public service function as an important part of the investigative role, our observations in departments across the country indicate that most police merely respond initially to the crime scene and file a cursory report; rarely do they subsequently contact the victims about the progress of the case. This is understandable, given the rising number of reported crimes and relatively constant police budgets.

Table 8.6
Presence of Information in Police Reports (in Percentages)

Case information desirable for prosecution	Jurisdiction A[a] information from at least one source[b]		Jurisdiction B[a] information from at least one source[b]	
1 What INTERVIEWS were reconducted?	100.0		100.0	
Offense				
2 Is there a verbatim report of the instant OFFENSE?	90.4		95.2	
3 Is there a verbatim report of the FORCE USED?	95.2		36.5	
4 What was the PHYSICAL HARM to the victim?	47.6	57.5%	18.5	36.2%
5 Is there a detailed description of the PROPERTY taken?	90.4		27.2	
6 What was the method of S(uspect)'s ESCAPE?	71.4		45.4	
7 What type of VEHICLE was used by S?	38.0		45.4	
8 What type of WEAPON was used by S?	85.7		63.6	
9 If a gun was used, was it LOADED?	19.0		13.5	
10 If a gun was used, when was it ACQUIRED?	28.4		.0	
11 Where is the LOCATION of the weapon now?	9.5		18.1	
Suspect				
12 Was S UNDER THE INFLUENCE of alcohol or drugs?	42.8		22.7	
13 What are the details of S's DEFENSE?	18.9		.0	
14 What is S's ECONOMIC STATUS?	14.2	39.3%	4.5	14.0%
15 Was S advised of CONSTITUTIONAL RIGHTS?	100.0		63.6	
16 If multiple suspects, what is their RELATIONSHIP?	42.7		.0	
17 Is there evidence of PRIOR OFFENSES by S?	66.6		9.0	
18 Is there evidence of S's MOTIVES?	47.6		18.1	
19 Is there evidence of past PSYCHIATRIC TREATMENT of S?	9.5		4.5	
20 What is S's PAROLE OR PROBATION status?	37.8		18.1	
21 Does S have an alcohol or drug ABUSE HISTORY?	23.8		9.0	
22 Where is S EMPLOYED?	28.5		4.5	
Victim/Witnesses				
23 What is the RELATIONSHIP between S and V(ictim)?	4.7		9.0	
24 What is the CREDIBILITY of the W(itnesses)?	9.5		.0	
25 Can the W make a CONTRIBUTION to the case prosecution?	23.8	31.1%	13.5	3.4%
26 Were MUG SHOTS shown to V or W?	51.7		4.5	
27 If shown, are the PROCEDURES and RESULTS adequately described?	30.0		.0	
28 Was a LINE-UP conducted?	53.0		.0	
29 If conducted, are the PROCEDURES and RESULTS adequately described?	40.0		.0	
30 Was an effort made to LIFT FINGERPRINTS at the scene?	41.0		4.5	

continued

Table 8.6 continued

31	If made, were USABLE FINGERPRINTS OBTAINED?	59.0	9.0
32	Were PHOTOS TAKEN at the crime scene?	35.0	4.5
33	Is the EXACT LOCATION from where the photos and prints were taken given?	29.0	.0
34	Did V VERIFY his statements in the crime report?	24.0	.0
35	Did V have IMPROPER MOTIVES in reporting the offense?	4.7	.0

Arrest

36	What was the legal BASIS FOR SEARCH AND SEIZURE?	23.8		36.3	
37	How was the LOCATION OF EVIDENCE learned?	33.3	52.3%	32.0	52.2%
38	How was the LOCATION OF S learned?	66.6		68.1	
39	How was the ARREST OF S made?	85.7		72.7	
	Overall	45.0%		26.4%	

Note: The percentages within the matrix refer only to the presence of information the police chose to record; they may not represent a complete picture of the information gathered by the police in the course of the investigation. It is possible that certain police officers record only "positive" information and assume that an omission of information automatically implies that the information is either not applicable or inappropriate in a specific case.

[a]Twenty-one robbery cases in each sample.

[b]Percentage of cases that presented this information from at least one source.

While it seems reasonable to suggest that local police departments might win more public confidence by notifying the victim when the perpetrator has been identified, such a policy of routine feedback could be self-defeating. For example, if the police were to inform a victim that the perpetrator of his crime had been apprehended and was not being charged with his offense but being prosecuted on another, the victim, rather than feeling more confident in the police or the criminal justice system, might in fact become disillusioned. And a resentful victim could become highly vocal about his dissatisfactions and cause other citizens to be negative about police performance.

How much information to give the victim and when to give it were the questions behind a telephone survey we made of robbery and burglary victims. This study must be regarded as exploratory; the survey was conducted simply as an initial attempt to explore victims' feelings about receiving information feedback and about which types of information are most important.

Table 8.7
A Comparison between A and B of Dispositions by Pleas of Guilty

Disposition	Percentage in Jurisdiction A	Percentage in Jurisdiction B
Plea of guilty to original charges	61.1	31.8
Plea of guilty to original charges but with special allegations stricken or not considered	27.7	22.7
Plea of guilty to 2d degree robbery reduced from 1st degree robbery	5.5	18.1
Plea of guilty to other lesser offense	5.5	4.5
Cases dismissed	—	22.7

The inquiry summarized by table 8.8 was accompanied by two pairs of questions, with the first question of each pair addressing the victim's desire to have feedback on a specific matter and the second eliciting his probable reaction if the feedback occurred. Table 8.9 displays the responses on whether or not the victim wanted to be told of a police decision to suspend or drop investigative effort on his case if such a decision were made: these responses suggest a consistent preference for knowledge about this police decision, but with an observable tendency to the contrary in cleared robbery cases (which involve a relatively small segment of the underlying population). Table 8.10 exhibits the victims' responses to the question of what their reactions would be if they were told that no further investigation was intended on their cases. We note that approximately one-third of our sample would react negatively to unfavorable feedback (and the proportion would be higher if the data were weighted to reflect the relative numbers of each crime type).

To the extent that our survey results may reach beyond the confines of our small sample, they broadly support the belief that there is a strong market for information feedback to victims from the police. But they also tend to confirm the view that some victims, if given unfavorable information, will develop undesirable attitudes toward the police. Finally, our results suggest that other repercussions from information feedback, of which the police are sometimes apprehensive, are of slight significance. Few victims, no matter how distressed by information coming from the police, indicated that they would act inimically to police interests.

PROACTIVE INVESTIGATION METHODS

In a departure from the typically reactive mode (so called, because the investigator does not focus on the case until after a crime has occurred) of most investigators assigned to Part I crimes, some police departments have shifted a small number of their investigators to more proactive investigation tactics. Proactive units usually deal with a particular type of offender, such as known burglars, robbery teams, or active fences. A number of such units have been supported on an experimental basis with funds from the Law Enforcement Assistance Administration.[22]

The proactive team members often work quite closely with other investigators, but, unlike regular investigators, they are not assigned a caseload of reported crimes. Instead, they are expected to generate other sources of information to identify serious offenders. These other sources may include informants they have cultivated, their own surveillance activities, or undercover fencing operations operated by the police themselves.

The primary objective in establishing these units is to reduce the incidence of the target crime. The reduction is supposed to result from the containment achieved by successfully arresting and prosecuting offenders and from the deterrent effect on others of the publicity given the proactive programs. Therefore, the arrest rates of these units are typically used as a measure of their primary effect; and changes in the rate of incidence of the target crime are also cited. The chief problem in using these two measures is the difficulty of isolating the unique effects of the proactive unit from other activities of the police department and from external factors affecting crime or arrest rates.

Table 8.8
Kind of Information Wanted by Victims

Survey question: As a victim, did you want the police to inform you?	Yes	No	Indifferent	If your answer was "yes," how important was it to you to be informed?	
				Very	Somewhat
If your case was solved?	32 (89%)	1 (3%)	3 (8%)	26	6
If a suspect was arrested?	32 (83%)	5 (14%)	1 (3%)	22	8
If a defendant was tried?	27 (75%)	4 (11%)	5 (14%)	15	12
If a defendant was sentenced?	27 (75%)	4 (11%)	5 (14%)	16	11
What sentence was imposed?	27 (75%)	4 (11%)	5 (14%)	16	11
If the defendant was released from custody?	18 (50%)	11 (31%)	7 (19%)	11	7

Table 8.9
Respondent's Desire to Be Told of Police Decision to
Suspend Investigation of His Case

Victim's response	Burglary	Robbery	Total
Yes	16	10	26 (72%)
No	3	4	7 (19%)
Indifferent or no answer	1	2	3 (8%)
Total	20	16	36 (100%)

In the course of our study we looked at several such units by either examining evaluation reports or making direct observations. In general, they all seemed to produce a much higher number of arrests for the officers assigned than did other types of patrol or investigative activities. Consistent effects on targeted crime rates could not be identified.

In order to determine which activities of these units actually resulted in arrests, we examined in considerable detail a sample of cases from two units, the Miami Stop Robbery unit and the Long Beach (California) Suppression of Burglary unit.

From the sample of robbery cases in Miami, we determined that, although the Stop officers averaged 4 arrests per man-month, half of which were for robbery, in 10 out of 11 of these arrests the Stop officer was simply executing a warrant obtained by some other unit or accompanying another officer to make the arrest. In Long Beach, the Suppression of Burglary officers averaged 2.4 arrests per man-month, half of which were for burglary or for receiving stolen property. An analysis of 27 of the arrests disclosed that just half (13) resulted from the unit's own work; the remaining arrests were by referral or were the result of routine investigation that could have been handled by any other unit.

Our general conclusion was that proactive techniques can be productive in making arrests, particularly for burglary and fencing. To be effective, however, the units must be staffed with highly motivated and innovative personnel. And the officers' efforts must be carefully monitored to preclude their diversion to making arrests for other units and to ensure that their tactics do not become so aggressive as to infringe on individual liberties.

POLICY IMPLICATIONS

We have identified several distinguishable functions performed by investigators: preparing cases for prosecution after the suspects are in custody; apprehending known suspects; performing certain routine tasks that may lead to identifying unknown suspects; engaging in intensive investigations when there are no suspects or when it is not clear that a crime has been committed; and conducting proactive investigations. In addition, investigators engage in various administrative tasks and paperwork related to these functions.

Table 8.10
Victim's Predicted Reaction to Information that Police Will Suspend
Investigation of His Case

Victim's prediction of his own reaction	Burglary	Robbery	Total
Appreciative of being told and agreeable to police decision	3	1	4 (12%)
Understanding and resigned	11	7	18 (53%)
Disturbed and resistant	4	1	5 (15%)
Angry and resentful	2	5	7 (21%)
			34[a] (100%)

[a]Two victims were omitted: the response of one was not applicable, and the other declined to answer.

We have enough information about the effectiveness of each function to begin asking whether the function should be performed at all and, if so, who should do it. The notion that all these functions must be performed by a single individual, or by officers having similar ranks or capabilities, does not stand up to scrutiny; in fact, many police departments have begun to assign distinguishable functions to separate units. Our own suggestions, to be presented below, support this development and extend it in certain ways. If a function now assigned to investigators can be performed as well or better, but at lower cost, by patrol officers, clerical personnel, or information systems, it should be removed from the investigators; if it serves the objectives of the prosecutor, then it should be responsive to the needs of the prosecutor; and, if especially competent investigators are required, the function should be assigned to a unit composed of such officers.

In this section we describe the implications of our findings for changes in the organization of the investigative function, the processing of physical evidence, and the role of the public.[23]

PREPARING CASES FOR PROSECUTION

Postarrest investigative activity—not only important for prosecution but also one of the major activities now performed by investigators—can perhaps be done in a less costly or more effective manner.

Our observations indicate that the current coordination, or lack thereof, between the police and prosecutorial agencies does not support a healthy working relationship. It allows for a situation in which each can blame the other for outcomes in court that it views as unfavorable.

Most prosecutors do not have investigators on their staff. If they do, these investigators are usually occupied with "white-collar" offenses rather than street crimes. Generally, then, the prosecutor relies on police investigators to provide the evidence needed to prosecute and convict arrestees. But inherent in this situation is a conflict between prosecutor and police. An arrest is justified by *probable cause*—that is, by an articulable, reasonable belief that a crime was committed and that the arrestee was the offender. Often, the police are satisfied to document the justification for the arrest rather than expend further investigative effort to strengthen the evidence in the case. The prosecutor, on the other hand, may be reluctant to file the charges preferred by the police, or to file at all, if he believes the evidence would not suffice for a conviction, that is, as *proof beyond a reasonable doubt*. Many cases appear to be affected by the conflicting incentives of police and prosecutor, as reflected in failures to file and in lenient filing, early dismissals, or imbalanced bargaining.

One way of ameliorating this problem is to make explicit the types of information that the prosecutor and police agree are appropriate to collect and document, given the nature of the crime. The form we designed for robbery cases (summarized in table 8.6) gives an example of how such information can be made explicit. Each jurisdiction should develop appropriate forms for major categories of crimes. Such written documents would assist the police in becoming more knowledgeable about the type and amount of information that a prosecutor requires to establish guilt for each type of offense and in allocating their investigative efforts to provide this information.[24]

We observed that the prosecutor's strictness with respect to filing decisions can affect the thoroughness of case preparation. In turn, the thoroughness of documentation may affect the percentage of cases subsequently dismissed and the degree of plea bargaining. We suggest, therefore, that prosecutors be mindful of the level of investigative documentation in their jurisdictions, especially in offices where the officer presenting the case may not have participated in the investigation.

One rationale advanced in some police departments for minimizing the factual content of formal investigative reports is that these reports are subject to discovery by defense counsel and thereby facilitate the impeachment of prosecution witnesses, including policemen. Such departments believe that the results of detailed investigations are better communicated orally to the prosecutor's office. The results of our research, while not conclusive, tend to refute this argument. In the jurisdiction ("A") where detailed documentation is prepared, no such negative consequences were noted; but in the jurisdiction ("B") having less information in the documentation, oral communication failed in some instances to reach all the prosecutors involved in the case.

Above and beyond merely improving coordination between police and prosecutors, it is worthy of experimentation to assign the prosecutor responsibility for certain investigative efforts. We feel that a promising approach would be to place nearly all postarrest investigations under the authority of the prosecutor, either by assigning police officers to his office or by making investigators an integral part of his staff, depending on the local situation. A test of this arrangement would show whether it is an effective way of assuring that the evidentiary needs for a successful prosecution are met.

APPREHENDING KNOWN SUSPECTS

We have noted that, in a substantial fraction of the cases ultimately cleared, the perpetrator is known from information available at the scene of the crime. If he or she is already in custody, the case becomes a matter for postarrest processing, as discussed above. If the perpetrator is not in custody, it is important for the responding officer(s), whether from investigative or patrol units, to obtain and make a record of the evidence identifying the suspect. This requires that the responding officers be permitted adequate time to conduct an initial investigation, including the interviewing of possible witnesses, and that the crime-reporting form be designed in such a way that the presence of information identifying a suspect is unmistakably recorded.

Apprehending a known suspect may or may not be difficult. Assigning all such apprehension to investigators does not appear to be cost-effective, especially if the investigators are headquartered at some distance from the suspect's location and a patrol officer is nearby. We believe that certain patrol officers, whom we shall call generalist-investigators, could be trained to handle this function in such a way that the arrests are legally proper and a minimum number of innocent persons are brought in for questioning. Only when apprehension proves difficult should investigative units become involved.

ROUTINE INVESTIGATIVE ACTIONS

For crimes without initial identification of a suspect, we found that many of those eventually cleared are solved by routine investigative actions—for example, listing a stolen automobile in the "hot car" file, asking the victim to view a previously assembled collection of mug shots for the crime in question, checking pawnshop slips, awaiting phone calls from the public, and tracing ownership of a weapon.

One implication of this finding is that any steps a police department can take to convert investigative tasks into routine actions will increase the number of crimes solved. Technological improvements, especially in information systems, produced many of the clearances we identified as "routine." In the absence of good information systems, such clearances might never have occurred or might have been difficult to achieve. The ability of patrol officers to check rapidly whether a vehicle is stolen or, more important, whether the owner is wanted for questioning produced numerous case solutions in our samples. Well-organized and maintained mug-shot, *modus operandi*, or pawn-slip files also led to clearances.

A second implication is that it may not be necessary for investigators, who are usually paid more than patrol officers or clerks, to perform the functions that lead to routine clearances. We believe that an experiment should be conducted to determine the cost and effectiveness of having lower-paid personnel perform these tasks.

Once clerical processing is complete, some action by a police officer may still be needed; for example, the suspect may still have to be apprehended. Such action should be assigned to generalist-investigators.

INVESTIGATING CRIMES WITHOUT SUSPECTS

Two basic objectives are served by taking more than routine investigative action when the suspect is unknown. One objective is to solve the crime; the other is to demonstrate that the police care about the crime and the victim. The latter objective can be carried out by generalist-investigators who are responsible to a local commander concerned with all aspects of police-community relations. This type of investigative duty does not require specialized skills or centralized coordination. The officers performing it could readily shift between patrol and investigative duties. In departments with team policing, such investigations could be a task rotated among team members.

If the objective is actually to solve the crime, police departments must realize that the results will rarely be commensurate with the effort involved. An explicit decision must be made that the nature of the crime itself or public concern about the crime warrants a full follow-up investigation. A significant reduction in investigative efforts would be appropriate for all but the most serious offenses. If, in a less serious offense, a thorough preliminary investigation fails to establish a suspect's identity, then the victim should be notified that active investigation is being suspended until new leads appear (as a result, for example, of an arrest in another matter).

Serious crimes (homicide, rape, assault with great bodily injury, robbery, or first-degree burglary) warrant special investigative efforts. These efforts can best be provided by a Major Offenses Unit, manned by investigators who are well trained and experienced in examining crime scenes, interpreting physical evidence, and interrogating hostile suspects and fearful witnesses, and who are aided by modern information systems. One reason for establishing such a unit is to identify the investigative positions that require special skills and training and that demand knowledge of citywide crime patterns and developments. Our observations suggest, by way of contrast, that current staffing patterns rarely allow most investigators to see these highly serious cases. Therefore, when such cases arise, the investigators are frequently ill equipped to cope with them and unduly distracted by the burden of paperwork on their routine cases.

A Major Offenses Unit would concentrate its efforts on a few *unsolved* serious felonies. The team would consist of a relatively small number of experienced investigators closely supervised by a team commander. From our observations, it appears that the most serious impediment to high-quality investigative work is the traditional method of case assignment and supervision. In nearly every department, a case is normally assigned to an individual investigator as his sole responsibility, whether he is a generalist, specialist, or engaged in team policing. Supervisors do not normally review the decisions he makes on how to pursue the investigation, and his decisions are largely unrecorded in the case file. Consequently, the relative priority an investigator gives to the tasks on a given case assigned to him depends largely on the number and nature of his other case assignments and on his personal predilections and biases. Caseload conflicts and personal predilections frequently lead an investigator to postpone unduly or perform improperly the critical tasks of a particular case assignment.

Assigning cases to investigative teams rather than to individuals could eliminate this problem. For effective operations, the team should include approximately six men and be led by a senior investigator knowledgeable about the local crime situation, criminal law, and police management. The leader's primary responsibility would be to keep informed of progress on the cases assigned to his team and to make the broad tactical decisions on the team's expenditure of effort. Each day the subordinate investigators would perform individually assigned tasks. A clerk delegated to the team would prepare progress reports to document the daily accomplishment on open cases and to assist the leader in making the allocation for the following day. These reports would also help the leader identify which of his men were most effective at which tasks. Such an approach should assure that significant steps in an investigation are objectively directed by an experienced senior investigator.

PROACTIVE INVESTIGATIONS

Our research into proactive units—let us call them "strike forces"—leads us to conclude that they can be relatively productive. In instances where such units were successful, they were manned by motivated and innovative personnel. The gain in employing them becomes illusory when mere quantity of arrests is emphasized, for then their efforts tend to be diverted into making arrests that are not the result of unique capabilities. We feel that departments should employ strike forces selectively and judiciously. The operation of strike forces necessitates careful procedural and legal planning to protect the officers involved and to ensure that the defendants they identify can be successfully prosecuted. These units also require close monitoring by senior officers to ensure that they do not become overly aggressive and infringe on individual privacy.

In all likelihood, the relative advantage of strike force operations in a particular department will not persist over a long period of time. The department must accustom itself to creating and then terminating strike forces, as circumstances dictate.

PROCESSING PHYSICAL EVIDENCE

Most police departments collect far more evidence (primarily fingerprints) than they can productively process. Our work shows that cold searches of inked fingerprint files could be far more effective than routine follow-up investigations in increasing the apprehension rate.

Fingerprint-processing capabilities should be strengthened as follows. First, the reference print files should be organized by geographic area, with a fingerprint specialist assigned to each area; no area should have more than 5,000 sets of inked prints. Second, to assure a large number of "request searches," which imply a cooperative effort between investigator and fingerprint specialist, some communication links should be devised to help motivate and facilitate the reciprocal exchange of information between these two parties. Third, the fingerprint specialists should be highly trained, highly motivated, and not overloaded with other tasks that might detract from their primary function.

Several existing systems for storing and retrieving inked prints with specified characteristics (of the latent print or the offender) appear useful and were widely praised by departments that have them. However, further research might contribute a major technological improvement in the capability of police departments to match latent prints with inked prints.

ROLE OF THE PUBLIC

Our research persuaded us that actions by members of the public can strongly influence the outcome of cases. Sometimes private citizens hold the perpetrator at the scene of the crime. Sometimes they recognize the suspect or stolen property at a later time and call the investigator. Sometimes the victim or his relatives conduct a full-scale investigation on their own and eventually present the investigator with a solution. Collectively, these types of citizen involvement account for a sizable fraction of cleared cases.

Police departments should initiate programs designed to enhance the victim's desire to cooperate fully with the police. Such programs might both increase apprehension rates and improve the quality of prosecutions. Specifically, when major crimes are solved, police departments should announce the particular contribution of members of the public (respecting, of course, any person's desire for anonymity). A realistic picture of how crimes are solved will help eliminate the public's distorted image of detectives and will impress on them the importance of cooperating with police.

REALLOCATION OF INVESTIGATIVE RESOURCES

Ultimately, our suggestions imply a substantial shift of police resources from investigative to other units. However, such reallocations cannot be justified on the basis of current knowledge alone; they must await testing and evaluation of each of our recommendations. If we prove correct, most initial investigations would be assigned to patrol units under the direction of local commanders. To improve the quality of initial investigations, the patrol force would have to be augmented with a large number of generalist-investigators. These officers would also perform certain follow-up work, such as apprehending known suspects and improving communications with victims and witnesses of crimes. The resources needed to field generalist-investigators would be obtained by reducing the number of investigators.

Additional major reallocations of resources away from "traditional" reactive investigative units are implied by our suggestions to have clerical personnel and generalist-investigators perform routine processing of cases, to increase the use of information systems, to enhance capabilities for processing physical evidence, to increase the number of proactive investigative units, and to assign investigative personnel to the prosecutor for postarrest preparation of cases. If all these changes were made, the only remaining investigative units concerned with Part I crimes would be the Major Offenses Units. The number of investigators assigned to such units would ordinarily be well under half the current number of investigators in most departments.

In no way does our study suggest that total police resources be reduced. On the contrary, our analysis of FBI data suggests that such a reduction might lower arrest and clearance rates. Reallocating resources might lead to somewhat increased arrest and clearance rates, but our suggestions are intended primarily for the more successful prosecution of arrestees and for improved public relations.

We know that most of the changes we advocate are practical, because we observed them in operation in one or more departments. For example, a number of departments have recently introduced "case screening," whereby each crime report is examined to determine whether or not a follow-up investigation should be conducted. Our findings indicate that the decision rule for case screening can be quite simple. If a suspect is known, the case should be pursued; if no suspect is known after a thorough preliminary investigation, the case should be assigned for routine clerical processing unless it is serious enough to be assigned to the appropriate Major Offenses Unit. The definition of "serious" must be determined individually by each department, since it is essentially a political decision.

Another current innovation is "team policing," in which investigators are assigned to work with patrol officers who cover a specified geographical area. While there are many organizational variations of team policing, most forms would permit the introduction of generalist-investigators having the functions we describe, and some already include such personnel.

We know of no jurisdiction in which the prosecutor currently administers postarrest investigations, although investigators have been assigned to several prosecutors' offices (for example, in Boston, New Orleans, and San Diego) to facilitate interactions with the police. Only a careful experiment will determine the feasibility and effectiveness of making the prosecutor responsible for postarrest investigations.

The National Institute of Law Enforcement and Criminal Justice has funded the introduction of revised investigative procedures in five jurisdictions. The experimental changes, which are based partly on the findings of our study, will be carefully evaluated to determine whether, to what extent, and under what circumstances they actually lead to improved effectiveness.

NOTES

1. Part I crimes are criminal homicide, forcible rape, robbery, aggravated assault, burglary, larceny, and auto theft. Except in the case of homicide, the FBI definitions of these crimes include attempts.

2. The complete results of the Rand survey are reported in Jan M. Chaiken, *The Criminal Investigation Process. Volume 11. Survey of Municipal and County Police Departments*, R-1777-DOJ (Santa Monica, Calif.: The Rand Corporation October 1975).

3. See, for example, National Criminal Justice Information and Statistics Service, "Expenditure and Employment Data for the Criminal Justice System" (Washington, D.C.: U.S. Government Printing Office, updated annually).

4. A crime is *cleared* when a perpetrator is apprehended or is identified as unapprehendable. The latter possibility is intended to apply in "exceptional" circumstances, such as when the perpetrator is dead.

5. Peter W. Greenwood, An Analysis of the Apprehension Activities of the New York City Police Department, R-529-NYC (New York: New York City-Rand Institute, September 1970). For the reader unfamiliar with this field, let us explain that more than one clearance can be claimed for a single arrest if the person arrested for a specific crime is then charged with, or admits to, crimes he committed elsewhere.

6. Bernard Greenberg et al., *Enhancement of the Investigative Function, Volume I. Analysis and Conclusions Volume III. Investigative Procedures—Selected Task Evaluation, Volume IV: Burglary Investigative Checklist and Handbook* (Menlo Park, Calif.: Stanford Research Institute, 1972). (Volume II is not available.)

7. Chaiken, *Criminal Investigation Process: Volume II*, pp. 36, 37.

8. In some jurisdictions, persons may be arrested "for investigation" without a crime being charged. In all jurisdictions, persons are occasionally arrested by error and are subsequently released by a prosecutor or magistrate without any clearance being claimed by the police.

9. Instances in which several perpetrators are arrested for a single crime may also explain an arrest/clearance ratio of over 1.

10. Herbert H. Isaacs, "A Study of Communications, Crimes, and Arrests in a Metropolitan Police Department," Appendix B of Institute of Defense Analyses, *Task Force Report: Science and Technology, A Report to the President's Commission of Law Enforcement and Administration of Justice* (Washington, D.C.: U.S. Government Printing Office, 1967).

11. John Conklin, *Robbery and the Criminal Justice System* (Philadelphia, Pa.: J.B. Lippincott Co, 1972).

12. After initial publication of the Rand study, this finding was further confirmed by a Police Foundation study, "Managing Investigations: The Rochester System," by Peter B. Bloch and James Bell (Washington, D.C., 1976). While that study was intended primarily to compare team policing with nonteam policing, the report presents data that make it possible to calculate the ratio of on scene arrests to all clearances by arrest for three crimes. The data show that, in Rochester, 31.7 percent of burglary clearances by arrest, 31.1 percent of robbery clearances by arrest, and 28.7 percent of larceny clearances by arrest were the result of on-scene arrests.

13. See Peter W. Greenwood, Jan M. Chaiken, Joan Petersilia, Linda Prusoff, Bob Castro, Konrad Kellen, Eugene Poggio, and Sorrel Wildhorn, *The Criminal Investigation Process: Volume III Observations and Analysis*, R-1778-DOJ (Santa Monica, Calif.: The Rand Corporation, October 1975), chap. 6.

14. See Chaiken, *Criminal Investigation Process: Volume II*, pp. 38-47.

15. The 1972 data revealed a linear relationship between arrests per officer and crime work-load, up to the threshold, but the intercept of the straight line fit was at a positive value of arrests per officer. After 1972, crime rates in the United States generally increased. Since we did not perform any longitudinal analyses, we do not know whether the thresholds also increased or remained at the same levels.

16. "Worked-on" means that at least half an hour was spent on the case. The types of cases assigned to each unit are described in Greenwood et al., *Criminal Investigation Process: Volume II*, PP 53-55. For example, the homicide unit handles not only homicides but also suicides and unattended deaths from natural causes.

17. Activities after the case is cleared can include processing the arrestees, vouchering property, meeting with prosecutors, appearing in court, contacting victims, and completing paperwork.

18. See Brian Parker and Joseph Peterson, "Physical Evidence Utilization in the Administration of Criminal Justice" (Berkeley, Calif.: School of Criminology, University of California, 1972).

19. President's Commission on Crime in the District of Columbia, *Report of the President's Commission On Crime in the District of Columbia* (Washington, D.C.: U.S. Government Printing Office, 1966).

20. The six departments are those in Berkeley, Long Beach, Los Angeles, and Richmond, California; in Miami, Florida; and in Washington, D.C. For further details, see Greenwood et al., *Criminal Investigation Process: Volume* II, chap. 7.

21. Peter W. Greenwood et al., *Prosecution of Adult Felony Defendants in Los Angeles County: A Police Perspective*, R-l127-DOJ (Santa Monica, Calif.: The Rand Corporation. March 1973) led us to expect significant differences in police investigative effort and prosecutorial posture between the two selected jurisdictions.

22. For a description of five antirobbery units of this type, see Richard H. Ward et al., *Police Robbery Control Manual* (Washington, D.C.: National Institute of Law Enforcement and Criminal Justice, 1975).

23. For an expanded discussion of the policy implications, see Peter W. Greenwood and Joan Petersilia, *The Criminal Investigation Process: Volume I. Summary and Policy Implications*, R-1776-DOJ (Santa Monica, Calif.: The Rand Corporation, October 1975).

24. Alternatives that might accomplish some similar aims include having the prosecutor provide the investigators with periodic evaluations of their case preparation efforts; training new investigators in case preparation; or having on-call attorneys assist in the preparation of serious cases.

25. See, for example, Peter B. Bloch and David Specht, *Neighborhood Team Policing* (Washington, D.C.: National Institute of Law Enforcement and Criminal Justice, December 1973).

Patterns of Police Investigation of Urban Crimes 9

William B. Waegel

The response of police investigators to citizen complaints of serious crimes constitutes a neglected area in the sociological literature of the police. Yet these activities are crucial to an understanding of the operation of the criminal justice system, for in most jurisdictions it is the exclusive task of detectives to investigate serious crimes. An examination of the interaction between police investigators, crime victims, witnesses, and perpetrators can enhance our understanding of the administration of justice and the functioning of the social control system.

Studies of uniformed police through participant observation are central among the works which have contributed to an understanding of day-to-day police activities. Skolnick (1967), Bittner (1967), Reiss (1971), Rubinstein (1973), Lundman (1974, 1979), Sykes and Clark (1975), Van Maanen (1978), and Manning (1978) have produced field studies which have examined and clarified the social world of the police, police-citizen encounters, and routine police practices.

However, few participant observation studies have focused on the critical area of detective work. Skolnick (1967) does devote some attention to specialized divisions, such as vice and detective bureaus, but much of his attention centers around police relationships with informers. This article utilized data obtained through participant observation to examine the patterned activities involved in police investigations of urban crimes.[1]

Source: William B. Waegel. "Patterns of Police Investigation of Urban Crimes." Reprinted from *Journal of Police Science and Administration* 10(4):452-465, 1982. Copyright held by the International Association of Chiefs of Police, 515 Washington Street, Alexandria, VA 22314 USA. Further reproduction without express written permission from IACP is strictly prohibited.

CASE HANDLING ORIENTATION

The organizational context in which detective work is carried out places significant constraints on investigative activities. In the department studies, the salient constraints are not rooted in supervisory surveillance, which generally is minimal, but rather in the bureaucratic requirements of producing completed investigative reports for each case within a rigid time frame while also producing an expected number and type of arrests.

For every case assigned, the detective must produce a completed investigative report within 14 days. In this report, there must be a description of the relevant information about the incident, the investigative activities undertaken, and a classification of the status of the investigation. Three classifications are available: (1) *closed*, which indicates that an arrest has been made and no further activity will be devoted to the case; (2) *suspended*, where the available information is such that further investigation is not warranted; and (3) *open*, which indicates that a continued investigation beyond the 14-day period holds some promise of resulting in an arrest. However, generally only "major cases" may remain classified as open, and special justification is always required. Supervisors seldom challenge the content of these reports, but compliance with time deadlines is closely monitored and used as a basis for evaluating individual performance. Detectives experience paperwork deadlines as a central source of pressure in their work, and view these deadlines as a fundamental constraint on how thoroughly any case can be investigated.

Detectives must also produce arrests, especially in burglary cases which comprise the majority of cases handled. While there is no formal arrest quota in the detective division, an informal understanding exists that one should produce at least two arrests per week if one desires to remain a detective and avoid transfer "back to the pit" (that is, back into uniform in the patrol division). Assignment to the detective division is the most prestigious position in the department, and it entails the additional benefit of rotating between only two, rather than three, work shifts. Although salary scales of patrol officers and detectives are the same for each rank, the latter have the luxury of wearing plain clothes and are free from the requirement of being available to handle radio calls. There is additionally the sense that detectives are engaged primarily in the "real police work" (that is, crime control as opposed to peace-keeping). The novitiate detective soon learns that he must produce an acceptable number and type of arrests, while at the same time comply with paperwork deadlines, if he is to remain a member of the detective division.

These features of the work setting generate an orientation to case handling which detectives refer to as "skimming." Skimming refers to selecting out for vigorous investigative effort those cases from one's workload which appear likely to result in an arrest, while summarily suspending or performing only a cursory investigation in the remainder of one's ordinary cases. Supervisors are certainly aware of this practice and of the fact that it ensures that the majority of ordinary cases will never receive a thorough investigation. However, supervisors themselves find their performance assessed in crude quantitative terms and are likely to be questioned by superiors if arrest levels drop from previous norms.

Within this context, understanding detective work thus requires an examination of the processes by which cases are attended to and assessed with regard to their likelihood of producing an arrest. Case-handling decisions are not guided by formal procedures for allocating time and effort to cases having different configurations of information. Rather, a set of informal interpretive schemes are used by detectives to manage the twin practical problems of paperwork deadlines and producing arrests. Through experience in working cases and through interaction with other members, detectives employ an instrumental short-hand for recognizing potentially productive cases which warrant vigorous investigative effort, and unproductive cases which are viewed as consuming time but having no tangible rewards. Because all the detectives experience similar problems in managing their caseloads, and because of the recognized utility of this case assessment shorthand, the interpretation and handling of cases by different detectives tend to be quite similar.

Burglary and robbery cases which are viewed as having little likelihood of producing an arrest are termed "routine cases" and receive minimal investigative effort. Assault, rape, and homicide cases generally receive a somewhat higher level of investigative effort. However, these latter offenses frequently involve acquainted parties,[2] and information is readily available to the investigator identifying the perpetrator. Such straightforward personal offense cases are also referred to as routine cases, for little effort is required to close the case. However, since no great investigative acumen is involved, less credit is accorded arrests in this type of case. Assault, rape and homicide cases involving nonacquainted parties ordinarily are designated major cases by supervisors, and methodical investigative work is called for. In general, the police are rather unsuccessful in solving this latter type of case.[3]

Case Interpretation Schemes

The preceding has suggested that detectives are constrained in their conception and handling of cases, not by the formal organization of their work or by supervisory surveillance, but rather by the bureaucratic pressure of writing reports and producing the proper number and quality of arrests. Given the case-working orientation previously described, an understanding of detective work requires an examination of the shorthand schemes which link typical case patterns with specific investigative activities.[4]

Table 9.1
Incident Features and Investigative Patterns

Crime	Readily Available Information	Case Interpretation	Case Handling
Burglary	Identifies suspected perpetrator	Nonroutine	Vigorous effort, arrest anticipated
	No concrete identifying information	Routine, "pork chop" burglary	Case suspended; level of effort varies according to victim characteristics
Robbery	Potentially identifying	Nonroutine	Vigorous effort
	Does not identify	Routine robbery	Case suspended; level of effort varies according to victim characteristics and whether weapon used
Assault	Identifies perpetrator	Routine "Mom and Pop," "barroom" assault	Arrest made; minimal investigative effort
	Does not identify	Nonroutine	Level of effort varies depending on severity of injury and victim characteristics; may be major case
Rape	Acquaintance of victim identified as perpetrator and victim seen as having certain characteristics	"Suspect," "morning after" rape	Vigorous effort to test veracity of victim's account
	Unknown perpetrator	Nonroutine	Major case
Homicide	Identifies perpetrator acquainted with victim	"Killing"	Perfunctory investigation
	Does not identify perpetrator	"Murder"	Major case

Observation of detective-victim interviews and examination of written case reports provide the data for specifying the content of the interpretive schemes used by detectives. In the victim interview, the kinds of questions asked and the pieces of information sought are revealing of the case patterns recognized as typical for different offenses. However, in attempting to make sense of the incident at hand, the detective attends to much more than is revealed in his explicit communication with the victim. His interpretation of the case is also based upon his understanding of the victim's lifestyle, racial or ethnic group, class position, and possible clout or connections, as these factors bear upon such concerns as the likelihood of the victim inquiring into the progress of the investigation, the victim's intentions regarding prosecution, and the victim's competence and quality as a source of information.

The interpretive schemes employed also receive partial expression in the written investigative reports which must be produced for each case. These reports contain a selective accounting of the meaning assigned to a case, the information and understandings upon which this interpretation is based, and the nature of the investigative activities undertaken.[5]

The following sections examine typical case patterns and associated investigative activities for the five offenses commonly dealt with by detectives: burglary, robbery, aggravated assault, rape, and homicide. Table 9.1 provides a summary of case-handling patterns.

"Pork Chop" Burglaries

Routine burglary incidents which are seen as warranting only low-effort treatment are commonly referred to as "pork chop" burglaries. Where an instant case displays sufficient correspondence with this general category, detectives understand that appropriate ways of handling the case are to summarily suspend it, suspend it after a brief victim interview or perfunctory investigation, or reclassify it to a lesser offense.

Since burglary cases constitute roughly two-thirds of all cases handled, the interpretive schemes for these cases tend to be the most crystalized and non-problematic. A burglary victim's ability or inability to provide information identifying the perpetrator or a probable perpetrator constitutes the single feature of burglary cases which is given greatest interpretive significance. In those few cases where the victim provides the name of a suspected perpetrator (often an ex-boyfriend, a relative, or a neighboring resident,[6] the case is a nonroutine one. When burglary cases are distributed at the beginning of each work shift, detectives quickly scan the original report prepared by a patrol officer and select out any cases having named suspects for immediate attention.

However, less than 10 percent of the patrol reports list a suspect by name. For the remaining cases, the initial inclination is to treat them as routine burglaries deserving of only minimal investigative effort.[7] In these cases, the social characteristics of the victim, particularly the victim's class position and race, have a decisive impact on the particular handling strategy adopted.

For example, where the victim is a low-status individual, detectives generally feel that it is safe and appropriate to summarily suspend the case or suspend it after briefly contacting the victim by telephone. A personal visit to the crime scene and a neighborhood canvass seldom are undertaken. Detectives assume that the patrol officer probably got all the information that was available from "the kind of people in that area."

When the victim is middle-class or when the burglary occurred in a "respectable" commercial establishment, detectives will commonly inspect the crime scene in person, interview the victim at some length, inquire of neighboring residents if they witnessed anything unusual, and, in general, sponsor the appearance of a reasonably thorough investigation. A more detailed investigative report is prepared explaining and justifying why the case has been suspended. This higher-effort handling strategy is employed largely because of a belief that this latter type of victim is more likely to inquire as to the progress of the investigation or complain to superiors about the detective's lack of success in solving the case. Detectives speak of cases "coming back on them" when they have not taken sufficient steps to impress victims that the case is being thoroughly investigated.

THE VICTIM INTERVIEW

The detective's fundamental concern upon receiving burglary cases centers around an effort to assess the typicality of the incident. This assessment is made on the basis of information contained in the original patrol report and/or information obtained during an interview with the victim.

Two contrasting types of victim interviews for routine burglary cases will be examined. In cases 1 and 2, the incidents are initially interpreted as routine and the detectives structure interviews with the victims accordingly. In case 3, the available information generates an understanding that appropriate handling of the case must include a rather lengthy victim interview and an attempt to sponsor the impression that the incident is being investigated thoroughly.

Case 1

A burglary had occurred at a disreputable bar located in a low-income area of the city. A few bottles of liquor were the only items taken. The fingerprint report from the evidence detection unit had not been received, so the detective introduced himself to the proprietor of the bar and asked to see the point of entry. He examined the area around the door which had been dusted for fingerprints and concluded that no useful prints had been obtained. Turning to the proprietor, the detective asked three questions: Do you have any idea who broke into your place? Do you think any of the neighbors around here might have seen anything when this occurred? Have you seen or heard about anyone suspicious hanging around here? After receiving negative replies to all three questions, the detective informed the proprietor that he would be contacted if anything came up and left the bar. Approximately 6 to 8 minutes were spent with the victim. As we got back into the car the detective told me he was suspending the case and remarked, "This (referring to the victim interview) is basically public relations work."

Case 2

A detective drove to the scene of a residential burglary in the same area of the city. The stolen items were noted, the victim stated that she had no idea who was responsible, and we left the victim's residence less than 4 minutes after we had arrived. "Kids," the detective remarked as he made some notes for future use in writing the investigative report. "I'll break it down to a criminal mischief." In the investigative report, the case was reclassified from burglary (a felony) to a misdemeanor and suspended. This handling strategy is encouraged by superiors, for it deletes both the incident and the fact that an arrest was never made from Part 1 crime statistics and the felony clearance rate.

Some burglary cases, in spite of the fact that the detective has interpreted the incident pattern as routine and unproductive, nevertheless are seen as requiring a different kind of victim interview and handling strategy.

Case 3

A detective was assigned a residential burglary in a transitional area of the city. He stopped in front of the address, read the original patrol report, and mentioned that this was the only white family on the block and that the row houses on either side of the victim's were vacant. An evidence detection report showed that four cards of fingerprints had been obtained from the scene. The detective asked the victim to show him the point of entry, and we were led through comfortably furnished rooms to the basement, where a large hole had been made in the brick wall separating her basement from the basement of the vacant house next door. The victim, a middle-aged woman who had lived in the house for over 20 years, stated that the loss was substantial and consisted mostly of jewelry, coin collections, camera equipment, and cash.

After returning upstairs, the detective pulled out his notebook and explained that he wished to record as much information about the incident as the victim could provide. She replied that an older group of males had come into the area recently, and she thought they were an organized group of house burglars. "I see them every morning when I leave for work. There's one guy who stands on either corner, and they're the lookouts. Apparently, they work with whoever is doing these burglaries, and they sit there and watch to see who works during the day, what time they leave, and what time they come back. Then they have all day to break into a place and rob it blind." The detective asked if she knew the names, or even nick-names, of any of these persons. She replied that she didn't and that she would have trouble pointing out specific persons because the group was new in the area. The detective listened to her extended response to his original question, but did not record any of it.

A complete listing and description of all items taken in the burglary was then compiled. The detective took voluminous notes, paying particular attention to items with recorded serial numbers and to pieces of jewelry which had identifying engraving. He assured the victim that this information would be followed up, and that she would be contacted if any of the articles were recovered or there were any other developments. The interview lasted 1 hour and 40 minutes.

Once outside, I asked the detective what he thought of the case. He replied by asking whether I had noticed that the burglars ignored two color television sets which were sitting out in plain view. He remarked, "The guys who did this weren't kids. They knew what they were doing."[8]

The detective's superficial handling of this case differed considerably from the handling strategies employed in cases 1 and 2. However, the minor nature of the subsequent investigative activities undertaken by the detective indicate that his interpretation of the case was that it was routine and unproductive. He entered serial numbers and other identifying information regarding the stolen articles into the computerized stolen property file "to cover myself, just in case." Later in the week he asked another detective assigned to the same sector if he had heard anything from his informants about anyone involved in daytime burglaries in that particular area of the city. The other detective replied that he had not, and at the end of the second week the investigator suspended the case and concluded his investigative report by stating that "all avenues of investigation have been exhausted."

The above discussion has presented contrasting examples of the handling of routine burglary cases. Handling strategies for such cases range from essentially no investigative effort, where a detective simply contacts the victim and inquires if the person has any idea who committed the burglary, to a perfunctory investigation in which weak information or minimal leads are pursued in a casual manner. The latter handling strategy usually involves an effort to convince the victim that "something is being done" about the incident in question. These different methods of handling routine burglary cases stem largely from differences in the characteristics of, and assumptions made about, the victims.

THE INVESTIGATIVE REPORT

Further clarification of the relationship between typical case patterns and associated handling strategies may be gained by examining the content of the formal investigative reports produced by detectives. This section will also serve to highlight the general nature of the organizational constraints and demands which form the context in which case assessments are made.

The case reports presented here are reproduced verbatim.[9]

Case 4

CORRECT OFFENSE: Burglary. Total value stolen: $280.

INVESTIGATIVE PROCEDURE: At [time, date] this investigator spoke with the victim in this complaint, at her residence. [She] gave this investigator the same basic information as is stated in the original report. Also, adding that she does not have any serial numbers on the stolen items, and that she has a few suspects from the neighborhood, some boys that live in the east 10th Street area, between Poplar and Wilson Streets. The victim does not know the names of these individuals, but stated that they frequent the area of the 900 block of Wilson Street.

CONCLUSION: This complaint is to be *SUSPENDED* at this time, N.I.L.

N.I.L. is an acronym for "no investigative leads" that is often used regarding routine burglary cases. The detective suspended this case after simply contacting the victim by telephone. Less than 2 minutes were spent speaking with the victim, and another 3 to 4 minutes dictating the report.

Case 5

CORRECT OFFENSE: Burglary, 2nd degree. Total value stolen: $110.

SUMMARY: This is a burglary that occurred between [date, time] at [address in a public housing project] where unknown person(s) entered that location by removing a board from the rear door, and once inside, removed the below described article.

PROPERTY STOLEN: One (1) Sharp 19-inch portable color TV in a brown and black cabinet. The television had a dial broken from off the side. [Victim] said value was $100. Miscellaneous frozen meats at $10.

PHYSICAL EVIDENCE: No physical evidence was obtained at this time.

VICTIM INTERVIEW: [Name], black female, [address]. On [date, time] this investigator spoke with the victim who informed me that between the above dates, some unknown person(s) entered her house by knocking a board from the rear door and once inside removed the above TV and frozen meats. [Victim] had no serial or model numbers on the TV and has no suspects in this investigation. The victim stated she did not wish any prosecution in this case. She is only concerned about recovering her TV.

On [date, time] the investigator made a canvass of the neighborhood for possible witness, but met with negative results.

A check of pawn sheets has been made with negative results.

CONCLUSION: Due to the fact that all avenues of investigation have been exhausted, and the victim does not want to prosecute, this case is SUSPENDED.

The detective who wrote the report fabricated both the neighborhood canvass and check of the pawn sheets to impress his supervisor that he had done as much as possible in a case where only meager information was available. For all practical purposes, the decision to suspend the case was made at the conclusion of the victim interview. The detective took for granted that in this neighborhood no one would volunteer that they witnessed the incident and that a search through the pawn sheets would be fruitless.

Cases 1 through 5 highlight the basic features of routine burglary cases and the associated patterns of investigative activity. The feature of burglary cases which is accorded primary interpretive significance is the availability of information which identifies a suspected perpetrator. Any case having an identified suspect is selected out for vigorous effort. Since there are no named suspects in the great majority of burglaries, most are interpreted and treated as routine. The amount of effort devoted to such cases is most directly linked to the victim's social status. Additional interpretive features include: (1) the victim's expressed or presumed attitude toward prosecution; (2) whether the offense was committed in such a way that physical evidence is available which could conclusively link a suspect to the crime; and (3) the area in which the incident occurred, particularly as this bears on the detective's beliefs about the inclinations of potential witnesses in that area.

The discussion of routine burglary cases and their handling illustrates the content of the shorthand schemes used by detectives in working burglary cases. Discussion of the remaining four types of routine offense patterns is based on the same kind of observation and documents, although space considerations will not permit the same volume of illustrative material to be presented.

ROUTINE ROBBERIES

The majority of persons who are apprehended for robbery are caught within 10 to 15 minutes after the commission of the crime. Those cases in which a suspect is not apprehended shortly after the incident are assigned to detectives for investigation. Detectives have less latitude in the handling strategies they may employ when a firearm is used in a robbery and the victim is a business establishment or a middle-class individual. Where a robbery incident has these features, the detective must conduct at least a perfunctory investigation and produce a very detailed investigative report. There is an assumption of offense repetition in armed robberies, and detectives anticipate that information in the report may have future value if a person is apprehended for a similar robbery incident.

Greater latitude exists in the handling of strong-arm robberies or muggings. Routine purse-snatching incidents usually receive either a perfunctory investigation or are suspended after an unproductive victim interview; the former strategy tends to be employed when the victim is middle-class and the latter when the victim is a poor person. When the victim of a strong-arm robbery is seen as a thoroughly "disreputable type" (such as a skid-row resident who has been "rolled"), the incident may be reclassified to a simple theft and suspended.

The feature accorded primary interpretive significance in assessing the routine or nonroutine nature of robbery incidents is the ability of the victim or witnesses to provide potentially identifying information regarding the perpetrator. Robbery occurs in a face-to-face setting, although masks are occasionally worn and perpetrators sometimes strike quickly from behind the victim. Victims and witnesses are often stunned by the speed and shock of the incident and, accordingly, the nature of the information they are able to provide varies widely. When this information takes the form of a simple clothing description, the incident is likely to be treated as a routine one. Regardless of the victim's characteristics, where potentially identifying information is provided which holds out the possibility of making an arrest, the case is defined as nonroutine, and a vigorous investigation is conducted. The crucial question asked during the victim or witness interview is "Would you recognize the guy if you saw him again?" or "Would you recognize the guy if you saw a picture of him?"

The interpretation of robbery incidents is also based on the manner in which the offense was committed. The typical armed robbery is seen as involving one or two young males wearing nondistinctive clothing and masks who enter a small business establishment (generally a corner grocery store, liquor store, or convenience store) for less than 2 minutes and do not leave fingerprints or other physical evidence behind. The typical mugging incident is seen as involving a middle-aged or elderly female victim and one or more teenage males who approach the victim from behind and then quickly move to a place where they are out of view of searching police. Further, detectives take into consideration the area of the city in which the incident occurred and, as in burglary cases, make assumptions about residents with regard to their cooperation with the police and the likelihood of a neighborhood canvass.

Cases 6 and 7 are illustrative of the interpretation and handling of routine and nonroutine robbery incidents.

Case 6

A young cab driver who was new to the job had been robbed by two males who hailed the cab and then displayed a gun and ordered the driver to take them to a street bordering the city reservoir. They took the cash box and the driver's wallet, pulled out the cab's microphone cord, and ordered the driver to lay down in the seat as they fled.

In the detective hall, the victim was questioned at length regarding a description of the two males. He could only provide a general clothing description since they had been in the back seat. It was noted that they had worn gloves during the incident. The driver was shown "hot" mugshots of persons recently involved in armed robberies, but none of these was identified as the perpetrator. Still visibly shaken by the incident, the driver was unclear about where he had picked the two up and the precise location where they had exited the cab. The driver stated that he thought he would be able to identify the male with the gun, and he was asked to come back the next day to look through additional mugbooks.

After the driver had left, and approximately 2½ hours after the robbery had occurred, the detective remarked: "That kid doesn't know what he is doing. And what kind of witness would he make. I'm ready to suspend the case right now."

Arrangements were never made for the victim to return to look through mugbooks because it was assumed that this would be fruitless (mugshots are very small (2" x 3") and are commonly several years old; identification through mugshots is rare). Nor was a neighborhood canvass for witnesses conducted, for it was assumed that residents in that area would be unlikely to volunteer information. The case was suspended 3 days later.

Robbery cases in which an arrest is not made shortly after the incidents are solved either through luck or gross incompetence on the part of the perpetrator, or through a major and time-consuming investigation involving informants and stakeouts. The latter situation occurs when an individual or group of persons is believed responsible for a series of robberies. The former situation is more common than one might suspect, as illustrated in the following case:

Case 7

An armed robbery had occurred at a small cleaning establishment when only one female clerk was present. Two males entered, placed a jacket on the counter, and asked to have it cleaned. As the clerk was filling out the slip, one male displayed a gun, ordered the clerk into a backroom, emptied the cash register and fled.

Two detectives responded and one began questioning the clerk. As she was describing the incident, she pointed to the jacket on the counter which the perpetrators had not taken with them when they fled. The second detective casually picked up the jacket and began looking through the pockets. In a small inside pocket was a document from the public defender's office containing a person's name. The case was solved simply by obtaining a photograph of this person and showing it to the clerk.

In summary, case features which constitute the basic interpretive framework for robbery incidents include:

1. The availability of information potentially identifying a suspect from the victim or witnesses

2. The social characteristics of the victim and witnesses which, within the interpretive schemes employed by detectives, make different categories of people more or less consequential as victims and more or less reliable sources of information

3. The victim's actual or presumed attitude toward spending the time and effort necessary in prosecuting the case

4. Whether the incident was carried out in such a way that physical evidence is obtainable

5. The area in which the incident occurred and the perceived likelihood of obtaining useful information from residents of that area through such procedures as a neighborhood canvass.

ROUTINE ASSAULTS

The majority of aggravated assault incidents observed occurred between persons who knew one another. Detectives use the term "Mom and Pop assault" or "barroom assault" to refer to incidents which involve acquainted parties. Unlike burglary and robbery cases, in assault incidents the victim frequently is able to provide the name of the perpetrator to responding police. Therefore, routine assault cases—those which are dealt with by means of low-effort handling strategies—generally result in an arrest. Where the victim and assailant were not previously acquainted in an assault incident, the case generally is defined as a nonroutine one requiring vigorous investigative effort.

There are no formal guidelines for handling assault incidents having different statutorily defined degrees of severity. Thus, an attempted murder incident involving a husband and wife in which the victim tells police that she was shot by her spouse is commonly handled in a purely routine manner. The detective takes written statements from both parties and any witnesses, attempts to locate and confiscate the weapon if one was used, orders photographs taken of the crime scene, and collects any relevant physical evidence. However, these tasks are performed in a casual, almost mechanical way, for the detective does not feel that he is actively seeking information about what happened, but merely collecting information and evidence which is largely superfluous. This casual investigative approach is partly traceable to a belief among detectives that their investigative methods will seldom come under court scrutiny in routine assault cases because most cases of this type will be resolved through a negotiated plea of guilty.

Since the time lag between the occurrence of the offense and the police response is seen as critical, detectives usually respond directly to the scene of felony assaults. Thus, within a short period of time detectives are able to ask the questions and seek out the basic information enabling them to make sense of the event and assess its routine or nonroutine nature.

The feature of assault cases having primary interpretive significance is the existence and nature of a prior social relationship between the involved parties. Detectives obtain a sense of what happened and what needs to be done in an assault incident when they learn that it involved a man and woman who have been living together, acquaintances who got into an argument outside a bar, or strangers.

The following incident, although involving an assault with a deadly weapon, was understood by the detective as requiring essentially no investigative effort.

Case 8

During the early morning hours, a man had assaulted his common-law wife with a knife, inflicting a laceration which required hospital treatment. During the drive to the public housing project where the parties lived, the detective remarked, "the drunks over here are always fightin' and cuttin' one another." It was noted from the patrol report that uniformed officers had advised the woman to sign a warrant and she had done so. The detective found the man standing in front of his residence and called out, "C'mon John, come with me. I gotta lock you up." No questions were asked about the incident during the drive to the station or during the handling of the arrest paperwork. No attempt was made to obtain a statement from the man for use in prosecuting the case. I later expressed surprise that the man had been released on his own recognizance for a felony assault, but the detective matter-of-factly replied, "Why not? She'll never show up in court and prosecute it anyhow. Why waste my time and everybody else's on it?"

No investigation was conducted. In assault cases of this type, detectives ordinarily write a brief report detailing the victim's account of the incident and "let the courts sort it out."

Detectives also attend to whether the precipitating circumstances were normal for the parties involved. Domestic assaults are seen as typically growing out of a heated, verbal argument over any number of personal issues. With regard to barroom-type assaults between males, one detective expressed the opinion that "money, booze, and women are the main reasons the natives go at it." If the precipitating circumstances are not seen as corresponding to such normal motives, but are found to lie in a dispute over stolen goods or a drug deal, a more vigorous investigation may be undertaken.

Detectives also base their interpretation on the life-styles and social characteristics of the involved parties. A shared belief exists among detectives that physical violence is a normal aspect of the lifestyles of lower-class persons and especially members of minority groups. As one detective remarked during the early stage of my field work, "There's one thing you've got to understand. These people are savages, and we're here to keep peace among the savages." On the other hand, where physical confrontation is not seen as a normal aspect of the lifestyle of the parties involved, a detective is likely to interview the parties at greater length in an effort to determine why the assault occurred. Photographs of the victim's injuries may be ordered and an interview with the attending physician conducted, for parties having different social characteristics and lifestyles are seen as having different likelihoods of resolving the matter through plea bargaining or through formal judicial procedures.

Routine assault cases are constructed from the following elements. The existence and nature of a prior social relationship between the involved parties constitutes the feature of assault incidents which is accorded primary interpretive significance. The interpretation and handling of assault incidents is also contingent upon:

1. Understanding of the lifestyles and social characteristics of the parties involved

2. The victim's attitude toward prosecution, which may derive from explicit statements made by the victim or which may be assumed on the basis of understandings about the relationship between, and the lifestyle of, the involved parties

3. Whether the precipitating circumstances are seen as normal for the type of incident in question.

The seriousness of the injury to the victim has little bearing on the assessment of the incident as routine or nonroutine, but it has substantial impact on whether the case will be summarily suspended or whether some investigative activities will be performed.

"MORNING AFTER" RAPES

Rape generally is viewed as so serious an offense that it warrants an intensive investigation. If the victim is attacked by an unknown assailant, supervisors almost invariably impose a major case definition on the incident, assign several detectives to the case full time, and sometimes play an active role in the investigation themselves. Where the victim is a poor person or a member of a minority group, the police response is typically of a lesser magnitude, although initially one or two detectives are likely to be assigned to the case full time. In other words, rape complaints generally receive a vigorous investigative effort.

However, there is one commonly recognized pattern of features regarding rape complaints which elicits a qualitatively different police response. When this configuration of features exists in a specific allegation of rape, detectives refer to the incident as a "morning after" or "suspect" rape, their initial reaction to the complaint is one of suspicion. Initial police efforts are concerned with and concentrate on attempting to establish the legitimacy of the complainant's allegations. Among detectives, it is viewed as a mark of investigative competence and acumen to "see through" a suspect rape complaint. This status dimension is sustained by frequent recounting of past cases in which a female did in fact falsely allege rape, in combination with the oft-repeated caution that "rape is the only crime where a person's word can send a guy to jail for life."[10]

The following case displays typical features of incidents categorized as "morning after" rapes.

Case 9

Two detectives were assigned to investigate a rape complaint which had been reported at approximately 3:00 A.M. After notifying police, the victim was immediately taken to a hospital for a medical examination. The physician indicated that the test for ejaculate was negative, but the victim had noticeable bruises on her vulva and inner thighs. The complainant was returned to the detective hall and questioned for over 4 hours. She stated that she had been alone walking to her residence at about 11:30 P.M. when a car pulled up to the curb beside her. She recognized the driver as a person she had known in high school and, after some discussion, agreed to ride around with him as he attempted to buy some marijuana. Some time later, she indicated that she needed to use a bathroom and asked to be taken home. The driver replied that she could use the one in his apartment. The complainant stated that when she arrived, she was sexually assaulted by the driver and three other males already in the apartment. She had difficulty expressing exactly what had happened, stating simply that they had "attacked her." One detective remarked that the victim appeared to be mentally retarded.

> At 8:00 A.M., I asked a supervising detective what he thought of the case. He replied, "It stinks. She keeps changing her story. She knows the guys who were supposed to have done it plus no sperm showed up in the test at the hospital. There is one guy locked up downstairs on a 2-hour detention, but it looks right now like there probably won't be any arrests made."

The case was eventually handled as an unfounded complaint, meaning that the investigators believed there was not sufficient evidence to warrant a criminal charge.

There is a shared belief among detectives that young, lower-class females are the most likely persons to falsely allege rape. Any indication of mental or emotional disturbance on the part of the victim heightens the detective's suspicion regarding the legitimacy of her allegation. Where a victim having these characteristics alleges that she has been raped by someone with whom she is acquainted, the initial orientation of detectives is to seek out information to categorize the event as a suspect or legitimate rape. It is standard procedure in rape investigations to transport the victim to a hospital immediately for a medical examination to test for the presence of ejaculate. Although there is an awareness that ejaculation within the victim does not occur in all rapes and that penetration and ejaculation are not statutorily required elements of the crime of rape, detectives nonetheless assign considerable interpretive significance to whether or not the rape has been "confirmed" by medical examination.

Additional information enabling detectives to categorize an incident as suspect or legitimate is sought out during the victim interviews. Where the victim possesses social characteristics believed to be typically associated with false allegations of rape, the questioning tends to take on a predictable form. Do you know the guy? How long have you known him? Have you ever had sexual relations with him before? Did he use a weapon or other means of force? Did you report this to the police as soon as you were able to? How did you come in contact with him prior to the incident? Did you voluntarily get into his car or accompany him home? Did you resist?

Where the victim provides the name of her alleged assailant, this person is brought in for questioning. The primary issue of interest is whether or not he indicates that the victim consented. At this point, sufficient information has usually been obtained to categorize the incident as suspect or legitimate. Investigative strategies differ radically depending on this assessment. Suspect rape incidents typically are unfounded or reduced to a lesser charge such as sexual assault or sexual misconduct.

"Morning after" rape cases consist of some combination of the features presented below. The feature assigned primary interpretive significance is whether a victim having specific social characteristics believed to be typical of females who falsely allege rape knew her assailant prior to the incident. An interpretation of a rape complaint as suspect is likely to be made when this feature exists in combination with some or all of the following elements:

1. Certain conduct by the victim prior to and during the incident may be construed as cooperative or consenting behavior. Voluntarily accompanying the alleged perpetrator to the place where the incident occurred, or voluntarily entering his vehicle, may be taken as indications of willingness on the part of the victim. The victim's failure to fight back to attempt to resist the assault may be seen as an indication that "she really didn't mind." Consumption of alcohol or other drugs by the two parties together prior to the incident is seen as cooperative and contributing behavior on the part of the victim.

2. Any delay in reporting the incident to police is seen as entailing the possibility that the victim has some ulterior motive in making the complaint. Revenge against the person named by the victim is seen as the most common motive for false allegations of rape.

3. An emotional state and attitude displayed toward the incident by the victim which are viewed as inappropriate for a female who has just been sexually abused raises suspicion. After listening to a rape complainant calmly and matter-of-factly describe the details of an incident, one detective expressed doubt regarding the victim's account, noting, "She should be more upset than this." Another detective stormed out of an interview with a 15-year-old resident of a juvenile group home who alleged that she had been raped by three other residents of the home and stated, "If she doesn't give a shit about what happened then why should I?"

4. Any contradictions or inconsistencies in the victim's account of the incident during extended questioning by different detectives are seen as indicative of a false complaint. One older, experienced detective expressed the opinion to the researcher that many investigators expect a clear, coherent, and consistent account of the incident in spite of the fact that the interview is being conducted within hours after the assault and in spite of the likelihood that many victims are embarrassed by, and are trying to forget, what has just happened to them. If the victim is asked to take a polygraph examination and declines for any reason, detectives are likely to conclude that a legitimate rape did not occur. If the victim consents to a polygraph examination and the results are termed "inconclusive" (a rather frequent outcome), the same inference is likely to be drawn.

5. A medical examination which does not confirm the presence of ejaculate within the victim is seen as reason for suspicion regarding the validity of the complaint.

6. The person named as the perpetrator provides an account of the incident in which the female consented to sexual relations.

KILLINGS

Detectives distinguish two types of homicides: killings and murders. In the former, the information and evidence available at the crime scene rather easily leads to the identification of the perpetrator. Commonly, such information is available from: (1) the perpetrator who remains at the scene of the crime when police arrive (such as the remorseful spouse); (2) persons who either witnessed the crime or have knowledge of a person who had threatened the victim, had been arguing with the victim, or had reason to assault the victim; or (3) a "dying declaration" provided by the victim.[11] Detectives recognize that most homicides occur between persons who know one another, and that often in such cases the perpetrator makes no serious attempt to conceal his or her deed. Where a particular case is seen as corresponding to the general category of routine killings, detectives view their task as a reasonably straightforward one involving apprehending the perpetrator, gathering any potential evidence, taking statements from any relevant parties, and writing a detailed report for use by the prosecutor.

In contrast, an incident is defined as a murder when available information does not readily identify the perpetrator. Different motives or precipitating circumstances are believed to be associated with this type of homicide, and methodical investigative work is deemed necessary.

The following case is typical of the interpretation and handling of routine killing incidents:

Case 10

Two detectives were assigned to a homicide case which had originally been handled by patrol officers as a routine assault case. The incident involved a lover's triangle between two males and a female who lived in the same block in one of the most deteriorated, skid-row type areas of the city. All three persons were described as long-term alcoholics. Patrol officers originally responded to the scene following a report of an assault in progress. Apparently the younger of the two males had argued with the female about her relationship with the other male. The female had been struck on the forehead during this argument and had suffered a serious scalp laceration. The older male was found lying in his apartment with a head laceration and was taken to a hospital where he was treated and kept for observation. He informed patrol officers that he had been beaten by the younger man, but he was highly intoxicated during this interview. Patrol officers arrested the younger man for assault on the female, and he was released on an unsecured bond. Three days later the older man died in the hospital.

The case was assigned to two detectives the following morning as a possible homicide. The detectives discussed possible classification of the incident: death from natural causes, homicide, or self-defense. It was decided that nothing further would be done until the medical examiner's office classified the death in the afternoon. When it was learned that the cause of death was a fractured skull, the detectives cursed and discussed what would have to be done "to cover ourselves." They obtained the victim's blood-stained clothing as possible evidence. An attempt was made to locate the suspect in the immediate area of his residence, but he was not found. After a brief inspection of the room where the victim was found, photographs were taken, and it was decided that a slipcover and a chair showing what appeared to be blood should be tagged as evidence. Both detectives repeatedly expressed their revulsion over the condition of the residence and the tasks they were performing. It was decided to make no further attempt to locate the suspect that day, but rather to wait and see whether he would show up for a scheduled court appearance the next day pertaining to the assault charge. "I could care less about this case, I'd be just as happy if drunks like these were left to kill each other off."

The following morning the suspect came into the detective hall to turn himself in. He was advised of his rights and told that he had an opportunity to make a statement about what happened. He stated that he had been extremely intoxicated that night, had passed out, and doesn't remember anything that happened. No further attempt was made to interrogate the suspect, and the interview lasted less than 30 minutes.

Obtaining a formal statement from the female assault victim about the incident and preparing a four-page investigation report concluded the detectives' work on the case. The total time and effort devoted to this investigation was comparable to that for a minor burglary case having a named suspect.

In homicide cases, primary interpretive significance is accorded a combination of two case features: (1) whether information available at the scene or in initial interviews identifies and links a person to the crime, and (2) whether there was a prior relationship between that person and the victim. Where both of these features are present in an instant case, the event ordinarily is interpreted as a killing and handled routinely.

The assessment of the routine or nonroutine nature of homicide incidents is also based on the social characteristics and lifestyles of the parties involved. In part, this assignment of identities to the principals in the case is made on the basis of territorial knowledge which includes assumptions and understandings about the typical inhabitants of an area and their likely patterns of behavior.

Detectives also attend to whether the motive and the circumstances precipitating the incident were normal for the parties involved. If the apparent motive and precipitating circumstances in a case map onto a common and understandable pattern for domestic killings or barroom-type killings, the incident tends to be readily categorized and treated as routine. In domestic killings, a heated argument regarding one party's sexual fidelity is seen as an ordinary precipitating circumstance. Similarly, for barroom-type killings involving two males, a verbal argument or challenge concerning a woman, money, or a number of other normal bases for heated arguments are seen as ordinary motives and precipitating circumstances. Further investigative effort is seen as necessary when such a common and readily understandable pattern is not evident in a case.

SUMMARY AND CONCLUSIONS

Police handling of criminal investigations is guided by a set of interpretive schemes through which cases having different configurations of information are seen as warranting different levels and methods of investigation. Organizational demands and constraints generate a distinctive work orientation for the frequently handled crimes of burglary and robbery. Detectives select out for vigorous effort readily solvable cases while devoting only cursory effort to the remaining cases. Case stereotypes also function to provide standard recipes for the handling of assault, rape, and homicide incidents which display typical features.

Investigative work in the department studied was vigorous and methodical in only a small percentage of the cases handled. Indeed an image of detective work as involving a special arsenal of sophisticated techniques is substantially misleading for most ordinary criminal investigations. If the victim or witnesses are able to provide potentially identifying information in burglary and robbery incidents, the case will be vigorously pursued. In the great majority of cases, such information is not available, and minimal effort is devoted to the case. The work orientation referred to as "skimming" enhances our understanding of the low clearance rates for burglary and robbery. The relatively small portion of incidents categorized as major cases receive a higher level of investigative effort and a wider variety of investigative techniques are used.

Case-handling methods also vary according to the victim's social status. The differential treatment of crime victims flows in part from a set of stereotypic assumptions about the detectives' concern with potential solvability. Thus, in certain neighborhoods methodical investigative procedures, such as an area canvass seldom are undertaken because of a belief that they would prove fruitless. A work orientation emphasizing practicality and productivity serves to encourage this substitution of assumptions for information gathering.

NOTES

1. The description and analysis presented here are based on 9 months of participant observation field work in a city police detective division. At the conclusion of the field work, the formulations contained in this article were discussed with various detectives in the context of "how the work is actually done." The patterned activities described here were recognized by experienced detectives as standard features of everyday practices. Further information about departmental characteristics, access problems, daily routines, and the field role adopted during the research is available from the author.

2. Statistics on the offender and victim relationship for personal offenses are broken down into categories for primary relationship, nonprimary (such as acquaintance, neighbor, sex rival, or enemy), stranger, other, and unknown. For homicide the respective figures are 33.7 percent, 28.1 percent, and 38.2 percent; for aggravated assault, 20.6 percent, 25.3 percent, and 55 percent; and for rape, 10.2 percent, 32.6 percent, and 57.2 percent (Dunn 1976:11).

3. This finding is also documented in survey research on police investigations. A recent study found that substantially more than half of all serious reported crimes receive no more than superficial attention from investigators. Further, if information identifying the perpetrator is not available at the time the crime is reported, the perpetrator generally will not be subsequently identified. See Greenwood et al. (1975).

4. A theoretical interpretation of the centrality of typificatory schemes in decision making by police and other legal agents is provided in Waegel (1981).

5. Garfinkel (1967:186-207) argues that organizational records are not to be treated as accurate or mirror reflections of the actual handling of a client or case by organizational members. However, these records can be employed to examine how members go about constructing a meaningful conception of a client or case and use it for their own practical purposes. Any valid sociological use of such records requires detailed knowledge on the part of the researcher regarding the context in which the records are produced, background understandings of members, and organizationally relevant purposes and routines.

6. Although "named suspects" (persons named in the original patrol report) are most commonly obtained from victims, other sources occasionally provide this information. A neighbor may come forward and volunteer that he or she witnessed the incident or has heard that a certain person or persons have been committing burglaries in the vicinity. Informants sometimes provide similar information.

7. There is a formal constraint on the detective's discretion regarding how much effort to devote to a burglary case. If the loss is in excess of $2,000, a lieutenant may impose a major case definition on the incident. The vast bulk of the city burglaries I observed involved much smaller losses.

8. There is a widespread misunderstanding concerning the utility of fingerprints obtained from a crime scene. Prior to my research, I had believed that a fingerprint obtained from a crime scene could automatically be used to identify the perpetrator. Unknown latent fingerprints from a crime scene cannot be identified from fingerprint files. The FBI fingerprint laboratory will only compare unknown latent prints with the file prints of identified suspects. Unknown prints from a crime scene and file prints of a suspect or suspects must be packaged together and sent to the FBI lab where technicians simply make comparisons. There are presently no automated procedures for comparing an unknown fingerprint against the millions of file prints.

9. The detectives dictate investigative reports through the desk telephones in the large detective room. The fact that this room is often crowded and noisy accounts for much of the fractured grammar in these reports. Identifying information has been deleted.

10. This statement means that rape cases are sometimes prosecuted successfully without corroboration of the victim's testimony and without direct evidence, such as fiber inter-mingling on clothing.
11. A surprising number of homicide victims do not expire immediately after receiving mortal injuries. Detectives immediately respond to any call involving a serious assault and, if the victim is conscious, ask two questions: Do you know who did this to you, and do you know why? If a dying declaration is obtained under the proper legal circumstances, the victim's statement will be admissible in court as an exception to the hearsay rule.

REFERENCES

Bittner, Egon. 1967. The police on skid row: A study of peace keeping. *Am. Social. Rev.* 32:699-715.

Dunn, Christopher S. 1976. *The patterns and distribution of assault incident characteristics.* Albany, NY: Criminal Justice Research Center.

Garfinkel, Harold. 1967. *Studies in ethnomethodology.* Englewood Cliffs: Prentice-Hall.

Greenwood, P; Chaiken, J.; Petersilia, J.; and Prusoff, L. 1975. *The criminal investigation process: Volume III.* Santa Monica, CA: Rand Corporation.

Lundman, Richard J. 1974. Routine arrest practices: A commonwealth perspective. *Social Problems* 22:127-141.

——————— . 1979. Organizational norms and police discretion: An observational study of police work with traffic law violators. *Criminology* 17:159-171.

Manning, Peter K. 1974. Police lying. *Urban Life* 3:283-306.

Reiss, Albert. 1971. *Police and the public.* New Haven: Yale Univ. Press.

Rubinstein, Jonathan. 1973. *City police.* New York: Ballantine.

Skolnick, Jerome. 1967. *Justice without trial.* New York: Wiley.

Sykes, Richard and Clark, John P. 1975. A theory of deference exchange in police-civilian encounters. *Am. J. Sociol.* 81:584-600.

Van Maanen, John. 1978. The asshole. In *Policing: A view from the street,* edited by Peter K. Manning and John Van Maanen. Santa Monica, CA: Goodyear.

Waegel, William B. 1981. Case routinization in investigative police work. *Social Problems* 28:263-275.

SOLVING CRIMES   10

John E. Eck

The detective occupies a prominent place in law enforcement lore and reality. An enduring popular image is that of the investigator who solves the most puzzling crimes through tenacity and intuition. For law enforcement administrators, the reality is far more complex. In recent years, the question of effective management of investigative work—a costly item in any department's budget—has ranked high on the list of concerns.

Given the importance of the criminal investigation process, it's not surprising that researchers, too, began to turn their attention to the study of detective work during the late sixties and seventies. One major work that homed in on the issues involved was the RAND study of the criminal investigation process, completed in the mid-seventies under the auspices of the National Institute of Justice. That research generated considerable controversy in the police world, but, at the same time, helped stimulate new thinking about how best to manage the investigation of crimes.

Now, a recent study funded by the National Institute of Justice and conducted by the Police Executive Research Forum has turned up valuable new information that can help departments get a better return on their investment in investigative operations. The study, *Solving Crimes: The Investigation of Burglary and Robbery,* is a comprehensive analysis of the actions of both patrol officers and detectives, the information obtained from their actions, and the results this information and these actions helped to produce.

Source: John E. Eck (1984). "Solving Crimes." *Research in Action, NIJ Reports* 184:4-8. Reprinted by permission of the National Institute of Justice.

Our findings shed considerable light on how burglary investigations are conducted, the relative importance of patrol officers' and detectives' action to investigative results, and how the management of investigations can be improved. The research revealed that investigations may be more productive than earlier studies suggested. In fact, our research concludes that follow-up investigations, usually conducted by detectives, *do* in fact contribute to solving the crimes studied. In addition, we found the activities of patrol officers and detectives equally important to investigations.

Our findings differ from previous studies. To put them in context it is useful to review briefly the evolution of research on solving crimes.

PREVIOUS RESEARCH ON INVESTIGATIONS

Researchers have paid much attention to the productivity of investigations, particularly to how investigators solve crimes and the relative contributions of patrol officers and detectives to crime solution. From this research have come two apparently contradictory hypotheses.

The first I will call the *Circumstance-Result Hypothesis.* It states that investigative results, such as arrests, are the result of circumstances that are essentially beyond police control: Is there a witness to the crime? Was stolen property marked and recorded by the owner? Is physical evidence present? Can the victim identify the suspect?

The patrol officer determines whether the necessary leads are present and whether the circumstances are favorable for an arrest. Detectives, on the other hand, do little investigative work in the normal meaning of the term. They are engaged in processing the case and completing paperwork. These activities may include calling the victim to verify that no leads exist, picking up and interrogating suspects identified by the patrol officer, and preparing cases to be turned over to the prosecutor.

Most previous research has offered this hypothesis as the predominant explanation of how crimes are solved. Evidence supporting it is provided by Isaacs (1967), Greenwood (1970), Greenberg, et al. (1975), Greenwood and Petersilia (1975), and Eck (1979). Although this idea predominates, the research supporting it is flawed. None of the studies that lend credence to this hypothesis actually examined the actions of detectives in dealing with solved and unsolved cases. Thus, there is no way of determining from these studies whether detectives' activities made a difference in the outcome of cases.

The second explanation of how crimes are solved is the *Effort-Result Hypothesis.* This view claims that investigative efforts of detectives contribute substantially to the success of the investigations.

Searching for witnesses, interviewing victims, checking records, cultivating informants, and other typical investigative activities can increase the chance of an arrest. Furthermore, actions taken based on initial leads can produce further leads and arrests.

Even less formal evidence has existed to support this notion, a view generally supported more by the investigators than researchers. Two studies—Ward (1971) and Folk (1971)—did describe such a model. Unfortunately, however, the research made no attempt to test the Effort-Result Hypothesis.

A NEW LOOK AT INVESTIGATIONS

To remedy the gaps in our understanding of how the investigative process really works, the Police Executive Research Forum and the National Institute of Justice launched a new in-depth study. We collected data on crimes that resulted in an arrest and crimes that did not. We documented the entire investigative process, from the arrival of the first patrol officer at the crime scene through termination of investigative efforts by detectives.

In all, data on 3,360 burglary and 320 robbery investigations were collected in three police agencies: the DeKalb County (Ga.) Department of Public Safety, the St. Petersburg (Fla.) Police Department, and the Wichita (Kan.) Police Department. Three sources were tapped for data: official reports, activity logs, and observations.

Official records included the patrol officers' incident reports, detectives' supplemental reports, case screening forms, and other documents. From these official reports we gleaned information on data describing the crime itself, the investigative information obtained, and the recorded investigative results.

The project also called for activity logs to be completed by patrol officers and detectives for each day they worked on a case. The logs described investigators' activities, the time they took, and the information they produced. Our researchers also observed patrol officers and detectives to ensure quality control of the data and to provide details that could not be obtained from activity logs and official reports.

One of the purposes of our research was to test the soundness of the two prevailing hypotheses about crime solving. Analysis of our data showed that both were partially correct, but neither told the full story.

Evidence to support the Circumstance-Result Hypothesis could be seen in the rapid attrition of cases from the investigative process. In our study, almost 50 percent of the burglary cases were screened out before assignment to a detective for follow-up investigation. While all robberies were assigned, 75 percent of them were dropped after one day. Assigned burglaries fared no better: 75 percent of burglary follow-up investigations were dropped after the first follow-up investigation day. Clearly, the lack of leads has a large effect early in the process.

More sophisticated data analysis confirmed the basic premise of the Effort-Result theory. We found that detective work on assigned cases *does* influence arrests. Actions such as witness and informant interviews, discussions with department members, and checking files were strongly related to arrests. These relationships held even when other variables, such as information collected by patrol officers, were accounted for. Surprisingly, though, victim interviews by detectives were found to be totally unrelated to arrests or other useful activities. In some respects they were even counterproductive—taking time from other, potentially more useful activities.

Since both of the prevailing notions fell short in providing a satisfactory explanation of how investigations produce arrests, we formulated a new hypothesis. We concluded that the investigative process implicitly works as a triage system, dividing cases into three groups:

- Cases that *cannot be solved* with a reasonable amount of investigative effort;

- Cases *solved by circumstances*, requiring only that suspects be arrested, booked, and interrogated, and a prosecutable case be prepared; and

- Cases that *may be solved* if a reasonable level of investigative effort is applied to them, but will not be solved otherwise.

The dividing of cases into groups is implicit because police agencies have no formal policies (with possibly one exception) promoting such a division. Case screening prior to assignment to detectives is the one exception. Detectives acting independently and using their knowledge and experience perform this sorting process without official procedures.

KEY FINDINGS

In addition to improving our understanding of how investigations produce arrests, our study produced other major findings with implications for policy and practice.

Length of Investigations. The vast majority of burglary and robbery cases are investigated for no more than 4 hours, counting both the preliminary work by patrol officers and the follow-up work by detectives. The investigations usually last for no more than 3 days (though the days are not necessarily consecutive), so that an average of 11 days elapses between the initial report of the crime and the suspension of all investigative activity.

Focus and Nature of Investigations Change. Preliminary investigations and the early stages of follow-up investigations focus on the victim and other sources of information outside the police department's control. Interviewing victims and checking crime scenes are routinely conducted. In cases that are pursued longer, the focus shifts to suspects and information sources within the department's control. In the later stages there is no single routine activity, as investigators take actions that are adapted to fit the leads developed earlier.

Sources of Information. The name of the suspect, the description of the suspect, and related crime information are the three most important types of information collected during the follow-up investigation. Unfortunately, the sources of this information are not used productively. The most used source of information that could lead to arrest of a suspect is the victim, but in any given case, *victims are the least likely source to have information that could lead to an arrest.* By contrast, four other information sources—witnesses, informants, other members of the department, and department records—are consulted far less often. But when they are consulted they are much more likely to produce useful information.

Role of Patrol Officers and Detectives. Preliminary investigations by patrol officers and follow-up investigations by detectives are equally important in determining whether cases will be solved with arrest. Patrol officers' conduct of preliminary investigations is important because most follow-up work is based on leads developed in the preliminary investigation. If few or no leads are developed, the case is likely to be screened out and never assigned for follow-up or, if assigned, the follow-up will be quickly suspended. But once a case is assigned, the investigative work of detectives is important for following up on leads. Even when the preliminary investigation did not develop suspect information, detectives can get the suspect's name in about 14 percent of these cases and make an arrest in almost 8 percent.

How the Research Differs from Earlier Studies

The major point of difference between the Forum's findings and those of earlier researchers concerns the role of detectives and the value of follow-up investigations, Earlier studies tended to emphasize the importance of patrol officers and preliminary investigations while downgrading the worth of follow-up. This study reaches the quite different conclusion that patrol officers and detectives contribute equally important work toward the solution of cases.

There are two explanations for the different conclusions. Unlike previous studies, this research documented the specific actions detectives take and the information they gather in follow-up investigations. The absence of such data made it impossible for previous researchers to measure the results of what detectives actually do.

A second explanation is that changes have occurred in investigative management as a result of the earlier studies. Five years have elapsed since publication of the last of those studies; all of them had a profound influence on investigative management today. For instance, there has been a greater emphasis on case screening and on improving the role of patrol officers' investigations—policy changes that were recommended by many of the earlier studies. It is possible that improvements made in investigative management have made follow-up investigations more useful than they were in the past. Further management improvement could have similar results.

RECOMMENDATIONS FOR POLICE MANAGERS

These research findings point the way to management changes that could make wiser and more efficient use of investigative resources. Recommendations for police investigation managers cover three areas: improving information collection, improving the management of follow-up investigations, and an alternative approach to investigations.

IMPROVING INFORMATION COLLECTION

Preliminary Investigations. Greater emphasis should be placed on collecting physical evidence when such evidence can be used, and patrol officers should devote greater efforts to searching for witnesses, checking department records, and using informants.

Follow-up Investigations. During follow-up investigations greater use should be made of agency records and more extensive use should be made of informants.

IMPROVING THE MANAGEMENT OF FOLLOW-UP INVESTIGATIONS

Regulating Case Flow. Three mechanisms should be used to ensure that resources are applied to those cases that are most likely to be solved. These mechanisms are: case screening, policies governing the length of time cases can remain open, and policies defining the maximum workload of detectives.

Monitoring Investigative Activities. To ensure that resources are used effectively on cases, supervisors must monitor investigations. There are three approaches: assign cases to investigators and monitor them when investigations are assigned and when they are terminated; assign cases to the investigative unit, assign tasks to investigators, and monitor activities when tasks are assigned and completed; or assign simple cases to investigators and complex cases to the unit, thus combining the first two approaches.

Measuring Investigative Unit Productivity. A system of productivity measures is needed to determine how units are meeting their goals. A measurement system is recommended that takes into account the number of cases assigned, number of suspects identified, number of arrests, number of arrests accepted by the prosecutor, number of arrests resulting in a conviction, and other measures.

Targeted Investigations

Investigations Work Is Primarily Reactive. Investigators react to citizens' reports of crime committed. Management improvements may increase the effectiveness of this approach but will not diminish its underlying weakness: the investigation takes place after the fact and forces investigators to respond to events outside their control. Managers seldom step back from the daily case flow to examine its sources, diagnose the problems, and design new and innovative programs and policies to deal with them. Targeted investigations are an attempt to do that.

An example of targeted investigation is the effort in an increasing number of departments to focus on a small number of repeat offenders and career criminals who commit a large number of crimes. But targeted investigation should not be limited to career criminals. For example, an analysis of crime patterns might reveal that truant juveniles commit a large proportion of the daytime residential burglaries in a particular section of a city. This could lead to specific investigative actions such as checking with school officials to determine which juveniles have been consistently absent from school on the days the burglaries occurred. And it could lead to broader law enforcement policies such as a joint effort by the police and the school system to enforce truancy laws strictly.

Targeted investigations are conducted by a team of investigators brought together to handle a problem. Targeted investigations can be divided into four stages: defining the problem and selecting the target; planning the strategy; conducting the investigations; and evaluating performance. The targeted investigations team should be temporary, operating long enough to alleviate the particular problem. Lessons learned from the evaluation of the targeted investigation can be applied to traditional investigations and to help design future targeted investigations.

CRIMINAL INVESTIGATIONS: ADAPTING RESEARCH TO PRACTICE

"What we thought was key has been confirmed," said George Kranda, Fairfax County (Va.) Police Department. Lt. Kranda, who participated in an Institute-sponsored work-shop conducted by the Police Executive Research Forum (PERF), offered this view of the PERF study, "Solving Crimes."

Lt. Kranda, as well as several other workshop participants, said that the research findings corroborated their own views about factors which contribute to arrest. PERF researchers presented the findings of their study and its recommendations to the managers of investigative units in police departments serving cities of 100,000 population or larger. The workshops were held in Los Angeles, Atlanta, Chicago, and Dallas. They drew police managers from 144 departments in the United States and 2 in Canada.

More emphasis on physical evidence, greater reliance on informants, and a greater use of department records—these were among the study's recommendations that conference leaders highlighted as key to improving the likelihood of arrest.

Lee Bacca, Los Angeles Sheriff's Department, spoke about case screening and related approaches for caseload management that his department has implemented. He urged other participants to adopt similar practices, including the recommendations by PERF. "This research is a model for more effective criminal investigations," Captain Bacca said.

Participants said that the study provided information and approaches that they, as managers, could put into practice. Several participants reported that they are now re-evaluating their procedures for managing cases after learning of the PERF research. "Now we can make the case that the public is better served by our adoption of these strategies," Lt. Kranda said. "We have this study as proof."

Observations on
Police Undercover Work   11

George I. Miller

Municipal police, like all formal organizations, are characterized by a division of labor. At the patrol officer level alone there are at least 50 separate forms of work to which an officer may be assigned (Van Maanen, 1984). While duties such as property clerk, jailer, or dispatcher are necessary for police departments to function, they rarely make headlines or inspire television or theater dramatizations. In contrast, undercover police work, because of its utilization of deception, improvisation, and entrepreneurship does generate such attention. Undercover work is arguably the most problematic form of policing undertaken by municipal police departments and little is known about it in operation. This paper focuses on police undercover work and examines it as a contribution to a sociology of work.

Most policing depends upon the authority of a uniform. It is empowering (Joseph and Alex, 1972; Bickman, 1974; Wilson, 1978). But, for obvious reasons, a uniform limits an officer's ability to gather information. When the police want to know about crimes or conduct not commonly brought to their attention and where the presence of a uniform is an impediment to acquiring that knowledge, they must initiate that inquiry. That form of investigation is often referred to as proactive policing (Reiss, 1971).

Like any intelligence-gathering organization, the police have a limited number of options: surveillance, eavesdropping, the recruiting of informants, and espionage. In police organizations, the practice of engaging in espionage is often called undercover work. The term "undercover" has been

Source: George I. Miller (1987). "Observations on Police Undercover Work." *Criminology*, 25(1):27-46. Reprinted by permission of the American Society of Criminology.

applied generically to much of nonuniform police work. Marx (1980), for instance, includes decoys, sting operations, and the use of informants as police agents. Undercover police work is defined herein as instances when a sworn officer, for organizationally approved investigative purposes, adopts an encompassing but fictitious civic identity and maintains it as a total identity over a defined and considerable period of time. The officer's new identity and private life are merged with the police identity in an attempt to discover and police conduct not commonly reported. While violations being investigated may include drugs, gambling, prostitution, or sales of illegal goods, false identities may also be adopted to investigate law-abiding citizens merely regarded as suspicious (for example, those advocating "radical" political views; see also Dix, 1975). They also may be adopted for "general fishing expeditions" (Iverson, 1967: 1,109). Officers who work undercover, like espionage agents, are useful only to the extent that their activities remain secret.

Even within the definition used here, two types of undercover work may be distinguished: light-cover and deep-cover.[1] The difference between them is the degree to which the officer's private life merges with the fictitious civic identity. Officers assigned to light-cover often work a regular daily tour of duty and otherwise maintain their private identity. Light-cover is limited in its investigatory scope since it allows the officer to only partially embrace a fictitious identity. For that reason, light-cover officers frequently depend upon the assistance of informants who provide introductions or pass information while going about their everyday business, which is frequently of a criminal nature. In contrast, officers assigned to deep-cover work become entirely submerged in the new identity for the duration of the assignment, and the work most fully approximates the definition of undercover. Deep-cover work is open-ended and may last for months or years (Girodo, 1984). The usefulness and ultimate power of the disguise is that the officer is able to circulate in areas where the police would not otherwise be welcome (Reiss, 1974).

DATA AND METHODOLOGY

This paper reports a pilot study on the police use of fictitious identities in gathering information about conduct external to the organization. The particular data for this paper are drawn from interviews with erstwhile undercover officers and supervisors of undercover operations. Some of the more general observations are informed by the personal experiences of the author, who was employed by a municipal police department as a sworn officer for over 8 years, the first 16 months of which were in a deep-cover capacity.

Eighteen interviews, ranging from one to three and one-half hours in duration, were conducted. Those interviewed are or were sworn police personnel acting in or directing undercover activities[2] at the municipal police level. Some of those interviewed are no longer members of police departments, but in no instance did the undercover assignment constitute their entire police career. Others are still police officers; some are patrol officers, others are detectives, and still others are supervisors or members of the command staff. The interviews were informal and open-ended, and took place in police departments, public places, or private homes.

A sample of this sort is very difficult to draw. Since undercover work, particularly deep-cover work, may not occur regularly in municipal police departments, the names and number of officers assigned to these duties is not always well known. For that reason, a snowball technique was employed to locate individuals. Before the snowball came to a rest, subjects had been drawn from six municipal police departments in two states in the Northeast. The officers had been assigned to undercover work at different times covering a 20-year period from the early 1960s to the early 1980s. Ten of the 18 officers interviewed had served in a deep-cover capacity. Only one of the officers interviewed was a female.[3]

FORMS OF UNDERCOVER WORK

The first strategy of deep undercover work treats the officer as an intelligence agent whose job it is to keep certain groups of individuals under surveillance and gather information about their activities rather than prepare criminal cases or make arrests. These assignments, by their very nature, do not involve any specific length of time. One officer, who spent 18 months infiltrating "subversive groups," said, "They told me I could stay undercover for as long as I wanted, for years, but if I felt I had to come out I could." That officer's work, however, did not place him in contact with criminal violators but primarily with otherwise respectable citizens and no arrests resulted from his investigation.[4]

The second deep undercover strategy involves "making cases"—that is, gathering intelligence for prosecution. The operation may not be focused on one violator but may be seeking to uncover a hierarchy of offenders (at least ideally) or a group of similar offenders at the same level (for example, street drug dealers). In that mode officers gather evidence of an individual's criminal violation by purchasing drugs, weapons, or by placing wagers, for example, and become the complainant seeking an arrest warrant (Hellman, 1975; Daley, 1971). The officer may secure arrest warrants for dozens of individuals for a variety of violations, and these warrants are served when the officer's official identity is revealed.

Light-cover strategies fall into the same two classifications as deep-cover but with one significant difference: the former involves the active participation of an informant. This strategy is far more common in municipal police departments than is deep-cover; it is more focused in time, activity, and intent. As Wilson (1978: 42) notes, "the dominant strategy of these investigations is not that of detecting or randomly observing a crime but of instigating one under controlled circumstances." The participation of an informant who is known and proven in the criminal milieu becomes part of the "cover" and affords officers easier access to violators without first having to fully establish their own credentials (Manning, 1980). One officer explained the plan:

> I was told to go out and attempt to buy drugs from known dealers who the informant knew and from whoever else was out there dealing. I worked mostly in the East Side of town buying heroin and coke . . . it was strictly through the informant who was right there 75% to 80% of the time acting as a go-between. . . . It resulted in 57 individual warrants for sales in 7 months.

A variant of the light-cover strategy involves using an informant for general introductions and establishment of a desired identity and then distancing oneself from that informant. Doing so is desirable for at least two reasons: it protects the informant's identity when arrests are later made and it removes the informant from possible participation in the illegal transaction. Only the female officer reported using that technique.

> I worked with an informant for a couple of months posing as his girlfriend but then I cut him loose. They brought in a male officer who then posed as my boyfriend. But I made the buys. . . . I made 59 arrests for heroin sales.

When the undercover officer is engaged in accumulating arrest warrants, time becomes a factor governing the length of the operation. One officer noted that

> The prosecutor made the decision [to end the operation]. He felt you damaged cases if you wait too long. The early cases would be jeopardized. The people had a legitimate right to be brought to trial.

The longer the elapsed time between the offense and the serving of the warrant, the more difficult it becomes for the arrested person to recall their activities and prepare a defense. The police, of course, maintain a daily log while citizens may not own an appointment book. And since legal questions involving the right to a speedy trial and other factors may become relevant, supervisors prefer to terminate operations of this type about one year after the first case is "made."

The decision to end an undercover operation, however, may be independent of the relative effectiveness of the officer. In a study of undercover operations in two different cities in the late 1960s and in 1970, Malkin (1971) showed that each operation could have been ended earlier with no appreciable loss of suspects. That is, the officer's effectiveness had peaked well before a year was up and suspects could have been brought to trial, or at least apprised of the charges against them, earlier than was done.

SELECTION

Deciding who will be chosen to join the department is a major problem for police administrators and the selection of who to assign to undercover work is a subset of that larger problem. The undercover officer is generally new to the organization and untrained. Of the 14 officers interviewed who worked undercover assignments, only two had any previous police experience.[5] Six were selected even before a civil service eligibility list was established and six were chosen at the beginning of their police training.[6] One officer said,

> I had no academy training. The Personnel Officer offered me the undercover assignment after I submitted my application. I took the civil service exam alone . . . and received mailed notification a week later that I had passed. I met with the Chief and [my supervisor] in a hotel room to get sworn in.

In the case of the single female in the study, undercover work was a way to get in the organization: Before she was assigned undercover, the leaders of the department had refused even to accept her application for employment.

> The police department came up with an informant but he would only work with a woman—he refused to introduce a strange man. The police department squeezed the informant and the informant squeezed the department. At the time they knew I wanted to get on the job (the department had no women and was not interested in hiring any). And the head of the drug unit said, "No, she won't work, she doesn't fit the mold." But they gave in and said they would try me out for one month—but not sworn. They said if it works they would make me a provisional police officer. I made a heroin buy my first night on the street.

This female officer was the only officer interviewed beginning her police career without being a sworn officer.

Undercover work may be perceived as a prerequisite for police employment for male officers as well—particularly when there are many applicants for new positions. When municipalities give preference to local residents for hiring, candidates from out of town may find the offered assignment a way to circumvent that policy. One officer reported,

> Hopefully they chose me because I'm bright. Probably they chose me because I didn't know [City A]. But I thought that if I turned [the assignment] down I might not have gotten onto the police department at all.

Police administrators select undercover officers based on the type of cases officers will investigate, the physical appearance of the officer, and the person's personality. One supervisor remarked, "We would never choose a guy six-six (6'6"), he'd stand out like a sore thumb." The black officers interviewed reported their selection was motivated by their race, and another supervisor observed that if he wanted to send someone to work in a Hispanic area he would need an Hispanic officer. The female officer, for example, was initially rejected because she did not fit a supervisor's notion of what a heroin user should look like. The use of such criteria is hardly a surprise, of course, as police in other assignments often rely on physical cues to evaluate suspects (Black, 1971). Another officer said,

> I was picked because I was Italian and looked like a gambler. I looked like a guinea punk. I never had a problem. I was always taken for a gangster and I have a "look of larceny" about me.

Not all of the supervisors agreed that mere appearance governed selection. One said, "It's a question of character," noting that what he was really looking for was the type of person "who doesn't really need anybody and can work alone" (Girodo, 1984). He went on to say, with sincerity, that the undercover, particularly the deep-cover "must have the ability to improvise" because "there are no rules" to deep-cover work and the person must be "basically deceitful."

Other supervisors took the position that how the officer felt about the work itself was more consequential than external factors. A supervisor asked, "Is the nature of the work contrary to what they believe? Are they afraid? These individuals have no expertise in law enforcement." Girodo (1984: 171) indicated that the supervisor must spend "considerable time detailing the hazards and range of difficulty the prospective candidate will have to endure. Occasionally, he may even try to dissuade the applicant from volunteering." Among the officers interviewed for this study, no such discussion was reported. If anything, conversations which took place prior to beginning an undercover assignment only stressed the positive—what a successful operation could mean for the officer's career, for instance.

The officers in this study accepted undercover assignments for two primary reasons: it assured them of selection to the department, or it promised a later benefit such as choice of assignment or preference at promotion time. The female officer previously mentioned was told that if she did a good job she would later get a desired plainclothes assignment. Another officer was assured that he would be assigned to the precinct of his choice; several were promised immediate promotion to detective. Not all of these promises were kept, however. Few of the supervisors involved were truly in a position to keep the promises they made, and what a "good" job is becomes subject to interpretation. None of the promises, of course, were in writing. But, for some officers, the assignment itself—to "pass" in a new identity—was sufficient to secure cooperation. To quote one officer, whose comments were similar to those of three others, "Someone is offering me a chance to become a spy—really a neat thing."

TRAINING

Formal academy training, which includes socialization into the police occupation as well as technical instruction, and which ranges from two months to one year in duration depending upon the municipality (Pike, 1981), is an experience the officer may not benefit from until the undercover assignment has ended. Police organizations that were observed evidence a preference for assigning newly recruited members to undercover work—particularly deep-cover work.[7]

> The rationale for this is that the Department does not want to have an agent identified while entering or leaving the academy or participating in training activities; further, as [the officer interviewed] said, "We don't want our undercover agents to react to situations like a cop" (Malkin, 1971: 14; also see Manning, 1980, especially pp. 49-52).

The undercover assignment, in this view, is more civilian than police, and it would be counterproductive to socialize a person to be a police officer and then ask them to adopt a false identity. Although instruction about rules of evidence, rights of suspects, and chains of custody would certainly be relevant for the undercover officer, the absence of that and other instruction is argued to be justified. One very experienced supervisor observed, "Maybe the training was inadequate, but if you want somebody to operate as an effective undercover person, do you really want them to have police training? I don't think so."

One of the officers interviewed as well as several supervisors provided a different explanation for the failure to provide police training, related more to organizational structure than to socialization. The officer contended that assigning trained personnel to undercover work would be sabotaged by other police officers. When asked about the benefits of training the officers in the academy before assigning them undercover, he said,

> If you did that you would probably get fucked by the other cops. Somebody who has a good informant would probably protect [the informant] by selling out the undercover.

A good informant, of course, keeps the police officer productive by generating information and arrests, and if the police department evaluates or rewards officers for making arrests (Miller, 1983), this suspicion is worth taking seriously. The fact may be that police solidarity, the vaunted "closed fraternity" often noted in police studies (Ahern, 1972), may not include new officers or those in organizationally marginal roles.[8]

The kind of investigation to which an undercover officer is assigned also affects whether training and socialization may be seen as dysfunctional to the work. Informants generally agreed that entry into the illegal drug market, for example, particularly at the level of street sales, involved fewer problems than other types of investigations. Most undercover officers assigned to street-level drug traffic were simply told to "hang around" specified areas and let themselves be seen. One officer observed, "Everybody was suspicious . . . but they dealt with a lot of people," so making drug purchases wasn't particularly difficult. Investigating "subversive" groups is seen as being more difficult and requiring a more detailed "cover story." Gambling investigations are seen as the most difficult to conduct as the structures of the enterprise are more formalized and durable. A supervisor pointed out that

> Gamblers are smarter. They question more. "Where are you from? Where are your parents from? What are you doing here?" So [your] cover has to be more solid than for drugs—the structure of gambling operations is tighter.

Officers were told to create their own cover stories utilizing as much of their identity as possible. A complete set of fictitious credentials was prepared for only two of the 14 officers interviewed.

The extent to which the officer receives training prior to assuming the fictitious identity varies from deep- to light-cover work. All of the officers interviewed who had worked deep-cover (eight) reported structured training of less than one day. As one officer remembered,

> I began on a Monday, hooked up with another more experienced undercover and was told what the job was like, what it consisted of, what you could do—should do—to make gambling cases. We

rode around a few places . . . where they believed gambling activities were taking place. The training lasted only a day. The next day I went on the street alone.

This officer, like the other seven, did not enter the police academy until the undercover assignment ended. Those assigned to purchasing narcotics reported "training" for about two hours, focusing on identifying different drugs, packaging, terminology, and prices. The work, progressing on a moment-to-moment schedule, gets its momentum from the officer's success in gaining confidence and confidences (Manning, 1980: Chapter Six). The officer is further taught through a series of informal and unstructured conversations and learns to adjust and improvise rather than to follow strict guidelines (Dix, 1975).

SUPERVISION

It is difficult to supervise undercover operations since direct control over the officer's activities is precluded by the nature of the work, and the "deeper" the cover the more limited the supervision possible (Williams and Guess, 1981). One officer said,

> They might tell me something to do, but the supervision was really minimal. They didn't have a real clear idea of what was going on—but that is what they had me out there for.

The supervisors reported that they were always aware of what their officers were doing, but there were general indications in the interviews that supervision was considered less important as undercover officers gained experience. A supervisor explained,

> . . . as the operation got going, surveillance lessened. The supervisors learned to trust the officer's competence and integrity—that they were doing what they were supposed to do.

The ideal model of how an undercover operation should be organized and supervised and the reality of how they actually run may be far apart.

The supervisor is also a counselor and stresses the law-enforcement orientation of the assignment: the officers must be constantly reminded that they are on the street and in the masquerade precisely because it is a masquerade and part of the job. In the undercover assignment, officers appear to sometimes lose sight of that fact. If the officer fails to maintain perspective, the police department's integrity is compromised. An officer in light-cover noted that the supervisor "keeps you from getting too close [emotionally]; he reminds you that the guy is a scum-bag."

Maintaining perspective may require close supervision, and the interviewed officers report exceptional independence which is all the more remarkable given their general inexperience. Two of the officers reported meeting with their police contact only once a week, although telephone contact was more frequent. One of those officers, however, was actively buying drugs and cases were being prepared for prosecution on the basis of the information and evidence supplied. This type of casual supervision of untrained operatives is especially questionable in terms of evidentiary chain of custody (Malkin, 1971). Evidence in the possession of the officers accumulates and is turned over en masse: it may be lost, misplaced, or mixed with contraband acquired from another source (Manning, 1980). It may also become a temptation for the officer to use, sell, or give away evidence. Novice officers, uninstructed in the correct procedures for handling evidence and writing reports, may ruin a case. The remainder of the undercover officers reported contact with their supervisors once a day, still an infrequent occurrence if multiple illegal transactions occur.

Undercover officers may not receive much feedback from their supervisors, and a one-way flow of information combined with a wholly new occupation and a fictitious identity can be problematic indeed. The officers, particularly those in deep-cover, are a valuable source of oftentimes unique information for the department, but rarely are they privy to organizational plans or analyses. As one supervisor remarked, there are

> no rewarding experiences. You don't know how your work is being received. You don't know what happens as a result of your work. [You] may work hard and get a guy good but then see him back on the street quickly—because supervisors can just turn him into an informant and you don't know what is going on.

The supervisors, however, felt that the officers had enough to worry about just concentrating on their day-to-day street activity and rejected the idea of including undercover officers in the formulation of strategy. The result, then, was that undercover officers reported little supervision in general and virtually none in the field. One informant stated that "I was supervised only to the extent [I] went back to headquarters and did paper work." Infrequent meetings with supervisors, ostensibly done to protect the officer's official identity, unintentionally exposes the novice officer to additional pressures and temptations.

DANGER

Except in the very well-planned and organized light-cover assignment, there is almost no way to protect undercover officers in the field in the event their true identity is suspected or becomes known (see Girodo, 1984, for an examination of a well-planned undercover operation). The untrained officer is mainly left to his or her own devices. A supervisor explained,

> You can't have surveillance unless you are running multiple agents, one in deep-cover and one in light as a back-up. Plus there is no need to as they are there for information only (while in deep-cover). In this case the undercover becomes the known, reliable informant (who detectives reference when applying for search or arrest warrants).

The difficulty in providing field security for the officer does not prevent the promise of coverage, however. An officer said,

> I was not scared in the beginning because I was lied to. I was told there would be at least two policemen watching me at all times and I believed it for two weeks. When I realized there was no one watching I asked about it and the supervisor told me that there was surveillance but I couldn't see them. But then I got hold of a gun and carried it with me for protection—first a .22 [caliber] and then a .25 automatic.

Several of the undercover officers carried handguns, some privately owned and some issued by the police department. But only in two cases were these officers trained in the use of those weapons. All, however, carried guns with the knowledge and tacit approval of their supervisors. A supervisor said he provided "weapons but no identification" and that the weapons were ones they had confiscated and were "private handguns not [police] service connected revolvers." What might happen if an untrained officer shot a citizen remains unknown and problematic.

Undercover work is seen by police officers as something akin to a game. The officers are playing a part and if they do it well, they believe they will do fine. In the beginning, the main problem is being thought to be a police officer.

> I was called a cop on my first day [on the street] because of being a new person. I laughed at the guy. After hanging around awhile I managed to fit in.

As a new person in an environment likely to be wholly new to the officer, and if no informant is used to provide an introduction, the undercover may feel uncomfortable and conspicuous. An officer remarked,

> Everybody is looking at you and can tell you are a cop. How could they not know it? That was what was in my mind. But I didn't think they would do anything—beat me up or anything—just tell me to get out of there.

The thought that the work might be dangerous does occur to the officers, but the threat is not regarded as being particularly credible. As one officer observed, "I was too stupid to be scared." But the threat and danger is quite real; five officers reported shooting incidents involving undercover officers and two reported the shooting deaths of colleagues.

After a short period of settling in and establishing a cover story, the officers under deep-cover cease to believe "cop" is written across their forehead. An officer with 18 months of deep-cover experience said,

> I could not have been more securely established than I was. I was well liked—trusted. I didn't need a partner, surveillance, or anything. I simply couldn't have been more secure than I was.

The female officer, too, felt secure. There had never been a female undercover in the city before and no one ever suggested she might constitute a threat. She reported taking chances and constantly trying to extend herself in ways which she now looks back upon in amazement. A light-cover officer, with substantial police experience prior to his undercover assignment, felt that routine patrol work was more dangerous than undercover work. He said,

> In patrol you come upon the unexpected. Here you knew you were dealing with felonies and individuals with guns. The awareness of what you were doing made it less dangerous.

The greater the penetration of an undercover officer into illicit activities, the greater the risk or threat was in reality but the perception was the opposite. The officer gets comfortable with the fictitious identity, feels secure, and, correspondingly, may take greater and perhaps unnecessary risks. Several officers, for example, noted they were constantly trying to test themselves to see how much they could get away with. None of the officers interviewed recognized the magnitude of the risk they took while the assignment was in progress. One officer stated, "Police work was all new to me—it seemed exciting and dangerous but I didn't know—like I do now—how dangerous it was." During the course of the interviews, all but one officer paused at some point to express astonishment at some aspect of what they had done in some situation.

In addition to situationally dangerous interactions, undercover assignments in general are extremely taxing emotionally on the officer; this is especially true for the deep-cover officer who is constantly "on" (Marx, 1982), always an actor on the stage.

> I was getting tired and was looking for a few days off. I called my supervisor to explain it. Instead of just asking for the time off straight out I began by telling him that I go to bed at night and dream of buying drugs. He got very excited—thought "this is great." He said he dreams of search warrants. He thought I was getting into it. I didn't get the time off.

For the officer infiltrating groups alleged to be "subversive," the strain can be enormous. Not only does the assignment require officers to work 24 hours a day, but they are not "making cases" and thus are unable to see a concrete product resulting from their work. Even relating feelings several years old was difficult:

> In order to be effective, I had to live and breathe socialism. And all my old friends are gone. You can live on your police contacts but you have to have friends and they are the ones I was writing reports about. But I knew they weren't [really friends]. So I asked to get out [of the assignment].

The effective intelligence operative clearly is subject to psychological strain and may be "turned" by those under investigation (Marx, 1974; Girodo, 1984). But, despite a general recognition of these problems, none of the officers in the study had been the subject of any special psychological evaluation prior to selection, after selection, or upon terminating the assignment.

TEMPTATION

Undercover officers face a variety of temptations since they are posing as and interacting with violators and doing so with little supervision (Williams and Guess, 1981; Wilson, 1978; Marx, 1974, 1982). Using, selling, or simply giving away[9] the drugs they come in contact with (Girodo, 1984) is one such problem. Undercover officers posing as users may be maneuvered into situations where their failure to inhale, ingest, or inject substances places them in grave danger. Supervisors offered no real recommendations to guide the officers beyond encouraging them to arrange transactions, meetings, and other activities in public places. One supervisor, however, said he would rather see the officer "shoot up" than get hurt for failing to do so and would cover up the act and make sure the officer did not become addicted. None of the officers involved in buying drugs admitted any personal use during their operations, but two of the three deep-cover "intelligence" operatives reported smoking marijuana. The nature of their assignments, of course, made the suggestion to remain in public places largely impossible.

Another temptation involves how cases are "made" or activity reports are written (Marx, 1982). Entrapment is always a possibility when police adopt a fictitious identity in the undercover assignment. While one supervisor remarked, "It's always better not to commit perjury," it is clear both that exculpatory information is not included in warrant applications emanating from undercover operations and, given the supervisor's observation, at least some forms of perjury may be deemed "acceptable." In other studies (Manning, 1974; Skolnick, 1975), it has been observed that officers' reports adhere to the letter of the law even if their actions do not. The interviews reported here indicate that officers' official reports may differ from those originally submitted.

The undercover officer, like the researcher, faces the problem of "going native." Citizens are not only candidates for arrest, they are social companions, confidants to some extent, and perhaps lovers. Moreover, given the nature of the work, a distinct possibility exists that friendships may develop with those same individuals the officer has made a case against. In other instances, officers can experience changing values and grow to identify with a "radical" point of view. As an officer said,

> I started with drugs and [the relationships were] clearly evident—white hats and black hats. Then I switched to subversive activities and it was more like white hats and grey hats. And my hat got grey. But they were my only friends. I didn't have any other friends. [You] develop a closeness that is psychologically difficult to close off.

Since undercover officers must spend a lot of time trying to blend into their new environment and open a circle of acquaintances, they need "tremendous self-discipline and self-awareness," according to supervisors. The extent to which the officers selected for this work are capable of handling the associated difficulties is reasonably open to question, and incidents where former undercover officers are later found to have become violators themselves are common (Marx, 1982; Girodo, 1984). As Donner (1971, quoted in Marx, 1974: 421) argues, "The infiltrator's secret knowledge that he alone in the group is immune from accountability for his acts dissolves all restraints on his zeal." Given the amount of contact these officers have with their "criminal" environment and the fact that they maintain this contact while misrepresenting their true identity with a modicum of supervision and training, it is surprising that more problems do not appear.

COMING OUT

Undercover assignments end when the officer can no longer continue the work (for example, they "burn out" or become identified as police officers) or when the officer's services have ceased to be necessary (for example, the "case has been made"). For light-cover officers there may be few or no problems attached to ending the masquerade as the style of work did not greatly intrude on their private identity. But, for the officer in a deep-cover assignment, the completion of an often lengthy masquerade may be intensely emotional (Girodo, 1984).

The deep-cover assignments of the officers interviewed averaged more than one year in duration; the range was 8 to 18 months. Its end required abruptly abandoning the fictitious identity they had lived and embracing a police identity with which they were largely unfamiliar. The officers looked forward to becoming a "regular" member of the police department, although they largely did not know what that meant, and to resuming "normal lives" with greater separation between work and private life. They were glad to "surface" and sought to renew old friends and acquaintances long abandoned. One officer reported,

> At the end I felt good, I felt real good. I went out and bought an M.G.—didn't change my appearance—and went to people [I had been friends with before the undercover assignment] with a badge and a gun to tell them what I had been doing for the past year and a half—to make friends again.

Only one of the officers reported any difficulty reestablishing abandoned relationships; this was an officer whose investigation involved bookmaking arrests. But as novice officers often go directly into the police academy for conventional training after the undercover assignment ends, they have an opportunity to establish a new circle of friends, which minimizes transition problems.[10]

For officers whose work activities involved "making cases," the end of the assignment coincided with a "round-up" of accused individuals for whom arrest warrants had been prepared. As all officers interviewed were employed by municipal police organizations and their work was primarily done within that municipality, the arrests generated focused hostility toward them for tricking those arrested. As a result, the former undercover officer was instructed to take unusual safety precautions upon shedding the fictitious identity. In addition to altering physical appearances (for example, cutting hair, shaving beards, growing mustaches), they were told to be alert for someone following them while driving to and from work. If they had used their own car during the assignment, they were encouraged to purchase a new automobile, although at their own expense. One officer, who had infiltrated the highest levels of a local organized crime group, was assigned a bodyguard The officer was still living with his parents and the bodyguard, armed with a shotgun, stayed in the house during the evening hours. The female officer noted she received far more protection and attention after the assignment ended than while it was ongoing. She said,

> For almost a year afterwards, I drove to another officer's house in the morning and I rode into work with him. Later they put a police radio in my personal car. They checked my gun [for cartridges] and the battery in my [portable] radio every day. They were very protective. This is not because they felt I wasn't capable, they weren't sure what to do so they were careful.

Finally, the supervisors must, in some fashion, "debrief" outgoing undercover officers and help them adjust to their new public identity as police officers. As a supervisor noted,

> They come to feel they are special and . . . are not treated specially. This is the biggest drawback. They feel they deserve things like promotion and very quickly get bitter when they do not get promoted.

Recall, however, that promises of promotion and other special treatment were reported by officers to have been among the inducements offered for undertaking the masquerade to begin with. Additionally, officers leave a rather unstructured setting for perhaps the most structured of all police settings, the academy. That socializing experience may be even more extreme for those officers with undercover experience. These interviews, albeit limited in number, indicate that former police undercover officers do face significant and immediate disappointments often due to inflated expectations of what awaits them upon termination. It may be true that the more successful the officer is in the undercover assignment, the greater will be the problems of readjustment.

DISCUSSION

Municipal police departments continue to assign police officers to undercover investigations as a strategy to learn about criminal and other activities of citizens. While police departments also use covert tactics internally, this paper has focused only on investigations external to the organization The intent here has been to seek understanding of a particular form of police work through the experiences of knowledgeable practitioners.

Undercover police work is used to locate and arrest persons involved in illegal activity. It is also used for intelligence gathering purposes, which means investigating persons even when there exists no intention or expectation of initiating any criminal prosecution. In that latter form, undercover operations are frequently questioned as they extend police activity to perhaps unreasonable lengths and directly threaten constitutionally protected behaviors (Dix, 1975; Lundy, 1969). Importantly, police departments do not initiate undercover operations only when other investigative techniques fall: agencies that use them tend to do so regularly. Thus, undercover operations may not be bounded by time and events; when one officer's masquerade ends, another officer's begins.

As opposed to being an investigation assigned to the most highly trained, competent, and knowledgeable officers in the organization, undercover work tends to be carried out by newly recruited and inexperienced members.[11] The undercover assignment, problematic as a police enforcement strategy, is even more problematic as an introduction and technique for newly appointed members. While Manning (1980: 52) pointed out that narcotic officers' freedom from the constraints of law loosens the commitment of the officer to both the law and the police role," the even greater freedom afforded the undercover operative, as yet untrained and a police officer in name only, is even more troublesome.

Supervisors, although experienced police officers, may be no more knowledgeable of undercover tactics and problems than are the novice officers. One supervisor, commenting on an undercover operation in which one of the two novice officers was shot and killed, observed, "We had never done anything like this before. We were flying by the seat of our pants." The officer's death terminated only one part of the undercover project and did not prompt changes in supervision, selection, or training. The supervisors merely sought to salvage the cases yielded by the operation without questioning policies which contributed to the officer's death.

These interviews revealed that officers learn one of the most questionable police tactics principally through informal and unstructured conversations which address only specific immediate problems and work-related concerns. Undercover work constitutes a problematic introduction to law enforcement as it stresses flexibility and creativity (Girodo, 1984) which are at odds with the bureaucratic and quasi-military orientation of the enterprise. The most important characteristic of the successful undercover operative, according to supervisors, is to dissemble. As one officer said, one must be a good liar—actor. This goes without saying. You wouldn't get to step one if you weren't. I guess I don't think of myself so much as a liar as an actor because I think of myself as basically a trustworthy person. You know they can't trust you but they think they can trust you and do.

The freedom and creativity inherent in the work, however, is potentially at odds with legal guidelines and leads to an investigatory-centered operation (Manning, 1980) run by untrained officers. With virtually no guidelines or standards to refer to, untrained officers may not know the standard against which their conduct must be judged (Dix, 1975).

Although undercover policing appears to be a useful strategy, officers and supervisors indicate several problems. There are few standards governing selecting and qualifying "agents," supervision may be lax, informants may assume wholly inappropriate responsibilities, and inexperienced officers are exposed to significant dangers with little preparation. There is little information about how effective undercover investigations are, what they cost (economically, psychologically, or constitutionally), or why they fail. Similarly, the extent to which police departments use the strategy is unknown. And there is a general absence of information regarding the adjustment problems officers experience either during an assignment or after the assignment has ended (but see Marx, 1982; Girodo, 1984), what these adjustment problems mean to the employing organization, or to what extent they result in damaging innocent citizens (Dix, 1975).

Hellman (1975: 69) notes that "once the use of undercover agents is accepted as a legitimate tool of law enforcement, distinctions among crimes tend to be forgotten." Successful operations encourage repetitions and foster a reliance on a tactic which becomes a regular investigative tool as opposed to a strategy of last resort. As an operation which relies on deception, an adherence to rules and careful supervision and oversight is imperative because the lives of inexperienced police officers and the rights of citizens hang in the balance.

NOTES

1. Williams and Guess (1981) have used a similar distinction of "partial" and "deep" cover.
2. In one case the officer did both, but at different times.
3. Two other women with undercover experience of the type explored here were located but declined to be interviewed. The absence of females in this study should come as no surprise, females only entered conventional police roles in the early 1970s and their main function outside of uniform assignments most frequently was in decoy type work (Martin, 1980). The number of female police officers in any police department remains small even in the mid-1980s, and the likelihood of women being assigned to undercover work at the municipal police level is smaller still.

4. Marx (1974, 1981) argues that police involvement in political intelligence situations may serve to increase or even instigate violations. But there was no indication of such provocative behavior on the part of the officers in this study. Intelligence-based investigations are also commented on by Lundy, 1969; Hellman, 1975; and Dix, 1975.
5. One officer was selected when his recruit training class ended and one had worked in uniform patrol for four years.
6. This mode of selection apparently occurs in the New York City Police Department also (Seedman, 1974).
7. Girodo's (1984) study indicates an exception. Still, since this research is principally exploring municipal police departments carrying out undercover operations largely within their own boundaries, recruitment of newly appointed members may continue to be the norm.
8. Officers assigned to "internal affairs," for example, may also be excluded.
9. Giving narcotics or controlled drugs is technically viewed as a sale at law.
10. Girodo's (1984) more experienced operatives lacked this type of support.
11. The most recent undercover operation reported in these interviews (1982) indicates some movement away from this practice. See also Girodo, 1984.

REFERENCES

Ahern, James F.
1972 *Police in Trouble*. New York: Hawthorn.

Bickman, Leonard
1974 Social roles and uniforms: Clothes make the person. *Psychology Today* 7:49-51.

Black, Donald
1971 The social organization of arrest. *Stanford Law Review* 23: 1,087-1,111.

Daley, Robert
1971 *Target Blue*. New York: Dell.

Dix, George E.
1975 Undercover investigations and police rule making. *Texas Law Review* 53: 203-294.

Donnelly, Richard C.
1951 Judicial control of informants, spies, stool pigeons, and agent provocateurs. *Yale Law Journal* 60: 1,091-1,131.

Girodo, Michel
1984 Entry and re-entry strain in undercover agents. In Vernon L. Allen and Evert van de Vliert (eds.), *Role Transitions*. New York: Plenum

Hellman, Arthur D.
1975 *Laws Against Marijuana*. Chicago: University of Illinois Press.

Iverson, William D.
1967 Judicial control of secret agents. *Yale Law Journal* 76: 994-1,019

Joseph, Nathan and Nicholas Alex
1972 The uniform: A sociological perspective. *American Journal of Sociology* 77: 719-730.

Lundy, Joseph P.
1969 Police undercover agents: New threat to first amendment freedoms. *George Washington Law Review* 37: 634-668.

Malkin, Joseph
1971 Justice before trial: Undercover narcotics investigations. Unpublished Manuscript. New Haven: Yale University Law School.

Manning, Peter K.
1974 Police Lying. *Urban Life and Culture* 3: 283-306.
1980 *The Narcs' Game*. Cambridge, MA: MIT Press.

Martin, Susan Ehrlich
1980 *Breaking and Entering: Policewomen on Patrol*. Berkeley: University of California Press.

Marx, Gary T.
1974 Thoughts on a neglected category of social movement participants: The agent provocateur and the informant. *American Journal of Sociology* 80: 402-442.
1980 The new undercover police work. *Urban Life* 8: 399-446.
1981 Ironies of social control: Authorities as contributors to deviance through escalations, non-enforcement and covert facilitation. *Social Problems* 28: 221-246.
1982 Who really gets stung: Some issues raised by the new police undercover work. *Crime and Delinquency* 8: 165-193.

Miller, George I.
1983 On the construction and production of ideology: The question of police civility. Presented at the annual meeting of the American Society of Criminology.

Pike, Diane L.
1981 Making rookies: The social organization of police academy training. Unpublished Ph.D. dissertation. New Haven: Yale University.

Reiss, Albert J., Jr.
1971 The Police and the Public. New Haven: Yale University Press.
1974 Citizen access to criminal justice. *The British Journal of Law and Society* l: 50-74.

Seedman, Albert A.
1974 *Chief*. New York: Arthur Fields.

Skolnick, Jerome
1975 *Justice Without Trial*. New York: Wiley.

Van Maanen, John
1984 Making rank: Becoming an American police sergeant. *Urban Life* 3: 155- 176.

Williams, Jay R. and L. Lynn Guess
1981 The informant: A narcotics enforcement dilemma. *Journal of Psychoactive Drugs* 13: 235-245.

Wilson, James Q.
1978 *The Investigators*. New York: Basic Books.

Modern Criminal Investigation: Innovations and Applications 12

Larry K. Gaines & Gary W. Cordner

Introduction

Criminal investigation has long been a primary tactic in the police arsenal to combat crime. Detecting criminality had its roots with the Bow Street runners when, in 1751, Sir Henry Fielding conceived the idea that officers or "runners" should be dispatched to crime scenes in an effort to apprehend criminals. This was not an insurmountable task considering that, at the time, London literally had thousands of robbers and burglars, and crime was a very common occurrence. Detecting has made substantial progress since Fielding's time, when runners merely observed for criminality and made arrests. More recently, the detective has come to be seen as a professional who doggedly pursues criminals using reasoning, persistence, and the latest scientific techniques to catch and convict lawbreakers.

The criminal investigation function within policing has evolved over 200+ years to its current professional standing. Kuykendall (1986) traces the progression of criminal investigation using three overlapping periods: the detective as secretive rogue (1850s-1920s), the detective as inquisitor (1890s-1960s), and the detective as bureaucrat (1940s-1980s). The secretive rogue refers to a period when there was little difference between the police and criminals. Detectives basically were thugs who arrested former colleagues or competitors, while allowing their friends to continue to commit criminal acts. Police practices often bordered on criminality. The detective as inquisitor refers to the police use of the "third degree." During this period, the police overly depended on confessions to obtain convictions and generally neglected evidence collection and case development. The detective as bureaucrat refers to a period when detectives tended to over-emphasize case management, the completion of reports, and deadlines as opposed to collecting evidence, solving cases, and satisfying victims. Detective work became more clerical than anything else and detectives were more likely to be found in the office than on the street.

Scientific criminal investigation, although in existence for a number of years (Thorwald, 1964), did not become vitally important until the due process revolution of the 1960s and 1970s, when the United States Supreme Court outlawed many questionable police techniques and specified narrower guidelines for searches, seizures, and interrogations. Changes in criminal procedures forced the police to do a better job of "making" cases, as opposed to depending on coerced confessions or questionably obtained evidence to obtain convictions.

Historically, there has been substantial mystery surrounding criminal investigations and detectives. The public often views detectives as the stalwarts of policing, with all other divisions, personnel, and activity secondary to criminal investigation. Much of this mystique has been generated by television, movies, and novels in which detectives are portrayed as being able to solve even the most complex crimes with no clues or a mere pittance of evidence. The police themselves have contributed to this image by making general promises to the public about crime fighting, crime reduction, and solving criminal cases (Klockars, 1985). The result has been that detectives have received a great deal of latitude when applying their craft. For years, detectives were fairly independent of police management. Because investigation was considered or treated as a craft or art, individual detectives made decisions about what leads to follow, what evidence was important, and how to manage and present cases.

During the 1970s and 1980s, police practitioners and researchers became interested in criminal investigations. This interest led to a substantial amount of research in an effort to eliminate the mystique surrounding criminal investigation. Researchers attempted to understand how detectives worked or applied their craft and how cases were solved, e.g., what role do evidence and investigative effort play in solving cases? Researchers also were interested in making criminal investigations more effective while giving police managers more control over investigators and what they did.

One of the first major studies to illuminate the interplay between detectives, evidence, and investigative activities, the Rand study, found that detectives did not generally solve cases by hard work, inspiration, or science, but instead focused on and solved easy cases. Only about three percent of solved cases were solved by detectives exerting extraordinary effort (Greenwood, Chaiken and Petersilia, 1977). Subsequent statistical examinations of how evidence affects case outcomes substantiated that with only a few exceptions, cases were solved as a result of specific suspect information provided by victims and witnesses; other information or evidence had little effect on whether a case was solved (Eck, 1979; Gaines, Lewis and

Swanagin, 1983). Upon closer examination of criminal investigations, Eck (1983) concluded that there were three separate categories of cases: weak cases which will not be solved regardless of the investigative effort (unsolvable cases); cases with moderate levels of evidence which can be solved with considerable investigative effort (solvable cases); and cases with strong evidence which will be solved with minimum effort (already solved cases). Eck noted that already solved cases did not need additional investigative time, and that time spent on unsolvable cases was wasted effort, whereas in those cases with moderate levels of evidence (solvable cases), additional investigative effort would potentially result in increased arrest rates. Brandl and Frank (1994) reexamined Eck's hypothesis and also found that increased numbers of solvable cases could be solved when additional investigation effort was applied to them.

RECENT DEVELOPMENTS

Since the first serious research into the effectiveness of criminal investigation in the 1970s, improvement efforts have been concentrated in three general areas: (1) managing investigations, (2) targeting investigations, and (3) modern technology. Managing investigations includes using case screening and so-called solvability factors to ensure that detectives focus on cases which have the capability of being solved, and second, ensuring that they collect and analyze the most promising types of evidence in each case. Managing investigations also requires supervisors to play a larger role in criminal investigation, reducing the historically unbridled discretion and independence of detectives. Finally, managing investigations includes reconsidering the role of patrol officers in criminal investigation, and possibly enlarging their role. Potentially, at least, patrol officers might conduct complete investigations of some categories of crimes, or at least more in-depth preliminary investigations, instead of being limited to superficial preliminary investigation or mere report taking.

Targeting investigations attempts to move criminal investigation from a reactive, scatter-shot strategy to a more proactive and targeted strategy. One of the most interesting developments in targeting investigations has been repeat offender programs, in which the focus of investigation shifts from crimes already committed to suspected high-rate offenders. Investigators target these offenders with surveillance, informants, sting operations, and enhanced prosecution in order to maximize the chances of arrest, conviction, and incarceration. Another targeted approach uses task forces to focus attention on major crimes or other types of offenses, such as drug trafficking, instead of relying completely on the efforts of individual detectives. Finally, targeting investigations can also include focusing on non-traditional offense categories that traditionally have not received special attention, such as domestic violence, corruption, or white-collar crime.

Modern technology has the potential to dramatically affect the nature of detective work and the effectiveness of criminal investigation. One line of development has been in the area of information technology—improving sharing of information among different law enforcement agencies on unsolved homicides possibly committed by serial killers, for example (Keppel and Weis, 1993), or using expert systems to draw conclusions about unsolved burglaries, including possible suspects. The other principal type of technology development influencing criminal investigation has been in the area of forensic science. Technological developments continue to improve the ability of the police to find and analyze physical evidence, making criminal investigation more and more scientific.

The remainder of this chapter examines two scientific innovations, automated fingerprint identification systems (AFIS) and DNA (deoxyribonucleic acid) testing, that have affected criminal investigation. AFIS and DNA testing are two recent innovations which extend or enhance the amount of information derived from certain types of physical evidence.

AFIS AND DNA

AFIS is a system whereby large numbers of fingerprints can be stored and automatically searched for matches. Prior to AFIS, police officials had to have either a suspect to compare to latent fingerprints from a crime scene or a full set of prints to send to a state agency or the Federal Bureau of Investigation in order to make an identification. Even though fingerprints could be used to conclusively associate a suspect with a crime scene, they were of limited use unless that suspect had first been identified through some other means. Consequently, substantial numbers of latent prints languished in police files waiting for a suspect for comparison. Fingerprints, essentially, were of limited value in identifying perpetrators.

Prior to DNA testing, body fluids such as semen or blood had long been used in criminal investigations, especially in rape, homicide, and assault cases. Frequently, when a violent crime occurred, there was an exchange of body fluids. The victim would leave blood or saliva on the perpetrator, or the perpetrator would leave semen, saliva, or blood on the victim. When investigators were able to locate and collect fresh samples of these fluids in an adequate volume, criminalists were able to identify the blood type of the perpetrator. Body fluids allowed investigators to link classes of suspects to a crime and thus narrow the range of suspects, and they could help the investigator focus on an individual suspect, but they could not positively tie the suspect to the crime scene. Although such evidence was not conclusive, it did serve as strong circumstantial evidence. Also, body fluids, like fingerprints, required a suspect already identified to be useful.

Recent innovations in AFIS and DNA testing have allowed criminal investigations to become far more exacting, resulting in a larger number of offenders being identified and convicted. AFIS and DNA facilitate investigations by identifying specific suspects. If an AFIS database contains one print, or in some cases, a partial print, exact matches can sometimes now be made. In this sense, the AFIS not only associates suspects with a crime scene, but it also facilitates the identification of suspects. This was virtually impossible before the implementation of AFIS. DNA, on the other hand, does not usually help locate a specific suspect, but it does identify suspects within an acceptable statistical probability. Basically, there are three billion different combinations of DNA code (Osterburg & Ward, 1992), allowing DNA testing to obtain extremely high statistical probabilities.

AUTOMATED FINGERPRINT IDENTIFICATION SYSTEMS

The primary fingerprint classification system used throughout the world, the Henry system, was devised by Sir Edward Henry, who served as Inspector General of Police in India and as Commissioner of London's Metropolitan Police. The system is based on dividing prints into whorls or non-whorls. As such there are 1,204 different classification categories that can exist for a given set of prints. It would appear that ample categories exist. However, approximately 25 percent of all fingerprints fall within the most common category.

Fingerprint depositories or databases can be quite extensive. Ten years ago, the FBI system contained approximately 23 million criminal fingerprints and the State of California had over 7.5 million individuals in its system (Wilson & Woodard, 1987). Large volumes of fingerprints are not uncommon for state depositories and even many large municipal departments. For example, the Los Angeles Police Department processes approximately 13,000 fingerprint cards per month. When large amounts of fingerprint cards are involved, manual searches for partial prints or individual prints are cost-prohibitive except for the most heinous of crimes. Computers have now changed all this. For example, the Virginia AFIS system can search eight million fingerprints in 75 minutes, a feat that would take an examiner over 40 years.

The development of AFIS has spanned approximately 20 years. The following are some of the milestones in its development:

1963   Research for automated fingerprint systems began.
1967   As a result of a conference held at FBI headquarters, contracts were given to Rockwell International to engineer an automated fingerprint reader.

1974   Rockwell International was given a contract by the FBI to deliver five automated fingerprint readers.

1978   Minnesota became the first state to install a state-wide system.

1980   The FBI completed conversion of its approximately 14.3 million fingerprint cards to a digital database.

1986   A national standard for the electronic transfer of fingerprints is established by the National Bureau of Standards. Also, the FBI initiates NCIC 2000 which incorporates the electronic transfer of fingerprint images.

Klug, Peterson, and Stoney (1992) surveyed law enforcement agencies to evaluate AFIS, the costs of AFIS, and to determine how extensive fingerprint databases were. They found that it cost an average of $4.2 million to implement an AFIS system. The NEC Corporation found that in 1993, a total of $57 million was spent on public safety AFIS projects, and they projected that the amount would be $160 million by 1998. Klug and his colleagues also found that the average size of an AFIS data base was 800,000 subjects. The departments in their study reported performing approximately 300 ten-print searches in an average 24-hour period. Ninety percent of the agencies reported that they compared all new entries to an unsolved latent file. Such a comparison would identify offenders who had previously committed a crime as they are entered into the system. Also, along these same lines, the Los Angeles Police Department reports that approximately 15 percent of the persons they enter into their system provide incorrect names or aliases which are caught by the department's AFIS system.

The mechanical operation or configuration of AFIS systems varies across agencies. The Virginia State Police operate a system with 24 remote sites. Some areas are opting for regional AFIS programs rather than depending on state-wide systems. For example, 45 different police agencies created the Hamilton County Regional Crime Information Center in Cincinnati, Ohio. The system was later expanded to include neighboring Montgomery County, and departments in Clermont County, Ohio and Northern Kentucky have approached the Center about participating. Multi-state systems have also been implemented. The Western Identification Network (WIN) includes six states: Idaho, Nevada, Wyoming, Montana, Oregon, and Utah. The WIN system has over 1.3 million records. WIN agencies have processed over 950,000 fingerprint cards and identified over 89,000 criminals. Several systems in Washington, California, and federal law enforcement agencies have AFIS systems that can query the WIN system.

THE IMPACT OF AFIS

It is difficult to describe how effective AFIS systems are and what their impact on criminal investigations has been. Several questions can be posed when attempting to evaluate AFIS:

1. How widespread is the utilization of AFIS by police criminal investigators?

2. What has been the impact of AFIS on police investigative success as measured by clearances, arrests, etc.?

3. What has been the impact of AFIS on police utilization of fingerprint and other kinds of evidence?

4. What has been the impact of AFIS on police investigative practices such as crime scene processing, case screening, etc.?

The salience of these questions should not be underestimated. Police programming with respect to investigative management (i.e., solvability factors, case screening, etc.) is dominated by models developed before AFIS. Police training and folklore still seem to be influenced by the view that latent fingerprints have more public relations than crime-solving value. The literature on criminal investigation continues to primarily reflect views of detective work based on the Rand study and other 1970s-era research. These resilient practices, beliefs, and views may be indicative of insurmountable inertial forces, or merely reflections of a lag time before the effects of AFIS become more pronounced. Regardless, the early implementation and utilization shortcomings of some AFIS systems illustrate the folly of merely assuming that AFIS had, or automatically will have, the dramatic effects within its potential.

Despite optimistic projections about the successes of AFIS, there is evidence to suggest that AFIS has yet to reach its potential. First, many police departments have not sought to maximize the collection of latent prints by training and equipping generalist patrol officers or by extensive provision of specialist crime scene technician services. Although a number of departments have departed from tradition and have placed greater emphasis on the collection of latent prints, most police agencies have not and continue to approach crime scenes from a bureaucratic, case management philosophy.

Another brake on the crime-solving impact of AFIS is limited capacity to process items of physical evidence thought to contain latent prints. In Kentucky, for example, a backlog of such evidence in the state crime lab was found to be an important bottleneck, drastically slowing the delivery of latent prints to AFIS system personnel (Cordner, 1990). Given the generally limited capacities of crime labs in this country, in comparison to the amounts of physical evidence submitted to them, this practical problem could potentially place serious limits on AFIS productivity.

Yet another roadblock is limited AFIS processing capability, due either to hardware or software processing limitations or to inadequate AFIS staffing. The latter problem was found to have an extremely negative impact on AFIS processing at two of Kentucky's three AFIS terminal sites (Cordner, 1990), and in these difficult financial times, this problem might become more typical. Unfortunately, the emotional appeal of funding for AFIS personnel or system upgrading is unlikely to compare well with demands for more police officers on the street or more detectives to investigate sex crimes against children, despite rational arguments in favor of the productivity advantages of greater AFIS capability and use.

DNA TESTING

DNA technology, used to link evidence to a suspect, was developed by Alec Jeffreys in Great Britain in the mid-1980s. The National Institute of Justice began funding DNA research in 1986. In 1988, the Federal Bureau of Investigation's crime laboratory began accepting specimens for analysis. Additionally, a number of states have invested in DNA technology, and there are a number of private firms that perform DNA testing for law enforcement agencies. Although fairly complicated as a scientific test, the costs for equipping a crime lab for DNA testing are not overly expensive. Swanson, Chamelin, and Territo (1992) report that private DNA testing costs approximately $1,500 to $2,500 per case when private laboratories are used. DNA testing takes from four to fourteen weeks to conduct.

DNA provides the genetic code that determines the finite building blocks that contribute to our individuality. It is a three-foot-long chemical that is contained in the 46 chromosomes in each cell in the human body. Half of an individual's chromosomes come from the father, and the other half are attributable to the mother. No two individuals can have the same DNA signature except for identical twins. Identical twins have the same DNA structure because they are produced when a single fertilized egg splits. Otherwise, as noted above, the probability of two individuals having the same DNA pattern is approximately one chance in three billion.

The first appellate court decision relative to DNA testing was *Andrews v. State of Florida* in 1988. In November 1987, Tommie Lee Andrews was convicted of the aggravated battery, sexual battery and armed burglary of an Orlando woman. The police used DNA testing to compare blood and semen samples with Andrews which resulted in a conclusive match. The Appeals Court ruled that the results of the test were based on scientific principle and therefore, admissible. The Court's acceptance of DNA testing was based on the *Frye* standard whereby a new technology must be sufficiently established to have gained general acceptance in the field of application (NIJ, 1990).

Without a question, the trial of O.J. Simpson for the murders of his ex-wife, Nicole Simpson, and Ronald Goldman, was the most spectacular trial in American history. The trial became a daily news event with millions following each twist and turn. It also inserted DNA testing into the national arena, both in terms of law enforcement and public exposure. The trial could perhaps be considered the most comprehensive training that American police officers have ever had. As a result of the trial and subsequent media coverage, every police officer and citizen is, at a minimum, cognizant of how DNA testing works and what it can produce. During the trial, several experts testified about the blood and DNA analysis. Numerous experts were called to testify, and each gave several days of testimony as a result of examination and cross-examination. They testified that blood left at the scene was identical to Simpson's genetic type which occurred in only one out of 170 million African-Americans and only one in 1.2 billion caucasians. The prosecution used this testimony to directly link Simpson to the murder scene (Lexington Herald-Leader, May 12, 1995).

Even though the defense attorneys mounted a dauntless attack on the experts, its impact on the weight of the evidence is difficult to gauge. As a result of the DNA tests, Simpson's attorneys were left with constructing a conspiracy defense. Once the DNA evidence was presented, they attempted to show that the police had planted the evidence in an effort to frame Simpson. The DNA testing had considerable weight in associating Simpson with the crime scene, and it is perhaps the most effective associative evidence short of a credible eye witness.

DNA testing has also been used to free wrongfully convicted prisoners. For example, Edward Honaker had been imprisoned for almost 10 years as a result of a rape conviction before a DNA test showed that he did not commit the crime. Two witnesses testified that he abducted and raped a 19-year-old woman. He was convicted and received two life terms and a 34-year term. At the time of his conviction, DNA testing was not available. Honaker's case was taken up by the Innocence Project, operated at the Benjamin N. Cardozo School of Law at Yeshiva University in Manhattan, which eventually obtained his release. During the first four years of the Innocence Project, 15 to 20 people had been cleared as a result of DNA testing. One of the peculiarities of the Honaker case was that the semen sample taken from the victim contained sperm; Honaker had previously had a vasectomy (New York Times, Oct. 22, 1994). Thus, it appears that DNA testing will be as important to defendants as it will be to the prosecution.

For the most part, DNA tests are viewed as associative evidence whereby the results associate a suspect with a crime. However, in limited circumstances DNA testing can also serve to identify suspects. Several states, as well as the FBI laboratory, are creating DNA data banks. These data banks can be searched for DNA matches much like AFIS systems search for fingerprints. Some states are currently limiting entries to sex offenders, while others are entering the DNA characteristics of a range of offenders. These data banks are useful in identifying and eliminating suspects.

As an alternative to the data bank, a department may attempt to have a large number of suspects submit to DNA testing. Recently, the Ann Arbor, Michigan Police Department investigated a series of rapes that appeared to be committed by the same serial rapist. Based on a description of the rapist, officers requested a number of suspects to submit to DNA testing, and in some cases, obtained court orders for testing. Close to 200 suspects were eventually tested before a suspect was identified as a result of the DNA tests. There was a substantial amount of negative publicity surrounding the case because all of the tested subjects were African-American and therefore, the tactic gave the appearance of being racially motivated. There were also some concerns over Fourth Amendment rights being abridged.

THE IMPACT OF DNA TESTING

DNA testing is primarily applicable in crimes against persons, although some property crimes will result in DNA evidence. Many of the questions posed in evaluating the effectiveness of AFIS can be leveled at DNA testing. At this point there are no comprehensive studies to determine the extent to which DNA testing is used in a state or single jurisdiction. Therefore, overall effectiveness or impact on criminal investigations cannot accurately be determined.

However, the police have a much better track record of collecting evidence that can be analyzed by DNA testing than they do with collecting and comparing fingerprints. This is for several reasons. First, DNA evidence is generally associated with more serious crimes. The more serious the crime, the more comprehensive are the police efforts to collect and analyze evidence. Second, the police have been collecting DNA evidence for decades for rudimentary, pre-DNA analyses. The police, essentially, have not had to change procedures to facilitate DNA testing. Indeed, the opposite is true. DNA testing requires smaller amounts of evidence for analysis than did previous conventional testing methods. Third, DNA evidence is easier to collect. Basically, DNA evidence is obvious and police officers can readily recognize its existence and value. Fingerprints, on the other hand, must be searched for and then non-suspect prints must be eliminated from comparison. This necessitates considerable time and effort in cases that police officers generally have deemed not important (burglaries and larcenies).

Perhaps the greatest impediment to DNA testing is laboratory processing. First, the length of time required for analysis is several months. This may in some cases inhibit the collection and submission of DNA evidence as detectives decide to rely on other evidence or methods. Second, there is a question about whether crime laboratories are adequately funded and equipped to handle large volumes of DNA analyses. A number of states have implemented DNA testing, but are they equipped and staffed to handle the caseload? As more DNA evidence is collected and processed, this may become a critical problem.

SUMMARY

AFIS and DNA testing represent two technological innovations that potentially can have significant impact on criminal investigations. Our concern is whether they will reach their potential, and once this potential is reached, what impact they will have on the practice of criminal investigation. Manning (1978) has documented the police passion and even obsession for technology. He notes that the police too often rely on technology for its appearance, rather than its effective use. In conjunction with Manning's criticism, it must be noted that in many cases, the police do not have effective methods of technology transfer. Technology in law enforcement initially tends to develop within jurisdictional pockets, and adoption by remaining departments or jurisdictions tends to be somewhat haphazard and inconsistent. Indeed, at this point in history, DNA testing and AFIS systems, at least in some areas of the country, are more of a novelty than fully implemented technological strategies. Police in some rural areas have no notion of these advances.

DNA testing and AFIS both have been in existence for a number of years. Yet AFIS appears not to have come close to reaching its full impact, while it is anticipated that DNA testing will surge in the wake of the O.J. Simpson trial.

REFERENCES

Brandl, S.G. and Frank, J. (1994). The relationship between evidence, detective effort, and the dispositions of burglary and robbery investigations. *American Journal of Police*, 13(3): 149-168.

Cordner, G. (1990). *Estimating the Impact of Automated Fingerprint Identification in Kentucky*. Frankfort, KY: Kentucky Criminal Justice Statistical Analysis Center.

Eck, J. (1983). *Solving Crimes: The Investigation of Burglary and Robbery*. Washington, DC: Police Executive Research Forum.

Eck, J. (1979). *Managing Case Assignments: The Burglary Investigation Decision Model Replication*. Washington, DC: Police Executive Research Forum.

Gaines, L.K., Lewis, B., and Swanagin, R. (1983). Case screening in criminal investigations: A case study of robbery. *Police Studies*, 6: 22-29.

Greenwood, P., Chaiken, J., and Petersilia, J. (1977). *The Criminal Investigation Process*. Lexington, MA: Heath.

Keppel, R.D. and Weis, J.G. (1993). Improving the investigation of violent crime: The homicide investigation and tracking system. *Research in Brief*. Washington, DC: National Institute of Justice.

Klockars, C. (1985). *The Idea of Police*. Newbury Park, CA: Sage Publications.

Klug, D.J., Peterson, J.L., and Stoney, D.A. (1992). *Automated Fingerprint Identification Systems: Their Acquisition, Management, Performance, and Organizational Impact*. A report to the National Institute of Justice (89-IJCX0051). Washington, DC: National Institute of Justice.

Kuykendall, J. (1986). The municipal police detective: An historical analysis. *Criminology*, 24(1): 175-201.

Lexington Herald-Leader (May 12, 1995). Blood DNA probably Simpson's, expert says. Author, p. A3.

Manning, P.K. (1978). The police: Mandate, strategies, and appearances. In L. Gaines & T. Ricks (eds.), *Managing the Police Organization*. St. Paul: West Publishing Co., pp. 15-49.

New York Times (Oct. 22, 1994). DNA tests free man in jail for decade. Author, p.8L.

Osterburg, J.W. and Ward, R.H. (1992). *Criminal Investigation*. Cincinnati: Anderson Publishing Co.

Swanson, C.R., Chamelin, N.C., and Territo, L. (1992). *Criminal Investigation*. (5th Ed.). New York: McGraw-Hill.

Thorwald, J. (1964). *The Century of the Detective*. New York: Harcourt, Brace, & World.

Wilson, T.F. and Woodard, P.L. (1987). *Automated Fingerprint Identification Systems: Technology and Policy Issues*. Washington, DC: Bureau of Justice Statistics.

IV. SPECIAL OPERATIONS

Specific problems and issues in the community often necessitate special police operational responses. At any given time in history, the police have wrangled with specific enforcement or disorder issues. An examination of the literature, both academic and police, shows that among the primary issues confronting the police today are incapacitation of offenders who commit multiple serious crimes, *hot spots*—locations that generate large amounts of police activity, drug enforcement, DUI enforcement and domestic violence. Each of these areas is problematic to the police. They represent issues for which there is no clear, universally accepted solution and they represent areas that have received substantial public attention, necessitating a definitive, effective response by the police.

The first article, "Selective Apprehension: A Police Strategy for Repeat Offender Programs," by Martin and Sherman examines how police departments have attempted to identify and incarcerate offenders who commit large numbers of offenses in a community. It is reasoned that if these types of offenders are apprehended, it will have a disproportionately higher impact on the jurisdiction's crime rates. A variety of tactics have been used by the police, and Martin and Sherman discuss several of these tactics and their relative effectiveness. It should also be noted that repeat offender programs almost always operate parallel to patrol and are used to supplement other operational activities.

Lawrence Sherman and the Crime Control Institute helped focus attention on the idea of hot spots in police work. In a series of research studies in Minneapolis, Sherman and his colleagues examined the nature of the distribution of crime, disorder, and calls for police services. They found concentrations, or hot spots, of such activity. Hot spots sometimes consisted of a number of the same type of calls, and in other instances, a hot spot contained a variety of different types of calls. Once hot spots are identified, the police can attempt to deal with them through problem solving. That is, the police must examine each concentration of activity in terms of the nature of the activities, identify the causes of the activities, and then implement actions that attempt to reduce or eliminate the causes. By attacking hot spots, the police can have a more significant impact on crime and disorder.

Without question, the most significant enforcement problem for the police today is drug enforcement. Every jurisdiction in the United States is plagued with a drug problem that is not only a problem in itself, but also contributes to additional crime and public disorder. Drug dealing becomes intertwined with a multitude of intractable issues requiring the police to deploy multiple tactics and strategies. In many instances, the police do not attempt to eliminate the problem, but are satisfied if it can be contained. Hayeslip, in "Local-Level Drug Enforcement: New Strategies," provides a review of some of the more contemporary tactics used by the police today.

Mastrofski and Ritti, in "A Case Study of a Police Department's Response to Stricter Drunk Driving Laws," provide an in-depth examination of how the police enforce DUI laws. DUI enforcement has come of age in the last decade. Previously, many police officers and departments did not consider the offense particularly important—it was treated much like any other traffic violation. Indeed, many police officers would not enforce the law because of the additional paperwork and prisoner processing time that was required. During the last ten years, however, organizations like Mothers Against Drunk Drivers have placed considerable political pressure on the police to more strictly enforce DUI laws, and on legislative bodies to enact stricter legislation. In their comparative examination, Mastrofski and Ritti contrast different departments in terms of DUI enforcement. They found that some departments have higher rates of enforcement than others. They then attempt to explore the reasons for these differences.

Finally, Hirschel and his colleagues examine the police response to domestic violence in "The Law Enforcement Response to Spouse Abuse." Domestic violence is one of the central issues in policing today. It is an issue that creates substantial controversy. When police officers make an arrest, the offender decries the action as being too severe.

When the police fail to make an arrest or take definitive action, they may fail to protect the victim and they are more likely to incur civil action when subsequent encounters in the family occur. Even with the numerous studies of domestic violence, there currently is no clear answer as to how the police should respond. Hirschel and his colleagues attempt to sort through the research and information to provide a practical overview.

Selective Apprehension: A Police Strategy for Repeat Offenders   13

Susan E. Martin & Lawrence W. Sherman

Two facts stand out in modern crime control policy debates. One is that a small proportion of criminals commits a disproportionately large number of crimes. The other is that most prisons have become increasingly overcrowded. Both facts have led to growing interest in selectively focusing criminal justice system resources on the most active and dangerous chronic offenders.

In the past, police have rarely adopted a selective approach to apprehending street criminals. The Metropolitan Police Department of Washington, D.C., adopted that approach in May 1982 in establishing an 88-officer (later reduced to 60) Repeat Offender Project (ROP, pronounced "rope").

The creation of ROP offered a unique opportunity for research on the problems and effectiveness of operating a proactive police unit to carry out a selective apprehension strategy. The Police Foundation obtained the department's agreement to cooperate with a systematic evaluation.

The Police Foundation study addresses several questions which are in turn addressed in this paper: (1) How does ROP operate and what strategies do its officers use in selecting and apprehending the persons it targets? (2) Do ROP's tactics increase the likelihood of arrest for targeted repeat offenders? (3) Are the offenders that ROP arrests more active and serious than offenders arrested under routine police operations? (4) Are the ROP arrestees more likely to be prosecuted, convicted, and incarcerated? (5) How does ROP affect the arrest productivity of its officers?

Source: Susan E. Martin and Lawrence W. Sherman (1986). "Selective Apprehension: A Police Strategy for Repeat Offenders." *Criminology*, 21(1):155-173. Reprinted by permission of the American Society of Criminology.

POLICING CAREER CRIMINALS

Since the publication of research indicating that a small proportion of the criminals commits a disproportionate amount of crime (Wolfgang, Figlio, and Sellin, 1972; Petersilia, Greenwood, and Lavin, 1978; Williams, 1979; Chaiken and Chaiken, 1982; Greenwood with Abrahamse, 1982), a variety of criminal justice efforts have begun to selectively identify and incapacitate those persons who are "career criminals" or "repeat offenders"—although definitions of such persons vary. To date, most of those efforts have been undertaken by prosecutors and parole boards. But the police may also fruitfully adopt policies focused on repeat offenders.

The police may be mobilized to enforce the law either reactively or proactively (Reiss, 1971). Most police work is reactive; in responding to citizen complaints, the officer's primary task is to detect the occurrence of a crime and to identify and apprehend the perpetrator at the scene of the crime or through subsequent investigative tactics. Proactive law enforcement efforts traditionally have been limited to investigations of vice and other offenses in which there are no complaints or victims to call police (Black, 1973; Moore, 1983; Wilson, 1978; Williams, Redlinger, and Manning, 1979) In recent years, more diverse proactive enforcement by police has occurred as illustrated by Abscam, "stings," and efforts to control police and political corruption. The success of these police initiatives has stimulated suggestions that proactive tactics be more widely applied to efforts to reduce street crime.

Programs focused on career criminals may employ various combinations of reactive and proactive tactics. To date, the reactive tactics used in such programs have included prioritized service of warrants against identified "career criminals" (Gay, Beall, and Bowers, 1984), notification of the prosecutor when an identified career criminal is arrested, and more active case supplementation through development of additional witnesses, evidence, or information about the other cases against the offender (Gay, 1983; Felony Augmentation Program, 1981). Proactive tactics have included use of decoys, surveillance, buy-bust schemes, and phony fencing operations (Pate, Bowers, and Parks, 1976; Wycoff, Brown, and Petersen, 1980; Felony Augmentation Program, 1981; Bowers and McCullough, 1982; Gay, 1983).

Although there is broad interest in career criminal initiatives among police administrators few departments have adopted career criminal programs. A recent survey indicated the existence of only 33 existing programs in the entire country (Gay, 1983). Little is known about how such career criminal programs actually operate or how effective they are. Thus, when the Metropolitan Police Department created the Repeat Offender Project, there were many unanswered questions about how it would and should operate and few precedents to guide it.

ROP's Design and Initial Implementation

The initial plan for ROP called for a proactive, perpetrator-oriented unit. Its objective was the identification and apprehension of two types of active recidivists: those already wanted on one or more warrants who could be arrested on sight, and those believed to be criminally active but not currently wanted. The former were called "warrant targets"; the latter came to be called "ROP-initiated" targets.

The plan defined ROP's criterion for selecting both types of targets as "the belief that the person is committing five or more Part I offenses per week." It called for half of the officers' time and effort to be devoted to working on warrant targets and half on ROP-initiated targets. Active efforts to apprehend both types of targets were to be brief (72 hours or less). This was intended to focus ROP's resources on the most active criminals, since only very active offenders were likely to be observed committing a crime within a three-day period.

A captain and his three lieutenants selected a team of 88 officers from more than 400 applicants who varied in age, race, gender, appearance, and previous police experience. The ROP officers were organized into seven-member squads, each of which included a female and a detective. The squad, led by a sergeant, became the basic work group to which targets were assigned and credit for arrests given. Officers were allowed ample discretion over routine activities, but the sergeant was responsible for selecting the squad's targets from the Target Committee pool and worked on the street with the officers. Three experienced investigators constituted the Target Committee, responsible for developing new targets and reviewing target candidates generated by the squads.

The unit's resources included 20 old cars (which blended inconspicuously into inner-city neighborhoods), other surveillance and investigative equipment, and a computer terminal linked to the department's information system. To aid in target selection, ROP routinely received the department's daily major violators list, the criminal histories of recent arrestees, daily crime reports from each district, and specially prepared weekly printouts listing all persons wanted on three or more felony warrants.

To reduce rivalry with other police units that could inhibit the flow of information necessary for ROP to function effectively, ROP adopted an internal arrest log. This log listed all arrests for which ROP officers were responsible, even if the arrest was formally booked to another officer.

Difficulties encountered in the first several months led to several modifications of ROP's target practices, squad operations, and apprehension tactics. The design anticipated that surveillance would be the principal tactic used to apprehend ROP-initiated targets. When around-the-clock surveillance of ROP-initiated targets proved to be time-consuming, frustrating, and unproductive of arrests, the squads increased the proportion of warrant targets to about 75% of those selected. They also gradually broadened the officers' repertoire of investigative and undercover infiltration strategies and skills. After several months, surveillance became just one of a variety of tactics used to catch both types of targets. In addition, the expectation that work on a target would be completed in 72 hours was relaxed when it proved impractical.

Target development practices also changed. Initially the Target Committee selected and developed all targets, mostly on the basis of official record information. However, such information was regarded as an incomplete and unreliable indicator of criminal activity and far less desirable than "street" information. With strong encouragement from ROP managers, ROP officers built up their informal information networks. After several months, the unit acquired a reputation for responding to requests for assistance, suggestions for targeting, and "hot tips" from other police units and informants. These information sources in other departmental units, neighboring police agencies, and on the street (that is informants), led to an increase in the proportion of targets generated by the squads. Squads also initiated a number of joint investigations on targets with other agencies. These changes allowed ROP to stretch its resources and become a center of information about criminal activities in the metropolitan area. They also resulted in targeting persons who did not meet ROP's selection criteria, diverting limited resources away from a focus on persons actively committing Part I offenses.

At the end of six months of operation, ROP was reduced from 88 to 60 officers, its 12 squads were reorganized and reduced to eight, and administrative procedures were tightened in order to streamline operations.

ROP IN ACTION

Although officers were expected to select criminally active targets, no formally stated set of indicators of activity nor any system for prioritizing among potential candidates was established. Selection was based on informal understandings about what makes a "good" target. Common considerations affecting selection were found to be the target's "catchability," moral worth, longer-term yield, and the squad's working style. Catchability depended primarily on the quality, recency, type, and amount of information about a warrant target's whereabouts and a ROP-initiated target's activities. Moral worth was related to the officer's belief that the target deserved to be arrested and punished. Contributing to a target's moral worth were the seriousness and length of prior criminal history, apparent contempt for the law and police, and alleged current activity. Yield was measured in terms of a target's contribution to ROP's information network and public visibility and the likelihood that the target would pay off in additional arrests and in the immediate incarceration of the target when arrested. For example, persons already on pretrial release for another offense and persons on parole release for another offense were more likely to be kept in jail upon rearrest by ROP.

The primary task in apprehending warrant targets was locating them. That task ranged from simple to complex. When a squad had a current address, all that was required was to wait at that location and arrest the target. But often the officers did not have a good address. To find the target they usually reviewed police and other records or contacted persons likely to know the target's whereabouts. Some contacts were straightforward, such as a call to the target's parole officer. Others involved deception. For example, a target's relative might have been told that the target had just won a prize he or she should collect or was being considered for a job and needed to be reached.

Most of ROP's warrant targets were wanted in Washington, D.C., as fugitives from justice in neighboring jurisdictions or on felony bench warrants for violation of probation or parole or failure to appear in court. These types of warrant targets were frequently selected because they met each of the targeting considerations. They were more catchable than others for two reasons. First, when officers from neighboring jurisdictions asked ROP officers to arrest D.C. residents they were seeking, they often provided ROP with useful information. Second, other D.C. officers were less likely to seek out fugitives and persons wanted on bench warrants than those wanted for Part I crimes, despite the seriousness of the underlying charges against the former. Such targets also strengthened ROP's ties and information networks.

To arrest persons who were not wanted, ROP officers had to develop evidence about a specific crime in which they participated. This involved a variety of vice and investigative activities such as buy-and-busts, cultivating informants and investigating their "tips," surveillance of targets, and linking stolen property found in the possession of a target back to its rightful owner. Several prolonged investigations involved penetration of fencing operations and arrests of both the target and his or her criminal associates.

Analysis of ROP apprehension activities and their outcomes indicate there was no consistent formula for or primary tactic associated with arrests. Most of ROP's arrests were made quickly (80% within one week of targeting) and did not involve extensive investigative efforts.

RESEARCH DESIGN

EXPERIMENT

The research design to assess ROP's effectiveness included several components. An experiment was conducted to determine whether persons selected as "repeat offenders" by ROP were more likely to be arrested because of ROP's efforts than they would be in its absence. The experimental design required ROP officers to identify their constantly changing pool of targets to pair any two of the same target type (warrant targets or ROP-initiated targets), and to assign one target by a coin toss to the experimental condition and the other to control. Experimental targets were investigated by a ROP squad of officers for a seven-day period, control targets were off limits to ROP officers but could be arrested by any other police officer. The experiment lasted 26 weeks, during which time work on 212 pairs of randomly assigned targets was completed.[1]

As is common in field experiments, there was some evidence that some ROP officers manipulated the coin toss (which research staff did not always control) to assure immediate assignment of the targets they desired. Others avoided submitting a target to the coin toss, getting it treated as an authorized exception (which constituted 32% of all ROP arrests) even though it did not always fit the rules for an exception. In addition, there were difficulties in locating non-ROP arrests, which suggests the possibility that some we missed.[2] But for reasons discussed below, these problems did not seem to threaten the internal validity of the findings.

QUASI-EXPERIMENTAL NONEQUIVALENT CONTROL GROUP DESIGN

The second research approach used in a quasi-experimental non-equivalent control group design to compare ROP officers with other assignments in terms of: (1) the number and seriousness of the officers' arrests as a measure of overall arrest productivity; (2) the dispositions of their arrests by the courts; and (3) the prior criminal histories of their arrestees at two time periods. Time one extended from April 1 to September 30, 1981, prior to the 1982 establishment of ROP. Time two went from April 1 to September 30, 1983. On each of the above variables, the 40 ROP officers who had operational assignments in patrol, tactical/crime prevention, vice, and detective units prior to assignment to ROP (termed "ROP-81" and "ROP-83") were compared with a random sample of 95 officers drawn from patrol, vice, and detective assignments; all 60 officers in tactical/crime prevention units; and 14 officers with warrant squad duties (called "comparison-81" and "comparison-83").

Information regarding all arrests made by the ROP and comparison officers in both time periods was collected from station house arrest logs and from ROP's internal arrest log (n = 571 ROP-81; 1,908 comparison-81; 261 ROP-83; and 2,078 comparison-83 arrests). Then computer-generated samples of about 300 ROP-81, comparison-81, and comparison-83 arrests were drawn for comparison with all 261 ROP-83 arrests.[3] Arrest histories of the sample of arrestees were obtained from the Metropolitan Police Department. Information on case dispositions of the arrests in the sample was obtained from the Criminal Division of the Superior Court.

Three separate analyses were carried out with these data. First, to compare changes in individual ROP and comparison officers' arrest productivity, the dependent variable, arrests in 1983, was regressed on officers' 1981 arrest rates, first alone, then with the addition of controls for district and assignment. These regressions were rerun to obtain individual change scores on three different outcome measures: total arrests; Part I arrests; and "serious" arrests including Part I's, plus weapon and drug-dealing offenses and arrests on a bench warrant.

The second analysis examined the case dispositions of the samples of arrests selected for follow-up. Regression was used to determine whether ROP officers' cases in 1983 were more likely than their cases in 1981, and than the 1981 and 1983 comparison officers' cases, to result in prosecution, conviction, incarceration, and longer sentences after including arrest type, officer assignment, arrestee's age, and prior arrest record in the equation as controls.

The third analysis was designed to determine whether ROP officers arrested persons with longer and more serious prior arrest records than the arrestees of comparison officers in 1981 and 1983. One-way ANOVA, simultaneous tests of significance of pairs of means, and regression were used to compare the prior arrest histories of the samples of ROP and comparison arrestees. The regression analysis controlled for the observed differences in the age of arrestees and officers' assignments by including them in the equation.

Observation and Data Collection at ROP

A third component of the research, extensive observation of ROP officers at work, was conducted to provide information about ROP target selection, investigative techniques, and apprehension strategies. In addition, a variety of data items was collected from the case jackets of all persons targeted by ROP during the study period. This included the 289 persons involved in the experiment, the 100 targets that were authorized exceptions, and 85 persons whom ROP officers serendipitously arrested while working on another assigned target.[4]

FINDINGS

EXPERIMENT

The experimental results clearly showed that ROP increased the likelihood of arrest of targeted repeat offenders. As indicated in Figure 13.1, of the 212 experimentals, ROP arrested 106 (50%). In contrast, only 17 experimentals (8%) and eight controls (4%) were arrested by officers in other units. This difference was statistically significant. Strong differences in arrest rates were found for both warrant and ROP-initiated targets. Fifty-five percent of warrant targets eligible for ROP arrests were arrested by ROP, a sharp contrast to the 9% of warrant targets eligible for non-ROP arrests that were arrested by non-ROP officers. For ROP-initiated targets, the comparable figures were 47% and 6%.

Figure 13.1
Arrest of ROP Targets Randomly Assigned to Experimental
and Control Status*

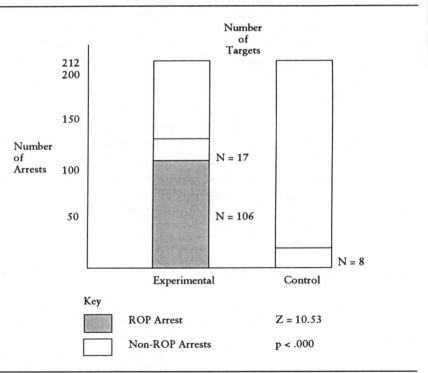

*The difference-of-proportions test normally would be calculated on the basis of the proportion arrested divided by the total number eligible for arrest. However, because many ROP arrests were made quickly, thereby effectively removing the target from the street, a more conservative measure was adopted. The 106 ROP arrests were subtracted from the 424 targetings so that the non-ROP proportion became 25/318 in calculating the proportion arrested and the variance.

The higher non-ROP arrest rate for experimentals than for controls supports the need for concern about possibilities of the manipulation of the coin toss or failure to detect control arrests discussed above. To test the potential impact of the manipulation of random assignment and of missed non-ROP arrests, the experimental findings were recalculated after making two adjustments. First, assuming that 20% of the coin tosses had not been random, 42 pairs of targets that resulted in ROP arrests but no non-ROP arrests were subtracted from both E and C totals. Second, assuming that ten control arrests were overlooked, ten arrests were added to the non-ROP totals.[5] These adjustments did not alter the significance of the experimental outcome (Z = 6.25, p < .001). Additional tests comparing experimental and control targets indicated that the latter had significantly more total arrests per year of exposure and that the former were significantly more likely to have been arrested in the six months prior to ROP targeting. This may have increased the experimentals' vulnerability to arrest by making recent data on their whereabouts available to police. Nevertheless, the magnitude of these findings suggests that, despite several problems in implementing and sustaining the experimental design, ROP made a difference by increasing the likelihood of arrest for both warrant and ROP-initiated targets.

PRIOR ARREST RECORDS OF ARRESTEES

The quasi-experimental comparative study examined the criminal histories of the samples of 1981 and 1983 ROP and comparison officers' arrestees, after making adjustments for district, assignment, and arrestee's age. In 1981, the differences between the number of prior arrests of each group's arrestees were minor. However, in 1983, ROP arrestees had significantly more total prior arrests than comparison officers' arrestees. As shown in Figure 13.2, ROP 1983 arrestees had an adjusted mean of 8.4 total prior arrests and comparison officers' arrestees only 4.2. ROP arrestees in 1983 also had significantly more arrests than comparison officers' arrestees for Part I and robbery offenses. Thus, in 1983, ROP officers' arrestees' prior arrest records had become longer and more serious than in 1981, whereas comparison officers' arrestees' records had become less serious. This finding suggests that assignment to ROP, rather than the individual characteristics of the officers, led to the change in arrestees' prior records.[6]

CASE DISPOSITIONS

The dispositions of the samples of arrests made by the ROP and comparison officers were examined to determine whether ROP officers' arrestees were more likely to be prosecuted, convicted, and incarcerated.[7] In general, in 1983, there were substantial differences between the case outcomes of ROP and comparison officers' arrests.

Figure 13.2
Mean Number of Prior Adult Arrests of Arrestees*

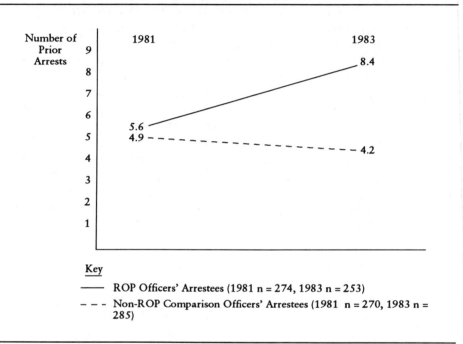

*Adjusted for officers' district and assignment and arrestee's age.

Although there was little overall change from 1981 to 1983 in the proportion of cases accepted for prosecution, as shown in Figure 13.3, there was a substantial increase in the proportion of the ROP officers' new cases accepted for prosecution as felonies. At the same time, the proportion of the sample of the comparison officers' cases prosecuted as felonies fell for officers in all assignments but casual clothes tactical units. As a result, 49% of ROP's new cases were accepted for prosecution as felonies, but comparison cases charged as felonies in 1983 ranged from 24% to 33%.[8]

Figure 13.3
Percentage of Eligible New Cases Prosecuted as Felonies*

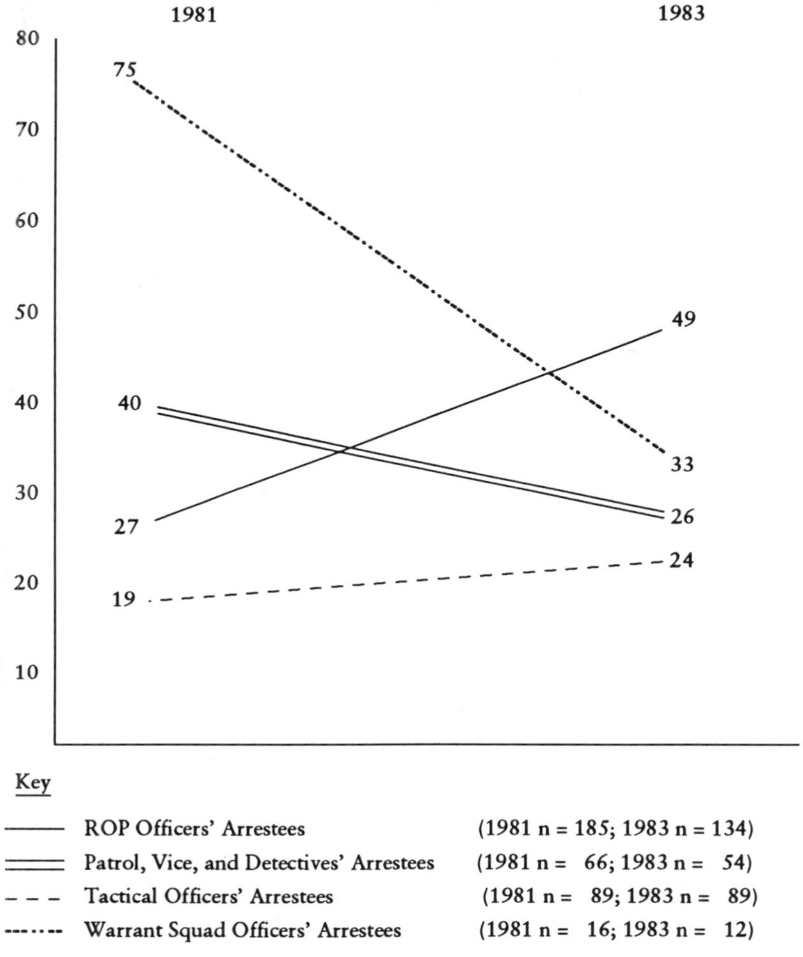

Key

———— ROP Officers' Arrestees   (1981 n = 185; 1983 n = 134)
═════ Patrol, Vice, and Detectives' Arrestees   (1981 n = 66; 1983 n = 54)
– – – Tactical Officers' Arrestees   (1981 n = 89; 1983 n = 89)
··–··– Warrant Squad Officers' Arrestees   (1981 n = 16; 1983 n = 12)

*Excludes arrests on bench warrants since a charge has already been filed.

Total convictions increased from 49% of all case outcomes in 1981 to 63% in 1983 for both ROP and comparison officer groups. For both groups the proportion of misdemeanor convictions increased as well. However, ROP officers also increased the proportion of felony convictions in comparison officers' case outcomes decreased for officers in patrol, vice, and detective assignments and increased for those assigned to tactical units and the warrant squad, leaving the overall proportion unchanged.

Incarceration rates must be interpreted cautiously, given the data limitation discussed below. As shown in Figure 13.4, incarceration rates for

ROP in 1983 remained at about the 1981 level; the rates for comparison officers in all other assignments fell, except for the warrant squad, whose rates rose substantially in 1983.[9]

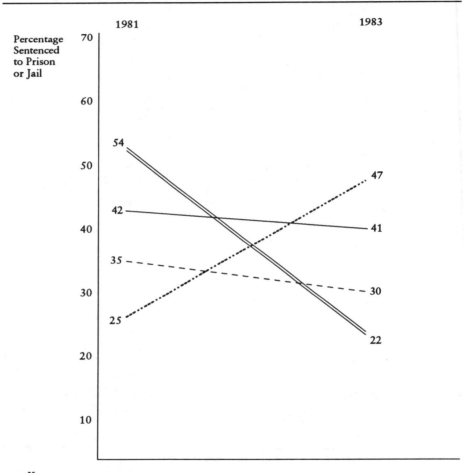

Figure 13.4
Proportion of Convicted Arrestees Sentenced to Some Incarceration*

Key

——— ROP Officers' Arrestees   (1981 n = 83, 1983 n = 70)
═══ Patrol, Vice, and Detectives' Arrestees   (1981 n = 28, 1983 n = 23)
– – – Tactical Officers' Arrestees   (1981 n = 37, 1983 n = 47)
······· Warrant Squad Arrestees   (1981 n = 12, 1983 n = 19)

*Includes all persons arrested on a bench warrant and both felony and misdemeanor convictions.

A further analysis regressed officer group on probability of incarceration and included officer assignment, offense type, offender's age. and prior arrest history in the equation. There was no difference between ROP-83 and comparison-83 cases in likelihood of conviction. However, prior total arrests was significantly associated with incarceration. Thus, the difference in the proportion of ROP and comparison convictees who were incarcerated in 1983 appears to stem from the previously noted greater seriousness of the prior history of ROP officers' arrestees in 1983.

Figure 13.5
Mean Number of Official Arrests by ROP and Comparison
Officers in 1983*

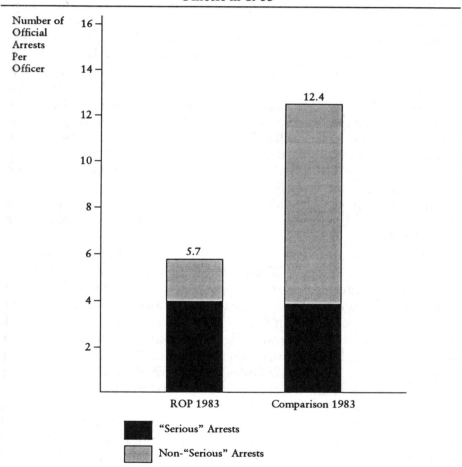

*Adjusted for district, assignment, time in ROP, and 1981 individual arrest rate. Analogous figures including total arrests are a mean of 5.9 total and 5.7 serious arrests for ROP officers and 13.1 and 4.1 total and serious arrests respectively for comparison officers.

Sentence length given incarceration was regressed on officer group after including controls for offense type, age, and criminal history. The data (not displayed) indicated that net of these controls, ROP arrestees that were sentenced to serve time in 1983 appear to be getting longer sentences than the comparison officer convictees. ROP's apparent effect on sentence length is probably a consequence of the more serious conviction offenses of its arrestees within each of the broad categories of offenses used in this study.

EFFECTS ON OFFICER ARREST PRODUCTIVITY

The third component in the quasi-experimental study was an examination of the effect of assignment to ROP on officers' arrest productivity. Using regression, changes were examined in the 1983 arrest rates of ROP and comparison officers after controlling for differences in their district and assignment and their 1981 arrest productivity using two different measures of ROP arrests. The first measure, total arrests, included both arrests officially credited to ROP as recorded in departmental arrest books and unofficial arrests that were recorded in ROP's internal arrest log. This latter group included arrests that ROP officers brought about but did not actually make (for example, those made by a D.C. detective who got a warrant on the basis of information provided by ROP regarding stolen property it recovered) and those in which ROP officers participated but which occurred outside the city limits. The second measure, official arrests, included only arrests formally credited to ROP officers in departmental arrest books.

Both measures introduce contrasting biases. The official arrest measure systematically depresses ROP officers' productivity by excluding cases the officers developed but were encouraged by their command officer to officially give away in order to foster cooperative relations. The total arrest measure, conversely, inflates ROP officers' arrest rates relative to those of comparison officers who may have contributed to others' arrests but got no such informal recognition for doing so. To be conservative, the data presented in Figure 13.5 are based on the official arrest measure, which understates to an unknown degree ROP officers' true arrest productivity while the analogous total arrest figures appear in a footnote in the figure.

Both measures indicate that ROP significantly depressed the overall arrest productivity of its officers. As shown in Figure 13.5, ROP officers in the six-month study period in 1983 made an adjusted mean of 5.7 arrests per officer while comparison officers had an adjusted mean of 12.4 arrests. ROP also had a significant depressive effect on the number of Part I arrests its officers made but had no effect on their productivity of "serious" arrests (Part I's plus arrests for distribution and possession with the intent to distribute drugs, weapons charges, and arrests on a felony bench warrant) using the official arrest measure. Statistical tests based on the total arrest measure, however found that the 1983 individual Part I rates of ROP and comparison officers did not differ from each other while the ROP officers' "serious" arrest rate was significantly higher than that of the comparison officers.

DISCUSSION

By most measures used to assess ROP, that unit appears to have succeeded in its goals of selecting, arresting, and contributing to the incarceration of repeat offenders. It increased the likelihood of arrests of targets, the seriousness of the criminal histories of its arrestees, the probability of prosecution for a felony, the chance of a felony conviction, and the length of the term of those sentenced to incarceration. However, several factors suggest a cautious interpretation of the findings and recognition of the potential dangers in adoption of the ROP model of perpetrator-oriented proactive policing by other departments.

COSTS

Creation and operation of ROP has involved some costs that should not be overlooked First, there were approximately $60,000 in direct expenses to equip the unit. Second, ROP has decreased its officer's overall arrest productivity. The arrests forgone, however, have tended to involve minor offenses such as disorderly conduct and traffic charges, while the rate at which ROP officers made arrests for "serious" offenses has been unaffected and may have increased if the less conservative measure is more nearly correct. Thus the trade-off appears to be a reduction in order-maintenance activities in exchange for an increase in crime-fighting activities.

THE CRIMINAL ACTIVITY OF TARGETS

Although ROP arrestees had longer criminal records than the comparison arrestees, one cannot be certain that they are the most active 20% of all offenders or are committing five or more Part I offenses per week. Other studies have found that prisoners with longer criminal records are more likely than those with short records to be among the highly active groups. But prediction instruments, particularly those resting on official record information, have been unreliable in selecting the high-rate criminals (Chaiken and Chaiken, 1982). It is likely that the street information on which ROP officers heavily rely enhances their ability to select the most criminally active targets. However, it was impossible for the present study to determine what proportion of the ROP targets actually met that unit's targeting criterion of committing five or more Part I offenses per week.

ROP's INCARCERATION AND CRIME REDUCTION EFFECTS

ROP's ultimate goal was the reduction of crime through incarceration of high-rate offenders. Unfortunately, no meaningful measures of ROP officers' conviction or incarceration productivity nor the unit's crime reduction effects could be developed due to data limitations. Necessary information on individual officer conviction and incarceration rates for their Time 1 arrests (and some non-ROP Time 2 arrests) were not available. The arrest productivity figures were based on individual change scores in each officer's arrests in both time periods. Due to the large number of arrests, it was possible to collect follow-up data for only a sample of cases. This made it impossible to calculate analogous conviction and incarceration productivity measures. Other data problems also limiting development of productivity measures included the high proportion of ROP arrests that were tried outside of Washington, D.C., for which disposition information was lacking (35% of all arrests), and the number of ROP's 1983 cases still pending December 31, 1984 (18, 17 of which were felonies, these constitute 12% of ROP's cases and 25% of its felony cases).

GENERALIZABILITY OF THE FINDINGS

One must be cautious about generalizing from the findings of a single case study. What worked for ROP may be related to the unique characteristics of Washington, D.C., its police department, or the personnel and leadership of ROP. Although ROP officers were not found to have made arrests at a higher rate than others prior to assignment to ROP, they may differ from them in other unknown ways. Furthermore, the impact of the ROP Captain's leadership cannot be overlooked. He is an unusually talented, charismatic leader who selected a superior supervisory team combining investigative and organizational skills, who flexibly adjusted ROP policies and practices, and who worked to sustain high officer morale and motivation. As an innovative unit, ROP faced ample internal and public scrutiny. This may have led officers to "try harder," producing a Hawthorne effect that may not be observed in a second generation of ROP officers. In the absence of other units or groups with which to compare the ROP experience, it is difficult to determine which aspects of its organization and tactics are idiosyncratic, which may be effectively replicated in a different setting, and which might better be altered.

This study leaves many questions unanswered. Further research is needed, for example, to determine the effectiveness of ROP's selection procedures and to estimate its crime control effect. Nevertheless, this study provides encouragement for police to develop a selective apprehension strategy. If street information does provide the best means of identifying and apprehending highly active offenders, then the Washington program and others like it might have a major impact on serious crime.

Notes

1. The changing target pool design was adopted to permit retargeting of persons, particularly those assigned to control. Consequently, some of the 289 persons targeted in the experiment were subject to random assignment more than once (n = 424 assignments).

2. Difficulties in carrying out the experiment resulted both from deliberate efforts to evade the rules governing target assignment (because ROP officers did not want to defer action on a target about whom they had information) and the unavailability of data (due to local record-keeping systems.) Manipulation of randomization was allowed to occur because authority to conduct the coin toss was gradually shifted for several reasons to two target committee members. It permitted squads to get new targets when the project director was unavailable. It eased the administrative burden the experiment put on the committee and increased squad compliance by coopting target committee members into the role of "rule enforcers." It also facilitated collection of structured observation data. However, it had a cost. Evidence of manipulation included after-the-fact admission by several ROP officers and observation of two squads "caught in the act."

   Data availability problems included delays in entering information about new warrants and the service of existing ones into the local computer system; the absence of any systematic information about arrests outside of D.C. and of juveniles in D.C.; and the lack of computerized data on D.C. arrests.

3. Differences between total included in sample and numbers reported in Figures 2-5 are due to missing data in criminal history and court records.

4. The 1983 arrests made by ROP officers that are included in the experimental and quasi-experimental data sets overlap substantially but are not identical because the data sets were developed independently. The experimental data include juvenile arrests and exclude several arrests that were eliminated from the experiment when the control mate subsequently was found to be incarcerated or otherwise ineligible for the coin toss. The additional data collected at the ROP office allowed comparison of exceptions and serendipitously arrested targets with those in the experiment. The quasi-experimental data did not distinguish among ROP arrestees by assignment type.

5. The 20% figure was selected because one ROP insider estimated that 10% of the tosses were nonrandom. To be conservative, that number was doubled. Furthermore, because there were more than twice as many arrests of experimentals (17) as controls (8) by non-ROP units, it was assumed that part of this difference was attributable to the lack of information about some non-ROP arrests.

6. Both the first author's observation and the data collected from the ROP office on all ROP targets support this finding. Examination of prior arrest history by target type

indicated that persons deliberately targeted by ROP (experimentals and authorized exceptions) had 7.5 prior arrests at the time they were initially targeted; those serendipitously arrested had only 3.7 such prior arrests. This difference is significant (t = 5.88, p < .001). However, comparisons of the prior records of experimentals and exceptions, using several different measures, found they did not differ. The simplest explanation of the change is conformity with the goals and norms of ROP. The ROP command staff made clear that officers were to concentrate efforts on investigations and apprehending targets selected on the basis of current and prior criminal activity and were expected not to arrest "targets of opportunity" for minor offenses. Officers also faced informal pressures such as teasing about "lowering ROP's standards" when they made an "inappropriate" arrest. Thus, it is hardly surprising that arrestees deliberately selected in part on the basis of their prior records would have longer histories than those arrested largely by chance.

7. The type of offense for which ROP and comparison officers made arrests also were compared. In 1981 they were similar and in 1983 they differed only with respect to cases not presented for prosecution in the D.C. courts. The proportion of ROP officers' arrests to persons as fugitives, escapees, and parole or probation violators increased from 1% to 26% of all arrests from the 1981 to 1983 time periods, while the proportion of "other" mostly minor, arrests fell from 35% to 15%. In contrast, 7% of comparison officers' arrestees in 1981 and 8% in 1983 were fugitives, escapees, and parole or probation violators, and "other" arrests increased from 24% to 30% of total arrests. Thus, overall, ROP-83 arrests tended to be for more serious crimes than comparison arrests although many of these are not included in the disposition analysis.

8. Figure 3 excludes arrests on bench warrants since the arrestee has previously been charged and failed to appear in court. Although there are misdemeanor and felony bench warrants, because the arrest logs did not distinguish between them, we were unable to do so at the arrest phase. These cases have been included in the conviction and sentencing analysis, however, because they make up an important proportion of the arrests of ROP officers in 1983 and the warrant squad officers in both 1981 and 1983 (16%, 50% and 64%, respectively) and often involve persons convicted of serious offenses. Unfortunately, this means that a meaningful control for differences in earlier outcomes cannot be employed, given the differences in the samples at different stages.

9. The incarceration and sentencing data are biased downward for both ROP and comparison cases in 1983 because 18 and 13 cases, respectively, were still pending as of December 31, 1984, when data collection for this study was terminated. Most of these cases involved serious felonies that are more likely to result in incarceration given convictions than those cases already disposed.

REFERENCES

Black, Donald
1973 The mobilization of law. *Journal of Legal Studies* 2: 125-149.

Bowers, Robert and Jack McCullough
1982 Assessing the "Sting": An Evaluation of the LEAA Property Crime Program. Washington, DC: University City Science Center.

Chaiken, Jan and Marcia Chaiken
1982 *Varieties of Criminal Behavior.* Santa Monica: The Rand Corporation.

Felony Augumentation Project.
1981 Felony Augumentation Project. New York: New York City Police Department.

Gay, William
1983 *Issues in law enforcement: Career criminal initiatives.* Unpublished. Washington, DC: University City Science Center.

Gay, William, Thomas Beall, and Robert Bowers
1984 *A multisite assessment of the integrated criminal apprehension program: final report.* Unpublished. Washington, D.C.: University City Science Center.

Greenwood, Peter with Alan Abrahamse
1982 *Selective Incapacitation.* Santa Monica: The Rand Corporation.

Moore, Mark
1983 Invisible offenses: A challenge to minimally intrusive law enforcement. In Gerald Caplan (ed.), *ABSCAM Ethics: Moral Issues and Deception in Law Enforcement.* Washington, DC: Police Foundation.

Pate, Tony, Robert A. Bowers, and Ron Parks
1976 *Three Approaches to Criminal Apprehension in Kansas City: An Evaluation Report.* Washington, DC: Police Foundation.

Petersilia, Joan, Peter Greenwood, and Marvin Lavin
1978 *Criminal Careers of Habitual Felons.* Santa Monica: The Rand Corporation.

Reiss, Albert J. Jr.
1971 *The Police and the Public.* New Haven: Yale University Press.

Williams, Jay, Lawrence Redlinger, and Peter R. Manning
1979 *Police Narcotics Control: Patterns and Strategies.* Washington, DC: National Institute of Law Enforcement and Criminal Justice.

Williams, Kristen
1979 *The scope and prediction of recidivism.* Unpublished paper. Washington, DC: INSLAW

Wilson, James Q.
1978 *The Investigators.* New York: Basic Books.

Wolfgang, Marvin, Robert Figlio, and Thorsten Sellin
1972 *Delinquency in a Birth Cohort.* Chicago: University of Chicago Press.

Wycoff, Mary Ann, Charles E. Brown, and Robert E. Petersen.
1980 *Birmingham anti-robbery unit evaluation report.* Unpublished. Washington, DC: Police Foundation.

Repeat Calls for Service: Policing the "Hot Spots"   14

Lawrence W. Sherman

Three percent of the estimated 115,000 addresses and intersections in Minneapolis were the subject of 50 percent of the 321,174 calls to police between December 15, 1985 and December 15, 1986. Sixty percent of the addresses and intersections produced no calls to police at all. Of the 40 percent with any calls, the majority (52 percent) had only one call, while 84 percent had less than five. The top 5 percent of locations with any calls produced 48.8 percent of the calls.

This highly skewed concentration of all police calls in relatively few locations raises substantial questions about current police strategies and suggests the need for focusing police resources on the chronic repeat call locations. This chapter reflects the first step in a research and development effort to create such a strategy, under National Institute of Justice (NIJ) funding, of a collaborative project of the Crime Control Institute and the Minneapolis Police Department.

911 Runs the Police Department

Much of the work sponsored by NIJ since 1982 has attempted to develop a variety of strategies for accomplishing police objectives. Prompted in part by Professor Herman Goldstein's landmark proposal for "problem-oriented policing" (Goldstein, 1979), NIJ's work has created and tested strategies focusing resources on specific, high-priority police targets. Implicit in these new strategies is a strong critique of the prevailing "dial-a-cop" system of allocating most police resources on the basis of the phone calls police receive.

Source: Lawrence W. Sherman (1987). "Repeat Calls for Service: Policing the 'Hot Spots.'" From "Repeat Calls to Police in Minneapolis," *Crime Control Reports* (4). Reprinted by permission of the Crime Control Institute.

With the recent growth of 911 systems and the steady increase in the number of calls to police, a virtual coup d'etat has taken over American policing. Gradually, with little public notice, police managers have lost control over how police spend their time. The usurper is the telephone, and a common policy that requires all calls to be answered rapidly.

In the words of one police chief, "911 runs the police department." This means that for all the orders headquarters may make, most police effort is directed simply on the basis of telephoned citizen requests for immediate service, almost all of which are now received in many cities at the emergency "911" number. This system is neither rational nor fair.

The dial-a-cop system is irrational because it prevents police from setting priorities and controlling crime more effectively. By letting each citizen decide whether a matter is appropriate for police work, we make it impossible for police to decide which matters deserve the most attention. In some cities, homicides literally go uninvestigated while police cars respond rapidly to help people locked out of their cars.

Of all the calls to police in the city of Minneapolis in 1986, for example, 5 percent were for car lockouts, 4 percent were for noise complaints, and 25 percent were for domestic and other arguments which generally had no violence (see Table 14.1). Meanwhile, scarce police resources permitted only limited efforts against narcotics pushers, repeat offenders, and serious domestic violence.

Dial-a-cop is irrational because, as NIJ-sponsored research has shown, rapid response by police makes little contribution to the apprehension of criminals or the prevention of victim injury, in the overwhelming majority of calls (Spelman and Eck, 1986). Other NIJ research shows that the calling public is generally happy to wait for a police response, or to receive no police car dispatched at all, as long as the telephone operators politely and accurately explain to the callers exactly what is going to happen (McEwen et al., 1984).

The dial-a-cop system also allocates resources unfairly across the problems that generate calls. Because all calls must be answered quickly, very little time can be spent on each call. The chronic locations are not given extra attention to try to reduce their heavy demands on police. Each call at the chronic locations receives the same limited attention that a call to a once-in-five years location receives. Dial-a-cop goes on putting out the fire, but it never takes away the matches.

Recognizing these problems, the National Institute of Justice has funded tests of a variety of police efforts to focus resources proactively (Reiss, 1971)—not waiting for telephone calls for direction—on high-priority police problems: repeat offenders (Martin and Sherman, 1986), unjustified community fear of crime (Pate, Wycoff, Skogan, and Sherman, 1986), and area patterns of street crime (Spelman and Eck, 1986). We now add to the list of these proactively policed, high-priority targets the chronic repeat-call locations that generate the majority of police patrol dispatches.

Table 14.1
Nature of Calls to Police in Minneapolis, All Addresses, 1986*
(unadjusted data)

CATEGORY	NUMBER	PERCENT**
Conflict Management:	104,354	32.5%
Domestics	24,948	7.8
Other Disturbances	55,568	17.3
Noise	12,204	3.8
Assault	11,634	3.6
Property Crime-Related:	91,055	28.4%
Theft	35,741	11.1
Burglary-related	33,384	10.4
Vandalism	11,197	3.5
Alarms	10,733	3.3
Traffic Problems:	59,630	18.6%
Traffic Enforcement	27,992	8.7
Property Damage Accident	10,296	3.2
Parking	8,007	2.5
All Other Traffic	13,335	4.2
Service:	42,473	13.2%
Lockouts	17,389	5.4
Medical Aid	9,008	2.8
Emergencies	6,986	2.0
Assistance	6,308	2.0
Persons—Lost/Found	1,578	0.5
Fires	1,204	0.4
Miscellaneous:	17,591	5.4%
Arrests and Bookings	5,059	1.6
Other	12,532	4.0
Stranger to Stranger Crime Against Persons:	6,071	1.9%
Robbery	4,219	1.3
Criminal Sexual Conduct	1,852	0.6
TOTALS:	321,174	100.0%

*December 15, 1985 to December 15, 1986.
**Percentages do not total 100 due to rounding.

The purpose of this chapter is to demonstrate the concentration of police work at a small number of locations, and the justification for assigning extra resources to those locations as a way of reducing total calls to police. While it is true that much of that concentration may simply reflect concentrations of people using or living at those locations, that does not alter the logic of police identifying and focusing their efforts on those locations. Whether extra resources can succeed in reducing repeat calls will be the subject of a later report on the Minneapolis RECAP (repeat call address policing) experiment.

RESEARCH METHODS

In order to develop the RECAP alternative to the dial-a-cop system, the Crime Control Institute obtained NIJ support for two tasks. One task was analyzing the patterns and concentrations of repeat calls. The other task was selecting, training, and evaluating the effectiveness of a small RECAP unit of police officers devoting full time to proactive policing of the most chronic locations in the city.

The analysis was intended to identify those locations as the targets for the unit's efforts. But it also serves to demonstrate the need for the unit, which would have been abandoned if the analysis showed little concentration of calls.

The analysis proved to be far more difficult than anticipated. Most police departments will experience similar or greater difficulties in undertaking the same analysis. The problem is that a full year of call data is needed to develop a reasonably complete picture of the distribution of repeat calls. But such a large data base seems to be beyond the current capacity of most big-city police departments.

We have not surveyed this issue systematically, but we can offer some examples to illustrate the problem. The minimum requirement for this kind of analysis is that police call records must be computerized. In some big cities like Milwaukee, this is still not the case (although it is changing rapidly). Even among the computerized dispatch systems, few if any have sufficient data storage capacity for analyzing a full year of calls.

The subject address and call nature code data punched into the computer—as distinct from a tape recording of the words exchanged between the caller and the police telephone operator—is generally removed from the computer and recorded on tape as soon as the computer's capacity is reached. In Minneapolis, the data are removed to tape about every seven days, depending on the volume of calls. In Colorado Springs, with an advanced computer-aided-dispatch system, the on-line storage capacity is reportedly three months. Other cities, like Dallas, have multiyear storage and retrieval capacity.

In order to identify the most active Minneapolis addresses over the course of a year, a new data base had to be constructed specifically for that purpose. Such an extensive task was not something the Minneapolis city government computer programmers had time to do. Nor, with a high hourly use cost, was it economical for the Crime Control Institute to use the city's mainframe computer. Both of these problems were handled, at the city's recommendation, by the Crime Control Institute's buying a microcomputer and retaining a programming firm familiar with the city's dispatch system.

THE UNADJUSTED DATA BASE

The analysis proceeded by our agreeing on a few data "fields" in the computerized "record" of each call that would be transferred from the weekly tapes into the microcomputer data base. The fields included street name, address, floor number, apartment number, nature code of call, date and time of call, and officer's disposition (which would tell whether a report was filed from the call). The total information taken from each record was 80 "bytes." With an estimated 300,000 calls, we purchased a microcomputer that could handle at least 24 million bytes. We then used a tape drive attached to the micro to read those fields off of each weekly dispatch tape and into the hard disk data file.

The original plan had been to define addresses down to the level of apartment, but the programmers advised us that the complications involved in creating that definition would be enormous and very expensive. The "address" in the data base is no more specific than the building address, and the data base is thus biased towards addresses with large resident or user populations.

The data base was limited to calls to police, thus excluding fire department and ambulance calls. It also excluded administrative calls recorded in the system, such as police officers notifying the dispatcher that they are "out to lunch." We asked that calls be excluded if there was no police car dispatched. Finally, we directed that the address in question would always be an address where the problem was located, not the address from which the call came (if that was a different address).

Both of the last two definitions were difficult to impose, given the nature of police-dispatching systems. The address employed in the data base was generally the address to which a police car was dispatched; but there was no way to insure that the problem had actually occurred at that address. Thus the "unadjusted" number-one call location in the city is the Hennepin County Medical Center, because police respond there to take a crime report whenever medical staff notify police (as Sherman required by law) that a crime victim has arrived in the emergency room. The crime, of course, happened elsewhere, but the dispatch computer does not record the address of occurrence.

The address in the data base is only "generally" the address to which a car is dispatched because some of the included calls—we do not know how many, but believe it to be relatively few—did not result in a police car being dispatched at all. There was an exclusion made of one code indication showing that the call was screened out, or handled by the telephone operator. But other non-dispatched calls slipped in because they had a "closed" disposition at the time they were received.

The "closed" disposition means that the purpose of the call is to create a record of an event rather than to request police service. When an off-duty police officer working as a retail security officer apprehends a shoplifter, for example, he can fill out all the paperwork to charge and release the suspect right at the scene. But he must still call the police operator to receive a case number for the arrest report. Such a call is listed as a closed call under the "event" disposition field, as distinct from the "officer" disposition field, on each call record.

At the time the data base fields were selected, we were not aware of this distinction. It only emerged as we analyzed the preliminary report from the last six months of 1986. We had omitted it in trying to conserve computer storage space, since including it would have taken close to a million bytes. But when we discovered how crucial it was to determining whether cars were actually dispatched, we decided to rebuild the data base from scratch. That effort will begin shortly and will provide the basis for the final evaluation of the RECAP unit's effectiveness at reducing calls to which police are actually dispatched.

The data base as described to this point will be defined as the "unadjusted" data base, which included 321,174 calls. The following exclusions describe how the "adjusted" data base was constructed for the purposes of identifying the most active addresses in the city.

THE ADJUSTED DATA BASE

In order to limit the target list more closely to addresses where problems actually occurred, the RECAP commander and officers went through a printout of the top 2,000 addresses in the last six months (approximately) of 1986. The time period was selected merely on the rounds of moving speedily, at a time when the data base was only half built. They tried to eliminate all addresses, such as all hospitals, city hall, police precinct stations, the St. Joseph's Shelter for lost, abandoned and abused children, and the courthouse, which were clearly not the locations of the problems but rather the locations to which police were dispatched to take a report. (Unfortunately, two small hospitals slipped through, but were deleted from the target list described below.)

They also decided, after a three-day planning retreat with Crime Control Institute staff and extensive debate for a week thereafter, to eliminate *intersections.* The problem with intersections from the standpoint of proactive police work is that there is very little chance of finding a stable group of people who generate or deal with the problems. Recurrent traffic accidents at bad intersections are already being mapped by another unit; so the remaining problems of muggings, fights, car lockouts, etc., could not be dealt with conveniently by a small unit.

For similar reasons, the RECAP unit also decided to eliminate parks and schools (which have their own special police units), and the one-block area downtown in which an enormous amount of vice consumption is concentrated: pornography stores, movies, and the most active bar in the city for calls to police. The city council was debating the future of that block heavily at the time, and even considered condemning it and tearing it down. When this analysis found that the twelve addresses and four intersections of the "E" block, as it is known, were the subject of 3,230 police calls in the unadjusted data base—more than 1 percent—the finding was the subject of a detailed story in the *Minneapolis Star and Tribune* (January 15, 1987).

The fact that 0.001 percent of the addresses and intersections produced 1 percent of the calls, or 1,000 times more calls than would be expected by an equal distribution, is a striking part of the overall concentrations reported here. But it also suggested a problem so major that it was prudent for the RECAP unit to exclude it from its work

The final categorical exclusion was the check-cashing establishments, which generate many calls for arrests of felonious bad-check passers. These arrests have a high conviction rate, and the RECAP officers did not want to discourage the arrests. One such establishment, however, slipped by into the adjusted data base reported here

In addition to these categorical exclusions, the officers dealt with two other issues. One issue, which will affect any police department attempting to identify repeat call locations, is the fact that police telephone operators enter the same address in different ways on different occasions. A good example comes from the most active bar on the "E" block, Moby Dick's, which is entered in at least these different ways:

- 620 Hennepin Ave.
- 620 Hennepin Ave.—Moby's
- 620 Hennepin Ave.—Moby Dick's
- 620 Hennepin Ave.—Moby's Bar

These different listings made the address appear to have fewer calls than it actually had, because the true total was split among the different ways of labeling the address.

Other buildings may have entrances and addresses on different streets, or have similar variations in the description of the premises following the address. We had asked the programmer to suppress those descriptions in the analysis, but it was not possible to combine the multiple listings without far more complex programming. Thus, both the unadjusted and adjusted data bases show *less* concentration of calls than actually exists.

The problem was somewhat reduced for the top 2,000 addresses. The RECAP officers read the address listings for the full year data set. They instructed the programmer to merge the remaining addresses that were presented under multiple labels, to the extent that they were able to detect them.

In addition, less than twenty addresses were deleted for reasons related to the evaluation research design, which will be described in later reports.

COMMERCIAL AND RESIDENTIAL ADDRESSES

The preliminary inspection of the top 2,000 addresses showed that they were predominantly commercial addresses. In order to insure that the RECAP experiment would have enough residential addresses to explore the full range of police problems, we decided to stratify the study sample. The officers went through the top 2,000 locations, using the reverse telephone directory to supplement their formidable knowledge of city addresses, and labeled each location as residential or commercial.

Once the designations and all the exclusions were complete, the programmers rank-ordered the commercial and residential addresses in separate lists. The top 250 addresses in each category were then identified as the project targets. It is this final, adjusted list that is the basis for the data presented in Tables 14.2 and 14.3. For the purpose of the experimental phase of the unit, only half of each list will be assigned to RECAP. The other, randomly selected half of each list will be left alone as a control group against which to compare the frequency of calls at the experimental locations.

LETTING CALLS SET PRIORITIES

Table 14.1 presents the overall distribution of calls by nature code in the unadjusted data base of 321,174 calls. The distribution is a regrouping of 114 separate nature codes into six more general categories. The categories are guided by the proper literature on the nature of police work (e.g., Wilson, 1968; Goldstein, 1977). The results show what police work becomes when police priorities are determined by the calls that come in.

There is no question that police are needed to deal with angry conflicts that can erupt, or have already erupted, into violence. It is hard to criticize the fact that one-third of all calls fall into this category. It is also hard to argue that police should not attend to calls about actual or potential property crime, which comprise 29 percent of calls, or traffic control at 19 percent, or even some of the service calls, at 13 percent.

Table 14.2

Nature of Police Calls to the 250 Most Active Commercial and to the 250 Most Active Residential Addresses in Minneapolis, 1986
(adjusted data)

CATEGORY	Commercial		Residential	
	Number	%**	Number	%**
Conflict Management:	6,357	32%	11,427	59%
Domestics	462	2	3,703	19
Other Disturbances	4,919	25	5,560	29
Assault	919	5	1,254	6
Noise	57	—	910	5
Property Crime-Related:	7,857	40%	3,640	19%
Theft	5,757	29	1,583	8
Burglary-related	940	5	1,432	7
Vandalism	425	2	587	3
Alarms	735	4	68	—
Traffic Problems:	985	5%	519	3%
Traffic Enforcement	131	1	131	1
Property Damage Accident	130	1	130	1
Parking	251	1	251	1
Service:	3,006	15%	2,584	13%
Lockouts	1,993	10	706	4
Medical Aid	700	4	1,025	5
Emergencies	435	2	940	5
Assistance	486	2	640	3
Persons—Lost/Found	88	—	206	1
Fires				
Miscellaneous:	756	4%	882	4%
Arrests and Bookings	304	2	460	2
Other				
Stranger to Stranger Crime Against Persons:	722	3%	548	2%
Robbery	616	3	371	2
Criminal Sexual Conduct	106	1	177	1
TOTALS:	19,564	100%	19,462	100%

*December 15, 1985 to December 15, 1986.
**Percentages do not total 100 due to rounding.

Table 14.3
Distribution of Calls to Police by Locations Generating Police Calls
in Minneapolis, 1986* (unadjusted data base)

Percentile of Call Addresses	% of Calls	Raw % of Calls	Cumulative % of Calls**
5	156,076	48.58	48.58
10	40,040	12.46	61.04
15	24,142	7.51	68.55
20	17,106	5.32	73.87
25	13,216	4.11	77.98
30	10,449	3.25	81.23
35	8,456	2.63	83.86
40	6,966	2.17	86.03
45	6,966	2.17	88.20
50	5,845	1.82	90.02
55	3,483	1.08	91.10
60	3,483	1.08	92.18
65	3,483	1.08	93.26
70	3,483	1.08	94.34
75	3,483	1.08	95.42
80	3,483	1.08	96.50
85	3,483	1.08	97.58
90	3,483	1.08	98.66
95	3,483	1.08	99.74
100	3,352	1.04	100.78

*December 15, 1985 to December 15, 1986.
**Percentages do not total 100 due to rounding.

It is possible to argue that police should not be providing a free car lockout service (5 percent of calls), when private locksmiths could do the same on a fee-for-service basis, a plan that is under much discussion in Minneapolis. But there are few such categories of calls that police could reasonably abandon altogether. The problem is not one of need, but one of balance.

The fact that only 2 percent of all calls concern the most serious crimes, stranger-to-stranger crimes against persons, suggests that the balance does not match citizen priorities. The Minneapolis police do expend other resources on street crime besides patrol car responses to citizen calls. But the total resources dedicated to stranger crime are probably minimal in comparison to the high priority many citizens would place on such offenses.

Bittner (1980) has defended the picture of police work presented in Table 14.1 by defining policing as the intervention in "situations-about-which-somebody-must-do-something-now." That is no doubt the common theme that runs through all of these calls. But it is arguable that police work can and should be more than just immediate responses. A good analogy is found in medicine, which is increasingly moving away from just treating the sick towards the preventive maintenance of health.

The analogy of public health is even more compelling, with the recent growth of proactive efforts to identify carriers of Acquired Immune Deficiency Syndrome (AIDS) to stop them from spreading the disease. Far more lives may be saved by such efforts than by doctors treating sore throats and the flu. Similarly, far more lives may be saved by focusing police resources on serious crime problems than by simply waiting for calls on minor crime problems to come in.

Whatever the merits of the priorities reflected in this distribution of calls in the unadjusted data base, it is important to note how it differs from the nature of calls about the top 250 commercial and residential locations in the adjusted data base. As Table 14.2 shows, both commercial and residential addresses are relatively free of traffic problems. But commercial addresses have proportionally more property crime calls than addresses in general, and residential addresses have proportionally twice as many conflict management calls as addresses in general.

Solving the problems that produce the high concentrations of repeat calls at these locations will not necessarily reduce street crime, but they may free up other police resources to concentrate on such crimes.

THE CHRONIC CALL LOCATIONS

And the concentration is substantial indeed. Each of the locations in the two adjusted lists of most active addresses generates an average of about 80 calls per year, slightly less than two a week Each list of 250, with only two-tenths of one percent of the city's addresses, produces 6 percent of the calls in the city. These addresses are thus 30 times more likely to produce a call to police on any given day than the average address in the city.

The concentrations are even more clearly demonstrated by the data from the unadjusted list. Analysis shows a steep decline in the total percentage of calls produced by addresses ranked below the top 5 percent of addresses in call frequency. The second 5 percent of addresses produce only 13 percent of the calls, the third 5 percent of addresses only 7 percent of the calls, and so on.

Table 14.3 shows a similar distribution among the 60 percent of addresses and intersections that had any calls at all, with almost 49 percent of the calls concentrated in the top 5 percent of those addresses.

Table 14.4 shows the distribution of places with calls by the number of calls at each place. The majority of those addresses had only one call, and 85 percent had less than five. Thus, the concentration of most calls in the few most active addresses is clearly intense.

These statistical concentrations raise the obvious question: What kinds of locations are consuming the lion's share of police patrol responses? The answer is not just low-rent apartments or tough bars, although they are well represented. The lists also include major commercial locations, which attract large numbers of people for many hours of the day.

Table 14.4
Number of Locations Responded to by Number of Police Calls per Address
in Minneapolis, 1986* (unadjusted data base)

Number of Calls	Number of Locations
0	45,353
1	35,926
2	11,329
3	5,691
4	3,511
5	2,304
6	1,680
7	1,253
8	964
9	817
10	655
11	508
12	417
13	358
14	302
15	301
16	260
17	203
18	225
19	175
20	162
Over 20	2,606

*December 15, 1985 to December 15, 1986.

Table 14.5 lists in rank order the top 50 addresses, both commercial and residential, in the adjusted list, showing the frequency of calls and the generic type of location at each address. An analysis of these locations shows that 21 are apartment buildings, of which four are public housing projects. Twelve are retail or grocery stores, and the grocery stores are generally open 24 hours a day. Five are bars, three are 24-hour convenience stores with the same national company, three are hotels, one is a fast-food hamburger chain (not McDonald's), and five others are of varied character.

Table 14.5
Top 50 Addresses in Minneapolis by Nature of Location and Number of Calls, 1986* (adjusted data base)

Rank	Nature of Location	Number of Calls
1	Large discount store	810
2	Large department store	686
3	24-hour convenience store and bar	607
4	Apartments—Public housing	479
5	Large discount store	471
6	Large discount store	449
7	Homeless center—former hotel	379
8	Transportation center	343
9	Large department store	319
10	Downtown business mall	251
11	Bar	244
12	Large department store	242
13	High-priced hotel	240
14	Bar	237
15	Apartments	233
16	Bar	222
17	Community center	209
18	Apartments	208
19	Apartments	207
20	Apartments	195
21	Grocery store—24-hour	195
22	Medium-priced hotel	193
23	Supermarket	192
24	Apartments	190
25	Supermarket	190
26	Small apartment	187
27	24-hour convenience store	183
28	Apartments—high rise	181
29	Apartments	177
30	Apartments	175
31	Apartments	168
32	Halfway house	163
33	Bar	158
34	Apartments	156
35	Apartments	156
36	Low-priced hotel	152
37	Apartments	149
38	Apartments—public housing	149
39	Apartments—public housing	148
40	Bar and 24-hour restaurant	147
41	Social service center	147
42	Fast food restaurant	146
43	24-hour convenience store	145
44	Grocery store—24-hour	145
45	Liquor store	143
46	Apartments	142
47	Apartments	142
48	Apartments	142
49	Apartments	142
50	Apartments—public housing	136
	TOTAL CALLS	11,870

*December 15, 1985 to December 15, 1986.

It is fairer to say that these addresses usually attract trouble rather than cause it. The role of the late-night hours, when many people are intoxicated and more vulnerable to committing or being victimized by crime, appears to be substantial. Yet, the profits from all-night operations are also reported to be substantial and a strong incentive for businesses to stay open.

It is also interesting to note the role of big business in these demands for local police service. While many of the locations are owned by local small businesses, especially the apartments, six of the top ten are operated by Fortune 500 companies.

USER FEES

Whether they simply attract trouble along with large numbers of customers by offering the public a needed service, or in the case of certain bars, cause trouble by serving intoxicated customers, these addresses do place major demands upon the police. Whether they pay disproportionately larger taxes than other police users is unclear. If not, then one implication might be to create a system of user fees for calling the police, restricted to commercial addresses—just as garbage collection is charged to commercial, but not residential, addresses in many cities.

THE RECAP STRATEGY

A less extreme approach is simply focusing police resources on the chronic use locations, in order to reduce their use. The goal of such a strategy should not be merely to reduce calls to police, and certainly not to discourage people from making calls in emergencies. The goal should be solving or reducing the problems generating the repeat calls.

One way to accomplish that goal might be to assign a small unit of officers to spend full time on proactive police work at these locations. These officers would not answer radio calls, but would work flexible hours to accomplish the following tasks at the high-volume locations identified through the computer-generated analysis described in this report:

- Description of the nature and use of the premises.
- Diagnosis of the problems generating the calls.
- Planning police or user action for reducing those problems.
- Implementing the action plan.
- Following up on repeat call rates to measure success.

The description can generally be done on the basis of existing officer knowledge or merely driving by the location. The diagnosis should be based upon a review of a computer printout of the nature, days, and time of the calls at the location, as well as the narratives in the crime and arrest reports previously filed for those locations. The diagnosis may also include personal contact with owners, managers, users, or residents of the locations.

The planning could be done after discussion with colleagues or supervisors, and possibly after consultation with other community resources, such as social service agencies. The action plan can then be implemented by the RECAP officers, other police units, social welfare organizations, or persons on the premises. The important point of departure from conventional police work is the *follow-up:* the RECAP officers' efforts to insure that the action plan was indeed implemented, and their monitoring of weekly computer reports on subsequent calls at the addresses they have worked upon. These reports, ideally, will take the form of a trend line showing how many calls were dispatched each week, with a vertical line through the trend showing the date the action plan was implemented.

This RECAP strategy began in Minneapolis in 1987 with four hand-picked volunteer officers and one sergeant commanding them. These officers were among the most experienced, hardest-working and creative officers in the department. Two were college graduates in social science, and they averaged over fifteen years of patrol experience. They were intentionally chosen for their excellence, as they would be in normal operational circumstances.

Whether even such a high-quality team can implement the complex strategy described here remains to be seen. If it is implemented properly, the experimental design being employed will give a fairly clear answer to the question of whether such a unit can reduce repeat calls at these chronic locations.

The ultimate success of such a strategy may depend as much upon the tactics used as upon the strategy itself. Negative results would not necessarily disprove the value of the strategy. But it would show that the methods used by the Minneapolis RECAP team failed to deal with the problems producing the calls, and raise serious doubt about whether any tactics could have made a difference.

The Minneapolis RECAP team is well aware that, perhaps for the first time in the history of the department, there is a "bottom line," profit-or-loss statement that they will show at the end of the experiment. With approximately 400 patrol officers handling 321,000 calls a year, each officer on patrol will handle roughly 800 calls per year, or about four per day worked. In order to justify their removal from patrol to RECAP, the officers must reduce calls by five times 800, or 4,000 calls, on an annualized basis. Anything more than that will be considered "profit"; anything less can be considered a "loss."

An annualized reduction of 4,000 calls amounts to about 20 percent fewer calls at the target addresses than in the previous year. Such a goal is not easy to attain, but neither does it seem unrealistic. Given the high quality of the group, there is good reason for optimism.

REFERENCES

Bittner, E. (1980). *The Functions of the Police in Modern Society*. Cambridge, MA: Oegelschlager, Gunn and Hain.

Goldstein, H. (1977). *Policing a Free Society*. Cambridge, MA: Ballinger.

————— (1979). "Improving Policing: A Problem-Oriented Approach." *Crime and Delinquency*, 25:236-258.

McEwen, J., E. Connors, and M. Cohen (1984). *Evaluation of the Differential Response Field Test*. Alexandria, VA: Research Management Associates.

Martin, S. and L. Sherman (1986). "Selective Apprehension: A Police Strategy for Repeat Offenders." *Criminology*, 24(1).

Pate, A., M. Wycoff, W. Skogan, and L. Sherman (1986). *Reducing Fear of Crime in Houston and Newark*. Washington, DC: Police Foundation.

Pierce, G., S. Spaar, and L. Briggs (1984). *The Character of Police Work: Implications for the Delivery of Services*. Boston: Northeastern University.

Reiss, A. (1971). *The Police and the Public*. New Haven: Yale University Press.

Spelman, W. and D. Brown (1981). *Calling the Police: A Replication of the Citizen Reporting Component of the Kansas City Response Time Analysis*. Washington, DC: Police Executive Research Forum.

Spelman, W. and J. Eck (1986). *Problem Oriented Policing*. Washington, DC: National Institute of Justice.

Wilson, J. (1968). *Varieties of Police Behavior*. Cambridge MA: Harvard University Press.

LOCAL-LEVEL DRUG ENFORCEMENT: NEW STRATEGIES 15

David W. Hayeslip, Jr.

Faced with growing drug-related violence, crime, and mounting public concern, police departments across the country are devising new approaches for combating drug dealing. The strategies include enlisting the support of community groups, seizing assets of both sellers and users, and cracking down on street sales.

The National Institute of Justice has begun to take a look at some of these new strategies. This article shares some preliminary information gathered in discussions with metropolitan police departments, and it concludes with questions that need to be answered concerning the impact of these approaches.

PUBLIC CONCERN MOUNTS

The magnitude of drug dealing activity has increased public pressure for police to take stronger action. A May 1988 *New York Times*—CBS News Survey found that 16 percent of respondents considered drugs to be the Nation's number one problem.[1] That is in sharp contrast to a 1985 Gallup Poll in which only 2 percent said drug abuse was number one.[2]

Police share the public's concern. They are especially worried about the rise in cocaine use, particularly in its most potent form known as "crack" or "rock." In many jurisdictions police report that crack has become the street drug of choice.

Crack's popularity is relatively new but has been building for several years. NIJ Drug Use Forecasting (DUF) tests have shown significant

---

Source: David W. Hayeslip Jr. (1989). "Local-Level Drug Enforcement: New Strategies." *Research in Action, NIJ Reports,* 213:2-5. Reprinted by permission of the National Institute of Justice.

increases in cocaine use among arrestees in a number of major cities over a 3-year period.[3] In Washington, D.C., cocaine use more than tripled.[4]

Crack is considered highly addictive. It is also readily available, trafficked in the open, of high quality (not significantly cut), and cheap. Crack users come from all social strata, and many turn to both property and street crime to finance their habits.

Police and other experts think that rising crime is linked to crack sales. Indeed, threatened and actual violence by drug dealers is a growing concern. Homicides associated with the control of drug markets are up in many cities, with residents of high-crime drug-sales areas living in constant fear. In some places, community residents are afraid to call the police because of threatened retaliation by drug dealers. Some drug dealers are reported to have forced public housing residents out of their homes so they could use the vacated apartments for temporary drug distribution or consumption.

The importation and distribution of illegal drugs appear to be well organized and to follow a basic four-step process. Producers of illegal drugs, or "kingpins," funnel narcotics to midlevel distributors. These in turn pass the drugs to lower level distributors who control street sellers.

Actually, the entire importation and distribution process is far more complex. Many individuals are involved as drugs move from stage to stage in a series of complicated relationships that vary according to geographical location and type of drug distributed. In many cities, gangs control street sales, like the "Bloods" and the "Crips" of the West Coast, or Jamaican "posses" and other ethnic minority gangs in other areas.

Street sales of powdered cocaine and crack follow several patterns. One of the most common means of distribution is though "crack houses." Typically, these are abandoned houses, some highly fortified against police intrusion and easily identified by both police and local citizens. In "open" crack houses, users can purchase and consume crack or other drugs on the premises. Hotels, motels, and apartments in rental buildings or public housing projects form yet another distribution avenue. On-the-corner street sales are also commonplace.

Because of the high volume and high visibility of illegal drug sales, police in many jurisdictions have been besieged with complaints from residents of neighborhoods where drug dealers and "dope houses" operate. In addition, there has been significant political and media pressure for metropolitan police departments and Federal law enforcement agencies to "do something" about drug sales in U.S. cities.

In response, Congress has recently stiffened the penalties for those who traffic in or use drugs, and it has committed greater resources to aid the war against drugs. The 1988 Anti-Drug Bill signed into law on November 18, 1988, provides Federal assistance to communities for treatment, prevention, education, and drug enforcement programs.

LAW ENFORCEMENT RESPONDS

At all levels, law enforcement agencies are stepping up their activities. They are joining hands with schools to help children resist drugs in prevention efforts such as Project DARE. Local law enforcement agencies are cooperating with each other in the fight. The International Association of Chiefs of Police recently reported, for example, that approximately 72 percent of the departments they surveyed participated in multijurisdictional drug enforcement task forces.[5]

A number of police departments, particularly in large metropolitan areas, are using new approaches in conjunction with more traditional ones. They are targeting alternative strategies against street sales and users and retaining traditional strategies for enforcement efforts against the kingpins and producers.

Control of drug supplies is generally a Federal responsibility, but Federal law enforcement agencies regularly receive help from State and local personnel through regional, statewide, or citywide task forces. Supply control efforts at the Federal level include source crop eradication, shipment interdiction, asset seizure and forfeiture, and investigations into organized crime and money laundering. These strategies are often interrelated.

In dealing with midlevel distribution, local law enforcement agencies use some of these same traditional approaches. They form task forces and employ interdiction strategies. They also use the traditional undercover and surveillance techniques that lead to search and arrest warrants against midlevel distributors. Where midlevel distribution is controlled by gangs, police emphasize gang enforcement investigations.

Street sales enforcement is almost exclusively a local responsibility. Among such traditional tactics are undercover surveillance and "buy busts," in which undercover officers buy drugs on the street and then arrest the sellers. Arresting drug dealers for possession and for possession with intent to distribute is another strategy traditionally employed at this stage.

Finally, at the end of the distribution chain, police arrest individual users for possession.

NEW STRATEGIES JOIN THE OLD

A number of new approaches are being tried against street sales and users, primarily by larger metropolitan police departments under funding from the Bureau of Justice Assistance and the National Institute of Justice. The newer approaches are not necessarily discrete; some departments combine several to mount a comprehensive attack on drug sales.

Nor are all of the "new" techniques entirely new. Some, like crackdowns and civil abatement procedures, are refinements of techniques police have long been using to deal with prostitution, for instance. The innovation is their application to combating drug sales. The new approaches, like the old ones, are designed to disrupt drug distribution through incapacitation and deterrence, with the ultimate goal of reducing drug consumption, street and property crime, and violence.

At the street-sales level, the new efforts can be roughly categorized as street enforcement, crack enforcement, problem-oriented policing, and citizen-oriented enforcement. Asset seizure and forfeiture also play a role, most often as integral parts of these other strategies. Figure 15.1 presents a summary of both traditional and innovative strategies for local enforcement of drug laws.

STREET AND CRACK ENFORCEMENT

Both street enforcement and crack enforcement are street-sales oriented; street programs deal with all types of drug sales, and crack programs focus on sales of this increasingly popular drug. These programs target drug sales locations and the street distributors themselves. Police use surveillance, informants, and information from drug hotlines to locate street sales and identify sellers.

Undertaking street enforcement and crack enforcement programs means increasing police personnel hours for narcotics control. Narcotics staff or tactical squads may work overtime, or patrol officers may be assigned to street-sales enforcement duty.

Specific police strategies depend on the nature of the drug problem. In cities where distribution takes place primarily through fortified crack houses, tactical or narcotics squads use search and arrest warrants, sometimes gaining entry by using heavy construction equipment. Where street sales are commonplace, the police may conduct saturation patrols or periodic large-scale arrests of suspected dealers in drug hot spots. These are frequently referred to as "sweeps" or "roundups."

Civil enforcement procedures are gaining acceptance as well, and police are relying more and more on asset seizure at the distribution level. For example, if a house is being used as a crack house, the police typically notify the owner—through the public works department or the city attorney's office—that the property is being used for illegal drug sales. If the owner fails to take action, civil seizure of the property takes place and the house may be forfeited or even destroyed.

Street and crack enforcement strategies make use of building and fire code enforcement, along with tenant eviction if the property is rented. In jurisdictions where public housing projects are the center of drug sales, the police and public housing authorities cooperate in securing tenant evictions and enforcing lease conditions.

Many innovative street enforcement programs focus on the purchaser and user of illegal narcotics. Police keep drug sales hotspots under surveillance and arrest both purchasers and sellers. Where it is permitted, police seize user assets, such as automobiles.

Another innovative approach is the "reverse sting," in which undercover police pose as drug dealers and arrest users who ask to buy narcotics or actually engage in what they assume is a drug transaction. User arrests may take place at the time of the sale or later in large-scale roundups of suspects, depending on the users' transience. This strategy is not as common as some of the others because of legal and operational concerns about police posing as dealers and engaging in what look like actual drug sales.

Some 17 cities across the United States are using street and crack enforcement programs administered by the Institute for Law and Justice and funded by the Bureau of Justice Assistance through its Narcotics Control Technical Assistance Program.

PROBLEM-ORIENTED POLICING

Problem-oriented approaches apply the model successfully developed in Newport News, Virginia.[6] Under this approach, police collect and analyze data on individuals, incidents, and police responses to crimes as the first step in developing particular prevention or enforcement strategies. The Police Executive Research Forum is currently managing the implementation of this approach in five cities with funds from the Bureau of Justice Assistance.

Instead of relying on subjective or anecdotal assessments of their local drug problem, police departments employing problem-oriented policing techniques collect and analyze objective data like crime statistics and citizen surveys. By looking at drug-arrest data, police in some cities have found that young adults are the group most actively involved in the drug trade; in other cities they have found juveniles to be the more heavily involved group.

Problem analysis often shows that many conditions that are not the responsibility of the police—such as the presence of abandoned buildings and the lack of recreational facilities—contribute to a city's drug problem.[7]

CITIZEN-ORIENTED POLICING

The premise of the citizen-oriented model of policing is that the police cannot solve the drug problem alone but must join with the community in controlling crime and ensuring public safety. The National Institute of Justice is evaluating implementation of the citizen-oriented approach to fighting drugs in several jurisdictions.

Local citizens establish community groups to eliminate the conditions that contribute to neighborhood drug sales. In Seattle, for example, citizens have set up their own drug hotline, pressured the legislature for new abatement laws and jail space, and conducted neighborhood cleanup projects.[8] The distinctive feature of this approach is that a major responsibility for breaking the drug distribution chain rests not just with the police but also with neighborhood groups who work hand in hand with the police.

EVALUATING THE STRATEGIES

While research in the 1970's examined conventional narcotics enforcement in selected jurisdictions,[9] little is known about the effect of more recent police innovations. A number of primarily descriptive assessments of the evolution or implementation of particular programs exist,[10] but scientific and professional law enforcement literature contains only limited quantitative evidence on program effects.

Reports of program outputs (actions of police) rather than program outcomes (reduction in crime) have been published. Some authors report that local enforcement efforts have resulted in more drug confiscation, seizures, and arrests.[11] These findings are not surprising. When greater resources are focused on a problem, higher program output can be expected.

Yet recent evaluations of some specific programs in several cities indicate that innovative law enforcement may indeed be affecting drug distribution. In Lynn, Massachusetts, a vigorous street-level enforcement program attacked an open, active heroin trade in the city.

Six State troopers and a detective from the Lynn Police Department were assigned to a drug task force to crack down on street sales by making such transactions more difficult. By using undercover operations, surveillance, and information gathered from a drug hotline, police made more arrests and executed more search warrants in the targeted area. Following this crack-down, heroin consumption appeared to decline, robberies and burglaries decreased sharply, and the very visible street sales traffic disappeared with no evidence of displacement into substitute markets in the city.[12]

New York City implemented Operation Pressure Point—a vigorous street-level enforcement program in Manhattan.[13] During the operation's initial phase, narcotics enforcement was strengthened and a highly visible saturation patrol was initiated, leading to a substantial increase in narcotics and misdemeanor arrests. Traffic and parking enforcement efforts in the area were also stepped up. The results resembled Lynn's: many open markets were closed and crime was reduced. It was unclear, however, if displacement of the markets occurred.[14]

Evaluations of other street-level efforts, however, showed different outcomes. In Lawrence, Massachusetts, for example, a program similar to Lynn's did not seem to affect robbery and burglary rates, and alternative street markets in neighboring jurisdictions appeared to draw purchasers away from Lawrence so that the trade did not decline in real terms.[15]

While the research conducted thus far is limited and the findings mixed, evaluations currently under way hold promise of useful findings. The Police Foundation, under a National Institute of Justice grant, is assessing the effects of community-oriented street-level enforcement in Birmingham, Alabama and Oakland, California.[16]

In both these cities, research in measuring the effects of street enforcement and police-community contact on crime, on citizens' perceptions and fears of crime, and on other attitudes. In one area of Oakland, police implemented a door-to-door campaign to stimulate police-citizen interaction. In a second area they implemented a rapid undercover response to drug hotline calls, and in a third they used both strategies. The effects in these areas are being compared to those in a control area.

In Seattle, a study is evaluating the implementation of the citizen-oriented policing strategy. The research will examine the problems incurred and the reactions of the public, the police, and other agencies.

Figure 15.1
Local Law Enforcement Strategies Against Drugs

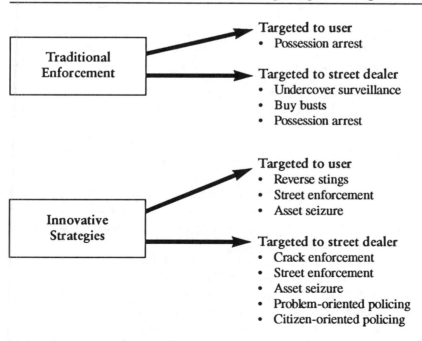

More and more, local law enforcement agencies are diversifying their strategies for combating drugs, variably targeting users and street sellers, and combining traditional techniques with newer approaches.

QUESTIONS FOR FUTURE STUDY

Upcoming research must address a number of issues so that sound conclusions can be drawn about the utility of the innovative approaches discussed in this article. Answers to the following questions will aid informed policy choices:

- What is the exact nature and extent of the drug problem in our cities? Many departments implementing new strategies lack baseline data or the analysis capability to assess the problem.

- What is the link between drug use and crime and what is meant by drug-related crime?

- To what extent is implementation of innovative strategies coopted in favor of "tried and true" traditional methods?

- Some of the new approaches call for quite different police responses from the reactive ones developed over the past few decades. Are there particular organizational or management factors that contribute to the potential success or failure of these new approaches?

- What are the long-term consequences, if any, of these new programs?

- How do these programs compare in cost and effectiveness with other approaches, such as education, interdiction, and traditional narcotics investigation techniques?

- Do the programs reduce drug sales? Or do they just disperse them to other locations?

NIJ PROMOTES INFORMATION SHARING

The foregoing summary describes some of the innovations in drug-law enforcement now taking place. Other new approaches, such as information system development and cooperative programs with prosecutors' offices, are also currently being tried.

The National Institute is planning to study some of the more innovative programs in a number of cities. The effort will begin with visits to several jurisdictions to discuss new drug enforcement efforts with police officials and operational personnel and observe some of these approaches in operation. By comparing these programs and their effects with traditional strategies, the Institute can give useful information to local agencies considering such innovations.

Agencies planning or currently implementing additional innovative approaches to drug enforcement are invited to share information. Contact David Hayeslip at the National Institute of Justice, 633 Indiana Avenue NW., Washington, DC 20531, telephone 1-202-724-2962.

NOTES

1. *Time*, May 30, 1988. "Thinking the Unthinkable." p. 14.
2. George Gallup, Jr., 1985. *The Gallup Report*, Report No. 235. Princeton, New Jersey, The Gallup Poll, pp. 20-21.
3. National Institute of Justice, 1988. "Attorney General Announces NIJ Drug Use Forecasting System," *NIJ Reports*, No. 208. March/April 1988. Washington, D.C., NIJ, p. 8.
4. Ibid.
5. International Association of Chiefs of Police, June 1988. *Reducing Crime by Reducing Drug Abuse: A Manual for Police Chiefs and Sheriffs*. Gaithersburg, Maryland, IACP, p. 65.
6. William Spelman and John E. Eck, 1987. "Newport News Tests Problem-Oriented Policing," *NIJ Reports*, No. 201, January/February 1987. Washington, D.C., NIJ, p. 2.
7. Tia Clark, 1988. "Cuyler: A Joint Effort," *Problem Solving Quarterly*, Vol. 1, No. 3, p. 4.
8. For additional information concerning the South Seattle Crime Reduction Project, contact George D. Shollenberger, Program Manager, Public Safety and Security, National Institute of Justice, 1-202-724-2596.
9. See for example: L.B. DeFleur, 1975, "Biasing Influences on Drug Arrest Records: Implications for Deviance Research," *American Sociological Review*, 40, pp. 88-103; P. Manning, 1980, *The Narc's Game: Organizational and Informational Limits on Drug Law Enforcement*, Cambridge, Massachusetts, MIT Press; W.F. McDonald, 1973, "Administratively Choosing the Drug Criminal: Police Discretion in the Enforcement of Drug Laws," *Journal of Drug Issues*, Spring, pp. 123-124; M. Moore, 1977, *Buy and Bust: The Effective Regulation of an Illicit Market in Heroin*, Lexington, Massachusetts, D.C. Heath; J. Skolnick, 1975, *Justice Without Trial*, New York, John Wiley and Sons; and J. Williams et al., 1979, *Police Narcotics Control: Patterns and Strategies*, Washington, D.C., U.S. Government Printing Office.
10. For example, Jack Crowley, 1986. "A Community Helps Put a 'CAP' on Drug Pushers," *Law and Order*, December, pp. 136-139.
11. For example, Institute for Law and Justice, 1988, "Crack Enforcement Program: Minneapolis," *Narcotics Control Technical Assistance Program Newsletter*, Vol. 2, No. 3, p. 1.
12. Mark Kleiman, *Bringing Back Street-Level Heroin Enforcement*, summarized in NIJ Reports, No. 202, March/April 1987, Washington, D.C. NIJ, p. 5.
13. Bocklet, Richard, 1987. "Operation Pressure Point," *Law and Order*, February, pp. 48-52.
14. Mark Kleiman, 1988. "Crackdowns: The Effects of Intensive Enforcement on Retail Heroin Dealing" in *Street Level Drug Enforcement: Examining the Issues*, Marcia Chaiken (ed.), Washington, D.C. NIJ.
15. Ibid.
16. For additional information, contact Dr. Craig Uchida, National Institute of Justice, 1-202-724-2959.

A CASE STUDY OF A POLICE DEPARTMENT'S RESPONSE TO STRICTER DRUNK-DRIVING LAWS

16

Stephen D. Mastrofski & R. Richard Ritti

> Glendower: I can call spirits from the vasty deep.
> Hotspur: Why, so can I, or so can any man;
> But will they come when you do call for them?
> –Shakespeare, *Henry IV, Part I,* III.i (53)

From time to time legislatures struggle mightily to produce major changes in the criminal law in response to popular or professional pressures. Sometimes an act that once was legal is made criminal, such as the manufacture and distribution of alcoholic beverages (the Volstead Act.). Sometimes the penalties for an existing crime are increased, such as the so-called "Rockefeller drug laws" in New York State in the early 1970s. And sometimes what once was criminal is decriminalized, or at least made a less serious offense (e.g., public drunkenness). Such enactments often represent the culmination of an important political drama, but one that is essentially symbolic, because the struggle to pass the law is a struggle about what shall be *written* into law. Like Glendower's summons, these laws evoke powerful forces—law enforcement agencies in this case, instead of demons. In the case of criminal laws passed by *states* for enforcement by *local* police, the metaphor of "vasty deep" seems apt because the latter are often far removed from the former, both geographically and in orientation to the issue at hand. Like Hotspur, then, we are led to wonder what police agencies will do when called to implement major changes in the criminal law.

Source: Stephen D. Mastrofski and R. Richard Ritti (1992). "A Case Study of a Police Department's Response to Stricter Drunk-Driving Laws." *Justice Quarterly,* 9(3):465-491. Reprinted by permission of the Academy of Criminal Justice Sciences.

In this paper we are concerned with the police reaction to changes in drunk-driving, or driving-under-the-influence (DUI), laws. Recent changes in drunk-driving laws around the nation have created an expectation of increased DUI enforcement. We argue that the police implementation of the new laws lacks uniformity because the organizations responsible for enforcement are local and are influenced heavily by local extralegal considerations. We briefly discuss the characteristics of local police organizations and their relationship to DUI enforcement levels. Then we illustrate the play between these characteristics and police DUI enforcement practices in a case study analysis of one police department.

DUI LEGAL REFORM IN THE 1980s

During the 1980s most states passed tougher drunk-driving laws following the "Scandinavian model": 1) a per se standard of evidence requiring only proof that the driver's blood alcohol level exceed a given threshold, 2) vigorous enforcement using breath and blood tests, and 3) severe sentences, including mandatory incarceration and loss of license (Jacobs 1989:123-26). Rationales for these changes included just deserts, deterrence, incapacitation, and even rehabilitation. Whatever the rationale, however, successful implementation requires higher drunk-driving arrest rates.

A number of scholars have pointed out that before the 1980s American criminal justice officials, reflecting widespread popular values, rarely treated drunk driving as a serious offense (Brown 1981; Gusfield 1981; Jacobs 1989; Reinarman 1988). Yet there are many reasons to expect police to respond dramatically after the flurry of drunk-driving legislation that swept the United States in the first half of the last decade. This issue achieved nationwide attention with astounding speed. Grass-roots campaigns by Mothers Against Drunk Drivers (MADD), Remove Intoxicated Drivers (RID), Students Against Drunk Drivers (SADD), and other groups received a great deal of attention from the press. A 1982 Gallup national survey showed that 89 percent of respondents favored stricter DUI laws, and 77 percent favored a two-day jail term for first offenders (Flanagan and McLeod 1983:287). A 1987 National Punishment Survey showed that the public rated a drunk driver who killed someone as commiting a crime slightly more serious than someone who raped a victim without causing other physical injury. Someone who drove drunk but did not cause an accident was rated as a slightly more serious offender than an unarmed robber who took $10 from a victim without causing bodily harm. In the case of death due to the DUI accident, 91 percent of respondents favored incarcerating the offender; in the case of the drunk driver who caused no accident, 54 percent favored incarceration (Flanagan and Jamieson 1988:150-51).

Not only have public attitudes shifted significantly, but the antidrunk-driving movement has been institutionalized in the proliferation of grass-roots citizen groups, state-supported anti-DUI programs, and federal interest in drunk driving as a national problem (Jacobs 1989:196). The availability of state and federal funds to undertake DUI enforcement is an incentive to local police departments to field special DUI enforcement programs; these programs endure despite fluctuations in the public's concern about drunk driving. Perhaps most important for local police, the rapid growth of citizens' antidrunk-driving groups means that local special interest groups are paying attention to drunk driving in their communities, thus increasing the likelihood that drunk driving remains on the local political and law enforcement agenda (Reinarman 1988).

Several features of the drunk driving offense itself should make rigorous enforcement attractive to police. Compared to other types of offenses, especially those occurring in private places, enforcement opportunities are plentiful and accessible to police (see Jacobs 1989:43-47 for estimates). The law affords police greater power to stop and question drivers of automobiles than to intervene with pedestrians and citizens in private places. Also, in view of the kind of evidence provided by breath and blood tests, a conviction is far more likely. In addition, because DUI arrests can be (and usually are) accomplished without a citizen complainant or a witness, the administrator can consider an officer's DUI arrests to be mostly the product of his or her own initiative and skill. Consequently, administrators who want to increase arrest rates presumably can exert some direct control over officers whose DUI activity is subpar. Thus police departments can use the DUI law to demonstrate their commitment to law enforcement in a manner that features organizational productivity.

Despite several indicators of a climate favoring DUI enforcement over the last decade, the police response appears to be quite variable. According to the Uniform Crime Reports, different types of communities show substantially different changes in DUI arrest rates. Between 1975 and 1985, for example, the DUI arrest rate per capita increased 69 percent in cities of 100,000 to 249,999 population, but only 38 percent in communities of fewer than 10,000 persons (U.S. Department of Justice 1989:169). In 1985 the DUI arrest rate per 100,000 population ranged from 78 in Delaware of 1,260 in California (Flanagan and Jamieson 1988:398).[1]

A FRAMEWORK FOR UNDERSTANDING THE IMPLEMENTATION OF DUI LAWS

The enactment of legislation raises questions of implementation, and that implementation has been described metaphorically as a system of "games" involving a variety of players who have some stake in how the legislation is carried out (Bardach 1977). The stakes in the games associated with the implementation of any law will vary. Control of the implementation process is the principal object of these games, which consist of various tactics and strategies by stakeholders. Several types of games disrupt successful implementation: those involving the diversion of resources to carry out the law, the deflection of goals from the lawmakers' original intent, disruptions to effective administrative control of the implementation process, and the dissipation of energies in other games. Such an analytic framework invites a particular approach to analyzing the implementation of legislation:

> It directs us to look at the players, what they regard as the stakes, their strategies and tactics, their resources for playing, the rules of play (which stipulate the conditions for winning), the rules of "fair" play (which stipulate the boundaries beyond which lie fraud or illegitimacy), the nature of the communications (or lack of them) among the players, and the degree of uncertainty surrounding the possible outcomes. The game metaphor also directs our attention to who is not willing to play and for what reasons, and who insists on changes in some of the game's parameters as a condition for playing (Bardach, 1977:56).

Who are the players in the DUI enforcement games? State agencies are not irrelevant, but their impact is usually quite limited. States characteristically do *not* set up special agencies to monitor the local enforcement of criminal laws, as they often do with various civil and regulatory laws (e.g., equal employment, environmental, labor, antitrust).[2] Indeed, states rarely provide additional funds for the enforcement of new criminal laws (Casper and Brereton 1984).[3] Even though the nationalization of drunk driving as an issue and the passage of tougher laws undoubtedly have stimulated enforcement,[4] a great deal of scholarship on law enforcement in America, directs our attention to *local* players to predict DUI enforcement levels (Gardiner 1969; Goldstein 1977; Langworthy 1985; Ostrom, Parks, and Whitaker 1978; Slovak 1986; Wilson 1968; Wilson and Boland 1978). Local factors are the screen through which the effects of the broader trend must be filtered.

The "DUI enforcement game," then, is played on local turf and dominated by local players. Elsewhere we have argued that precisely who plays, how they play, and the consequences for DUI enforcement levels are determined largely by several environmental and organizational factors: 1) the local demand for drunk-driving enforcement, 2) the police administration's priority for DUI and control of the organization, and 4) the disposition of the local police culture regarding drunk driving and related work issues (Mastrofski, Ritti, and Hoffmaster 1987).

DEMAND FOR DUI ENFORCEMENT

The everyday work of police is determined mostly by the demands placed on the department by its citizens through "calls for service" (Goldstein 1990:20). Virtually every American police department places top priority on responding to calls for service; unless a routine crime comes to police attention through this mechanism, a special effort by the department's leader is required to divert resources for DUI enforcement. Drunk-driving offenses rarely come to police attention because of a citizen's complaint; *police*-initiated enforcement is needed to achieve arrest levels beyond the relatively few offenses made known to police from reported accidents (Jacobs 1989:110). Making a DUI arrest is time-consuming, however; sometimes it takes four hours to process. An officer can commit this kind of time only if resources are adequate to handle the calls for service workload or if the department is willing to reduce the level of response to calls for service. From the rational administrator's perspective, it seems risky to fail to respond to a specific request for service. Nonresponse produces a disgruntled citizen, whereas the failure to stop or arrest a potential drunk driver rarely generates a specific complaint about police service.

Because the police rarely experience demand for DUI enforcement through calls for service, the principal source of pressure, when it is experienced at all, is the demand for action by politically salient local "players." Characteristically, such pressure originates with citizens' groups, elected officials, candidates for local office, heads of human service agencies, and the press. The nature and the extent of external pressure for DUI enforcement establish the stakes of the DUI enforcement game and determine the risks associated with the tactics employed by the players.[5] When these pressures are sufficiently high, the police chief ignores or opposes them only at great peril. Where the political pressures about drunk driving are not strong, the risks of ignoring the problem or assigning it a low priority are modest. A police administrator, however, may seize upon DUI in entrepreneurial fashion, crusading to create an issue, solve a problem, and help establish an identity for himself and the department (Bullington and Block 1990). In this way, someone in the police organization fashions a benefit from initiating DUI enforcement, even when the stakes (initially at least) are low. This strategy is risky, however, because the crusading chief must quickly develop community support or else face any opposition that arises without allies.

PRIORITIES OF THE POLICE ADMINISTRATION

Setting agency priorities is one of the key functions of top administrators. Wilson (1968) argued that the selection of the chief is the most significant influence that local elected officials can exert on their police department. It is the chief who articulates the department's general goals, sets its operational priorities, and establishes an ethos for accomplishing them (e.g., through professionalism). Gardiner (1969) found that the principal determinant of traffic enforcement was management policy, but a number of subsequent analyses have called these findings into question. Managerial priorities appear not to play a dominating role in directing arrest patterns generally (Aaronson, Dienes, and Musheno 1984; Brown 1981; Klockars 1985; Manning 1977; Muir 1977) or in DUI arrest patterns specifically (Mastrofski et al. 1987). Still, a police administrator rarely states publicly that enforcement of *any* offense is a low priority, because such a statement would belie the convenient fiction that the law is being enforced fully (Klockars 1985).

POLICE ADMINISTRATORS' COMMAND AND CONTROL CAPACITY

A chief who wishes to give drunk-driving enforcement a high priority must do so by shaping patrol officers' street-level discretion. Probably the most frequent management approach to persuading the rank and file is simply exhortation—arguing for a particular perspective and providing what the chief believes are compelling reasons for that view. For example, the chief may highlight the threat to highway safety posed by drunk drivers and may even invite citizen advocate groups to address officers, giving the victim's perspective on drunk driving.

The department also may influence the socialization of those people it selects as police by the way it trains them—both initially and throughout their careers. The amount and quality of recruit training devoted to DUI enforcement not only signals the department's commitment; it also provides the basic knowledge and skills necessary to do the job correctly and in a way that will not embarrass the officer in court. Assigning rookies to work with experienced officers who have a commitment to DUI enforcement is another way of reinforcing DUI efforts.

A third major way in which administrators shape their subordinates' behavior is to reward and punish them on the basis of their adherence to policies, rules, and priorities. The chief can issue policies and directives specifying the procedures for identifying, arresting, and processing drunk drivers, and he can order his subordinates to commit their efforts to this purpose. To make those policies meaningful, the chief must have the capacity to monitor officers' DUI arrest productivity, and he must have sufficient influence over factors that matter to officers, namely job benefits and career opportunities. The chief also must have control over disciplinary actions: He must be able to withhold significant work benefits and to censure, suspend, and even dismiss officers who fail to perform adequately or who misbehave. Few chiefs, however, especially in large departments, enjoy this kind of power.[6] Their capacity to offer positive reinforcement is typically limited to distributing desirable job assignments and training opportunities. The capacity to offer direct financial rewards for arrests is constrained severely by personnel rules, although administrators sometimes can offer *indirect* financial rewards by influencing the disbursement of over-time pay (often this is a factor in time-consuming DUI arrests). Yet because administrators' capacity to influence all of these factors is modest at best, the real power of the top administrator and the rest of the supervisory hier-archy is to make the officers' work environment the least onerous possi-ble. They can do so by protecting officers from outside censure and internal discipline when their enforcement initiatives generate complaints (Muir 1977; Van Maanen 1983). They also can make it as easy and effi-cient as possible to process DUI arrests.

In view of the widely acknowledged importance of the street-level offi-cer's discretion in determining actual enforcement practices, the police administrator's command and control capacity depends on his power to recruit and indoctrinate officers with his priorities and to reward and dis-cipline them accordingly. The stronger the command and control capacity, the greater the likelihood that the administrator will secure enforcement practices consistent with his priority for DUI enforcement—whatever that priority might be. Some literature suggests that strong interaction effects sometimes exist between external pressure for police practice and the com-mand and control capacity; police chiefs who are willing and able to take advantage of strong crisis-generated pressure to change practices control-ling lethal force and corruption have enjoyed some success in reducing the level of undesired incidents (Sherman 1977; 1983; Fyfe 1979).

INFORMAL SOCIAL CONTROL

In addition to the formal system of hierarchical control, police organi-zations have informal systems that influence the exercise of street-level dis-cretion on matters such as DUI enforcement. A number of scholars have noted this bifurcation of control in police departments, and refer to the loosely structured informal system as a police subculture reflecting the val-ues, beliefs, and orientations of the rank and file (Manning 1977; 1989; Reuss-Ianni, 1983; Rubinstein 1973; Skolnick 1966; Van Maanen 1974). Evi-dence suggests that the rank and file vary considerably in their law enforce-ment priorities (Broderick 1977; Brown 1981; Muir 1977; Worden 1989); patterns in these belief systems may reflect a particular *local* police cul-ture, much as members of the courtroom work group have been found to vary in their local legal culture (Eisenstein, Flemming, and Nardulli 1988).

The tendency of the rank and file to be actively engaged in DUI enforcement has been found to influence the level of DUI arrests in depart-ments, independent of management directives (Mastrofski et al. 1987). Particularly interesting is the prospect that increasingly heterogeneous police forces will not show a single, uniform orientation to a task such as DUI enforcement, but rather will demonstrate diversity through cliques that reinforce divergent enforcement perspectives (Mastrofski 1990;8-17). Perhaps strong support (or opposition) by a small group of officers will have a disproportionate effect on the department's performance in DUI enforcement.

Although the values, beliefs, and orientations of the rank and file are explicit objects of the police hierarchy's formal system of command and control, the local police culture clearly responds very slowly, if at all, if only because it is easier to change police administrators (by firing, hiring, and demotion) than the rank and file. The local police culture therefore is always a potential force in shaping a department's DUI enforcement practices, particularly when the formal command and control capacity is weak. This is the chronic state of police departments that Wilson characterized as having the "watchman" style (1968:ch.5).

We have suggested that several local factors determine how vigorously the new DUI laws will be enforced. Much of the literature on police organizations suggests that a causal chain links these factors, beginning with the political environment and ending with the performance of the rank and file, as reflected in patterns of arrest (Gardiner 1969; Langworthy 1985; Slovak 1986; Wilson 1968; Wilson and Boland 1978). In his volume on drunk driving in America, James Jacobs argued that this model indeed operates for DUI enforcement:

> [T]he police do respond to pressure; they do shape their priorities according to the wishes of the public; interest groups and public opinion have succeeded in making drunk driving enforcement a higher priority (1989:112).

Most research on policy implementation, however, suggests that the causal link between political climate, formal policy, and actual practice are very weak (Palumbo and Calista 1990). Therefore we are inclined to suspect that these factors interact in more complex, less predictable ways. Thus, even in the face of strong environmental pressure for vigorous implementation of laws such as the drunk driving reforms, the impetus for change will be dissipated. Where external pressure for more DUI enforcement is weak or nonexistent, such links would appear to be even more tenuous. These, in fact, are the conditions of the case study we will present; we suspect that the relatively low level of pressure for DUI enforcement in this case is typical of communities that account for the majority of the country's population. Under these conditions, we would expect the formal policies and actions of the government leaders and police administration to be less relevant to determining enforcement levels than the agency's less visible but more pervasive *informal* social system.

Drunk-Driving Enforcement in Pennsylvania

In 1983 Pennsylvania instituted a DUI law similar to those being passed in other states in the early 1980s. It included a per se rule of evidence, mandatory jail sentences for convicted offenders,[7] a mandatory one-year license suspension, and severe restrictions on prosecutorial and judicial discretion to reduce charges (other than dismissal for cause).

The new law and the publicity surrounding its development seem to have stimulated DUI arrests in Pennsylvania: they increased 40 percent between 1981 and 1987. Yet except for a one-year decline following passage of the law, the number of alcohol-related fatal accidents has moved upward (Pennsylvania Commission on Crime and Delinquency 1988). In addition, comparison of DUI arrest rates to those of other northeastern states shows that Pennsylvania rates are among the lowest.

A 1989 survey of Pennsylvania police agencies with one or more full-time sworn officers revealed tremendous variation in the DUI arrest rate for that year.[8] Table 16.1 shows that on average, the arrest rate in departments in the smallest size category (one to five sworn) was more than three times that of the largest department (more than 100 sworn). The table also shows considerable within category variation in the DUI arrest rate: some categories ranged from zero to 20 DUI arrests per officer. So it appears that Pennsylvania police organizations react in quite different ways when "summoned from the vasty deep" to enforce drunk-driving laws.

Table 16.1
Pennsylvania DUI Arrests per Officer, by Department Size, 1989

Number of Officers In Department	Number of Departments	Mean Number of Arrests	Standard Deviation
1-5	373	4.50	4.80
6-10	168	3.66	3.24
11-25	135	3.06	2.54
26-50	36	2.50	1.60
51-100	11	2.58	1.69
>100	12	1.31	.64
Entire Sample	735	3.86	3.99

In the remainder of the paper we report the findings of a case study of Melville (a fictional name), one of these Pennsylvania police departments. Focusing on the organizational characteristics discussed earlier, our analysis will show that in order to understand Melville's response to Pennsylvania's DUI law, we must consider in detail the complex ways in which features of the police organization and its environment interact. In this case the interaction produces results that would not be predicted from a routine statistical analysis of organizational characteristics.

METHODS

We conducted intensive field research in Melville during late 1989 and early 1990. Two field researchers spent more than two weeks on site, during which they conducted in-depth interviews with department administrators, supervisors, police officers, court officials, representatives of citizens' groups, and the press. More than 30 such interviews were conducted, and varied in length from 20 minutes to two hours.[9] We also held casual discussions with police around the station house and observed officers at work, including the arrest and processing of drunk drivers. In addition, we administered an anonymous survey questionnaire to more than 100 uniformed officers to obtain their views and experiences regarding drunk driving.[10] The department provided a variety of documents, records, and reports. In 1990 we also conducted a telephone survey of 232 randomly selected licensed drivers over age 21.[11]

DUI ENFORCEMENT IN MELVILLE

Melville is one of a dozen Pennsylvania departments with 100 or more full-time police officers. From 1982 (the year before the state's new DUI law took effect) to 1985, DUI arrests per officer in Melville climbed from 1.3 to 1.6, an average annual increase of more than 7 percent. By 1988, however, the department's arrest rate had returned to 1.3. Melville, though well below the average for all departments in Pennsylvania, was average for its size category (1.3) and nearly three times greater than the line of best fit would predict from a regression of arrest rate on department size. The most intriguing finding is that Melville's DUI arrest rate is as *high* at it is, in view of the department's and certain other organizational and environmental features. Indeed, the analysis that follows suggests that a substantial number of drunk driving arrests in Melville were made *despite* a number of organizational policies and informal norms that conspired against it.

Melville's police appear to have ample opportunity to apprehend drunk drivers. Melville has a great variety of roadways: state and federal highways, commercial strips, a downtown, and residential neighborhoods. The city has a large number of public drinking establishments; its wine and spirit consumption is well above that of most counties in the state. Melville has a significant college student population in residence. The city also attracts many out-of-town visitors to various sports, cultural, and business events. The absolute number of alcohol-related fatalities reported is typically among the highest in the state.

Demand for DUI Enforcement

Melville feels little pressure from the state to pursue DUIs. In the 1970s the department had received state funds for overtime associated with DUI enforcement, but its administrators were unable to recall any such state or federal support in the years since the 1983 law. State law allows local jurisdictions to receive some of the funds generated by its DUI offenders' fines, but the department was unable to point to any such funds in its treasury. The state Department of Transportation, the principal source of state DUI-related enforcement funds, does not routinely monitor individual police agencies' DUI arrest productivity. Indirectly the state makes a variety of DUI training programs available to Pennsylvania police, but each department may choose the extent of participation. The only state requirement for DUI training is found in the minimum requirements for municipal officers' recruit training, approximately 10 of the required 520 hours.

At the local level the demand for drunk-driving enforcement in Melville is not particularly strong. Other matters dominate the police-related political agenda: drugs, relations with poor and minority citizens, hiring practices, maintaining levels of service, and the distribution of services to various segments of the community. Drunk-driving enforcement has not been an issue in recent or earlier campaigns for local elected office. From time to time the local press discusses the subject in its editorials, and occasionally it features stories in which the courts seem to downplay the seriousness of a case.

Local court officials are proud of the county's high conviction rate in drunk-driving cases, but the district attorney pointedly avoids publicity campaigns to heighten citizens' concern about specific crimes. The DA prides himself on running a very "professional" office; his chief assistant stated, "We don't have a crime of the month or year!" The prosecutors pay attention mainly to technical issues. The prosecutor's office tries to be consistent in its decisions on individual cases: "We preach to out people not to get into a persecution mode. We don't want improper prosecutions." The office is very influential in determining who is offered pretrial diversion from the criminal process (for rehabilitative purposes) and on what terms. Most first offenders receive diversion; the restrictiveness of the terms is determined on a scale reflecting the blood-alcohol level of the offender. Thus the district attorney's office strives to provide a measured, deliberate, and professional climate for DUI enforcement, one that avoids inflaming public passions.

The most sharply focused support for DUI enforcement comes from a county chapter of Mothers Against Drunk Drivers (MADD). Formed in the early 1980s, this chapter spent its first few years publicizing the issue and lobbying state policy makers for changes in the law. By 1989 the membership had grown considerably and the organization's objectives became more diverse; victim assistance played an increasingly central role. Recently the organization had participated in a "red ribbon" public awareness campaign, in which drivers were urged to tie ribbons to their car door handles to signify their concern about the drunk driving problem and their support for vigorous enforcement of the DUI laws. Melville's mayor served as the chair of this campaign. The chapter also routinely provides lectures and presentations regarding drunk driving to schools, businesses, and civic groups.

The group's monitoring of DUI enforcement is focused on the court. The chapter does not attempt to monitor all cases, but relies on tips from callers that an offender may be receiving undue leniency or inattention. Volunteer members who specialize in this function then call the district attorney's office and ask about the status of the case. The MADD chapter and the DA's office report a good working relationship. The chapter rarely investigates police enforcement practices. Indeed, the group avoids any action that appears to be adversarial or confrontational with the police departments in the county; it prefers to nurture a "cooperative relationship" that emphasizes shared concern about drunk driving. A recent example is the chapter's purchase of video cameras for county area police departments, including Melville, to tape DUI arrests.

The quiescence of most of Melville's public about the need for drunk-driving enforcement was mentioned consistently in interviews with administrators, supervisors, and patrol officers. The need for increased DUI enforcement is hardly ever raised at community meetings and gripe sessions. Other issues appear to be more important to the public; most frequently they complain about violent crime, drugs, theft, vandalism, and minor disorders (e.g., unruly juveniles). Neighborhoods are more interested in obtaining foot patrols than in drunk driving enforcement. The telephone survey of Melville's licensed drivers reinforces the picture presented by police: only 5 percent stated that DUI enforcement was their top priority, compared to more than 50 percent who cited violent crime or drugs.[12]

The workload demand on the Melville police appears to be higher than in other departments in the state. The number of Part 1 and Part 2 UCR offenses per officer is among the highest in Pennsylvania. Administrators and officers repeatedly mention the difficulty of meeting a heavy citizen demand for a variety of services, many of which require special details that do not show up in calls-for-service statistics (e.g., regulating traffic for special events). The demand for these services is mentioned frequently by officers and administrators as a significant constraint on their capacity to look for, arrest, and process drunk drivers.

THE CHIEF'S PRIORITIES

DUI enforcement is not a departmental priority in Melville. Violent crimes, burglary, auto theft, drug dealing, and simply keeping up with the demand for service are the leading concerns of top management. The principal issues for local elected officials are economic development and race relations. The police role is that of contributing to a safe, stable, and progressive environment for economic development and community harmony. Several officers in the patrol division suggested that the chief "took care of" the criminal investigations division (in which he himself had spent much of his career), and that the patrol function therefore received inadequate support. The criminal investigations division accounts for 13 percent of the sworn force and 33 percent of the full-time civilian employees. We did not attempt to determine whether that fact and other departmental policies constitute favoritism, but it is clear that drugs and the traditional major street crimes occupy the chief's mind.

In the chief's words, DUI enforcement is "in the middle." That is, he believes DUI deserves police attention, but resources are simply inadequate in view of the need to respond to other, more serious problems:

> If I pull my guys off of answering calls for service to do more DUI, then the mayor has to answer all the citizens' complaints that we're not answering their demands for service. And then the mayor lets me know about it. I don't need that. So I keep those complaints from getting to the mayor by giving the citizens what they want.

The chief believes his officers would arrest a drunk driver if they observed something flagrant, but most would not be inclined to seek out DUI violations because of their heavy, citizen-initiated workload. Under the severe constraints on resources that the chief perceives to be hindering his department, he reluctantly finds this approach acceptable. Consequently the department has not used any special squads, blitzes, or sobriety checkpoints except for stepped-up traffic enforcement during the holidays. The chief would consider special measures only if external funding were made available.

One important factor of the city's perspective on its drunk-driving problem is how it handles court overtime for DUI arrests. The contract with the police union provides that officers who must go to court when not on regular duty will receive time-and-a-half pay; if an officer is in court more than 15 minutes, he or she will receive a minimum of three hours' overtime pay. Drunk-driving arrests frequently involve two or three court appearances, costing the city an extra $250 to $300 per arrest. In past years, enterprising officers could plan their arrests so that they had overtime nearly every day of the week. As a result, some of the most aggressive patrol-rank officers were bringing home larger paychecks than mid-level administrators. To reduce the expense of overtime pay, the city consolidated its DUI court cases into one day per week, thus restricting sharply the amount of overtime an officer could accumulate. In the following year the DUI arrest rate fell almost 13 percent, although a decline had begun two years earlier.

Another indicator is the lack of DUI enforcement training provided by the department. Indeed, the department provides only the state-required minimum for recruits. In-service training also is offered at the state-mandated minimum level. A few officers in the traffic division have been trained in the use of breath-testing equipment, but no effort has been made to train comprehensively in the new law. Further, the department provides no training in conducting field sobriety tests. A median time of one hour of DUI-related training was reported by the sample survey of officers since the new law had been passed. Only one-fourth of the officers rated their DUI training as excellent or good.

Other indicators also are revealing. The department places a low priority on traffic enforcement and on related services generally. The most important priority for the traffic division is in the *regulation* of traffic flow to ensure orderly and efficient entry and exit in the downtown area, especially during the city's many special events. The traffic division operates the department's only breath-testing machine but otherwise spends relatively little time on traffic enforcement. Training on traffic accident investigation is minimal. Consequently, many supervisors encourage officers not to assign blame when writing accident reports; this advice results in statements such as "Two cars collided." Traffic citations are issued infrequently. Homicide detectives conduct investigations of all fatal accidents, but they have no training in accident reconstruction. As a result, they produce reports based on witness interviews—"he-says-she-says" reports, as one officer wryly observed.

A final indicator of the administration's perspective on DUI enforcement is its relationship with the local MADD chapter, particularly its treatment of the video camera donated by the chapter. Administrators accepted the gift camera in a publicized ceremony, but it has not been put to its intended use, nor are there any plans to do so. Administrators feel that the camera will require extra time to use; will involve too much extra paperwork to document evidence, and will only provide defense attorneys with another means of attacking police procedures on technical grounds (a view supported by the district attorney's office). Leaders of the MADD chapter know that the department has not deployed the camera, but the group has exerted no pressure to use it. They prefer to emphasize the "positive," cooperative aspects of their relationship with the police rather than engage in confrontation. Thus the presentation of the camera fulfilled the symbolic function of demonstrating that the MADD group did something to further DUI enforcement and showed that the police are appreciative, but it has had no impact on actual police enforcement practices. In general, department administrators are positive about MADD and describe good relations with the group. They are pleased that MADD expends its energies on public awareness, education, and victim assistance projects, but they express some wariness of involvement by this or any citizen organization in matters relating directly to how the police do their work.

COMMAND AND CONTROL CAPACITY

Melville's command and control capacity appears to be severely constrained by a number of factors. Its ability to shape officers' attitudes through selection processes is limited by the hiring restrictions of previous years. Between 1983 and 1988 the size of the sworn force decreased 17 percent and began to inch up again only in 1989. During the cutback period, officers with the greatest seniority were more likely to remain in the department, thus producing a force heavily skewed toward older officers. In the random-sample survey of uniformed officers, 56 percent have served more than 15 years and 79 percent have served nine or more years. Many officers and administrators note that older officers tend to be more tolerant toward drunk drivers because they themselves are more likely than the younger officers to come from the "shot-and-a-beer" crowd. Further, the older officers joined the force and formed their work habits long before the emergence of popular pressure to treat DUIs more seriously. The department is further constrained in its hiring practices by a court order establishing quotas for hiring females and members of racial minorities. Under these circumstances, hiring officers who might be aggressive in DUI enforcement is neither a priority nor feasible.

Policies on handling specific aspects of DUI enforcement do not seem to most officers to be well articulated. For example, only 12 percent of those surveyed stated that the department's policies and guidelines on when to pull over a potential drunk driver were "very helpful"; 11 percent gave this response about when to conduct field sobriety tests; 15 percent about when to take a driver into custody to determine the level of intoxication; and 9 percent about when to use an alternative to arrest in dealing with a drinking driver. In all cases, the largest proportion responded that the department has no policy (from 33 to 46% depending upon the policy).

The Melville department also is limited in its capacity to reward selectively those officers who pursue management priorities. Although the department has a significant number of supervisory and management positions, few of these have opened up because of financial cutbacks in past years. Written examination scores heavily affect prospects for promotion, although several officers believe that outside political influences occasionally have forced even a resistant chief to promote on other considerations. Patrol assignments to different parts of the city are determined by periodic bids; the more senior officers receive preference.

The rank-and-file bargaining unit is aggressive and is willing to challenge the administration in matters that traditionally have been viewed as management's prerogative. Further, many officers believe that the administration is cowed by external pressure regarding female and minority officers and subjects them less frequently to discipline for poor performance.

The major incentive at the chief's disposal is the assignment of officers to specialist duties and units. Almost one-third of the department works in specialist (nonpatrol) divisions. Assignment to the criminal investigations division, the largest of these, is particularly prized. Training and facilitating educational opportunities also are incentives within the control of department administrators, but are not used much. Another incentive available to the department hierarchy is the assignment of officers to "details," which are additional duties paid for by private organizations requiring police service.

The department's capacity to monitor officers' performance is not well developed. Centralized activity statistics on individual officers are not available, although some mid-level supervisors maintain their own records. Only one of these collects DUI arrests specifically, and he pays no special attention to them. The traffic division, which is responsible for maintaining the results of breath test, finds it difficult to provide information of individual officers' productivity in DUI arrests because this record system is not computerized.

LOCAL POLICE CULTURE

Overall, Melville police do not hold attitudes conducive to a high level of DUI enforcement. None of the officers who completed the anonymous survey said that drunk driving should be a top enforcement priority; only 6 percent said it should be the second priority; and 13 percent said it should be the third.

Forty-one percent of the sample agreed that "Police should concentrate on highly intoxicated drivers rather than those who are slightly over the legal limit." Although 83 percent of the officers reported an inclination to intervene when they spotted someone who *might* be driving while intoxicated, nearly 50 percent expressed a preference for an alternative to arrest.

According to the survey, about one officer in three believes that citizens of the community place a "high" or "very high" priority on DUI enforcement, and one in four perceives the same for the department's administrators. About one in five thinks that local elected officials want increased DUI enforcement, one in four states that officials are satisfied with the current enforcement level, and one in two says that local officials have expressed no opinion or that the respondent does not know that opinion.

Although a significant fraction of the department perceives a community climate of concern about DUI enforcement, very few translate that perception into personal views that DUI should be a high priority. This may be the case because very few officers regard pursuing DUI arrests as improving their chances for professional advancement. None indicate that it "greatly improves chances"; only 1 percent say that it "somewhat improves chances." Further, only about 7 percent of the officers anticipate receiving formal or informal recognition when they do a good job, again reinforcing the previous observation that the department's capacity (or willingness) to reward on the basis of performance is quite limited. Officers do not seem to perceive overwhelming peer pressure against officers who produce high arrest figures, but nearly half believe that at least some officers would resent such productivity.

Perhaps more revealing than the survey results are the comments of officers, supervisors, and administrators in interviews and casual conversation. The following section contains a distillation of comments made by these individuals.

WHY OFFICERS AVOID MAKING DUI ARRESTS

Incompetence and laziness. Because of ineptitude or laziness, some officers simply try to avoid any police work that may increase their visibility in the department (e.g., having to go to court) or may require much time in dealing with citizens or handling paperwork. They view overtime as an intrusion on their time off, find going to court a hassle or intimidating, and allow their distaste or frustration in dealing with drunks to overpower any sense of the good that might derive from their intervention. This approach corresponds closely to the "avoider" style described by Muir (1977).

Opinion that drunk driving is not serious. Some officers rank DUI as a low priority, either because of personal belief or on the basis of the perceived priorities of authoritative sources, such as community and department leaders. Acknowledging that they themselves occasionally committed this offense, some officers commented, "There but for the grace of God go I." Some suggest that the punishment for DUI is often too severe. Others believe that handling assigned calls should be the top priority and that there is little time for proactive work. Still others want to focus exclusively on more "glamorous" crimes: robbery, burglary, drugs, and auto theft.

Lack of faith in the utility of arrest. Two views fall into this category. One is that the courts and correctional programs do not succeed, so there is no point in initiating a formal process. A second perspective is that arrest is not necessarily the most effective and most efficient police response. Officers holding this view will arrest the falling-down drunk, but they handle the less inebriated in alternative ways—following them home, providing them with alternative transportation, or taking their car keys. These officers regard arrest as *a means, not an end*. They are concerned about the amount of time they must spend "out of service" to process drunk-driver arrests, and define their leniency as a more efficient form of ensuring the public's safety.

WHY OFFICERS MAKE DUI ARRESTS

Professional productivity. The opposite of the "avoider" mentioned above, this officer sees his or her role in terms of the amount of activity generated. Law enforcement, especially making arrests, is considered a key part of that role. Arrests are an end of police work, not the means. Drunk driving is just one of many violations that this officer, like Brown's (1981) "clean-sweep crimefighter," is eager and willing to enforce.

DUI as serious crime. This officer, a moral specialist, takes two forms: the drunk hater and the utilitarian. The drunk hater is motivated by personal experience with a drunk driver or alcohol abusers. The utilitarian calculates what offenses cause the greatest harm and concludes that the loss of life, limb, and property to drunk drivers is too great.

DUI as bounty. The bounty hunter engages in DUI enforcement strictly for the money it brings in overtime pay. These officers are few and are isolated from most of their colleagues, unless they find a like-minded partner. Administrators would like to keep them from tapping the city's budget for overtime pay, but they cannot denounce them formally for fear of appearing soft on drunk driving and opposed to full enforcement of the laws. Administrators and most rank-and file officers say that bounty hunting is contrary to their image of police officers as professionals, who should be motivated by a spirit of public service rather than private gain. In Melville, the term "bounty hunter" is nearly always used disdainfully.

One of our field research experiences illustrates the intensity of feelings, both pro and con, about bounty hunting. While waiting to administer the survey to an oncoming shift, one of our researchers was approached by Officer Jones (a pseudonym). Jones said that he had received orders to stay away from us, but that he intended to talk to us anyway because he had heard that we wanted to talk to him and others who made a lot of DUI arrests. Officer Jones was known as a bounty hunter and readily admitted, "I am in it for the money. I have made more money than X [his boss, a mid-level administrator]. They even posted this fact with hopes of discouraging my activities." This tactic only spurred him on, however. He made a large number of arrests generally, and he caught many drunk drivers because he made stops frequently, hoping to discover some violation. First the department tried to suppress this effort by transferring Jones to areas offering less opportunity, but he just "sat on stop signs, stopping everyone who rolled through them" until he found his DUI for the day. Then the department transferred him to a desk job at the station house, but that did not stop him either. He arrested people who came in drunk to ask questions about someone's arrest or who simply wanted information. When they left, he followed them to their car; as soon as they started the engine, he arrested them. Finally when Jones was ordered to remain in the station house, he arrested persons for trespassing or disorderly conduct when they "stumbled in."

Jones's antagonistic and defiant relationship with the department hierarchy was reiterated in various ways by other bounty hunters we interviewed. It is most remarkable that in the face of departmental discouragement and peer group scorn, this small group of officers accounts for a substantial share of the department's DUI arrests. In 1989 the leading bounty hunter (not Jones, by a long shot) made 41 DUI arrests and had 48 "assists," in which he was recorded as the second officer. The top 4.6 percent of the DUI arresters accounted for 42 percent of all DUI arrest. Nearly all of these officers were identified as bounty hunters by themselves or by others. At the other extreme, 58 percent of the officers made no DUI arrests, and 79 percent made two or fewer. The irony here is that the department's subcultural outcasts account for so substantial a share of the department's drunk driving arrests.

DISCUSSION

In some respects, Melville is close to the ideal type of department with a low DUI enforcement. Although the opportunity to arrest drunk drivers appears to be ample, the demand for this activity is quite low. The Melville community's political leaders find other concerns more pressing. Management's priorities too are elsewhere, and generally reflect the community's demands. The department actually has undertaken a number of strategies to *limit* drunk driving enforcement. The dominant local police culture reinforce this view for a variety of reasons—in part as a reaction to specific management policies, and in part because of the large proportion of "older" officers still on the force. The most interesting aspect is the hierarchy's rather limited and underdeveloped command and control capacity. This, in fact, probably accounts for management's inability to *restrict* drunk driving arrests even further. Bounty hunting as a police method is costly, unprofessional, and unpopular among police generally—yet it appears to produce results, and its proponents pursue it stubbornly in the face of formal and informal obstacles.

A theoretical perspective requires us to examine the department's reaction to the DUI law at three levels: outward appearances to the public, internal policies, and the reactions of the major street-level decision makers, namely the patrol officers.

OUTWARD APPEARANCES

Earlier we stated that the extent to which the new state law on drunk driving is enforced depends heavily on features of local police organizations and their local environments. Without some compelling external threat or incentive, police departments have great leeway in determining the scope of their enforcement efforts for particular violations. In this, the most common, situation, police administrators pay more attention to those laws which afford them the greatest opportunity to demonstrate their (and their organization's) worth to key local constituencies. In Melville, DUI enforcement does not present such opportunities. Further, police leaders see no benefit in making an issue of DUI to establish their identity as agents of change. Their priorities are simply elsewhere. Yet the administration does not care to antagonize the local MADD chapter, a small but active segment of the community concerned about drunk driving. Open acknowledgment of the department's low priority for DUI enforcement could bring unwanted publicity, expose the myth of full enforcement, and stimulate a more active and more broadly based citizens' movement that would try to influence department policies and practices, and might even become adversarial.

Consequently the department's administrators "play it safe" by resorting to symbolic responses to the DUI issue. Outward appearances are managed through several of what Manning (1977) calls "presentational strategies." A sizable traffic division operates the breath-testing machine, but has little time for traffic enforcement because its officers are too busy with special events. A symbiotic relationship with the local MADD chapter is established, in which each party exchanges symbolic gestures. The mayor's and the department's participation in MADD's red-ribbon campaign and the video camera donation gives the citizen's group essential publicity and signals that it is doing something about the drunk-driving problem. By engaging in these activities the department signals that it, too, cares about this problem. Even more to the point, it placates a citizen's group *without really intruding on internal department policies and day-to-day practices.*

From the perspective of the police administrators, the department's legitimacy and value can be nurtured best by focusing on other issues: "serious street crime," drug dealing, and service delivery. The large number of police specialists available to address these problems provides ample opportunity to employ other presentational strategies that signify departmental effectiveness. Station houses, symbols of service distribution, also serve this purpose. Elaborate hierarchies and written rules and directives also provide the image of a department responsive to the chief and to the city's direction.

INTERNAL POLICIES

At the second level, internal policies are implemented to allow the agency to deal with the nuts and bolts of administering the agency, which is dominated by the concern for providing services to a demanding public with limited resources. Undoubtedly the department could do more to support drunk-driving enforcement: it could provide more training at relatively low cost, could press for more efficient allocation of personnel to shifts, and could require more productivity from officers on those shifts. Such tactics, however, are certain to generate stiff resistance from the union, thus forcing the administration to expend precious energy and political goodwill. All of this would result from pressing an enforcement initiative in an area for which there is currently no compelling external political demand. Thus, as bad as the situation in Melville may appear to advocates of strict drunk-driving enforcement, the department's policies seem perfectly rational from a practical administrator's perspective.

THE STREET-LEVEL DECISION MAKERS

Finally, the directives and policies of the administration seem to have had only limited impact on street-level practice. Because the formal hierarchy has a very limited capacity to alter patterns of street-level decision making, the administration has experienced only modest success in suppressing overtime (and thus DUI arrests). Many officers continue to make DUI arrests for reasons related to their view of the public interest, but a small core of "bounty hunters" does so for purely personal economic gain. Most of these officers persist in this activity despite the reduced opportunities for overtime. This street-level resistance to top-down influence is all the more remarkable because it requires that officers *take action* to be productive, thus reversing the traditional roles of management and labor. Ultimately this situation exacerbates the difficulty of inducing police officers to do what management wants.

CONCLUSION

A case study cannot test theory, but it can be used to suggest ways to develop it. Our study of Melville indicates that drunk driving is not a significant local political issue, that the police administration has no interest in pursuing it beyond symbolic gestures, and that the great majority of police officers also are not committed. The remarkable point about Melville is that in the face of all these forces conspiring against aggressive DUI enforcement, a few outcasts—bounty hunters—can generate a disproportionately high number of drunk driving arrests, making the department's DUI arrest rate much higher than would otherwise be expected. The irony is that this group, insulated from the formal hierarchy by the hierarchy's weak capacity for command and control, actually works aggressively to fulfill the ostensible objectives of the state's new DUI law. Another irony is that the impetus for this enforcement effort comes not from policy concerns about reducing a social problem, but from these officers' desire for pecuniary gain. Melville is the case of the horse led to water that drank in spite of itself. It demonstrates the risks of assuming that there is a rational progression from political environment to public policy, and ultimately to performance. It cautions us to examine closely cases of apparent implementation of state laws, because any success may be due to factors entirely independent of efforts to accomplish political and administrative accountability.

Future research might attempt to determine how frequently street-level police enforcement practices occur independent of, or in opposition to, formal policy. To what extent can small numbers of self-styled specialists in police departments determine how vigorously laws are enforced? For example, would we find this pattern of implementation in police enforcement practices where there was strong external pressure for DUI enforcement? Under such circumstances would the processes of accountability between the community, the police administration, and the rank and file be linked more strongly, or would there simply be greater pressure to produce even more dramatic symbolic responses?

NOTES

1. Some of this disparity may accrue to differences in the laws, although surveys of current DUI laws show a rather consistent pattern across most states in the key elements of the Scandinavian model.
2. States have set up antidrunk-driving task forces and agencies (Jacobs, 1984:197), but they, like the national drug "czar," characteristically lack the authority or power to establish implementation standards and monitor compliance.
3. Federal legislation has linked highway funds to a state's passage of antidrunk-driving countermeasures, but the receipt of funds has not been tied to actual levels of DUI

enforcement. Some states provide for the return of some portion of DUI fines to the government of the arresting police department, but no systematic data are available on the scope of this incentive system and on whether these funds are earmarked for future DUI enforcement.

4. Between the mid-1970s and mid-1980s the nation's drunk-driving arrest rate increased 55 percent. It peaked in 1983 and has declined somewhat since then (Greenfield 1988:2).

5. Although conceivably there could be external pressure *not* to enforce DUI laws (e.g., from bar and restaurant owners), we have not found this in the literature or in our own research. Visible pressure groups have coalesced to seek more enforcement, not less.

6. Bardach (1977:139) calls this centralization of the administrator's power the "management game" and notes that despite recurring campaigns in government for "better management," this strategy cannot overcome the structural limitations of control of major programs and the agencies that must administer them.

7. A mandatory minimum of 48 hours was required for first offenders, 30 days for second offenders, 90 days for third offenders, and one year for the fourth offenders.

8. We conducted a mail survey of Pennsylvania police departments with one or more full-time sworn officers drawn from the list of departments reporting Uniform Crime Statistics. The response rate was 79.2 percent. See Mastrofski and Ritti (1990:20) for survey details.

9. We interviewed all administrators in the chain of command responsible for units with DUI enforcement, from the chief down to the patrol and traffic division levels. One supervisor in each patrol section and two supervisors in the traffic division were interviewed; we selected them on the basis of availability. We selected patrol-rank officers by asking line supervisors to identify two types of officers: those who were strongly committed to DUI enforcement and those who were not, but were highly regarded as good police officers (15 in all). Respondents provided information on their peers as well as about themselves during the interviews.

10. To protect Melville's identity, we do not report the precise number of surveys completed. The survey was administered to patrol officers at roll call, and took about 10-15 minutes. All work shifts and stations were sampled; we returned to each shift more than once to reach officers who had had days off. More than 95 percent of the officers who were given a survey completed it. The sample is considered to be representative of the officers whose routine responsibilities include DUI enforcement.

11. We identified respondent households by using a modified random-digit-dialing method; we randomly selected telephone numbers from the directory and replaced the last two digits with random numbers to give unlisted numbers an equal chance of selection. Only residences were surveyed. We used a four-callback procedure. Respondents were informed that the survey was about traffic laws and enforcement of those laws. The topic of drunk driving was not mentioned until respondents had been asked open-ended questions about what the law enforcement priorities of their local police should be. The response rate was 52 percent. We considered this rate good, given the deterioration of response rates to telephone surveys over the years, especially in large cities such as Melville.

12. Respondents were asked, "Given the kinds of public safety problems faced by your community, please describe in your own words what should be the MOST IMPORTANT priority for your local police . . . that is, preventing what kind of crime?"

REFERENCES

Aaronson, D. E., C. T. Dienes, and M.C. Musheno (1984). *Public Policy and Policy Discretion: Processes of Decriminalization*. New York: Clark Boardman.

Bardach, E. (1977). *The Implementation Game: What Happens after a Bill Becomes a Law*. Cambridge, MA: MIT Press.

Broderick, J. J. (1977). *Police in a Time of Change*. Morristown, NJ: General Learning Press.

Brown, M. K. (1981). *Working the Street: Police Discretion and the Dilemmas of Reform*. New York: Russell Sage Foundation.

Bullington, B. and A. Block (1990). "A Trojan Horse: Anti-Communism and the War on Drugs." *Contemporary Crises: Law, Crime and Social Policy* 14:39-55.

Casper, J. D. and D. Brereton (1984). "Evaluating Criminal Justice Reforms." *Law and Society Review* 18:121-44.

Eisenstein, J., R. Flemming and F. Nardulli (1988). *The Contours of Justice: Communities and Their Courts*. Boston: Little, Brown.

Flanagan, T. J. and K. M. Jamieson (1988). *Sourcebook of Criminal Justice Statistics-1987*. Washington, D.C.: U.S. Department of Justice.

Fyfe, J. J. (1979). "Administrative Interventions on Police Shooting Discretion: An Empirical Examination." *Journal of Criminal Justice* 7:300-23.

Gardiner, J. A. (1969). *Traffic and the Police: Variations in Law Enforcement Policy*. Cambridge, MA: Harvard University Press.

Goldstein, H. (1977). *Policing a Free Society*. Cambridge, MA: Ballinger.

————— (1990). *Problem-Oriented Policing*. New York: McGraw-Hill.

Greenfield, L. A. (1988). *Drunk Driving*. Bureau of Justice Statistics Special Report. Washington, D.C.: U.S. Department of Justice.

Gusfield, J. (1981). *The Culture of Public Problems: Drinking-Driving and the Symbolic Order*. Chicago: University of Chicago Press.

Jacobs, J. B. (1989). *Drunk Driving: An American Dilemma*. Chicago: University of Chicago Press.

Klockars, C. B. (1985). *The Idea of Police*. Beverly Hills: Sage.

Langworthy, R. H. (1985). "Wilson's Theory of Police Behavior: A Replication of the Constraint Theory." *Justice Quarterly* 2:89-98.

Ostrom, E., R. B. Parks, and G. P. Whitaker (1978). *Patterns of Metropolitan Policing*. Cambridge, MA: Ballinger.

Manning, P. K. (1977). *Police Work: The Social Organization of Policing*. Cambridge, MA: Ballinger.

————— (1989). "The Police Occupational Culture in Anglo-American Societies." In W. G. Bailey (ed.), *Encyclopedia of Police Science*, pp. 384-88. New York: Garland.

Mastrofski, S. D. (1990). "The Prospects of Change in Police Patrol: A Decade in Review." *American Journal of Police* 9:1-79.

Mastrofski, S. D. and R. Ritti (1990). *More Effective DUI Enforcement in Pennsylvania: Final Report*. University Park, PA: Pennsylvania State University.

Mastrofski, S. D. and R. Ritti, and D. Hoffmaster (1987). "Organizational Determinants of Police Discretion: The Case of Drinking-Driving." *Journal of Criminal Justice* 15:387-402.

Muir, W. K., Jr. (1977). *Police: Streetcorner Politicians.* Chicago: University of Chicago Press.

Palumbo, D. J. and D. J. Calista (1990). *Implementation and the Policy Process: Opening Up the Black Box.* New York: Greenwood.

Pennsylvania Commission on Crime and Delinquency (1988). "The Effort to Reduce Drunken Driving in Pennsylvania: The Effects on the Criminal Justice System and Highway Safety." *The Justice Analyst* October.

Reinarman, C. (1988). "The Social Construction of an Alcohol Problem: The Case of Mothers Against Drunk Drivers and Social Control in the 1980s." *Theory and Society* 17:91-120.

Reuss-Ianni, E. (1983). *The Two Cultures of Policing: Street Cops and Management Cops.* New Brunswick, NJ: Transaction Books.

Rubinstein, J. (1973). *City Police.* New York: Farrar, Straus and Giroux.

Sherman, L. W. (1977). "Police Corruption Control: Environmental Context vs. Organizational Policy." In D. H. Bayley (ed.), *Police and Society,* pp. 107-26. Beverly Hills: Sage.

_____ (1983). "Reducing Police Gun Use: Critical Events, Administrative Policy, and Organizational Change." In M. Punch (ed.), *Control in the Police Organization,* pp. 98-125. Cambridge, MA: MIT Press.

Skolnick, J. H. (1966). *Justice Without Trial: Law Enforcement in a Democratic Society.* New York: Wiley.

Slovak, J. S. (1986). *Styles of Urban Policing: Organization, Environment, and Police Styles in Selected American Cities.* New York: New York University Press.

U.S. Department of Justice (1989). *Uniform Crime Reports—1987.* Washington, D.C.: U.S. Department of Justice.

Van Maanen, J. (1974). "Working the Street: A Developmental View of Police Behavior." In H. Jacob (ed.), *The Potential for Reform of Criminal Justice,* pp. 83-130. Beverly Hills: Sage.

_____ (1983). "The Boss: First-Line Supervision in an American Police Agency." In M. Punch (ed.), *Control in the Police Organization,* pp. 275-317. Cambridge, MA: MIT Press.

Wilson, J. Q. (1968). *Varieties of Police Behavior: The Management of Law and Order in Eight Communities.* Cambridge, MA: Harvard University Press.

Wilson, J. Q. and B. Boland (1978). "The Effect of Police on Crime." *Law and Society Review* 12:267-390.

Worden, R. E. (1989). "Situational and Attitudinal Explanations of Police Behavior: A Theoretical Reappraisal and Empirical Assessment." *Law and Society Review* 23-663-711.

THE LAW ENFORCEMENT RESPONSE TO SPOUSE ABUSE: PAST, PRESENT AND FUTURE   17

J. David Hirschel, Ira W. Hutchison,
Charles W. Dean & Anne-Marie Mills

For many centuries husbands had the right to use force to coerce their wives to conform to their expectations. Until very recently, spouse abuse has been considered more a problem of public order than a criminal matter.

Societal acceptance of spouse abuse as criminal has been slow and inconsistent, and attitudes favoring nonintervention have been slow to change. Competition for resources occurs when the criminal justice system is asked to assign higher priority to this problem. On the felony level the battle has been won; there is no dispute that felonious spouse abuse is considered a matter for the criminal justice system. This is not the case, however, on the misdemeanor level. Because domestic violence accounts for a significant proportion of all calls for police service, assigning a higher priority to such calls requires a major reallocation of police resources. Although many people do not question the morality of arresting a man for assaulting his wife or partner, the real question is whether to arrest and prosecute those who commit this crime at the expense of other governmental responsibilities or of law enforcement and judicial responses to other crimes.

This article examines the historical treatment of wives and the evolution of the law enforcement response to spouse abuse. We first address the issue of definition: some confusion exists between the generic concept of spouse abuse and other types of family disturbance that may or may not be similar. Both conceptual and practical problems are present in defining abuse. The definitional problem is particularly noteworthy in view of the fact that most domestic calls for police service involve situations which are

Source: J. David Hirschel, Ira W. Hutchison, Charles W. Dean and Anne-Marie Mills (1992). "The Law Enforcement Response to Spouse Abuse: Past, Present and Future." *Justice Quarterly*, 9(2):247-283. Reprinted by permission of the Academy of Criminal Justice Sciences.

either shouting matches or in which there are no victims with apparent injuries. Verbal abuse seldom qualifies as criminal behavior, so police can do little in this respect.

It is important to address current social attitudes towards spouse abuse and to discuss how we reached this point. An examination of the historical treatment of wives helps us to understand why hostile behavior, now viewed as spouse abuse, was acceptable for so long, why it is currently an unresolved public policy issue, and why both the public and the legal system resist in treating all spouse abusers as criminals.

In this article we also address different estimates of the prevalence of spouse abuse, and then focus on that segment of spouse abuse which is reported to police. We examine problems of definition, different data sources, and varying probabilities of calling the police in order to explain the difficulties in measuring the extent to which spouse abuse actually constitutes a law enforcement problem.

The basic question at the center of the current public debate is the proper role of law enforcement in spouse abuse. Significant research now has been conducted on the police response to spouse abuse, but the findings are not entirely consistent with each other or with the position of advocacy groups. Nationwide there has been considerable momentum toward the adoption of pro-arrest policies. We explore the rationale for such policies and examine the empirical studies that test the effectiveness of arrest in reducing subsequent recidivism by spouse abusers. We conclude by discussing the multiple issues involved in achieving a more comprehensive understanding of the place of law enforcement as only one possible societal response to spouse abuse.

DEFINITIONS

A preliminary issue involves an understanding of the key concepts that are the focus of this article: *spouse* and *abuse*. Although these words have apparent common sense meanings, each may be used in a variety of ways which makes effective comparisons more difficult.

The common, popular understanding of *spouse* is congruent with dictionary definitions, and focuses on married couples. The more common definition of spouse in research literature, however, pertains to persons in conjugal or conjugal-like relationships, including married, separated, and cohabiting couples (Berk and Loseke 1981; Buzawa and Buzawa 1990; Ford and Regoli forthcoming; Goolkasian 1986; Williams and Hawkins 1989). This difference is relatively important because a large proportion of abusive incidents reported to police involve cohabiting couples, an issue that we will examine later in greater detail.

The term *spouse* is gender-free and may erroneously imply a parity between men and women. At we will discuss later, husbands often are the targets of abuse, but their probability of being injured is much lower than that of wives. Morley and Mullender (1991) note that the gender-specific term *woman-battering* has given way to the androgynous terms *domestic, spouse, marital,* and *family* violence. It is unclear whether the broadening of this concept has had a positive or a harmful effect on family violence studies. The variation both in concepts and in their references (i.e., who is included) creates some confusion.

A second major issue is whether to define *abuse* as measured by aggressive actions or as measured by the outcome of such acts (i.e., injuries; Straus 1990). According to Berk et al. (1983), there is little consensus on the kinds of behavior to which the term *abuse* refers. Feld and Straus (1989:143) define violence as "an act carried out with the intention or perceived intention of causing physical pain or injury to another person." Schulman (1979), Straus (1979), and Straus, Gelles, and Steinmetz (1980) also use acts as a definition of abuse. On the other hand, Berk et al. (1983) emphasize the severity of injuries as the focus of their study.

This article defines spouse abuse to include married, separated, divorced, cohabiting, and formerly cohabiting couples, and focuses primarily on female victims unless noted otherwise. The literature we include here encompasses abuse as defined either by act or by outcome. In general we concentrate on physical aggression because of the paucity of data on verbal aggression such as threats. Although we recognize both the frequency and the seriousness of threats, this type of abuse is less likely to produce a law enforcement response.

EVOLVING ATTITUDES TOWARD SPOUSE ABUSE

HISTORICAL OVERVIEW

Wife abuse appears to be a cultural universal that has been approved implicitly or explicitly until very recently. From an anthropological perspective it may be observed that a large proportion of societies have given adult males authority to coerce the behavior of dependent females. This authority appears to be an integral part of a monogamous marriage relationship, which involves differential power between the partners in a setting culturally defined as private. When formal governments emerged and legal codes developed, the wife consistently was treated as telltale subordinate to the husband; wife beating either was not considered criminal or was formally approved.

Roman law, which has been served as a basis for many legal systems in the Western world, originally gave a husband sovereign authority over his wife, who acquired the status of daughter at marriage. This authority, known as *patria potestas*, included the power of life and death and the right to unrestrained physical chastisement of the wife and other family members (Hecker 1914:13; Pleck 1987:9).

A modified form of *patria potestas* was incorporated into English common law (Oppenlander 1981:386) under the guise of family protection (Gamache, Edleson, and Schock 1988:194; Sigler 1989:2; Walker 1990:124-27; Smith 1989:3). In 1768 Blackstone described the husband's right to chastise his wife moderately in order to enforce obedience (1897:147). The criterion for "moderate" was the "rule of thumb," which allowed a husband to use any reasonable instruments, including a rod no thicker than his thumb, to correct his "wayward" wife.

The English heritage was brought to the American colonies; husbands in America, as in England, retained the power to chastise their wives. Although the Puritans enacted the first laws against wife beating in 1641 with the passage of the Massachusetts *Body of Laws and Liberties,* the integrity and privacy of the family still were considered more important that the protection of victims. This orientation contributed greatly to tolerance and indifference toward wife beating (Pleck 1987:21-2; 1989). Between 1633 and 1802, for example, only 12 cases involving wife beating are to found in the court records of Plymouth Colony (Pleck 1989:25).

Although it is debatable how accurately these cases represent the law in the United States in general (Pleck 1989:32-33), a number of appellate court decisions in this period upheld a husband's right to chastise his wife physically. In 1824 the Mississippi State Supreme Court declared in *Bradley v. State* that "the husband be permitted to exercise the right of moderate chastisement." The Court emphasized that "family broils and dissentions" were not proper matters to bring before a court of law, but were best left inside the walls of the home (158).

Other cases reinforced this position, holding that a wife was incompetent to testify against her husband in a case where "a lasting injury or great bodily harm" was not inflicted or threatened (*State v. Hussey* 1852:128); that "the law gives the husband power to use such a degree of force as is necessary to make the wife behave herself and know her place," and that bruises left by a horse-whip or switch may be justified by the circumstances so as not to give a wife a right to abandon her husband and "claim to be divorced" (*Joyner v. Joyner* 1862:252-53); that the effect, not the instrument, was the standard to be used in determining whether the husband had exceeded his authority (*State v. Black* 1864; *State v. Rhodes* 1865); and that a husband was permitted to use the force necessary to control an unruly wife, even if they were living apart by agreement. The court would "not invade the domestic forum unless some permanent injury be inflicted" except in cases of excessive violence to "gratify . . . bad passions" (*State v. Black* (1864:163)).

The Puritan attitude of indifference or outright approval was maintained until the late 1830s (Pleck 1989). Working initially through churches and later through the temperance societies, the women's rights movements gained momentum during the nineteenth century. Whereas the Puritans placed family preservation ahead of women's rights, the temperance movement reversed the order (Pleck 1989).

Women's growing activism evolved in the 1850s into a push for women's rights which helped to sponsor legislation regarding married women's property, conventions on women's rights, and recommendations on divorce (Pleck 1989). The interest in women's rights, however, did not peak until the 1870s. After the Civil War, state intervention in the family was viewed as more acceptable than in the past because of the broader governmental control allowed by the war (Pleck 1987:89). As a consequence, state legislatures began to pass Married Women's Acts, which allowed married women to enter contracts, sue, and own property in their own right, and liberalized the divorce laws, thus eroding men's absolute dominance over women.

A focus on law and order and a humanitarian concern for the victims of spouse abuse led to attempts to enact legislation that expressed a more serious view of this problem (Pleck 1989:35). Between 1876 and 1906 bills were introduced in 12 states, and were passed in three, to punish wife beaters with a whipping (Pleck 1989:40). Passing a statute and enforcing it, however, are not the same. After Maryland enacted a law in 1882 to punish wife beaters with either a whip or a year in jail, no one was prosecuted under that statutory provision for a year and only two convictions occurred in three years. Although unused, the provision remained on the books until 1948 (Pleck 1989:41).

During this period dicta and holdings in court cases likewise became less supportive of a husband's right to exercise physical control over his wife. In the Alabama case of *Fulgham v. State* (1871) the court denied the right, declaring that wife whipping was "at best, but a low and barbarous custom" (147). Three years later, in *State v. Oliver* (1874), a lower court found guilty a husband who had whipped his wife with two thin switches, leaving bruises. The North Carolina Supreme Court affirmed this judgment, stating that the old "rule of thumb" no longer was the law in North Carolina. Yet despite the legal rejection of the right to chastise, the belief that spouse abuse belonged within the privacy of the home continued to be very much a part of American culture. Physical cruelty was disapproved, but it was not grounds for a woman to obtain a divorce especially because nagging women were regarded as having provoked their husbands (Pleck 1987:25).

The de facto decriminalization of spouse abuse was reinforced by the emergence of family courts in the second decade of the twentieth century. These courts tended to view family violence as a domestic problem rather than as a crime, and urged reconciliation whenever possible (Pleck 1987:136-37). From 1920 until the late 1970s, relatively little occurred, legislatively or judicially, in the area of spouse abuse.

Because law both reflects and shapes societal values, we can expect its development and enforcement to be inconsistent over time among jurisdictions and among agencies within a given jurisdiction. The legislation and court rulings discussed above trace the uneven evolution of law regarding spouse abuse. Generally the changes in legislation and in enforcement were roughly parallel. Yet in spousal relationships, moderate force that otherwise would be treated as criminal often went unpunished.

PAST AND CURRENT ATTITUDES

A certain ambivalence toward spouse abuse always has existed and still persists today. A number of reasons are advanced for this attitude: the privacy of the home, the social approval of violence, the inequality of women in society, and noninvolvement by criminal justice officials (Gelles and Straus 1988:25; Oppenlander 1981:385; Pleck 1989:20-21).

Spouse abuse has been viewed differently from "ordinary" assault between other principals because spouse abuse has been regarded as less serious on the grounds that the wife belongs to the husband and the home is his castle; therefore what happens in the castle is not a concern for his neighbors or the criminal justice system (Belknap 1990:248; Dobash and Dobash 1991; Fyfe and Flavin 1991; Pleck 1989:21). Although the state can punish violators, it continues to give family members special immunity to protect family life and the marriage (Oppenlander 1981:385; Pleck 1989:20). Senator Jesse Helms argued against federal funding of domestic violence shelters because they constituted "social engineering," removing the husband as the "head of the family" (126 Cong. Rec. 24, 12058, 1980).

The cultural belief in the sanctity of the family privacy prevents societal, legal, or personal intervention (Balos and Trotzky 1988:83; Berk and Loseke 1981:319; Buda and Butler 1984:366; Gelles and Straus 1988:27; Roy 1977:138; Sigler 1989:2; Waits 1985:299). Modern industrial societies—characterized by urbanization, anonymity, high residential mobility, neolocal monogamous family patterns, and religiously reinforced family privacy—seem to have difficulty in developing and enforcing effective community standards that would limit wife abuse.

Because "violence is as American as apple pie" (Gelles and Straus 1988:26), some researchers suggest that abuse in the family is a result of the approval given to other forms of violence (Breslin 1978:298; Gelles and Straus 1988:26; Oppenlander 1981:394; Sigler 1989:98). The family is less authoritarian and more egalitarian than in the past; spouse abuse continues, however (Pleck 1989).

Men receive implicit social permission to beat their wives when nothing is done to stop abuse (Buzawa and Buzawa 1985:143; Roy 1977:138, Walker 1990:48). The problem is convincing the police to arrest, the prosecutors to prosecute vigorously, and the court system to sanction (Balos and Trotzky 1988:106; Goolkasian 1986:3). The criminal justice system is reluctant to punish batterers (Watts 1985:271), thus giving the impression that the abuser faces very little risk (Gelles and Straus 1988:24). Although spouse abuse is condemned in theory, the law still allows it to continue (Waits 1985:299).

THE EXTENT OF THE PROBLEM

The empirical study of family violence is relatively recent; only since the 1970s has it been studied in depth and extensively. Accurate prevalence and incidence data remain beyond reach, however. Both official records, such as those based on calls to police, and self-report data are best regarded as rough estimates of the extent of actual abuse.

SCOPE AND PROBABILITY OF ABUSE

Despite 20 years of empirical research, estimates of the number of women abused by their partners each year vary greatly, ranging from 2.1 million (Langan and Innes 1986) to more than 8 million (Straus 1989). It has been estimated that violence occurs each year in approximately one relationship in six (Straus et al. 1980). The probability estimate is that between 25 and 30 percent of couples will experience a violent incident in their lifetime (Gelles and Straus 1988; Nisonoff and Bitman 1979; Straus et al. 1980).

The widespread variation in numerical estimates is due to four factors. First, definitional differences are great; they range from any threat of unwanted touching to the infliction of serious injuries. Straus and Gelles (1990-96) estimate rates of *any* husband-to-wife violence at 116 per 1,000 couples per year (6,250,000 women), whereas they estimate any *severe* husband-to-wife violence at 34 per 1,000 couples per year (1,800,000 women). Second, estimates are based on different data sources: police data, shelter intakes, injuries reported to police or hospitals, and extrapolations from surveys. Even if there were no definitional differences, the different sources of data would produce widely varying parameters because they capture different segments of the abused population. Third, the time factor varies: published reports do not always make clear whether authors are using a data base to project estimates for a given year or for a lifetime probability of ever-abuse. In a given year, an estimate for that year will include those who entered the pool of abused women in a previous year, as well as those who are "new" to the pool. Fourth, although everyone agrees that abuse is underreported, nobody agrees about the extent of underreporting; this issue is discussed in greater detail below.

Predictors associated with spouse abuse. In review of characteristics associated with spouse abuse, Hotaling and Sugarman (1986) investigated more than 400 empirical studies of husband-to-wife violence. Their review produced a total of 97 potential risk markers; a risk marker is defined as "an attribute or characteristic that is associated with an increased probability to either the use of husband-to-wife violence, or the risk of being victimized by husband-to-wife violence" (1986:102). Because this review unquestionably is the most comprehensive available, we rely on it for our overview.

Of the 97 characteristics investigated, Hotaling and Sugarman found very few to be consistent risk markers. In particular, attributes of women associated with being abused by men were rare. Of the 42 female-related characteristics investigated, only one appeared as a consistent risk marker: witnessing violence between parents while growing up. All of the other female characteristics investigated were determined to be inconsistent or nonrisk markers: for example, experiencing violence as a child (although this trait almost qualified), age, race, educational level, income, traditional sex role expectations, alcohol use, and self-esteem.

Far more predictive of spouse abuse in Hotaling and Sugarman's (1986) review were the characteristics associated with men. Of the 38 potential risk markers attributed to men, nine appeared as consistent predictors of abuse: being sexually aggressive toward their wives, violence toward their children, witnessing violence as a child, witnessing violence as an adolescent, occupational status, alcohol use, income, assertiveness, and educational level. Hotaling and Sugarman (1986) also investigated risk markers associated with the couple, and found five variables associated with higher levels of spouse abuse: Frequency of verbal arguments, religious incompatibility, family income/social class (primarily through the husband's income), marital adjustment, and marital status. In sum, it is far more difficult to predict victimization of women in spouse abuse situations on the basis of any characteristic of the woman than on the basis of her male partner's attributes. Hotaling and Sugarman (1986) conclude that the psychiatric model of spouse abuse receives strong support from their review.

As new research is conducted, other factors may emerge as consistent risk markers; perhaps some of those now identified as increasing the probability of abuse will emerge as less accurate predictors. One dilemma is that comparisons (both within and across studies) include men who have abused a woman only once as well as those who are chronic batterers. We should not expect to find to find a consistent set of predictors when the entire range of wife abuse is reduced to the threshold requirement of a single incident. Greater progress on the question of prediction would be made if more attention were given to developing typologies of abusers, victims, and relationships and then to determining predictor variables associated with particular types. For example, it may be that chronic abusers (of one or more female partners) are differentiated from occasional abusers by particular characteristics associated with both personality and situational variables.

Social class characteristics. As documented by both police reports and numerous researchers, marital violence exists in every class and income group, regardless of race and social class (Finesmith 1983; Lockhart 1987; Schulman 1979; Straus et al. 1980) Years of research, however, have failed to produce clear-cut and convincing documentation on the degree to which spouse abuse is distributed *equally* across various demographic groups. The most accurate current conclusion is that spouse abuse is comparable across social class variables; that is, more similarity than difference exists between groups. Yet although intragroup differences are greater than intergroup differences, we simply cannot conclude that demographic differences are absent. Some studies have discovered an inverse relationship between income and violence: as income increases, violence decreases (Finesmith 1983; Yllo and Straus 1981).

Schulman (1979) found, however, that although abusive families tend to be urban, young, and nonwhite, these violent families are not differentiated easily from similar nonabusive families. In a study of 307 black and white women from various social classes, Lockhart (1987) found no significant intergroup difference in victimization by domestic violence.

We speculate that researchers and the interpreters of research sometimes may bend over backward in their efforts to avoid any bias, and thus may distort results unwittingly by down playing any intergroup differences. It is clear that spouse abuse is not characteristic of any particular group. It is less clear whether all groups are truly equal in both prevalence and incidence of abusive behavior.

Abusive incidents reported to the police. The proportion of spouse assaults reported to the police differs widely, depending on how the study was conducted (Bowker 1984). According to estimates, from one-tenth to two-thirds of abused women call the police to report an incident. In a survey of 1,793 Kentucky women, Schulman (1979) found that women called police in only 9 percent of the incidents. Compared to findings from other studies, this figure implies an extremely high proportion of unreported incidents. The generally accepted estimate (based in particular on national samples) is that approximately one-half of all incidents are reported to the police. Analysis of 1973-1976 National Crime Panel Survey data revealed that approximately 55 of every 100 incidents of intimate violence went unreported to law enforcement (U.S. Department of Justice 1980). Analysis of 1978-1982 data showed that 48 percent of the incidents were not reported to the police (Langan and Innes 1986). In a study of 420 women who sought treatment in a domestic abuse program in Washington State, Kuhl (1982) discovered that 66 percent of the women had not filed a report.

Characteristics of persons calling police. Much of the dilemma in understanding demographic material in abuse rates is due again to data sources; there is no way to reconcile somewhat disparate information. As in some other areas of the criminal justice system, citizens who call the police to report a particular criminal action are not representative of all who experience that particular crime. An inherent self-selection process is present in the use of police services. Thus no one concludes that abused women who call the police are a representative demographic sample of all women who experience abuse.

Although domestic disturbances cut across all demographic boundaries, police are involved most often in domestic disturbances among the poor and uneducated (Hamberger and Hastings 1988; Moore 1979; Parnas 1967). Bowker (1982, 1984) reports that the police are more likely to come into contact with couples of relatively low socioeconomic status, with low-quality marital relationships, and suffering or inflicting severe violence. Nonwhite and lower-income women (under $7,500) are more than twice as likely to report an incident to the police as are white, high-income women (over $15,000) (Schulman 1979). Underreporting occurs at all socioeconomic levels but is particularly likely among middle- and upper-income persons.

Reasons for underreporting. A clear relationship between selective perception and underreporting has emerged in various studies. An unknown number of victims do not consider their assault to be a crime, or, if they do so, they do not report the incident or disclose to any official how they received their injuries (Breslin 1978). Because spouse abuse is so common in society, many victims to not view it as a crime and therefore do not report it to the police. As Langley and Levy (1978:5) note, these are the missing persons of official statistics.

Some women do not perceive a slap in the face as abuse, and so do not report it; others perceive such an action as abusive, but only a fraction of those women report it. The more severe the behavior, the more likely it is to be both perceived as abusive and reported often; often, however, even very severe abuse is never reported to the police. Langan and Innes (1986) found that the primary reason offered by women for not reporting an abusive incident to the police was that they considered it a private or personal matter (49 percent of respondents). A further 12 percent of the victims did not report because they feared reprisal. Similar proportions failed to report because they thought the crime was not important enough, or because they believed the police could not or would not do anything.

Some women report most incidents of abuse, some report some incidents, and some never report any incident that takes place. Unfortunately, the accumulation of studies does not tell us how many of each type are found in the reported and in the unreported incidents.

Abuse reported in surveys. Other than police reports, surveys provide the most comprehensive data on spouse abuse. Yet these, too, must be interpreted with some caution for a number of reasons. First, the perception of what constitutes abuse remains a problem. As Straus (1989:27) points out, victims and suspects may not view abuse as a crime and therefore may not report it in a crime survey. National Crime Surveys (NCS) estimates of the crime of woman battering are one-fiftieth of the rate revealed in a national survey produced by Straus (1990). Second, national surveys face the problem of distilling spouse abuse from other forms of domestic violence as well as from nonfamily violence. National crime surveys find family offenses a difficult subject to quantify; neither the Uniform Crime Reports (UCR) nor the NCS are designed to measure family violence specifically (Rose and Goss 1989). As a result, an assault on a spouse is counted among the other nondomestic assaults (Miller 1979). Third, surveys such as the NCS can be problematic because interviews may be conducted with both the victim and the offender present. It is reasonable to assume that many victims would not report violence because of fear of reprisal by the offender (Straus 1989).

Nonwife abuse. The common perception of spouse abuse involves a husband and a wife, with the latter as the victim. Although wife abuse is the modal adult domestic violence, there is a growing recognition of the abuse of husbands, cohabitants, and—to a lesser extent—gay or lesbian partners. Offenders are not always men, nor are the victims always women; instead the problem is one of "spouse" abuse because men also are victims (Dobash and Dobash 1991:350).

The same elements in society that explain violence against wives cause women's violence towards men (Straus 1980). Violence against men, however, was and still is perceived as unusual in patriarchal societies, where men are expected to dominate and control the female (Dobash and Dobash 1991). Many women hit and beat their husbands, but the data have been "misreported, misinterpreted, and misunderstood" (Gelles and Straus 1988:90).

Steinmetz (1977) estimated that of 47 million married couples, more than a quarter-million husbands experience several beatings from their spouses. In Straus, Gelles, and Steinmetz's 1975 study (Gelles and Straus 1988), 2 million men were victims of violence inflicted by their wives. Straus and Gelles (1986, 1990) showed that the rate of wife-to-husband assault is slightly higher than that of husband-to-wife assault, but an attack by a woman is less severe and less likely to cause injury. In addition, men are much less likely to report an attack by a woman (Dutton 1988; Edleson and Brygger 1986; Jouriles and O'Leary 1985; Stets and Straus 1989; Straus 1989; Szinovacz 1983).

Gelles and Straus (1988) concluded that violence against women has received more publicity because men's greater strength causes more damage and because the women are acting in self-defense in about three-quarters of the cases. Some feminists, however, have tried to maintain a low profile on battered husbands so that battered women would receive funding (Gelles and Straus 1988:188).

Any discussion of spouse abuse must also include some attention to cohabitants. The number of cohabitants has increased almost fourfold in the past 20 years, and such individuals are primarily young: two-thirds of males and three-fourths of females are less than 35 years old (Spanier 1983). There is increasing evidence that cohabitants are particularly prone to abusive relationships. In their comparison of married, dating, and cohabiting couples, Stets and Straus (1989) report that the highest rates of assault and the most severe assaults are found among cohabiting couples. Hutchison, Hirschel, and Pesackis (1988) found that the number of calls for abusive situations to police by cohabitants equaled the number of similar calls by married couples, although the latter group made up a far greater proportion of the population. Stets concluded that cohabitants experience more aggression than married couples because of a combination of factors: youth, minority status, problems including depression and alcohol use, and the lack of "social control associated with participation in organizations and being tied to their relationships" (1991:678).

FAMILY AND SPOUSE HOMICIDES

Murder data are more systematic, more extensive, and more reliable than abuse data. Because such data have been collected nationally for many years, it is possible to determine both patterns and changes with some degree of precision. Nonetheless, distilling spouse abuse data from national data sources, such as the Uniform Crime Reports, presents possibilities of misinterpretation and confusion.

In 1984 the Attorney General's Task Force on Family Violence found that almost 20 percent of murders involve family members and that nearly one-third of female homicide victims are murdered by their husbands or boyfriends (U.S. Department of Justice 1984:11). A review of FBI Uniform Crime Reports data (1985-1990) shows that the percentage of all murder victims who were killed by a spouse or boyfriend/girlfriend has remained relatively constant over the past few years. In the five-year period 1986-1990, 28 to 30 percent of all female murder victims were killed by husbands or boyfriends; in the same period, 4 to 6 percent of all male victims were killed by wives or girlfriends. Despite the escalation of homicide rates, some consistency remains in homicide rates of offenders and victims. In the past few years, 75 percent of the murder victims have been male. In addition, just as males are killed primarily by other males, females also are killed by males: approximately 90 percent of female victims are murdered by men (U.S. Department of Justice 1986-1991).

FBI homicide data disclose that women make up only 14 percent of the homicide offenders; the relationship between offender and victim varies, however (Straus 1989). In contrast to women's low representation as offenders in stranger homicide, Straus (1989) found a much higher proportion in family homicide: women murder male partners 56 to 62 percent as often as men murder female partners. It appears that men kill "across the board," but women are more likely to kill husbands or boyfriends. Zahn and Sagi (1987:395-95) found that although males were the predominant offenders in family homicides, a much higher proportion of family homicides than of any other homicide type involved a female offender. Males were almost equally likely to offend against males and against females in the family. In contrast, female offenders' victims were almost exclusively male.

These data do not suggest any kind of murder "parity" between husbands and wives; the cold facts disguise the family dynamics. Wives are seven times more likely than husbands to have killed in self-defense (Jolin 1983) or in response to an assault initiated by the male partner (Straus 1989). In a study of 144 women who killed a mate in a domestic incident, Mann (1986:10) found that 58.6 percent stated self-defense as a reason for the killing. Recognition of the family dynamics involved in these killings is evidenced by wives on trial for killing their husbands.

THE ROLE OF LAW ENFORCEMENT

HISTORICAL BACKGROUND

In the past, domestic violence calls often were assigned low priority (Fleming 1979; Parnas 1971; U.S. Commission on Civil Rights 1982). Police responded reluctantly to abuse calls, attempted to restore peace and order between the disputants, and typically left without taking more formal action.

Explanations for the long-term avoidance of formal action are manifold. First, violence within the family had been considered to be essentially a private matter; this view allowed adults to use force to solve personal disputes (Breslin 1978; Martin 1976). Second, female victims had been perceived as uncooperative; this situation, it was claimed, made arresting and prosecuting abusers a waste of time (Parnas 1967:931; U.S. Commission on Civil Rights 1982). Third was a concern that taking action against abusers hurt their families, especially members financially dependent on the offenders (Parnas 1967:931 U.S. Department of Justice 1984). Fourth, intervening in family disputes was not regarded as "real police work" (Buzawa and Buzawa 1990:29; Fyfe and Flavin 1991:4; Parnas 1971:542). Finally, Martin (1976) and others argued that responding officers, who usually were male, typically sided with offenders. This taking of sides reinforced a cultural norm stressing male superiority; this norm was exemplified, as discussed in an earlier section, by laws in colonial and later times that allowed a man to chastise his wife.

The police response to spouse abuse changed little until the 1960s. Under the influence of social scientists, psychologists, and a developing women's movement, the order maintenance approach received a professional twist. Mediation and crisis intervention were promoted as the appropriate tools for dealing with family violence. This development led to police training is crisis intervention techniques (Bard 1970, 1973, 1975; Spitzner and McGee 1975), the establishment of police family crisis intervention units (Bard 1970, 1975), and mixed police crisis teams composed of police officers and social workers (Burnett et al. 1976).

Despite the added training and the use of specialized units, there is little evidence that crisis intervention and mediation have had much success in reducing abuse. Oppenlander (1982), for example, reported that police tended to make more arrests in abusive situations than in other cases, even though crisis intervention approaches often took precedence over arrest. Relatively few evaluations were made, however (see e.g., Pearce and Snortum 1983; Wylie et al. 1976), to assess the effects of these changes; most of the innovations occurred before controlled experimental research on the effects of police policy was conducted.

In addition, many police officers did not welcome these changes. Mediation seemed more like social work than police work. Moreover, some commentators (e.g., Langley and Levy 1978) thought that the police were inadequately prepared to perform family crisis intervention. Others were concerned about applying crisis intervention. Others were concerned about applying crisis intervention techniques and mediation to abuse situations. Loving (1980), for example, wrote that techniques designed for situations involving verbal abuse were being applied inappropriately to situations involving physical assaults.

The Attorney General's Task Force on Family Violence (U.S. Department of Justice 1984) identified what may well be a fundamental flaw in the mediation approach. The process of mediation assumes some equality of culpability between the parties to a dispute. The assumption of equal culpability and the failure to hold the offender accountable for his actions give him no incentive to reform. Thus, "rather than stopping the violence and providing protection for the victim, mediation may inadvertently contribute to a dangerous escalation of violence" (U.S. Department of Justice 1984:23).

These concerns about crisis intervention and mediation, coupled with arguments that female victims' rights were violated by the failure of police enforcement, produced demands for the arrest of abusers as the appropriate police response (Langley and Levy 1978; U.S. Commission on Civil Rights 1982). In some jurisdictions, women's groups filed suits to effect this change in policy (see e.g., *Bruno v. Codd* 1977; *Scott v. Hart* 1976; *Thurman v. City of Torrington* 1984). The rationale for advocating arrest was clear. As the Attorney General's Task Force on Family Violence stated unequivocally, "*The legal response to family violence must be guided primarily by the nature of the abusive act, not the relationship between the victim and the abuser*" (U.S. Department of Justice 1984:4).

CONTEMPORARY PREFERRED ARREST POLICIES

Many vexing issues are raised by the meaning, implementation, and effects of the preferred arrest movement, but the current trend toward preferred arrest policies is indisputable. In recent years we have seen a major increase in the number of police departments that apply such policies. It is uncertain to what extent this increase is attributable to changes that have taken place in state statutes. Lerman, Landis, and Goldzweig observed in 1983 that "twenty-seven of the recent state laws on domestic violence expand(ed) police power to arrest in domestic abuse cases" (1983:44). Ferraro notes that as of 1986, six states had passed laws requiring arrest with a positive determination of probable cause and the presence of the offender on the scene (1989:61). By 1988, 10 states had enacted such laws (Victim Services Agency 1988:3).

Often, however, the potential of such statutory provisions is limited by the existence of requirements that must be satisfied before the laws can be invoked. Some state laws, for example, require the existence of a visible injury and/or the elapsing of only a short time between the commission of the offense and the arrival of the police. In their survey of police departments with preferred arrest policies, Hirschel and Hutchison (1991) reported that although all of the departments applied such a policy in cases of visible injury or a threat with a deadly weapon, only in a minority of the departments was such a policy in effect for situations involving verbal threats or property damage. Moreover, there is evidence that (subject to jurisdictional variation) about half of all offenders leave the scene before the police arrive (Hirschel and Hutchison 1987:11), and thus would not be arrested unless the victims swore out arrest warrants. Finally, policy trends favoring either preferred or mandatory arrest decisions do not necessarily include all abuse victims. It is known, for example, that cohabiting women call police disproportionately more than married women for domestic assault (Hutchison et al. 1988:14). Nonetheless, in at lease some states nonmarried couples are not included in preferred arrest policies (Ferraro 1989).

The police also are asked to take action against abusers who have violated provisions of protective orders granted to abused women by the courts. Such orders currently are available in 48 states and in Washington, DC (Finn and Colson 1990:1). Suspected violation of the provisions of these orders may (and in 10 states must; Victim Services Agency 1988:4) result in arrest of the offender.

Preferred arrest (also called pro-arrest or presumptive) policies are far more common than mandatory policies. A 1986 study by the Crime Control Institute ("Roughening Up" 1987; Sherman and Cohn 1989) investigated arrest policies and found that the number of departments with such policies had increased fourfold since 1984. The study, however, did not include police departments in cities with populations of less that 100,000, so we cannot determine the extent to which the trend in large cities is being replicated elsewhere.

In general, the literature does not examine whether police departments adopted these arrest policies on their own initiative or as a result of changes in state law. It is clear that a number of factors have prompted police departments to change their policies. The same forces that operated on state legislatures also have influenced police departments. Foremost among these are various women's groups, including the National Coalition Against Domestic Violence, state chapters of this organization, and local coalitions that formed to alter existing policy and practice.

Although it is difficult to unravel the various factors that have motivated police departments to move toward preferred arrest policies, it is important to gauge the extent to which departments have adopted these policies willingly. This point is important because the orientation of top administrators influences rank-and-file enforcement of the policies. Available information suggests that police departments generally have not played a leading role in adopting arrest policies, and occasionally have been very reluctant to do so. In 1980, for example, Arizona's legislature passed a law that expanded police arrest powers. The chief of the Phoenix Police Department, however, adopted a presumptive arrest policy for his department only when faced with the possibility of legislation *mandating* arrest (Ferraro 1989:63). Miller (1979:16) in Oregon, Bell (1985:532) in Ohio and Buzawa (1988:174-75) in New Hampshire have noted a similar reluctance on the part of police departments to change their policies to conform with new statutory provisions.

The success of formal policies depends upon the support of both command and line personnel. The impact of negative attitudes among chiefs of police regarding the use of arrest in abuse cases is demonstrated clearly by Buzawa's (1988) research in New Hampshire. She found that a lack of support by chiefs was associated with low enrollments in the voluntary state-administered training program, the absence of written departmental policies, low or nonexistent arrest rates for domestic violence incidents, and a feeling among officers that responding to abuse calls was usually a waste of time (Buzawa 1988:175-78). In one jurisdiction the chief even said that "he could not recall a 'genuine' call for domestic violence in his numerous years as an administrator," and consequently "did not highly value" (undoubtedly an understatement) "the role of police intervention in this area" (Buzawa 1988:175).

Whatever policy might be, police officers are accustomed to making their own decisions on the street and traditionally are antagonistic to policies that limit their discretion. In his survey of Minneapolis officers, conducted after the Sherman and Berk experiment, Steinman found a strong indication of independence: 99 percent of respondents voiced the belief that they "should make their own decisions about problems that arise on duty," 77 percent reported that they "usually do what they think necessary even if they expect supervisors to disagree," and 43 percent declared that "they should use their own standards of police work even when department procedures prohibit them from doing so" (1988:2).

In the only available in-depth study of police response to a new presumptive arrest policy, Ferraro (1989) provides a fascinating study of the Phoenix Police Department. Even though the State of Arizona passed such legislation in 1980, little actual change occurred until 1984, when the Phoenix Police Department finally adopted a presumptive arrest policy. On the basis of ride-along observational data, Ferraro reports that in spite of this policy, arrests were made in only 18 percent of the battering incidents to which her research team responded. One problem was that in interpreting probable cause, officers were employing "a level of evidence high enough for felony arrests" (1989:64). In the face of opportunity and discretion to interpret both policy and circumstance, there is no reason to expect that police in general suddenly will reverse their traditional reluctance to arrest.

Research shows that certain factors are associated with positive attitudes toward preferred arrest policies. Not surprisingly, an officer's general orientation toward domestic violence is likely to affect his or her attitude (Berk and Loseke 1981:320-21; Ferraro 1989:66-67; Homant and Kennedy 1985; Walter 1981). Female police officers tend to be more supportive of arrest policies than male police officers (see e.g., Ferraro 1989; Homant and Kennedy 1985). Training also influences police attitudes; studies have found that training is associated positively with both officers' perception and citizens' evaluation of officers' handling of disturbance calls (Pearce and Snortum 1983), with improvement in officers' attitudes toward domestic situations (Buchanon and Perry 1985), and with officers' willingness to arrest domestic violence offenders (Buzawa 1982:4212-22).

Two final issues that affect police officers' attitudes toward domestic violence calls arise from their perceptions of the danger posed by such calls and from their fear of being sued at civil law for false arrest of an alleged offender. First, there persists a common perception that domestic disturbances are unusually dangerous for police in regard to frequencies of both assaults and homicides (Buzawa and Buzawa 1990:29). This perception has been "transmitted largely through police folklore" (Konstantin 1984:32). Such a perception has been supported by the interpretation of FBI "disturbance calls" data. These data grouped family quarrels with other types of disturbances, such as bar fights and "man with gun" calls, and were easily misinterpreted by some individuals, who took all of the disturbance calls to be domestic disturbance calls (see e.g., Bard 1974:foreword; Stephens 1977:164). In addition, it has been suggested that crisis intervention trainers projected this perception of danger deliberately to attract the attention of antagonistic recruits (Fyfe and Flavin 1991:8). It is clear, however, that only a small percentage of police officers killed in the line of duty died while responding to abuse calls (see e.g., Konstantin 1984; Margarita 1980a). An in-depth analysis by Garner and Clemmer (1986) concluded that domestic disturbances are one of the least frequent contributors to police homicide. The danger of assault and injury likewise has been exaggerated (see e.g., Geller and Karales 1981; Margarita 1980b). Recent studies, however, suggest that in some locations, domestic calls still may constitute the most dangerous category both in assault (see e.g., Uchida, Brooks, and Kopers 1987) and in injury (see e.g., Stanford and Mowry 1990; Uchida et al. 1987).

In addition, the fear of being sued (at least successfully) in civil court for wrongful arrest of an alleged offender has been exaggerated greatly. Although this concern is raised frequently by officers in police departments that adopt preferred arrest policies, in reality this is a rare occurrence. It is possible that officers and police departments in fact are as likely to be sued successfully for failure to arrest an alleged offender (see, e.g., *Nearing v. Weaver* 1983; *Thurman v. City of Torrington* 1984) as for wrongful arrest of an alleged offender. Such suits for failure to arrest have been based on allegations of denial of due process or equal protection of the law (see, e.g., *Balistreri v. Pacifica Police Department* 1990; *Dudosh v. City of Allentown* 1987; *Thurman v. City of Torrington* 1984) or infringement of rights granted victims by state statutes (see, e.g., *Nearing v. Weaver* 1983; *turner v. City of North Charleston* 1987). Yet despite some large awards (e.g., $2.3 million in *Thurman*), not many suits have been successful. It has been suggested that recent Supreme Court case law (*Deshaney v. Winnebago County Department of Social Services* 1989) will make it more difficult for abused women to win civil suits in federal court against police departments that failed to protect them (Zalman forthcoming).

DETERRENCE AND PREFERRED ARREST POLICIES

An argument that has been raised both for and against arresting spouse abusers arises from the findings of research studies designed to test the deterrent effect of arrest in such cases. Although the deterrence argument generally is not considered necessary to justify the arrest of the alleged perpetrators of other criminal offenses, such as rape, robbery, burglary, and auto theft, it has played a central part in the debate about the role of arrest in the social measures adopted to combat spouse abuse.

The Minneapolis Study. The formulation of social policy involves at best an amalgam of competing interests, viewpoints, and resources. Maintenance of the status quo is likely except in the face of compelling evidence that seems to justify a change. Extant procedures are likely to remain in effect unless policy makers are convinced that an alternative is either essential or better. Experimental research offers both the scientific community and policy makers a plausible basis for policy recommendations. Experimental methodology, in brief, is the most convincing of methodologies. Perhaps the major contribution of the Minneapolis experiment lies not in its substantive findings but in its reception by those involved in spouse abuse policies. We speculate that neither police departments nor advocates of change would have paid so much attention if the Minneapolis study had not been a controlled scientific experiment.

The Minneapolis experiment, conducted by Sherman and Berk in 1981-1982, was the first study to test the deterrent effect of arrest in spouse abuse cases—more accurately domestic violence cases, because the research design also included same-sex and other familial relationships (Sherman and Berk 1984a, 1984b). In that study certain predefined misdemeanor domestic assault cases, in which both the offender and the victim were present when the police arrived on the scene, were assigned randomly to one of three treatment responses: 1) advising the couple (including informal mediation in some cases); 2) separating the couple by ordering the offender to leave for eight hours; and 3) arresting the offender, which meant that he stayed overnight in jail. The selected cases then were tracked for six months: official record checks were made on offenders, and interviews were conducted with victims every two weeks to determine whether subsequent abuse occurred. A "police recorded failure" occurred when the offender generated a written offense or arrest report for domestic violence. A "victim reported failure" occurred when a victim reported "a repeat incident with the same suspect, broadly defined to include an actual assault, threatened assault or property damage" (Sherman and Berk 1984b:266).

During the course of the study, the participating officers (about 52 in number) produced a total of 330 eligible cases; three officers turned in 28 percent of the cases (Sherman and Berk 1984b:263-64). Sixteen cases were excluded from analyses because no treatment was applied or because reports had been generated on cases with victim-offender relationships that were outside the ambit of the study.[1] Whereas 99 percent of the cases targeted for arrest received the "arrest" treatment, only 78 percent of the "advise" cases and 73 percent of the "separate" cases were treated as assigned. All 12 follow-up interviews were obtained from 161 victims, for an interview completion rate of 49 percent (Sherman and Berk 1984b).

Analysis of the data showed that arrest was more effective than the other two responses in deterring subsequent abuse. According to police data, the overall failure rate was 18.2 percent; the arrest treatment returned the lowest failure rate (13%), and the separate treatment the highest (26%; Sherman and Berk 1984b).[2] Only the difference between the arrest and the separate treatments, however, was significant at the .05 level. The victim data showed a failure rate of 19 percent for those assigned the arrest treatment, as compared to 33 percent for those assigned the separate treatment and 37 percent for those assigned the advise treatment. Here the only significant difference was between the advise and the arrest treatments (Sherman and Berk 1984a, 1984b).

Both the researchers themselves (e.g., Sherman and Berk 1984b:263-66, 269) and others (e.g., Binder and Meeker 1988; Elliot 1989:453-54; Lempert 1989:152-54) have pointed out problems with the study. These problems include inadequate sample size; the submission of a disproportionate number of cases by a few officers; inadequate controls over the treatments actually delivered; the possibility of surveillance effects caused by multiple follow-up interviews; and lack of generalizability of the findings due to attributes of the city in which the sample was obtained, and of the sample itself.

Despite these methodological problems, the Minneapolis study received unprecedented national attention and is credited with helping to promote the nationwide movement toward arrest as the preferred response in abuse cases ("Roughening Up" 1987; Sherman and Cohn 1989). Yet if fundamental policy changes were to be undertaken with a clear (i.e., generalizable) basis for estimating the effects of an arrest policy, additional field experiments based on random assignment were needed. Accordingly, in order to test the validity of the results obtained in the Minneapolis experiment, the National Institute of Justice funded additional experiments in Omaha, Atlanta, Colorado Springs, Dade County (Florida), Milwaukee, and Charlotte (North Carolina).

Subsequent studies. Like the Minneapolis study, the six later studies examined whether arrest is the most effective law enforcement response for deterring spouse abusers from committing subsequent acts of abuse. Certain elements were common to the six projects: all employed an experimental design in which cases that met predefined eligibility requirements were assigned randomly to treatment responses; all used arrest as one of the treatment responses; all focused on the misdemeanor range of cases, in which the police were empowered but not required to make an arrest; and a six-month follow-up was conducted on all eligible cases through use of police records and interviews with victims.

The Omaha study, which was funded about two years before the others, employed a two-part research design that focused on whether the offender was present when the officers arrived on the scene. If the offender was present, the case was assigned randomly to one of the treatments employed in the Minneapolis study; arrest, separate, or mediate. If the offender had gone when the police arrived, the case was assigned randomly either to receive or not to receive a warrant for the offender's arrest. Like the Minneapolis and the Milwaukee studies (but not the other four), the Omaha study extended beyond heterosexual couples who were or had been married or cohabiting. It also included same-sex couples as well as victims and offenders in other familial relationships.

Analysis of the 330 eligible cases in which the offender was present revealed no significant differences between the failure rates of the three treatments, whether official measures or victim-reported measures of recidivism were employed (Dunford, Huizinga, and Elliot 1990). Analysis of the 247 cases in the offender-absent part of the experiment, however, showed that cases in which warrants were issued were both less likely and slower to result in further abuse than cases in which no warrant was issued (Dunford et al. 1989; Dunford 1990).

The Charlotte Project was the only one to employ the entire patrol division in round-the-clock and citywide sampling for the full duration of the project. It used three treatment responses: 1) advising and possibly separating the couple; 2) arresting the offender; and 3) issuing a citation to the offender (an order requiring the offender to appear in court to answer specific charges). Analysis of the 650 eligible cases obtained by the project produced only two significant findings: the differences between the effects of the advise/separate and the citation treatments and between the effects of the informal (advise/separate) and the formal (arrest and citation) treatments on the official incidence (but not the prevalence) measures of arrest recidivism. In no case, whether official- or victim-reported measures of recidivism were employed, did the failure rate of the arrest treatment differ significantly from those of the other two treatments (Hirschel et al. 1991; Hirschel, Hutchison and Dean, 1992).

The Milwaukee Project also employed three treatment responses: 1) full arrest accompanied by a relatively long period of detention in jail (a mean of 11.1 hours); 2) short arrest, which resulted in the release of the offender within a few hours (a mean of 2.8 hours); and 3) no arrest (warning only). Analysis of the 1,200 eligible cases revealed, in general, no significant differences between the treatments. However, according to interviews and one official measure (the commission of subsequent violence against *any* victim), short arrest had a substantial initial (30-day) deterrent effect in relation to warning only, although this deterrent effect dissipated over a longer follow-up period. These data highlight the importance of both multiple measures of recidivism and an adequate follow-up period to determine treatment effects. On the basis of the official measure that the authors consider to be their most comprehensive indicator of official recidivism (police reports to the local shelter's hotline concerning all probable-cause domestic violence cases), the short-arrest group consistently showed significantly higher rates of long-term recidivism than the warning-only group (Sherman et al. 1991).

Comments. The results of these three studies (Omaha, Charlotte, and Milwaukee) present an unambiguous picture: arrest of misdemeanor spouse abusers is no more or less effective in preventing recurrence of abuse than the other responses examined. These results, coupled with the concerns that have been raised about the validity of the Minneapolis findings (e.g., Binder and Meeker 1988), suggest a lack of adequate support for a mandatory or presumptive arrest policy based on specific deterrence. Possibly this picture will be modified when the three other sites present their findings. At this point, the hope that arrest alone could contribute significantly to solving the problem of spouse abuse is unfulfilled.

We offer several possible explanations why arrest has not been found to deter subsequent abuse. First, the majority of offenders in these studies have previous criminal histories: 59 percent in Minneapolis (Sherman and Berk 1984b:266), 65 percent in Omaha (Dunford et al. 1990:194), 69 percent in Charlotte (Hirschel et al. 1991:37) and 50 percent in Milwaukee (Sherman et al. 1991:827). Thus in many cases, arrest is neither a new nor an unusual experience.

Second, for many of the couples in these studies, abuse is a common rather than an occasional occurrence. Indeed, for some, abuse is chronic. For offenders who have criminal histories or who have been offenders in chronically abusive relationships, it is unrealistic to imagine that arrest will have much impact.

Third, arrest alone, which was a focal point of the research projects, may not constitute as strong a societal response as commonly perceived. The popular conception is that the arrested person is put in jail and that that punitive action is sufficient to change behavior. The fact is that "time in jail" is often minimal beyond the booking time required: it is estimated to have averaged about 16 hours in Omaha (Dunsford et al. 1990:191), nine hours in Charlotte (Hirschel et al. 1991:151), and three hours for short and 11 hours for long arrest in Milwaukee (Sherman et al. 1991). Thus arrest with immediate release simply may not mean much, particularly when the offenders have been arrested before.

Fourth, although not technically within the scope of the project, some information was gathered on the processing of offenders through the criminal justice system. The data support the conclusion that a spouse very rarely is found guilty and ordered to spend any significant time in jail. In Minneapolis "only 3 (2%) of the 136 arrested offenders were formally punished by fines or subsequent incarceration" (Sherman and Berk 1984b:270). In Charlotte only four (1%) of all the men who had been issued a citation or arrested spent time in jail beyond the initial arrest; another eight (2%) received credit for time served before going to trial (Hirschel et al. 1991:147). In Milwaukee initial charges were filed in 37 (5%) of the 802 arrest cases, and only 11 (1%)) resulted in convictions (Sherman et al. 1991). In Omaha, however, 64 percent of those arrested were sentenced to jail, probation or fine (Dunford, Huizinga and Elliot 1989:31).

Fifth, these studies focus on whether arrest constitutes a deterrent for spouse abusers as a whole. For the most part they do not examine whether there is any particular subgroup of spouse abusers for whom arrest may serve as a deterrent. In a study in southern California, Berk and Newton (1985) generally confirm the deterrent value of arrest (on the basis of an ex post facto analysis of 783 wife-battering incidents) but argue carefully that a conditional effect is present. They note in particular, that arrest is most effective for batterers whom police ordinarily would be inclined to arrest. In subsequent analyses of the Milwaukee data, Sherman et al. (1992) found, however, that arrest exerted a deterrent effect on those with high stakes in social conformity (the employed, married, high school graduates and whites), but an escalation effect on those with the opposite attributes (the unemployed, etc.) as measured by reports of subsequent abuse to the domestic violence hotline.

PREFERRED ARREST POLICIES AS PART OF A COORDINATED COMMUNITY RESPONSE

In some jurisdictions, police departments has moved to a preferred arrest policy without the involvement of other agencies. In other jurisdictions the movement to such a policy has been part of a new, coordinated, community response to the problem of abuse. In general it is the latter departments that have reported positive results with their new policies. Gamache et al. (1988) report that after the introduction of community intervention projects in three Minnesota communities, rates of both arrests and successful prosecutions increased; similar results are recorded by Steinman (1988:2) in Lincoln, Nebraska, by Ferguson (1987:9) and Goolkasian (1986:37-38) in Seattle, by Pence (1983:257-57) in Duluth, and by Burris and Jaffe (1983:312) in London, Ontario. After noting that police policies in Lincoln, Seattle, Duluth, and London are coordinated with community wide support, Steinman suggests that "this is probably not the case in most communities where departments have adopted arrest policies" (1988:2).

In addition, with the exception of Seattle, the cities that have been studied most closely are small, with relatively modest crime and domestic violence rates. In the three Minnesota communities studied by Gamache et al., the populations range from 15,000 to 36,000 inhabitants and recorded five or fewer domestic violence arrests a month per community during the research period (1988:195, 201). Duluth has received considerable national attention for its Domestic Abuse Intervention Project, which coordinates the efforts of nine law enforcement, criminal justice, and human service agencies; this city has a population under 100,000 and recorded only some 10 arrests a month during the research period reported by Pence (1983:258-59). These observations suggest that postarrest coordination can be achieved more easily in smaller communities with relatively modest crime and domestic violence rates. Yet even this type of coordinated community response, however commendable for other purposes, provides no evidence that abuse rates are affected.

SUMMARY AND DISCUSSION

Describing the law enforcement response to spouse abuse requires some understanding of the social and legal foundations. In this article we have presented a brief review of the historical attitudes toward wife abuse, the evolution of the response by the legal system to such abuse, the contemporary scope of the problem, the traditional law enforcement role of the past, and the current and sometimes controversial movement toward the arrest of spouse abusers. We have focused primarily on the abuse of women who are in marital or spouselike (e.g., cohabitant) relationships. Although we recognize that the abuse of men in both marital and cohabitant relationships falls clearly within the parameters of spouse abuse, both the research literature and social concern regarding abused men are quite limited.

As we have shown in this article, the United States has a long and inglorious tradition, inherited from our English origins, of ignoring and minimizing spouse abuse. Indeed, only recently has our society begun to consider such behavior as "abuse," much less as a social "problem." Males' rights to chastise and abuse females are rooted deeply in our social and legal traditions.

Although protective laws had been passed as long ago as the latter part of the seventeenth century, they hardly were enforced. The predominant patterns, lodged in the perceived rights of male power and primacy, reflected highly permissive attitudes toward spouse abusers. Legal intervention was minimal, at least as may be determined through extant court records; serious laws, with serious enforcement, were not initiated until the latter part of the twentieth century. We have identified some of the reasons for the traditional police reluctance to intervene in family disputes. As described above, we have traced such reluctance to a combination of factors including traditional values of family privacy, the perception that family disputes are inappropriate as police work, and the perception of danger in responding to domestic violence calls. In addition, many police simply do not believe that intervening in spouse abuse does much to address the problem—either for a particular couple or for the larger social issue. In this regard, such sentiments may be typical of much work that police do for a variety of criminal offenses.

Our review concludes with a significant focus on the current scene: perhaps it can be summarized adequately as a gradual strengthening of spouse abuse laws by state legislatures, but it is marked by a continued and pervasive reluctance of police to do more than is absolutely required by law. We also review the original movement toward pro-arrest policies, and discuss the nearly conclusive current evidence that arrest for misdemeanor spouse abuse has little unique deterrent effect in reducing further abuse.

A number of issues remain to be addressed, ranging from the interpretation of data to the design and implementation of effective social policies.

First, as made clear by this review and by comprehensive assessments of the scope of spouse abuse, there is much room for misinterpretation, distortion, and manipulation of data. Because spouse abuse itself (finally) raises social concern, if not anger, it almost begs for exaggeration. Estimates both of the number of people affected and of probabilities of abuse vary widely, depending on definitions, data sources, and the quality of work performed by the researchers, interpreters, and disseminators of results. One cannot dispute that spouse abuse is an immense social problem: the scope needs no exaggeration in order to warrant concerted, unrelenting action in search of solution. We believe that carelessness or exaggeration in reporting estimates actually may contribute to less rather than more concern for the problem. There is no reason to expect policy makers, often already jaded by causes, to believe exaggerated claims or to act on them.

Second, some confusion exists about the true extent of popular support for taking significant action to combat spouse abuse. Like any cause for any social problem, this cause has ardent supporters who are in the forefront of change. Most communities know by now that spouse abuse is a major problem and that there is a great need for social support services such as shelters, victims' assistance agencies, treatment programs for men, and employment and relocation services for abused women. It is beyond the scope of this article to determine whether the generally inadequate level of social services represents weariness of community support or reflects the reality that limited resources must be allocated to multiple and therefore competing programs.

Third, the law enforcement role in spouse abuse is hinged inevitably to both state law and community pressures. In this review we have documented the gradual change in state laws, which have moved toward giving police more authority and more responsibility for intervening in abusive situations. Police authority always is defined and limited by state law; the fact is that such law, although stronger that 50 or even 20 years ago, still leaves much to be desired. Law is influenced in turn by pressure brought to bear on lawmakers; such pressure often has developed from women's groups within communities, with varying degrees of success at the state level. Thus, what police ultimately are empowered to do (or are prohibited from doing) derives from state laws, most of which were enacted originally by men and now are under attack primarily by women. It is an unequal battle, and real successes in changing state laws typically come only after much pressure. Ironically although not surprisingly, in this situation (as in others) it is primarily women who are battling for the rights of other women, to protect them against a social and personal problem inflicted largely by men (at least in cases of serious injury).

Fourth, one can make a case that the recent movement toward pro-arrest policies for police, although motivated nobly by the sincere (but perhaps futile) hope that arrest will make a difference, also reflects a "quick fix" mentality by both activists and sympathizers. Placing hopes on the success of arrest as a deterrent to spouse abuse removes pressure from other possible responses, such as the social support services mentioned above. It would be satisfying and simple if the fact of arrest had made a difference in the Minneapolis replication studies, but unfortunately, the hoped-for results have not yet materialized.

Fifth, study of the role of arrest of spouse abusers has been limited. All of the experiments funded by the National Institute of Justice focused on the misdemeanor range of spouse abuse, in which police are empowered, but not required, to make warrantless arrests on the scene. Only the Omaha study examined situations in which police obtained warrants, located offenders, and made arrests off-scene. A significant issue is the degree to which police officers may interpret the facts of a situation (upon their arrival at the scene of a reported incident) so as to find that it does not meet the criteria for an on-the-scene arrest for an offense committed in their absence. State law stipulates the general conditions for a finding of the legal authority to make such an arrest, but interpretation always depends on the responding officers. When the threshold requirements are high, it is virtually guaranteed that the great majority of reported incidents will not be subject to official police action beyond a simple response to the incident because many police officers will decide subjectively that the minimum requirements have not been met.

If state laws were to cast a wider net so as to encompass a broader range of abusive behavior, and if local police departments stood solidly behind pro-arrest policies, far more abusers would be arrested. In the Charlotte study, for example, only a minority (approximately 18%) of domestic calls to which police responded were classified as misdemeanors and hence as subject to the discretionary power of police to make an arrest. A very small minority were felony-type cases, in which police almost always make an arrest. Thus in the great majority of calls to which police responded, the incident was evaluated by responding officers as not meeting the legal criteria for either a felony or a misdemeanor. Very simply, officers decided that no crime had been committed.

Sixth, spouse abuse is probably the only area of criminal behavior in which it has been considered necessary to justify the arrest of offenders on the grounds that such arrests will serve as a deterrent. To our knowledge, it has never been suggested that drug dealers, thieves, or rapists not be arrested because arrest had failed to reduce subsequent recidivism for these crimes. Ironically, the great hope placed in the arrest of spouse abusers as a deterrent ultimately may be counterproductive if either police or lawmakers react to the replication experiments with diminished concern for making such arrests. As we argue elsewhere (Hirschel et al. 1991), one can make a strong case that spouse abusers should be arrested for a variety of other reasons beyond any deterrent value of arrest. Even if arrest may not have much punitive value, it still may constitute a more conscionable choice than nonarrest. Not to arrest may communicate to men the message that abuse is not serious and to women the message that they are on their own. It may communicate to children, who very often witness abuse of their mothers, that the abuse of women is tolerated, if not legitimated. It may communicate to the public at large that a level of violence which is unacceptable when inflicted by a stranger is acceptable when inflicted by an intimate.

Seventh, the law enforcement role, on which this article has focused, inevitably is shaped by the response of the judicial system. It is a reasonably human response of police to question the efficacy of arresting spouse abusers when they already are reluctant to do so because of traditional beliefs, and when they know that little will happen to such abusers as they enter the judicial system. As we stated earlier, the popular perception is that arrest means time in jail, in this case time in jail for spouse abusers. In fact, as we pointed out, actual time in jail (beyond booking time) is extremely rare. For the many men who already have been in jail for other offenses, such nonaction hardly can be expected to be punitive. Indeed, the impotence of the criminal justice system in sentencing abusers to active time could even have a reinforcing effect on the norm held by some males, that abusing one's partner simply does not matter very much. We have received the impression, although it is well beyond the scope of this article, that creative sentencing for spouse abusers is an option used infrequently by the courts. Thus neither police nor offenders have reason to believe in either the deterrent or the punitive powers of arrest.

Finally, as jail space becomes even more crowded and as communities are hard pressed to confine offenders for other crimes viewed as more "serious," some hard decisions must be made and alternatives to jail (e.g., mandated treatment for offenders) must be imposed.

What, then might realistically be the most suitable law enforcement role in dealing with spouse abuse? A number of avenues seem both plausible and appropriate. The law enforcement role must be integrated more carefully with the social support systems within communities. Although we do no believe that such coordination provides a measurable deterrent to further abuse, it creates both real and symbolic support for abuse victims.

Although we do not suggest a return to the now-discarded crisis mediation approach, there is some evidence that police characteristics and the manner in which police manage incidents influence women's perceptions of the adequacy of the police response. In those departments which can afford to assign specialized teams to respond to abuse calls, it is likely that women will feel more strongly supported (even if they are not, in fact, protected any better) by the existence of such teams. There is some evidence that simply calling the police to report an abusive incident is an advantage in reducing subsequent incidents (Langan and Innes 1986). We speculate that if women felt that they were supported more strongly when reporting incidents to police, some change might occur in the long run for some couples. The problem of spouse abuse is so intractable that no single approach will have a major impact; the accumulation of small successes is the most that can be anticipated.

In addition, it is both incredible and quite baffling that neither social science researchers nor the police have developed more sophisticated ways of profiling and responding to spouse abusers. To our knowledge, the ordinary police policy in responding to a reported incident is to treat it as a new event and to respond (except for information that the responding officer may possess) only on the basis of that event. For many couples, such a response is perfectly appropriate. For many other couples, however, abuse is both serious and chronic. There is no logical reason why these couples should be treated as one would treat a new couple in the initial stages of abusiveness. It would seem that researchers and police could cooperate to identify "high-risk" couples, if for no other reason than that police receive the most virulent criticism when often-reported abuse terminates in a murder.

Finally, we are left with the question "What should be the law enforcement response to spouse abuse?" The only answer is quite simple, if unsatisfactory: to enforce the law. Police deserve some criticism for their laxity in enforcing the existing laws, but much of the criticism is undeserved because it disregards the reality that police are limited severely in what they can and cannot do. Responsible communities will look as critically at strengthening the prosecutorial, judicial, and social support systems as they have viewed the police for their apparent inability to solve this problem; it is a police problem only insofar as it is a law enforcement problem. Police do not possess the legal mandate, the credentials, or the resources to solve the problem by themselves. They have the responsibility to enforce the law, however. Beyond that, it is the responsibility of concerned citizens and lawmakers to address the multiple legal and social service issues encompassed by the problem of spouse abuse.

NOTES

1. Later changed to 17 (see Berk, Smyth, and Sherman 1988; Berk and Sherman 1988:71).
2. The failure rate for the advise treatment is not reported here, but is reported elsewhere as 19 percent (Sherman and Berk 1984a). This figure is slightly high in view of the overall failure rate reported in the publication cited in the text (Sherman and Berk 1984b). Furthermore, discrepancies exist between the failure rates reported in different publications. For example, Sherman and Berk (1984a) report official failure rates of 10 percent for cases in the arrest treatment, 19 percent for cases in the advise treatment, and 24 percent for cases in the separate treatment.

REFERENCES

Balos, Beverly and Katie Trotzky (1988) "Enforcement of the Domestic Abuse Act in Minnesota: A Preliminary Study." *Law & Inequality* 6:38-125.

Bard, Morton (1970) *Training Crisis Intervention: From Concept to Implementation.* Washington, DC: U.S. Department of Justice.

_____ (1973) *Family Crisis Intervention: From Concept to Implementation.* Washington, DC: U.S. Government Printing Office.

_____ (1975) "Role of Law Enforcement in the Helping System." In Alan R. Coffey and Vernon E. Renner (eds.) *Criminal Justice as a System: Readings* pp. 56-66. Englewood Cliffs, NJ: Prentice-Hall.

Belknap, Joanne (1990) "Police Training in Domestic Violence: Perceptions of Training and Knowledge of the Law." *America Criminal Justice Society* 14 (2):248-67.

Bell, Daniel (1985) "Domestic Violence: Victimization, Police Intervention, and Disposition." *Journal of Criminal Justice* 13:525-34.

Berk, Richard A., Sarah F. Berk, Donileen R. Loseke, and David Raume (1983) "Mutual Combat and Other Family Violence Myths." In David Finkelhor, Richard J. Gelles, Gerald Hotaling, and Murray V. Straus (eds.), *The Dark Side of Families: Current Family Violence Research* pp. 197-212. Beverly Hills: Sage.

Berk, Sarah and Donileen R. Loseke (1981) "Handling Family Violence: Situational Determinants of Police Arrest in Domestic Disturbances." *Law and Society Review* 15:317-46.

Berk, Richard and Phyllis Newton (1985) "Does Arrest Really Deter Wife Battery?" An Effort to Replicate the Findings of the Minneapolis Spouse Abuse Experiment." *American Sociological Review* 50:253-62.

Berk, Richard A., and Lawrence W. Sherman (1988) "Police Responses to Family Violence Incidents: An analysis of an Experimental Design with Incomplete Randomization." *Journal of the Statistical Association* 83:70-76.

Berk, Richard, Gordon Smyth, and Lawrence Sherman (1988) "When Random Assignment Fails: Some Lessons from the Minneapolis Spouse Abuse Experiment." *Journal of Quantitative Criminology* 43:209-23.

Binder, Arnold and James W. Meeker (1988) "Experiments as Reforms." *Journal of Criminal Justice* 16:347-58.

Blackstone, William (1987) *Commentaries on the Laws of England,* edited by W. Hardcastle Browne. St. Paul: West.

Bowker, Lee (1982) "Police Services to Battered Women: Bad or Not So Bad?" *Criminal Justice and Behavior* 9:476-94.

_____ (1984) "Battered Wives and the Police: A National Study of Usage and Effectiveness." *Police Studies* 7:84-93.

Breslin, Warren J. (1978) "Police Intervention in Domestic Confrontations." *Journal of Police Science and Administration* 6:293-302.

Buchanon, Dale R. and Patricia A. Perry (1985) "Attitudes of Police Recruits towards Domestic Disturbances: An Evaluation of Family Crisis Intervention Training." *Journal of Criminal Justice* 13:561-72.

Buda, Michael A. and Teresa L. Butler (1984) "The Battered Wife Syndrome: A Backdoor Assault on Domestic Violence." *Journal of Family Law* 23:359-90.

Burnett, Bruce B., John J. Carr, John Sinapi, and Roy Taylor (1976) "Police and Social Workers in a Community Outreach Program." *Social Casework* 57:41-49.

Burris, Carole A. and Peter Jaffe (1983) "Wife Abuse as a Crime: the Impact of Police Laying Charges." *Canadian Journal of Criminology* 25:309-18.

Buzawa, Eve S. (1982) "Police Officer Response to Domestic Violence Legislation in Michigan." *Journal of Police Science and Administration* __:415-24.

_____ (1988) "Explaining Variations in Police Response to Domestic Violence: A Case Study in Detroit and New England." In Gerald T. Hotaling, David Finkelhor, John T. Kirkpatrick, and Murray A. Straus (eds.), *Coping with Family Violence* pp. 162-82. Beverly Hills: Sage.

Buzawa, Eve S. and Carl G. Buzawa (1985) "Legislative Trends in the Criminal Justice Response to Domestic Violence." In Alan J. Lincoln and Murray A. Straus (eds.), *Crime and the Family* pp. 134-47. Springfield, IL: Thomas

_____ (1990) *Domestic Violence: The Criminal Justice Response.* Newbury Park, CA: Sage.

Dobash, Russell P. and R. Emerson Dobash (1978) "Wives: The 'Appropriate' Victims of Marital Violence." *Victimology* 3-4:426-42.

_____ (1991) "Gender, Methodology, and Methods in Criminological Research: The Case of Spousal Violence," Paper presented at the British Criminology Conference, York.

Dunford, Franklyn W. (1990) "System Initiated Warrants for Suspects of Misdemeanor Domestic Assault: A Pilot Study." *Justice Quarterly* 7:631-53.

Dunford, Franklyn W., David Huizinga and Delbert S. Elliot (1989) *The Omaha Domestic Violence Police Experiment: Final Report,* Washington DC: National Institute of Justice.

_____ (1990) "The Role of Arrest in Domestic Assault: The Omaha Police Experiment." *Criminology* 28:183-206.

Dutton, Donald G. (1988) *The Domestic Assault of Women: The Psychological and Criminal Justice Perspectives.* Boston: Allyn & Bacon.

Edleson, Jeffrey L. and Mary P. Brygger (1986) "Gender Differences in Reporting of Battering Incidences." *Family Relations* 35:377-82.

Elliot, Delbert S. (1989) "Criminal Justice Procedures in Family Violence Crimes." In Lloyd Ohlin and Michael Tonry (eds.), *Family Violence* pp. 427-80. Chicago: University of Chicago Press.

Feld, Scott L. and Murray A. Straus (1989) "Escalation and Desistance of Wife Assault in Marriage." *Criminology* 27:141-61.

Ferguson, Harv (1987) "Mandating Arrests for Domestic Violence." *FBI Law Enforcement Bulletin* 56:6-11.

Ferraro, Kathleen J. (1989) "Policing Woman Battering." *Social Problems* 36:61-74.

Finesmith, Barbara K. (1983) "Police Response to Battered Women: A Critique and Proposals for Reform." *Seton Hall Law Review* 14:74-109.

Finn, Peter and Sarah Colson (1990) *Civil Protection Orders: Legislation, Current Court Practice, and Enforcement.* Washington DC: U.S. Department of Justice.

Fleming, Jennifer B. (1979) *Stopping Wife Abuse: A Guide to the Psychological and Legal Implications for the Abused Woman and Those Helping Her.* Garden City, NY: Anchor.

Ford, David A. and Mary J. Regoli (forthcoming) "The Preventive Impacts of Policies for Prosecuting Wife Batterers." In Eve S. Buzawa and Carl G. Buzawa (eds.), *Domestic Violence: The Changing Criminal Justice Response to Domestic Violence.* Westport, CT: Greenwood.

Fyfe, James J. and Jeanne Flavin (1991) "Differential Police Processing of Domestic Assault Complaints." Paper presented at the annual meeting of the Academy of Criminal Justice Sciences, Nashville.

Gamache, Denise J., Jeffrey L. Edleson, and Michael D. Schock (1988) "Coordinated Police, Judicial, and Social Service Response to Woman Battering: A Multiple-Baseline Evaluation across Three Communities." In Gerald T. Hotaling, David Finkelhor, John T. Kirkpatrick, and Murray A. Straus (eds.), *Coping with Family Violence* pp. 193-209. Beverly Hills: Sage.

Garner, Joel and Elizabeth Clemmer (1986) *Danger to Police in Domestic Disturbances: A New Look.* Washington, DC: U.S. Department of Justice.

Geller, William A. and Kevin J. Karales (1981) Split-Second Decisions: Shoots of and by Chicago Police. Chicago: Chicago Law Enforcement.

Gelles, Richard J. and Murray A. Straus (1988) *Intimate Violence*. New York: Simon and Schuster.

Goolkasian, Gail A. (1986) *Confronting Domestic Violence: A Guide for Criminal Justice Agencies*. Washington, DC: U.S. Department of Justice.

Hamberger, L. Kevin and James Hastings (1988) "Characteristics of Male Spouse Abusers Consistent with Personality Disorders." *Hospital and Community Psychiatry* 39:763-70.

Hecker, Eugene A. (1914) *A Short History of Women's Rights*. Westport, CT: Greenwood.

Hirschel, J. David, Ira W. Hutchison, Charles W. Dean, Joseph J. Kelley and Carolyn E. Pesackis (1991) *Charlotte Spouse Assault Replication Project: Final Report*. Washington, DC: National Institute of Justice.

Hirschel, J. David, Ira W. Hutchison (1991) "Police-Preferred Arrest Policies." In Michael Steinman (ed.), *Wife Battering: Policy Responses* pp. 49-72. Cincinnati: Anderson.

Hirschel, J. David, Ira W. Hutchison, and Charles W. Dean (1992) "The Failure of Arrest to Deter Spouse Abuse" (1992) *Journal of Research in Crime and Delinquency* 29:7-33.

Homant, Robert J. and Daniel B. Kennedy (1985) "Police Perception of Spouse Abuse: A Comparison of Male and Female Officers." *Journal of Criminal Justice* 13:29-47.

Hotaling, Gerald T. and David B. Sugarman (1986) "An Analysis of Risk Markers in Husband to Wife Violence: The Current State of Knowledge." *Violence and Victims* 1:101-24.

Hutchison, Ira W., J. David Hirschel, and Carolyn E. Pesackis (1988) "Domestic Variations in Domestic Violence Calls to Police." Paper presented at the annual meeting of the Southern Sociological Association, Nashville.

Jolin, Annette (1983) "Domestic Violence Legislation: An Impact Assessment." *Journal of Police Science and Administration* 11:451-56.

Jouriles, Ernest N. and K. Daniel O'Leary (1985) "Interspousal Reliability of Reports of Marital Violence." *Journal of Consulting and Clinical Psychology* 53:419-21.

Konstantin, David N. (1984) "Homicides of American Law Enforcement Officers 1978-1980." *Justice Quarterly* 1:29-45.

Kuhl, Anna F. (1982) "Community Responses to Battered Women." *Victimology* 7:49-59.

Langan, Patrick and Christopher Innes (1986) *Preventing Domestic Violence against Women*. Washington, DC: U.S. Department of Justice.

Langley, Roger and Richard G. Levy (1978) "Wife Abuse and the Police Response." *FBI Law Enforcement Bulletin* 47:4-9.

Lempert, Richard (1989) "Humility Is a Virtue: On the Publicization of Policy Relevant Research." *Law and Society Review* 23:145-61.

Lerman, Lisa G., Leslie Landis, and Sharon Goldzweig (1983) "State Legislation on Domestic Violence." In J. J. Costa (ed.), *Abuse of Women: Legislation, Reporting and Prevention* pp. 39-75. Lexington, MA: Heath.

Lockhart, Lettie L. (1987) "A Reexamination of the Effects of Race and Social Class on the Incidence of Marital Violence: A Search for Reliable Differences." *Journal of Marriage and the Family* 49:603-10.

Loving, N. (1980) *Responding to Spouse Abuse and Wife Beating*. Washington, DC: Police Executive Research Forum.

Mann, Coramae R. (1986) "Getting Even: Women Who Kill in Domestic Encounters." Paper presented at the Annual Meeting of the American Society of Criminology, Atlanta.

Margarita, Mona (1980a) "Killing the Police: Myths and Motives." *Annals of the American Association of Political and Social Science* 452:63-71.

_____ (1980b) "Criminal Violence against Police." Doctoral dissertation, University of New York at Albany.

Martin, Del. (1976) *Battered Wives*. San Francisco: Glide.

Miller, Marilyn G. (1979) *Domestic Violence in Oregon*. Salem: Governor's Commission for Women, State of Oregon Executive Department.

Moore, Donna M. (1979) *Battered Women*. Beverly Hills: Sage.

Morley, Rebecca and Audrey Mullender (1991) "Preventing Violence against Women in the Home: Feminist Dilemmas Concerning Recent British Developments." Paper presented at the British Criminology Conference, York.

Nisonoff, Linda and Irving Bitman (1979) "Spouse Abuse: Incidence and Relationship to Selected Demographic Variables," *Victimology* 4:131-40.

Oppenlander, Nan (1981) "The Evolution of Law and Wife Abuse." *Law and Police Quarterly* 3:382-405.

_____ (1982) "Coping or Copping Out: Police Service Delivery in Domestic Disputes." *Criminology* 20:449-65.

Parnas, Raymond I. (1967) "The Police Response to the Domestic Disturbance." *Wisconsin Law Review* (Fall):914-60.

_____ (1971) "Police Discretion and Diversion of Incidents of Intra-Family Violence." *Law and Contemporary Problems* 36:539-65.

Pearce, Jack B. and John R. Snortum (1983) "Police Effectiveness in Handling Disturbance Calls: An Evaluation of Crisis Intervention Training." *Criminal Justice and Behavior* 10:71-92.

Pence, Ellen (1983) "The Duluth Domestic Abuse Intervention Project." *Hamline Law Review* 6:247-75.

Pleck, Elizabeth (1987) *Domestic Tyranny: The Making of Social Policy against Family Violence from Colonial Times to the Present*. New York: Oxford University Press.

_____ (1989) "Criminal Approaches to Family Violence 1640-1980." In Lloyd Ohlin and Michael Tonry (eds.), *Crime and Justice: A Review of Research* pp. 19-58. Chicago: University of Chicago Press.

Rose, Kristina and Janet Goss (1989) *Domestic Violence Statistics*. Rockville, MD: Justice Statistics Clearinghouse.

"Roughing Up: Spouse Abuse Arrests Grow (1987) *Law Enforcement News* 13:1-13.

Roy, Maria (1977) "Some Thoughts Regarding the Criminal Justice System and Wife-Beating." In Maria Roy (ed.), *Battered Women: A Psychosociological Study of Domestic Violence* pp. 138-39. New York: Van Nostrand Reinhold.

Schulman, Mark A. (1979) *A Survey of Spousal Violence against Women in Kentucky*. Washington, DC: Police Foundation.

Sherman, Lawrence W. and Richard A. Berk (1984a) *The Minneapolis Domestic Violence Experiment.* Washington, DC: Police Foundation.

————— (1984b) "The Specific Deterrent Effects of Arrest for Domestic Assault." *American Sociological Review* 49:261-72.

Sherman, Lawrence W. and Ellen G. Cohn (1989) "The Impact of Research on Legal Policy: The Minneapolis Domestic Violence Experiment." *Law and Society Review* 23:117-44.

Sherman, Lawrence W., Janell C. Schmidt, Dennis P. Rogan, Patrick R. Gartin, Ellen G. Cohn, Dean Collins, and Anthony R. Bacich (1991) "From Initial Deterrence to Long Term Escalation: Short Custody Arrest for Poverty Ghetto Domestic Violence." *Criminology* 29:821-50.

Sherman, Lawrence W., Janell D. Schmidt, Dennis P. Rogan, Douglas A. Smith, Patrick R. Gartin, Ellen G. Cohn, Dean J. Collins and Anthony R. Bacich (1992) "The Variable Effects of Arrest on Criminal Careers: The Milwaukee Domestic Violence Experiment." *The Journal of Criminal Law and Criminology* 83:forthcoming.

Sherman, Lawrence W., Douglas A. Smith, Janell D. Schmidt, and Dennis P. Rogan (1991) *Ghetto Poverty, Crime and Punishment: Legal and Informal Control of Domestic Violence.* Washington, DC: Crime Control Institute.

Sigler, Robert T. (1989) *Domestic Violence in Context: An Assessment of Community Attitudes.* Lexington, MA: Heath.

Smith, Lorna J. F. (1989) *Domestic Violence: An Overview of the Literature.* London: Her Majesty's Stationery Office.

Spanier, Graham B. (1983) "Married and Unmarried Cohabitation in the United States: 1980." *Journal of Marriage and the Family* 45:277-88.

Spitzner, Joseph H. and Donald H. McGee (1975) "Family Crisis Intervention Training, Diversion, and the Prevention of Crimes of Violence." *Police Chief* 42:252-53.

Stanford, Rose M. and Bonney L. Mowry (1990) "Domestic Disturbance Danger Rate." *Journal of Police Science and Administration* 17(4):244-49.

Steinman, Michael (1988) "Anticipating Rank and File Police Reactions to Arrest Policies Regarding Spouse Abuse." *Criminal Justice Research Bulletin* 4:1-5.

Steinmetz, Suzanne K. (1977) *The Cycle of Violence: Assertive and Abusive Family Interaction.* New York: Praeger.

Stephens, Darrell V. (1977) "Domestic Assault: The Police Response." In Maria Roy (ed.), *Battered Women: A Psychosociological Study of Domestic Violence* pp. 164-72. New York: Van Nostrand Reinhold.

Stets, Jan E. and Murray A. Straus (1989) "The Marriage License as a Hitting License: A Comparison of Assaults in Dating, Cohabiting and Married Couples." *Journal of Family Violence* 41:33-52.

Straus, Murray A. (1979) "Measuring Intrafamily Conflict and Violence: The Conflict Tactics (CT) Scales." *Journal of Marriage and the Family* 41:75-88.

————— (1980) "Victims and Aggressors in Marital Violence." *American Behavioral Scientist* 23:681-704.

————— (1989) "Assaults by Wives on Husbands: Implications for Primary Prevention of Marital Violence." Paper presented at annual meetings of the American Society of Criminology, Reno.

_____ (1990) "Conceptualization and Measurement of Battering: Implication for Public Policy." In Michael Steinman (ed.), *Woman Battering: Policy Responses* pp. 19-47. Cincinnati: Anderson.

Straus, Murray A. and Richard J. Gelles (1986) "Societal Change and Change in Family Violence from 1975 to 1985 as Revealed in Two National Surveys." *Journal of Marriage and the Family* 48:465-79.

_____ (1990) *Physical Violence in American Families*. New Brunswick, NJ: Transaction Books.

Straus, Murray, Richard Gelles, and Suzanne Steinmetz (1980) *Behind Closed Doors: Violence in the American Family*. Garden City, NY: Anchor.

Szinovacz, Maximiliane (1983) "Using Couple Data as a Methodological Tool: The Case of Marital Violence." *Journal of Marriage and the Family* 45:633-44.

Uchida, Craig D., Laure W. Brooks, and Christopher S. Kopers (1987) "Danger to Police during Domestic Encounters: Assaults on Baltimore County Police, 1984-1986." *Criminal Justice Policy Review* 2:357-71.

U.S. Commission on Civil Rights (1982) *Under the Rule of Thumb: Battered Women and the Administration of Justice*. Washington, DC: U.S. Government Printing Office.

U.S. Department of Justice (1980) *Intimate Victims: A Study of Violence among Friends and Relatives*. Washington, DC: U.S. Government Printing Office.

_____ (1984) *Attorney General's Task Force on Family Violence: Final Report*. Washington, DC: Author.

_____ (1986-1991) *Crime in the United States: 1985-1990*. Washington, DC: U.S. Government Printing Office.

Victim Services Agency (1988) *The Law Enforcement Response to Family Violence: A State by State Guide to Family Violence Legislation*. New York: Author.

Waits, Kathleen (1985) "The Criminal Justice System's Response to Battering: Understanding the Problem, Forging the Solutions." *Washington Law Review* 60:267-329.

Walker, Gillian A. (1990) *Family Violence and the Women's Movement: A Conceptual Politics of Struggle*. Toronto: University of Toronto Press.

Walter, James D. (1981) "Police in the Middle: A Study of Small City Police Intervention in Domestic Disputes." *Journal of Police Science and Administration* 9:243-60.

Williams, Kirk R. and Richard Hawkins (1989) "The Meaning of Arrest for Wife Assault." *Criminology* 27:163-81.

Wylie, Peter B., Louis F. Basinger, Charlotte L. Heinecke and Jean A. Rueckert (1976) *An Approach to Evaluating a Police Program of Family Crisis Intervention in Six Demonstration Cities: Final Report*. Washington, DC: U.S. Government Printing Office.

Yllo, Kersti and Murray A. Straus (1981) "Interpersonal Violence among Married and Cohabiting Couples." *Family Relations* 30:339-47.

Zahn, Margaret A. and Philip C. Sagi (1987) "Stranger Homicides in Nine American Cities." *Journal of Criminal Law and Criminology* 78(2):377-97.

Zalman, Marvin (forthcoming) "The Court's Response to Police Intervention in Domestic Violence." In Eve S. Buzawa and Carl G. Buzawa (eds.), *Domestic Violence: The Changing Criminal Justice Response*. Westport, CT: Greenwood.

CASES CITED

Balistreri v. Pacifica Police Department 901 F.2d 696, 9th Cir. (1990)

Bradley v. State 2 Miss. 156 (1824)

Bruno v. Codd 396 N.Y.S. 974 (1977)

Deshaney v. Winnebago County Department of Social Services 489 U.S. 189 (1989)

Dudosh v. City of Allentown 665 F. Supp. 381, E.D. Pa. (1987)

Fulgham v. State 46 Ala. 143 (1871)

Joyner v. Joyner 59 N.C. 322 (1862)

Nearing v. Weaver 295 Or. 702 (1983)

Scott v. Hart No. 6-76-2395, N.D. Cal. (1976)

State v. Black 60 N.C. 262 (1864)

State v. Hussey 44 N.C. 124 (1852)

State v. Oliver 70 N.C. 44 (1874)

State v. Rhodes 61 N.C. 452 (1865)

Thurman v. City of Torrington 595 F. Supp. 1521, D. Conn. (1984)

Turner v. City of Charleston 675 F. Supp 314, D.S.C. (1987)

V. COMMUNITY POLICING AND PROBLEM-SOLVING

No subject has dominated the policing field during the past decade quite so much as community policing. In fact, so much analysis and evaluation has been directed toward community policing that little capacity has been left over for the examination of more traditional police operations and administration topics. Consequently, the next study of criminal investigation you hear about will probably focus on the role of police detectives in community policing; the latest police administrative studies focus on supervision and performance evaluation within a community policing framework. Moreover, the billions of dollars in grants attached to the 1994 federal crime bill pretty well guarantee that community policing will continue to dominate the police research and evaluation agenda for some years to come.

In the first chapter in this section, George Kelling, who was the lead researcher in the Kansas City Preventive Patrol Experiment over 20 years ago, argues that "a quiet revolution is reshaping American policing." He reviews several forces driving this change, including much of the research presented earlier in this text. He describes the characteristics of community policing and problem solving, and offers four reasons to be optimistic at this juncture: citizens like the new strategy, its effectiveness is supported by recent research, police departments have gained experience with innovation over the last two decades, and a new breed of police leadership is in charge. He con-

365

cludes that "policing is changing dramatically . . . citizens and police are joining hands to defend communities."

Chapter 19 looks systematically at one of the immediate precursors to community policing—community crime prevention. Dennis Rosenbaum classifies the wide range of community crime prevention efforts into three basic categories—personal, household and neighborhood protection behaviors—and also reviews the evidence on the effectiveness of physical environment alterations to community policing. He finds that community participation in community crime prevention efforts is often weak and inconsistent, so that hoped-for increases in social interaction and informal social control are rarely observed. Personal and household measures often work to reduce victimization, but at a cost—sometimes in the form of lifestyle restrictions, sometimes in actual dollar costs of security hardware. The effectiveness of neighborhood-level strategies is not as well documented, and more rigorous evaluations discover beneficial effects less often. Overall, Rosenbaum's exhaustive review of community crime prevention in the 1970s and 1980s should serve as a cautionary tale for those inclined to draw premature conclusions about the effectiveness of the panacea of the 1990s, community policing.

From the outset of the debate and discussion about community policing, many observers and police practitioners have asked, "Where's the beef?" Early forms of community policing mainly emphasized changing the police organization's relationship with the community and putting police officers back into closer contact with citizens. "But for what purpose?" critics asked, worried that this new strategy might be all rhetoric and no reality. Eventually, problem-solving came to be seen as the central operational element of community policing—police officers should work closely with citizens to identify and solve community problems. Bill Spelman and John Eck, who conducted the first major study of problem-oriented policing in Newport News, Virginia, describe this approach and its underlying rationale in their chapter "Sitting Ducks, Ravenous Wolves, and Helping Hands." They advocate a form of policing that concentrates attention on hot spots, chronic victims and repeat offenders, and that draws upon a wide range of community resources and support.

In the next chapter, Webster and Connors explore in detail the first step in police problem-solving, that of identifying community problems. They draw on the specific experiences of several police agencies to illustrate promising methods as well as stumbling blocks and limitations. Among the sources of information for problem identification that they discuss are officer observations and experience, citizen complaints, crime analysis, police reports, call-for-service analysis, crime mapping, community groups and surveys. They also discuss several practical steps that must be taken in most police agencies in order to support patrol officer problem-solving, including overcoming negative attitudes, developing information systems, allocating sufficient blocks of time and providing leadership.

In Chapter 22, Cordner seeks to provide a coherent framework for analyzing and evaluating community policing and problem-solving. So much has been written on these subjects since the early 1980s, and so many police departments have implemented such widely varying programs, that we are at a point where the term "community policing" can mean almost anything or everything. He identifies three basic dimensions of community policing—philosophical, strategic and programmatic—and describes common components within each. One value of this framework is that variations in community policing from one jurisdiction to the next can be understood in terms of differences in specific components or in the emphasis given to the different dimensions. Another value is that the framework provides a format for considering the evidence on the effectiveness of community policing. Thus far, according to Cordner, we have many studies of specific programmatic elements of community policing, but no evidence concerning the impact of underlying strategic and philosophical dimensions. The programmatic elements of community policing seem to have had their most consistent beneficial effects in reducing disorder and improving police officer and community attitudes; their effects on crime, fear, overall police workload and police officer behavior have been less consistent and generally mixed.

The prevailing mood of enthusiasm for community policing, and our culturally inherited belief in the inevitability of progress, are challenged in the final chapter by Williams and Wagoner. They dispute the assumption that policing in America should become, or even can become, more proactive, whether in the form of community policing or any other strategy. They point out that a serious commitment to proactive community policing will require substantial organizational changes in police departments and new power relationships between police agencies and the community. Their view is that tradition, inertia and bureaucratic interests will win and that policing will remain primarily reactive in nature. Williams and Wagoner predict that "through the end of this decade [the 1990s], there will be minor modifications in policing, all of which will be strongly resisted, or modified to such an extent that the consequences will be minimal or nonexistent." Only time will tell whether this rather pessimistic outlook, or George Kelling's rosier "quiet revolution" scenario, comes closer to hitting the mark.

POLICE AND COMMUNITIES: THE QUIET REVOLUTION

18

George L. Kelling

INTRODUCTION

A quiet revolution is reshaping American policing.

Police in dozens of communities are returning to foot patrol. In many communities, police are surveying citizens to learn what they believe to be their most serious neighborhood problems. Many police departments are finding alternatives to rapidly responding to the majority of calls for service. Many departments are targeting resources on citizen fear of crime by concentrating on disorder. Organizing citizens' groups has become a priority in many departments. Increasingly, police departments are looking for means to evaluate themselves on their contribution to the quality of neighborhood life, not just crime statistics. Are such activities the business of policing? In a crescendo, police are answering yes.

True, such activities contrast with popular images of police: the "thin blue line" separating plundering villains from peaceful residents and storekeepers, and racing through city streets in high-powered cars with sirens wailing and lights flashing. Yet, in city after city, a new vision of policing is taking hold of the imagination of progressive police and gratified citizens. Note the 1987 report of the Philadelphia Task Force. Dismissing the notion of police as Philadelphia's professional defense against crime, and its residents as passive recipients of police ministrations, the report affirms new police values:

> Because the current strategy for policing Philadelphia emphasizes crime control and neglects the Department's need to be accountable to the public and for a partnership with it, the task force recommends: The police commissioner should formulate an explicit

Source: George L. Kelling (1988). "Police and Communities: The Quiet Revolution." *Perspectives on Policing*, 1:1-7. Reprinted by permission of the National Institute of Justice.

mission statement for the Department that will guide planning and operations toward a strategy of *"community"* or *"problem solving"* policing. Such a statement should be developed in consultation with the citizens of Philadelphia and should reflect their views. (Emphases added.)

These themes—problem solving, community policing, consultation, partnership, accountability—have swept through American policing so swiftly that Harvard University's Professor Mark H. Moore has noted that "We in academe have to scramble to keep track of developments in policing." Professor Herman Goldstein of the University of Wisconsin sees police as "having turned a corner" by emphasizing community accountability and problem solving.

THE NEW MODEL OF POLICING

What corner has been turned? What are these changes that are advancing through policing?

BROKEN WINDOWS

In February 1982, James Q. Wilson and I published an article in *Atlantic* known popularly as "Broken Windows." We made three points.

1. **Neighborhood disorder**—drunks, panhandling, youth gangs, prostitution, and other urban incivilities—creates citizen fear.

2. **Just as unrepaired** broken windows can signal to people that nobody cares about a building and lead to more serious vandalism, untended disorderly behavior can also signal that nobody cares about the community and lead to more serious disorder and crime. Such signals—untended property, disorderly persons, drunks, obstreperous youth, etc.—both create fear in citizens and attract predators.

3. **If police are to deal** with disorder to reduce fear and crime, they must rely on citizens for legitimacy and assistance.

"Broken Windows" gave voice to sentiments felt both by citizens and police. It recognized a major change in the focus of police. Police had believed that they should deal with serious crime, yet were frustrated by lack of success. Citizens conceded to police that crime was a problem, but were more concerned about daily incivilities that disrupted and often destroyed neighborhood social, commercial, and political life. "We were trying to get people to be concerned about crime problems," says Darrel Stephens, former Chief in Newport News and now Executive Director of the Police Executive Research Forum, "never understanding that daily living issues had a much greater impact on citizens and commanded their time and attention."

Many police officials, however, believed the broken windows metaphor went further. For them, it not only suggested changes in the focus of police work (disorder, for example), it also suggested major modifications in the overall strategy of police departments. What are some of these strategic changes?

DEFENSE OF A COMMUNITY

Police are a neighborhood's primary defense against disorder and crime, right? This orthodoxy has been the basis of police strategy for a generation. What is the police job? Fighting crime. How do they do this? Patrolling in cars, responding to calls for service, and investigating crimes. What is the role of citizens in all of this? Supporting police by calling them if trouble occurs and by being good witnesses.

But using our metaphor, let us again ask the question of whether police are the primary defense against crime and disorder. Are police the "thin blue line" defending neighborhoods and communities? Considering a specific example might help us answer this question. For example, should police have primary responsibility for controlling a neighborhood youth who, say, is bullying other children?

Of course not. The first line of defense in a neighborhood against a troublesome youth is the youth's family. Even if the family is failing, our immediate answer would not be to involve police. Extended family— aunts, uncles, grandparents—might become involved. Neighbors and friends (of both the parents and youth) often offer assistance. The youth's church or school might become involved.

On occasion police will be called: Suppose that the youth is severely bullying other children to the point of injuring them. A bullied child's parents call the police. Is the bully's family then relieved of the responsibility? Are neighbors? The school? Once police are called, are neighbors relieved of their duty to be vigilant and protect their own or other neighbors' children? Does calling police relieve teachers of their obligation to be alert and protect children from assault? The answer to all these questions is no. We expect families, neighbors, teachers, and others to be responsible and prudent.

If we believe that community institutions are the first line of defense against disorder and crime, and the source of strength for maintaining the quality of life, what should the strategy of police be? The old view was that they were a community's professional defense against crime and disorder:

Citizens should leave control of crime and maintenance of order to police. The new strategy is that police are to stimulate and buttress a community's ability to produce attractive neighborhoods and protect them against predators. Moreover, in communities that are wary of strangers, police serve to help citizens tolerate and protect outsiders who come into their neighborhoods for social or commercial purposes.

But what about neighborhoods in which things have gotten out of hand—where, for example, predators like drug dealers take over and openly and outrageously deal drugs and threaten citizens? Clearly, police must play a leading role defending such communities. Should they do so on their own, however?

Police have tried in the past to control neighborhoods plagued by predators without involving residents. Concerned, for example, about serious street crime, police made youths, especially minority youths, the targets of aggressive field interrogations. The results, in the United States during the 1960's and more recently in England during the early 1980's, were disastrous. Crime was largely unaffected. Youths already hostile to police became even more so. Worst of all, good citizens became estranged from police.

Citizens in neighborhoods plagued by crime and disorder were disaffected because they simply would not have police they neither knew nor authorized whizzing in and out of their neighborhoods "takin' names and kickin' ass." Community relations programs were beside the point. Citizens were in no mood to surrender control of their neighborhoods to remote and officious police who showed them little respect. Police are the first line of defense in a neighborhood? Wrong—citizens are!

DEFENDING COMMUNITIES—FROM INCIDENTS TO PROBLEMS

The strategy of assisting citizens maintain the quality of life in their neighborhoods dramatically improves on the former police strategy. To understand why, one has to understand in some detail how police work has been conducted in the past. Generally, the business of police for the past 30 years has been responding to calls for service.

For example, a concerned and frightened citizen calls police about a neighbor husband and wife who are fighting. Police come and intervene. They might separate the couple, urge them to get help, or, if violence has occurred, arrest the perpetrator. But basically, police try to resolve the incident and get back into their patrol cars so they are available for the next call. Beat officers may well know that this household has been the subject of 50 or 100 calls to the police department during the past year. In fact, they have known intuitively what researchers Glenn Pierce in Boston and

Lawrence Sherman in Minneapolis have confirmed through research: fewer than 10 percent of the addresses calling for police service generate over 60 percent of the total calls for service during a given year.

Indeed, it is very likely that the domestic dispute described above is nothing new for the disputing couple, the neighbors, or police. More likely than not, citizens have previously called police and they have responded. And, with each call to police, it becomes more likely that there will be another.

This atomistic response to incidents acutely frustrates patrol officers. Herman Goldstein describes this frustration: "Although the public looks at the average officer as a powerful authority figure, the officer very often feels impotent because he or she is dealing with things for which he or she has no solution. Officers believe this makes them look silly in the eyes of the public." But, given the routine of police work, officers have had no alternative to their typical response: Go to a call, pacify things, and leave to get ready for another call. To deal with the problem of atomistic responses to incidents, Goldstein has proposed what he calls "problem-oriented policing."

Stated simply, problem-oriented policing is a method of working with citizens to help them identify and solve problems. Darrel Stephens, along with Chief David Couper of Madison, Wisconsin, and Chief Neil Behan of Baltimore County, Maryland, has pioneered in problem-oriented policing. Problems approached via problem-oriented policing include sexual assault and drunk driving in Madison, auto theft, spouse abuse, and burglary in Newport News, and street robbery and burglary in Baltimore County.

Stephens' goal is for "police officers to take the time to stop and think about what they were doing." Mark Moore echoes Stephens: "In the past there were a small number of guys in the police chief's office who did the thinking and everybody else just carried out their ideas. Problem solving gets thousands of brains working on problems."

THE DRIVE TO CHANGE

Why are these changes taking place now? There are three reasons:

1. Citizen disenchantment with police services;

2. Research conducted during the 1970's; and,

3. Frustration with the traditional role of the police officer.

1. Disenchantment with police services—At first, it seems too strong to say "disenchantment" when referring to citizens' attitudes towards police.

Certainly citizens admire and respect most police officers. Citizens enjoy contact with police. Moreover, research shows that most citizens do not find the limited capability of police to prevent or solve crimes either surprising or of particular concern. Nevertheless, there is widespread disenchantment with police tactics that continue to keep police officers remote and distant from citizens.

Minority citizens in inner cities continue to be frustrated by police who whisk in and out of their neighborhoods with little sensitivity to community norms and values. Regardless of where one asks, minorities want both the familiarity and accountability that characterize foot patrol. Working- and middle-class communities of all races are demanding increased collaboration with police in the determination of police priorities in their neighborhoods. Community crime control has become a mainstay of their sense of neighborhood security and a means of lobbying for different police services. And many merchants and affluent citizens have felt so vulnerable that they have turned to private security for service and protection. In private sector terms, police are losing to the competition—private security and community crime control.

2. Research—The 1970's research about police effectiveness was another stimulus to change. Research about preventive patrol, rapid response to calls for service, and investigative work—the three mainstays of police tactics—was uniformly discouraging.

Research demonstrated that preventive patrol in automobiles had little effect on crime, citizen levels of fear, or citizen satisfaction with police. Rapid response to calls for service likewise had little impact on arrests, citizen satisfaction with police, or levels of citizen fear. Also, research into criminal investigation effectiveness suggested that detective units were so poorly administered that they had little chance of being effective.

3. Role of the patrol officer—Finally, patrol officers have been frustrated with their traditional role. Despite pieties that patrol has been the backbone of policing, every police executive has known that, at best, patrol has been what officers do until they become detectives or are promoted.

At worst, patrol has been the dumping ground for officers who are incompetent, suffering from alcoholism or other problems, or simply burned out. High status for police practitioners went to detectives. Getting "busted to patrol" has been a constant threat to police managers or detectives who fail to perform by some standard or judgment. (It is doubtful that failing patrol officers ever get threatened with being busted to the detective unit.)

Never mind that patrol officers have the most important mission in police departments: They handle the public's most pressing problems and must make complex decisions almost instantaneously. Moreover, they do this with little supervision or training. Despite this, police administrators treat patrol officers as if they did little to advance the organization's mission. The salaries of patrol officers also reflect their demeaned status. No wonder many officers have grown cynical and have turned to unions for leadership rather than to police executives. "Stupid management made unions," says Robert Kliesmet, the President of the International Union of Police Associations AFL-CIO.

THE BASIS FOR NEW OPTIMISM

Given these circumstances, what is the basis of current optimism of police leaders that they have turned a corner? Optimism arises from four factors:

1. Citizen response to the new strategy;

2. Ongoing research on police effectiveness;

3. Past experience police have had with innovation; and

4. The values of the new generation of police leaders.

1. Citizen response—The overwhelming public response to community and problem-solving policing has been positive, regardless of where it has been instituted. When queried about how he knows community policing works in New York, Lt. Jerry Simpson responds: "The District Commanders' phones stop ringing." Simpson continues: "Commanders' phones stop ringing because problems have been solved. Even skeptical commanders soon learn that most of their troubles go away with community policing." Citizens like the cop on the beat and enjoy working with him/her to solve problems. Crisley Wood, Executive Director of the Neighborhood Justice Network in Boston—an agency that has established a network of neighborhood crime control organizations—puts it this way: "The cop on the beat, who meets regularly with citizen groups, is the single most important service that the Boston Police Department can provide."

Testimonies aside, perhaps the single most compelling evidence of the popularity of community or problem-solving policing is found in Flint, Michigan, where, it will be recalled, citizens have twice voted to increase their taxes to maintain neighborhood foot patrols—the second time by a two-to-one margin.

2. New research on effectiveness—Research conducted during the early and mid-1970's frustrated police executives. It generally showed what did not work. Research conducted during the late 1970's and early 1980's was

different. By beginning to demonstrate that new tactics did work, it fueled the move to rejuvenate policing. This research provided police with the following guidance:

> Foot patrol can reduce citizen fear of crime, improve the relationship between police and citizens, and increase citizen satisfaction with police. This was discovered in Newark, New Jersey, and Flint. In Flint, foot patrol also reduced crime and calls for service. Moreover, in both cities, it increased officer satisfaction with police work.
>
> The productivity of detectives can be enhanced if patrol officers carefully interview neighborhood residents about criminal events, get the information to detectives, and detectives use it wisely, according to John Eck of PERF.
>
> Citizen fear can be substantially reduced, researcher Tony Pate of the Police Foundation discovered in Newark, by police tactics that emphasize increasing the quantity and improving the quality of citizen-police interaction.
>
> Police anti-fear tactics can also reduce household burglaries, according to research conducted by Mary Ann Wycoff, also of the Police Foundation.
>
> Street-level enforcement of heroin and cocaine laws can reduce serious crime in the area of enforcement, without being displaced to adjacent areas, according to an experiment conducted by Mark Kleiman of Harvard University's Program in Criminal Justice Policy and Management.
>
> Problem-oriented policing can be used to reduce thefts from cars, problems associated with prostitution, and household burglaries, according to William Spelman and John Eck of PERF.
>
> These positive findings about new police tactics provide police with both the motive and justification for continued efforts to rejuvenate policing.

3. Experience with innovation—The desire to improve policing is not new with this generation of reformers. The 1960's and 1970's had their share of reformers as well. Robert Eichelberger of Dayton innovated with team policing (tactics akin in many ways to problem solving) and public policymaking; Frank Dyson of Dallas with team policing and generalist/specialist patrol officers; Carl Gooden with team policing in Cincinnati; and there were many other innovators.

But innovators of this earlier era were handicapped by a lack of documented successes and failures of implementation. Those who experimented with team policing were not aware that elements of team policing were simply incompatible with preventive patrol and rapid response to calls for service. As a result, implementation of team policing followed a discouraging pattern. It would be implemented, officers and citizens would like it, it would have an initial impact on crime, and then business as usual would overwhelm it—the program would simply vanish.

Moreover, the lessons about innovation and excellence that Peters and Waterman brought together in *In Search of Excellence* were not available to police administrators. The current generation of reformers has an edge: They have availed themselves of the opportunity to learn from the documented successes and failures of the past. Not content with merely studying innovation and management in policing, Houston's Chief Lee Brown is having key personnel spend internships in private sector corporations noted for excellence in management.

4. New breed of police leadership—The new breed of police leadership is unique in the history of American policing. Unlike the tendency in the past for chiefs to be local and inbred, chiefs of this generation are urbane and cosmopolitan.

Chief Lee Brown of Houston received a Ph.D. in criminology from the University of California-Berkeley; Chief Joseph McNamara of San Jose, California, has a Ph.D. from Harvard University, and is a published novelist; Hubert Williams, formerly Director of the Newark Police Department and now President of the Police Foundation, is a lawyer and has studied criminology in the Law School at Harvard University; Benjamin Ward, Commissioner of the New York City Police Department, is an attorney and was Commissioner of Corrections in New York State.

These are merely a sample. The point is, members of this generation of police leadership are well educated and of diverse backgrounds. All of those noted above, as well as many others, have sponsored research and experimentation to improve policing.

PROBLEMS

We have looked at the benefits of community policing. What is the down side? What are the risks?

These questions led to the creation of the Executive Session on Community Policing in the Program in Criminal Justice Policy and Management of Harvard University's John F. Kennedy School of Government. Funded by the National Institute of Justice and the Charles Stewart Mott, and Guggenheim Foundations, the Executive Sessions has convened police and political elites with a small number of academics around the issue of community policing. Francis X. Hartmann, moderator of the Executive Session, describes the purpose of the meetings: "These persons with a special and important relationship to contemporary policing have evolved into a real working group, which is addressing the gap between the realities and aspirations of American policing. Community policing is a significant effort to fill this gap."

Among the questions the Executive Session has raised are the following:

1. Police are a valuable resource in a community. Does community policing squander that resource by concentrating on the wrong priorities?

2. How will community policing fit into police departments given how they are now organized? and,

3. Will community policing open the door to increased police corruption or other inappropriate behavior by line officers?

WILL COMMUNITY POLICING SQUANDER POLICE RESOURCES?

This question worries police. They understand that police are a valuable but sparse resource in a community. Hubert Williams, a pioneer in community policing, expresses his concern. "Are police now being put in the role of providing services that are statutorily the responsibilities of some other agencies?" Los Angeles's Chief Gates echoes Williams: "Hubie's (Williams is) right—you can't solve all the problems in the world and shouldn't try." Both worry that if police are spread too thin, by problem-solving activities for example, that they will not be able to properly protect the community from serious crime.

This issue is now being heatedly debated in Flint. There, it will be recalled, citizens have passed two bills funding foot patrol—the second by a two-to-one majority. A report commissioned by city government, however, concludes: "The Cost of the Neighborhood Foot Patrol Program Exceeds the Benefit It Provides the Citizens of Flint," and recommends abandoning the program when funding expires in 1988.

Why, according to the report, should foot patrol be abandoned? So more "effective" police work can be done. What is effective police work? Quick response to calls for service, taking reports, and increased visibility by putting police officers in cars. "It is simply wrong," says Robert Wasserman, noted police tactician and Research Fellow in the Program in Criminal Justice at Harvard, "to propose abandoning foot patrol in the name of short response time and visibility vis-a-vis patrolling in cars.

Every shred of evidence is that rapid response and patrolling in cars does-n't reduce crime, increase citizen satisfaction, or reduce fear. Which is the luxury," Wasserman concludes, "a tactic like foot patrol that gives you two, and maybe three, of your goals, or a tactic like riding around in cars going from call to call that gives you none?" Experienced police executives share Wasserman's concerns. Almost without exception, they are attempting to find ways to get out of the morass that myths of the efficacy of rapid response have created for large-city police departments. It was Commissioner Ben Ward of New York City, for example, who puts a cap on resources that can be used to respond to calls for service and is attempting to find improved means of responding to calls. Commissioner Francis "Mickey" Roache expresses the deep frustration felt by so many police: "I hate to say this, but in Boston we run from one call to another. We don't accomplish anything. We're just running all over the place. It's absolutely insane."

A politician's response to the recommendation to end Flint's foot patrol program is interesting. Daniel Whitehurst, former Mayor of Fresno, California, reflects: "I find it hard to imagine ending a program that cit-izens not only find popular but are willing to pay for as well."

"The overwhelming danger," Mark Moore concludes, "is that, in the name of efficiency, police and city officials will be tempted to maintain old patterns. They will think they are doing good, but will be squandering police resources." "Chips" Stewart emphasizes the need to move ahead: "As comfortable as old tactics might feel, police must continue to exper-iment with methods that have shown promise to improve police effec-tiveness and efficiency."

WILL COMMUNITY POLICING FIT WITHIN POLICING AS IT IS NOW ORGANIZED?

Many police and academics believe this to be the most serious prob-lem facing cities implementing community policing. Modern police depart-ments have achieved an impressive capacity to respond quickly to calls for service. This has been accomplished by acquiring and linking elaborate automobile, telephone, radio, and computer technologies, by centralizing control and dispatch of officers, by pressing officers to be "in service" (rather than "out of service" dealing with citizens), and by allocating police in cars throughout the city on the basis of expected calls for service.

Community policing is quite different: it is not incident- or technology-driven; officers operate on a decentralized basis, it emphasizes officers being in regular contact with citizens, and it allocates police on the basis of neighborhoods. The question is, how reconcilable are these two strategies? Some (Lawrence Sherman of the University of Maryland in one example) have taken a strong stance that radical alterations will be required if police are to respond more effectively to community problems. Others (Richard Larson of the Massachusetts Institute of Technology, for example) disagree, believing that community policing is reconcilable with rapid response technology—indeed Professor Larson would emphasize that current computer technology can facilitate community policing.

WILL THE COMMUNITY POLICING STRATEGY LEAD TO INCREASED POLICE CORRUPTION AND MISBEHAVIOR?

The initial news from Houston, New York, Flint, Newark, Los Angeles, Baltimore County, and other police departments which have experimented with community policing is good. Community policing has not led to increased problems of corruption or misbehavior.

Why is it, however, that policymakers fear that community policing has the potential to increase the incidents of police running amok? The answer? Community policing radically decentralizes police authority; officers must create for themselves the best responses to problems; and, police become intimately involved with citizens.

These ingredients may not sound so troublesome in themselves—after all, many private and public sector organizations radically decentralize authority, encourage creativity, and are characterized by relative intimacy between service providers and consumers. Nevertheless, in police circles such ingredients violate the orthodox means of controlling corruption. For a generation, police have believed that to eliminate corruption it is necessary to centralize authority, limit discretion, and reduce intimacy between police and citizens. They had good reason to: Early policing in the United States had been characterized by financial corruption, failure of police to protect the rights of all citizens, and zealotry.

But just as it is possible to squander police resources in the name of efficiency, it is also possible to squander police resources in the quest for integrity. Centralization, standardization, and remoteness may preclude many opportunities for corruption, but they may also preclude the possibility of good policing. For example, street-level cocaine and heroin enforcement by patrol officers, now known to have crime reduction value, has been banned in cities because of fear of corruption. It is almost as if the purpose of police was to be corruption free, rather than to do essential work. If, as it appears to be, it is necessary to take risks to solve problems, then so be it: police will have to learn to manage risks as well as do managers in other enterprises.

Does this imply softening on the issue of police corruption? Absolutely not. Police and city managers will have to continue to be vigilant: community policing exposes officers to more opportunities for traditional financial corruption; in many neighborhoods police will be faced with demands to protect communities from the incursions of minorities; and, police will be tempted to become overzealous when they see citizens' problems being ignored by other agencies.

These dangers mean, however, that police executives will have to manage through values, rather than merely policies and procedures, and by establishing regular neighborhood and community institution reporting mechanisms, rather than through centralized command and control systems.

Each of these issues—use of police resources, organizational compatibility, and corruption—is complicated. Some will be the subject of debate. Others will require research and experimentation to resolve. But most police chiefs will begin to address these issues in a new way. They will not attempt to resolve them in the ways of the past: in secret, behind closed doors. Their approach will reflect the values of the individual neighborhoods as well as the community as a whole.

Policing is changing dramatically. On the one hand, we wish policing to retain the old values of police integrity, equitable distribution of police resources throughout a community, and police efficiency which characterized the old model of police. But the challenge of contemporary police and city executives is to redefine these concepts in light of the resurgence of neighborhood vitality, consumerism, and more realistic assessments of the institutional capacity of police.

The quiet revolution is beginning to make itself heard: citizens and police are joining together to defend communities.

COMMUNITY CRIME PREVENTION: A REVIEW AND SYNTHESIS OF THE LITERATURE 19

Dennis P. Rosenbaum

The "war against crime" in the United States and other Western countries has been fought on the battlefield of the criminal justice system; on the whole, the strategies employed have produced very limited effects on community crime rates. A major study by Jacob and Lineberry (1982) found that the primary response to crime by governmental agencies over the past three decades has been to increase the budgets and personnel rosters of criminal justice agencies. Although research and management decisions have increased the efficiency of many criminal justice operations over the past two decades (see Petersilia 1987), these changes have not dramatically affected the "bottom line." As a result, the theories and policies underlying these practices have been called into question. Whether one examines traditional police practices (Eck and Spelman 1987a), selective incapacitation of career criminals (Gottfredson and Hirschi 1986, 1988; Greenwood 1979), deterrence through criminal sanctions (Cook 1980), or rehabilitation (Lipton, Martinson, and Wilks 1975), there have been widespread disillusionment and sometimes wholesale rejection of strategies that may be effective under certain conditions (e.g., see Cullen and Gilbert 1982). Despite the raging debates over the effectiveness and appropriateness of different strategies for reducing crime in Western societies, there is a consensus that the criminal justice system, as generally conceived, is inherently limited in its capacity to prevent crime.

What is the alternative? Expanding the role of ordinary citizens in the "war on crime" has been recommended by no less than three national commissions in the United States, which assessed the nation's response to crime. As disappointment with the formal mechanisms for maintaining

Source: Dennis P. Rosenbaum (1988). "Community Crime Prevention: A Review and Synthesis of the Literature." *Justice Quarterly*, 5(3):323-395. Reprinted by permission of the Academy of Criminal Justice Sciences.

order increases, community-based crime prevention strategies have emerged as a promising alternative to reactive, offender-oriented approaches. This alternative is based on the premise that private citizens play a major role in maintaining order in a free society, and therefore should be encouraged to accept more responsibility for the prevention of crime (Hope and Shaw 1988; Lavrakas 1985; Rosenbaum 1986). Thus community crime prevention programs have focused on increasing the participation of individual citizens, small groups, and voluntary community organizations in activities designed to reduce crime and to improve the quality of neighborhood life. Because society cannot afford a "cop on every corner" or a parole officer for every parolee, criminal justice scholars and policy makers must take a closer look at the costs and benefits of this relatively cheap alternative.

Growing interest in community crime prevention was not simply the result of academic and professional dissatisfaction with traditional crime control strategies. Beginning with the Kennedy administration and the civil rights movement in the early 1960s, the United States federal government has encouraged citizen participation in policy decisions regarding community action, health, and the environment (Grant 1981; Kramer 1969). During this period there was a major increase in the number of community organizations in the United States (Bell and Held 1969). Citizen interest in the crime issue was a logical extension of this grass-roots activity because of changes in the magnitude of the crime problem. In the United States, rising crime rates during the 1970s meant that more people were victimized by crime than ever before. Not surprisingly, public concern about crime and fear of crime also were on the rise (DuBow, McCabe, and Kaplan 1979), thus providing more citizens with motivation to seek some type of effective preventive action. With the advent of victimization surveys in several Western countries has come a substantial shift of political attention away from offenders to the victims of crime, including a concern about what can be done to protect the public from the threat of crime. Also, because fear of crime is believed to accelerate neighborhood decline and to increase crime rates (cf. Skogan 1986), numerous fear-reduction programs have been developed recently, which are oriented strongly toward citizen-police partnerships in the coproduction of public safety (e.g. Pate, Wycoff, Skogan, and Sherman 1986; Rosenbaum 1986).

Community crime prevention has evolved continually from the standpoint of the practitioner. In the late 1960s and early 1970s, "crime prevention" was largely a public relations tactic by law enforcement to improve the community's image of what the police were doing (DuBow and Emmons 1981). In the mid-1970s, with a push from several national commissions and the availability of grants from the Law Enforcement Assistance Administration (LEAA), police departments began to educate the public about individual crime prevention measures for protecting themselves and their property. Within a few years, law enforcement officials felt comfortable in promoting collective crime prevention measures such as "Block Watch," but only as the "eyes and ears" of the police in a crime-reporting capacity. Not until 1977 was it recognized through national crime control policy that the "community" should play the central role in defining "community crime prevention" (DuBow and Emmons 1981; Lavrakas 1985). Two federal initiatives—the Community Anti-Crime Program in 1977 (Krug 1983) and the Urban Crime Prevention Program in 1980 (Roehl and Cook 1984)—provided funds directly to community organizations (rather than to law enforcement) to help mobilize neighborhood residents in the fight against crime. To some extent, community scholars in the early 1980s rejected the role of the criminal justice system in the maintenance of order and placed their confidence in the efficacy of voluntary organizations. We have learned since, however, that community groups are quite limited in preventing urban crime without the support of law enforcement, adequate funding, and considerable technical assistance (Bennett 1988; Lewis, Grant, and Rosenbaum 1988; Roehl and Cook 1984; Yin 1986). Thus, starting in the mid 1980s, the pendulum began to swing back to a more realistic position, namely that formal and informal means of crime reduction and order maintenance are complementary and should work together to define "community crime prevention."

In this article I will attempt to review what is known currently—on the basis of social science research—about the nature, extent, and efficacy of community crime prevention strategies. This article will describe what most citizens do, both individually and collectively, to prevent crime in their neighborhoods. More important, it will provide a critical assessment of the research literature pertaining to the effectiveness of these behaviors in reducing crime, "incivilities," and fear of crime, and in building a sense of community. This review also will cover research on modifications of the physical environment and innovations in policing as they pertain to neighborhood-based crime prevention. Community crime prevention has been advocated in hundreds of cities as a "highly effective" means of preventing crime (e.g. National Crime Prevention Council 1987). Whereas the media, the politicians, and law enforcement agencies find it a very appealing strategy for attacking both fear and crime, the task here is to "separate the wheat from the chaff." This task entails drawing conclusions on the basis of data gathered by acceptable social science methods rather than on the basis of opinion and speculation.

THE THEORETICAL AND EMPIRICAL RATIONALE

Informal Social Control. Although community crime prevention embodies more than one model of social intervention, its primary intellectual heritage can be traced to the "Chicago School" in the 1920s and

1930s, where urban scholars examined the impact of "community" on crime (Shaw and McKay 1931,1942). This exploration was the beginning of a long line of research showing that high rates of crime can be found in neighborhoods characterized by a heterogeneity of class and ethnicity, high levels of transiency, and disproportionate number of youths, among other factors (see Greenberg, Rohe, and Williams 1985). Shaw and McKay (1942) concluded that high crime rates were the result of "social disorganization"; that is, a weakened capacity of local institutions and organizations (because of the erosion of shared norms and values) to regulate or control the behavior of local residents. Families, churches, schools, and ethnic groups that once held the community together and dictated appropriate social behavior had been weakened. Although this view has been challenged and refined over the years (see Carey 1975; Matza 1969), it serves as the foundation for today's renewed interest in the study of "community crime careers" (Reiss 1986) and as a rationale for certain community crime prevention programs.

The argument for intervention through community crime prevention runs as follows: If social disorganization is the problem and if traditional agents of social control no longer are performing adequately, we need to find alternative ways to strengthen informal social control and to restore a "sense of community." From the classic Chicago Area Project (by Shaw and McKay) to modern crime prevention, collective citizen action—via voluntary community organizations—has been proposed as a primary strategy for dealing with the problem of eroding informal social control (Greenberg, Rohe, and Williams 1985; Skogan 1987a). Today the objective is to "organize" the neighborhood and thus to encourage the types of behaviors that are believed to provide the basis for regulating or controlling social behavior, beginning with the encouragement of more frequent social interaction (Rosenbaum 1987). Social control can be defined as "the use of rewards or punishments to insure that members of a group—such as a family, organization, neighborhood, or society—will obey the group's rules or norms" (Greenberg et al. 1985:4). Whereas formal social control is derived from written rules and laws and is enforced by the police and the courts, informal social control is based on custom or social norms and is enforced by the citizenry through behaviors such as surveillance, verbal reprimands, rejection, warnings, and other pressures to encourage conformity.

Organizing a disorganized neighborhood and encouraging behaviors by residents that help to enforce social norms sound like a logical strategy but can it be done? This is an empirical question that community crime prevention practitioners and researchers must address. The central hypothesis to be tested in this field is what I call the "implant hypothesis" (Rosenbaum 1987); namely, that informal social control and related processes can be "implanted by collective citizen action in neighborhoods where they are naturally weak or nonexistent. Even this hypothesis is based on the assumption that informal social control is an important mechanism for controlling crime, disorder, and fear of crime. Evidence relevant to this assumption will be assessed as well.

Opportunity Reduction. Modern "community crime prevention" involves much more than direct attempts to improve social integration and community cohesion. Crime prevention has been practiced for thousands of years by individuals seeking to reduce their risk of victimization. "Crime prevention" has been defined internationally as "the anticipation, recognition, and appraisal of a crime risk and the initiation of some action to remove it" (National Crime Prevention Institute 1978). In practice, crime prevention generally focuses on removing or reducing specific opportunities for crime rather than attempting to change the offender's motivation to commit crime. Along these lines, a substantial portion of the theorizing about crime prevention is derived from scholarship in environmental criminology (cf. Brantingham and Brantingham 1981), and is based on the premise that the physical environment can determine the opportunities for criminal behavior. Jacobs (1961) was a pioneer in proposing that changes in urban design (e.g., widening sidewalks) could be used to encourage more high density social interaction, to increase the natural surveillance of public spaces (i.e., more "eyes on the street"), and therefore to reduce the opportunities for criminal conduct. Newman (1972) later expanded these design concepts to develop a theory of "defensible space," which placed heavy emphasis on how architecture could be used to increase the "surveillability" of public areas and to give residents a sense of "territoriality" for these areas.[1] The concept of territoriality, in which a protective, ownership-like position is adopted with regard to specific areas, is central to crime prevention theorizing and has stimulated the development of special territorial theories focusing on the perspective of the offender (Brown and Altman 1981) as well as the resident (Taylor, Gottfredson, and Brower 1981).

One of the most significant developments in community crime prevention is the application of territoriality and surveillance concepts to social (rather than physical) interventions. The common organizing strategies that encourage residents to "watch out" for suspicious or criminal activity are attempting to increase intentional surveillance through social influence rather than to increase natural surveillance through changes in the physical environment (Rosenbaum 1987). The primary objective is the same, whether the intervention is social or physical namely, to reduce the opportunity for criminal activity in specific settings by increasing the risk of detection and apprehension. Hence this approach to crime prevention often is referred to as "opportunity reduction in the United States (Bennett 1988; Rosenbaum 1986) and "situational crime prevention" in England (Clarke 1983; Hough, Clarke, and Mayhew 1980).

The opportunity-reduction approach is sufficiently broad to incorporate a variety of crime prevention strategies, including one of the oldest and most widely used tactics—target hardening. From castle moats to deadbolt locks, these measures are designed to remove access to or to increase the physical security of certain property.

CONCEPTUALIZATION OF CRIME PREVENTION BEHAVIORS

Whether people are responding to the threat of crime, the introduction of crime prevention programs, or other stimuli, the fact remains that many residents engage in a wide range of crime prevention behaviors. National surveys indicate that between one-half and two-thirds of adults in the United States limited or changed their behavior because of crime (Garofalo 1977a; Mendelsohn, O'Keefe, and Liu 1981). The problem is how to conceptualize or group these behaviors in a manner that allows for a meaningful discussion of their prevalence and their effectiveness in preventing crime. The academic literature is filled with typologies and categorizations (see DuBow et al. 1979; Lavrakas and Lewis 1980) As noted above, the concepts of "access control," "surveillance and "territoriality" have been used extensively to describe citizen crime prevention behaviors in the context of environmental design applications (Tien, Reppetto, and Hanes 1976) and in general models of "situational" crime prevention (Hough et al. 1980). Other popular descriptions include "avoidance" versus "mobilization" behaviors (Furstenberg 1972), "individual" versus "collective" behaviors (Conklin 1975), and "private-minded" versus "public-minded" behaviors (Schneider and Schneider 1978). Unfortunately there has been little empirical work to establish the validity of these constructs (Lavrakas and Lewis 1980). Hence, although these terms will be used here as needed for descriptive purposes, an alternative scheme—proposed and validated empirically by Lavrakas and his colleagues (Lavrakas and Lewis 1980; Lavrakas, Normoyle, Skogan, Hertz, Salem, and Lewis 1980)—will be used to categorize crime prevention behaviors.

Crime prevention behaviors can be classified as one of three types, depending on whom or what the behavior is intended to protect: 1) personal protection behaviors, intended to protect oneself from victimization; 2) household protection behaviors, intended to protect one's property (and persons residing in one's home) by seeking to prevent illegal entry; and 3) neighborhood protection behaviors, intended to protect a specific geographic area (e.g., residential block) and to prevent criminal activity in that territory. For simplicity of presentation, this conceptualization will be limited to changes in personal and social behavior, even if these changes result in a modification of the physical environment (e.g., buying and installing locks). More ambitious changes in the physical environment will be treated in a separate section.

This review is limited to community crime prevention behaviors and programs directed primarily at residential crime. The main focus of this analysis is the behavior of ordinary citizens in residential settings and programs designed to modify such behavior. Excluded are preventive efforts directed at commercial crime, white-collar crime, and other specific types of criminal activity. The literature on the prevention of juvenile delinquency also is outside the scope of this review. Finally, this assessment gives greater attention to what citizens actually do than to what experts think they should be doing. An effort was made, however, not to overlook promising innovations that lack public recognition or endorsement because of their age.

PERSONAL PROTECTION BEHAVIORS

NATURE AND EXTENT OF SELF-PROTECTION

Individual citizens have employed a variety of behaviors for self-protection such as avoiding threatening situations, taking self-defense classes, and buying large dogs and handguns. Essentially there are two basic types of individual protective measures (cf. Suttles 1972): a) those intended to reduce the risk of victimization by avoiding threatening situations and b) those intended to manage risk (when it is unavoidable) either by making victimization more difficult or by minimizing the loss when victimization occurs. (Precautionary measures that serve a dual purpose of self-protection and property protection, such as locking doors and windows, will be covered later under "household protection behaviors.")

Risk-avoidance Behaviors. The most widely employed and discussed individual reactions to crime are "risk-avoidance" behaviors (Lavrakas et al. 1980). Many residents believe that staying at home, especially at night, is a good way to avoid being victimized by crime. The frequency of staying at home at night varies dramatically from only eight percent of the residents in a small Ohio town (Gorse and Beran 1973) to 80 percent of the residents in a high-crime Philadelphia neighborhood (Savitz, Lili, and Rosen 1977) Most surveys of big cities or urban neighborhoods show that the percentage of residents who stay off the streets at night ranges from 25 to 45 percent (Biderman, Johnson, McIntyre, and Weir 1967; Harris 1969; Reiss 1967; Skogan and Maxfield 1981).

Avoiding certain parts of the city or neighborhood is another common risk-avoidance behavior. Victimization surveys in eight large U.S. cities found that 36 percent of the respondents would not go into certain areas of the city at night and 20 percent would avoid certain areas during the day

(Garofalo 1977a). The tendency to avoid certain parts of the city has been show to be substantially higher in separate studies of Detroit (52%, Institute for Social Research 1975), Kansas City (68%, Kelling, Pate, Dieckman, and Brown 1974), and Chicago (70%, Lavrakas et al. 1980). In addition to avoiding downtown areas, people often report staying away from public parks (Malt Associates 1971; Springer 1974), and places where they are likely to encounter strangers or other threatening persons. For example, 75 percent of the respondents from four Portland neighborhoods said they would cross the street when they saw a gang of teenagers (Yaden, Folkstand, and Glazier 1973); 67 percent of Chicago residents report that they avoid walking near strangers in the neighborhood (Lavrakas et al. 1980).

If these and other crime prevention behaviors are deemed ineffective or undesirable, the most drastic means of avoiding crime risk is to move to a safer area. Most research suggests that the primary reason for moving is improved housing or greater convenience rather than avoiding crime (see DuBow et al. 1979). Unfortunately, most of the research is based on self-report data that are limited by recall problems and by the respondent's motivation to give "socially desirable" answers. We know, however, that mobility from the inner city of the suburbs is largely a response by white residents and one that is not available to low-income and minority residents who share the same motivation to relocate (Skogan and Maxfield 1981).

Risk-management Behaviors. If citizens cannot avoid certain areas or times of the day that are considered "high-risk," often they will take protective actions to make crime more difficult or less costly to them. Overall, survey research suggests that seven of ten urban residents avoid carrying a lot of cash when out in the neighborhood (Lavrakas et al. 1980); nearly half choose to travel in a car rather than walk to avoid risk (Skogan and Maxfield 1981); 25 to 50 percent take an escort when going out at night (Biderman et al. 1967; Kleinman and David 1973; Reiss 1967; Skogan and Maxfield 1981); and almost 15 percent take something with them that could be used as a weapon such as a dog, a whistle, a knife, or a gun (Kelling et al. 1974; Kennedy and Associates n.d.; Kleinman and David 1973; Mangione and Noble 1975; McIntyre 1967). In addition, pedestrians engage in certain behaviors (e.g. dress, demeanor) that are intended to create an image of self-assured aggressiveness, or having limited possessions (DuBow et al. 1979), which hopefully, will make them less attractive to offenders. Research has yet to document the prevalence of these impression-management behaviors.

Also, there are numerous responses to an offender after a confrontational crime has been initiated. Data from the 1985 National Crime Survey show that victims of violent crime (rape, robbery, assault) took some self-protective action in approximately three-quarters of the incidents (Bureau of Justice Statistics 1987). The most commonly used self-protective measure is nonviolent resistance (31%), including evasion, followed by the use of force (22%), threatening or reasoning with the offender (20%), and trying to get help or frightening the offender (18%). Finally, one of the most hotly debated measures employed for self-protection and crime deterrence is the purchase, carrying, and use of firearms by citizens. National survey data indicate that approximately half of all U.S. households possess a firearm (Erskine 1972; Wright and Marston 1975). The estimated number of weapons in private hands increased by a dramatic 40 million from 1968 (80 million) to 1978 (120 million), with handguns accounting for approximately 25 to 30 percent of the weapons at both times (Wright, Rossi, and Daly 1983). In their review of the literature, Wright and his colleagues rely on citizens' self-reported reasons for gun ownership to reach their conclusion that in most cases, fear and self-protection are not the driving motives for weapon purchases. Approximately three-quarters of gun owners report that their guns are primarily for sport and recreation, while only one-quarter (or 45 to 50% of handgun owners) report that self-defense and protection are the primary reasons for gun ownership.

Given the human tendency to give socially desirable answers, we can assume that the percentage of citizens who own firearms for "self-defense" is underestimated. Additional data that are consistent with the self-protection hypothesis can be found in a national increase in female gun ownership, a disproportionate increase in handgun (vs other firearm) purchases in recent years, and local evidence that purchases by females are correlated positively with changes in area crime rates (Bordua and Lizotte 1979). Nevertheless, the deployment of weapons in violent crime confrontations remains rather limited. The use or brandishing of a weapon accounted for only four percent of the self-defense methods used by victims of violent crime in the United States during 1985; only one percent of the victims' self-defense measures involved a firearm (Bureau of Justice Statistics 1986).

Strategy Effectiveness. How effective are the above-mentioned behaviors in reducing the probability of victimization and/or reducing fear of crime? Because these are largely self-protective behaviors, this assessment will be limited primarily to a discussion of their effects on the individual rather than on the levels of crime or fear in the community.

In the extreme, there is little doubt that risk-avoidance behavior is effective in reducing one's risk of victimization. Unless one lives with a violent family member, staying at home behind locked doors and not venturing outside should lower a person's risk of personal victimization because most violent crime occurs outdoors (Bureau of Justice Statistics 1986). More generally, studies have shown that persons who engage in high levels of risk-avoidance activity—especially women and older citizens who avoid going out at night, bring along escorts, or avoid certain areas or persons—are less likely to be victimized than persons who report fewer such behaviors (Biderman et al. 1967; Garofalo 1977b; Kleinman and David

1973; Lavrakas 1982; Rifai-Young 1976; Skogan and Maxfield 1981). Exposure to crime, however, tends to encourage avoidance behavior. Such behavior generally is more frequent among persons who live in high-crime areas (Boggs 1971; Clotfelter 1977; Furstenberg 1972) and who have been victimized by confrontational crimes (Conklin 1971; Garofalo 1977a). Although this research is complicated by questions about the direction of causality, nevertheless there is clearly a limit on the effectiveness of avoidance as a victimization prevention measure, as demonstrated in higher-crime areas.

The research on victimization and "routine activities" offers additional support for the notion that an individual's behavior can influence his or her probability of victimization (Cohen and Felson 1979; Garofalo 1987; Maxfield 1987). One of the most basic observations gleaned from the National Crime Survey over the past decade is that crime is not a random set of events, distributed evenly across all segments of American society. Rather, personal characteristics and individual lifestyles (i.e., "routine daily activities") play a major role in determining one's chances of criminal victimization (Hindelang, Gottfredson, and Garofalo 1978). The "typical" victim of crime is young, black, single or divorced, male, and unemployed, with an income level that is below poverty (Bureau of Justice Statistics 1983). Although routine activities per se do not entirely explain individual differences in victimization (Garofalo 1987), a lifestyle characterized by a fast night life and contact with drugs, gangs, or related forms of deviance should dramatically increase a person's chances of being victimized. Lifestyle is a prime candidate for explaining why, in 1984, homicide was the leading cause of death among black males between the ages of 15 and 24 (Centers for Disease Control 1987). More generally, persons who live in, frequent, or walk through high-crime areas have a higher probability of victimization than persons without this exposure to risk.

Collectively these data demonstrate that the risk of crime is not distributed evenly across persons and settings; and thus they suggest that persons who can avoid high-risk behaviors and high-risk situations are considerably less likely to experience criminal victimization than persons who follow a risky lifestyle or whose daily activities bring them into close proximity with offenders. Yet these observations in no way suggest that such risk-avoidance behaviors are under the individual's control or can be modified through social intervention (e.g., crime prevention education). Many people have little choice but to live and work in high-risk environments, and lifestyle patterns often are shaped by years of social influence.

Even if avoidance behaviors were easily modifiable, a policy of encouraging withdrawal from social interaction would be viewed with suspicion today. Avoiding risk by restricting one's behavior often is viewed as a major loss of freedom and opportunity for a better life. Many elderly citizens have become prisoners in their own homes; more than two-thirds of those studied report that they "never" go out at night (Rifai-Young 1976, 1977). Shopping, visiting friends, and attending social activities have been restricted for many older citizens. Risk avoidance also may have a long-term detrimental effect on local crime rates. When a large number of residents withdraw from the streets, this reaction may undermine the community's ability to exercise informal social control and surveillance over public behavior, thus lowering the constraints against deviant and criminal behavior.

The decision to move out of the neighborhood is another example of extreme risk-avoidance behavior that can be highly effective in reducing the mover's exposure to crime (Skogan and Maxfield 1981). Here again, however, the flight of high-income whites to the suburbs tends to exacerbate the problems of poor housing, unemployment and crime in the inner-city neighborhoods they leave behind (Kasarda 1976; Skogan 1977). In sum, individual protection may be increased, but often the price is heavy in terms of personal freedom and/or long-term collective safety.

If certain avoidance behaviors are generally effective in lowering one's risk of victimization, are they also effective in lowering fear of crime? If fear is influenced by an objective assessment of risk or by feelings of efficacy in preventing victimization, lower levels of fear would be predicted for persons who take self-protective actions (see Rosenbaum and Heath in press). The opposite is true, however—a wide range of studies has found that persons who restrict their behavior (e.g., avoid going out in the evening, take escorts when they do go out, avoid areas regarded as dangerous) are significantly more fearful of crime than persons who do not engage in these behavioral restrictions (Gordon and Riger 1979, 1988; Lavrakas 1982; Maxfield 1977, 1987; Savitz et al. 1977; Skogan and Maxfield 1981; Tyler 1980). Again, these correlational studies are problematical in discerning the direction of causality. Most researchers believe that fear is the driving force behind increases in personal protection behaviors rather than the reverse. Rosenbaum and Heath (in press), although not rejecting this conventional wisdom, argue that the repetition of self-protective behaviors could strengthen the fear response. In any event, the fact remains that the positive relationship between these self-protective behaviors and fear is the opposite of what many crime prevention strategists would like to see. A pattern of avoidance behavior implies that citizens are fearful of offenders, prefer to withdraw from threatening situations, and feel a lack of control over crime in their environment (cf. Cohen 1978; Lavrakas et al. 1980). In contrast, many residents realize that offenders cannot be avoided completely, and therefore choose to protect themselves with self-defense strategies in the event of confrontation. The effectiveness of two categories of self-defense is considered here: firearms and rape prevention.

Possession of Firearms. If firearms often are purchased to provide additional security, one might expect that owning a weapon would reduce fear of crime. In fact, most surveys that examine fear have found that gun owners are less fearful than the rest of the population (Maxfield 1977). Although it might be tempting to conclude that gun ownership decreases fear, Stinchcombe and his colleagues have shown that this relationship is spurious: gun owners typically are males, who are much less fearful than females, and live in rural areas where crime and fear are low (Stinchcombe, Heimer, Iliff, Scheppele, Smith and Taylor 1978) More research is needed to determine the relationship between gun ownership and fear of crime for persons whose primary reason for ownership is self-protection.

What is the effect of private weapon ownership on crime and on individual victimization rates? Although firearms usually are purchased either for self-defense or for recreation, many people believe that the wide availability of weapons contributes significantly to the level of crime and violence in our society. Wright et al. (1983) conclude that there is "little evidence" to support this hypothesis because there is no research that links the acquisition of firearms directly with subsequent criminal behavior. Even so, the general statistics on handguns and violence reviewed by these authors are provocative. As homicide rates increased from 1960 to 1978, for example, so did the percentage of homicides committed with firearms (53% to 63%); roughly three-quarters of these firearm murders involved handguns. The same pattern of covariation and increasing firearm usage was evident for robberies, aggravated assaults, and suicides during this period. Another noteworthy statistic is that an estimated 275,000 handguns fall into criminal hands each year from residential theft or burglary. Finally, there is the problem of accidental death and injury due to firearms. Although reliable statistics are not available, Wright et al. estimate that there were approximately 170 thousand (plus or minus 75) firearms accidents in 1975. In sum, an estimated 30,000 deaths occur each year because of criminal, accidental, or suicidal uses of firearms; in another 900,000 incidents firearms are present, fired, or involved in some other capacity. One cannot help asking what the overall picture might be if the opportunities for using firearms were curtailed dramatically.

Researchers also have asked whether weapons serve to deter crime and/or protect individual gun owners. Clearly, deterrence (whether specific or general) and self-defense are separate objectives (cf. Green 1987). At this point there is little evidence that guns serve to deter crime. Many studies show how gun ownership rates and new gun laws are related to crime rates (see Green 1987; Wright et al. 1983, for reviews). These findings will not be reviewed here for lack of space and because much of the data are inherently uninterpretible on account of uncertain causal ordering. As Green (1987) notes, natural quasi-experiments may provide more informative data. Kleck and Bordua (1983) found that the rate of forcible rape dropped significantly in Orlando, Florida (relative to control areas nearby) after 6,000 women were trained in the safe use of firearms. Yet considerably more research would be needed, with considerably better controls, to substantiate a general deterrent effect. Furthermore, the logic of general deterrence with gun ownership is questionable in many cases. There is little reason for offenders to fear being shot in many criminal circumstances (e.g., burglary of unoccupied premises). Research on the perceptions of convicted offenders (e.g. Wright and Rossi 1985) suggests that these individuals fear and avoid armed victims, but it is not especially useful for generalizing to the larger criminally inclined population that is not behind bars. Also, the actual risk of injury to the offender is not great, even though it is similar to other criminal justice deterrents. Kleck (1979) estimates that the risk of being shot by the victim is similar to the risk of being apprehended, convicted, and imprisoned—roughly one to two percent.

What about the possibility of self-protection with a firearm? As Wright et al. (1983) point out, most research shows no relationship between gun ownership and criminal victimization. There is some evidence that possessing a weapon decreases the probability of a "successful" victimization, but the probability of injury or death to the victim increases under these circumstances (Block and Skogan 1984). Thus persons who use guns to protect themselves and/or their property are incurring additional risks.

In sum, whether the "domestic arms buildup" in the United States serves to deter or to stimulate crime and violence has not been answered definitively, even though the available data have been used on both sides of this hotly debated issue. At the personal level, there is little evidence to suggest that owning a weapon reduces one's chances of victimization; some evidence suggests that possession of a weapon increases one's chances of injury when confronting an offender as well as the chances of gun-related accidents. Gun ownership may give some citizens an added feeling of security (although this point is undocumented), but in the final analysis it may exact a price at both the individual and the societal levels. Unfortunately, citizen gun ownership is a complex political and criminal justice issue that cannot be covered fully here.

Rape Self-defense. The possibility of confronting a rapist is a fear-arousing thought for most women (Gordon and Riger 1988) and causes them to consider how they should respond if assaulted. Hence there is considerable interest in whether some self-defense strategies are more effective than others for avoiding rape. Furby and Fischhoff (1986) conducted a meta-analysis of 24 empirical studies that address this question and found a fairly consistent pattern of results, regardless of the victim's relationship to the offender: *forceful* strategies, such as screaming, yelling, and physical resistance (as well as fleeing) were deemed effective in that they were associated with a lower probability of rape, while *nonforceful* strategies, such as pleading, crying, reasoning, and moral appeals were considered ineffective in that they were associated with a higher probability of rape. More forceful strategies, however, were more likely to be associated with physical injury other than the rape itself.

Furby and Fischhoff recognize that these sexual assault studies present potentially serious methodological problems; thus caution is needed in interpreting the results. First, attempted rapes are less likely to be reported (to anyone) than completed rapes, so we do not know the full range of strategies employed in many cases where rape was avoided. Second, the direction of causality between self-defense strategy and outcome is unclear for certain strategies (e.g., crying may be an effect rather than a cause of unsuccessful rape avoidance) For most strategies, however, the proposed causal order seems more plausible. Finally, a word of caution is needed about drawing general conclusions at this time. We cannot establish from this research "what works when" until the conditions that determine strategy effectiveness are understood more fully. The effectiveness of a given strategy varies depending on the characteristics of the offender, the victim, and the setting (e.g. presence of a weapon).

Beyond the effects on victimization prevention per se there is a small amount of evidence on the relationship between women's self-defense skills and their perceptions and fears regarding crime. Women who describe themselves as strong and fast are less fearful of victimization than women who describe themselves as weak and slow (Gordon and Riger 1988). Self-defense training programs have emerged across the United States to correct this perception of physical vulnerability and to give women a feeling of self-efficacy in threatening situations. There is some evidence to indicate that such programs are effective. A quasi-experimental evaluation of one self-defense program found that women enrolled in the course felt more control over their bodies and less fear of crime afterward than women who were not enrolled in the course (Cohen, Kidder, and Harvey 1978).

SUMMARY

Many citizens report that crime has caused them to change their behavior, and most citizens have taken some crime prevention measures to reduce their chances of victimization. Personal protection (or self-protection) behaviors are a common form of crime prevention activity; the most pervasive type of self-protection is avoidance behavior. There are many ways to avoid situations that present a high risk of criminal victimization, ranging from not talking to strangers on the street to moving out of a high crime neighborhood. At the level of self-protection, most residents respond to the threat of crime simply by restricting their mobility (i.e., not going out at night, avoiding strangers, avoiding areas perceived as dangerous).

Research supports common sense regarding the effects of avoidance on victimization: persons who engage in high levels of behavioral restriction are much less likely to be victimized by crime than persons who show little interest in avoidance behaviors and lead more "risky" lives. Moreover, simple arithmetic tells us that extreme behaviors such as never going outside or moving to a safer neighborhood reduce one's chances of victimization. The present review, however, suggests that avoidance behaviors have a downside. The gain in personal protection is purchased at a high price: a loss of behavioral freedom, a lower quality of life, and/or a possible increase in community-level crime rates. Moreover, there is substantial evidence that engaging in avoidance behavior is associated with higher levels of fear of crime. The only evidence that personal protective behaviors contribute to a reduction in fear comes from the literature on rape self-defense training.

From a policy standpoint, these data provide little basis for encouraging the already common risk-avoidance behaviors that remove citizens from the streets and contribute to a "fortress" mentality. Unfortunately, the available research cannot identify less extreme avoidance behaviors that also are effective at reducing risk. Even if the current knowledge was sufficient to identify these precautionary measures, we still have no evidence that such behaviors can be modified through crime prevention programming.

The self-defense and rape literatures can be interpreted to suggest that more attention should be paid to aggressive mobilization measures and less to behavioral restriction. Carrying a handgun is highly controversial, but less radical mobilization strategies, such as self-defense training, may improve feelings of self-efficacy and reduce fear of victimization. Considerably more research is needed, however, to substantiate these preliminary conclusions and to address the issue of the effect on victimization rates.

HOUSEHOLD PROTECTION BEHAVIORS

NATURE AND EXTENT OF HOUSEHOLD PROTECTION

In addition to self-protection outside the home, another major concern of most citizens is the protection of their property and loved ones. Consequently citizens engage in a wide range of behaviors to protect their homes from unlawful entry. One's home is considered a uniquely private place ("one's castle") where one can retreat from the world of crime and other problems that lie outside (cf. Lavrakas 1981). Consequently burglary and home invasion by unknown offenders represent more than a financial loss; victims often view these criminal acts as a psychological invasion or violation (Rosenbaum and Lurigio in press).

As with other prevention activities, household protection measures are intended either to prevent victimization entirely or to reduce the amount of loss that occurs when victimization is not prevented. Many preventive measures create *physical barriers* to access (e.g., locks), while others are designed to create *psychological barriers* (e.g., leaving lights on). "Target hardening" is the primary strategy employed for household protection, and it has a long history of application. Target-hardening measures, whether locks, window bars, fences, alarms, or other devices, are designed to eliminate physical intrusion or to make it more difficult, thus reducing the probability that a crime can be committed.

Many studies have measured the extent and nature of home protection activities (Christian 1973; Clotfelter 1977; Courtis and Dusseyer 1970; Ennis 1967; Harris 1969; Kelling et al. 1974; Lavrakas 1981; Maxfield 1977; Percy 1979; Rosentraub and Harlow 1980; Schneider 1975; Schwartz and Clarren 1978; Skogan and Maxfield 1981). The following general conclusions can be drawn: the most common hardware change is the purchase and installation of better locks on doors in the "last few years" (between 25% and 50% of urban residents). Most other devices—including window locks and bars, special outside lights, and alarms—are installed by a much smaller segment of the population (often under 10%), although 30 to 40 percent of the residents in some cities report installing special outdoor lights and window locks. A one-time supplement to the National Crime Survey found that roughly seven percent of the U.S. households interviewed in 1984 had burglar alarms (Whitaker 1986).

Many security devices are of little value unless they are used. More prevalent than one-time purchases are the repetitious behaviors often associated with these devices. Locking doors and windows when going out is the most common target-hardening response—75 to 95 percent of the public report these behaviors. On the basis of the empirically supported notion that burglars view full-time occupancy as a strong deterrent to residential burglary (Reppetto 1974), citizens sometimes create psychological barriers that give the impression of occupancy. Leaving on lights when one is away is by far the most common strategy (65 to 90% of residents), followed by stopping mail deliveries (50 to 60%), the use of timers on indoor lights and radios (20 to 40%), and notifying the police (8 to 12%). When going away for several days or more, residents often request that neighbors keep an eye on their house (60 to 80%); this surveillance response will be discussed in the following section as part of "neighborhood protection behaviors." The frequency of other "occupancy" behaviors, such as hiring a "house-sitter," having the lawn mowed, and having sidewalks shoveled, has not been researched.

If theft of property cannot be prevented, the conventional strategy for minimizing losses is to purchase insurance that covers theft (60 to 75%). In addition, many citizens today engrave their valuables with unique identification numbers, hoping to increase their chances of recovering the stolen property (see discussion below).

Beginning in the early 1970s, local, state, and federal support was provided to help citizens identify security vulnerabilities at home and to encourage them to take appropriate preventive action (including many of the above-mentioned activities). Two programs were initiated in response to the growing problem of residential burglary: Crime Prevention Security Surveys and Operation Identification. These two strategies, along with Neighborhood Watch, make up the "Big Three" programs (Feins 1983) that have shaped the mainstream of citizen crime prevention activities in the United States over the past decade. Because these programs have been publicized widely and have been adopted by law enforcement agencies here and in other countries, they deserve a brief description (Neighborhood Watch will be discussed under "Neighborhood Crime Prevention Behaviors").

Security Surveys. The security survey has long been recognized in the security field as a fundamental tool for identifying and responding to crime risks (Kingsbury 1973). In the crime prevention field, it gained visibility as a potential strategy for encouraging citizen participation in home protection activities. In residential settings, the security survey is a detailed on-site inspection of the dwelling unit and the surrounding area by a crime prevention expert (usually a police officer specialist) to "identify deficiencies or security risks; to define the protection needs; and, to make recommendations to minimize criminal opportunity" (Mombiosse 1968: 13) A national study in late 1975 identified more than 300 survey-performing agencies, but most agencies did not keep data on the extent of citizen participation and compliance with security recommendations (International Training, Research, and Evaluation Council 1977). Our 1983 survey of randomly selected residents in Chicago found that 13 percent had undergone a home security survey (data from Rosenbaum, Lewis, and Grant 1985).

Operation Identification. The "Operation Identification" program started in Monterey Park, California in 1963 and became one of the "Big Three" crime prevention strategies marketed in the United States during the mid-1970s. The fundamental idea behind this approach is that engraving or marking property with a unique identifying code will: 1) deter potential burglars by lowering the economic gain and increasing the risk of apprehension (by linking recovered property to specific crimes), and 2) increase the probability of recovery and return of stolen property to the victim. A national study conducted in 1975 found that despite broad public awareness of Operation Identification created through media campaigns and other educational efforts, most local projects were unable to recruit more than ten percent of their target populations. (Heller, Stenzel, Gill, Kolde, and Schimeman 1975). Nearly a decade later (1984), however, the participation level stood at 25 percent of all U.S. households (Whitaker 1986).

Finally, the characteristics of those who participate in household protection behaviors should be noted. The distribution of these behaviors in the population is substantially different from the distribution of personal protection behaviors. Persons who engage in household protection activities generally are from higher income brackets, older, more educated, and more likely to be homeowners (Lavrakas et al. 1980; Whitaker 1986). Home ownership and income clearly are the strongest predictors of home protection activities. This segment of the population has the financial resources and the protective motivation to install rather expensive target-hardening devices to protect their private property.

STRATEGY EFFECTIVENESS

The effectiveness of home protection behaviors and of target hardening in particular has been studied more thoroughly than other citizen crime prevention strategies. Although the research is weak and inconclusive in many respects, some consistent findings have emerged. Various research findings are summarized below in relationship to victimization rates, crime rates, and fear of crime.

Psychological Barriers. Before reviewing the research on target hardening or restrictions on physical access to property, it should be noted that we know very little about the effects of *psychological* barriers or efforts to give the appearance of occupancy (e.g., leaving lights on, stopping mail). Research on residential burglary and on perceptions of convicted burglars, however, provides indirect support for the effectiveness of this strategy. Specifically, houses that are occupied more frequently are less likely to be burglarized (Lentzner 1981; Waller and Okihiro 1978; Winchester and Jackson 1982); burglars, when interviewed, place more importance on occupancy status than on conventional target-hardening measures in deciding whether to select a particular house as a burglary target (Bennett and Wright 1984; Reppetto 1974). It is unknown whether these perceptions from older, convicted burglars match the perceptions of younger burglars who are still on the street.

Target Hardening. The effectiveness of locks, bars, grills, markings, alarms, and other devices for "hardening" the target has been examined either directly or indirectly in diverse studies. Although the effect of these measures often is unclear in residential settings, their ability to reduce specific types of criminal activity in specific situations has been demonstrated clearly. Clarke (1983) cites some compelling examples in Great Britain: thefts from public telephones were made virtually impossible after the Post Office replaced aluminum coin boxes with less vulnerable steel boxes in the late 1960s. Also, the opportunity for government employees to make unauthorized long-distance calls was reduced dramatically when devices were installed that required callers to seek operator assistance.

The situation can be quite different in residential settings, where the implementation of security measures often is a choice of individual households and varies substantially from one house to the next. Even so, quasi-experimental evaluations of government-funded crime prevention programs in public housing provide some reasonable tests of target-hardening strategies (see Rubenstein, Murray, Motoyama, and Rouse 1980). The available evidence is consistent with the hypothesis that reducing access to property through target-hardening measures will reduce the level of residential burglary. In Seattle, researchers observed a significant reduction in the number of burglaries at three of four public housing sites after the installation of deadbolt locks, solid-case doors, short walls, and nine-inch window-opening restrictions (Seattle Law and Justice Planning Office 1975). In Chicago's Cabrini Green Public Housing Project, the introduction of new locks and intercoms, the enclosure of lobbies, and the placement of security personnel at doors paralleled a 29 percent decrease in index crimes in the experimental buildings over two years, while control buildings experienced a 21 percent increase (Arthur Young and Company 1978). The most fundamental problem with the latter demonstration is that the effects cannot be attributed to target-hardening activities because other crime prevention strategies were introduced at the same time. This is a widespread problem with evaluation research in the field of community crime prevention.

Alarms are marketed widely in commercial and residential settings, but surprisingly few studies of their effectiveness have been conducted. Even *ex post facto* analyses of alarms in residential burglaries are rare and inconclusive. The only quasi-experimental evidence comes from the use of alarms in businesses and schools in Cedar Rapids, Iowa (Cedar Rapids Police Department 1972). Schools that received alarm systems experienced a 75 percent reduction in burglaries during the year, compared to a 25 percent reduction in schools without the alarms. Although businesses did not show a similar reduction in burglaries, alarms were associated with a significant decline in attempted burglaries and with significant increases in the rates of arrest and clearance.

Research on patterns of residential burglary provide another data base for testing the notion that burglary prevention measures are effective. With few exceptions (e.g. Winchester and Jackson 1982), the bulk of these studies across several countries shows that burglary victims are more careless and less well-protected by hardware than nonvictims (Pope 1977; Reppetto 1974; Scarr 1973; van Dijk and Steinmetz 1982; Walsh 1980). Furthermore, as Mayhew (1984) noted, the sizable number of *unsuccessful* burglaries may indicate the efficacy of household security efforts, although other preventive factors may be operating as well. In the United States, roughly 22 percent of all residential burglaries in 1985 were classified as "attempted forcible entries" (Jamieson and Flanagan

1987); in Great Britain, nearly one-third of the burglaries fall into this category (Hough and Mayhew 1983).

Although certain home protection behaviors are quite prevalent (as noted earlier), the burglary/victimization literature highlights some sizable gaps in security, especially among those who are victimized (e.g., inadequate locks, leaving doors and windows unlocked). For example, 45 percent of the residential burglaries in 1985 were entries without force (Bureau of Justice Statistics 1987) This research raises the question of whether home protection behaviors can be increased through programmatic intervention. The national evaluations of property-marking and security survey programs are summarized below because they address this question and because interventions usually provide stronger tests of behavior-change hypotheses than the (largely) correlational findings cited above, in which self-selection plays a major role.

Property-marking Programs. Evaluations of Operation Identification projects in the United States (Heller et al. 1975) and Canada (Jones 1982; Zaharchuk and Lynch 1977) have produced similar results. On the positive side, households that participated in the program (by engraving their valuables and posting warning stickers for offenders) generally experienced significantly lower burglary rates than nonparticipants. In some of the better pre- versus post-program analyses of burglary rates, participants were found to experience a 32.8 percent reduction in Seattle (Seattle Law and Justice Planning Office 1975) and a 24.9 percent reduction in St. Louis (Schimerman 1974). However, whether reduced burglary rates were due to the property-marking program or to other factors cannot be determined from these data. For example, there is some evidence that participants engage in more target-hardening activities than nonparticipants (perhaps indicating that they are more security-conscious to begin with) and may have had a lower risk of victimization before participation. Even so, a rare longitudinal study by Wilson and Schneider (1978) found that although prior victimization is a good predictor of future victimization in the absence of intervention, displaying a property-marking sticker in the window appears to lower significantly a victim's risk of future burglary, even though previous nonvictims who do not participate in the program still have a slightly lower risk of victimization than participants.

On the negative side, there is little evidence that property-marking programs influence citywide burglary rates, even in smaller towns. In Illinois, 255 cities with property-marking programs did not experience reductions in citywide burglary rates relative to 389 cities without such programs (Mattick, Olander, Baker, and Schlegel 1974). This finding should not be surprising because the vast majority (85%) of programs studied in the United States were unable to recruit more than ten percent of the residents in the target population (Heller et al. 1975); when implementation areas were defined carefully, some evidence of geographic displacement of burglary was observed. The low levels of participation also may help to explain why property-marking programs have been unable to achieve their other goals of increasing the rates of apprehension, conviction, property recovery, or property return, although the theory behind these expectations is suspect as well. Data on fear of crime either were not collected or were not reported.

Security Surveys. The national evaluation of crime prevention security survey programs (ITREC 1977) produced surprisingly little quantitative information to assess program effects. Fewer than a dozen of the 206 programs studied could produce evaluation reports: only five used burglary-rate data to evaluate effects. Nevertheless, some favorable findings were reported; when residents participate in the program and comply with survey recommendations for improving home protection, they are less likely to be victimized. These findings were replicated later in Santa Ana, California, along with a 17 percent drop in burglary (an 11% increase citywide) (California Crime Resistance Task Force 1982). As in the property-marking programs, however, participation levels in security surveys tend to be quite low. In the national evaluation, only four of the 20 programs visited by the research staff had conducted security surveys with more than ten percent of their target area population; the level of citizen compliance with security recommendations often was unknown. Also, the research designs generally were weak in a number of respects.

One of the frequently stated goals of the initial security survey programs—other than burglary reduction—was to improve police-community relations. Today, fear reduction can be added to this list of goals. Although attitudinal and perceptual data usually were not collected as part of the evaluations, Rosenbaum and Bickman (in preparation) conducted a randomized experiment to evaluate the effect of security surveys on the perceptions and fears of recently burglarized residents—the group most likely to request such services. The results were surprising: burglary victims who, through random assignment, received a crime prevention security survey by a trained police officer were significantly more fearful of crime, angrier, and more upset about the incident and experienced less emotional recovery than victims who did not receive a security survey. While fear and other negative feelings increased as a direct result of this intervention, so did home protection behaviors. Thus a security survey may enhance the safety of participating households, but at the cost of arousing fear.

SUMMARY

Home protection behaviors are common; most people engage in protective behaviors that are simple and relatively inexpensive (e.g., locking doors when going out), leaving the more comprehensive security programs (e.g., elaborate alarm and surveillance systems) to those who can afford such protection (cf. Schneider 1987; Skogan and Maxfield 1981). There is some evidence to suggest that persons who engage in household protection behaviors are less likely to be victimized by property crime than persons who do not take such actions. Although the evidence is not always clear about whether the relationship is causal or spurious, it is suggestive.

NEIGHBORHOOD PROTECTION BEHAVIORS: COLLECTIVE ACTIONS

NATURE AND EXTENT OF COLLECTIVE ACTION

Strategies to "organize" the community and to provide a collective response to crime have become the cornerstone of community crime prevention activities in recent years. Neighborhood protection behaviors, as defined here, are collective attempts to prevent crime and disorder in a geographically defined residential area, such as a block or neighborhood.

There are many types of collective citizen actions and many ways of conceptualizing these responses to crime (see Bickman, Lavrakas, Green, North-Walker, Edwards, Vorkowski, DuBow, and Wuerth 1976; DuBow et al. 1979; Yin, Vogel, Chaiken and Both 1976). Research has taught us that local voluntary organizations often are the primary vehicle for neighborhood crime prevention activities in urban areas (Lavrakas et al. 1980; Podolefsky and DuBow 1981). Neighborhood-level surveys in a number of major U.S. cities show that between 11 and 20 percent of the population participate in local voluntary organizations and that seven to 20 percent participate in crime prevention activities associated with these organizations (Ahlbrandt and Cummingham 1979; Lavrakas et al. 1980; Rohe and Greenberg 1982; Skogan and Maxfield 1981; Taub, Surgeon, Lindholm, Otti, and Bridges 1977). National data from 1981 indicate that 12 percent of the adult population were involved in a neighborhood group with crime prevention activities (O'Keefe and Mendelsohn 1984).

Community groups often are the mechanism for organizing community action, but wide variation exists in their organizational structure, objectives, and approaches to crime prevention (Lewis et al. 1988). Citizen groups range from stable, multi-issue organizations with "crime" as one of many items on their agenda to single issue ad hoc groups that focus on a particular type of criminal activity (DuBow et al. 1979; Skogan 1987). Nevertheless, the anticrime strategies pursued by voluntary citizen groups show some degree of commonality. Two distinct approaches to crime prevention have been identified in the literature with corresponding behaviors: the most publicized orientation is referred to as the "opportunity reduction" or "victimization prevention" approach, while the alternative orientation is called the "social problems" or "root causes" approach

Bennett and Lavrakas 1988; Lewis and Salem 1981; Podolefsky and DuBow 1981).

Opportunity Reduction Approach. Collective anti-crime measures that emerge from the opportunity reduction approach often involve surveillance, crime reporting, and target-hardening activities designed to control or deter crime in specific settings. Neighborhood Watch is the prototype of this approach, and often serves as a vehicle for encouraging a range of opportunity-reduction behaviors (Bennett and Lavrakas 1988; Garafolo and McLeod 1986; Rosenbaum 1987). Through a national survey of 550 Neighborhood Watch programs, Garafolo and McLeod (1986) found that in addition to being the "eyes and ears" of the police, most programs included property marking (81%), home security surveys (68%), meetings to plan and exchange information (61%), and the distribution of newsletters (54%). More than one-third also were involved in crime tip hotlines and efforts to improve the physical environment (e.g., better street lighting).

In terms of social impact, Neighborhood Watch is billed by program advocates as more than an opportunity-reduction program (National Crime Prevention Council 1987). By encouraging social interaction (beginning with local meetings), this strategy is considered to be one of the primary mechanisms available to community residents who are interested in restoring informal social control processes or creating a sense of "community" (see Rosenbaum 1987, 1988).[2]

Despite widespread publicity and public awareness of Neighborhood Watch, participation levels remain rather modest. Resident surveys in areas that have been the target of substantial organizing activity show that attendance at a Block Watch or Neighborhood Watch meeting is reported by 10 percent of the households in Portland, Oregon (Schneider 1986), 16 percent in Chicago (Rosenbaum et al 1986) and nearly 18 percent in Minneapolis (McPherson and Silloway 1987). At the national level, two national crime surveys conducted in 1984 provide some reliable data on this topic: in the United States, seven percent of the nation's households had participated in Neighborhood Watch (Whitaker 1986), while in England, where the concept was newer, less than one percent were involved (Hope 1988). The opportunity to participate is one factor that restricts participation levels. The U.S. data (Whitaker 1986) show that 38 percent of the households in neighborhoods that *have* Neighborhood Watch are participants in the program. Central-city areas are more likely to have programs than either suburban or nonmetropolitan areas, but people living in the latter areas are more likely to participate in the program when one is available.

For citizens who prefer a more aggressive and more structured approach to area surveillance, civilian patrols have become a popular alternative to passive watching. Citizen patrols have a long history that predates the creation of public law enforcement and includes an extended period of vigilantism in the United States (see DuBow et al. 1979). Over the past 25 years, a variety of patrols have emerged in urban areas, serving a variety of functions (see Garofalo and McLeod 1986; Pennell, Curtis and Henderson 1985; Podolefsky and DuBow 1981; Yin et al. 1976). In the 1960s, for example, blacks used citizen patrols to protect themselves against police abuses in urban areas and against racist groups in the south (Garofalo and McLeod 1986; Marx and Archer 1971). In the 1970s, citizen patrols in urban areas became a popular supplement to police patrols, and were initiated to deter residential criminal activity and to detect crimes in progress. Patrols differ in function (e.g. community protection vs crime prevention), surveillance area (e.g., buildings, neighborhood streets, public transportation, college campuses), mode of transportation (e.g., foot, bicycle, or motorized patrol), policies about intervention, and other dimensions (Yin et al. 1976) Whereas most patrols are local groups with local interests, the Guardian Angels are a national network of patrols serving more than 50 U.S. cities (see Pennell et al. 1985).

The prevalence of civilian patrols is difficult to estimate from the available data. In 1975 a national study estimated that there were more than 800 patrols throughout the United States (Yin et al. 1976). In 1984 a national mail survey of Neighborhood Watch Programs revealed that 12 percent had a formal surveillance component and that most of these were motorized patrols (Garofalo and McLeod 1986). At the city level, Pennell et al. (1985) cite reports that an estimated 150,000 Philadelphia residents participated in mobile patrols in the first half of 1980, and a similar number did so in New York City. There is some evidence, however, that the number of newly created citizen patrols (and Neighborhood Watches) peaked in 1983-84 and then declined significantly in 1985 (Garofalo and McLeod 1986). Yet this conclusion must be viewed with caution because it is based on a mail survey with a moderately low return rate (26%).

Who participates in collective anti-crime activities? The pattern of participation in community crime prevention groups is quite similar to that of voluntary community organizations in general. A number of studies have found that those who participate in voluntary organizations are more likely to be middle or upper middle class, homeowners, well-educated, middle-aged, married with children, and less transient than nonparticipators (for reviews see Greenberg et al. 1985; Skogan 1987). Certainly, residents who participate in Neighborhood Watch fit this description, as shown in both a national survey of Neighborhood Watch programs (Garofolo and McLeod 1986) and in the one existing national survey of U.S. households (Whitaker 1986). The limited research on organizations sponsoring anti-crime programs also confirms this pattern of middle-class participation for a variety of crime prevention activities (Lavrakas et al. 1980; Podolefsky and DuBow 1981). Also, unlike self-protection and even household protection behaviors, participation in collective neighborhood anti-crime activities often is motivated by "civic-mindedness" rather than by fear of crime (Lavrakas et al. 1980).

Who participates in formal citizen patrols is less well documented, but the available evidence suggests a similar pattern to that of Watch-type programs, except that men are more involved than women in patrolling activities (Lavrakas et al. 1980; Pennell et al. 1985; Troyer 1988). There is also some evidence that citizen patrols are more likely to emerge in racially heterogeneous areas (Yin et al. 1976) and in gentrifying areas among newcomers (McDonald 1986), but this observation is true of participation in Watch programs as well (Henig 1984).

Social Problems Approach. The social problems approach to collective anti-crime activities is based on the belief, held by many citizens (Erskine 1974), that crime is caused by the "social ills" of society, especially by social conditions that cause youth to become delinquent (Podolefsky and DuBow 1981). Hence many citizens participate in community crime prevention activities that address a variety of social problems or "root causes" of crime. The nature and extent of collective participation in such activities are not well documented in the literature, but two major projects at Northwestern University provide some data on this topic. The "Reactions to Crime" project collected random survey data in three large cities and ten neighborhoods, giving persons associated with voluntary organizations an open-ended chance to describe anything their group had ever done about crime. Podolefsky and DuBow (1981) identified 946 activities and placed them into 47 categories. Of these 47 types of activities, the most common was "providing positive youth activities (14% of the activities), followed by holding meetings to discuss crime (9%), improving or cleaning up the neighborhood (8%), and putting pressure on the police about policy (6%)." In total, youth-related activities constituted nearly 20 percent of the total anti-crime responses.

More recently, Bennett and Lavrakas (1988) completed a process evaluation of ten community crime prevention programs in nine large U.S. cities as part of the Eisenhower Neighborhood Program. Four neighborhood-based programs emphasized the "causes-of-crime" (i.e. social problems) approach, three emphasized "opportunity reduction," and three showed an even balance. Youth-oriented activities were the backbone of the social problems approach; communitywide surveys (including residents who were not community group members) revealed that participation in such activities ranged from 1 to 15 percent across the ten sites (with a mode of 6%), and from 6 to 15 percent in neighborhoods with groups that emphasized the "causes-of-crime" approach. Youth activities included athletic programs, employment programs (e.g., job training, development, counseling, referral), drug prevention programs, computer clubs, troops (Girl Scouts, Boy Scouts, Explorers), tutorial and literacy programs, youth councils, and many others. Generally speaking, youth-oriented programs often seek either a) to take youths off the streets by giving them "something else" to do, on the assumption that removing them from the streets will reduce their chances of "getting into trouble," or b) to give them specific skills and opportunities that will improve their competence, self-respect, and likelihood of self-sufficiency. Boys have been the target of nearly all neighborhood-based programs, although there is a growing interest in developing programs for adolescent girls (e.g., pregnancy and drug prevention), and adults (e.g., parenting and employment skills).

In sum, a variety of collective anti-crime activities have been initiated by community residents; these efforts tend to focus either on reducing opportunities for crime in particular settings or on alleviating social problems that are believed to be the "root causes" of crime. Both approaches seek to strengthen informal social controls in the neighborhood, but through different processes (i.e., social interaction and surveillance vs job market stability, values clarification, and self-sufficient role models). Voluntary community organizations are the primary vehicle for citizen participation in collective anticrime activities. Neighborhood Watch is the prototype of the "opportunity reduction" approach; participants in this program tend to be middle-class homeowners with an investment in the neighborhood. A wide range of social problems has been addressed under the "social problems" approach, but the community effort has been concentrated primarily on youth activities, with special attention to removing employment barriers at the individual level and keeping youths off the streets. Participation in collective anticrime activities is less prevalent than participation in either self-protection or household protection activities although reliable measures are not available regarding the extent of social-problems activities at the national level.

STRATEGY EFFECTIVENESS

Social Problems Approach. Nearly all of the evaluation research on collective anticrime strategies focuses on opportunity reduction activities (i.e., "victimization prevention" behaviors and programs). At present we know little about the effectiveness of neighborhood-based strategies that focus on social problems, especially youth-oriented activities organized by voluntary community organizations. The available data on the effects of the "social problems" approaches come from evaluations of large-scale government employment and training programs in the 1960s and 1970s—programs designed to improve local labor market experience and to reduce crime. After reviewing this literature, McGahey (1986) concludes that "analyses of individual employment and criminal behavior show little or no effect on labor market status or recidivism" (256). One exception was the Job Corps, whose success McGahey attributes to the fact that participants were "physically and socially removed from their high-crime neighborhoods and crime-prone peer groups" (257). The empirical evidence regarding the success or failure of anti-poverty programs in the United

States is a hotly-debated and politically-charged topic. Murray (1984) argues that American social-welfare policies over the past 20 years have contributed to a *worsening* of poverty and related social problems, but Jencks (1985) offers a compelling critique of Murray's analysis and his interpretation of the data.

Despite the debatable success of earlier social problems approaches, Lynn Curtis and Betsy Lindsay of the Eisenhower Foundation (Curtis 1985, 1987) have remodeled this strategy for the 1980s, emphasizing the importance of "bubble-up" planning by grass-roots community groups who seek "financial self-sufficiency" rather than continuing the traditional "trickle-down" approach to funding and program development. A four-year demonstration called the "Neighborhood Anti-Crime Self-Help Program" was initiated in 1982 in ten urban neighborhoods. The preliminary results from a major impact evaluation show that local programs had little effect on official crime rates and possibly a negative effect on victimization rates (Lavrakas and Bennett 1988; Curtis 1987), for a more positive view of the results). Fear of crime was largely unaffected in neighborhoods served by organizations with a social problems orientation but showed some evidence of decline in several sites with a strong opportunity reduction orientation, especially citizen patrols. The strongest evidence of effects appeared at the individual level. Fischer's (1988) analysis of these data, controlling for self-selection variables in a panel design, revealed that persons who participated intensively and directly in block-level meetings showed an increased sense of community, greater perceived efficacy of crime prevention activities, more household protective behaviors, less fear of crime, and stronger perceptions of informal social control (i.e., willingness to help others or to intervene). Although controlling for self-selection through statistical procedures does not entirely rule out self-selection effects, the use of panel data makes a stronger case than usual.

The "models of success" (Curtis 1987) that served as the theoretical foundation for the Eisenhower demonstration defined their success in terms of the individual youths who participated in their programs. The Argus Community, Inc. in the South Bronx (Sturz and Taylor 1987) and the House of Umoja in Philadelphia (Fattah 1987) offer extended-family environments for high-risk youths or adjudicated offenders. Argus graduates have been found to have lower recidivism rates than other high-risk offender programs in New York City; Umojan participants have substantially lower rates of recidivism than youths released from juvenile correctional facilities (see Curtis 1987). Although these data are encouraging, the adequacy of the comparison groups and the type of recidivism measures employed remain unknown without a review of the original research reports. Also, these programs are not entirely community-focused; their objective is to serve high-risk youth citywide rather than to change the local neighborhood or to assist local youths through mobilized citizen actions.

Another widely publicized "model" program that fits better the description of a community-based strategy is the Center for Orientation and Services (also known as "Centro") in Puerto Rico (Ferre 1987; Siberman 1978). Working with ten full-time "advocates," Sister Ferre has managed to organize the neighborhood to improve local services, offer extended-family activities, and provide employment opportunities for youth. Curtis (1987:13) reports that "over a 15-year period the number of adjudicated delinquents in the La Playa neighborhood where Centro is located was reduced by 85 percent and the delinquency rate was cut in half, despite a rapid increase in the population of high-risk youth." Again, this does not constitute a controlled evaluation whether these observed changes are due to Centro or to other forces in the local or citywide environment cannot be determined.

In summary, there is little *hard* evidence to show that the social problems approach to community crime prevention is effective in reducing community crime rates or building community cohesion, although several strategies are seen as conceptually attractive and are lauded as model programs for helping poor neighborhoods help themselves. To say that there is "little hard evidence" does not mean that this approach is ineffective, only that there have been few strong evaluations of program effects in this rediscovered policy area. The one major evaluation of programs addressing "root causes" showed few promising results, but we should not expect communitywide effects in two years when these programs touch so few residents. Future evaluations may need to focus only on participating individuals (both service providers and recipients) and to use more sophisticated research designs than we have seen to date in the popular models of success." Unfortunately the community benefits can be called into question if researchers and practitioners begin to limit their attention to the individual benefits to be derived from such programs. Perhaps a redeeming feature of collective crime prevention programs (and one to which I will return later) is their potential for producing communitywide benefits that are not captured easily in quantitative measures of crime and crime-related perceptions (see Bennett and Lavrakas 1988; Grant, Lewis, and Rosenbaum in press).

Opportunity Reduction: Natural Covariation. Various research literatures can be used to examine whether collective anticrime efforts—directed at reducing criminal opportunities and strengthening informal social control—constitute effective strategies for dealing with crime-related problems in urban areas. The summary below will begin with the relevant findings of neighborhood studies that document natural covariation between prevention-related social processes and crime-related outcomes, and then will proceed to examine evaluation research on the effects of collective social interventions. Although the latter research shows considerable variation in scientific rigor, it provides a more direct test of the central hypotheses in community crime prevention.

Several theoretical models have been proposed to help articulate the social processes involved in the prevention of residential crime through collective citizen action (e.g., Greenberg et al. 1985; Hunter 1974; Lavrakas et al. 1880; Podolefsky and DuBow 1981; Rosenbaum 1987; Rubenstein et al. 1980; Skogan and Maxfield 1981; Taub, Taylor, and Dunham 1984; Taylor and Gottfredson 1986) In the interest of parsimony and space, Figure 1 represents the author's attempt to synthesize these works, at the risk of oversimplification. Essentially this model identifies the basic causal links that are posited as intervening processes between the initial attempts to "organize" neighborhood residents and the final outcomes of reduced crime and fear of crime. Organizers can seek to reduce crime *directly* by educating residents about possible crime prevention measures and by encouraging participation in these anti-crime activities, or *indirectly* by encouraging social interaction and friendship patterns that serve as the basis for exercising informal social control. Although the variable domain is more extensive than what is presented in Figure 19.1 (see Rosenbaum et al. 1986), the bulk of the literature is concerned with only three primary outcomes: crime (and, to a lesser extent, disorders), fear of crime and community cohesion (or informal social control). Hence the literature summary that follows will focus on these outcome variables as they relate to community crime prevention activities and neighborhood social behavior.

The findings of various neighborhood studies and psychological research on small groups can be construed as supportive of collective crime prevention programs, or at least of certain causal links in this model. Over the years a number of studies have explored the factors that contribute to the development of social cohesion and informal social control in group settings. In addition to physical proximity (Festinger, Schachter, and Back 1950) and group size (Zander 1979), a critical factor in the development of group cohesion (and therefore of a group's ability to exercise social control) is the *frequency of social contact* (Shaw 1981). The importance of social interaction as a predictor of informal social control also has been confirmed in the literature on social networks (Fischer, Jackson, Stueve, Gerson, and Jones 1977). Taken as whole, these studies suggest that frequent social interaction contributes to informal social control and hence they provide justification for crime prevention programs that seek to increase the amount of social contact in the neighborhood. Finding covariation between social interaction and informal social control, however, is not the same as demonstrating a) that levels of social interaction in the community can be modified through social intervention, and b) that more social interaction will help to reduce criminal activity, and will do so through the processes specified in Figure 19.1.

According to theory, community organizations provide neighbors with opportunities to interact more frequently. This added social interaction should lead to increased familiarity, a greater exchange of information,

Figure 19.1
Simplified Impact Model of Collective Citizen Crime Prevention Behaviors

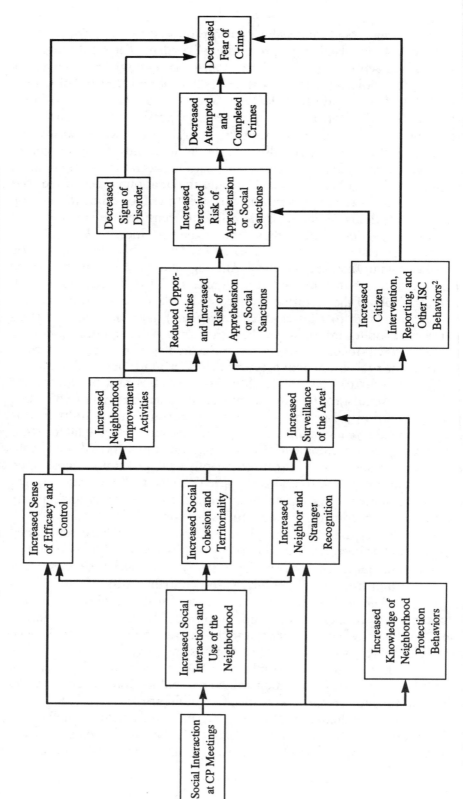

1   Refers to both natural and planned surveillance of either criminal or normative violations.
2   Refers to informal social control behaviors, including subtle pressures to conform to social expectations.

and a stronger feeling of integration into the community (DuBow and Podolefsky 1981; Greenberg et al. 1985; Rosenbaum 1987; Skogan 1987a). There is considerable evidence that participating in community organizations is associated with higher levels of social interaction (Ahlbrandt and Cunningham 1979; Axelrod 1956; Bell and Boat 1957; Fellin and Litwak 1963; Greer 1956; Hunter 1975; Kasarda and Janowitz 1974). There is little evidence, however, that social interaction in the community is related to the prevention of crime; this possible link represents a key test for informal social control theory.

The literature on pedestrian traffic and crime is one way of examining the social interaction hypothesis; it does not require the many assumptions needed in informal social control models. Increased pedestrian traffic is viewed by straight opportunity reduction theorists as a means of enhancing surveillance in public areas ("eyes on the street") and increasing the risk of detection and apprehension. Research testing this hypothesis has shown mixed results. Consistent with the notion that surveillance can have a deterrent effect, several studies have found that the presence of more people on the street is associated with a lower rate of criminal activity (Leudtke and Associates 1970; Ley and Cybriwsky 1974). Yet other studies have shown otherwise, namely that larger volumes of pedestrian traffic are associated with higher crime rates (Dietrick 1977) or that pedestrian traffic levels are unrelated to crime (Reppetto 1974). Even so, the world is not entirely uninterpretable; to clarify matters, there is some evidence that the deterrent capacity of increased pedestrian traffic depends on the *type* of pedestrians on the street. If the pedestrians are largely gang members or criminally minded persons, the surveillance effect will be negated (Brill and Associates 1977). Also, if the traffic is composed of dissimilar persons and if the neighborhood is not socially integrated, more traffic is likely to increase fear of crime (Hunter and Baumer 1982). Finally, because crime and fear are higher in both low- and high-traffic areas, a simple curvilinear relationship could be tested.

Other researchers have examined the crime prevention value of specific behaviors and perceptions which are viewed as more direct indicators of informal social control processes. On the positive side, crime rates and related crime problems are lower in areas where residents express attachment to the neighborhood (Taub et al. 1984; Warren 1969), perceive a sense of responsibility for what happens in the neighborhood (Taylor, Gottfredson, and Brower 1981), express a willingness to intervene in observed criminal activity (Maccoby, Johnson and Church 1958), and believe that their neighbors are inclined to intervene (Newman and Franck 1980). On the negative side, crime rates do not appear to be associated consistently with "neighboring" activities (e.g., surveillance), having friends in the neighborhood, or being able to recognize strangers (see Greenberg et al. 1985). A major problem with the "positive results" is that the direction of causality remains unclear. In fact, it is quite plausible that living in a low-crime area engenders feelings of neighborhood attachment and control of local behavior, rather than the reverse. Again, this problem highlights the need for experimental intervention.

Other research suggests that informal social control processes are important to citizen responsiveness in certain crime situations. Controlled experiments show that witnesses to a crime are more likely to intervene or to call the police if they know or are acquainted with the victim, if they know the witnesses, if they are encouraged to intervene by other witnesses, or if they are familiar with the environment where the incident occurred (Bickman and Rosenbaum 1977; Gillis and Hagan 1982; Latane and Darley 1970; Moriarity 1975; Ross 1971). Although these findings suggest that getting to know one's neighbors may improve citizen responsiveness in emergency situations, they do not suggest any direct link to crime reduction, especially because the observation of incidents in progress is rare. Also, the decision to intervene in a criminal or suspicious event is complex, and usually results in bystanders electing *not* to become involved (cf. Latane and Darley 1970).

In sum, many behavioral indicators of informal social control have *not* been linked directly to lower crime rates. Nevertheless there is some evidence to suggest that a) certain control-related attitudes and perceptions are associated with lower crime rates; b) informal pressures can be used to encourage citizen intervention; and c) surveillance by pedestrians may serve as a deterrent to crime if the pedestrians are largely "good citizens."

Beyond the direct link between informal social control and crime, one of the more interesting hypotheses is that informal social control may influence the level of disorder or incivility, which can escalate to more serious crime. "Incivility" refers to a wide range of social deviance and physical conditions, including graffiti, litter, vandalism, boarded-up buildings, abandoned autos, poorly maintained homes, groups of youths "hanging out," public drunkenness, prostitution, drug sales, and harassment of local residents. The often-used reference to these conditions as "signs of disorder" suggests that they are visual evidence of social disorganization and indicators that residents are unable to maintain order (Skogan 1987b; Wilson and Kelling 1982). This perception supposedly is shared by residents and by offenders. Residents become fearful and withdraw while offenders see new opportunities and move in, thus creating more crime. Research testing these hypothesized links among informal social control, disorder, and crime is virtually nonexistent, but Skogan (1987) has completed an important reanalysis of data from 13,000 residents in 40 neighborhoods across six major U.S. cities. The results indicate that higher levels of disorder are associated with "less frequent social interaction between neighbors, withdrawal from community life, lower levels of community solidarity, less informal cooperation between neighbors to prevent crime, and less household crime prevention activity" (73). These findings are consistent with the argument that disorders or incivilities weaken informal social controls and impair a community's capacity to respond to emerging problems; in turn, this situation opens the door to further neighborhood deterioration.

Can this process be reversed? The most fundamental question in this field is whether community organizers can "implant" social interaction and other informal social control activities in neighborhoods where currently they are weak or nonexistent and where crime rates are high (Rosenbaum 1987). The implant hypothesis can be tested only through social intervention and evaluation, and not through studies that describe the natural covariation between variables in urban settings.

Opportunity Reduction: Interventions and Evaluations. This section summarizes what is known currently about the effectiveness of collective anticrime activities directed at reducing opportunities for crime, building community cohesion, and reducing fear of crime. There can be little doubt that community crime prevention involving collective citizen actions has been depicted as highly effective by the mass media, politicians, researchers, and program advocates. In recent years hundreds of success stories have been told about how these programs, especially Neighborhood Watch, reduced crime and fear of crime, and were responsible for restoring a sense of community (e.g., National Crime Prevention Council 1987). What is the empirical basis for these reports of success? Sometimes the "I-believe-it-works" testimony of surveyed police officials, community leaders, and program staff is used as evidence that the programs are effective in achieving these outcomes (National Crime Prevention Council 1987; Washnis 1976). Many of the success stories, however, are based on actual crime statistics and sometimes on fear-of-crime data (see California Crime Resistance Task Force 1982; Feins 1983; Linden, Barker, and Frisbie 1984; National Crime Prevention Council 1987; Titus 1984). The literature is filled with claims that collective citizen action has reduced residential burglary from 20 to 60 percent. Unfortunately these reports often represent a significant misuse of the terms "research" and "evaluation research." As I have noted elsewhere, many of the "evaluations" are seriously flawed on methodological grounds (Lurigio and Rosenbaum 1986; Rosenbaum 1987); consequently the findings should not be taken very seriously. Evidence regarding the efficacy of the two major types of surveillance programs is reviewed below—citizen patrols and Neighborhood Watch.

Effects of Citizen Patrols. Although citizen patrols are common in urban neighborhoods and have been praised as partially effective in reducing street crime (Castberg 1980; Russell 1982; Washnis 1977), there has been very little evaluation research that measures their impact (for a review, see Pennell et al. 1985). The national evaluation of citizen patrols (Yin et al. 1977) used anecdotal evidence to reach the conclusion that building patrols (one of four patrol types) may be effective in preventing crime and in increasing residents' sense of safety at home and when patrols are visible. The evidence regarding other forms of patrols was less certain at the time. Neighborhood patrols were able to report numerous crime incidents to the police, but occasionally made residents feel uneasy about the legitimacy of their activities. Although Yin and his colleagues found some evidence of vigilante-like behavior by patrols (especially when members grew bored or were recruited from youth factions in the neighborhood), generally there was little support for this common concern.

Crime and perception data have been collected in two separate studies. In Columbus, Ohio, Latessa and Allen (1980) found that a well-organized walking patrol was associated with a decline in several types of reported crime in the target area; the largest decreases occurred in burglary and auto theft. As part of a national evaluation of the Guardian Angels, Pennell and her colleagues conducted an impact assessment in San Diego and found that this patrol group had little effect on violent crime but may have contributed to short-term decline in property crimes during peak visibility periods (Pennell et al. 1985). In terms of perceptions, surveys of San Diego residents and eastern transit riders showed that citizens perceive the Guardian Angels as effective in reducing crime and report feeling more safe when the Angels are patrolling.

At this point, citizen patrols have not been studied sufficiently to produce any conclusions about possible deterrent effects, but there is little reason to think that this type of formal surveillance would be more effective than uniformed police officers on foot patrol. The evidence showing crime reduction through police foot patrols is rather limited (e.g. Trojanowicz 1986), but a more consistent finding has been a reduction in residents' fear of crime (e.g. Pate 1986).

Effects of Neighborhood Watch. Several observations can be made regarding the general research on Watch-type programs. On the positive side, a number of studies reveal that persons who participate in such programs are less likely to be victimized by property crime than nonparticipants, and show some evidence (although considerably less) that target areas experience lower burglary rates after program implementation (see Greenberg et al. 1985; Titus 1983). Still, many of these evaluations are methodologically weak and cannot be defended against numerous threats to validity (for a listing of these weaknesses see Lurigio and Rosenbaum 1986; Skogan 1979; Yin 1979). Even some of the more carefully designed evaluations—showing positive effects on crime and fear levels in New York (Rich, Chavis, Florin, Perkins, and Wandersman 1987; Wandersman, Florin, Chavis, Rich, and Prestby 1985) and St. Louis (Kohfeld, Salert, and Schoenberg 1981)—report only cross-sectional data, leaving room for preprogram characteristics to account for the observed differences between treated and untreated areas. Some of the stronger evaluations of community crime prevention programs, with pretests and strong measurement, found evidence of success in reducing property crime victimization and fear of crime (see Rosenbaum 1986). Unfortunately, many of these evaluations do not isolate the effect of collective citizen action per se because the programs typically were comprehensive and often included changes in police practice, citizen activities, and/or the physical environment (e.g. Fowler and Mangione 1986).

By far the best empirical evidence regarding the efficacy of collective citizen action can be found in four large-scale quasi-experimental evaluations of Neighborhood Watch programs in Seattle (Cirel, Evans, McGillis, and Whitcomb 1977; Lindsay and McGillis 1986), Chicago (Rosenbaum et al. 1985,1986). Minneapolis (Pate, McPherson and Silloway 1987), and London, England (Bennett 1987). These evaluations collected panel and/or independent sample data on residents in experimental and carefully selected control areas, and employed state-of-the-art measurement to examine program effects on a wide variety of intervening and outcome variables. In addition to using rigorous evaluation designs, these projects are noteworthy because of the resources and effort devoted to systematic implementation of the program in most target areas. As evidence, the evaluators were able to report significant increases over time (relative to control groups) in residents' awareness of and participation in the program.

Table 19.1 summarizes the impact results for crime, fear, and community cohesion. Clearly the pattern of findings from these four studies is dramatically different from those in dozens of other Neighborhood Watch evaluations that claim success. The programs generally showed either no effect or increases in crime rates in the experimental areas after the intervention. Two marginally significant decreases in crime were found: a reduction in residential burglary in Seattle (based on a liberal analysis of the data) and a reduction in overall victimization rates in one of four Chicago neighborhoods. The pattern of results for fear of crime was similar. With the exception of one neighborhood in London, fear of personal crime and property crime either were unaffected by neighborhood organizing or showed significant increases relative to controls. Three of four Chicago neighborhoods experienced increases in fear of personal crime, but the more typical finding across these evaluations was "no difference." Finally, social cohesion generally was not affected by the programs; the one increase in London was offset by one decrease in Chicago. Notably, the only favorable outcomes with respect to social cohesion and fear of crime (reported in one London neighborhood) were based on the weakest subset of data, namely a pretest-posttest comparison on independent samples without a control group. All other findings were based on much stronger research designs. Finally, there was little evidence of program effects on various subgroups of the target population.

Perhaps the most important set of findings to emerge from these evaluations is that community organizing was unable to activate the intervening social behaviors that are hypothesized as necessary (according to informal social control and opportunity reduction models) to produce the desired changes in crime, fear, and social integration. Specifically, the researchers reported very few changes in social interaction, surveillance, stranger recognition, crime reporting, home protection behaviors, feelings of control, efficacy, and responsibility, satisfaction with the neighborhood, and attitudes toward the police.

One of the basic conclusions to be drawn from this work is that organizing the community through watch-type programs, which emphasize surveillance and target-hardening activities, has been oversold as a stand-alone strategy in the war against crime (see Rosenbaum 1987 for a detailed critique of this approach and its underlying assumptions). A more comprehensive approach that involves changes in citizen behavior, police activity, and the physical environment appears to increase the probability of impact (e.g. Fowler and Mangione 1986), but the causal variables in these multifaceted interventions are difficult to isolate.

Table 19.1
Major Evaluations of Collective Citizen Crime Prevention[1]

		Major Outcomes		
		Fear		Social
Authors/Sites	Crime[2]	Personnel	Property	Cohesion
Bennett (1987)				
London, England				
Target Area 1	Increase	No change	Decrease	Increase
Target Area 2	No change	No change	No change	No change
Cirel et al. (1977)				
Seattle	Marginal decrease in burglary	Marginal increase	—	—
Pate et al. (1987)				
Minneapolis	No change[3]	No change	No change	No change
Rosenbaum et al. (1985)				
Chicago				
Target Area 1	Marginal decrease	Increase	No change	No change
Target Area 2	Increase	Increase	No change	Decrease
Target Area 3	Increase	Increase	Increase	No change
Target Area 4	No change	No change	No change	No change

[1]   Findings are significant at p < .05 unless otherwise indicated.
[2]   Survey data include a composite index of property and personal crime unless otherwise indicated.
[3]   Both survey and police data

Another major lesson from these experimental programs is that organizing and sustaining community interest in activities directed at reducing opportunity and creating informal social control are considerably more difficult in low-income, heterogeneous areas that are most in need of crime prevention assistance. Participation levels generally are much lower in these areas (Bennett, Fisher, and Lavrakas 1986), even after a much stronger organizing effort (McPherson and Silloway 1987). Asking residents to "join together" and "watch out for suspicious persons" is asking a great deal in neighborhoods characterized by high levels of fear and distrust, a disproportionate number of "strangers," and a host of other problems. In fact, local voluntary organizations in these areas often express a preference for the social problems approach to community crime prevention rather than opportunity reduction (Bennett and Lavrakas 1988; Podolefski 1983), recognizing that crime is not caused by "strangers" from outside the neighborhood but by local problems that affect local residents, such as drug abuse, unemployment, and poor housing.

THE PHYSICAL ENVIRONMENT

The field of community crime prevention would be incomplete if it failed to recognize the role of the physical environment in preventing or encouraging criminal activity. In the context of residential crime prevention, the "physical environment" can include the design and location of single-family and multi-family dwelling units, the layout of residential streets, landscaping, street lighting, security hardware, signs of physical deterioration or property destruction, and many other characteristics of the physical environment. In his influential book *Defensible Space*, Oscar Newman (1972) argued that architects and urban planners can prevent crime by designing buildings and grounds with "defensible space" that encourages feelings of "territoriality" among residents and users of the environment. The physical environment may influence crime in two basic ways: 1) It can work *directly* to reduce crime by reducing access to property and removing criminal opportunities. In this case, "target hardening" via security hardware is the classic method of limiting an offender's access to property and persons.[3] 2) The physical environment can work *indirectly* to reduce crime, fear, and related problems by influencing the social behavior and social perceptions of residents and/or potential offenders. This hypothesized connection between the built environment, social behavior, and crime has been the source of considerable debate and research over the past 15 years and provides the focus of the review that follows.

The research literature on "defensible space" theory and "crime prevention through environmental design" (CPTED) applications is now rather sizable and diverse. (For reviews, see Mayhew 1979; Rubenstein et al. 1980; Taylor and Gottfredson 1986; Taylor, Gottfredson, and Brower 1980.) The basic elements of the theories are captured in the generalized model depicted earlier in Figure 19.1. Statements about how the built environment might influence residential behavior and perceptions generally are based either on a simple surveillance approach (i.e., creating environments that encourage natural "watching" and intervening) or on a territoriality/informal social control approach (i.e., creating environments that encourage "community building"). The objective of the surveillance approach is to increase the number of "eyes on the street" and to heighten the visibility of potential crime targets. Proposals to accomplish this goal include widening sidewalks, improving street lighting, reducing concealment near dwelling units, placing outdoor activities in plain view of dwelling unit windows, and many other physical design features. As noted earlier, the assumption is that local residents will be more likely to notice and respond to suspicious or criminal activity in such environments. In turn this responsiveness by citizens should increase the chances of arrest or of stopping crimes in progress. Crime prevention through environmental design, however, cannot be predicted simply from *residents'* behavior, but requires assumptions about the *offender's* perceptions and behavior. Potential offenders must become aware of the risks associated with targets that are subject to high levels of surveillance and then must decide either to select targets with greater opportunity or not to commit a crime. Because of the importance of offenders' perceptions in this area, social psychologists have developed models to explain how criminally minded persons make decisions about potential target sites (e.g. Brown and Altman 1981; Taylor and Gottfredson 1986).

Beyond the surveillance hypothesis, the territorial/informal social control approach is based on the notion that a properly designed environment can increase social interaction and social cohesion among local residents, which in turn will reduce crime and fear in the manner described earlier. In addition to the design examples listed above, proposals for achieving these objectives include reducing the number of families per entrance and the number of apartments per floor in multifamily dwelling units, increasing the maintenance and aesthetic appeal of public places, and restricting vehicular traffic with cul-de-sacs. The major objective of these efforts is to "privatize" public and semipublic areas so that "territorial" motivation is aroused, strangers are more easily recognizable, and residents develop a sense of personal responsibility for maintaining a clean and safe environment.

What evidence exists to support the notion that crime can be prevented through the proper design of residential environments? First, various correlational studies provide "circumstantial evidence" of the importance of the physical environment in crime prevention. Much of this work relates to the environmental opportunity for *human surveillance* of the target area. For example, there is some evidence that crime is more likely if offenders have the physical opportunity for concealment, such as a place to hide near doors or windows (Molumby 1976). Also, the accessibility of the target location to outside traffic appears to be related to criminal activity. The probability of victimization is higher on streets that are most accessible, such as cross intersections rather than cul-de-sacs (Bevis and Nutter 1977), in dwelling units near parking lots, streets, or recreational areas (Brill and Associates 1977), and in dwelling units and commercial units located on the border of the neighborhood or near street corners (Brantingham and Brantingham 1978; Luedtke and Associates 1970; Reppetto 1974). Accessibility results also have been found when comparing neighborhoods (Greenberg and Rohe 1984; Greenberg, Rohe, and Williams 1982). Finally, the research on pedestrian traffic cited earlier provides some support for the surveillance hypothesis, although too many people on the street or the wrong type of pedestrians can eliminate the crime-deterrent and fear-reduction effects created by the presence of more "eyes on the street."

Recent research on physical signs of disorder or incivilities supports the notion that the physical appearance of the environment can influence behavior and perceptions. In contrast to earlier findings by Taylor and his colleagues in Baltimore (Taylor, Gottfredson, and Shumaker 1984), a multisite analysis by Skogan (1987b), controlling for social status variables, revealed that physical deterioration and vandalism of property are associated with high levels of crime, greater fear of crime, less social interaction, and less community cohesion. Thus residents seem to withdraw when the physical environment provides threatening signs of disorder. These data also suggest that criminally minded persons see these physical signs as opportunities for crime (i.e., suggesting a probability of detection and apprehension), but actual offender data unfortunately are lacking.

Much of the research that provides a more direct test of "defensible space" theory and CPTED principles was conducted in public housing in the United States and England. This topic is somewhat controversial; researchers, after reviewing the available research literature, sometimes arrive at different conclusions about the effectiveness of environmental design strategies (e.g., Mayhew 1979; Rubenstein et al. 1980; Taylor and Gottfredson 1986). On the positive side, Newman and Franck (1980) studied 63 public housing developments in three major U.S. cities and found relationships between a number of physical characteristics and crime rates that were consistent with defensible space principles. For example, burglary rates were correlated positively with building and apartment accessibility, and fear of crime was lower in smaller buildings. Newman's research, however, has been criticized heavily on methodological and analytical grounds (e.g., Bottoms 1974; Mayhew 1979; Rubenstein et al. 1980). Nevertheless, further support for defensible space theory can be found in British research. A study of residential burglary by Winchester and

Jackson (1982) found that physical site characteristics were better predictors of victimization than were social/behavioral variables. Also, Wilson's (1978) assessment of 285 housing blocks in 38 public housing projects in London revealed that vandalism was higher at sites where certain aspects of the physical design did not allow for defensible space. These design effects, however, were evident only when there was not a high density of children; that factor was the primary determinant of vandalism rates.

Indeed, researchers have learned that social/demographic variables usually are more important in predicting crime rates than are the characteristics of the physical environment. In contrast to his earlier writings (Newman 1972), Oscar Newman acknowledged later the importance of social variables after finding that the proportions of low-income and teenage residents were strong predictors of burglary rates (e.g., Newman and Franck 1980). In a study of 66 neighborhoods in Baltimore, Taylor et al. (1984) found that the apparent strong link between design and crime disappeared after they controlled for the social status of the neighborhood. The importance of social variables also was illustrated in Merry's (1981) 18-month qualitative look at a multiethnic housing project in Boston. Merry found that although the project had strong defensible space features, it experienced high levels of crime and incivility, which she attributed to the ethnic fragmentation of the community. Merry brought attention to an important observation in this field: physical design may establish the preconditions for citizens to exercise social control ("defensible space) but it cannot guarantee such behaviors ("defended space").

Although the social composition of the neighborhood is important in preventing crime, researchers have yet to demonstrate that physical design characteristics can produce the types of social control behaviors that defensible space theory posits as mediators in the design-crime link. In a comparison of carefully matched low- and high-crime neighborhoods in Atlanta, Greenberg and her colleagues (Greenberg et al. 1982; Greenberg and Rohe 1984) found that physical design differences which created a more private, less accessible environment (e.g., fewer major through streets, less nonresidential land use, less public parking) were associated with lower crime rates. Yet, they did not find that informal social control variables (e.g., levels of informal surveillance, social ties) were predictive of differences in crime rates. Thus in some settings, physical design may reduce opportunities for criminal behavior directly without altering the territorial behaviors of local residents.

The introduction of better street lighting is one of the most widely implemented environmental design changes that does not require the social assumptions of territorial and informal social control theories. Improved street lighting should increase visibility in lighted areas, which in theory should increase the probability that crime will be observed and thus should deter offending behavior. Tien and his colleagues (Tien,

O'Donnell, Barnett, and Mirchandani 1979) conducted a national evaluation of 41 street lighting projects and reached two general conclusions: 1) improved lighting decreases fear of crime, but 2) it does not have any measurable effects on levels of crime. The authors caution, however, that the local evaluations on which these conclusions are based suffer from numerous methodological shortcomings. In a sizable CPTED demonstration project in Portland, Oregon with two consecutive evaluations, significant reductions in crime were noted after the installation of high-intensity lighting along a commercial strip, but improved lighting was only one of several physical and social interventions in the target area (see Lavrakas and Kushmuk 1986).

As in other areas of crime prevention, much of the research on environmental design is based on cross-sectional data and therefore offers only weak evidence that redesigning the residential environment will produce changes in crime, fear of crime, and community cohesion. A major exception to this conclusion is the demonstration and the two consecutive evaluations conducted in a low-income neighborhood in Hartford, Connecticut (Fowler and Mangione 1982, 1986; Fowler, McCalla, and Mangione 1979). The Hartford program employed a comprehensive three-pronged approach to reducing crime and fear: 1) changes in the physical environment (especially the elimination of several through streets); 2) changes in police activities (e.g., permanent assignments, decentralization, improved crime analysis, improved relationships with local residents); and 3) changes in citizen crime prevention activities (e.g., creation of voluntary community organizations and encouragement of anti-crime activities reflecting community needs). The first evaluation in 1977 found reductions in crime on the redesigned streets, but the re-evaluation in 1979 found that crime had increased. Between the first and second evaluation, the community organizing activities had declined and the team policing activities had been largely withdrawn. Thus one possible conclusion from the Hartford project is that physical changes in the environment do not have stand-alone effects on crime (cf. Taylor and Gottfredson 1986). The findings with regard to residents' behavior and perceptions were mixed. The first evaluation did not find changes in the most critical perceptions and behavior, such as fear of crime or informal social control, but improvements were noted in some areas (e.g., increased stranger recognition and watching of neighbors houses). The second evaluation showed reduction in fear and increased use of environment, but at a time when crime was on the rise. The evaluators interpret these improvements as evidence of informal social control, but others (Taylor and Gottfredson 1986) suggest that it may be nothing more than a lag in perceptions in view of an earlier decline in crime rates. Although Hartford is hailed as a major success story for community crime prevention, the program achieved only limited success in demonstrating that design changes (or other changes, for that matter) achieve crime reduction to theories of community crime prevention. Pedestrian activity, social cohesion, willingness to intervene, and related variables were largely unaffected by the interventions.

SUMMARY

In sum, a variety of evidence exists to suggest that the physical environment has a direct effect on the level of crime in residential settings, as well as some evidence that it affects fear of crime. Crime rates are higher when criminals have easier access to buildings and neighborhoods and when buildings are marred with graffiti, broken windows, litter, and other signs of disorder. Fear is higher when streets are poorly lighted and when property shows signs of deterioration or damage.

Although a link has been established between the physical environment and crime, researchers have been unable to identify changes in key social behaviors that are expected (in theory) to serve as intervening variables. In many situations the layout of the physical environment simply may reduce the offender's access to the target area or perceived opportunities for crime, but may have little effect on residents' perceptions and behaviors related to territoriality or informal social control. Other than the mixed results in Hartford, there is little evidence that physical design increases residents' use of the local environment, social interaction, natural surveillance, sense of community, sense of responsibility for behavior in public places, desire to intervene in criminal situations, or various behavioral expressions of informal social control. Part of the problem is the scarcity of good evaluation research in this area (as opposed to cross-sectional research) and the absence of good measures of informal social control.

Yet we know that social behavior is important to environmental design programs. Other than security hardware, the physical environment is nothing but wood, metal, and concrete if we do not understand how it influences social behavior *or* how its effects are limited or enhanced by social behaviors. At present we know more about the latter. Research suggests that the stand-alone effects of design on crime are limited in the absence of certain residential behaviors. The Hartford program demonstrated that residents and police play important mediating roles; without their help, the behaviors sought through design interventions are less likely to be achieved or sustained. Furthermore, the effects of design on crime (and presumably on residential behaviors) are especially difficult to demonstrate when the social environment is characterized by poverty, a large proportion of youths, and/or ethnic heterogeneity. Thus physical design is not a panacea that can produce a social environment where one is lacking completely, but it does appear to help in certain conditions. The task ahead is to identify environmental design options that are practical as well as politically and economically feasible.

COMMUNITY POLICING

To speak of community crime prevention without discussing law enforcement would be to forget that the citizenry and its government have "conspired" over the years to define the police as the primary means for preventing and controlling crime at the neighborhood level. With few exceptions, the money and the responsibility for neighborhood crime control programs have been given to law enforcement agencies rather than directly to the community. This section examines the role of the police in community crime prevention efforts and tries to assess the direction and the promise of these strategies.

Earlier, the evolution of *modern* "community crime prevention" was described briefly; it was mentioned that police crime prevention activities were little more than a public relations function to improve the community's image of law enforcement. Since that time crime prevention officers have played a critical role in educating the public and stimulating their participation in standardized programs such as Neighborhood Watch, Operation Identification, and Security Surveys (e.g., Garofalo and McLeod 1986). Even so, most law enforcement administrators continue to view these police activities as auxiliary and tangential to "real" police work; for this reason police crime prevention programs never have received the status or the resources needed to function adequately. Thus if crime prevention activities are to receive the attention they deserve, they are unlikely to do so through these traditional roles. Such attention is more likely to come as a result of some fundamental changes in the definition of "real" police work. Although the history of modern police reform and innovation is characterized by a sequence of failures and false starts, there is some reason to be optimistic that such changes are beginning to take shape; they are referred to commonly as "community policing" or "problem-oriented policing."

Community policing is emerging from a growing recognition that the police are extremely dependent on local residents to achieve their goals of reducing crime and fear of crime in urban neighborhoods. Research over the past 15 years has highlighted the limitations of traditional police practices (see Eck and Spelman 1987a for a review). Armed with evaluation data, researchers have challenged the crime-control effectiveness of random motorized patrols (Kelling et al. 1974), rapid police response to the crime scene (Kansas City Police Department 1980; Spelman and Brown 1984), criminal investigations (Eck 1982; Greenwood, Petersilia, and Chaiken 1977), and traditional crime analysis (Gay, Beall, and Bowers 1984). In essence, considerable time and effort have been expended to improve police management and efficiency, but the fundamental approach to policing has remained the same: namely, responding to and investigating individual citizen calls for service in a reactive fashion (rather than seeking to identify and address community problems) and treating local citizens as passive recipients of police services (rather than as co-producers of public safety). More of the same thing with greater efficiency does not translate into more effectiveness.

Police research not only suggests that improvements in traditional policing have had little, if any, effect on crime and public perceptions; it also points to the importance of the citizen's role in solving crime. Information provided by ordinary citizens—not fancy detective work—is the basis for most criminal arrests (Skogan and Antunes 1979), and clearance rates are low because police receive few good leads from the public (Eck 1982; Spelman, Oshima, and Kelling 1985). Also, police are learning that local residents are the main source of information about the many neighborhood problems that concern the community (Pate et al. 1986). In sum, innovative police agencies are beginning to see that a "new" approach to policing is needed, one that brings police officers back into the neighborhoods where they started in 1829 and that seeks to strengthen the cooperation between police and citizens in solving local problems.

Some of the key elements of community or problem-oriented policing include an emphasis on improving the number and quality of police-citizen contacts, a broader definition of "legitimate" police work, decentralization of the police bureaucracy, and a greater emphasis on proactive problem-solving strategies, which often include crime prevention activities (Eck and Spelman 1987b; Goldstein 1979, 1987; Murphy and Muir 1984; Pate et al. 1986; Skolnick and Bayley 1986, 1988). Although a distinction has been made between "community policing" and "problem-oriented policing" (e.g., Eck and Spelman 1987b; Skolnick and Bayley 1988), both approaches seek to improve the partnership between the police and the community. "Community policing" is an umbrella term for a wide variety of community-oriented police activities that share a common set of principles or values (e.g., Murphy and Muir 1984), whereas "problem-oriented policing" has been defined as a more prescribed approach to addressing neighborhood concerns through the identification and analysis of specific problems, followed by the development, implementation, and evaluation of specific solutions (Eck and Spelman 1987a, 1987b; Goldstein 1979).

EVIDENCE OF EFFECTIVENESS

Elements of community policing strategies have been implemented not only in the United States but also in Australia, Canada, Great Britain, Denmark, Norway, Sweden, Finland, Singapore, and Japan (for an international perspective see Skolnick and Bayley 1988). To date, however, there has been little evaluation research on the effectiveness of these strategies in preventing crime, reducing fear of crime, and achieving other desired outcomes. Foot patrols probably are the most widely used method of community policing in the United States, and have been evaluated in Flint, Michigan (Trojanowicz 1986) and Newark, New Jersey (Pate 1986). As noted earlier, it remains uncertain whether police foot patrols can reduce crime, but they seem to be effective in reducing fear of crime and engendering positive citizen attitudes toward the police.

The Fear Reduction Project in Houston and Newark conducted by the Police Foundation, represented a sizable demonstration and evaluation of several community policing strategies (see Pate et al. 1986). The results at these two sites were mixed. Programs focusing on individual residents— such as the distribution of a police-community newsletter (with crime prevention news and tips) and recontacting victims of crime to offer sympathy and services—showed virtually no effects, but the more community-oriented programs that encouraged officers to become familiar with local residents and the neighborhood demonstrated more positive results. For example, two programs were associated with reductions in perceived social disorder, reductions in perceived crime levels and improved citizen evaluations of the police. These were fairly comprehensive programs involving a variety of police-citizen contacts and diverse crime prevention activities, ranging from neighborhood cleanups to community "storefront" centers.

One noticeable failure in the Houston-Newark Fear Reduction project was the "Signs of Crime" program, which attempted a) to reduce fear and related problems by reducing social disorder (through foot patrols and aggressive order maintenance) and b) to reduce physical deterioration (through more intense city services and a youth cleanup program). The lack of positive police-citizen contact and the random implementation of the program may help to explain the complete lack of effects, but in view of the amount of resources devoted to this strategy, some might question the "incivility" theory and the "crime attack" model that served as the rationale for this approach (cf. Wilson 1983; Wilson and Kelling 1982).

To date, comparable evaluations of problem-oriented policing programs do not exist, although preliminary studies have yielded some encouraging results. The early case studies in Madison, Wisconsin (Goldstein and Susmilch 1982) and in London, England (Hoare, Stewart, and Purcell 1984) demonstrated that problem-oriented approaches can yield useful information about specific problems, but that implementation is more difficult and more time-consuming than thought previously. The first impact data were collected through larger field studies in Baltimore (Cordner 1986) and Newport News, Virginia (Eck and Spelman 1987b). The Citizen Oriented Police Enforcement (COPE) project in Baltimore involved 45 officers whose mission was to reduce citizens' fear of crime by identifying and resolving fear-arousing problems. Activities were extremely diverse and ranged from exerting multiagency pressure on an apartment house manager (to correct disrepair and violations of housing, health, and fire codes) to demolishing a tree house that served as a hangout for youths using drugs and alcohol. Three waves of community surveys in the target areas showed evidence of reductions in fear of crime (Cordner 1986), but the evaluation was quite limited. Methodological limitations include the absence of any usable control groups, the absence of statistical tests, the use of police officers as interviewers for a portion of the data collection, and the possibility of regression to the mean because a high level of fear was a main criterion for site selection.

In Newport News, a more ambitious departmentwide program was implemented; the types of problems ranged from minor disorders to robbery. The Police Executive Research Forum (PERF) conducted a thorough process assessment and collected some impact data (Eck and Spelman 1987b; Spelman and Eck 1986). Time series analyses showed significant declines in personal robberies (down 39%) and larcenies from autos (down 53%) in the downtown area after implementation; household burglaries declined 35 percent in a targeted housing unit. The Newport News evaluation was limited to reported crime statistics, and thus, a more comprehensive impact assessment is needed, with additional outcome measures.

LIMITATIONS AND CAUTIONS

Community or problem-oriented policing is currently a "hot" idea that may permanently alter policing as we know it. Its promise lies in its capacity to address a wide range of social and physical problems that contribute to neighborhood crime and fear of crime, and to mobilize individual citizens and numerous agencies in this effort. Unfortunately, the list of potential pitfalls is long (see Bayley in press; Goldstein 1987). When the police are asked to address the social problems of racism, poverty, and unemployment, someone beside Herman Goldstein will ask, "What are the limits on the role of the police in our society? Should we be concerned again about police accountability, police corruption, and political abuse?" Leaving aside these tough questions, this author is more concerned about the other extreme—the potential trivialization of problem-oriented policing. Arresting a few prostitutes or eliminating a few locations where youth hang out may serve as a temporary solution for local residents, but it does little to address the underlying causes of these problems. Furthermore, such problems are likely to be displaced to nearby locations. Another concern is that the issue of "co-production" will be lost in this race to implement community policing. Without a full appreciation of community dynamics, many police departments may feel that officers can collect a little data and then proceed to develop and implement solutions on their own. In sum, the future of this course remains uncertain but promising.

CONCLUSIONS AND IMPLICATIONS

ASSESSING THE BENEFITS AND THE COSTS

The gains achieved by citizen crime prevention behaviors (although still somewhat tentative) often carry a price tag. At the individual level, persons who engage in high-risk avoidance behaviors generally are less likely to be victimized, but this response amounts to a loss of behavioral freedom; it also may enhance fear and, if practiced widely, may contribute to a rise in community-level crime rates. Self-defense training, resistance by potential victims, and even carrying a weapon may lower the risk of successful victimization and increase feelings of safety (although the effects of weapons are uncertain) but these actions also may increase the risk of injury.

In regard to household protection behaviors, there is consistent evidence that target-hardening actions are associated with a lower risk of victimization for residential burglary. Yet the benefits of these security measures (if we assume that the relationship is causal) are enjoyed only by those who can pay for security hardware; participation tends to be restricted to persons with higher incomes. Furthermore, although home protection behaviors are expected to reduce fear of crime, there is evidence that home security surveys have the opposite effect.

As for collective anti-crime programs, nearly one hundred reports indicate that Neighborhood Watch reduces crime, but a closer look uncovers a curious inverse relationship: the stronger the research design, the weaker the program effects observed. Although neighborhood studies have underscored the importance of social interaction in developing informal social control, neighborhood crime prevention programs have been unable to set in motion the social interaction, territoriality, surveillance, and other behaviors that theoretically are expected at the block or neighborhood level. Furthermore, the price of attending neighborhood meetings may be an increase in fear of crime unless one is involved intensively as a regular participant.

Research on the physical environment has yielded a similar pattern of results: correlational research suggests that certain design features are associated with lower rates of crime and fear. Although evaluations of CPTED programs show some direct effects on crime, they have not been able to produce the mediating social behaviors posited in Newman's (1972) popular "defensible space" theory.

Overall, a diverse set of research literature suggests that crime prevention theories have identified some of the key variables on which to build effective interventions; yet the evaluation literature has produced only mixed results, and the gains carry some possible liabilities. There is no single reason for this less-than-perfect outcome—weak implementation, poor research, and a few unjustified theoretical assumptions all contribute.

KNOWLEDGE GAPS AND SUBSTANTIVE ISSUES

We have learned a great deal over the past 20 years, but many questions remain unanswered. Several major issues must be addressed if community crime prevention is to establish itself as a viable set of strategies for combating crime and related neighborhood problems. A few of the most critical knowledge gaps and substantive issues are addressed below.

Crime Displacement. Because community crime prevention emphasizes the reduction of criminal opportunities in specific situations, one of the most challenging problems for this set of anti-crime strategies is crime displacement. When the motivation for offending is not modified and when crime prevention measures are not practiced widely, neighborhoods are full of alternative opportunities for criminal behavior when a particular opportunity has been blocked or removed. As Clarke (1983) observes, "Within easy reach of every house with a burglar alarm or car with an antitheft device are many others without such protection" (246). There are many different types of displacement, including geographic, temporal, tactical, target, and activity displacement (Garber 1978; Reppetto 1976). Unfortunately, existing research tells us very little about the extent and nature of crime displacement. This problem is difficult to study properly and rarely is taken seriously by evaluators, but it remains an important issue. Some evidence of displacement has been documented in programs to increase police manpower in particular areas (Chaiken, Lawless and Stevenson 1974; Press 1971; Schnelle, Kirchner, McNees, and Lawler 1975; Schwartz and Clarren 1978), to improve street lighting (Wright, Heilweil, Pelletier, and Dickinson 1974), to engrave property (Heller et al. 1975), and to prevent auto theft (Mayhew, Clarke, Sturman, and Hough 1976). No displacement efforts were observed, however, in the widely discussed Seattle (Lindsay and McGillis 1986) and Hartford (Fowler et al. 1979) crime prevention programs.

Because of the (largely unknown) problem of displacement, we are hard pressed to estimate the *collective benefit* to the community from crime prevention activities. Clarke (1983) argues that a certain amount of crime and especially certain types of crime are likely to be prevented rather than displaced. Yet in view of the virtually unlimited possibilities for criminal activity, overall citizen participation levels will need to be increased substantially before displacement problems can be contained.

Participation and Maintenance. The research literature gives us some reason to think that if citizens participated in certain prevention activities, they would be less likely to be victimized, and if there was a greater prevalence of participation in the community, less displacement would occur. Inducing people to participate, however and maintaining their interest or involvement are the major problems facing community crime prevention practitioners. Participation in collective neighborhood activities is especially low even after strong organizing efforts have been made; perhaps for this reason organizers often resort to "you-could-be-a-victim" scare tactics (Rosenbaum and Heath in press). Clearly there is a need for more effective social influence techniques in community crime prevention strategies.

Although crime and fear are sufficient to stimulate initial participation for some residents, we have learned that these are not adequate motives to *maintain* participation. The evaluation literature is filled with complaints about the difficulties of maintaining participation levels in community crime prevention programs (Bennett and Lavrakas 1988; Garofalo and McLeod 1986; Krug 1983; Lindsay and McGillis 1986; Rosenbaum 1987). Numerous solutions have been proposed, with varying degrees of success. Organizers have learned that crime in itself is a "no-win" issue (Skogan 1987) and that successful maintenance requires a continuous group structure, strong leadership, links to outside resources, a full agenda (including social activities and noncrime issues), decentralized planning, and extensive efforts to communicate with and reward participants (Bennett and Lavrakas 1988; Chavis, Florin, Rich, Wandersman, and Perkins 1987; Garofalo and McLeod 1986). In this respect, community policing programs will be no better off than the typical single-issue block watch: both lack the mechanisms for *continuous* citizen participation in neighborhood improvement activities.

Despite organizers' efforts to stimulate participation and fight waning interest, there are good reasons to expect an upper limit on citizen participation levels (see Skogan 1981). If low participation and high dropout rates are, to some extent, intransigent problems, perhaps policy analysts should give more serious attention to crime prevention strategies that "shortcut" the social process by seeking to create either psychological or physical barriers to crime *which do not require increased citizen participation.* To be effective, this approach would require substantially more research on how offenders perceive these anticrime tactics. Crime prevention practitioners already use many of these tactics (e.g., stickers on windows and Watch signs on street corners) but without the benefit of research support.

Program Generalizability. The biggest challenge facing crime prevention today is to implement effective programs in high-crime neighborhoods. Crime prevention programs have "proven themselves" in middle-class areas where residential burglary is the major problem and where participation is easier to achieve, but heterogeneous, low-income, high-crime neighborhoods present a entirely different picture. For example, participation in collective Watch-type programs is not only a middle-class phenomenon (as noted earlier) but also requires moderate levels of social integration in the community before it can be implemented effectively. Hope (1988) documented a curvilinear relationship between neighborhood social cohesion and participation in Neighborhood Watch in Great Britain; that is, low program participation was observed in neighborhoods that had either very low or very high social cohesion. The implication is that attempts to strengthen informal social control through surveillance programs will succeed only in areas that already possess some degree of informal social control. This is the dilemma of community crime prevention in tough urban neighborhoods. Considerable research, using both ethnographic and survey data, shows that informal social controls are weaker in low-income, minority, and heterogeneous neighborhoods (for a review, see Greenberg et al. 1985). Indeed, heterogeneity is a key problem for establishing social cohesion and allowing residents to enforce a set of shared norms regarding appropriate social behavior. Research shows that dissimilarity along ethnic, racial, religious, or economic lines stands as a barrier to social interaction and social cohesion (Eames and Goode 1977; Maccoby, Johnson, and Church 1958; Shaw 1981; Zander 1979). From a social policy standpoint, the Neighborhood Watch research suggests that community organizers face major obstacles when they seek to "implant" informal social control by using a strategy that does not match the needs and problems of the local community and is based on assumptions about social relations that do not apply in that environment (Rosenbaum 1987). Policy makers and funders should be cautious about prepackaged programs and should recognize the importance of interventions that are tailored to the needs of the local community.

In the absence of effective crime prevention programs in poor neighborhoods, we can assume that a certain amount of crime will be displaced from nearby areas that can afford better protection. Crime prevention can become a political issue regarding the provision of collective goods (Schneider 1986, 1987). Because household protection behaviors, for example, are associated strongly with income, strategies must be pursued which help to "redistribute" public safety in a manner that benefits those who can least afford this protection. Government-supported programs to purchase and install hardware would address two main obstacles to household protection in high-crime areas: money and citizen participation in repetitious crime prevention behaviors.

High Expectations. For years, community crime prevention programs have suffered from unrealistic expectations. Frequently programs are expected to reduce "crime" (all crime) in an entire city or a large neighborhood, as well as reduce fear and restore a sense of community. Furthermore, because of funding constraints, this goal is to be accomplished within 6 to 12 months, with one or two persons responsible for the program. Until policy makers and funding agencies decide to commit adequate resources to these demonstration programs and to set realistic expectations, the effectiveness of community crime prevention strategies will remain unknown. We are fooling ourselves if we think that small amounts of money for short periods of time are sufficient to make a difference in tough neighborhoods where the crime problem is complex and deeply rooted. Neighborhood self-sufficiency, if at all possible, will take several years to achieve and will require a substantial amount of planning, technical assistance, and funding. Also, politicians must be disabused of the notion that community "self-help" and "volunteerism" are free.

Programs must narrow their focus to a few specific crimes or problems in a small target area and must direct their limited resources in this area in order to maximize the impact. Without a stronger dosage of the treatment, there is little reason to expect that most interventions will make a difference (Rosenbaum 1987). Furthermore, to date there is little evidence that crime prevention programs can have effects which reach beyond their immediate participants or small geographic areas, despite theoretical claims that the program should affect nonparticipants as well. Perhaps program advocates should be happy with small victories at this point, in view of the dangers of pursuing larger, neighborhood-wide effects without the proper backing and without a sound theory as to how these larger changes will take place.

Strategy Type. Recently there has been a push for greater attention to the "social problems" approach to crime prevention and for less attention to "opportunity reduction" strategies (Currie 1988; Curtis 1987). Although the social problems approach deserves a fair test, there is no need for communities to choose *a priori* between these two approaches to crime prevention; each has its purpose and they can be used jointly as complementary tactics (see Bennett and Lavrakas 1988). Generally speaking, opportunity reduction may be sufficient for middle-class, low-to-moderate crime areas, while more troubled areas could use anything that works.

The social problems approach is theoretically enticing because of its focus on "root causes," but several words of caution are in order. First, the problems of low citizen participation and low "dosage" apply equally well to this approach. Citizens' desire to participate will not be increased magically, nor will helping a handful of high-risk youth influence the quality of life in the entire neighborhood. Second, when conducted properly, this program is considerably more expensive than simple opportunity reduction programs, but this consideration should not deter us from funding intensive strategies of this type. All too often social policy regarding preventive programs is "a penny wise and a pound foolish." Finally, these programs must be community-based and community-focused, representing a true partnership between the government and local residents. The typical government-run poverty programs or the popular individual-focused (high-risk youth) programs will not be adequate this time around.

Finally, a note of caution on community policing. Although the implications of community policing for enhancing the police-citizen partnership seem promising, the bureaucratic and political obstacles to full-scale implementation are substantial. This change will require decentralization (which is threatening to upper middle management), "permanent" assignments or beats, entirely new supervision and performance evaluation standards, specialized training in a wide range of social service areas, and many other changes in law enforcement. Because the money for preventing crime already has been allocated to the police budget, however, the community has a vested interest in seeing that some of these changes take place.

RESEARCH AND EVALUATION ISSUES

Both the quantity and the quality of evaluation research in this field are inadequate for building a solid body of knowledge regarding the nature, extent, and effectiveness of community crime prevention initiatives. A few thoughts on this topic and a research agenda are outlined below.

Quantity and Quality of Data. Researchers in this field should be astonished that we still do not have a national data base on citizen crime prevention behaviors. The one-time supplement to the National Crime Survey in 1984 covered only a few behaviors; other local data bases are now dated. In addition, in spite of all the theorizing about how social behavior influences neighborhood conditions, there is surprisingly little data on the mediating processes that have been proposed.

The primary reason why we do not know "what works" in community crime prevention is the quality of the evaluation research. The one hundred or more evaluations that lack control groups and proper measures of key variables are not worth a penny. Unless evaluations are funded adequately and conducted by trained researchers, they should not be conducted at all because the results usually are untrustworthy. Individuals who are not familiar with basic methods of research (e.g., Babbie 1986), techniques for program evaluation (e.g., Rossi and Freeman 1988), and critical threats to research validity (Cook and Campbell 1979) should not be in the business of evaluating community crime prevention programs.

The importance of conducting experiments and quasi-experiments must be understood by both practitioners and researchers. There is a pressing need to move beyond studies of natural covariation to experimental interventions if we are interested in testing theories of crime prevention and documenting program impact. For example, knowing that a neighborhood with a high level of disorder also has a high level of fear tells us very little about whether a program to reduce fear can do so by reducing disorder. We must begin to document 1) that a program can reduce levels of disorder, and 2) that these changes in disorder are associated with changes in fear level. This particular example has not been demonstrated to date.

Future work in this area could benefit significantly from several methodological improvements: 1) reducing the present reliance on police crime statistics in favor of victimization surveys; 2) collecting more longitudinal data to assist with cause-and-effect inferences when experimentation is not possible; 3) using survey measures of perceptions and behavior that have known reliabilities and developing new observational measures of behavior, especially formal social control; and 4) using experimental and quasi-experimental designs more frequently to test whether crime prevention programs are having any effect on the hypothesized intervening social variables.

Measuring "Success". Ten years ago, when anti-crime programs were unable to achieve success while using crime rates as their main (and only) criterion, interest shifted to quality-of-life measures such as social cohesion and fear of crime. Yet even this approach is relatively narrow and limits the number of ways in which community groups and other actors can demonstrate success. Recently, evaluators have suggested expanding the realm of measurement and incorporating qualitative indicators of neighborhood gains (Bennett and Lavrakas 1988; Grant et al. in press). For example, Block Watch may not reduce local crime rates, but it may serve as an organizing tool for community groups to boost their membership and to respond to a variety of problems. One community group in Chicago, although it had little effect on crime or residents' perceptions, succeeded in pressuring landlords, local businesses, and the police to make desired changes in the neighborhood (Grant et al. in press). Thus organizations should receive credit for achieving certain intermediate outcomes, especially when evaluations are conducted within a short period of time.

Research Agenda. Because research suggestions have been offered throughout this article, only a few directions for research will be suggested here. First, there is a compelling need to open up the "black box" of community crime prevention and test the many presumed causal links in our theoretical models. If we assume good interventions, quantitative measures must be supplemented by good field work to pinpoint the social processes that are operating: what are the effects on social interaction, discussion, perceptions, surveillance, and informal social control behaviors? Also, environmental and social conditions must be documented carefully. We are past the point of wanting to report that crime prevention does or does not work, and now are interested in *specifying the conditions* under which particular outcomes are observed.

Because of the paucity of knowledge in this area, numerous small-scale experiments are needed to test the many assumptions about the deterrent effects of various crime prevention measures. In this regard, more research is needed on offender perceptions and decision making. A simple example of our ignorance is found in Garofalo and McLeod (1986), who specify the assumptions about deterrence that underlie the posting of Neighborhood Watch signs: 1) potential offenders will see the signs; 2) they will know what Neighborhood Watch is; 3) they will believe that residents practice Neighborhood Watch; 4) they will believe that Neighborhood Watch activities increase their risk of detection; and 5) they will view this increased risk as a sufficient deterrent from criminal behavior. In fact, currently we do not know whether any of these assumptions are true; yet they *all* must be true if the program is to have a deterrent effect.

At the individual level, we need more compelling evidence that engaging in certain behaviors reduces one's chances of victimization. Regular supplements to the National Crime Survey, with panel data collected before and after victimization, would answer this question more clearly than the current array of one-time local surveys.

Neighborhood-based programs that seek to correct social problems in the community should receive a *fair* test. This type of intervention would require considerable funding, but this investment would be very small when viewed in the context of the potential gains. The usual methods of evaluating crime prevention programs should be modified if the immediate objective is to alter the behavior of youths and their families rather than to produce communitywide effects.

Collectively, previous evaluations suggest that interventions which are the joint produce of police and citizen input are more likely to affect crime and residents' perceptions than interventions which are initiated by one or the other (Yin 1986). Demonstrations and evaluations of "coproduction" activities are needed, especially in the context of community policing, where new roles and responsibilities are being defined for all parties. Research can help to document this developing process and to identify major obstacles.

Finally, in my opinion, we are reaching a point in the development of community crime prevention where policy makers, practitioners, and researchers are beginning to realize that the goal is to *prevent crime* rather than to advocate (or challenge) a particular type of program. With this idea in mind, researchers should pay more attention to the full range of social or physical variables in the environment that may influence levels of crime and/or the quality of neighborhood life. When all the attention is given to individual and collective behaviors, we can forget easily that macro-level structural variables, such as community racial composition income, occupation, and marital status, can explain much of the variability in crime rates (see Byrne and Sampson 1986). The larger policy decisions that contribute to these patterns of social behavior deserve more "watching" by a "vigilant" public. If housing policies, for example, have a significant impact on patterns of crime (Bottoms and Wiles 1988), such decisions should be of interest to crime prevention researchers and policy makers. The closer crime prevention practice and research can come to the root causes of crime, the better the chances of enhancing both the magnitude and the duration of the effects.

NOTES

1. In the crime prevention field, the application of design principles often is referred to as "crime prevention through environmental design," or CPTED (Jeffrey 1971).
2. Informal social control is not identified here as a separate crime prevention orientation because it is a major objective of both orientations.
3. The purchase, installation, and use of security hardware for residential crime prevention ("target hardening") was covered earlier under "household protection behaviors." Here attention is given to other aspects of the physical environment that have been studied in relation to crime prevention.

REFERENCES

Ahlbrandt, R.S., Jr. and J.V. Cunningham (1979) *A New Public Policy for Neighborhood Preservation*. New York: Praeger.

Axelrod, M. (1956) "Urban Structure and Social Participation." *American Sociological Review* 21:13-18.

Babbie, E. (1986) *The Practice of Social Research*. 4th edition. Belmont, CA: Wadsworth.

Bayley, D.H. (in press) "Community Policing: A Report From the Devil's Advocate." In J. Greene and S. Mastrofski (eds.), *Community Policing: Rhetoric or Reality*. New York: Praeger.

Bell, W. and M.D. Boat (1957) "Urban Neighborhoods and Informal Social Relations." *American Journal of Sociology* 62:391-98.

Bennett, S.F. with P.J. Lavrakas (1988) *Evaluation of the Planning and Implementation of the Neighborhood Program*. Final process report to the Eisenhower Foundation. Evanston, IL: Northwestern University, Center for Urban Affairs and Policy Research.

Bennett, S.F., B.S. Fisher, and P.J. Lavrakas (1986) "Awareness and Participation in the Eisenhower Neighborhood Program." Paper presented at the annual meeting of the American Society for Criminology, Atlanta.

Bennett, T. (1987) *An Evaluation of Two Neighborhood Watch Schemes in London*. Executive summary of final report to the Home Office Research and Planning Unit. Cambridge, England: Cambridge University, Institute of Criminology.

Bennett, T. and R. Wright (1984) *Burglars on Burglary: Prevention and the Offender*. Aldershot, England: Gower.

Bevis, C. and J.B. Nutter (1977) *Changing Street Layouts to Reduce Residential Burglary*. St. Paul: Governor's Commission on Crime Prevention and Control.

Bickman, L., P.J. Lavrakas, S.K. Green, N. North-Walker, J. Edwards, S. Vorkowski, S.S. DuBow, and J. Wuerth (1976) *Citizen Crime Reporting Projects*. National Evaluation Program, Phase I Summary Report. Washington, DC: Department of Justice.

Bickman, L. and D.P. Rosenbaum (1977) "Crime Reporting as a Function of By-stander Encouragement, Surveillance, and Credibility." *Journal of Personality and Social Psychology* 35:577-86.

Biderman, A.D., L.A. Johnson, J. McIntyre, and A.W. Weir (1967) *Report on a Pilot Study in the District of Columbia on Victimization and Attitudes toward law Enforcement.* Washington, DC: U.S. Government Printing Office.

Block, R. and W.G. Skogan (1984) The Dynamics of Violence between Strangers: Victim Resistance and Outcomes in Rape, Assault, and Robbery. Final report to the National Institute of Justice. Evanston, IL: Northwestern University, Center for Urban Affairs and Policy Research.

Boggs, S. (1971) "Formal and Informal Crime Control: An Exploratory Study of Urban, Suburban, and Rural Orientations." *Sociological Quarterly* 12:319-27.

Bordua, D.J. and A.J. Lizotte (1979) "Patterns of Legal Firearms Ownership: A Cultural and Situational Analysis of Illinois Counties." *Law and Policy Quarterly* 12:147-75.

Bottoms, A.E. (1974) Review of O. Newman's *Defensible Space, British Journal of Criminology,* 14:204-6.

Bottoms, A.E. and P. Wiles (1988) "Crime and Housing Policy: A Framework For Crime Prevention Analysis." In T. Hope and M. Shaw (eds.) *Communities and Crime Reduction.* London: Her Majesty's Stationery Office, pp. 84-98.

Brantingham, P.L. and P.J. Brantingham (1978) "A Theoretical Model of a Crime Site Selection." In M. Krohn and R.L. Akers (eds.), *Crime, Law and Sanction.* Beverly Hills: Sage, pp. 105-18.

————— (1981) "Notes on the Geometry of Crime." In P.J. Brantingham and P.L. Brantingham (eds.), *Environmental Criminology.* Beverly Hills: Sage, pp. 27-54.

Brill and Associates (1977) *Comprehensive Security Planning: A Program for William Nickerson Gardens, Los Angeles, California.* Washington, DC: Department of Housing and Urban Development, Office of Policy Development Research.

Brown B. and I. Altman (1981) "Territoriality and Residential Crime: A Conceptual Framework." In P.J. Brantingham and P.L Brantingham (eds.), *Environmental Criminology.* Beverly Hills: Sage, pp. 55-76.

Bureau of Justice Statistics (1988) *Report to the Nation on Crime and Justice: The Data.* Washington, DC: U.S. Department of Justice.

————— (1986) *Sourcebook of Criminal Justice Statistics.* Washington. DC: U.S. Government Printing Office.

————— (1987) *Criminal Victimization in the United States, 1985.* Washington. DC: U.S. Department of Justice.

Byrne, J. and R. Sampson, eds. (1986) *The Social Ecology of Crime.* New York: Springer-Verlag.

California Crime Resistance Task Force (1982) *Crime Prevention Exemplary Programs.* Sacramento, CA: California Office of Criminal Justice Planning.

Carey, J. T. (1975) *Sociology and Public Affairs: The Chicago School.* Beverly Hills: Sage.

Castberg, A.D. (1980) "Assessing Community Based Citizen Anti-Crime Programs." *USA Today,* 108:33-35.

Cedar Rapids Police Department (1972) *Evaluation of the Effects of a Large-Scale Burglar Alarm System.* Report prepared for the U.S. Department of Justice. Cedar Rapids, IA: Author.

Centers For Disease Control (1987) *1986 Annual Report*. Atlanta Center for Environmental Health, Division of Injury Epidemiology and Control.

Chaiken, J.M., M.W. Lawless, and K.A. Stevenson (1974) *The Impact of Police Activity on Crime: Robberies on the New York City Subway System*. New York: Rand.

Chavis, D.M., P. Florin, R.C. Rich, A. Wandersman, and D.D. Perkins (1987) *The Role of Block Associations in Crime Control and Community Development: The Block Buster Project*. Final report to the Ford Foundation. New York: Citizens Committee for New York City, Inc.

Christian, T.F. (1973) "The Organized Neighborhoods, Crime Prevention, and the Criminal Justice System." Ph.D. dissertation, Michigan State University.

Cirel, P., P. Evans, D. McGillis, and D. Whitcomb (1977) *Community Crime Prevention Program: Seattle, Washington*. Washington, D.C.: U.S. Department of Justice, National Institute of Justice.

Clarke, R.V. (1983) "Situational Crime Prevention: Its Theoretical Basis and Practical Scope." In M. Tonry and N. Morris (eds.), *An Annual Review of Research*. Chicago: University of Chicago Press, pp. 225-256.

Clotfelter, C.T. (1977) "Urban Crime and Household Protective Measures." *Review of Economics and Statistics* 59:499-503.

Cohen, E.S. (1978) "Fear of Crime and Feelings of Control: Reactions to Crime in an Urban Community." Ph.D. dissertation. Philadelphia: Temple University.

Cohen, E.S., L. Kidder, and J. Harvey (1978) "Crime Prevention vs. Victimization: The Psychology of Two Different Reactions." *Victimology* 3: 285-96.

Cohen, L.E. and M. Felson (1979) "Social Change and Crime Rate Trends: A Routine Activities Approach." *American Sociological Review* 44: 588-608.

Conklin, J.E. (1971) "Dimensions of Community Response to the Crime Problem." *Social Problems* 18: 373-84.

Conklin, J.E. (1975) *The Impact of Crime*. New York: Macmillan.

Cook, P.J. (1980) "Research in Criminal Deterrence: Laying the Groundwork for the Second Decade." In N. Morris and M. Tonry (eds.), *Crime and Justice: An Annual Review of Research*, Vol. 2. Chicago: University of Chicago Press, pp. 211-68.

Cook, T.D. and D.T. Campbell (1979) *Quasi-Experimentation: Design and Analysis Issues for Field Settings*. Chicago: Rand McNally.

Cordner, G.W. (1986) "Fear of Crime and the Police: An Evaluation of a Fear-Reduction Strategy." *Journal of Police Science and Administration* 14(3): 223-33

Courtis, M. and I. Dusseyer (1970) "Attitudes towards Crime and the Police in Toronto: A Report on Some Survey Findings." Toronto: Centre of Criminology, University of Toronto.

Cullen, F.T. and K.E. Gilbert (1982) *Reaffirming Rehabilitation*. Cincinnati: Anderson.

Currie, E. (1988) "Two Visions of Community Crime Prevention." In T. Hope and M. Shaw (eds.), *Communities and Crime Reduction*. London: Her Majesty's Stationery Office, pp. 280-86.

Curtis, L. (1987) "The Retreat of Folly: Some Modest Replications of Inner-City Success." *The Annals* 494: 71-89.

_____ ed. (1987) "Policies to Prevent Crime: Neighborhood, Family, and Employment Strategies." *The Annals* Volume 494.

Dietrick, B. (1977) "The Neighborhood and Burglary Victimization in Metropolitan Sub-urbs." Presented at the annual meeting of the Society for the Study of Social Problems, Chicago.

Dijk, J.J.M. van and C. Steinmetz (1981) *An Evaluation of the National Publicity Campaigns*. The Hague: Research and Documentation Centre, Ministry of Justice.

DuBow, F. and D. Emmons (1981) "The Community Hypothesis." In D.A. Lewis (ed.), *Reactions to Crime*. Beverly Hills: Sage, pp. 167-81.

DuBow, F., E. McCabe, and G. Kaplan (1979) *Reactions to Crime: A Critical Review of the Literature*. Washington, DC: U.S. Department of Justice, National Institute of Justice.

Eames, E. and J.G. Goode (1977) *Anthropology of the City*. Englewood Cliffs, NJ: Prentice-Hall.

Eck, J.E. (1982) *Solving Crimes: The Investigation of Burglary and Robbery*. Washington, DC: Police Executive Research Forum.

Eck, J.E. and W. Spelman with D. Hill, D.W. Stephens, J.R. Stedman, and G.R Murphy (1987a) *Problem Solving: Problem-Oriented Policing in Newport News*. Washington DC: Police Executive Research Forum.

————— (1987b) "Who Ya Gonna Call? The Police as Problem Busters." *Crime and Delinquency* 33: 31-52.

Ennis, P.H. (1967) *Criminal Victimization in the United States: A Report of a Nationwide Survey*. Washington DC: U.S. Government Printing Office.

Erskine, H. (1972) "The Polls: Gun Control." *Public Opinion Quarterly* 36: 455-69. (1974) "The Polls: Fear of Violence and Crime." *Public Opinion Quarterly* 38: 131-45.

Fattah, D. (1987) "The House of Umoja as a Case Study for Social Justice." *The Annals* 494:37-41.

Feins, J.D. (1983) *Partnerships For Neighborhood Crime Prevention*. Washington, DC: Department of Justice, National Institute of Justice.

Fellin, P. and F. Litwak (1963) "Neighborhood Cohesion under Conditions of Mobility." *American Sociological Review* 28:364-76.

Ferré, M.I. (1987) Prevention and Control of Violence Through Community Revitalization, Individual Dignity, and Personal Self-Confidence. *The Annals* 494: 27.

Festinger, L., S. Schachter, and K. Back (1950) *Social Pressures in Informal Groups*. Stanford: Stanford University Press.

Fischer, B.S. (1988) "Participatory Democracy in Action: Crime Prevention Activities." Unpublished Ph.D. dissertation, Northwestern University, Department of Political Science.

Fisher, C.S., R.M. Jackson, C.A. Stueve, K. Gerson, and L.M. Jones with M. Baldassare (1977) *Network and Places: Social Relations in the Urban Setting*. New York: Free Press.

Fowler, F.J., Jr. and T.W. Mangione (1982) *Neighborhood Crime, Fear, and Social Control: A Second Look at the Hartford Program*. Washington, DC: U.S. Department of Justice.

————— (1986) "A Three-Pronged Effort to Reduce Crime and Fear of Crime: The Hartford Experiment." In D.P. Rosenbaum (ed.), *Community Crime Prevention: Does It Work?* Beverly Hills: Sage, pp. 87-108.

Fowler, J.J., Jr., M.E. McCalla, and T.W. Mangione (1979) *Reducing Residential Crime and Fear: The Hartford Neighborhood Crime Prevention Program.* Washington, DC: U.S. Department of Justice.

Furby, L. and B. Fischoff (1986) *Rape Self-Defense Strategies: A Review of Their Effectiveness.* Eugene, OR: Eugene Research Institute.

Furstenberg, F.F. Jr. (1972) "Fear of Crime and Its Effects on Citizen Behavior." In A. Biderman (ed.), *Crime and Justice: A Symposium.* New York: Nailburg.

Garber, T. (1978) "Crime Displacement: The Literature and Strategies for Its Investigation." *Crime and Delinquency* 6: 100-06.

Garofalo, J. (1977a) *Public Opinion about Crime: The Attitudes of Victims and Nonvictims in Selected Cities.* Washington, DC: U.S. Government Printing Office.

_____ (1977b) "Victimization and the Fear of Crime in Major American Cities." Paper presented at the annual meeting of the American Association for Public Opinion Research, Buck Hills Falls, PA.

_____ (1987) "Reassessing the Lifestyle Model of Criminal Victimization." In M. Gottfredson and T. Hirschi (eds.), *Positive Criminology: Essays in Honor of Michael J.* Beverly Hills: Sage, pp. 23-42.

Garofalo, J. and M. McLeod (1986) *Improving the Effectiveness and Utilization of Neighborhood Watch Programs.* Draft final report to the National Institute of Justice. Albany: State University of New York at Albany, Hindelang Criminal Justice Research Center.

Gay, W.G., T.M. Beall, and R.A. Bowers (1984) *A Four-Site Assessment of the Integrated Criminal Apprehension Program.* Washington, DC: University City Science Center.

Gills, A.R. and J. Hagan (1982) *Bystander Apathy and the Territorial Imperative.* Toronto: University of Toronto, Centre for Urban and Community Studies.

Goldstein, H. (1979) "Improving Policing: A Problem-Oriented Approach." *Crime and Delinquency* 25:236-58.

_____ (1987) "Toward Community-Oriented Policing: Potential, Basic Requirements, and Threshold Questions." *Crime and Delinquency* 33:6-30.

Goldstein, H. and C.E. Susmilch (1982) *Experimenting with the Problem-Oriented Approach to Improving Police Service: A Report and Some Reflections on Two Case Studies.* Madison: University of Wisconsin Law School.

Gordon, M.T. and S. Riger (1979) "Fear and Avoidance: A Link between Attitudes and Behavior." *Victimology* 4: 395-402.

_____ (1988) *The Female Fear.* New York: Free Press.

Gorse, W.J. and N.J. Beran (1973) *The Community Criminal Justice System of Lincoln.* Columbus: Ohio State University, Program for the Study of Crime and Delinquency.

Gottfredson, M. and T. Hirschi (1986) "The True Value of Lambda Would Appear to Be Zero: An Essay on Career Criminals, Criminal Careers, Selective Incapacitation, Cohort Studies, and Related Topics." *Criminology* 24: 213-33.

_____ (1988) "Science, Public Policy, and the Career Paradigm." *Criminology* 26: 37-55.

Grant, J.A. (1981) "National Policy, Citizen Participation and Health System Reform: The Case of Three Health Systems Agencies in the San Francisco Bay Area." Unpublished Ph.D. dissertation. Berkeley: University of California.

Grant J.A., D.A. Lewis, and D.P. Rosenbaum (in press) "Political Benefits of Program Participation: The Case of Community Crime Prevention." *Urban Affairs.*

Green, G.A. (1987) "Citizen Gun Ownership and Criminal Deterrence: Theory, Research, and Policy." *Criminology* 25: 63-81.

Greenberg, S. and W. Rohe (1984) "Neighborhood Design and Crime: A Test of Two Perspectives." *Journal of the American Planning Association* 49: 48-61

Greenberg, S., W.M. Rohe, and J.R. Williams (1982) "Safety in Urban Neighborhoods." *Population and Environment* 5:141-65.

————— (1985) *Informal Citizen Action and Crime Prevention at the Neighborhood Level: Synthesis and Assessment of the Research.* Washington, DC: U.S. Department of Justice, National Institute of Justice.

Greenwood, P. (1979) "Rand Research on Criminal Careers." In *Progress to Date.* Santa Monica, CA: Rand Corporation.

Greenwood, P., J. Petersilia, and J. Chaiken (1977) *The Criminal Investigation Process.* Lexington, MA: Heath.

Greer, S. (1956) "Urbanism Reconsidered: A Comparative Study of Local Areas in a Metropolis." *American Sociological Review* 21:19-25.

Harris, R. (1969) *Fear of Crime.* New York: Praeger.

Heller, N.B., W.W. Stenzel, A.D. Gill, R.A. Kold, and S.R. Schimerman (1975) *Operation Identification Projects: Assessment of Effectiveness.* National Evaluation Program, Phase I. Washington, DC: U.S. Department of Justice, National Institute of Law Enforcement and Criminal Justice.

Henig, J.R. (1984) "Citizens Against Crime: An Assessment of the Neighborhood Watch Program in Washington D.C." Unpublished manuscript. Washington DC: Washington University, Center for Washington Area Studies.

Hindelang, M.J., M.R. Gottfredson, and J. Garofalo (1978) *Victims of Personal Crime.* Cambridge, MA: Ballinger.

Hoare, M.A, G. Stewart, and C.M. Purcell (1984) *The Problem-Oriented Approach: Four Pilot Studies.* London, England: Management Services Division, Metropolitan Police.

Hope, T. (1988) "Support for Neighborhood Watch: A British Crime Survey Analysis." Her Majesty's Stationery Office, pp. 146-61.

Hope, T. and M. Shaw (eds.) (1988) *Communities and Crime Reduction.* London: Her Majesty's Stationery Office.

Hough, J.M. R.V.G. Clarke, and P. Mayhew (1980) "Introduction." In R.G.V Clarke and P. Mayhew (eds.), *Designing Out Crime.* London: Her Majesty's Stationery Office.

Hough, J.M. and P. Mayhew (1983) *The British Crime Survey.* First report. London: Her Majesty's Stationery Office.

Hunter, A (1974) *Symbolic Communities.* Chicago: University of Chicago Press.

————— (1975) "The Loss of Community: An Empirical Test through Replication." *American Sociological Review* 40:537-52.

Hunter, A. and T.L. Baumer (1982) "Street Traffic, Social Integration, and Fear of Crime." *Sociological Inquiry* 52: 122-31.

Institute for Social Research (1975) *Public Safety: Quality of Life in the Detroit Metropolitan Area*. Ann Arbor: University of Michigan, Survey Research Center.

International Training, Research, and Evaluation Council (ITREC) (1977) *National Evaluation Program Phase I Summary Report: Crime Prevention Security Survey*. Washington, DC: National Institute of Law Enforcement and Criminal Justice.

Jacob, H. and R.L. Lineberry (1982) *Government Responses to Crime*. Executive summary report to the National Institute of Justice. Evanston, IL: Northwestern University, Center for Urban Affairs and Policy Research.

Jacobs, J. (1961) *The Death and Life of Great American Cities*. New York: Vintage.

Jamieson, K.M. and T.J. Flanagan, eds. (1987) *Sourcebook of Criminal Justice Statistics—1986*. Washington, DC: U.S. Department of Justice, Bureau of Justice Statistics.

Jeffrey, C.R. (1971) *Crime Prevention through Experimental Design*. Beverly Hills: Sage.

Jencks, C (1985) "How Poor are the Poor?" A Review of C. Murray (1984) *Losing Ground: American Social Policy*, 1950-1080. New York Review of Books. (May 9): 41-48.

Jones, D. (1982) *Evaluation of the Portage la Prairie Project*. Ottawa: Royal Canadian Mounted Police Crime Prevention Centre.

Kansas City Police Department (1980) *Response Time Analysis: Volume II—Part I*, Crime Analysis. Washington, DC: U.S. Government Printing Office.

Kasarda, J.D. (1976) "The Changing Occupational Structure of the American Metropolis." In B. Schwartz (ed.), *The Changing Face of the Suburbs*. Chicago: University of Chicago Press, pp. 113-36.

Kasarda, J.D. and M. Janowitz (1974) "Community Attachment in Mass Society." *American Psychological Review* 39:328-39.

Kelling, G.L., T. Pate, D. Dieckman, and C. Brown (1974) *The Kansas City Preventive Patrol Experiment: A Technical Report*. Washington, DC: The Police Foundation.

Kennedy, R.L. and Associates (n.d.) *A Survey of Public Attitudes toward the Criminal Justice System in Multnomah County, Oregon*.

Kingsbury, A. (1973) *Introduction to Security and Crime Prevention Surveys*. Springfield, IL: Thomas.

Kleck, G. (1979) "Guns, Homicide, and Gun Control: Some Assumptions and Some Evidence." Paper presented at the annual meeting of the Midwest Sociological Society, Minneapolis.

Kleck, G. and D.J. Bordua (1983) "The Factual Foundation for Certain Key Assumptions of Gun Control." *Law and Policy Quarterly* 5:271-98.

Kleinman, P. and D. David (1973) "Victimization and Perception of Crime in a Ghetto Community. *Criminology* 11,3:307-43.

Kohfeld, C.W., B. Salert, and S. Schoenberg (1981) "Neighborhood Associations and Urban Crime." *Community Action* :37-44.

Kramer, R.J. (1969) *Participation and the Poor: Comparative Case Studies in the War on Poverty*. Englewood Cliffs, NJ: Prentice-Hall.

Krug, R.E. (1983) *Community against Crime: Two Federal Initiatives*. Washington, DC: U.S. Department of Justice, National Institute of Justice.

Latane, B. and J. Darley (1970) *The Unresponsive Bystander: Why Doesn't He Help?* New York: Appleton-Century-Crofts.

Latessa, E.J. and H.F. Allen (1980) "Using Citizens to Prevent Crime: An Example of Deterrence and Community Involvement." *Journal of Police Science and Administration* 8(1)-.69-74.

Lavrakas, P.J. (1981) "On Households." In D.A. Lewis (ed.), *Reactions to Crime*. Beverly Hills: Sage, pp. 67-86.

_____ (1982) "Fear of Crime and Behavioral Restrictions in Urban and Suburban Neighborhoods." *Population and Environment* 5:242-64.

_____ (1985) "Citizen Self-Help and Neighborhood Crime Prevention Policy." In L.A. Curtis (ed.), *American Violence and Public Policy*. New Haven, CT: Yale University Press, pp. 87-115.

Lavrakas, P.J. and S. Bennett (1988) *Cross-Site Impact Evaluation Report for the Neighborhood Anti-Crime Self-Help Program*. Draft final impact report to the Eisenhower Foundation. Evanston, IL: Northwestern University, Center for Urban Affairs and Policy Research.

Lavrakas, P.J. and J.W. Kushmuk (1986) "Evaluating Crime Prevention through Environmental Design: The Portland Commercial Demonstration Project." In D Rosenbaum (ed.), *Community Crime Prevention: Does It Work?* Beverly Hills: Sage, pp. 202-227.

Lavrakas, P.J. and D.A. Lewis (1980) "The Conceptualization and Measurement of Citizens' Crime Prevention Behaviors." *Journal of Research in Crime and Delinquency*: 254-72.

Lavrakas, P.J., J. Normoyle, W.G. Skogan, E.J. Hertz, C. Salem, and D.A Lewis (1980) *Factors Related to Citizen Involvement in Personal, Household, and Neighborhood Anti-crime Measures*. Final report to the National Institute of Justice. Evanston, IL: Northwestern University. Center for Urban Affairs and Policy Research.

Lentzner, H.R. (1981) "No-Force Residential Burglaries: The Consequences of Negligence" In J. Stoik (ed.), *Building Security*. Philadelphia: American Society for Testing and Materials.

Lewis, D.A., J.A. Grant, and D.P. Rosenbaum (1988) *The Social Construction of Reform: Community Organizations and Crime Prevention*. New Brunswick, NJ: Transaction.

Lewis, D.A. and G. Salem (1981) "Community Crime Prevention: An Analysis of a Developing Perspective." *Crime and Delinquency* 27:405;21.

Ley, D. and R. Cybriwsky (1974) "The Spatial Ecology of Stripped Cars." *Environment and Behavior* 6: 53-67.

Linden, R., I. Barker, and D. Frisbie (1984) *Working Together to Prevent Crime*. Ottawa: Solicitor General Canada.

Lindsay, B. and D. McGillis (1986) "Citywide Community Crime Prevention: An Assessment of the Seattle Program." In D.P. Rosenbaum (ed.), *Community Crime Prevention: Does It Work?* Beverly Hills: Sage, pp. 46-67.

Lipton, D., R. Martinson, and J. Wilks (1975) *Effectiveness of Correctional Treatment—A Survey of Treatment Evaluation Studies*. New York: Praeger.

Luedtke, G. and Associates (1970) *Crime and the Physical City: Neighborhood Design Techniques for Crime Reduction*. Springfield, VA: National Technical Information Council.

Lurigio, A.J. and D.P. Rosenbaum (1986) "Evaluation Research in Community Crime Prevention: A Critical Look at the Field." In D.P. Rosenbaum (ed.), *Community Crime Prevention: Does It Work?* Beverly Hills: Sage, pp. 19-44.

Maccoby, E.E., J.P. Johnson, and R.M. Church (1958) "Community Integration and the Social Control of Juvenile Delinquency." *Journal of Social Issues* 14:38-51.

Malt Associates, H.L. (1971) *An Analysis of Public Safety as Related to the Incidence of Crime in Parks and Recreation Areas in Central Cities.* Phase I report submitted to the Department of Housing and Urban Development. Washington, DC: Author.

Mangione, T.W. and C. Noble (1975) *Baseline Survey Measures Including Update Survey Information for the Evaluation of a Crime Control Model.* Hartford, CT: Center for Survey Research, University of Massachusetts.

Marx, G.T. and D. Archer (1971) "Citizen Involvement in the Law Enforcement Process: The Case of Community Police Patrols." *American Behavioral Scientist* 15: 52-72.

Mattick, H., C.K. Olander, D.G. Baker, and H.E. Schlegel (1974) *An Evaluation of Operation Identification as Implemented in Illinois.* Chicago: University of Illinois at Chicago, Center for Research in Criminal Justice.

Matza, D. (1969) *Becoming Deviant.* Englewood Cliffs, NJ: Prentice-Hall.

Maxfield, M.G. (1977) "Reactions to Fear," Working paper based on an examination of survey data from Portland (OR), Kansas City, and Cincinnati. Evanston, IL: Northwestern University, Center for Urban Affairs and Policy Research.

———— (1987) *Explaining Fear of Crime: Evidence from the 1984 British Crime Survey.* London: Her Majesty's Stationery Office.

Mayhew, P.M. (1979) "Defensible Space: The Current Status of a Crime Prevention Theory." *Howard Journal* 18: 150-59.

———— (1984) "Target-Hardening: How Much of an Answer?" In R.V.G. Clarke and T. Hope (eds.), *Coping with Burglary.* Boston: Kluwer-Nijhoh, pp. 29-44.

Mayhew, P.M., R.V. Clarke, A. Sturman, and J.M. Hough (1976) *Crime as Opportunity.* London: Her Majesty's Stationery Office.

McDonald, S.C. (1986) "Does Gentrification Affect Crime Rates?" In A.L. Reiss, Jr. and M. Tonry (eds.), *Communities and Crime*, vol. 8 of M. Tonry and N. Morris (eds.), *Crime and Justice: A Review of Research.* Chicago: University of Chicago Press, pp. 163-201.

McGahey, R.M. (1986) "Economic Conditions, Neighborhood Organization, and Urban Crime." In A.J. Reiss, Jr. and M. Tonry (eds.), Communities and Crime, vol. 8 of M. Tonry and N. Morris (eds.), *Crime and Justice: A Review of the Research.* Chicago: University of Chicago Press, pp. 231-311.

McIntyre, J. (1967) "Public Attitudes toward Crime and Law Enforcement." *Annals of the American Academy of Political and Social Science* 374: 34-36.

McPherson, M. and G. Silloway (1987) "The Implementation Process: Effort and Response." In A. Pate, M. McPherson, and G. Silloway (eds.), *The Minneapolis Community Crime Prevention Experiment.* Draft Evaluation Report. Washington, DC: Police Foundation, pp. 4-1 to 4-83.

Mendelsohn, H., G.J. O'Keefe, and J. Liu (1981) "Public Communications and the Prevention of Crime: Evaluations and Strategies." Denver: University of Denver, Center for Mass Communications Research and Policy.

Merry, S.E. (1981) Urban Danger: Life in a Neighborhood of Strangers. Springfield, IL: Mombiosse.

Molumby, T. (1976) "Patterns of Crime in a University Housing Project." *American Behavioral Scientist* 20: 247-59.

Moriarity, T. (1975) "Crime, Commitment, and the Responsive Bystander: Two Field Experiments." *Journal of Personality and Social Psychology* 31, 2:370-76.

Murphy, C. and G. Muir (1984) *Community Based Policing: A Review of the Critical Issues.* Ottawa, Canada: Ministry of the Solicitor General of Canada.

Murray, C. (1984) *Losing Ground: American Social Policy, 1950-1980.* New York: Basic Books.

National Crime Prevention Council (1987) "The Success of Community Crime Prevention." Washington, DC: Author.

National Crime Prevention Institute (1978) *Understanding Crime Prevention: Volume 1.* Lexington, KY: National Crime Prevention Institute Press.

Newman, O. (1972) *Defensible Space: Crime Prevention Through Urban Design.* New York: Macmillan.

Newman, O. and K.A. Franck (1980) *Factors Influencing Crime and Instability in Urban Housing Developments.* Washington, DC: U.S. Government Printing Office.

O Keefe, G.J and H. Mendelsohn (1984) *"Taking a Bite out of Crime": The Impact of a Mass Media Crime Prevention Campaign.* Washington, DC: U.S. Department of Justice, National Institute of Justice.

Pate, A.M. (1986) "Experimenting With Foot Patrol: The Newark Experience." In D.P. Rosenbaum (ed.), *Community Crime Prevention: Does It Work?* Beverly Hills: Sage, pp. 137-56.

Pate, A.M., M. McPherson, and G. Silloway, eds., (1987) *The Minneapolis Community Crime Prevention Experiment.* Draft evaluation report. Washington, DC: Police Foundation.

Pate, A.M., M.A. Wycoff, W.G. Skogan, and L. Sherman (1986) *Reducing Fear of Crime in Houston and Newark.* U.S. Department of Justice, National Institute of Justice. Washington, DC: Police Foundation.

Pennell, S., C. Curtis, and J. Henderson (1985) *Guardian Angels: An Assessment of Citizen Responses to Crime.* Volume 2. Technical report to the National Institute of Justice. San Diego: San Diego Association of Governments.

Percy, S. L. (1979) "Citizen Coproduction of Community Safety." In R. Baker and F.A. Meyer, Jr. (eds.), *Evaluating Alternative Law Enforcement Policies.* Lexington, MA: Heath, pp. 125-34.

Petersilia, J. (1987) *The Influence of Criminal Justice Research.* Santa Monica, CA: Rand Corporation.

Podolefsky, A.M. (1983) *Case Studies in Community Crime Prevention.* Springfield, IL: Thomas.

Podolefsky, A.M. and F. DuBow (1981) *Strategies for Community Crime Prevention: Collective Responses to Crime in Urban America.* Springfield, IL: Thomas.

Pope, C.E. (1977) *Crime Specific Analysis: The Characteristics of Burglary Incidents.* Washington, DC: U.S. Department of Justice.

Press, J.S. (1971) *Some Effects of an Increase in Police Manpower in the 20th Precinct of New York City*. New York: Rand.

Reiss, A.J. Jr. (1967) *Studies in Crime and Law Enforcement in Major Metropolitan Areas*. Field Survey III, vol. 1. Presidential Commission on Law Enforcement and the Administration of Justice. Washington, DC: U.S. Government Printing Office.

_____ (1986) "Why Are Communities Important in Understanding Crime?" In A.J. Reiss Jr. and Michael Tonry (eds.), *Communities and Crime*. Volume 8. Chicago: University of Chicago Press, pp. 1-33.

Reppetto, T.A. (1974) *Residential Crime*. Cambridge, MA: Ballinger.

_____ (1976) "Crime Prevention and the Displacement Phenomenon." *Crime and Delinquency* 22: 166-77.

Rich, R.C., D.M. Chavis, P. Florin, D. Perkins, and A. Wandersman (1987) "Block Associations and the Community Development Approach to Crime Control: A Preliminary Analysis." Paper presented at the annual meeting of the American Society of Criminology, Montreal.

Rifai-Young, M.A. (1976) *Older Americans' Crime Prevention Research Project*. Portland OR: Multnomah County Division of Public Safety.

_____ (1977) "The Response of the Older Adult to Criminal Victimization." *Police Chief* (February) : 48-50.

Roehl, J.A. and R.F. Cook (1984) *Evaluation of the Urban Crime Prevention Program*. Washington, DC: Department of Justice, National Institute of Justice.

Rohe, W. and S. Greenberg (1982) *Participation in Community Crime Prevention Programs*. Chapel Hill: University of North Carolina, Department of City and Regional Planning.

Rosenbaum, D.P., ed. (1986) *Community Crime Prevention: Does It Work?* Beverly Hills: Sage.

_____ (1987) "The Theory and Research Behind Neighborhood Watch: Is It a Sound Fear and Crime Reduction Strategy?" *Crime and Delinquency* 33:103-34.

_____ (1988) "A Critical Eye on Neighborhood Watch: Does It Reduce Crime and Fear?" In T. Hope and M. Shaw (eds.), *Communities and Crime Reduction*. London: Her Majesty's Stationery Office, pp. 126-45.

Rosenbaum, D.P. and L. Bickman (in preparation) "Scaring People into Crime Prevention: The Results of a Randomized Field Experiment." Manuscript in preparation based on a paper presented at the 91st annual convention of the American Psychological Association, Anaheim.

Rosenbaum, D.P. and L. Heath (in press) "The 'Psycho-Logic' of Fear Reduction and Crime Prevention Programs." In J. Edwards, E. Posavac, S. Tindale, F. Bryant, and L. Heath (eds.), *Applied Social Psychology Annual*. Volume 9. New York: Plenum.

Rosenbaum, D.P., D.A. Lewis, and J.A. Grant (1985) *The Impact of Community Crime Prevention Programs in Chicago: Can Neighborhood Organizations Make a Difference?* Evanston, IL: Northwestern University, Center for Urban Affairs and Policy Research.

_____ (1986) "Neighborhood-Based Crime Prevention: Assessing the Efficacy of Community Organizing in Chicago." In D.P. Rosenbaum (ed.), *Community Crime Prevention: Does It Work?* Beverly Hills: Sage, pp. 109-33.

Rosenbaum, D.P. and Lurigio, A.J. (in press) "The Psychological Effects of Criminal Victimization: Past and Future Research." *Victimology*.

Rosentraub, M.S. and K.S. Harlow (1980) "The Coproduction of Policy Services: A Case Study of Citizens' Inputs in the Production of Personal Safety." Unpublished manuscript. Arlington, TX: Institute of Urban Studies.

Ross, A.S. (1971) "Effect of Increased Responsibility on Bystander Intervention: The Presence of Children." *Journal of Personality and Social Psychology* 19(3):306-10.

Rossi, P.H. and H.E. Freeman (1988) *Evaluation: A Systematic Approach*. 3rd edition. Beverly Hills: Sage.

Rubenstein, H., C. Murray, T. Motoyama, and W.V. Rouse (1980) *The Link between Crime and the Built Environment: The Current State of Knowledge*. Volume 1. Washington DC: U.S. Department of Justice, National Institute of Justice.

Russell, R.F. (1982) "Neighborhood Security Patrols Are Working in Anne Arundel County, Maryland." *Police Chief* May: 42-43.

Savitz, L.D., M. Lalli, and L. Rosen (1977) *City Life and Delinquency—Victimization, Fear of Crime and Gang Membership*. Washington DC: National Institute for Juvenile Justice and Delinquency Prevention, Office of Juvenile Justice and Delinquency Prevention.

Scarr, H.A. (1973) *Patterns of Burglary*. 2nd edition. Washington, DC: National Institute of Law Enforcement and Criminal Justice.

Schimerman, S.R. (1974) *Project Evaluation Report: Operation Identification*. St. Louis: Missouri Law Enforcement Assistance Council.

Schneider, A.L. (1975) *Evaluation of the Portland Neighborhood-Based Anti-Burglary Program*. Eugene, OR: Institute of Policy Analysis.

————— (1986) "Neighborhood-Based Anti-Burglary Strategies: An Analysis of Public and Private Benefits from the Portland Program." In D.P. Rosenbaum (ed.), *Community Crime Prevention: Does It Work?* Beverly Hills: Sage, pp. 68-86.

————— (1987) "Coproduction of Public and Private Safety: An Analysis of Bystander Intervention, 'Private Neighboring,' and Personal Protection." *Western Political Science Quarterly* 40-611-30.

Schneider, A.L. and P.R. Schneider (1978) *Private and Public-Minded Citizen Responses to a Neighborhood-Based Crime Prevention Strategy*. Eugene, OR: Institute of Policy Analysis.

Schnelle, J.F., R.E. Kirchner, M.O. McNees, and J.M. Lawler (1975) "Social Evaluation Research: The Evaluation of Two Police Patrolling Strategies." *Journal of Applied Behavior Analysis* 8, 4:353-66.

Schwartz, A.I. and S. Clarren (1978) *The Cincinnati Team Policing Experiment*. Washington, DC: The Police Foundation.

Seattle Law and Justice Planning Office (1975) *Burglary Reduction Program*. Final report prepared for the Law Enforcement Assistance Administration. Seattle, WA: Author.

Shaw, C.R. and H.D. McKay (1931) *Social Factors in Juvenile Delinquency*. Volume 2, No. 13. Washington, DC: U.S. Government Printing Office.

————— (1942) *Juvenile Delinquency and Urban Areas*. Chicago: University of Chicago Press.

Shaw, M.E. (1981) *Group Dynamics*. 3rd edition. New York: McGraw-Hill.

Silberman, C.E. (1978) *Criminal Violence, Criminal Justice*. New York: Random House.

Skogan, W.G. (1977) "The Changing Distribution of Crime: A Multi-City Time-Series Analysis." *Urban Affairs Quarterly* 13:33-48.

_____ (1979) "Community Crime Prevention Programs—Measurement Issues in Their Evaluation." In National Criminal Justice Reference Service (ed.) *How Well Does It Work ?* Washington, DC Government Printing Office, pp. 135-70.

_____ (1981) "On Attitudes and Behaviors." In D.A. Lewis (ed.) *Reactions to Crime.* Beverly Hills: Sage, pp. 19-45.

_____ (1986) Fear of Crime and Neighborhood Change." In A.J. Reiss, Jr. and M. Tonry (eds.), *Communities and Crime.* Volume 8 of M. Tonry and N. Morris (eds.), *Crime and Justice: A Review of Research.* Chicago: University of Chicago Press, pp. 203-29.

_____ (1987a) "Community Organizations and Crime." In M. Tonry and N. Morris (eds.), *Crime and Justice: A Review of Research.* Volume 10. Chicago: University of Chicago Press, pp. 39-78.

_____ (1987b) *Disorder and Community Decline.* Final report to the National Institute of Justice. Evanston, IL: Northwestern University, Center for Urban Affairs and Policy Research.

Skogan, W.G. and G. Antunes (1979) "Information, Apprehension, and Deterrence: Exploring the Limits of Police Productivity." *Journal of Criminal Justice* Fall: 217-42.

Skogan, W.G. and M.G. Maxfield (1981) *Coping with Crime: Individual and Neighborhood Reactions.* Beverly Hills: Sage.

Skolnick, J.H. and D.H. Bayely (1986) *The New Blue Line: Police Innovation in Six American Cities.* New York: Free Press.

_____ (1988) *Community Policing: Issues and Practices around the World.* Washington, DC: National Institute of Justice.

Spelman, W. and D.K. Brown (1984) *Calling the Police: Citizen Reporting of Serious Crime.* Washington DC: U.S. Government Printing Office.

Spelman, W. and J.E. Eck (i986) "Problem-Oriented Policing." *Research in Brief.* Washington, DC: U.S. Department of Justice. National Institute of Justice.

Spelman, W., M. Oshima, and G.L. Kelling (1985) *Crime Suppression and Traditional Police Tactics.* Final report to the Florence V. Burden Foundation. Cambridge, MA: Harvard University, Program in Criminal Justice Policy and Management.

Springer, L. (1974) "Crime Perception and Response Behavior: Two Views of a Seattle Community." Ph.D. dissertation, Pennsylvania State University.

Stinchcombe, A.L., C. Heimer, R.A. Iliff, K. Scheppele, T.W. Smith, and D.G. Taylor (1978) *Crime and Punishment in Public Opinion: 1948-1974.* Chicago: National Opinion Research Center.

Sturz, E.L. and M. Taylor (1987) "Inventing and Reinventing Argus: What Makes One Community Organization Work." *The Annals* 494:19-26.

Suttles, G.D. (1972) *The Social Construction of Communities.* Chicago: University of Chicago Press.

Taub, R.P., G.P. Surgeon, S. Lindholm, P.B. Otti, and A. Bridges (1977) "Urban Voluntary Associations: Locality Based and Externally Induced," *American Journal of Sociology* 83: 425-42.

Taub, R.P., D.G. Taylor, and J. Dunham (1984) *Patterns of Neighborhood Change: Race and Crime in Urban America.* Chicago: University of Chicago Press.

Taylor, R.B. and S. Gottfredson (1986) "Environmental Design, Crime, and Prevention: An Examination of Community Dynamics." In A.J. Reiss Jr. and M. Tonry (eds.), *Communities and Crime.* Volume 8. Chicago: University of Chicago Press, pp. 387-416.

Taylor, R.B., S. Gottfredson, and S. Brower (1980) "The Defensibility of Defensible Space." In T. Hirschi and M. Gottfredson (eds.), *Understanding Crime*. Beverly Hills: Sage, pp. 53-72.

———— (1981) *Informal Control in the Urban Residential Environment*. Final report to the National Institute of Justice. Baltimore: Johns Hopkins University.

Taylor, R.B., S. Gottfredson, and S.A. Shumaker (1984) *Neighborhood Responses to Disorder*. Unpublished final report. Baltimore: Johns Hopkins University, Center for Metropolitan Planning and Research.

Tien, J.M., V.F. O'Donnell, A. Barnett, and P.B. Mirchandani (1979) *Street Lighting Projects*. National Evaluation Program Phase I report. Washington, DC: U.S. Government Printing Office.

Tien, J., T. Reppetto, and L. Hanes (1976) *Elements of CPTED*. Arlington, VA: Westinghouse.

Titus, R.M. (1984) "Residential Burglary and the Community Response." In R.V.G Clarke and T. Hope (eds.), *Coping with Burglary*. Boston: Kluwer-Nijhoh, pp. 97-130.

Trojanowicz, R.C. (1986) "Evaluating a Neighborhood Foot Patrol Program: The Flint, Michigan Project." In D.P. Rosenbaum (ed.), *Community Crime Prevention: Does It Work?* Beverly Hills: Sage, pp. 157-78.

Troyer, R.J. (1988) "The Urban Anti-Crime Patrol Phenomenon: A Case Study of a Student Effort." *Justice Quarterly* 5:3.

Tyler, T.R. (1980) "The Impact of Directly and Indirectly Experienced Events: The Origin of Crime-Related Judgments and Behaviors." *Journal of Personality and Social Psychology* 39:13-28.

Waller, I. and N. Okihiro (1978) *Burglary: The Victim and the Public*. Toronto: University of Toronto Press.

Walsh, D. (1980) *Break-in: Burglary from Private Homes*. London: Constable.

Wandersman, A., P. Florin, D.M. Chavis, R.C. Rich, and J. Prestby (1985) Getting Together and Getting Things Done." *Psychology Today* (November) ;65-71.

Warren, D.I. (1969) "Neighborhood Structure and Riot Behavior in Detroit: Some Exploratory Findings." *Social Problems* 16: 464-84.

Washnis, G.J. (1976) *Citizen Involvement in Crime Prevention*. Lexington, MA: Heath.

Whitaker, C.J. (1986) "Crime Prevention Measures." Bureau of Justice Statistics Special Report. Washington, DC: U.S. Department of Justice.

Wilson, S. (1978) "Vandalism and 'Defensible Space' on London Housing Estates." In R.V. Clarke (ed.) *Tackling Vandalism*. London: Her Majesty's Stationery Office.

Wilson, J.Q. (1983) *Thinking About Crime*. New York: Basic Books.

Wilson, J.Q. and G.L. Kelling (1982) "Broken Windows." *Atlantic Monthly* (March); 29-38.

Wilson, L.A., and A.L. Schneider (1978) "Investigating the Efficacy and Equity of Public Initiatives in the Provision of Private Safety." Paper presented at the annual conference of the Western Political Science Association meetings, Los Angeles.

Winchester, S. and H. Jackson (1982) *Residential Burglary: The Limits of Prevention*. London: Her Majesty's Stationery Office.

Wright, J.D. and L.I. Marston (1975) "The Ownership of the Means of Destruction: Weapons in the United States." *Social Problems* 23:93-107.

Wright, J.D. and P.H. Rossi (1985) *The Armed Criminal in America*. Washington, DC: U.S. Government Printing Office.

Wright, J.D., P.H. Rossi, and K. Daly (1983) *Under the Gun: Weapons, Crime, and Violence in America*. New York: Aldine.

Wright, R., M. Heilweil, P. Pelletier, and K. Dickinson (1974) *Impact of Streetlighting on Crime*. Report to the National Institute of Law Enforcement and Criminal Justice. Ann Arbor: University of Michigan.

Yaden, D., S. Folkstand, and P. Glazer (1973) *The Impact of Crime in Selected Neighborhoods: A Study of Public Attitudes in Four Portland Census Tracts*. Portland, OR: Campaign Information Counselors.

Yin, R.K. (1979) "What is Citizen Crime Prevention?" In National Criminal Justice Reference Service (ed.) *How Well Does It Work?* Washington, DC: U.S. Government Printing Office, pp. 107-34.

————— (1986) "Community Crime Prevention: A Synthesis of Eleven Evaluations." In D.P. Rosenbaum (ed.), *Community Crime Prevention: Does It Work?* Beverly Hills: Sage, pp. 294-308.

Yin, R.K., M.E. Vogel, J.M. Chaiken, and D.R. Both (1976) *Patrolling the Neighborhood Beat: Residents and Residential Security*. Santa Monica: Rand.

————— (1977) *Citizen Patrol Projects (Phase I Summary Report)*. National Evaluation Program, Washington, DC: U.S. Department of Justice.

Young, Arthur and Company (1978) *Second Year Report for the Cabrini Green High Impact Project*. Chicago: City Department of Development and Planning

Zaharchuk, T. and J. Lynch (1977) *Operation Identification: A Police Prescriptive Package*. Ottawa: Communication Division, Ministry of the Solicitor General of Canada.

Zander, A. (1979) "The Psychology of Group Process." In M.R. Rosenzweig and L.W. Porter (eds.), *Annual Review of Psychology*, Palo Alto: Annual Reviews, pp. 417-51.

Sitting Ducks, Ravenous Wolves, and Helping Hands: New Approaches to Urban Policing 20

William Spelman & John E. Eck

Drug dealers have taken over a park. Neighborhood residents, afraid to use the park, feel helpless. Foot patrols and drug raids fail to roust the dealers.

A city is hit with a rash of convenience store robberies. Stakeouts, fast response to robbery calls, and enhanced investigations lead to some arrests—but do not solve the robbery problem.

Disorderly kids invade a peaceful residential neighborhood. Although they have committed no serious crimes, they are noisy and unpredictable; some acts of vandalism have been reported. The kids are black and the residents white—and the police fear a racial incident.

Problems like these plague cities everywhere. Social incivilities, drug dealing and abuse, and violent crime hurt more than the immediate victims: they create fears among the rest of us. We wonder who will be next, but feel incapable of taking action.

Until recently, there was little the criminal justice system could do to help. Police continued to respond to calls for service, and attempted (usually without success) to arrest and punish the most serious criminals. Sometimes they tried to organize a neighborhood watch. But research conducted in the 1970s and early 1980s showed repeatedly that these strategies were severely limited in their effectiveness.

Source: William Spelman and John E. Eck (1989). "Sitting Ducks, Ravenous Wolves, and Helping Hands: New Approaches to Urban Policing." *Public Affairs Comment,* XXXV (2):1-9. Reprinted by permission of the University of Texas at Austin, Lyndon B. Johnson School of Public Affairs.

Since the mid-1980s, some innovative police departments have begun to test a new approach to these problems. This "problem-oriented" approach differs from the traditional methods in several ways:

- Police actively seek ways to prevent crime and better the quality of neighborhood life rather than simply react to calls for service and reported crimes.

- Police recognize that crime and disorder problems arise from a variety of conditions and that thorough analysis is needed before they can tailor effective responses to these conditions.

- Police understand that many crime and disorder problems stem from factors beyond the control of any single public or private agency. If these problems are to be solved, they must be attacked on many different fronts, with the police, other agencies, and the public "coproducing" neighborhood security.

Recent research shows that when police adopt a proactive stance, analyze local conditions, and recognize the value of coproduction in framing and implementing a response, they can reduce crime and fear of crime. This new approach has profound implications for the management and operations of police agencies, and for the relationship between the police and the communities they serve.

The Problem: The Incident-Driven Approach

Problem-oriented policing is the culmination of more than two decades of research into the nature of crime and the effectiveness of police response. Many strands of research led to the new approach, but three basic findings were particularly important:

- Additional police resources, if applied in response to individual incidents of crime and disorder, will be ineffective at controlling crime.

- Few incidents are isolated; most are symptoms of some recurring, underlying problem. Problem analysis can help police develop effective, proactive tactics.

- Crime problems are integrally linked to other urban problems, and so the most effective responses require coordinating the activities of private citizens, the business sector, and government agencies outside the criminal justice system.

In short, "incident-driven policing," the prevailing method of delivering police services, consistently treats symptoms, not diseases. By working with others to identify, analyze, and treat the diseases, police can hope to make headway against crime and disorder.

ADDING POLICE RESOURCES WILL BE INEFFECTIVE

Most police work is reactive—a response to crimes and disorders reported by the public. And current reactive tactics may be effective at controlling crime, to a point. For example, by maintaining some threat of apprehension and punishment, current police actions may deter many would-be offenders.[1]

Nevertheless, twenty years of research into police operations suggest that the marginal value of additional police resources, if applied in the traditional, reactive ways, will be very small.[2] For example, preventive patrol tactics probably will not deter offenders unless the patrol force can be increased dramatically—perhaps by a factor of thirty or more.[3] Only 10 percent of crimes are reported to the police within five minutes of their being committed; thus even the fastest police response to the scene will not result in apprehension of a suspect for the vast majority of crimes.[4] And case solution rates are low because detectives rarely have many leads to work with; even if the number of detectives could be doubled or tripled, it would have virtually no effect on the number of cases solved.[5]

Research has also revealed that alternative deployment methods—split force, investigative case screening, differential response to calls—can succeed in shifting scarce resources to those incidents where they are most needed.[6] In the cases studied, these schemes, often directed by crime analysis, made police operations more efficient and freed up resources for other activities. But they did not make operations more effective.

CRIME ANALYSIS CAN LEAD TO MORE EFFECTIVE TACTICS

Three elements must generally be present before a crime will be committed: someone must be motivated to commit the crime; a suitable target must be present; and the target must be (relatively) unguarded, providing the offender with an opportunity to commit the crime.[7] These elements are more likely to be present at some times and places than at others, forming crime patterns and recurring crime problems. The removal of just one of the elements can alter a crime pattern. Thus, by identifying the elements that are easiest to remove and working to remove them, police can make crime prevention tactics more efficient and effective.

The most obvious crime patterns are spatial. Since the 1930s, researchers have shown that crime types and offender methods of operation—not to mention gross crime rates—differed substantially among neighborhoods.[8] One reason for these differences is that some kinds of neighborhoods have fewer unguarded targets than others. For example, neighborhoods with diverse land uses, single-family houses and garden apartment buildings, and intense street lighting provide criminals with fewer opportunities and incur lower crime rates.[9] Social characteristics such as residential stability, homogeneity of lifestyle, and family orientation empower residents of a neighborhood to "handle" bad actors without calling the police.[10]

Another reason crime rates differ between neighborhoods is that some areas have more potential offenders and victims than others. Adolescents, the poor, and members of minority groups commit property crimes at higher rates. Also, poor youths have few sources of transportation, so it is not surprising that burglary and robbery rates are highest in neighborhoods with many poor black and Hispanic youths. Some neighborhoods attract more than their share of offenders because open-air drug markets or bars that cater to the especially rowdy or criminal are located there. Potential victims who have the money to do so can make themselves unattractive to offenders by keeping valuables in safe deposit boxes or safes, garaging their cars, and buying houses with sturdy locks and alarms.

Thus neighborhood crime patterns differ in predictable ways, for comprehensible reasons. The implications for crime prevention policies are obvious: if our aim is to reduce the crime rate in a given neighborhood, it is clearly important to know what crimes are committed there, and what might be done either to reduce the number of available offenders or victims or to increase the number of willing and able guardians. Since neighborhoods differ, the best crime prevention strategies will differ from one neighborhood to the next. Officers assigned to an area must study the social and physical conditions there before developing and implementing strategies.

These strategies are given a focus by one regularity that seems to hold for crime problems in all neighborhoods: crime is concentrated. Suppose we took all the criminals active in a community and lined them up in order of the frequency with which they committed crimes. Those who committed crimes most often would go to the head of the line; those who committed crimes only occasionally would go to the end. If all offenders were alike, then it would not matter much where we lined the offenders up; the offenders at the front of the line would commit about as many crimes as those at the end. For example, the "worst" 10 percent of criminals would account for about 10 percent of all crimes. But if there were significant differences among offenders, those at the head of the line would account for far more than their share of all crimes committed; the worst 10 percent would account for much more than 10 percent of all crimes. Analysis of arrest records and offender interviews shows that offenders differ substantially, and that the worst 10 percent of criminals commit about 55 percent of the crimes (see Figure 20.1).[11]

Figure 20.1
Ducks, Wolves, and Dens: Crime is Concentrated

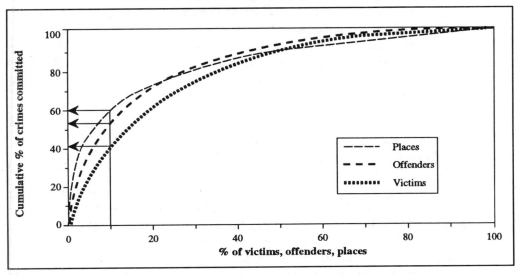

The same principle applies to victims and places. A few particularly vulnerable people run risks of victimization that are much higher than average—the most vulnerable 10 percent of victims are involved in about 40 percent of all crimes.[12] And over 60 percent of crimes are committed at a few particularly dangerous locations.[13] Research suggests that there are usually good reasons why these offenders, victims, and locations account for so many crimes. If something can be done about these "ravenous wolves," "sitting ducks," and "dens of iniquity," the crime problem can, in theory, be reduced dramatically.

This is all the more true because current police policies systematically overlook the most crime-prone people and places. For example, until recently, police gave little attention to cases of family violence—even though abused family members suffer particularly high risks of being abused again.[14] If repeat calls to a single location are made at different times of the day, they will be distributed over several shifts; thus even the beat officers may not recognize the continuing nature of the problem. The most frequent offenders are also the most successful at evading arrest.[15]

These concentrations of crimes among victims, locations, and offenders are important handles for proactive crime-prevention activity. They are the "problems" that are the focus of problem-oriented policing. Government and private agencies have mounted a wide variety of programs aimed at preventing these most predictable of crimes. For example, police, prosecutors, judges, and parole boards have adopted programs and policies aimed at deterrence and incapacitation of frequent, serious offenders.[16] Especially vulnerable people—abused spouses and children, the elderly, the mentally disabled—have been the subject of many recent crime prevention efforts. Through directed patrols[17] and environmental and situational crime prevention,[18] police and other agencies have begun to deal with crime-prone locations as well.

But because the nature of these concentrations is different for every problem, standardized responses will not generally succeed. Previous experience can be a guide, but police must study and create a somewhat different response for each problem they take on.

NEIGHBORHOOD PROBLEMS ARE LINKED TO OTHER URBAN PROBLEMS

Knowing whether a given crime or disorder problem results from frequent offenders, high-risk victims, vulnerable locations, or some combination of the three may be helpful, but it is often insufficient to allow the police to identify a workable solution. To solve many problems, the police need the help of outside agencies, the business sector, or the public.

Often this cooperation is necessary because the police lack the authority to remove the offending conditions. If a rowdy bar produces many assaults, it can be closed down—by the state alcoholic beverage control board. If a blind corner produces many automobile accidents, a stop light can be installed—by the city traffic department. If a woman is continually beaten by her husband, she can move out—by her own volition, perhaps with the assistance of a battered women's shelter; the police cannot force her to do so, however.

Perhaps a more important reason for cooperative solutions is that recurring problems have many parts, and no single agency is responsible for all of them. A run-down apartment complex may look like a serious burglary problem to the police. But the fire department sees burnt-out, vacant apartments and a high risk of fire. The housing department sees code violations and the health department sees an abundance of trash and rats. The bank sees a bad risk and refuses to loan the apartment owner the money needed to renovate the vacant apartments taken over by the drug addicts who commit the burglaries. The residents, beset on all sides, see no hope—they cannot afford cleaner and safer housing.

Clearly, no single agency will be able to solve this problem, because the various parts feed off one another. On the other hand, if all the parts could be addressed at the same time, it is possible that the conditions could be removed and the problem solved. This would require the cooperation of the police, fire, housing, and health departments, the bank, and the apartment owner. It might also require the help of the residents, to ensure that the appropriate agencies are notified should the problems start to return.

There is evidence that citizens in particular "coproduce" crime control with public agencies. In addition to cooperating with the police and pressuring public and private agencies to deliver the goods and services the neighborhood needs, citizens sometimes intervene directly in disorderly or criminal incidents. Although some experts maintain that these informal interventions are the most important determinants of a neighborhood's crime rate, they are difficult to maintain in high-crime areas. The physical design of urban neighborhoods—public housing, in particular—discourages surveillance and intervention by neighbors.[19] Often the residents of these poor neighborhoods are fearful of cooperating with the police; they have little in common with one another; they do not expect to stay long; and they do not even recognize one another. These characteristics make it hard for neighbors to control the minor disorders that may contribute to crime. When families are headed by single parents who must work, parents may not even be able to control their own children.[20] On the other hand, the physical and social environment of high-crime neighborhoods can be improved by governments and businesses, in turn increasing the prospects for intervention and cooperation.

All this suggests that crime prevention strategies are incomplete and possibly ineffective unless they recognize the close links between crime, the physical environment, neighborhood culture, and other factors. In general, these links require that the public and outside agencies work with the police to eliminate or ameliorate the conditions that cause the problem.

A SOLUTION: PROBLEM-ORIENTED POLICING

Police could be more effective if they reduced their reliance on traditional methods and instead relied on tailor-made responses that coordinate the activities of people and agencies both inside and outside the criminal justice system. How would such a police department work? How would it be structured? How well would it control crime and disorder? The problem-oriented approach is new, but the experiences of innovative departments suggest some intriguing answers.

DESIGNING PROBLEM-ORIENTED POLICING

The heart of problem-oriented policing is systematic thinking. Although problem solving has been conducted in very different ways in different departments, the most methodical approach has been adopted in Newport News, Virginia.

The Newport News Police Department bases its problem-solving system on three principles. First, officers of all ranks, from all units, should be able to use the procedures as part of their daily routine. Second, the system must encourage officers to collect information from a broad range of sources and not limit themselves to conventional police data. Finally, the system should encourage "coproduction" solutions not limited to the criminal justice process.

After several months of work, a department task force developed a problem-solving process that fit these criteria. It consists of four parts:

- **Scanning.** As part of their daily routine, officers are expected to look for possible problems.

- **Analysis.** Officers then collect information about the problem. They rely on a Problem Analysis Guide, developed by the task force, which directs officers to examine offenders, victims, the social and physical environment, and previous responses to the problem. The goal is to understand the scope, nature, and causes of the problem.

- **Response.** The knowledge gained in the analysis stage is then used to develop and implement solutions. Officers seek the assistance of other police units, public and private organizations, and anyone else who can help.

- **Assessment.** Finally, officers evaluate the effectiveness of their response. They may use the results to revise the response, collect more data, or even redefine the problem.

Newport News's systematic process has since been adopted by other agencies interested in problem solving, including San Diego, Tulsa, Madison, and New York City. Similar approaches have been adopted, although less explicitly, by other police agencies that have experimented with problem-oriented policing.

PROBLEM SOLVING IN PRACTICE

Since the early 1980s, police agencies have applied the problem-solving approach to a wide variety of problems. To illustrate the breadth of problems and solutions that are possible, three case studies are described here. The first two are serious and complex problems—one affecting a residential neighborhood, the other an entire city—that succumbed to careful analysis and comprehensive responses. The third case is an apparently difficult neighborhood problem that was solved in only a few hours through careful observation and a little thought.

New York Retirees Sting Drug Dealers. When out-of-towners think of New York City, they think first of the Empire State Building, Wall Street, and Broadway—the glitz and glitter of Manhattan. But New Yorkers tend to think first of districts like Sunset Park in Brooklyn, a neighborhood of row houses and small businesses peopled by a mix of working- and middle-class Irish, Italians, Puerto Ricans, and blacks. Contrary to the national stereotype, Sunset Park is clean. Many streets are lined with trees. The district is dotted with vest-pocket parks containing some amenities as handball and basketball courts for the vigorous, sandboxes and swings for the young, and sunny benches for the relaxed.

Despite these amenities, for years the neighborhood park at the corner of 49th Street and 5th Avenue had lured only drug users looking for a quick score. Respectable residents avoided the park, fearing confrontations with the drug traffickers. The New York Police Department tried to respond to the problem, directing its officers to patrol the park and issue loitering citations to apparent dealers. This dispersed the dealers and users—until the patrol car had turned the corner and disappeared from view. Then business returned to normal. Not surprisingly, the problem persisted.

In May 1986, Officer Vinny Esposito was assigned to the 49th Street beat. As one of the first members of New York's innovative Community Patrol Officer Program (CPOP), Esposito was expected to do more than just handle individual incidents on his beat. His job was to identify and solve recurring problems. The drug-ridden 49th Street park clearly fit the bill, and Esposito went to work.

At first, Esposito used the old tactics. He spent as much time in the park as he could, dispersing dealers and making arrests whenever possible. Unfortunately, his beat was large and the time he could spend in the park was limited. Worse yet, every arrest took him away from the park for an hour or more—and whenever he left, the junkies returned. Weeks passed with no apparent effect on the drug trade. Esposito considered the problem further, and decided to take a different tack.

He began by recognizing that loitering citations and even drug arrests were at worst minor inconveniences to the dealers and users, since few arrests led to jail or prison terms. On the other hand, Esposito reasoned, the threat of losing hundreds or thousands of dollars worth of drugs could be a serious deterrent. Dealers, recognizing their vulnerability in the event of a police field stop, typically hid their stashes in the park. Esposito could seize the dope if he knew where it was hidden—but that required the assistance of local residents.

Esposito held meetings of the tenants in the apartment buildings that overlooked the park. Many tenants were elderly and spent most of their days at home. Esposito asked them to watch the dealers from their windows and report the locations of any drug stashes they saw to the local precinct station. Reassured that their tips would remain completely anonymous, the frustrated tenants readily agreed to help.

Calls began coming in. For each one, a CPOP officer at the precinct station took down the information and radioed the location of the stash to Officer Esposito, who then confiscated the drugs and took them to the station. Within twenty minutes of each time, Esposito was back on the beat and the dealers were a little bit poorer.

This new strategy had several effects. Some dealers found themselves having to explain to unsympathetic suppliers where their goods had gone. Others began keeping their stashes on their person, making them more vulnerable to arrest. Others simply quit the park. Within one month, all the dealers had gotten the message—and the park was free of drugs.

Today, the park is a different place. Children play on the swings, youths play basketball. Many of the older residents who once sat at home, phoning in anonymous tips, now spend their days sunning themselves on the benches of "their" park. They show no signs of giving it back to the dealers.

The actions taken by Officer Esposito and local residents may not work as well anywhere else. But the thinking that led to their actions can. Like the Sunset Park case, many persistent problems affect residents of small neighborhoods the most. As Officer Esposito's actions illustrate, these problems can often be solved with the resident's help. But other such problems are not restricted to small localities—they affect residents throughout the city. For problems like these, citywide changes in policies and practices are necessary. Sometimes there is a citywide "community of interest" that can be relied upon to assist the police in much the same way that the elderly residents of Sunset Park helped clear the drug dealers out of their vest-pocket park. Merchant associations, chain retail stores, and citywide community groups may all be of assistance. Even when these communities are uncooperative, however, the police may still be able to solve the problem.

Gainesville Puts the Brakes on QuikStop Crime. When the university town of Gainesville, Florida, was hit with a rash of convenience store robberies in spring 1985, the police recognized that they were dealing with more than just a series of unrelated incidents. The department's crime analysts expected to find that one or two repeat offenders were responsible for the robberies, but suspect description provided by the victims proved otherwise—many different offenders were responsible. Word had apparently spread that convenience stores were an easy target. Police Chief Wayland Clifton, Jr., wondered why, and detailed several members of his department to find out.[21]

Gainesvillle police officers compared the stores that were robbed to others that were not. Their conclusions were revealing. Many of the stores that had been robbed had posted large advertisements in their front windows, blocking the view from the street. Often, the checkout stand could not be seen by a passing car or pedestrian. Many stores failed to light their parking lots, further limiting visibility. Others kept large sums of money in the cash register, and some provided only one inexperienced employee during the late night hours. The stores that had not been robbed tended to provide better visibility, limit the amount of cash in the register, and train their employees in crime prevention techniques. Thus the criminals seemed to be focusing on the most lucrative and vulnerable targets.

To confirm their findings, the Gainesville Police arranged for a psychologist at a local university to interview sixty-five offenders who were serving sentences for convenience store robberies. This independent analysis provided even clearer results: would-be robbers avoided stores staffed by two clerks. Many of the robbers were simply taking advantage of available opportunities; if they had had trouble finding stores with only one clerk on duty, many of the robberies might never have been committed at all.

The police department presented these findings to an association of local merchants that had been established to develop a response to the problem. The police asked for a commitment to change the conditions that made robberies easy to commit. They were disappointed: the merchants felt that the solution lay in more frequent police patrols, and they refused to agree to voluntary crime prevention standards. In effect, the merchants argued that the costs of convenience store crime prevention should be borne by the public as a whole rather than by the stores themselves.

Chief Clifton knew that he could not stop the robberies with police presence unless he assigned his officers to stand guard at every convenience store in the city. Instead, he directed his officers to search for another way of mandating crime prevention measures. Their research revealed that the cities of Akron, Ohio, and Coral Gables, Florida, had passed ordinances requiring merchants to take certain crime prevention measures, and that these ordinances had reduced the incidence of robbery. Clifton and his officers began drafting such an ordinance for Gainesville.

By the summer of 1986, the department was ready to present its findings to the City Commission. The proposed ordinance would require convenience stores to remove window advertising, place cash registers in full view of the street, install security cameras and outside lighting, and limit the amount of cash available in the register. Most important, it would require two or more employees, trained in crime prevention techniques, to work late at night. In July, the City Commission overruled the objections of the convenience store owners and passed the ordinance.

The stores fought the ordinance in court, arguing that the crime prevention measures would be costly and ineffective. But the judge found the police department's research to be persuasive. The store owners' injunction was denied, and the ordinance took effect on schedule.

The first year after the adoption of the new ordinance brought encouraging results: convenience store robberies were down by 65 percent overall, and by 75 percent at night. Best of all, the robbery rate was reduced far below its pre-1985 levels. Convenience stores continue to do a land-office business in Gainesville, and many store owners now admit—a bit grudgingly—that the police department's city-wide approach has solved a difficult problem.

Persistent problems are natural targets of problem solving. It is easy to see how time-consuming research and complex crime prevention measures can be worth the effort if they will help to remove a longstanding problem. But many crime and disorder problems are temporary and nagging, rather than persistent and severe; they do not merit lengthy analysis and complicated responses. Still, thinking systematically about even a minor problem can often reveal quick solutions that are easy to implement.

Newport News Skates out of Trouble. The quiet nights of a middle-class Newport News neighborhood were spoiled when groups of rowdy teenagers began to frequent the area on Fridays and Saturdays. There had been no violence, and the kids' primary offenses were loud music, horseplay, and occasional vandalism. But residents felt the teenagers were unpredictable, particularly since they came from the city's mostly Black south-east side, several miles away. The neighborhood became a regular stop for officers working the evening shift.

Sergeant Jim Hogan recognized that responding to these calls took time but accomplished little except to irritate everyone involved. One Friday night he asked the beat officer, Paul Summerfield, to look into the problem and develop a better solution.

Summerfield suspected that the source of the problem might be a roller skating rink. The rink had been trying to increase business by offering reduced rates and transportation on Friday and Saturday nights. As he drove north toward the rink later that night, Summerfield saw several large groups of youths walking south. Other kids were still hanging around the rink, which had closed shortly before. Summerfield talked to several of them and found that they were waiting for a bus. The others, he was told, had become impatient and begun the three-mile walk home. Then Summerfield talked to the rink owner. The owner told him he had leased the bus to pick up and drop off kids who lived far from the rink. But he said there were always more kids needing rides at the end of the night than the bus had picked up earlier.

When Officer Summerfield returned to the skating rink early the next evening, he saw about fifty youngsters get out of the bus rented by the skating rink. But he saw others get out of the public transit buses that stopped running at midnight, and he saw parents in pajamas drop kids off, then turn around and go home. Clearly the rink's bus would be unable to take home all the kids who would be stranded at closing time.

Summerfield consulted Sergeant Hogan. They agreed that the skating rink owner should be asked to bus the kids home. Summerfield returned to the rink Monday and spoke with the owner. When informed of the size of the problem he had unwittingly created, the owner agreed to lease more buses. By the next weekend, the buses were in use and Summerfield and Hogan saw no kids walking home.

Elapsed time from problem identification to problem solution: one week. Resources used: about four hours of an officer's time. Results: fewer calls, happier kids, satisfied homeowners.

INSTITUTIONALIZING PROBLEM-ORIENTED POLICING

Problem-oriented policing is a state of mind, not a program, technique, or procedure. Problem-solving procedures and analysis guides can be helpful, but only if they encourage clear-headed analysis of problems and an uninhibited search for solutions. Moreover, there are any number of ways of implementing the approach. The New York Police Department established a special unit to focus on neighborhood problems full time; in Newport News, all officers are obliged to spend some of their time identifying and working out problems. There is a place for problem solving in any agency's standard operating procedures. In the long run, however, it is likely that the problem-oriented approach will have its most dramatic impact on the management structure of American policing and on the relationship between the police, other city agencies, and the public.

Changes in Management Structure. As the case studies considered above suggest, crime and disorder problems are fundamentally local and specialized in nature. As a result, they are best analyzed and responded to on a case-by-case basis by the line officers and detectives assigned to the problem neighborhood or crime type. Implementing this approach will require changes in the centralized, control-oriented organizational structure and management style of most police agencies. Command staff and mid-level managers can structure problem-solving efforts by creating standard operating procedures, such as the problem-solving process created in Newport News. They can also encourage effective and innovative efforts by regarding the officers who undertake them. But they cannot make the many individual decisions that are required to identify, analyze, and solve problems.

Inevitably, the changes in structure and style will affect line supervisors—sergeants—the most. Problem solving puts a dual burden on supervisors. On the one hand, they must make many of the tough, operational decisions: setting priorities among different problems, facilitating communication and cooperation with other divisions of the police department and outside agencies, and making sure their officers solve the problems they are assigned. On the other hand, sergeants must also provide leadership, encouraging creative analysis and response. As the sergeant's role shifts from taskmaster to team leader, police agencies must take greater care in selecting, training, and rewarding their line supervisors.

As the structure and style of police agencies change, managers must also shift their focus from internal management problems to the external problems of the public. When a few routine procedures such as preventive patrol, rapid response, and follow-up investigations formed the bulk of an agency's activity, the manager's job was mostly to remove barriers to efficient execution of these routines. Good managers streamlined administrative procedures and reduced paperwork; they implemented new resource deployment schemes; they structured officer discretion.[22] They did not need to emphasize crime and disorder reduction, since crimes and disorders would presumably take care of themselves if the routines were implemented properly.

On the other hand, problem-solving activities are inherently nonroutine; it is far more important to choose the correct response from among many possibilities—to "do the right thing"—than it is to "do things right." Thus managers must shift their attention from internal efficiency measures to external effectiveness measures. And they must shift from global, city- and precinct-wide measures to carefully defined, problem-specific measures. Instead of city-wide clearance and arrest rates, police must emphasize neighborhood crime rates; Instead of counting the number of tickets written by all officers, they must count the number of auto accidents on particular stretches of road. Implicitly, police must recognize that problem-specific crime rates, accident rates, and the like are partly within their control. Whereas no agency can be held accountable for citywide crime and accident rates, police managers and officers must accept partial responsibility for conditions in their areas.

Changes in Police Role. Of course, crime, disorder, and other evils are only partly the responsibility of the police. As the three case studies illustrate, police cannot solve these problems by themselves; they need help from other public service agencies, the business community, and the public. The need to obtain cooperation and assistance from these "coproducers" of public safety requires that the role of the police agency must change.

One fundamental change will be in the autonomy of the police relative to other public service agencies. Urban bureaucracies are currently structured along functional lines—public works maintains roads and sewers, codes compliance ensures that building codes are met, and so on. But if urban problems are interrelated and concentrated, as the research and case studies presented above suggest, then these functional distinctions begin to blur. The activities of the public works, codes, and other departments affect (and perhaps worsen) the problems of all the other departments, so at a minimum they must communicate to one another what they are doing about a problem and why. A more ambitious and effective strategy would be for them to develop and implement a common response. In the short run, each agency gives up some of its "turf"; in the long run, each agency saves itself a lot of work.

Problem-oriented police agencies have found that line personnel in other agencies can be "hidden allies," bending procedures to get the job done. For example, one police agency attempted to solve a recurring traffic accident problem at a blind corner by convincing the traffic engineer to install a stop sign. The engineer refused to comply until he had conducted his own study; unfortunately, many similar problems were already awaiting study, so the engineer would not be able to consider the corner for several months. Then a police officer discovered that the public works personnel who actually installed the signs could replace a missing or deteriorated sign within a few days, and that the roadworkers would by happy to install the "missing" stop sign. The work order was placed, and the sign was installed within a week. Now police officers in this jurisdiction regularly bypass the traffic engineer and deal directly with public works officials.

Hidden allies may help get the job done, but in the long run turf difficulties are best surmounted when top managers—city managers and department heads—recognize the value of a cooperative, problem-solving approach and urge their managers and line personnel to comply. This puts the onus on problem-oriented police administrators to educate and lobby their colleagues, running interference for their officers. As will be discussed later, such an education effort may ultimately result in substantial changes in the city bureaucracy.

Problem-oriented policing also requires that police take on a different role with regard to the public it serves. At present, police ask little more of citizens than that they report crimes, be good witnesses, and stand aside to let the professionals do their job. As with public service agencies, however, problem solving requires that the police and the public communicate and cooperate more frequently, on a wider variety of issues. In particular, problem-oriented police agencies recognize that sometimes citizens know better what must be done.

This raises many difficult questions. Just as different public service agencies see different aspects of a problem, so do different groups of citizens. If there is no consensus among the community of interest as to the nature of the problem, but public cooperation is necessary to solve it, the police must play a role in forging this consensus. Few police agencies are well equipped for such essentially political activities.

The dilemma is even more serious when the conflict is of values, not just perceptions. Quiet residents of an urban neighborhood may see nothing wrong with police harassment of their rowdier neighbors; the rowdies may legitimately claim that they have the right to be raucous so long as they end their loud parties before midnight and do not threaten other residents. In dealing with such a problem, police must balance the rights and needs of the two groups. This is hardly new—police have always had to balance the goals of serving the majority while guarding the liberties of the minority. Because the problem-oriented approach encourages police to seek such difficult situations, however, they may find themselves making such tough choices more often. On the other hand, problem solving also emphasizes the power of information and cooperative action over the power of formal, unilateral authority. If police can develop a broader repertoire of solutions to conflicts like these, they may find that these tough choices are easier to make.

It remains to be seen how the limits on police authority will be set, but it is certain that problem solving will require a new consensus on the role, authority, and limitations of the police in each jurisdiction that adopts it.[23]

THE FUTURE: BEYOND PROBLEM-ORIENTED POLICING

Problem-oriented policing is new. Traditional procedures die hard, problem solving methods are still under development, and no one knows for sure how successful the approach will be. As a result, no police agency has adopted the approach fully, and it will be a long time before many agencies do. On the other hand, problem-oriented policing is a realistic response to the limitations of traditional, incident-driven policing. It relies on our growing knowledge of the nature of crime and disorder, and it has been successful in a wide variety of police agencies, for a wide variety of urban crime and disorder problems. The problem-oriented approach seems to be where police work is going.

It also seems to be where other urban service agencies are going. Problem-oriented approaches have been implemented on an experimental basis in electric utilities,[24] urban transit authorities, [25] and recreation and parks departments. [26] Over the next few years, it makes sense to expect dramatic growth in the use of problem-solving techniques not only in municipal policing but in other areas as well. It is likely, then, that problem-oriented police officers will find problem-oriented firefighters, housing inspectors, and others to work with.

This seems to be the case in Madison, Wisconsin, where city agencies have been working on problem solving since 1984. The city has implemented a program of quality and productivity improvement, a form of problem solving originally developed in the private sector to improve the quality of manufactured goods. Project teams have been established within most city agencies, consisting of line personnel, supervisors, and managers, often working with a statistical consultant. They identify a recurring problem within their agency, usually an administrative bottleneck, and use methods successful in private industry to analyze and solve it.[27] Although most Madison city agencies have concentrated on administrative problems, some—including the Madison Police Department—are beginning to extend the methods to public problems. When Madison police officers take on a public problem, chances are they will find sympathetic and experienced problem solvers to work with in other agencies.

The growing use of problem-oriented approaches should help to reduce turf problems. As standard operating procedures become more flexible and decisionmaking becomes decentralized, line officials may find that they owe as much allegiance to their colleagues from other agencies as they do to their own bureaucracies. One natural method of institutionalizing these developments would be to adopt a matrix organizational structure. Neighborhood teams, consisting of members of the police, fire, public works, and other departments, would work together on a formal basis to deliver urban services. Although full implementation of a matrix is a long way off, the foundation for such a structure has already been laid in New York City. All urban service agencies are decentralized into eighty-eight districts with identical boundaries; citizens participate in agency decisionmaking through community boards, a permanent part of the city government structure.[28]

A central element of problem-oriented policing is that administrative arrangements are less important than the activities that line officers undertake. But just as the centralized, control-oriented police structure helped police administrators to institutionalize incident-driven policing, so might a decentralized, team-based matrix help city managers to institutionalize problem-oriented urban service provision.

Such an interagency team approach would also provide long-term benefits for the relationship between city government and the public. More problem solvers would be available, with different backgrounds, viewpoints, and opportunities for contact with the public; this would improve the chances of early identification and complete analysis of problems. Because they would report to different bureaucracies, members of problem-solving teams would act as a check on one another, reducing many of the potential dangers of community problem solving. Finally, the teams would provide a unified contact point for frustrated citizens who would otherwise be unable to negotiate their way through the city bureaucracy. If problem-solving teams can be linked to community organizations, the opportunities for cooperative efforts would increase dramatically.

Such benefits, like the interagency team or matrix structure, are speculative. Problem-oriented policing is not. It provides a tested, practical approach for police agencies frustrated with putting Band-Aids on symptoms. By responding to recurring problems, and by working with other agencies, businesses, and the public whenever possible, innovative police agencies have begun to develop an effective strategy for reducing crime and other troubling conditions in our cities.

NOTES

1. Philip J. Cook, "Research in Criminal Deterrence: Laying the Groundwork for the Second Decade," in *Crime and Justice: An Annual Review of Research,* vol. 4, ed. Michael Tonry and Norval Morrris (Chicago: University of Chicago Press, 1980).
2. John E. Eck and William Spelman, *Problem Solving: Problem-oriented Policing in Newport News* (Washington, D.C.: Police Executive Research Forum, 1987).
3. J. Schnelle, R. Kirchner, J. Casey, P. Uselton, and M. McNees, "Patrol Evaluation Research: A Multiple-Baseline Analysis of Saturation Police Patrolling during Day and Night Hours," *Journal of Applied Behavior Analysis* 10 (1976): 33-40; George L. Kelling, Tony Pate, Duane Dieckman, and Charles E. Brown, *The Kansas City Preventive Patrol Experiment: A Technical Report* (Washington, D.C.: Police Foundation, 1974).
4. William Spelman and Dale K. Brown, *Calling the Police: Citizen Reporting of Serious Crime* (Washington, D.C.: U.S. Government Printing Office, 1984).
5. John E. Eck, *Solving Crimes: The Investigation of Burglary and Robbery* (Washington, D.C.: Police Executive Research Forum, 1982); William Spelman, Michael Oshima, and George L. Kelling, *Crime Suppression and Traditional Police Tactics,* final report to the Florence V. Burden Foundation (Cambridge, Mass.: Program in Criminal Justice Policy and Management, Harvard University, 1985).
6. James M. Tien, James A. Simon, and Richard C. Larson, *An Alternative Approach in Police Patrol: The Wilmington Split-Force Experiment* (Washington, D.C.: U.S. Government Printing Office, 1978); John E. Eck, *Managing Case Assignments: The Burglary Investigation Decision Model Replication* (Washington, D.C.: Police Executive Research Forum, 1979); J. Thomas McEwen, Edward F. Connors, and Marcia I. Cohen, *Evaluation of the Differential Police Response Field Test* (Alexandria, Va: Research Management Associates, 1984).
7. Lawrence E. Cohen and Marcus Felson, "Social Change and Crime Rate Trends: A Routine Activity Approach," *American Sociological Review* 44 (August 1979): 588-608.
8. For example, Clifford R. Shaw and Henry E. McKay, *Juvenile Delinquency and Urban Areas* (Chicago: University of Chicago Press, 1942); and Thomas A. Reppetto, *Residential Crime* (Cambridge, Mass.: Ballinger, 1974).
9. Jane Jacobs, *The Death and Life of Great American Cities* (New York: Vintage, 1961); Floyd J. Fowler, Jr., Mary Ellen McCalla, and Thomas W. Mangione, *Reducing Residential Crime and Fear: The Hartford Neighborhood Crime Prevention Program* (Washington, D.C.: U.S. Government Printing Office. 1979).
10. Stephanie W. Greenberg, William M. Rohe, and Jay R. Williams, *Safe and Secure Neighborhoods: Physical Characteristics and Informal Territorial Control in High and Low Crime Neighborhoods* (Washington, D.C.: U.S. Government Printing Office, 1984).

11. Alfred Blumstein, Jacqueline Cohen, Jeffrey A. Roth, and Christy A. Visher, *Criminal Careers and "Career Criminals,"* vol. 1 (Washington, D.C.: National Academy Press, 1986).

12. James F. Nelson, "Multiple Victimization in American Cities: A Statistical Analysis of Rare Events," *American Journal of Sociology* 85 (1980): 870-91.

13. Glenn L. Pierce, Susan Spaar, and LeBaron R. Briggs, *The Character of Police Work: Strategic and Tactical Implications* (Boston: Center for Applied Social Research, Northeastern University, 1986); Lawrence W. Sherman, "Repeat Calls to Police in Minneapolis," in *Crime Control Reports Number* 4 (Washington, D.C.: Crime Control Institute, 1987).

14. Albert J. Reiss, Jr., "Victim Proneness in Repeat Victimization by Type of Crime," in *Indicators of Crime and Criminal Justice: Quantitative Studies,* ed. Stephen E. Fienberg and Albert J. Reiss, Jr. (Washington, D.C.: U.S. Government Printing Office, 1980), pp. 41-53.

15. William Spelman, "The Incapacitation Benefits of Selective Criminal Justice Policies," Ph.D. diss., Harvard University, 1988.

16. Mark H. Moore, Susan R. Estrich, Daniel McGillis, and William Spelman, *Dangerous Offenders: The Elusive Target of Justice* (Cambridge, Mass.: Harvard University Press, 1985).

17. Tien, Simon, and Larson, *Alternative Approach.*

18. C. Ray Jeffery, *Crime Prevention through Environmental Design* (Beverly Hills, Cal.: Sage, 1971); Ronald V. Clarke and Derek B. Cornish, "Modeling Offenders' Decisions: A Framework for Research and Policy," in *Crime and Justice: An Annual Review of Research,* vol. 6, ed. Michael Tonry and Norval Morris (Chicago: University of Chicago Press, 1985, pp. 147-85).

19. Oscar Newman, *Defensible Space: Crime Prevention through Urban Design* (New York: Macmillan, 1972).

20. Greenberg, Rohe, and Williams, *Safe and Secure Neighborhoods.*

21. Wayland Clifton, Jr., "Convenience Store Robberies in Gainesville, Florida: An Intervention Strategy by the Gainesville Police Department," reported by the Gainesville Police Department, Gainesville, Florida, 1987.

22. Herman Goldstein, "Improving Policing: A Problem-oriented Approach," *Crime and Delinquency* 25 (April 1979): 236-58.

23. Herman Goldstein, "Toward Community-Oriented Policing: Potential Basic Requirements and Threshold Questions," *Crime and Delinquency* 33 (January 1986): 1-30.

24. John Francis Hird, "An Electric Utility," in *Out of the Crisis,* ed. W. Edwards Deming (Cambridge, Mass.: Center for Advanced Engineering Study, Massachusetts Institute of Technology, 1986).

25. Harvey J. Brightman, *Group Problem Solving: An Improved Managerial Approach* (Atlanta: Business Publishing Division, College of Business Administration, Georgia State University, 1988).

26. Joseph J. Bannon, *Problem Solving in Recreation and Parks* (Englewood Cliffs, N.J.: Prentice-Hall, 1972).

27. William Hunter, Jan O'Neill, and Carol Wallen, *Doing More with Less in the Public Sector: A Progress Report from Madison, Wisconsin,* report no. 13 (Madison: Center for Quality and Productivity Improvement, College of Engineering, University of Wisconsin, 1986).

28. John Mudd, *Neighborhood Services* (New Haven, Conn.: Yale University Press, 1984).

POLICE METHODS FOR IDENTIFYING COMMUNITY PROBLEMS 21

Barbara Webster & Edward F. Connors

The results of a recent national survey of criminal justice agencies shows a tremendous interest among police chiefs in community and problem-oriented policing. Eighty percent of chiefs report needing technical assistance or research on the subject, and 69 percent are interested in applying problem-solving techniques specifically to drug problems (McEwen et al., 1991).

Technical distinctions can be made between community policing (also known as neighborhood policing) and problem-oriented policing, and police managers often ask about the differences between the two. Both approaches recognize a need to draw the community and the police closer together, and they have several common elements: consultations between police and residents, development of strategies to fit neighborhood needs, and mobilization of community resources (Bayley, 1991). But problem-oriented policing as conceptualized by Herman Goldstein encourages (among other things) a higher level of community problem identification and analysis (Goldstein, 1990a). It represents a "fine-tuning approach" found in "the most advanced community-oriented policing programs" (Goldstein, 1990b). The operational term, then, is leaning toward community policing, with problem-oriented policing viewed as a specific enhancement to community policing.

Community policing is often described as both a philosophy and an organizational strategy. As a philosophy, it broadens the police mandate by placing an increased emphasis on involving community members in identifying problems and exploring creative solutions to them. Problems of interest to both the police and the community include not only crimes but

Source: Barbara Webster and Edward F. Connors (1993). "Police Methods for Identifying Community Problems." *American Journal of Police,* 12(1):75-102. Reprinted by permission of MCB University Press Ltd.

also fear of crime, crime prevention, disorder, and neighborhood deterioration. The community policing philosophy recognizes the apparent link between blighted neighborhood conditions and the level of crime in a community. It suggests that if the police can address the conditions that breed crime, they may be able to reduce crime and fear (Wilson & Kelling, 1989; New York City Police Department and Vera Institute of Justice, 1988).

Within the past few years, the community policing plans devised by many police departments reflect a common philosophy, although it varies somewhat in emphasis. For example, the Portland, Oregon community policing plan (Portland Police Bureau, 1990) identifies "partnership, empowerment, problem solving, accountability, and service orientation" as key factors. The Montgomery County, Maryland, Police Department echoes Portland's view but concludes that ultimately, the definition of community policing "is what the Department and the Community agree it to be." (Montgomery County Police, 1991). Seattle, Washington, stresses community policing as "an operating philosophy (values and attitudes) rather than specific tactics" and sees it as "a proactive complement to the traditional (reactive) approach of answering emergency calls." Seattle also includes an emphasis on crime prevention; problem solving; and cooperation between the police, the community, and other agencies (Seattle Police Department, 1991). Tempe, Arizona, stresses that community policing is a partnership between the police and citizens to "improve the quality of life in our city by identifying and resolving public safety concerns . . . not a program or addition to traditional policing. It is an umbrella that encompasses a broad range of techniques and resources." (Tempe Police Department, 1991).

There is also considerable agreement on what community policing is *not*—or should not be. It is often discussed as *not* an attempt to turn police officers into social workers; *not* a return to unprofessionalism, payoffs, and political manipulation of police business; and *not* a public relations ploy or a limited community relations unit.

While there seems to be agreement among police practitioners about what a community policing philosophy means, there is a great deal of diversity in how the philosophy is making the leap into action. Departments that have articulated community policing goals may be using any number of tactics in a variety of combinations—long-term assignments of officers to neighborhood beats, special squads of community police officers, neighborhood police offices, foot patrol assignments, training in problem-solving skills, and many others. These tactics may or may not be part of a master plan for organizational change or decentralization.

Some researchers at times seem to straddle a line between a desire to observe, hands-off, the community policing phenomenon, and a need to offer guidelines. Trojanowicz and Bucqueroux (1990) express concern about "pinning it [community policing] down in ways that might inhibit its continued growth," but they also offer specific community policing tenets to introduce a book that is largely prescriptive (Kelling, 1990). Goldstein worries that taking a cookbook approach to instruction in problem-solving runs the risk of discouraging innovation and oversimplifying the concept; but he concludes that guidelines are needed and provides some (Goldstein, 1990c).

There are four main steps to the problem-solving process as discussed by Herman Goldstein and others: problem identification or scanning, analysis, response and assessment (Eck & Spelman, 1987). This article focuses on one aspect of this process: identifying community problems. In our experience, this aspect of community policing has proved more difficult than anticipated for some departments new to the problem-solving approach. The intent is not to write a prescription, but to review and expand upon some of the problem identification techniques discussed by Eck and Spelman (1987), Goldstein (1990c), and others.

There is now a considerable body of experience on which to draw. Since the late 1970s, many law enforcement agencies have experimented with special community policing squads or programs, and some have used problem-solving techniques in a structured way. Some of the best known include the foot patrol program in Flint, Michigan (Trojanowicz & Bucqueroux 1990), and community policing experiments in Madison, Wisconsin (Goldstein, 1990c), Edmonton, Canada (Koller, 1990), and in Houston and Newark (Pate et al., 1986); New York City's Community Patrol Officer Program (CPOP) (Farrell, 1988); and Baltimore County, Maryland's, Citizen Oriented Police Enforcement (COPE) program, which was created to address problems that contributed to fear of crime (Cordner, 1985).

Further, in just the past two years since Goldstein's comprehensive work on problem-oriented policing was published (Goldstein, 1990c), the U.S. Department of Justice has greatly increased its commitment to community-oriented policing. Eight large and medium-sized cities are currently implementing programs with funding from the Bureau of Justice Assistance (BJA) under its innovative Neighborhood-Oriented Policing (INOP) program, and four rural sites will soon develop demonstration projects under a rural INOP initiative. The BJA-sponsored "Weed and Seed" effort, which includes a strong emphasis on community policing, will soon involve 19 sites in implementing a comprehensive attack on violent crime and drug trafficking. There are an even greater number of law enforcement agencies that have made public commitments to implement a community policing approach without federal funding.

Some of these departments are still contemplating the best ways to put the community policing philosophy into operation. Others, such as Portland, Oregon, have developed detailed, time-phased plans. Still others have implemented special projects, but have not yet made the types of organizational changes needed to support a major shift to community policing. A few departments have gained considerable experience in implementing the concept department-wide. The Newport News, Virginia, Police Department is one of the first police agencies in the country to attempt this (Eck & Spelman, 1987). New York City's community-oriented approach includes eventually integrating CPOP into all precincts.

The Baltimore County, Maryland, Police Department in 1987 introduced problem solving to 350 patrol officers in one patrol area. The department viewed this experiment as a step toward department-wide problem solving (Webster et al., 1989). The Institute for Law and Justice (ILJ) and the Police Executive Research Forum (PERF) evaluated the Baltimore County experiment, making many site visits to observe and discuss the problem-solving process. Thus, this paper draws many of its examples from Baltimore County.

Although the literature contains many accounts of crimes and problems solved through community policing efforts, few, if any, comprehensive community policing efforts have been rigorously evaluated. Many must simply stand the test of time before a meaningful impact evaluation is possible. Nevertheless, patrol officers throughout the country are now being called upon to bear significant responsibilities for identifying, analyzing, and solving community problems. To have any chance at success, they must have meaningful training, strong leadership, and systems throughout the department that support their efforts to identify and solve problems when they are not answering calls.

ISSUES INVOLVED IN IDENTIFYING PROBLEMS

Identifying problems can be a stumbling block for several reasons. Some of the obstacles relate to officer attitudes about change in general and about community policing in particular. Other difficulties relate to the department's overall readiness to support community policing.

OFFICER ATTITUDES

Many officers, including supervisors, may see community policing as yet another program—a fad that will come and go if they can just wait it out. In addition, community policing generally calls for a new emphasis on disorder problems such as juveniles hanging out, or on environmental conditions that facilitate crime (e.g., abandoned buildings). Involvement in projects that deal with these issues may conflict with many officers' views of themselves as crime-busters.

Of course, patrol officers are not the only police employees who may resist change. Personnel who prepare budgets, purchase equipment and supplies, or perform crime analysis, for example, may hold back the support needed for successful problem solving. In short, a shift to community policing is subject to all the considerations inherent in making any major change in a police organization (Sparrow, 1988).

A survey of Baltimore County officers in the experimental patrol area revealed that before the project began, about 25 percent agreed with problem solving and community policing objectives, half were neutral, and 25 percent were opposed. An earlier study compared the attitudes of Baltimore County COPE officers with a control group of officers who had routine patrol duties. The conclusion was that officers implementing community-oriented strategies tend to have more job satisfaction, more positive attitudes toward the community, and a broader view of the police role (Hayeslip & Cordner, 1987).

It is typical, and perhaps easier, for departments to begin community policing with individual programs rather than to introduce the concept department-wide (Brown, 1989). While it makes sense to test a new approach with a limited program, it is also important to foster an understanding of that program among officers in the field. This was demonstrated in Baltimore County, where some commanders were concerned that officers would resist problem solving because it was closely associated with COPE. There was a negative perception of COPE among many patrol officers and supervisors. COPE officers did not respond to calls, provide backups, or work rotating shifts, factors that contributed to officers' low opinion of COPE. Poor communication between COPE and regular patrol was also a problem. Efforts were made to improve communication during the patrol experiment by involving COPE officers in training sessions.

DEPARTMENT PREPARATION AND SUPPORT

Other difficulties with problem identification relate to the department's preparation for community policing. This includes ensuring that officers have enough time for problem solving. Time may not be an issue for special squads in which officers have limited call-handling responsibilities and a clear problem-solving mission. Well-staffed departments in low crime areas may also find that there is sufficient patrol down time that can be used for problem solving. But time is an issue for department-wide problem solving in a busy department that is still at the mercy of 911.

Officers who spend more than 40 percent of their available time answering calls are not likely to have the blocks of time needed for problem solving or, for that matter, for many other types of directed patrol activities.[1] This can be expected to affect officers' willingness (although not their ability) to identify problems, since they may believe they will not have enough time to follow up.

Patrol supervisors must assume responsibility for freeing up as much time as possible for problem solving. However, other department systems, resources, and policies must be in place if they are to do this. For example, a review of the department's differential police response (DPR) policies may reveal several types of calls that could be handled by a telephone report unit or some other means. Full use of all available DPR options can free up additional time for problem solving, or at least enable officers to gain more control of their work day (McEwen et al., 1986). Similarly, the department may need to use other methods (e.g., civilian police aides) to reduce officer time spent on certain types of calls, such as minor traffic accidents.

In addition, many patrol supervisors are not accustomed to soliciting information about community problems from patrol officers. The Baltimore County study suggested that few officers would identify problems unless shift supervisors provided leadership and guidance. Officers also needed clear procedures for taking action once problems were identified. Details like forms, resource checklists, and monitoring procedures need to be in place. In addition, crime analysts will need the capability—computer software and hardware, experience, training, and time to handle officers' special requests.

An absence of rewards for problem solving may also inhibit problem identification. If evaluations and pay increases still depend exclusively on traditional performance measures (e.g., number of arrests, traffic tickets issued), officers without a great deal of internal motivation are likely to hold their participation in problem solving to a minimum.

In short, administrators may expect only a limited amount of problem solving to occur by decree. The department must provide the leadership and make the organizational changes needed to support it. In the recent Baltimore County experiment, it appeared that leadership by precinct commanders and shift lieutenants was especially important to successful problem solving. A recent report on the Newport News experience also stresses the significant role that mid-level managers and first-line supervisors play in motivating officers to identify and work on problems (Mitchell, 1990).

DEFINING PROBLEMS: THE FIRST STEP

Training in problem identification often begins with the following working definition of a problem: *a group of incidents that are similar in one or more ways and are of concern to the police and the public.* Central to this definition is that public concern is paramount (Goldstein, 1979). The problem must be of some concern to a portion of the public, and not just a concern of the police. Thus, the definition eliminates issues that are strictly police administrative matters (e.g., the need for daily briefings). It also eliminates community concerns for which the police clearly do not have responsibility (e.g., the cost of school lunches).

However, if the public *expects* the police to be involved, then the problem becomes a police matter and a candidate for the problem-solving approach. The definition, therefore, does allow inclusion of many community problems that in the past technically have not been the responsibility of the police. These problems are appropriate for police action because they contribute to a crime, disorder, or fear of crime problem, or simply because the public believes the police ought to do something.

For example, a run-down building provides a haven for drug trafficking. Police have observed the activity and citizens have complained about it. A traditional police response might include arresting users and dealers and ordering intensified patrols in the area. If the drug activity persists despite these efforts, it may well be time to consider why. Part of the solution may lie in having the building either fixed up or condemned. The question then arises: is this a police responsibility?

The police are not general contractors, nor do they have the power to condemn buildings. But the community-oriented, problem-oriented view is that the police can, and probably should, inspire the appropriate agencies, groups, or individuals to act. In this instance, action may be required of the health department, zoning department, citizen groups, a private property owner, the housing authority, or some combination of these entities.

Similarly, a lack of sports programs may contribute to a problem with teenagers loitering, or poor lighting may contribute to muggings at an apartment parking lot. While it may not be appropriate for police to organize a team or install new street lights, it would be appropriate for them to pursue these options with others who have a stake in solving the problem.

WAYS TO IDENTIFY PROBLEMS

When the Baltimore County experiment began, officers used three main sources of information to identify problems: their own observations, citizen complaints, and police department data. Other methods were used to clarify the scope of these problems (and could also have been used initially to identify problems). These included door-to-door neighborhood surveys, officer participation at community meetings, and consultations with other agencies and police department units. Problem-solving in Newport News also relied heavily on these methods (Eck & Spelman, 1987). As a department gains more experience with problem solving, and as crime analysis capabilities improve, many more information sources can be developed. This section discusses a range of options. Some require a considerable expenditure for computer software, data entry, and data analysis. Others are as simple as a conversation over a cup of coffee.

OFFICER OBSERVATION AND EXPERIENCE

One of the easiest and best ways to learn of problems is to listen to patrol officers recount their experiences and observations. Often, they have a greater stake and interest in problems than police officials further removed from the street.

Most officers have responded to, or know about, repeat domestic calls to particular addresses, repeat false alarm calls to commercial establishments, street corners overtaken by drug activity, bars where violence regularly occurs, and many other recurring problems.

Officers on routine patrol can also identify opportunities to prevent crime or accidents. For example, an officer may notice that an elementary school needs a crossing guard, or that political campaign signs are blocking the view at an intersection. Also important are officers' observations of neighborhood deterioration. Graffiti, trash, vandalism, junk cars and the like can all be signs that a public place is no longer under public control (Wilson & Kelling, 1989).

Officers on foot patrol and officers assigned to neighborhood police offices have additional opportunities to observe neighborhood conditions and activities. New York City CPOP officers, for example, are required to conduct foot patrol of some part of their beats each day, covering the entire beat at least twice a week. They are also expected to talk to residents and merchants, attend community meetings, and make personal observations (Farrell, 1988).

The problem identification task challenges the department to capture officers' information about crime and community problems so that it can be brought to the attention of supervisors and acted upon. The information can be harnessed in a number of ways. Officers may use a special form to report problems for further consideration. A focus group of patrol officers may brainstorm a list of problems, using the general definition noted earlier. An alternative is to form a problem identification task group with representatives from patrol, investigations, crime analysis, crime prevention, community relations, and other units. This type of multi-disciplinary group was used to launch problem-solving in Newport News (Eck & Spelman, 1987).

CITIZEN COMPLAINTS

Ideally, problem identification in a community policing department is a proactive, "bottom up" process in which officers, by virtue of their close contact with residents, are able to bring community concerns to the department's attention. Realistically, citizens and elected officials often bring problems directly to the attention of the chief of police, precinct captain, or other command staff. Complaints may be received in the form of phone calls, letters, or comments at public meetings. Many of these problems can be appropriately delegated to patrol officers for follow-up using the problem solving process.

In Oakland, California, the police department attempted to encourage citizens in the central district to report problems through the RID CARD program (Report Incidents Directly). The police, private developers, and city officials recognized that "soft crime" was a problem that contributed to fear and discouraged people from living, working, and patronizing businesses in the central district. Soft crime involved many behaviors that people felt threatened their safety, but which received low priority when reported to 911. Included were verbal and physical harassment, panhandling, drug sales, public intoxication, loitering, littering, bizarre and frightening behavior, soliciting, and similar matters.

Many of these incidents were either not reported, or were reported to private security personnel who had no mechanism for passing the information along to the police. The RID cards were intended to give complaints about soft crime higher priority. They took the form of postcard-sized incident reports and were distributed by officers, private security guards, and building managers. Citizens could mail the cards directly to the central district section or hand them to any Oakland police officer or uniformed private guard. Fliers encouraged use of the cards, stating that they were important for identifying crime patterns and potential suspects, and that they would be used to deploy officers and assist investigators.

After the initial promotion, the use of the cards declined, but they appear to have been valuable at least in the short run. They helped focus officers' attention on looking into soft crime issues, and they informed supervisors of the kinds of problems that residents and users of the central district considered important (Reiss, 1985).

CRIME ANALYSIS

Crime analysis has the potential to become increasingly useful to police engaged in problem solving. The value of crime analysis will depend, of course, on many factors, including the following:

- Extent and quality of data captured (garbage in, garbage out).

- Availability of software programs to sort and cross-reference data.

- Capacity to produce reports that describe crimes and disorder at the beat or neighborhood level, or by specific addresses.

- Ability to present data in useful formats.

- Accessibility of data to patrol officers.

Finally, the value of crime analysis to problem solving will depend on the time crime analysts are allotted to respond to individual officer requests and their ability to become problem analysts. This can mean devising new ways to collect and analyze information on disorder problems, and integrating information from concerned citizens with data from official police records.

The techniques discussed in this section include using various police reports to identify problems; using computer-assisted dispatch data to identify hot spots through repeat call analysis; and generating graphs and maps from crime data and information provided by citizen groups.

Police Reports

Police offense reports can be analyzed for suspect characteristics, MOs, victim characteristics, and many other factors. Offense reports are also a potential source of information about high-crime areas and addresses, since they capture exact descriptions of locations. However, there are considerable limitations to their use for this purpose.

First, they may not be programmed to be sorted by address. Second, the picture they present of high crime and disturbance locations will be incomplete, since police do not file offense reports for all crimes and activities reported to them. In a typical police department, patrol officers may write official reports on only about 25 to 30 percent of calls to which they respond.

Third, there may be a considerable lag between the time the officer files a report and the time data entry and analysis are complete. Departments with precinct-based crime analysts generally have an advantage over agencies that rely solely on a centralized crime analysis unit for all data analysis. The precinct analyst usually answers to the precinct commander and has an investment in meeting the needs of the officers assigned there. For example, the precinct analyst may develop special databases on activities of interest using offense reports (e.g., reported garage burglaries by time of day, day of week, patrol beat, and address).

Officers may also conduct manual searches of offense reports, field contact cards, and other records to uncover problems. In Baltimore County, for example, each precinct maintained a notebook of offense reports filed from that precinct. Two officers scanned the reports and found several on runaways from a girls home. Since various officers had responded from various shifts and had not talked about the situation, no one was aware that there was a pattern. Further investigation revealed frequent delays of more than 24 hours between the time a girl was noticed missing and the time the police were called. A problem-solving project was undertaken, resulting in more timely reporting and security improvements at the girls home.

Call for Service Analysis

With the advent of computer-assisted dispatch (CAD) systems, a more reliable source of data on crime and disorder has become available. Call for service data does have limitations, but it is more complete than offense reports, providing the most extensive account available of what the public tells the police about crime. The data captured by CAD systems can be sorted to reveal "hot spots" of crime and disturbances—specific locations from which an unusual number of calls to the police are made (Sherman et al., 1989).

One study on hot spots recently analyzed nearly 324,000 calls for service for a one-year period over all 115,000 addresses and intersections in Minneapolis. The results showed relatively few hot spots accounting for the majority of calls to the police:

- 50 percent of all calls came from 3 percent of places.

- All robbery calls came from 2.2 percent of places.

- All rape calls came from 1.2 percent of places.

- All auto thefts came from 2.7 percent of places (Sherman et al., 1989).

Using CAD runs for repeat call analysis requires an understanding of the CAD system's limitations. These may vary from department to department, but basic limitations include the following:

- Data may include calls made in error or as intentional lies.

- One event may generate more than one call.

- Information from police at the scene may be recorded as a separate call, rather than replacing the earlier call.

- There is often a considerable lag between the time an event occurs and the time the call is made.

- Some systems may allow entry of the caller's address and the address to which police respond, but not the actual location of the event.

- Hospitals and other public locations (e.g., phone booth in a public housing complex) may account for overreporting; the locations where those crimes occurred will be undercounted.

- Misspellings, omissions, and variations in the way place names are entered (e.g., Joe E.'s Tavern and Joey's Tavern) will result in undercounting crime at a location.

Many departments have the capability to use CAD data for repeat call analysis. The repeat call locations identified in this way can become targets of directed patrol efforts, including problem solving.

For example, early in the Baltimore County study, the test precincts received printouts of the top 25 call for service areas to review for problem-solving assignments. In a separate effort, the Baltimore County domestic assault unit developed its own list of repeat call locations. After the Minneapolis study noted earlier, the police department formed a five-officer unit to address crime problems at the most crime-ridden locations. In Houston, the police and Hispanic citizens were concerned about violence at cantinas. Through repeat call analysis, police learned that only 3 percent of the cantinas in the city were responsible for 40 percent of the violence. The data narrowed the scope of the problem and enabled a special liquor control squad to better target its efforts (Spelman, 1988).

Repeat alarm calls are another example of how CAD data can be used to support patrol officer problem solving. In fact, when the Baltimore County experiment began, some commanders preferred that officers start with alarm projects. There were several reasons for this. Data documenting repeat alarm calls by address were readily available. Commanders anticipated that solving alarm problems would be relatively simple, and that the benefits compared to the investment of time would be significant.

As in many jurisdictions, alarms were priority calls requiring an immediate response by two officers. At least 90 percent of commercial alarm calls were false alarms, generated by faulty equipment or employee error. Officers used CAD printouts to identify repeat alarm addresses; or, when they had already identified these addresses from their own experience, they requested the CAD printouts to use in their follow-up discussions with merchants. Few alarm problems took more than two hours of any officer's time to resolve, and all merchants contacted either eliminated or greatly reduced the number of false alarm calls from their establishments.

Crime Mapping

Traditional pin maps can aid police work by graphically representing crime locations; but with a high volume of crimes, they are too time-consuming to put together and update. Computer-generated crime maps can now display more information, do it more quickly, and present it in an easy-to-read format.

One sophisticated crime analysis and mapping system was developed by the Illinois Criminal Justice Information Authority under a grant from the Bureau of Justice Statistics. It involves a group of computer programs and analytical methods for detecting community crime patterns, and uses time as well as geographic data. Areas ranging from a city block to an entire town can be examined, and spot maps can be produced seconds after an incident has been entered into the computer (Illinois Criminal Justice Information Authority, 1987).

Another system developed in the Chicago Police Department's 25th district generates graphs, maps, and reports using crime data from both police and citizens. The Microcomputer Assisted Patrol Analysis and Deployment System (MAPADS) was funded by the National Institute of Justice and developed by the Chicago Police Department, University of Illinois, Northwestern University, the Chicago Alliance for Neighborhood Safety (CANS), and Apple Computer, Inc.

Input from citizens is obtained through CANS, a nonprofit organization comprised of many local community groups. CANS collects two types of data from citizens. The first is data on "incivilities" and quality of life concerns that do not usually require police intervention (e.g., youth loitering, abandoned buildings, noisy parties). The second is data on crime concerns about which police often lack good intelligence (e.g., gang and narcotics activity). One of the specific purposes of MAPADS is to "determine target areas for community based/problem oriented policing" (Casey & Muslik, 1988).

COMMUNITY GROUPS

Problem solving involves soliciting information from community groups and involving citizens in solving their own problems. Both police and scholars concerned with community organizations are still trying to answer two key questions: How can local organizations be encouraged to adopt a crime-fighting agenda; and how can new anticrime groups be developed in areas that have none? (Skogan, 1989).

One obvious source of information about problems is Neighborhood Watch. However, there are some limitations on this source. Considerable evidence suggests that anticrime groups like Neighborhood Watch are most likely to flourish in middle-class communities with moderate crime problems. In affluent and low-crime areas, citizens see little reason to organize in this way. At the other extreme, fear and distrust among neighbors in crime-ridden neighborhoods may paralyze collective action.

There are many accounts in the community policing literature of officers working closely with other types of citizen groups. These include civic associations, tenant groups in private apartment complexes and public housing areas, business organizations, parent-teacher organizations, churches, and issue-oriented advocacy groups such as Mothers Against Drunk Driving (MADD).

In Dallas, Operation CLEAN (Community and Law Enforcement Against Narcotics) provides one example of how police, public and private agencies, clergy, and community groups can combine efforts to combat drug problems. Based on police information and citizen complaints of high-profile drug trafficking, an area as small as one block is targeted. Next, narcotics officers are assigned to the area for about ten days. A police sweep is then made to provide immediate relief, followed by two weeks of 24-hour, intensified patrol. During the next six weeks, other city agencies begin rehabilitation, code enforcement, and demolition of unsalvageable properties.

Finally, a long-range rehabilitation process begins. This has involved such efforts as calling on ministerial alliances to assist agencies and counsel residents, obtaining corporate sponsors to "adopt a block," pursuing park department funds for after-school programs in a park, and moving church-donated houses into neighborhoods (Vines, 1989).

There are several cautions to keep in mind when working with community groups to identify problems. First, the group's priorities may not be those of the neighborhood as a whole. Second, the group's members are not necessarily representative of all those who would be affected by proposed solutions. Third, police who encourage input from citizens must be careful not to raise expectations that the problems identified will be solved immediately.

Fourth, information provided at citizen group meetings—like a report from a single citizen or an informant—usually needs to be expanded or corroborated. Much of this work may be done during the analysis phase of the problem-solving process. However, some initial information gathering is advisable to determine the scope of the problem. Police may do this by observing problem locations at various times of day and days of the week; using various types of traditional investigative techniques; holding a special neighborhood meeting on the situation; or conducting a survey.

Finally, a department's commitment to community policing suggests that a greater number of patrol officers—not just crime prevention or community relations specialists—will be expected to participate in community meetings. Police may also organize their own ad hoc groups around a particular crime problem. The group may disband when the problem is resolved, or it may continue to bring concerns to police attention. Police departments need to ensure that officers who organize or participate in community meetings are well prepared. Officers may benefit from training to develop skills in group process and facilitation. Experienced community relations, public information, or crime prevention officers may be able to assist, either by providing in-service training sessions, or in less formal ways. For example, in Baltimore County, two officers' efforts to restore an abandoned playground culminated in their having to present their proposal to a recreation department committee. To sharpen their oral presentation, the officers consulted with the precinct's administrative sergeant, who had many years' experience speaking before similar groups.

SURVEYS

There are a number of ways in which officers may conduct surveys to identify or clarify problems. For example, an officer may canvass all the business proprietors in a strip shopping center on his or her beat. The community policing approach encourages this type of face-to-face, proactive contact with merchants.

A variation on this theme occurred during the Baltimore County experiment. One officer was charged with telephoning businesses to update the department's after-hours business contact cards. Although he did not conduct a formal survey, he used this task to also inquire about problems the owners might want to bring to police attention.

On a somewhat larger scale, a team of officers may survey residents of a housing complex or neighborhood known to have particular crime problems. The survey could be of value in determining residents' priority concerns, gaining specific information about trouble spots, and learning more about residents' expectations of police. The process may also help officers identify allies and community leaders who can aid in solving the problems identified.[2] Residents may be more likely to contact the police about future problems when officers leave their cards and encourage residents to call them directly. A survey can also present a public relations opportunity for the department when officers inform citizens of the agency's new community policing objectives.

Another approach to the survey process involves developing a beat profile. In Tempe, Arizona, a special community policing squad began by conducting a detailed profile of a target beat. Surveys conducted by squad members involved both door-to-door surveys of residents and businesses and detailed observations of the environment. A survey instrument was developed and pilot tested, and all survey team members were trained and given a uniform protocol to follow. The survey instrument included questions about socio-demographic characteristics of residents, observed crime and drug problems, fear of crime, perception of city and police services, willingness to participate in and support community policing objectives, and other information.

Survey team members also recorded information about the surroundings—condition of buildings, homes, streets, and yards; presence of abandoned vehicles; possible zoning and other code violations; and existence of such problems as graffiti, trash, loiterers, gang members, and other signs of disorder. All the information obtained from the surveys and observation reports is being entered into a microcomputer and will be analyzed for trends and patterns. The information will also provide evaluators with "before" data needed to assess the impact of the Tempe community policing project.[3]

As noted earlier, officer surveys can also be conducted to clarify the scope of known problems. For example, in Baltimore County, a business proprietor called police about a shoplifting problem. By conducting a brief survey of other merchants in the shopping center, police learned that none of the other businesses had this problem. The solution, therefore, was a simple one that involved advising a single merchant on how to improve security.

In another Baltimore County project, a resident frequently called police about noisy customers at an all-night, self-service car wash. Officers conducted a door-to-door survey of other residents adjacent to the business. They learned that the vast majority were also disturbed by the situation. The solution involved several neighbors meeting with police, the business owner, zoning personnel, and others to negotiate construction of a sound barrier.

Finally, in connection with a department-wide shift to community policing, administrators may consider conducting a large-scale community survey to identify specific problems. This effort would differ from surveys that focus on police performance, citizen attitudes about the police, or victimization. A starting point might be to review the work done by the Lansing, Michigan, Police Department in cooperation with the National Neighborhood Foot Patrol Center. The Lansing Police Department Community Survey asks citizens to prioritize police services, functions, and responses to crime (Trojanowicz et al., 1987). The survey has a few drawbacks, however. It is a written survey that requires a fairly high reading level, and it does not ask about specific concerns. A survey that gathered more specific information about problems could prove useful in developing responsive community policing policies and programs (Patterson & Grant, 1988).

OTHER INFORMATION SOURCES

There is probably no special unit in a department that could not assist patrol officers to some degree with problem identification. The difficulty lies in tapping into this information. In small departments, the process for doing so may be quite informal. Larger agencies may want to consider developing processes, forms, and referral guidelines. Special units and divisions that contributed to problem identification in Baltimore County and Newport News included the office of the chief, crime analysis, crime prevention, community relations, detectives, vice/narcotics, communications and dispatch, and others.

Television, newspaper, and other media reports can be another source of information about community problems, and can help police identify organizations and individuals who may be allies in efforts to solve them.

Letters to the editor, editorials, and op-ed columns should not be over-looked, and media coverage of national or regional events can suggest problems that may be of local concern as well. Some departments may find it useful to maintain a clippings file, which can be used to suggest possible problem-solving projects. Maintaining such a file would be an appropriate task for department volunteers.

In summary, information sources about community problems are virtually unlimited for officers with initiative, creativity, and a commitment to the problem-solving approach. Conducting a formal survey may not be possible for all officers, but most can take advantage of a coffee break to ask a convenience store manager about problems, or stop and talk for a minute with a playground supervisor. In Tempe, some members of the community policing squad have begun to have lunch with schoolteachers on a regular basis. Simply by looking around an elementary school cafeteria, they saw that many new ethnic groups were represented, an observation that may help them anticipate changes in the community. As part of problem-solving training in Baltimore County, COPE officers assisted in preparing a checklist of resources that officers might use to gain information about problems. Such a list might include other law enforcement agencies; schools; churches and church councils; elected officials and other community leaders; local government agencies; nonprofit human service youth and recreation programs; business groups; local service clubs; and many others.

TYPES OF PROBLEMS APPROPRIATE FOR PATROL PROBLEM SOLVING

There does not appear to be any inherent limit on the types of problems patrol officers can work on successfully. If the problem is identified as being of concern to the community and the police, then it is legitimate to have a patrol officer address the problem (or in some instances, bring it to the attention of a special unit).

Officers can be expected to identify both crime and disorder problems. In Baltimore County, there was an emphasis on disorder problems, perhaps because problem solving was closely linked to community policing. To many of the officers and supervisors interviewed, community policing meant focusing on non-crime concerns. The training for patrol officers also placed considerable emphasis on building links with other agencies, residents, and business people. The applicability of problem solving to major crime problems was not as obvious, and was not emphasized by administrators or supervisors. In addition, Baltimore County has many special units designed to address crime problems.

If disorder and other quality-of-life problems are the most frequent types of problems in an area, and citizens are more concerned about them, then an emphasis on these problems seems well placed. However, this would not preclude applying a problem-solving approach to major crime problems. The list that follows demonstrates the diversity of problems identified and addressed in several jurisdictions.

EXAMPLES OF CRIME AND DISTURBANCE PROBLEMS

Some of the problems identified in Baltimore County included:

- A series of burglaries from trailers at a construction site

- Drug activity, drinking, and disorderly conduct at a community park

- Auto thefts at a shopping plaza

- Suspected drug activity at a private residence

- Thefts from autos at a shopping mall

- Large groups of young people drinking and trespassing at a quarry

- Juveniles loitering at a shopping center

- Juveniles loitering near a bar

- Adults drinking in public outside a tavern

- Vagrants panhandling at a shopping center

- Problems with false and faulty alarms at commercial addresses

- Conflicts within families

- Parking and traffic problems

Early problem-solving projects in Newport News, Virginia, included the following:

- Street prostitution and related robberies in a downtown neighborhood

- Thefts from autos at a parking lot used by employees of a shipbuilding company

- A high rate of burglaries at a run-down apartment complex

- Repeat domestic assault calls to certain addresses

In a project conducted by PERF for the Bureau of Justice Assistance, five police departments agreed to apply the problem-solving approach to drug crimes. The following are typical of the drug-related problems identified:

- Abandoned cars on public housing property created an eyesore and were used to stash drugs (Tampa)

- Repeat calls over a period of years involved drugs and violence at a private residence (San Diego)

- The absentee owner of a pool hall allowed drug-related activity and illegal gambling on the premises (San Diego)

- Poor outdoor lighting at a public housing complex facilitated street drug sales (Tampa)

- Juveniles sold drugs at a public housing complex (Tulsa)

- Repeat thefts from autos by a crack addict (Philadelphia) (Weisel, 1990).

As the list above suggests, few if any crime or disorder problems would be categorically inappropriate for patrol problem solving. Of course, some problems initially identified may need to be screened out for a variety of reasons. For example, the department may be addressing a problem at the administrative level, a special unit may be assigned exclusive responsibility for a particular type of problem, or a reported problem cannot be corroborated. But the experience of many departments suggests that officers, given enough support from the department, can successfully tackle problems ranging from double parking to homicide prevention.

SUMMARY

Community policing has been promoted as both a new approach to police work, and as a return to the good old days when officers knew the people they served. Either way, it involves improving a department's responsiveness to the law enforcement needs of a diverse community. It also involves listening more carefully to how the community defines those needs.

The obvious first step in this process is identifying crime and disorder problems that are of mutual concern to both the police and some portion of the public. On the surface, identifying problems should be an easy task for police. But for many officers, major problem means major crime. Indeed, much of their training involves preparing for the dangerous but relatively rare incident. Understandably, they may distrust the department's community policing approach, with its new emphasis on such citizen concerns as "incivilities" and signs of neighborhood decline.

Police departments vary in the resources they can provide to support problem identification. Large departments like Chicago have developed sophisticated computer-aided crime mapping systems; other departments may work with a university to analyze large call-for-service databases. Yet many sources of information about problems exist in even the smallest departments—officer knowledge and observation, citizen complaints, police reports and call data, surveys, information from community groups, and many others.

In addition to information sources, officers must have sufficient blocks of time to identify and work on problems. Before department-wide community policing can succeed, the agency will need to evaluate whether it is doing all it can to relieve officers of duties that do not require sworn authority. But the problem-solving experiences in Baltimore County and Newport News suggest that leadership—from the top, of course, but particularly at the precinct commander and supervisory levels—is even more important than time for ensuring that officers become actively involved in identifying and solving community problems.

Well-developed efforts to strengthen the police-community partnership must adapt and employ some type of systematic way to identify, analyze, and resolve problems. Comprehensive evaluations of community policing strategies—however necessary they may be—are expensive and lengthy propositions. There are other ways in which researchers might use their expertise to aid and shed light on what appears to qualify as a nationwide movement toward community policing. This article summarizes a range of methods that police can use to identify problems. There is much that remains to be discovered and communicated about the pros and cons of these methods and how to make them more effective.

Community surveys, for example, are of interest to many police agencies, yet they can be misused as well as useful. Experiences with crime mapping need to be explored more fully. The difficulties involved in using call-for-service data for identifying problems or in obtaining useful information from community groups have only been hinted at here. Exploring these and other problem identification methods in-depth could be of tremendous value to the field as police departments attempt to develop new ways of thinking about crime and community problems.

NOTES

1. Recent patrol resource allocation studies by ILJ have concluded that departments committed to community policing should set a goal of having officers spend about 35 to 40 percent of their time on community policing activities, including problem solving. This would allow for sufficient blocks of time to perform meaningful tasks, and would leave about one-third of patrol time for responding to calls and another third for other duties (court appearances, roll call, training, meals, etc.).
2. For an example of this type of survey process, see William H. Lindsey and Bruce Quint, *The Oasis Technique*, Fort Lauderdale, Florida, Florida Atlantic University/Florida International University Joint Center for Environmental and Urban Problems, 1986.
3. ILJ is currently studying the Tempe community policing project for the U.S. Department of Justice, Bureau of Justice Assistance.

REFERENCES

Bayley, D. (1991). "The Best Defense." *Fresh Perspectives*. Washington, DC: Police Executive Research Forum.

Brown, L. (1989). "Community Policing: A Practical Guide for Police Officials." *Police Chief*. Arlington, VA: International Association of Chiefs of Police (August).

Casey, M. and M. Buslik (1988). *Computerized Decision Support: Innovative Policing in Chicago*. Chicago, IL: Police Department (September).

Cordner, G. (1985). *The Baltimore County Citizen Oriented Police Enforcement (COPE) Project: Final Evaluation*. Baltimore County, MD: Police Department.

Eck, J. and W. Spelman (1987). *Problem-Solving: Problem-Oriented Policing in Newport News*. Washington, DC: National Institute of Justice.

Farrell, M. (1988). "The Development of the Community Patrol Officer Program: Community-Oriented Policing in the New York City Police Department." In J. Greene and S. Mastrofski (eds.), *Community Policing: Rhetoric or Reality?* New York: Praeger Publishers.

Goldstein, H. (1979). "Improving Policing: A Problem-Oriented Approach." *Crime and Delinquency*, 25.

Goldstein, H. (1990a). "Remarks." Police Executive Research Forum National Conference on Problem Oriented Policing. San Diego, CA (November).

Goldstein, H. (1990b). "Does Community Policing Work?" *The New York Times*, December 20:E11.

Goldstein, H. (1990c). *Problem-Oriented Policing*. New York: McGraw-Hill, Inc.

Hayeslip, D. and G. Cordner (1987). "The Effects of Community-Oriented Patrol on Police Officer Attitudes." *American Journal of Police*, 6(1).

Illinois Criminal Justice Information Authority (1987). "Spatial and Temporal Analysis of Crime." *Research Bulletin*, (April).

Koller, K. (1990). *Working the Beat*. Edmonton, Canada: Edmonton Police Service.

McEwen, J. et al. (1991). *1990 National Assessment Survey of Criminal Justice Agencies: Final Report*. Washington, DC: National Institute of Justice.

McEwen, J. et al. (1986). *Evaluation of the Differential Police Response Field Test*. Washington, DC: National Institute of Justice.

Mitchell, W. (1990). "Problem-Oriented Policing and Drug Enforcement in Newport News." *Public Management*. Washington, DC: International City Managers Association (July).

Montgomery County Police, Community Policing Project (1990). *An Overview of Community Policing*. Montgomery County, MD: Police Department.

New York City Police Department and Vera Institute of Justice, (1988). *The Community Patrol Officer Program Problem-Solving Guide*. New York: Police Department (September).

Pate, A. (1986). *Reducing Fear of Crime in Houston and Newark: A Summary Report*. Washington, DC: Police Foundation.

Patterson, R., Jr. and N. Grant (1988). "Community Mapping: Rationale and Considerations for Implementation." *Journal of Police Science and Administration*, 16(2).

Portland Police Bureau (1990). *Community Policing Transition Plan*. Portland, OR: Police Bureau.

Reiss, A. (1985). *Policing a City's Central District: The Oakland Story*. Washington, DC: National Institute of Justice.

Seattle Police Department, Planning Section (1990). *Community Policing in Seattle: A Descriptive Study of the South Seattle Crime Reduction Project*. Seattle, WA: Police Department.

Sherman, L. (1989). "Hot Spots of Predatory Crime: Routine Activities and the Criminology of Place." *Criminology*, 27(1).

Skogan, W. (1989). "Communities, Crime, and Neighborhood Organization." *Crime and Delinquency*, 35(3).

Sparrow, M. (1988). "Implementing Community Policing." *Perspectives on Policing*. Washington, DC: National Institute of Justice and the John F. Kennedy School of Government, Harvard University.

Spelman, W. (1988). *Beyond Bean Counting: New Approaches for Managing Crime Data*. Washington, DC: Police Executive Research Forum.

Tempe Police Department (1991). *Master Plan for Community Policing*. Tempe, AZ: Police Department.

Trojanowicz, R. (1987). *Community Policing: Community Input into Police Policy-Making*. East Lansing, MI: National Neighborhood Foot Patrol Center.

Trojanowicz, R. and B. Bucqueroux (1990). *Community Policing: A Contemporary Perspective*. Cincinnati, OH: Anderson Publishing Co.

Vines, M. (1989). "City of Dallas Implements Operation CLEAN." *NCTAP News*. Alexandria, VA: Institute for Law and Justice, 3(2): August.

Webster, B. (1989). *Evaluation of Community Crime/Problem Resolution Through Police Directed Patrol*. Final report to the National Institute of Justice.

Weisel, D. (1990). *Tackling Drug Problems in Public Housing: A Guide for Police*. Washington, DC: Police Executive Research Forum.

Wilson, J. and G. Kelling (1982). "The Police and Neighborhood Safety: Broken Windows." *Atlantic Monthly* (March).

Wilson, J. and G. Kelling (1989). "Making Neighborhoods Safe." *Atlantic Monthly* (February).

COMMUNITY POLICING:
ELEMENTS AND EFFECTS   22

Gary W. Cordner

In little more than a decade, community policing has evolved from a few foot patrol experiments to a comprehensive organizational strategy guiding modern police departments.[1] It is now seen almost universally as the most effective method available for improving police-community relations. Proponents also believe that it will ultimately prove to be an effective crime control strategy. Indicative of its stature in the 1990s, community policing is required of the 100,000 new police officers funded by the Crime Bill passed in 1994 by the U.S. Congress.

Four complicating factors have made it extremely difficult to determine the effectiveness of community policing, however:

- *Programmatic complexity*—There exists no single definition of community policing nor any mandatory set of program elements. Police agencies around the country (and around the world) have implemented a wide array of organizational and operational innovations under the label "community policing." Because community policing is not one consistent "thing," it is difficult to say whether "it" works.

- *Multiple effects*—The number of intended and unintended effects that might accrue to community policing is considerable. Community policing might affect crime, fear of crime, disorder, community relations, and/or police officer attitudes, to mention just a few plausible impacts. The existence of these multiple effects, as opposed to a single bottom-line criterion, severely reduces the likelihood of a simple yes or no answer to the question "Does community policing work?"

Source: Gary W. Cordner (1995). "Community Policing: Elements and Effects." *Police Forum*, 5(3): 1-8. Reprinted by permission of the Academy of Criminal Justice Sciences.

- *Variation in program scope*—The scope of community policing projects has varied from single-officer assignments to department-wide efforts. Some of the most positive results have come from projects that involved only a few specialist officers, small special units, or narrowly defined target areas. The generalizability of these positive results to full-scale department-wide implementation is problematic.

- *Research design limitations*—Despite heroic efforts by police officials and researchers, most community policing studies have had serious research design limitations. These include lack of control groups, failure to randomize treatments, and a tendency to measure only short-term effects. Consequently, the findings of many community policing studies do not have as much credibility as we might hope.

These complicating factors are offered not as excuses but rather to sensitize the reader to the very real difficulty of producing reliable knowledge about the effects of community policing. Additionally, they identify priority issues that such agencies as the National Institute of Justice and the Office of Community-Oriented Policing Services have addressed and are continuing to address.

WHAT IS COMMUNITY POLICING?

Community policing remains many things to many people. A common refrain among proponents is "Community policing is a philosophy, not a program." An equally common refrain among police officers is "Just tell me exactly what you want me to do differently." Some critics, echoing concerns similar to those expressed by police officers, argue that if community policing is nothing more than a philosophy, it is but an empty shell (Goldstein, 1987).

It would be easy to list several dozen common elements of community policing, starting with foot patrol and mountain bikes and ending with the police as organizers of, and advocates for, the poor and dispossessed. Instead, it may be more helpful to identify three major dimensions of community policing and the most common developments occurring within each. The three are:

- The Philosophical Dimension

- The Strategic Dimension

- The Programmatic Dimension

THE PHILOSOPHICAL DIMENSION

Many of its most thoughtful and forceful advocates emphasize that community policing is a new philosophy of policing, perhaps constituting even a paradigm shift away from professional-model policing. The philosophical dimension includes the central ideas and beliefs underlying community policing. Three of the most important of these are described below.

Broad Police Function. Community policing embraces a broad view of the police function rather than a narrow focus on crime fighting or law enforcement (Kelling and Moore, 1988). Historical evidence is often cited to show that the police function was originally quite broad and varied and that it only narrowed in recent decades, perhaps due to the influence of the professional model and popular media representations of police work. Social science data is also frequently cited to show that police officers actually spend relatively little of their time dealing with serious offenders or investigating violent crimes.

This broader view of the police function recognizes the kinds of non-enforcement tasks that police already perform and seeks to give them greater status and legitimacy. These include order maintenance, social service, and general assistance duties. They may also include greater responsibilities in protecting and enhancing "the lives of those who are most vulnerable—juveniles, the elderly, minorities, the poor, the disabled, the homeless" (Trojanowicz and Bucqueroux, 1990: xiv).

Citizen Input. Community policing takes the view that in a free society citizens should have open access to police organizations and input to police policies and decisions. Access and input through elected officials is considered necessary but not sufficient. Individual neighborhoods and communities should have the opportunity to influence how they are policed and legitimate interest groups in the community should be able to discuss their views and concerns directly with police officials.

Mechanisms for achieving greater citizen input are varied. Some police agencies use systematic and periodic community surveys to elicit citizen input (Bureau of Justice Assistance, 1994a). Others rely on open forums, town meetings, radio and television call-in programs, and similar methods open to all residents. Some police officials meet regularly with citizen advisory boards, ministry alliances, minority group representatives, business leaders, and other formal groups. These techniques have been used by police chief executives, district commanders, and ordinary patrol officers; they can be focused as widely as the entire jurisdiction or as narrowly as a beat or a single neighborhood.

The techniques used to achieve citizen input should be less important than the end result. Community policing emphasizes that police departments should seek and carefully consider citizen input when making policies and decisions that affect the community. Any other alternative would be unthinkable in an agency that is part of a government "of the people, for the people, and by the people."

Neighborhood Variation. Community policing supports differential enforcement and tailored policing based on local norms and values. An argument is made that the criminal law is a very blunt instrument and that police officers inevitably exercise wide discretion when making enforcement decisions. Presently, individual officers make arrest and other decisions based on a combination of legal, bureaucratic, and idiosyncratic criteria, while the police department maintains the myth of full or at least uniform enforcement (Goldstein, 1977). Under community policing, officers are asked to consider the "will of the community" when deciding which laws to enforce under what circumstances, and police executives are asked to tolerate and even encourage such differential policing.

Such differential or tailored policing primarily affects police handling of minor criminal offenses, local ordinance violations, and public disorder. Some kinds of behavior proscribed by state and local law, and some levels of noise and disorder, may be seen as less bothersome in some neighborhoods than in others. Similarly, some police methods, including such aggressive tactics as roadblocks and more prevention-oriented programs such as landlord training, may coincide with norms and values in some neighborhoods but not others.

Even the strongest advocates of community policing recognize that a balance must be reached between differential neighborhood-level policing and uniform jurisdiction-wide policing. Some crimes are so serious and some laws are so important that localized toleration in their policing would not be acceptable. Additionally, many aspects of police behavior are governed by constitutional, statutory, and case law; it would not be proper for police to act illegally or unconstitutionally just because they had community support for such behavior. Police executives also have a professional duty to run their agencies in ways that produce effective, efficient, and ethical police behavior; this responsibility sometimes conflicts with citizens' preferences and desires.

Striking a healthy and satisfactory balance between competing interests has always been one of the central concerns of policing and police administration. Community policing simply argues that neighborhood-level norms and values should be added to the mix of legal, professional, and organizational considerations that influences decision-making about policies, programs, and resources at the executive level as well as enforcement-level decisions on the street.

THE STRATEGIC DIMENSION

The strategic dimension of community policing includes the key operational concepts that translate philosophy into action. These strategic concepts are the links between the broad ideas and beliefs that underlie community policing and the specific programs and practices by which it is implemented.

Geographic Focus. Community policing strategy emphasizes the geographic basis of assignment and responsibility by shifting the fundamental unit of patrol accountability from time of day to place. That is, rather than holding patrol officers, supervisors, and shift commanders responsible for wide areas but only during their eight or ten hour shifts, community policing seeks to establish 24-hour responsibility for smaller areas.

Of course, no single officer works 24 hours a day, seven days a week, week in and week out. Community policing usually deals with this limitation in one or a combination of three ways: (1) community police officers assigned to neighborhoods may be specialists, with most call-handling relegated to a more traditional patrol unit; (2) each individual patrol officer may be held responsible for long-term problem solving in an assigned neighborhood, even though s/he handles calls in a much larger area and, of necessity, many of the calls in the assigned area are handled by other officers; or (3) small teams of officers share both call-handling and problem solving responsibility in a beat-sized area.

A key ingredient of this geographic focus, however it is implemented, is permanency of assignment. Community policing recommends that patrol officers be assigned to the same areas for extended periods of time, to increase their familiarity with the community and the community's familiarity with them. Ideally, this familiarity will build trust, confidence, and cooperation on both sides of the police-citizen interaction. Also, officers will simply become more knowledgeable about the community and its residents, aiding early intervention and timely problem identification and avoiding conflict based on misperception or misunderstanding.

It is important to recognize that most police departments have long used geography as the basis for daily patrol assignment. Many of these departments, however, assign patrol officers to different beats from one day to the next, creating little continuity or permanency. Moreover, even in police agencies with fairly steady beat assignments, patrol officers are only held accountable for handling their calls and maintaining order (keeping things quiet) *during their shift*. The citizen's question, "Who in the police department is responsible for *my area*, my neighborhood?" can then only truthfully be answered "the chief" or, in large departments, "the precinct commander." Neither patrol officers nor the two or three levels of management above them can be held accountable for dealing with long-term problems in any specific locations in the entire community. Thus, a crucial component of community policing strategy is to create some degree of geographic accountability at all levels in the police organization, but particularly at the level of the patrol officer who delivers basic police services and is in a position to identify and solve neighborhood problems.

Prevention Focus. Community policing strategy also emphasizes a more proactive and preventive orientation, in contrast to the reactive focus that has characterized much of policing under the professional model. This proactive, preventive orientation takes several forms. One is simply to encourage better use of police officers' time. In many police departments, patrol officers' time not committed to handling calls is either spent simply waiting for the next call or randomly driving around. Under community policing, this substantial resource of free patrol time is devoted to directed enforcement activities, specific crime prevention efforts, problem solving, community engagement, citizen interaction, or similar kinds of activities.

Another aspect of the preventive focus overlaps with the substantive focus of community policing and with problem-oriented operations. Officers are encouraged to look beyond the individual incidents that they encounter as calls for service and reported crimes in order to discover underlying problems and conditions (Eck and Spelman, 1987). If they can discover such underlying conditions and do something to improve them, officers can prevent the future recurrence of incidents and calls. While immediate response to in-progress emergencies and after-the-fact investigation of crimes will always remain important functions of policing, community policing seeks to elevate before-the-fact prevention and problem-solving to comparable status.

Closely related to this line of thinking, but deserving of specific mention, is the desire to enhance the status of crime prevention within police organizations. Most police departments devote the vast majority of their personnel to patrol and investigations, primarily for the purposes of rapid response and follow-up investigation *after* something has happened. Granted, some prevention of crime through the visibility, omnipresence, and deterrence created by patrolling, rapid response, and investigating is expected, but the weight of research over the past two decades has greatly diminished these expectations (Kelling, Pate, Dieckman, and Brown, 1974; Greenwood and Petersilia, 1975; Spelman and Brown, 1982). Despite these lowered expectations, however, police departments still typically devote only a few officers specifically to crime prevention programming, and do little to encourage patrol officers to engage in any kinds of crime prevention activity beyond routine riding around.

Moreover, within both informal and formal police cultures, crime solving and criminal apprehension are usually more highly valued than crime prevention. An individual officer is more likely to be commended for arresting a bank robber than for initiating actions that prevent such robberies. Detectives usually enjoy higher status than uniformed officers (especially in the eyes of the public), whereas, within many police agencies, crime prevention officers are seen as public relations functionaries, kiddie cops, or worse. To many police officers, crime prevention work is simply not real police work.

The preeminence of reactive crime fighting within police and popular cultures is understandable, given the dramatic nature of emergencies, crimes, and investigations. Much of police work is about responding to trouble and fixing it, about the contest between good and evil. Responding to emergencies and fighting crime have heroic elements that naturally appeal to both police officers and citizens. Given the choice, though, almost all citizens would prefer not being victimized in the first place to being dramatically rescued, to having the police successfully track down their assailant, or to having the police recover their stolen property. Most citizens would agree that "an ounce of prevention is worth a pound of cure." This is not to suggest that police should turn their backs on reactive handling of crimes and emergencies, but only that before-the-fact prevention should be given greater consideration.

A final element of community policing's preventive focus takes more of a social welfare orientation, particularly toward juveniles. An argument is made that police officers, by serving as mentors and role models, and by providing educational, recreational, and even counseling services, can affect peoples' behavior in positive ways that ultimately lead to reductions in crime and disorder. In essence, police are asked to support and augment the efforts of families, churches, schools, and other social service agencies. This kind of police activity is seen as particularly necessary by some in order to offset the deficiencies and correct the failures of these other social institutions in modern America.

Substantive Focus. The third key element of community policing strategy is a more careful and deliberate focus on substantive problems in the community (Goldstein, 1990). This substantive focus stands in contrast to three interrelated tendencies of professional model policing: (1) a tendency to regard law enforcement as *the* end of policing rather than as one of several means available to police officers; (2) a tendency to focus more attention on the process of policing than on substantive problems and outcomes; and (3) a tendency to focus more attention on administrative issues within police organizations than on substantive problems in the community.

Confusion in modern policing over the role of law enforcement reflects a common organizational pathology called goal displacement by which, over time, favored methods come to be seen as ends in themselves. To overcome this confusion, community policing emphasizes that in our society the law is but a means to the greater ends of life, liberty, and the pursuit of happiness. The particular ends of policing tie in to these societal goals and relate to the protection of life and property, the maintenance of public order, and the protection of individual rights. One of the primary *tools* given to police for accomplishing these ends is the law and its enforcement—use of this tool has no great value in its own right, however, except as it contributes to protection of life and property, maintenance of order, and protection of rights.

This distinction between means and ends has very significant practical implications. It reminds us, for example, that the best police department is *not* necessarily the one that enforces the law the most but rather the one that provides the best protection and order. Similarly, the best officers are not necessarily those who make the most arrests and issue the most tickets, but rather the ones who are most successful in controlling crime, maintaining order, and improving traffic safety in their assigned areas.

The distinction between means and ends also directs attention to the other means, besides law enforcement, that are available to police officers. The simple recognition that law enforcement is but one of several methods available to police officers then leads to the realization that effectiveness in policing requires choosing, in each instance, that method which maximizes attainment of police goals and objectives and adherence to important police values. This conception of policing not simply as law enforcement but rather as decision making has important implications for the selection, training, supervision, and evaluation of police officers.

Thinking of policing as involving choosing the most effective method for handling a situation or solving a problem also points out the need to focus greater attention on substance rather than process. That is, the body of policing knowledge that has been most highly developed and transmitted through formal education and training emphasizes the processes of call handling, reporting, mediating, enforcing, and investigating and largely ignores both information about substantive problems (e.g., domestic violence, drug abuse, fear of crime) and information about what works best in handling such problems. To be effective decision makers, however, police officers need information about substantive problems and about what works as well as skills to assist them in diagnosing and analyzing situations and selecting the most appropriate responses.

Police administrators similarly need to shift the focus of their attention. Under the professional model, the preeminent concern of police executives was seen as overseeing the efficient operation of the police department. Attention was directed inward toward the workings of the police organization itself. As a consequence of this focus, police management training and education came to be dominated by consideration of the processes of administration, with near total disregard for either the work performed by police officers or the substantive problems that police departments are expected to address. Without denigrating the importance of efficient administration, community policing emphasizes that the primary focus of police executives should be on the accomplishment of the police mission. This requires that police executives spend more time looking outward toward the substantive problems in the community and that they worry as much about effectiveness as about efficiency.

THE PROGRAMMATIC DIMENSION

The programmatic dimension of community policing ultimately translates ideas, philosophies, and strategies into concrete programs, tactics, and behaviors. Even those who insist that "community policing is a philosophy, not a program" must concede that unless community policing eventually leads to some action, some new or different behavior, it is all rhetoric and no reality (Greene and Mastrofski, 1988). Indeed, many commentators have taken the view that community policing is little more than a new police marketing strategy that has left the core elements of the police role untouched (see, e.g., Klockars, 1988; Manning, 1988; Weatheritt, 1988).

Reoriented Police Operations. An essential programmatic feature of community policing is a reorientation of police operations that entails less reliance on random motorized patrol, immediate response to all calls for service, and follow-up investigations by detectives. Studies over the past two decades have convincingly demonstrated the limitations of these traditional police practices and have suggested some promising alternatives.

Many police departments today have increased their use of foot patrol, directed patrol, door-to-door policing, and other alternatives to traditional motorized patrol (Cordner and Trojanowicz, 1992). Generally, these alternatives seek more targeted tactical effectiveness, more attention to minor offenses and "incivilities," a greater "felt presence" of police, and/or more police-citizen contact. Other police departments have simply reduced their commitment to any form of continuous patrolling, preferring instead to have their patrol officers engage in problem solving, crime prevention, and similar activities when not handling calls and emergencies.

Many police agencies have also adopted differential responses to calls for service (McEwen, Connors, and Cohen, 1986). Rather than attempting to immediately dispatch a sworn officer in response to each and every notification of a crime, disturbance, or other situation, these departments vary their responses depending upon the circumstances. Some crime reports may be taken over the telephone, some service requests may be referred to other government agencies, and some sworn officer responses may be delayed. A particularly interesting alternative is to ask complainants to go in person to a nearby police mini-station or storefront office, where an officer, a civilian employee, or even a volunteer takes a report or provides other in-person assistance. Use of differential responses helps departments cope with the sometimes overwhelming burden of 9-1-1 calls and frees up patrol officer time for other activities, such as patrolling, problem solving, and crime prevention.

Traditional criminal investigation has also been reexamined in recent years (Eck, 1992). Some departments have de-specialized the activity, reducing the size of the detective unit and making patrol officers more responsible for follow-up investigations. Many have also eliminated the practice of conducting an extensive follow-up investigation of every reported crime, focusing instead on the more serious offenses and on more "solvable" cases. Investigative attention has also been expanded to include a focus on offenders as well as on offenses, especially in the form of repeat offender units that target high-frequency serious offenders. A few departments have taken the additional step of trying to get detectives to expand their case-by-case orientation to include problem solving and crime prevention. In this approach, a burglary detective would be as concerned with reducing burglaries through problem solving and crime prevention as s/he was with solving particular burglary cases.

Not all contemporary alternatives to motorized patrol, rapid response, and criminal investigation are closely allied with community policing. Those specific operational alternatives, and those uses of the freed-up time of patrol officers and detectives, that are consistent with the philosophical and strategic foundations of community policing should be distinguished from those that conform to other philosophies and strategies of policing (Moore and Trojanowicz, 1988).

Problem Solving. Supporters of community policing are convinced that the very nature of police work must be altered from its present incident-by-incident, case-by-case orientation to one that is more problem-oriented (Goldstein, 1990). Certainly, incidents must still be handled and cases must still be investigated. Whenever possible, however, attention should be directed toward underlying problems and conditions. Following the medical analogy, policing should address causes as well as symptoms, and should adopt the epidemiological public health approach as much as the individual doctor's clinical approach.

This problem solving approach should be characterized by several important features: (1) it should be the standard operating method of policing, not an occasional special project; (2) it should be practiced by personnel throughout the ranks, not just by specialists or managers; (3) it should be empirical, in the sense that decisions are made on the basis of information that is gathered systematically; (4) it should involve, whenever possible, collaboration between police and other agencies and institutions; and (5) it should incorporate, whenever possible, community input and participation, so that it is the community's problems that are addressed (not just the police department's) and so that the community shares in the responsibility for its own protection.

The problem solving process consists of four steps: (1) careful identification of the problem; (2) careful analysis of the problem; (3) a search for alternative solutions to the problem; and (4) implementation and assessment of a response to the problem. Community input can be incorporated within any or all of the steps in the process. Identification, analysis, and assessment should rely on information from multiple sources. A variety of alternative solutions should be considered, including, but not limited to, traditional enforcement methods. Typically, the most effective solutions are those that combine several different responses, including some that draw on more than just the police department's authority and resources.

A crucial characteristic of the problem-oriented approach is that it seeks tailored solutions to specific community problems. Arrests and law enforcement are *not* abandoned—rather, an effort is made in each situation to determine which alternative responses best fit the problem. Use of the criminal law is always considered, as are civil law enforcement, mediation, community mobilization, referral, collaboration, alteration of the physical environment, public education, and a host of other possibilities. The common sense notion of choosing the tool that best fits the problem, instead of simply grabbing the most convenient or familiar tool in the tool box, lies close to the heart of the problem solving method.

Community Engagement. Participation of the community in its own protection is one of the central elements of community policing (Bureau of Justice Assistance, 1994c). This participation can run the gamut from watching neighbors' homes to reporting drug dealers to patrolling the streets. It can involve participation in problem identification and problem solving efforts, in crime prevention programs, in neighborhood revitalization, and in youth-oriented educational and recreational programs. Citizens may act individually or in groups, they may collaborate with the police, and they may even join the police department by donating their time as police department volunteers, reserves, or auxiliaries.

Under community policing, police agencies are expected not only to cooperate with citizens and communities but to actively solicit input and participation (Bureau of Justice Assistance, 1994b). The exact nature of this participation can and should vary from community to community and from situation to situation, in keeping with the problem-oriented approach. As a general rule, though, police should avoid claiming that they alone can handle crime, drug, or disorder problems, and they should encourage individual citizens and community groups to shoulder some responsibility for dealing with such problems.

Police have sometimes found it necessary to engage in community organizing as a means of accomplishing any degree of citizen participation in problem solving or crime prevention. In disorganized and transient neighborhoods, residents are often so distressed, fearful, and suspicious of each other (or just so unfamiliar with their neighbors) that police have literally had to set about creating a sense of community where none previously existed. As difficult as this kind of community organizing can be, and as far from the conventional police role as this may seem, these are often the very communities that most need both enhanced police protection and a greater degree of citizen involvement in crime prevention, order maintenance, and general watchfulness over public spaces.

One vexing aspect of community organizing and community engagement results from the pluralistic nature of our society. Differing and often conflicting interests are found in many communities, and they are sometimes represented by competing interest groups. Thus, the elders in a community may want the police to crack down on juveniles, while the youths themselves complain of few opportunities for recreation or entertainment. Tenants may seek police help in organizing a rent strike, while landlords want police assistance in screening or managing the same tenants. Finding common interests around which to rally entire communities, or just identifying common interests on which to base police practices, can be very challenging and, at times, impossible.

It is important to recognize that this inherent feature of pluralistic communities does not arise because of community policing. Police have long been caught in the middle between the interests of adults and juveniles, landlords and tenants, and similar groups. Sometimes the law has provided a convenient reference point for handling such conflicts, but just as often police have had to mediate, arbitrate, or just take the side of the party with the best case. Moreover, when the law has offered a solution, it has frequently been a temporary or unpopular one, and one that still resulted in the police taking sides, protestations of "we're just enforcing the law" notwithstanding.

Fortunately, nearly all citizens want to be safe from violence, want their property protected, and want some level of orderliness in their neighborhoods. Officers can usually find enough consensus in communities upon which to base cooperative efforts aimed at improving safety and public order. Sometimes, apparently deep conflicts between individuals or groups recede when attention is focused on how best to solve specific neighborhood problems. It would be naive to expect overwhelming community consensus in every situation, but it is equally mistaken to think that conflict is so endemic that widespread community support and participation cannot be achieved in many circumstances.

WHAT DO WE KNOW?

Despite the programmatic and evaluation complexities discussed earlier, we do have a substantial amount of information from empirical studies of community policing. Table 22.1 summarizes the "preponderance of the evidence" on the effects of community policing based on a review of over 60 such studies (recent reviews have also been completed by Normandeau, 1993; Bennett, 1994; Leighton, 1994; and Skogan, 1994).

Table 22.1
Preponderance of the Evidence on Community Policing

Effects/ Dimensions	Crime	Fear	Disorder	Calls for Service	Community Relations	Police Officer Attitudes	Police Officer Behavior
Philosophical: Broad Police Function Citizen Input Neighborhood Variation	UNK	UNK	UNK	UNK	UNK	UNK	UNK
Strategic: Geographic Focus Preventive Focus Substantive Focus	UNK	UNK	UNK	UNK	UNK	UNK	UNK
Programmatic: Re-oriented Operations Problem Solving Community Engagement	MIX	MIX	POS	MIX	POS	POS	MIX

Legend: POS = positive effects (beneficial effects)
          NEG = negative effects
          MIX = mixed effects
          UNK = unknown (completely or substantially untested)

The first thing to note in Table 22.1 is that two-thirds of the 21 cells—all those in the top two rows—are labelled "unknown." Nearly all of the evaluations conducted to-date have focused on the programmatic dimension of community policing (the bottom row of the table), leaving us with little or no information on the effects of philosophical and strategic changes. This gap in community policing research is undoubtedly caused by a combination of two factors: (1) most community policing efforts, at least until recently, have been limited programmatic and street-level initiatives rather than large-scale strategic or organizational-change initiatives; and (2) evaluation of narrowly-focused programmatic initiatives is much easier and more feasible than evaluation of philosophical and organization-wide change.

The most useful way to summarize the evidence on the effects of community policing is to scan the bottom row of Table 22.1.

CRIME

The evidence is mixed. Only a few studies have used experimental designs and victimization surveys to test the effects of community policing on crime; many others have relied on simple before-after comparisons of reported crime or single-item victimization questions drawn from community surveys. Overall, a slight majority of the studies have detected crime decreases, giving reason for optimism, but evaluation design limitations prevent us from drawing any authoritative conclusions.

FEAR OF CRIME

Again the evidence is mixed, but it leans more heavily in the positive direction. A number of studies have employed community surveys to make before-after comparisons of fear and related perceptions, some with experimental designs. Fear has typically been measured using a variety of survey items, lending the studies more credibility. The now widely-accepted view that community policing helps reduce levels of fear of crime and increases perceptions of safety seems reasonably well-founded, although some efforts have failed to accomplish fear reductions.

DISORDER

The impact of community policing on disorder, minor crime, incivilities, and signs of crime has not been subjected to careful testing as frequently as its impact on crime and fear. The available evidence suggests, though, that community policing, and especially foot patrol and problem solving, helps reduce levels of disorder, lending partial support to the "broken windows" thesis (Wilson and Kelling, 1982).

CALLS FOR SERVICE

Community policing might reduce calls for service in several ways: problem solving might address underlying issues that generate calls; collaboration might increase call referrals to other government agencies; foot patrols and mini-stations might receive citizen requests directly, thus heading off calls to central dispatch; and workload management might find alternative responses for some types of calls. Although the ability of the last approach (workload management) to reduce the volume of calls dispatched to sworn units for immediate response has clearly been demonstrated (McEwen et al., 1986), the rest of the evidence on the effects of community policing on calls for service is mixed. Several studies have found positive effects but several others have not.

COMMUNITY RELATIONS

The vast majority of the studies that have looked at the impact of community policing on citizens' attitudes toward the police have uncovered positive effects. Clearly, citizens generally appreciate mini-stations in their neighborhoods, foot patrols, problem-solving efforts, and other forms of community policing.

POLICE OFFICER ATTITUDES

A clear majority of the studies that have investigated the effects of community policing on officers' job satisfaction, perceptions of the community, and other related attitudes have discovered beneficial effects. Officers involved in community policing, especially if they are volunteers or members of special units, typically thrive on their new duties and responsibilities. What is somewhat less certain, however, is (1) whether these effects will survive the long term and (2) whether these benefits are as universal when *all* officers are required to engage in community policing. Whenever community policing is practiced only by specialists, as has generally been the case until recently in most departments, one condition that *is* nearly universal is conflict between the specialists and other members of the agency, frequently reflected in derogatory remarks about "the grin and wave squad."

POLICE OFFICER BEHAVIOR

Significant anecdotal evidence suggests that foot patrol, problem solving, permanent assignment, mini-stations, and other features of community policing lead to changes in some police officers' behavior, but these behavioral effects have only been lightly documented thus far. Evidence also suggests that many officers resist changing their behavior, out of opposition to the philosophical underpinnings of community policing, doubts that community policing really works, or just plain habit.

CONCLUSION

A great deal of energy has been invested since 1980 in determining the nature of community policing and its effects. These efforts have paid off to the extent that the scope and variation of community policing is much better understood today and some of its effects have been fairly well documented. Since community policing has evolved significantly during this period, however, some of its elements have been more carefully evaluated than others. In addition, programmatic complexity, multiple effects, variations in scope, and research design limitations have hampered many of the community policing evaluations conducted thus far. Nevertheless, the programmatic elements of community policing do seem to produce several beneficial outcomes for citizens and officers, and have the potential to impact crime and disorder. Whether the more philosophical and strategic elements of community policing will become firmly rooted, and whether they will ultimately have beneficial effects, is yet to be seen.

NOTE

1.   Preparation of this chapter was supported, in part, under award # 94-IJ-CX-0006 from the National Institute of Justice, U.S. Department of Justice. Points of view in this document are those of the author and do not necessarily represent the official position of the U.S. Department of Justice.

REFERENCES

Bennett, Trevor. 1994. "Community Policing on the Ground: Developments in Britain." In Dennis P. Rosenbaum, ed., *The Challenge of Community Policing: Testing the Promises*. Thousand Oaks, CA: Sage, pp. 224-246.

Bureau of Justice Assistance. 1994a. *A Police Guide to Surveying Citizens and Their Environment*. Washington, DC: author.

_____ . 1994b. *Neighborhood-Oriented Policing in Rural Communities: A Program Planning Guide*. Washington, DC: author.

_____ . 1994c. *Understanding Community Policing: A Framework for Action*. Washington, DC: author.

Cordner, Gary W. and Robert C. Trojanowicz. 1992. "Patrol," in Gary W. Cordner and Donna C. Hale, eds., *What Works in Policing? Operations and Administration Examined*. Cincinnati, OH: Anderson, pp. 3-18.

Eck, John E. 1992. "Criminal Investigation," in Gary W. Cordner and Donna C. Hale, eds., *What Works in Policing? Operations and Administration Examined*. Cincinnati, OH: Anderson, pp. 19-34.

_____ and William Spelman. 1987. *Problem Solving: Problem-Oriented Policing in Newport News*. Washington, DC: Police Executive Research Forum.

Goldstein, Herman. 1977. *Policing A Free Society*. Cambridge, MA: Ballinger.

_____. 1987. "Toward Community-Oriented Policing: Potential, Basic Requirements, and Threshold Questions," *Crime & Delinquency* 25: 236-258.

_____. 1990. *Problem-Oriented Policing*. New York: McGraw-Hill.

Greene, Jack R. and Stephen D. Mastrofski, eds. 1988. *Community Policing: Rhetoric or Reality?* New York: Praeger.

Greenwood, Peter W. and Joan Petersilia. 1975. *The Criminal Investigation Process, Volume I: Summary and Implications*. Santa Monica, CA: Rand Corporation.

Kelling, George L., Tony Pate, Duane Dieckman, and Charles E. Brown. 1974. *The Kansas City Preventive Patrol Experiment: A Summary Report*. Washington, DC: Police Foundation.

Kelling, George L. and Mark H. Moore. 1988. "The Evolving Strategy of Policing." *Perspectives on Policing* No. 4. Washington, DC: National Institute of Justice.

Klockars, Carl B. 1988. "The Rhetoric of Community Policing." In Jack R. Greene and Stephen D. Mastrofski, eds., *Community Policing: Rhetoric or Reality?* New York: Praeger, pp. 239-258.

Leighton, Barry N. 1994. "Community Policing in Canada: An Overview of Experience and Evaluations." In Dennis P. Rosenbaum, ed., *The Challenge of Community Policing: Testing the Promises*. Thousand Oaks, CA: Sage, pp. 209-223.

Manning, Peter K. 1988. "Community Policing as a Drama of Control." In Jack R. Greene and Stephen D. Mastrofski, eds., *Community Policing: Rhetoric or Reality?* New York: Praeger, pp. 27-46.

McEwen, J. Thomas, Edward F. Connors III, and Marcia I. Cohen. 1986. *Evaluation of the Differential Police Responses Field Test*. Washington, DC: National Institute of Justice.

Moore, Mark H. and Robert C. Trojanowicz. 1988. "Corporate Strategies for Policing." *Perspectives on Policing* No. 6. Washington, DC: National Institute of Justice.

Normandeau, Andre. 1993. "Community Policing in Canada: A Review of Some Recent Studies," *American Journal of Police* 12,1: 57-73.

Skogan, Wesley G. 1994. "The Impact of Community Policing on Neighborhood Residents: A Cross-Site Analysis." In Dennis P. Rosenbaum, ed., *The Challenge of Community Policing: Testing the Promises*. Thousand Oaks, CA: Sage, pp. 167-181.

Spelman, William and Dale K. Brown. 1982. *Calling the Police: Citizen Reporting of Serious Crime*. Washington, DC: Police Executive Research Forum.

Trojanowicz, Robert and Bonnie Bucqueroux. 1990. *Community Policing: A Contemporary Perspective*. Cincinnati, OH: Anderson.

Weatheritt, Mollie. 1988. "Community Policing: Rhetoric or Reality?" In Jack R. Greene and Stephen D. Mastrofski, eds., *Community Policing: Rhetoric or Reality?* New York: Praeger, pp. 153-176.

Wilson, James Q. and George L. Kelling. 1982. "Police and Neighborhood Safety: Broken Windows," *The Atlantic Monthly* (March): 29-38.

MAKING THE POLICE PROACTIVE: AN IMPOSSIBLE TASK FOR IMPROBABLE REASONS   23

Frank P. Williams III & Carl P. Wagoner

The standard position today, heard from both the public and the police, is that our crime problem is getting out of hand. Begging the question of whether we actually have a crime wave or a media-based crime-reporting wave (Fishman, 1977), we propose to discuss the issue of what society can do about crime in the context of police reform and police services. With some ideological exceptions, those who study crime and the police are fairly well agreed that police can be expected to have very little direct effect on crime and criminality and that, further, preventing crime is not really the function of the police.

Unfortunately, neither the public nor their quasi-elected officials share this opinion regarding the function of the police. Their position is grounded in a conservative ideology which stresses deterrence and "taking the handcuffs off police," in addition to advocating the adding of more police and more technological innovation, in order to increase the apprehension of offenders. However, there is abundant evidence to the effect that crime is not reduced nor apprehension increased by adding police or, for example, by eliminating the exclusionary rule (Walker, 1989).

This resistance to evidence that police, by themselves, can do little about crime is itself an interesting situation. As noted above, we suspect that it is based in the current conservative mentality and movement, the political utility of crime in providing a "mantle of law and order" and, ironically, the police themselves. This latter source is intriguing because both the rise and fall of crime rates have long been used as a political ploy by law enforcement to gain access to greater resources (Weis and Milakovich,

Source: Frank P. Williams III and Carl P. Wagoner (1992). "Making the Police Proactive: An Impossible Task for Improbable Reasons." *Police Forum*, 2(2):1-5. Reprinted by permission of the Academy of Criminal Justice Sciences.

1974). The latent function of such a ploy, however, is that police departments then invite the public to hold them accountable for crime itself.

The connection between "doing something" about crime and recent calls for proactive policing has created an expectation that police should, indeed, engage in proactive crime prevention. Historically, there is some merit to this expectation. The origins of modern policing lie in the private forces created by the Bow Street merchants of London and the Thames River police of the West Indies Merchants Association. These forces were clearly proactive in their approach to "crime." Yet, as police forces became public entities, they became more reactive in approach and lost their direct connection to citizens. This is further illustrated by the changing nature of the police role in the movement from mechanical to organic solidarity, and the corresponding changes in the nature of criminals and the increasing rates of crime (Lundman, 1980).

In short, police forces evolved concurrently with the state's emergence under the social contract in the dual role of victim and enforcer of restitution. This process resulted in a police role as chief enforcer of the social contract and, in modern times, placed the police directly as a servant of the government, not as a servant of the people. The point here is that modern police are reactive in nature and respond directly to government rather than to the citizenry. Indirectly, of course, police do respond to the people through the representatives of government.

This is not to suggest that the police are completely devoid of an ability to be proactive. It is the case that both in law enforcement situations and in order maintenance situations police can take the initiative. However, when they do so it is usually in response to internal pressure from top administration, which is often acting in response to external pressure.

When a call is issued to "do something about crime," government (local or otherwise) instructs its law enforcement agent to respond, either with action or with explanations. Unfortunately, the police are not for the most part, designed as proactive agents. This is illustrated in the limited success of community crime prevention programs ("neighborhood watch," "operation identification," and home security surveys) have had (Currie, 1985; Turk and Grimes, 1992). Even more problematic from our viewpoint is that the type of response which is demanded from law enforcement, and the form of response generated, varies by the type of "public" making the demand.

A common observation is that power (or potential power) defines the type of public and the form of response. Thus, demands that the police respond to crime take various forms and precipitate commensurate demands for change in police philosophy and structure.

The primary intent of this essay is to critique proactive policing and calls for police change. To do this, we will explore the relationship between crime, proactive policies, and three "ideal types" of public, which we will refer to as citizens, interest groups, and elites. A secondary intent is to stimulate discussion on the issue of police change in a proactive direction. As a result, we have chosen to eschew an objective and carefully documented approach in favor of a more subjective and controversial one.

PUBLIC POWER, PROACTIVE POLICING AND CHANGE

PROACTIVE POLICING

Our first concern is to determine the type of response that would be required in order to generate proactive policing under our three types of publics. A demand from citizens requires a more diffuse and broader response(s) than from the other types of publics. In fact, for such a demand to be made is itself an extraordinary event, since the "public" is not often united or does not often see the world through the same colored glasses, particularly in an heterogeneous, urban/industrial society. In keeping with the nature of the demand, the police response will likely result in substantial resource expenditure (if this is possible in an era of steady state or decreasing resources), perhaps even requiring major structural and philosophical changes. The likelihood of such changes is minimal since, as we will note later, law enforcement organizations are particularly resistant to change.

Demands from interest groups, on the other hand, are commonplace and often require little adaptation on the part of the police, other than the shifting of focus and resources from one area of concern to another. Our form of government is well-adapted to interest groups and, thus, one might even argue that police structure and philosophy are currently products designed to meet this form of public demand. The chief characteristic we expect here is that the demands are individualistic and specific.

The elite demand requires a non-specific response by the police. In fact, the nature of the response is unlikely to be directly generated by the police themselves. Instead, the response is likely to be in the form of police reaction to new laws or political philosophies. Such responses can be profound and far-reaching, but will tend to produce new enforcement strategies and/or directions of activity aimed at particular segments of society rather than changes in police philosophy or organizational structure. In short, we see citizen demands as resulting in a return to a more mechanical style of policing (as opposed to a contemporary organic style), interest group responses as service-oriented, and elite demands as selective repression.

CHANGE

Because of the changing nature of society, as well as the changing nature and increased amount of crime, many have argued that change of the police is both desirable and/or imminent (Currie, 1985; Germann, 1985; Wilson, 1985; Goldstein, 1979). If so, our second concern is to describe the form that changes might take under our three types of publics. Under the citizen type of demand we believe that any police change would be toward development into a more citizen-responsive force, and oriented to a closer relationship with the community. Such a change, if real rather than superficial, would require a substantial increase in new resources and recommitment of current resources, significant changes in philosophy, and potentially massive restructuring of police organizations.

The term interest group as used here refers to associations and coalitions of persons with a common concern which binds them together. Their effectiveness is determined by the degree of pressure they can bring to the police directly or indirectly through other governmental agencies. It needs to be noted that many such interest groups are transitory in nature, and are often issue specific. Interest-group demands would produce change oriented toward specific services such as peace-keeping and enclave protection. Further, because the nature of interest groups is both pluralistic and individualistic, change to meet their demands would entail a certain amount of decentralization in order to quickly respond to shifting priorities and allegiances. Critical variables influencing the extent of change are the degree of resources dispersed among the interest groups, the form of those resources, and the temporal nature of those resources.

Elite demands would result in selective repression of those who constitute a threat to the existing social order. Thus, change in policing requires a reordering of priorities and, potentially, some degree of new organizational structure. Because some older parts of the structure can be dispensed with, structural changes may merely mean a reshuffling of resources and reorganization. Centralized authority and the chain of command would remain important due to the necessity of ensuring the transmission of the new priorities and the preparation for, and the development of, new attitudes on the part of the rank and file in regard to the "new" threat. Critical variables here include the extent of police agreement with the values to be defended, perceptions police have of the newly criminalized community, and the relative threat to the existing social order.

THE IRONY OF CHANGE

Given these potential avenues of change, the question is not what police organizations will become but in what directions have the police already responded? A few brief examples will serve to demonstrate an irony that the triad of publics does indeed affect the nature of policing and, at the same time, produces conflict that results in little actual change.

CITIZEN-BASED CHANGE

The clearest example of reaction to this power source is the development of community policing. Although by 1990 more than 300 police departments in the United States had reported some form of community policing, there remains today a relative lack of understanding as to what constitutes community policing (Strecher, 1991). At times it has been substituted for what is still a community-relations approach, at times it has been synonymous with "problem-oriented policing," and at times foot patrol has been equated with community policing (Trojanowicz and Bucqueroux, 1990).

Instead, community policing requires a substantial change in both structure and form, including attitudinal, organizational, and subcultural change. It represents a "new" philosophy of policing whereby police officers and the community work together to solve community problems of crime and related social ills. This means giving citizens of the community a direct say in the solutions and activities that regulate crime. Community policing also requires an organizational structure which is flattened, with horizontal as well as vertical communication. Centralized authority is minimized, with area captains becoming "mini-chiefs" with full decision-making authority, and with individual community-policing officers sharing decision making, particularly on their own beat. Police officers are given authority to not only create their own solutions to problems but also contact and request assistance from other governmental agencies and private entities. In short, police officers become citizens of their own neighborhoods and combine with residents to produce a healthy neighborhood.

Thus the problems here are that real community policing requires a radical restructuring of police organizations and a new sense of function. All we know of organizational theory tells us that such change will be resisted. A project manager of one of the five sites for the national community policing experiment aptly described the adaptations required of police officers and the organization as "traumatic" (McPherson, 1992). Further, as Van Horn and Van Meter (1977), among others, have noted, the predisposition of the people in the agency to support the implementation of new policy is a crucial variable in determining the success of the policy.

Other governmental agencies also play a key role in the success of this transformation. If they have different agendas, or see the "citizen mandate" as conflicting, responses to the requests of individual community police officers will be problematic. These agencies can defeat community policing philosophies either by failing to participate or simply by dragging their feet on requests. The probability of all affected government agencies buying into the same citizen-oriented philosophy is exceedingly low.

Similarly, because police officers will come and go in neighborhoods (and of course there will be several shifts involved), officers themselves cannot be responsible for community policing — the community itself must be. Getting a community to realize this in today's specialized world is no small feat, in and of itself. In effect, the ultimate feasibility and success of community policing is beyond the control of the police. The five-site national experiment has demonstrated the way in which these difficulties have combined to effectively disassemble the citizen-oriented approach. Only one of the sites (San Diego) remains committed to community policing and that site had an existing heritage of a community orientation. The other four have not only fallen by the wayside, but in one case the experiment caused the downfall of the chief of police (McPherson, 1992).

INTEREST GROUP-BASED CHANGE

Reactions to this power source require the ability to make swift responses to potentially immediate concerns of changing interest groups. We suggest this can result in the creation of decentralized teams to police and protect the various interest groups. In operation such decentralized teams (such as an anti-gang task force with the responsibility of quickly moving into an area, conducting a sweep for possible law violators and then moving out) may be responding to interest groups such as the "public at large" or to the organized interests of a particular neighborhood. Further, such interest groups may demand or require other than purely law enforcement activities on the part of police. Wilson (1968) has written at length on the "interests" of particular communities centering around service functions.

While this service orientation may share appearances, and even some techniques, with community based-policing, or with problem-oriented policing, the reality is that the police organization is merely responding to various pressures brought about by various special-interest groups. Therefore, the result is policy based on short-term decisions and assignments, with ever-increasing resources devoted to immediate problems. Such a situation leads to relative chaos and the inability of police to respond to changing conditions in the community at large.

With squandered resources and a lack of organized policy and planning, a reasonable expectation is that geographic enclaves derived from the more powerful and long-term interest groups will develop. We refer to these as "enclaves" because the concept of enclaved and walled communities, whether based on cultural factors or on environmental design, is an excellent exemplar. Residents identify with the area and non-residents are seen as intruders and potential criminals. Emergent police responses to the enclave movement are concerned with maintaining the enclave community at the expense of the larger community. Examples of the form of policing required here include stopping of blacks who are in an enclave where they "do not ordinarily belong" (e.g., Jamal Wilkes, former Los Angeles Lakers basketball star being detained "on suspicion" while driving his Rolls Royce in the "Wilshire Corridor" in Los Angeles; an episode of LA Law where a black attorney jogging in an upper-class neighborhood was accosted and arrested by police).

Neighborhood Watch programs exemplify the response of police organizations to this source of governmental power. In a real sense, these programs are not oriented toward protecting citizens of the general community, but rather are a method of focusing service on selective areas. Those who have been in police departments operating neighborhood watch programs tell us that, when a "neighborhood" is advised of a possible displacement effect on crime, the invariable response from residents is that they don't care, they just want *their* neighborhood safe from crime. This is analogous to the NIMBY (Not In My Back Yard) phenomenon which routinely occurs in prison site selection.

The irony here is that as services are continually focused on the interest group enclaves, the proactive nature of police crime prevention can serve to displace crime into the larger non-enclaved community, thus creating a "battle-ground" and greater demands of protection from the enclaves. The cycle of demand for protection and focus of resources has the potential to render impotent the police organization and to destroy the enclaves themselves.

ELITE-BASED CHANGE

Changes in police derived from this power base require selective enforcement of laws, proliferation of special-interest laws, and order maintenance exerted on the masses. All are based on a re-emphasis of basic (elite) values in society and the emergence of a strident conservatism. A number of current modifications of police structure are predicated on the drug war and are, in some sense, a reorientation of the earlier war on crime of the 1970s. For example, resource allocations from the federal government, designed to encourage and reward police departments for their crime-fighting efforts, were moved into drunken-driving campaigns and now have been moved into the drug war. Police departments, as a result, have eliminated some older crime-fighting units and substituted drug enforcement programs.

This most recent phase, the war on drugs, has once again succeeded in connecting drug use with crime, thus providing a rationale for police to adopt the ideology of the new drug war. In addition, the war has succeeded in criminalizing (and thus delegitimizing) a major portion of those who might threaten the elite value system. In part because drug use has been associated with the liberal values of the 1960s, elite conservative values have been able to dominate the present era. Moreover, both an emphasis on the repression of drug-users and the advent of work place drug-testing have been used to resolve elite concerns about societal productivity.

It is likely that in a democratic society there will ultimately be a reaction, and there will be attempts to shift power (at least momentarily) in efforts to liberalize the laws concerning drug possession and use. Thus, it could be argued that repression contains the seeds of its own overthrow and may ultimately result in image problems for the police, as well as distrust and greater regulation of police activity. The police themselves have been placed in a quandary of having to eliminate a large number of otherwise desirable recruits because of a history of drug use. A recent recruiting solution has been to ask about the kind of drugs and make selective decisions while ignoring the presumptive illegality of all drug use.

CONCLUSIONS

While some change is undoubtedly taking place among police and in police organizations, the current situation leads us to believe that nothing substantial is taking place except, perhaps, in idiosyncratic circumstances and isolated instances. Further, our separation of the public into three types is misleading in the sense that each appears to be acting independently. Actually, all three types act in concert, with the more powerful having the greatest potential effect. Each one, however, tends to offset the others and dissipates the entire effect of change. The most probable approach to police change is that there will be a mixture of all these variations, in response to the mixture of the public types. This means that none of the potential approaches above will become commonplace, none will be logically and systematically approached, and in the end police will not become proactive. We predict that the police will maintain their current para-military form and bureaucratic structure. In the face of conflicting masters and differential demands, informal organizational goals serving survival will yield resistance to change and no viable new alternatives will emerge. We do not, however, rule out incremental change, particularly that change associated with larger societal concerns.

The most likely scenario is that crime will decrease by the turn of the century, largely due to demographic changes. The decrease in crime will, in turn, take pressure off the police to "do something about it." Thus, through the end of this decade, there will be minor modifications in policing, all of which will be strongly resisted, or modified to such an extent that the consequences will be minimal or nonexistent.

This, however, belies the function of the police and takes as granted the fact that police can affect crime. We believe there is sufficient evidence to support the assertion that any reduction of crime must come from outside the police. Therefore, the real question is not whether the police can prevent and control crime but, instead, whether and how efficiently and effectively the police can react to crime. Our constructed scenarios for proactive police roles are all unlikely, or else undesirable, in our present society. We would do well, then, to focus on the police as a reactive force and, if enhancement of this function is desirable, find methods of stripping proactive pretense from police organizations. If we must have a specific proactive force to control and prevent crime, a far better choice is to create an agency specifically responsible for that function and empower it to respond to crime on a far larger scope. Such an agency would presumably engage in the improvement of education, health, recreation, community renovation, and the myriad of other factors associated with the emergence of crime in our society. The police, however, should simply be assigned the task of reacting to crime as, or after, it is committed.

REFERENCES

Currie, E. (1985). *Confronting Crime: An American Challenge*. New York: Pantheon Books.

Fishman, M. (1977). Crime waves as ideology. *Social Problems,* 25: 531-543.

Germann, A.C. (1985). "Law Enforcement: A Look Into the Future." In *The Ambivalent Force: Perspectives on the Police*, Abraham Blumberg and Elaine Neiderhoffer (eds.), 3rd ed. New York: Holt, Rinehart and Winston.

Goldstein, A. (1979). Improving the Police: A Problem-Oriented Approach. *Crime and Delinquency,* 25: 236-258.

Inciardi, J. (1992). *The War on Drugs II*. Mountain View, CA: Mayfield Publishing Company.

McPherson, N. (1992). "Problem Oriented Policing in San Diego." Comments made during panel presentation at the annual meeting of the Western Society of Criminology, San Diego, CA.

Strecher, V.G. (1991). Histories and futures of policing: Readings and misreadings of a pivotal present. *Police Forum,* 1(1): 1-9.

Trojanowicz, R. and Bucqueroux, B. (1990). *Community Policing: A Contemporary Perspective*. Cincinnati: Anderson Publishing Company.

Turk, A.T. and Grimes, R. (1992). "Neighborhood Watch Committees: Participation and Impact." Paper delivered at the annual meeting of the Western Society of Criminology, San Diego, CA.

Van Horn, C.E. and Van Meter, D.S. (1977). "The implementation of inter-governmental policy." In *Policy Studies Review Annual*, Vol. 1, S.S. Nagel (ed.). Beverly Hills, CA: Sage.

Walker, S. (1989). *Sense and Nonsense About Crime: A Policy Guide.* 2nd ed. Pacific Grove, CA: Brooks-Cole Publishing Company.

Weis, K. and Milikovich, M.E. (1974). Political misuses of crime rates. *Transaction,* 11(5):27-33.

Wilson, J.Q. (1968). *Varieties of Police Behavior.* Cambridge, MA: Harvard University Press.

————— (1985). *Thinking About Crime.* Rev. ed. New York: Vintage Press.

Subject Index

Author Index

Greenfield, L., 325, 326
Greenwood, P., 19, 24, 25, 50, 133, 161,
    163, 186, 187, 211, 214, 242,
    252, 258, 275, 383, 425, 442,
    500, 511
Greer, S., 413, 437, 442
Grimes, R., 514, 521
Griswold, D., 126, 129
Gruber, J., 135
Gruenberg, B., 138
Guess, L., 229, 233, 240
Gusfield, J., 301, 325

Haaga, J., 129
Hagan, J., 414, 441
Halleck, H., 129
Halper, A., 123, 129
Hamberger, L., 338, 359
Hanes, L., 388, 450
Harlow, K., 398, 448
Harris, R., 389, 398, 442
Harvey, J., 396, 439
Hastings, J., 338, 359
Hawkins, R., 330, 363
Hayeslip, D., 293, 477, 493
Heath, L., 393, 431, 447
Hecker, E., 332, 359
Heilweil, M., 430, 451
Heimer, C., 394, 449
Heinecke, C., 363
Held, 384
Heller, N., 399, 402
Hellman, A., 223, 238, 239
Henderson, J., 446
Henig, J., 407, 442
Hertz, E., 444
Hill, D., 440
Hill, K., 135
Hindelang, M., 392, 442
Hird, J., 471
Hirschel, J., 329, 340, 343, 349, 350,
    359, 360
Hirschi, T., 383, 398, 441
Hoare, M., 427, 442
Hoffmaster, D., 306, 325
Hollister, 25
Homant, R., 345, 360
Hope, T., 384, 405, 432, 442
Hotaling, G., 336, 360
Hough, J., 387, 388, 402, 430, 442
Hser, Y., 24
Huizinga, D., 349, 351, 358

Hunter, A., 411, 413, 442
Hunter, R., 127
Hunter, W., 471
Hutchison, I., 329, 340, 343, 344, 349,
    360

Iliff, R., 394, 449
Inciardi, J., 521
Innes, C., 335, 338, 356, 360
Isaacs, H., 164, 186, 214
Iverson, W., 222, 239

Jackson, H., 400, 401, 422, 450
Jackson, R., 411
Jacob, H., 138, 383, 443
Jacobs, J., 304, 305, 310, 325, 326, 387,
    443, 470
Jaffe, P., 351, 358
Jamieson, K., 304, 305, 325, 401, 443
Janowitz, M., 413, 443
Jeffrey, C., 127, 129, 437, 443, 471
Jencks, C., 443
Johnson, J., 413, 432, 445
Johnson, L., 389, 438,
Jolin, A., 341, 360
Jones, B., 135
Jones, D., 402, 443
Jones, L., 411
Joseph, N., 221, 239
Jouriles, E., 340, 360

Kaplan, G., 384, 440
Karales, K., 346, 359
Kasarda, J., 393, 413, 443
Kaufman, C., 136
Kellen, K., 186
Kelley, J., 359
Kelling, G., 2, 3, 19, 24, 25, 50, 58, 59,
    61, 66, 70, 71, 115, 117, 118,
    127, 129, 130, 365, 367, 368,
    390, 398, 414, 425, 427, 443,
    449, 450, 470, 474, 475, 480,
    494, 497, 500, 508, 511
Kennedy, D., 345, 360
Kennedy, R., 443, 470
Keppel, R., 244, 252
Kidder, L., 396, 439
Kingsbury, A., 399, 443
Kirchner, R., 430, 448
Kleck, G., 394, 395, 443
Kleinman, M., 125, 129, 301, 443
Kleinman, P., 390, 391

Wilson, J., 19, 23, 24, 25, 50, 116, 118,
    221, 224, 233, 240, 258, 275,
    284, 292, 306, 310, 326, 370,
    414, 422, 427, 450, 474, 480,
    494, 508, 511, 516, 518, 522
Wilson, L., 402
Wilson, O., 23
Wilson, S., 450
Winchester, S., 400, 401, 421, 450
Wish, E., 24
Wolfgang, M., 23, 24, 258, 275
Worden, R., 131, 150, 309, 326
Wright, J., 390, 394, 395, 400, 430, 450,
    451
Wright, R., 451
Wuerth, J., 437

Wycoff, M., 25, 258, 275, 278, 292,
    384, 446
Wylie, P., 342, 363

Yaden, D., 451
Yin, R., 385, 404, 407, 415, 416, 436,
    451
Yllo, K., 363, 337
Young, A., 451

Zaharchuk, T., 402, 451
Zahn, M., 341, 363
Zalman, M., 346, 363
Zander, A., 411, 432, 451
Zimmer, L., 125, 126, 130